Human Dynamics in
Psychology
and Education

Human Dynamics in Psychology and Education

SELECTED READINGS

edited by

DON E. HAMACHEK

MICHIGAN STATE UNIVERSITY

Allyn and Bacon, Inc.   Boston

Library of Congress Catalog Card Number: 68–19473

PRINTED IN THE UNITED STATES OF AMERICA

First printing . . . June, 1968
Second printing . . . October, 1968

PREFACE

This is a book about people. It focuses on ideas and controversies concerning such things as how people learn, issues about teaching, testing and grading, growth processes and developmental consequences, child-rearing strategies and outcomes, maladaptive behavior and disadvantaged youth, questions about personal freedom, personality dynamics, and the importance of understanding one's self.

As I organized this anthology into its five major parts and thirteen chapters, I was guided by four basic ideas which I hoped would be expressed as a unified concept upon completion.

Number one, I wanted the organizational plan to reflect a kind of fluid pacing of ideas so that the ideas, or concepts, or theories, treated here are seen only as the beginning and indicate that there is more, much more, to know and think about than one book can offer. Hence, the emphasis in each of the five major parts on "Toward Understanding . . ." which, I hope, puts the emphasis where it properly should be, namely, on "we are moving toward," rather than on "we have arrived."

Number two, I was guided by the conviction that a book of this sort, which has as one of its aims to talk to interested students with divergent interests, does not have to reflect only a limited range of sources. The purely empirical or "scientific" sources have something to offer but so, too, do the purely "speculative," or interpretive, sources. Although there was no conscious attempt to restrict selections that might come from any single source, as it turns out only four papers come from any one journal. The 58 selections in this edition range over 25 different journals, eleven books, one monograph, and one unpublished paper. All in all, 64 different authors are represented.

Number three, I endeavored (but failed, I am sure, in some instances) to choose selections which seemed to be more than one psychologist or educator talking to another. For the most part, the articles included here are written in a language and style which most students in the various fields of psychology and education should be able to comprehend. This does not suggest that there is not some old-fashion, rigorous, "you've-got-to-dig-to-understand" material in this collection. Not at all. I have, however, attempted to avoid the tiny little studies which report tiny little problems in language only a select few can understand.

And number four, consistent with everything so far, I rather deliberately attempted to choose articles in which the emphasis is focused primarily on *human* behavior, *human* meanings, and *human* understandings which grow out of uniquely *human* experiences.

This anthology is designed to serve either as the sole text for a course or as a supplementary source. It is not designed to serve up easy answers or ready-made solutions. In fact, there are many instances where two different authors are placed back-to-back precisely because they offer diametrically opposing viewpoints about a similar problem. If we begin by agreeing that at least one of the purposes of education is to make us less like each other and more like ourselves, then the challenge here will be for student and teacher to think the ideas through, mull them over, discuss the differences and, in the best sense of the word, get involved to the extent that they make a personal difference so that, ultimately, they can have personal meaning.

It is hoped that this anthology can be a useful tool in courses concerned with the preparation of teachers, mental hygienists, counselors, social workers, and researchers interested in understanding man both as he sees himself and as he is acted on by forces outside self. I would hope that a volume of this nature can be more adventure-like than task-like and that it serves that ultimate end of being more challenging than dulling, more freeing than restricting.

The ideas and sweat of many people go into a book of this sort, and although acknowledgment is made, in separate credits, to the authors and publishers of the selections used, I once again express my indebtedness for the privilege of reprinting these significant papers.

D.E.H.

CONTENTS

vii

CHAPTER TWO

NATURE AND NURTURE OF MOTI-
VATION

CHAPTER THREE

DYNAMICS OF INTELLIGENCE AND
CREATIVITY

PART II   Toward Understanding the Nature
             of Instruction   185

CHAPTER FOUR

CLASSROOM DYNAMICS AND TEACH-
ING PROCESSES

CHAPTER TEN

EDUCATING AND UNDERSTANDING THE DISADVANTAGED

Human Dynamics in
Psychology
and Education

PART ONE

Toward Understanding the Nature of Learning and Cognitive Processes

"Learning, if rightly applied, makes a young man thinking and attentive, industrious, confident and wary; and an old man cheerful and useful. It is an ornament in prosperity, a refuge in adversity, and entertainment at all times; it cheers in solitude, and gives moderation and wisdom in all circumstances." R. Palmer (1808–1887)

The three chapters in this section are designed to introduce you to the complex processes involved in cognition and learning. The purpose here is to give you a general overview of some of the significant contemporary issues and theories related to learning, motivation, intelligence, and creativity.

Since there have always been endless controversies about what is fact and what is fiction in psychology, Chapter One begins with Dr. Watson's listing of fifty propositions or generalizations, crucial for understanding learning and behavior, with which psychologists of different theoretical camps would consistently agree. From here you will move to a brief look at some representative theories of learning which should give you a taste of the wide diversity of points of view when it comes to explaining and understanding how people learn.

Drs. Gagné and Bruner have back-to-back papers in Chapter One which discuss ideas and issues of major significance to those of us concerned with how to make learning more meaningful, more lasting, more active and less passive. Dr. Bruner suggests that "It matters *not* what we have learned but rather what we *do* with what we have learned." Both men have something to say about the "doing with" aspect of learning.

1

The final selection in Chapter One will help you see relationships between achievement strivings during the first four years of school and later achievement during adolescence and adulthood. It may be that a child's early performance in school is more related to how he achieves later in life than we thought.

Chapter Two is very much related to Chapter One because without motivation there can be little, if any, learning—at least learning of the kind which is associated with what goes on in classrooms. This chapter will expose you to a broad span of research and ideas related to motivation—what it is, what it isn't, and how to encourage it. In reading number eight, Dr. Farson raises some critical questions about the use of praise as a motivator, which may give you pause if you are inclined to think it is *always* the best way to motivate people.

Highly related to any discussion of learning and cognitive processes are the constructs, intelligence and creativity. We frequently associate the amount of intelligence one has with either heredity, or environment, or a bit of both. In Chapter Three, Dr. Combs explores the idea of intelligence as a function of one's perceptions. Is there a ceiling on intellectual development? Does intelligence change from the preschool years into adulthood? Selection nine in Chapter Three focuses specifically on these and related questions. And finally, what is creativity? What are its components? How can creative output be enhanced, encouraged, and developed? Dr. Guilford speaks eloquently to these and other issues, while Dr. Maslow concludes this section with some ideas about how self-actualization may, in fact, be the ultimate expression of personal creativeness.

Part I, then, will expose you to some of the basic issues associated with learning and cognitive processes. In the final analysis, the subtle innuendos and complexities actually involved in the learning process will be best demonstrated by instructors and students as they engage in discussion over the ideas presented in this section.

CHAPTER ONE

DYNAMICS OF LEARNING AND THE LEARNER'S TASK

1   What Psychology Can We Feel Sure About?*

BY GOODWIN WATSON

EDITOR'S NOTE: *Included in this article are fifty generalizations related to learning, social and group dynamics, growth and developmental processes, teaching and subject matter considerations with which psychologists from all theoretical "schools" of psychology would probably agree. Whether you intend to be a teacher, an administrator, a psychologist, or just a good parent, there is something here that each of us can learn from. In a general way, this article will set the stage and serve as the backdrop for many of the subsequent articles in this book.*

Educators and others who wish to apply psychology in their professional work have long been troubled by controversies among psychologists themselves. Behaviorism arose to challenge the introspective method; Thorndike's connectionism was controverted by Gestalt concepts; psychoanalysts talked an almost completely different language. It was natural for teachers to say, "Let's wait until the psychologists themselves straighten out their various systems!" It looked for a while as if one could support almost any educational practice by choosing which psychologist to cite.

Gradually, however, a body of pretty firm facts has accumulated. While it remains true that research findings will be somewhat differently

---

* Watson, Goodwin. "What Psychology Can We Feel Sure About?" *Teachers College Record* (1960), 253–257. Reprinted as a separate pamphlet under the title, *What Psychology Can We Trust?* (New York: Bureau of Publications, Teachers College, Columbia University, 1961). Reprinted by permission of the author and the publisher.

expressed and explained within different theoretical frameworks, the findings themselves are fairly solid.

A workshop of educators recently asked me to formulate for them some statements of what we really know today about children and learning. To my own surprise, the list of propositions with which few knowledgeable psychologists of any "school" would disagree, grew to fifty.

In no science are truths established beyond the possibility of revision. Einstein modified thinking about gravity, even though Newton's observations were essentially correct. Psychology is much younger and more malleable than physics. New facts are constantly accumulating in psychological research, and these will doubtless introduce some qualifications and modifications—conceivably even a basic contradiction. The educator who bases his program on these propositions, however, is entitled to feel that he is on solid psychological ground and not on shifting sands.

What follows is a listing of fifty propositions, important for education, upon which psychologists of all "schools" would consistently agree. These are presented in twelve classifications.

Nature-Nurture

1. Every trait in human behavior is a product of the interaction of heredity (as determined at conception by genes) and environmental influences. Some traits (preferences in food or clothing, for example) are easily influenced by nurture; others (height, rate of skeletal ossification) seem to be affected only by extreme differences in environment.

2. There are specific stages in individual development during which certain capacities for behavior appear. The manner in which these capacities are then utilized sets a pattern for later behavior which is highly resistant to change. If unutilized then, they are likely not to develop later (for example, visual perception, mother attachment, language pronunciation, sports skills, peer relations, independence from parents, heterosexuality).

3. The significance of the important biological transformations of pubescence (growth of primary sex organs, development of secondary sex characteristics, skeletal and muscular growth, glandular interaction) lies mainly in the *meaning* which cultural norms and personal history have given to these changes.

Learning Process

4. Behaviors which are rewarded (reinforced) are more likely to recur.

5. Sheer repetition without indications of improvement or any kind of reinforcement is a poor way to attempt to learn.

6. Threat and punishment have variable and uncertain effects upon learning; they may make the punished response more likely or less likely to recur; they may set up avoidance tendencies which prevent further learning.

7. Reward (reinforcement), to be most effective in learning, must follow almost immediately after the desired behavior and be clearly connected with that behavior in the mind of the learner.

8. The type of reward (reinforcement) which has the greatest transfer value to other life-situations is the kind one gives oneself—the sense of satisfaction in achieving purposes.

9. Opportunity for fresh, novel, stimulating experience is a kind of reward which is quite effective in conditioning and learning.

10. The experience of learning by sudden insight into a previously confused or puzzling situation arises when: (a) there has been a sufficient background and preparation; (b) attention is given to the relationships operative in the whole situation; (c) the perceptual structure "frees" the key elements to be shifted into new patterns; (d) the task is meaningful and within the range of ability of the subject.

11. Learners progress in any area of learning only as far as they need to in order to achieve their purposes. Often they do only well enough to "get by"; with increased motivation they improve.

12. Forgetting proceeds rapidly at first—then more and more slowly; recall shortly after learning reduces the amount forgotten.

Maturation: Life Tasks

13. The most rapid mental growth occurs during infancy and early childhood; the average child achieves about half of his total mental growth by the age of five.

14. Ability to learn increases with age up to adult years.

15. During the elementary school years (ages 6 to 12) most children enjoy energetic activity—running, chasing, jumping, shouting, and roughhouse. . . . Boys are generally more vigorous, active, rough, and noisy than girls.

16. Not until after eleven years of age do most children develop the sense of time which is required for historical perspective.

17. Readiness for any new learning is a complex product of interaction among physiological maturation, prerequisite learning, the pupil's sense of the importance of this lesson in his world, and his feeling about the teacher and the school situation.

Individual Differences

18. No two children make the same response to any school situation. Differences of heredity, physical maturity, intelligence, motor skills, health,

experiences with parents, siblings, playmates; consequent attitudes, motives, drives, tastes, fears—all these and more enter into production of each child's unique reaction. Children vary in their minds and personalities as much as in their appearance.

19. Pupils vary not only in their present performance but in their rate of growth and the "ceiling" which represents their potential level of achievement. Some "late bloomers" may eventually surpass pupils who seem far ahead of them in grade school.

20. Gains in intelligence test scores by children are positively related to aggressiveness, competitiveness, initiative, and strength of felt need to achieve.

21. Pupils grouped by ability on any one kind of test (age, size, IQ, reading, arithmetic, science, art, music, physical fitness, and so forth) will vary over a range of several grades in other abilities and traits.

Level of Challenge

22. The most effective effort is put forth by children when they attempt tasks which fall in the "range of challenge"—not too easy and not too hard—where success seems quite possible but not certain.

23. According to some studies, many pupils experience so much criticism, failure, and discouragement in school that their self-confidence, level of aspiration, and sense of worth are damaged.

Teaching Method

24. Children are more apt to throw themselves wholeheartedly into any project if they themselves have participated in the selection and planning of the enterprise.

25. Reaction to excessive direction by the teacher may be: (a) apathetic conformity; (b) defiance; (c) scape-goating; (d) escape from the whole affair.

26. Learning from reading is facilitated more by time spent recalling what has been read than by rereading.

27. Pupils *think* when they encounter an obstacle, difficulty, puzzle or challenge in a course of action which interests them. The process of thinking involves designing and testing plausible solutions for the problem as understood by the thinker.

28. The best way to help pupils form a general concept is to present the concept in numerous and varied specific situations, contrasting experiences with and without the desired concept, then to encourage precise formulations of the general idea and its application in situations different from those in which the concept was learned.

"Discipline" and Learning

29. Over-strict discipline is associated with more conformity, anxiety, shyness and acquiescence in children; greater permissiveness is associated with more initiative and creativity in children.

30. When children (or adults) experience too much frustration, their behavior ceases to be integrated, purposeful, and rational. Blindly they act out their rage or discouragement or withdrawal. The threshold of what is "too much" varies; it is lowered by previous failures.

Group Relations

31. Pupils learn much from one another; those who have been together for years learn new material more easily from one of their own group than they do from strangers.

32. When groups act for a common goal there is better cooperation and more friendliness than when individuals in the group are engaged in competitive rivalry with one another.

33. At age six, spontaneous groups seldom exceed three or four children; play groups all through childhood are smaller than school classes.

34. Children learn that peer consensus is an important criterion; they are uncomfortable when they disagree with their peers, and especially when they find themselves in a minority of one against all the others.

35. Groups which feel some need (internal coherence or external pressure) to work together try to influence deviates toward the group norm. If there is no felt need to stay together, the deviate may be ignored and thus excluded.

36. Leadership qualities vary with the demands of the particular situation. A good leader for a football team may or may not be a good leader for a discussion group, a research project, or an overnight hike; leadership is not a general trait.

37. In most school classes, one to three pupils remain unchosen by their classmates for friendship, for parties, or for working committees. These "isolates" are usually also unpopular with teachers.

Subject Matter

38. No school subjects are markedly superior to others for "strengthening mental powers." General improvement as a result of study of any subject depends on instruction designed to build up generalizations about principles, concept formation, and improvements of techniques of study, thinking, and communication.

39. What is learned is most likely to be available for use if it is learned in a situation much like that in which it is to be used and immediately preceding the time when it is needed. Learning in childhood-forgetting and relearning when needed is not an efficient procedure.

40. Television is the most frequently reported activity of elementary school pupils, occupying about the same number of hours per week as are given to school—far more than would voluntarily be given to school attendance.

Attitudes and Learning

41. Children (and adults even more) tend to select groups, reading matter, TV shows, and other influences which agree with their own opinions; they break off contact with contradictory views.

42. Children remember new information which confirms their previous attitudes better than they remember new information which runs counter to their previous attitudes.

Social Stratification

43. Attitudes toward members of "out-groups" are usually acquired from members of one's "in-group."

44. Children who differ in race, nationality, religion, or social class background, but who play together on a footing of equal status and acceptance, usually come to like one another.

45. Children who are looked down upon (or looked up to) because of their family, school marks, social class, race, nationality, religion, or sex tend to adopt and to internalize this evaluation of themselves.

46. Two thirds of the elementary school children of America come from lower-class homes; the one third who come from the lower-lower class usually find school very uncongenial.

47. Children choose most of their "best friends" from homes of the same socioeconomic class as their own.

48. More girls than boys wish, from time to time, that they could change their sex.

Evaluation

49. If there is a discrepancy between the real *objectives* and the *tests* used to measure achievement, the latter become the main influence upon choice of subject matter and method.

50. The superiority of man over calculating machines is more evident in the formulation of questions than in the working out of answers.

2   *Representative Theories of Learning and Their Implications for Education**

BY MORRIS L. BIGGE

EDITOR'S NOTE: There are so many points of view about the nature of learning and learning theory that it is sometimes difficult, even for psychologists, to sort out the differences among the various theoretical camps. This short outline article by Dr. Bigge will help you put people, emphases in teaching, and associated learning theories into better perspective. To which "camp" do you see yourself belonging? Conditioning, Stimulus-Response theory? Cognitive, Gestalt-Field theory? Each theory is implicitly related to some basic assumptions about the nature of man. What are your assumptions?

Since ancient times, most civilized societies have developed and, to some degree, tested theories about how man learns. As each new theory has gained support, it has seldom displaced its predecessors but merely competed with them. For this reason, the educational philosophies and practices of many teachers may include ideas from a variety of learning theories, some of which are basically contradictory in nature.

Each theory of learning is linked to a conception of the basic nature of man: In basic moral inclination, is he innately good, is he evil, or is he neutral? Then, in relation to his environment, is he active, passive, or interactive? Each of the different conceptions has its adherents, and each has its own approach to learning.

The accompanying chart outlines the concepts involved in ten major

* Reprinted from the *NEA Journal*, March, 1966, 18–19, by permission of the author and the publisher.

Representative Theories of Learning and Their Implications for Education

	I	II	III	IV	V	VI	VII
	Theory of Learning	Psychological System or Outlook	Assumption Concerning the Basic Moral and Psychological Nature of Man	Basis for Transfer of Learning	Main Emphasis in Teaching	Key Persons	Contemporary Exponents
MIND SUBSTANCE FAMILY	1. Theistic mental discipline	faculty psychology	bad-active mind substance continues active until curbed	exercised faculties, automatic transfer	exercise of faculties—the "muscles" of the mind	St. Augustine, John Calvin, J. Edwards	many Hebraic-Christian fundamentalists
	2. Humanistic mental discipline	classicism	neutral-active mind substance to be developed through exercise	cultivated mind or intellect	training of intrinsic mental power	Plato, Aristotle	M. J. Adler, St. John's College
	3. Natural unfoldment	romantic naturalism	good-active natural personality to unfold	recapitulation of racial history, no transfer needed	negative or permissive education	J. J. Rousseau, F. Froebel	extreme progressivists
	4. Apperception or Herbartionism	structuralism	neutral-passive mind composed of active mental states or ideas	growing apperceptive mass	addition of new mental states or ideas to a store of old ones in subconscious mind	J. F. Herbart, E. B. Titchener	many teachers and administrators
CONDITIONING THEORIES OF STIMULUS-RESPONSE (S-R) ASSOCIATION-ISTIC FAMILY	5. S-R bond	connectionism	neutral-passive or re-active organism with many potential S-R connections	identical elements	promotion of acquisition of desired S-R connections	E. L. Thorndike	J. M. Stephens, A. I. Gates
	6. Conditioning (with no reinforcement)	behaviorism	neutral-passive or re-active organism with innate reflexive drives and emotions	conditioned responses or reflexes	promotion of adhesion of desired responses to appropriate stimuli	J. B. Watson	E. R. Guthrie
	7. Reinforcement and conditioning	reinforcement	neutral-passive organism with innate reflexes and needs with their drive stimuli	reinforced or conditioned responses	successive, systematic changes in organisms' environment to increase the probability of desired responses (operants)	C. L. Hull	B. F. Skinner, K. W. Spence

I	II	III	IV	V	VI	VII
Theory of Learning	Psychological System or Outlook	Assumption Concerning the Basic Moral and Psychological Nature of Man	Basis for Transfer of Learning	Main Emphasis in Teaching	Key Persons	Contemporary Exponents
8. Insight	Gestalt psychology	naturally-active being whose activity follows psychological laws of organization	transposition of insights	promotion of insightful learning	M. Wertheimer, K. Koffka	W. Köhler
9. Goal insight	configurationalism	neutral-interactive purposive individual in sequential relationships with environment	tested insights	aid students in trial-and-error, goal-directed learning	B. H. Bode, R. H. Wheeler	E. E. Bayles
10. Cognitive-field	field psychology or relativism	neutral-interactive purposive person in simultaneous mutual interaction with environment, including other persons	continuity of life spaces, experience, or insights	help students restructure their life spaces—gain new insights into their contemporaneous situations	Kurt Lewin, E. C. Tolman, J. S. Bruner	R. G. Barker, A. W. Combs, H. F. Wright, M. L. Bigge

COGNITIVE THEORIES OF GESTALT-FIELD FAMILY

11

learning theories (Column I) either prevalent in today's schools or advocated by leading psychologists. Reinforcement and conditioning (No. 7), especially as represented by B. F. Skinner's "operant conditioning" and the cognitive-field theory (No. 10), first advanced by Kurt Lewin but refined by contemporary psychologists, are two leading contenders in the present scene.

Teachers may find this chart useful in thinking through and noting possible inconsistencies in their own educational outlook and how their outlook agrees or disagrees with that of their school administration. Although some of the theories have roots that go back to antiquity, they all still exert influence in presentday schools.

Each theory has its unique approach to education. However, some of them have enough in common to justify grouping them in families. Thus, in a more general sense, there are only five basic outlooks in regard to learning—the three families plus theories 3 and 4.

3   *The Learning of Concepts**[1]

BY ROBERT M. GAGNÉ

*EDITOR'S NOTE: We frequently talk about "learning concepts,"
but are we always certain what this means? Is there a difference, for
example, between the learning of concepts and the learning of principles? Dr. Gagné suggests that there are, indeed, differences and
goes on to cite the implications of these differences when it comes to
considering curriculum content and instructional methods. Before
you begin reading this article it might be useful to reflect a moment
on what you think the differences are between a concept and a
principle. In your mind, how do they differ? Would you teach for
one differently than for the other? As you read this article, keep in
mind the assumptions that you began with and then compare notes
at the end.*

For those interested in the design of effective instructional conditions
in the school situation, the learning of concepts is a matter of central
concern. School learning is preponderantly conceptual in nature. Nevertheless, there is great variation in the ways in which the term "concept" is
used by educational writers and, accordingly, a variety of descriptions of
the essential conditions for learning concepts by students. What *is* a
concept, anyhow, in a generic sense? How is it related to a "fact" or a
"principle" or a "generalization"? How is it related to methods of learning,
such as repetition, or to discovery?

Being a psychologist, I naturally think that one should attempt to seek

* Reprinted from *The School Review*, Autumn, 1965, Vol. 75, No. 3, 187–
196, by permission of the author and the publisher.

an answer to such basic definitional questions in that body of partially organized knowledge that has originated from controlled experimental research on behavior. For surely it is true that human learning of concepts can be studied in the framework of controlled laboratory experimentation. Whatever may be the variation in concepts of science, mathematics, language, art, or other content subjects, when people speak of concept-learning they must be referring to a kind of change in human performance that is independent of such content. And if it is independent, then it would seem possible to arrange a set of conditions under which the learning of a concept can be studied systematically.

When one examines the experimental literature on "concept forma-tion," "concept-learning," and related matters, it appears that here too the word "concept" is not being used with great consistency. Under the heading of concepts, one can find experimental studies dealing with such things as the learning of nonsense words, the acquiring of a new category word by children, the inferring of common functions of a set of objects, the combining of object qualities to achieve new categories, and even the solving of mathematical puzzles. All of these kinds of experiments un-doubtedly represent studies of learning. What is not entirely evident, however, is whether they reflect the learning of the same kinds of capabil-ities. It is truly difficult to describe what it is that these experimental studies have in common, or whether they are in fact devoted to the study of a common problem.

What does "learning a concept" mean? The approach I should like to take here is one that depends largely on observations of what happens in school learning. I do this, not to suggest that one can study the problem systematically in this way, but rather that perhaps one can begin to *define* the problem in such a manner. Perhaps if there can be agreement on what a concept is, and on how it is typically acquired in practice, then it will be possible to design experimental studies to find out the effects on its learning of various conditions of the learning situation.

An Initial Distinction

Some anticipation of my conclusions needs to be stated at the outset in order to spare you the details of a historical account. As a result of examining the kinds of situations that are said to represent concept-learning, I have arrived at the following propositions:

1. There are at least two different, important kinds of phenomena commonly referred to as concept-learning. One refers to the acquiring of a common response, often a name, to a class of objects varying in appearance. This may best be called *concept-learning*. The second refers to the combining of concepts into entities variously referred to as "ideas," "facts," "principles," or "rules." I prefer to call this *principle-learning*.

An example of these two different kinds of capabilities can perhaps be

illustrated by *number*. First of all, there are such things as number concepts. When a young child is able to correctly assign the name "three" to collections of any three objects, and at the same time not assign it to collections of two or four objects, it may be said that the child has learned the concept "three." But as mathematics educators will be quick to point out, this is only the most elementary meaning of what they have in mind when they speak of the child "knowing the concept three." Obviously, they want the child to know that three is a set that may be formed by joining the sets two and one, by taking one member away from the set four, by subtracting zero from the set three, by dividing six into two equal parts, by taking the square root of nine, and so on. Perhaps all of these together could form what might be called the "meaning of three." But each of these is a separate *idea* or *principle*. Each of them is achieved by *combining* the concept three (in the simple sense previously described) with some other concept, perhaps equally simple. There is, then, the concept three, the correct choosing of objects to which the name three can be legitimately assigned. And in addition there is a set of principles of three, which are actually combinations of simpler concepts.

2. The basic reason for the distinction between *concept* and *principle* is that they represent two different kinds of learned capabilities. In the first case, the criterion performance is simply being able to answer such a question as "Which of these collections of objects is three?" In the second case, the criterion performance is being able to *use* the concept three in combination, as in the question "What number added to two will give three?" These are quite different performances. Obviously, a child who is able to do the first may not have learned to do the second. If the second question is asked in a way which excludes the possibility of verbal parroting (as it needs to be), then it seems very likely that a child who does it correctly *will* be able to answer the simpler question correctly.

3. If it is true that knowing a concept and knowing a principle are two different capabilities, then it is also quite possible that the conditions for learning them are also different. I shall have more to say about this presently.

Learning Concepts

How is a concept learned? What are the conditions that need to obtain in the instructional situation in order for a new concept to be acquired? It should not be too difficult to identify these conditions. For one thing, we know that animals can acquire concepts. The Harlows' monkeys acquired the concept "odd" when they had learned to choose the odd one of any three objects presented, two of which were nearly identical. If two identical cubes and a sphere were presented, they would choose the sphere; if two boxes and a stick were presented, they would choose the stick.[2] It is instructive to note that what the monkeys learned was the capability of choosing an "odd" one, regardless of the physical appearances of the objects presented. They learned to respond to a *class* of situations which the experimenter could classify as "odd."

How did the animals learn the concept "odd"? Actually, it required a lot of practice with a variety of specific situations each containing "an odd one" which was correct and each differing from the preceding one in the actual objects it contained. Human beings, too, can learn concepts this same way. In fact, sometimes psychologists force them to learn concepts this way in order to analyze the phenomenon. But one should not be led to suppose that humans *have* to learn concepts this way. In one way or another, it is almost bound to be true that the process of concept-learning gets shortened by human beings. Language is one thing that operates to bring this about. For example, studies by the Kendlers indicate that four-year-olds learn a reversal problem by extended trial-and-error, whereas seven-year-olds learn to reverse a discrimination in virtually a single trial.[3] The strong suggestion is that seven-year-olds can say something like "opposite" to themselves, whereas four-year-olds do not yet have the language to do this.

Suppose the concepts "liquid" and "solid" are to be taught to a young child. It seems likely that the learning situation would be something like the following:[4]

1. Show the child a glass containing water and a glass containing a rock. Say "This is a solid" and "This is a liquid."

2. Using a different container, show the child some powdered substance in a pile in a container and some milk in another container. Say "This is a solid; this is a liquid."

3. Provide still a third example of solid and liquid, using different materials and containers.

4. Show the child a number of examples of liquids and solids which he has not seen before. Ask him to distinguish the liquids and the solids. (In this example, I assume the child has previously learned to repeat the words "liquid" and "solid" readily when he hears them; they are familiar in sound.)

The characteristics of this learning situation are, first, that several varieties of the class, themselves of varying physical appearance, were used to exemplify the class to be responded to. Second, words already familiar as responses were used to guide the learning. Under such circumstances, one might expect a child to learn a fairly adequate set of concepts of "liquid" and "solid." This is tested by asking the child to identify liquids and solids from a set that he has not seen before and that has not been used in the learning.

It is also important to note two things that were *not* present in this situation. First, this is not repeated trial-and-error learning. Only three examples are used, all different. The situation is not repeated identically over and over again. Second, although there is language here, it is by no means extensive. One has not tried to teach the concepts, for example, by making such verbal statements as "A liquid is a substance whose particles move freely over each other so that its mass assumes the shape of the container in which it is placed." This characteristic of a liquid is directly exhibited, rather than being verbally described.

Presumably, much the same sort of conditions may obtain when an older student learns a new technical term. Something like this must have to be done when a student learns a concept like "point of inflection" in mathematics, or when he learns concepts such as "cell," "nucleus," or "mitochondrion" in biology, or when he learns what a "simile" is in English. Sometimes, it is true, even more extensive verbalization is used, and I shall return to this point in a moment.

Learning Principles

What is meant by learning a principle (or rule)? And how does this differ from learning a concept? It needs to be recalled here that a principle is a combination of concepts.

Principles, being combinations, can become very complex. But let us start with an extremely simple one, such as "liquids pour." What kind of learning situation would be set up to bring about the learning of such a principle? Actually, there are two possibilities, and this does not make my task easier.[5]

Possibility one is this: After determining that the concepts "liquid" and "pour" can be identified, make the statement that "liquids pour." To test the learning, give the student a liquid in a container, and say, in effect, "Show me." This technique is what is often called *reception learning*, and there is little doubt that a very large proportion of school learning is basically of this sort, as D. P. Ausubel says.[6]

Possibility two is this: First determine that the concepts "liquid" and "pour" can be identified. Then, give the student a number of different liquids in a number of different containers. Ask him to demonstrate ways in which the liquids are alike and different from solids. One thing he will do is pour them; he may also make the verbal statement, "Liquids pour." This learning technique is called *discovery learning*, and there is some evidence, though not much, that the principle learned this way is better retained and transferred than is the case with reception learning.

Regardless of the learning technique, however, the important thing to note is that what is learned is a combination of concepts, called a principle. There is no particular reason to think that there are any important formal differences between a simple principle of this sort and the great variety of more complex principles that are learned at later ages, such as principles of using adjectives, or of dividing quantities into fractional parts, or of specifying the functions of a legislature, or of relating force and mass and acceleration.

The characteristics of the learning situation for principles are, first, that the concepts of which it is composed must be previously learned. Second, the principle is either stated verbally or discovered by the learner. The acquisition of the principle is tested by asking the student to demonstrate its application to a particular case which he has not encountered during the learning.

Note particularly that the conditions of learning for a principle are *not* the same as those for a concept. Perhaps the outstanding difference is that the concepts which make up the principle must already be learned; they are prerequisite to the learning. Second, there is no requirement to illustrate the principle by two or three examples (although of course this may be done *after* the learning, for other purposes). Third, it is possible to discover a principle, since the two or more concepts which make it up may be theoretically "combined" in a number of different ways. But pure discovery, without verbal guidance, does not usually occur as a process in the learning of concepts by human beings. One could more aptly describe what monkeys do in attaining concepts as "discovery." Since they cannot be guided by language, they must go through a rather lengthy trial-and-error procedure to get to the point where they can choose the odd one or go to the middle door. If human beings had to "discover" new concepts in this way, it would take them a very long time to learn all the things they have to learn. Using a familiar word accomplishes the instruction much more rapidly. But it also short-circuits the process of discovery.

Concept-Learning by Definition

While the distinction between concepts and principles in terms of conditions required for learning seems fairly clear, there is another source of confusion between them: When people are verbally sophisticated, they often learn concepts verbally, as pointed out by J. B. Carroll in a recent article.[7] That is to say, individuals learn concepts "by definition." If a person does not know the concept "caliche," he may learn what it is by reading or hearing the verbal statement, "a crust of calcium carbonate formed on stony soil in arid regions."

It is important to note that in this kind of learning situation, a *principle* is being used to provide instruction for the learning of a *concept*. The verbal statement itself is obviously a principle, because it contains several concepts: crust, calcium carbonate, stony soil, arid, region. And just as obviously, the learner will not be able to acquire "caliche" as a concept unless he does indeed know what each of these other concepts means, that is, unless he has previously learned each of them.

There can be little doubt that many new concepts are learned in this verbal manner by literate students and adults. Lest one think, however, that this method of learning concepts is a flawless one, a caution should be noted. A concept that is learned by way of verbally stated principles may have some inadequacies. For example, if an individual visits Texas for the first time in his life after hearing a verbal definition of caliche, will he make a certain identification of this material? Or will he be somewhat hesitant about it, and tend to confuse it with something else? Perhaps everyone would agree that for learning what caliche is, nothing can quite take the place of actually observing it.

This principle of "seeing is believing" is of more than passing importance to the problem of concept-learning. It is, for example, a fundamental reason why science educators are so firmly convinced of the value of the laboratory. If the student is to learn concepts like "power," "energy," "osmotic pressure," and many others, he can, to be sure, learn them in some sense by means of definitions. But there is a danger that the concepts he learns this way are inadequate in one way or another. Accordingly, most science educators would maintain that the performing of operations, including observation in the laboratory, is an essential part of the learning situation required for the learning of fully adequate, generalizable concepts. The role of the laboratory in school learning serves to remind us of the concrete basis for learning concepts and of the potential insufficiencies of concept-learning which is based solely upon verbally conveyed definitions. This is equally true in subjects other than science. The requirement for direct observation exists in all school subjects.

SUMMARY

In summary, it appears to be of some importance for the design of curriculum content and instructional method to recognize a distinction between concepts and principles. Different conditions are applicable to the learning of concepts and the learning of principles. Two differences that I have mentioned are perhaps of greatest importance. The first is that concepts are prior to principles and, in this sense, are simpler than principles. To learn a principle, one must have previously learned the concepts of which it is composed. A second difference pertains to verbal guidance versus pure discovery as a learning method. Learning concepts by pure discovery would appear to be an inhumanly inefficient thing to do, given the existence of language. But principles can be learned by discovery. There is some slight evidence to suggest that such a method of learning principles may be advantageous for retention and transfer, although it is likely to be more time-consuming for initial learning. Additional soundly designed research could well be devoted to this latter question.

FOOTNOTES:

[1] Paper given as part of a symposium on "Concept-Learning and the Curriculum" at the annual meeting of the American Educational Research Association, Chicago, Illinois, February 12, 1965.

2 H. F. Harlow, and M. K. Harlow, "Learning To Think," *Scientific American,* CLXXXI (1949), 36–39.

3 H. H. Kendler, and T. S. Kendler, "Effect of Verbalization on Reversal Shifts in Children," *Science,* CXLI (1961), 1619–20.

4 See my *The Conditions of Learning* (New York: Holt, Rinehart & Winston, 1965).

5 See *ibid.*

6 *The Psychology of Meaningful Verbal Learning* (New York: Grune & Stratton, 1963).

7 "Words, Meanings and Concepts," *Harvard Educational Review,* XXXIV (1964), 178–202.

4   *Learning and Thinking*[*][1]

BY JEROME S. BRUNER

EDITOR'S NOTE: In the previous article, Dr. Gagné discussed the different conditions applicable to the learning of concepts and the learning of principles. In this paper, Dr. Bruner goes a step further and describes the active pragmatic ideal of leaping the barrier from learning into thinking. Is it true that knowledge-getting is too often a passive activity in our classrooms? That we are better at teaching students how to answer questions than we are at teaching them how to ask questions? Too frequently, perhaps, we test students (at all levels) on what they know. What would happen if we attempted, as Dr. Bruner suggests, to judge students on the basis of what they can generate from what they know? Maybe, just maybe, we do separate learning from thinking. What do you think?

I have been engaged, these last few years, in research on what makes it possible for organisms—human and subhuman alike—to take advantage of past learning in attempting to deal with and master new problems before them now. It is a problem with a deceptively simple ring to it. In pursuit of it, my colleagues and I have found ourselves observing children in schoolrooms, watching them learning. It has been a revealing experience.

We have come to recognize in this work that one of the principal objectives of learning is to save us from subsequent learning. This seems a paradox, but it is not. Another way of putting the matter is to say that

[*] Jerome S. Bruner, "Learning and Thinking," *Harvard Educational Review,* Vol. 29, No. 3, Summer, 1959, pp. 184–192. Copyright © 1959 President and Fellows of Harvard College.

when we learn something, the objective is to learn it in such a way that we get a maximum of travel out of what we have learned. A homely example is provided by the relationship in arithmetic between addition and multiplication. If the principle of addition has been grasped in its deeper sense, in its generic sense, then it is unnecessary to learn multiplication. For, in principle, multiplication is only repeated addition. It is not, as we would say in our curricula, another "unit."

Learning something in a generic way is like leaping over a barrier. On the other side of the barrier is thinking. When the generic has been grasped, it is then that we are able to recognize the new problems we encounter as exemplars of old principles we have mastered. Once over the barrier, we are able to benefit from what William James long ago called "the electric sense of analogy."

There are two interesting features in generic learning—in the kind of learning that permits us to cross the barrier into thinking. One of them is *organization;* the other is *manipulation.* If we are to use our past learning, we must organize it in such a way that it is no longer bound to the specific situation in which the learning occurred. Let me give an example from the history of science. It would have been possible for Galileo to have published a handbook for the distances traversed per unit time by falling bodies. School boys for centuries thereafter could easily have been tortured by the task of having to remember the Galilean tables. Such tables, cumbersome though they might have been, would have contained all the necessary information for dealing with free-falling bodies. Instead, Galileo had the inspiration to reorganize this welter of information into a highly simplified form. You recall the compact expression $S = \frac{1}{2} gt^2$: it not only summarizes all possible handbooks but organizes their knowledge in a way that makes manipulation possible. Not only do we know the distances fallen, but we can use the knowledge for bodies that fall anywhere, in any gravitational field—not just our own.

One of the most notable things about the human mind is its limited capacity for dealing at any one moment with diverse arrays of information. It has been known for a long time that we can deal only with about seven independent items of information at once; beyond that point we exceed our "channel capacity," to use our current jargon. We simply cannot manipulate large masses of information. Because of these limits, we must condense and recode. The seven things we deal with must be worth their weight. A simple formula that can regenerate the distance fallen by any free body, past or future, is under these conditions highly nutritious for its weight. Good organization achieves the kind of economical representation of facts that makes it possible to use the facts in the future. Sheer brute learning, noble though it may be, is not enough. Facts simply learned without a generic organization are the naked and useless untruth. The proper reward of learning is not that it pleases the teacher or the parents, nor is it that we become "quiz kids." The proper reward is that we can now use what we have learned, can cross the barrier from learning into thinking. Are we mindful of these matters in our conduct of teaching?

What has been said thus far must seem singularly lacking in relevance to magic, to art, and to poetry. It appears to relate principally to the learning of mathematics, science, and the social studies. But there is an analogous point to be made about the learning of the arts and literature. If one has read literature and beheld works of art in such a way as to be able to think with their aid, then one has also grasped a deeper, simplifying principle. The underlying principle that gives one the power to use literature and the arts in one's thinking is not of the order of a generic condensation of knowledge. Rather it is metaphoric in nature, and perhaps the best way of describing this class of principles is to call them guiding myths.

Let me take an example from mythology. Recall when you read for the first time the story of Perseus slaying the hateful Medusa. You recall that to look directly upon the Medusa was to be turned to stone. The secret of Perseus was to direct the killing thrust of his sword by the reflection of Medusa on his polished shield. It is an exciting story, full of the ingenuity that Hercules had taught us to expect. Beneath the story, beneath all great stories, there is a deeper metaphoric meaning. I did not understand this meaning for many years, indeed, not until my son asked me what the myth of Perseus "meant." It occurred to me that the polished shield might symbolize all of the devices be which we are able to take action against evil without becoming contaminated by it. The law suggested itself as one such device, enabling us to act against those who trespassed against morality without ourselves having to trespass in our action. I do not wish to hold a brief for my interpretation of the Perseus myth. But I would like to make one point about it.

Man must cope with a relatively limited number of plights—birth, growth, loneliness, the passions, death, and not very many more. They are plights that are neither solved nor by-passed by being "adjusted." An adjusted man must face his passions just as surely as he faces death. I would urge that a grasp of the basic plights through the basic myths of art and literature provides the organizing principle by which knowledge of the human condition is rendered into a form that makes thinking possible, by which we go beyond learning to the use of knowledge. I am not suggesting that the Greek myths are better than other forms of literature. I urge simply that there be exposure to, and interpretation of, literature that deals deeply with the human condition. I have learned as much from Charley Brown of *Peanuts* as I have learned from Perseus. The pablum school readers, stripped of rich imagery in the interest of "readability," stripped of passion in the erroneous belief that the deeper human condition will not interest the child—these are no more the vehicles for getting over the barrier to thinking than are the methods of teaching mathematics by a rote parroting at the blackboard.

II

I should like to consider now some conditions in our schools today that promote and inhibit progress across the barrier from learning to thinking. I should point out in advance that I am not very cheerful on this subject.

The Passivity of Knowledge-Getting

I have been struck during the past year or so, sitting in classrooms as an observer, by the passivity of the process we call education. The emphasis is upon gaining and storing information, gaining it and storing it in the form in which it is presented. We carry the remainder in long division so, peaches are grown in Georgia, transportation is vital to cities, New York is our largest port, and so on. Can the facts or the methods presented be mimicked? If so, the unit is at an end. There is little effort indeed which goes into the process of putting the information together, finding out what is generic about it. Long division is a skill, like threading a needle. The excitement of it as a method of partitioning things that relates it to such matters as subtraction is rarely stressed. One of the great inventions of man—elementary number theory—is presented as a cookbook. I have yet to see a teacher present one way of doing division and then put it squarely to the class to suggest six other ways of doing it—for there are at least six other ways of doing it than any one that might be taught in a school. So too with algebra. Algebra is not a set of rules for manipulating numbers and letters except in a trivial sense. It is a way of thinking, a way of coping with the drama of the unknown. Lincoln Steffens, in his *Autobiography,* complains upon his graduation from the University of California that his teachers had taught him only of the known, how to commit it to mind, and had done little to instruct him in the art of approaching the unknown, the art of posing questions. How does one ask questions about the unknown? Well, algebra is one technique, the technique for arranging the known in such a way that one is enabled to discern the value of an unknown quantity. It is an enriching strategy, algebra, but only if it is grasped as an extended instance of common sense.

Once I did see a teacher specifically encourage a class to organize and use minimal information to draw a maximum number of inferences. The teacher modeled his technique, I suppose, on the tried method of the storyteller. He presented the beginnings of the Whiskey Rebellion and said to his pupils, much in the manner of Ellery Queen speaking to his readers, "You now have enough to reconstruct the rest of the story. Let's see if we can do it." He was urging them to cross the barrier from learning into thinking. It is unhappily true that this is a rare exception in our schools.

So knowledge-getting becomes passive. Thinking is the reward for learning, and we may be systematically depriving our students of this reward as far as school learning is concerned.

One experiment which I can report provides encouragement. It was devised and carried out by the research group with which I am associated at Harvard in collaboration with teachers in the fifth grade of a good public school. It is on the unpromising topic of the geography of the North Central States and is currently in progress so that I cannot give all of the results. We hit upon the happy idea of presenting this chunk of geography not as a set of knowns, but as a set of unknowns. One class was presented blank maps, containing only tracings of the rivers and lakes of the area as well as the natural resources. They were asked as a first exercise to indicate where the principal cities would be located, where the railroads, and where the main highways. Books and maps were not permitted and "looking up the facts" was cast in a sinful light. Upon completing this exercise, a class discussion was begun in which the children attempted to justify why the major city would be here, a large city there, a railroad on this line, etc.

The discussion was a hot one. After an hour, and much pleading, permission was given to consult the rolled up wall map. I will never forget one young student, as he pointed his finger at the foot of Lake Michigan, shouting, "Yipee, *Chicago* is at the end of the pointing-down lake." And another replying, "Well, OK: but Chicago's no good for the rivers and it should be here where there is a big city (St. Louis)." These children were thinking, and learning was an instrument for checking and improving the process. To at least a half dozen children in the class it is not a matter of indifference that no big city is to be found at the junction of Lake Huron, Lake Michigan, and Lake Ontario. They were slightly shaken up transportation theorists when the facts were in.

The children in another class taught conventionally, got their facts all right, sitting down, benchbound. And that was that. We will see in six months which group remembers more. But whichever does, one thing I will predict. One group learned geography as a set of rational acts of induction—that cities spring up where there is water, where there are natural resources, where there are things to be processed and shipped. The other group learned passively that there were arbitrary cities at arbitrary places by arbitrary bodies of water and arbitrary sources of supply. One learned geography as a form of activity. The other stored some names and positions as a passive form of registration.

The Episodic Curriculum

In a social studies class of an elementary school in a well-to-do suburb of one of our great eastern cities, I saw groups of twelve-year-old children doing a "project" on the southeastern states. Each team was gathering facts that might eventually end up on a map or a chart or some other graphic device. The fact-gathering was atomized and episodic. Here were the

industrial products of North Carolina. There was the list of the five principal cities of Georgia. I asked the children of one team what life would be
like and what people would worry about in a place where the principal
products were peanuts, cotton, and peaches. The question was greeted as
"unfair." They were gathering facts.

It is not just the schools. The informational environment of America
seems increasingly to be going through such an atomization. Entertainment
is in fifteen minute episodes on TV, to be taken while sitting down. The
school curriculum is built of episodic units, each a task to itself: "We have
now finished addition. Let us now move to multiplication." Even in our
humor the "gag" threatens to replace the shrewd observer of the human
comedy. I have seen an elementary school play fashioned entirely on a
parody of radio commercials. It was a brave effort to tie the 10-second
atoms together.

I do not wish to make it seem as if our present state of education is a
decline from some previous Golden Age. For I do not think there has ever
been a Golden Age in American public education. The difference now is
that we can afford dross less well than ever before. The volume of positive
knowledge increases at a rapid rate. Atomizing it into facts-to-be-filed is not
likely to produce the kind of broad grasp that will be needed in the world
of the next quarter century. And it is certainly no training for the higher
education that more and more of our children will be getting.

I have not meant the above as a plea for the "central subject" or the
"project" method of teaching. It is, rather, a plea for the recognition of the
continuity of knowledge. One hears professional educators speak of "coverage," that certain topics must be covered. There are indeed many things
that must be covered, but they are not unconnected things. The object of
learning is to gain facts in a context of connectivity that permits the facts to
be used generatively. The larger the number of isolated facts, the more
staggering the number of connections between them—unless one can
reduce them to some deeper order. Not all of them can be. Yet it is an ideal
worth striving for, be it in the fifth grade or in graduate school. As Robert
Oppenheimer put it in a recent address before the American Academy,
"Everything cannot be connected with everything in the world we live in.
Everything can be connected with anything."

The Embarrassment of Passion

I should like to consider now the guiding myth. Let me begin with a
summary of the young Christopher Columbus as he is presented in a
popular social studies textbook. Young Chris is walking along the water
front in his home town and gets to wondering where all those ships go.
Eventually he comes back to his brother's cobbler shop and exclaims, "Gee,
Bart, I wonder where all those ships go, whether maybe if they just kept
going they wouldn't come back because the world is round." Bart replies
with pleasant brotherly encouragement. Chris is a well-adjusted kid. Bart is

a nice big brother. And where is the passion that drove this obsessed man across uncharted oceans? What impelled this Columbus with such force that he finally enlisted the aid of Ferdinand and Isabella over the protest of their advisors? Everything is there in the story except the essential truth— the fanatical urge to explore in an age of exploration, the sense of an expanding world. Columbus did not have a schoolboy's whim, nor was he the well-adjusted grownup of this account. He was a man driven to explore, to control. The justification for the pablum that makes up such textbooks is that such accounts as these touch more directly on the life of the child.

What is this "life of the child" as seen by text writers and publishers? It is an image created out of an ideal of adjustment. The ideal of adjustment has little place for the driven man, the mythic hero, the idiosyncratic style. Its ideal is mediocentrism, reasonableness above all, being nice. Such an ideal does not touch closely the deeper life of the child. It does not appeal to the dark but energizing forces that lie close beneath the surface. The Old Testament, the Greek Myths, the Norse legends—these are the embarrassing chronicles of men of passion. They were devised to catch and preserve the power and tragedy of the human condition—and its ambiguity, too. In their place, we have substituted the noncontroversial and the banal.

Here a special word is needed about the concept of "expressing yourself," which is our conception of how one may engage the deeper impulses of the child. I have seen a book review class in a public school in which the children had the choice of reporting on any book they wished to choose, in or out of the school library, and where the discussion by the other children had to do entirely with the manner in which the reciting child presented his material. Nothing was said about the book in the discussion. The emphasis was on nice presentation, and whether the book sounded interesting. I have no quarrel with rewarding self-expression. I wonder simply whether it is not perhaps desirable, too, to make known the canons of excellence. The children in this class were learning to be seductive in their recounting; they were not concerned with an honest accounting of the human condition. The books they had read were cute, there was no excitement in them, none to be extracted. Increasingly the children in American elementary schools grow out of touch with the guiding myths. Self-expression is not a substitute. Adjustment is a worthy ideal, if not an ennobling one. But when we strive to attain it by shutting our eyes to the turmoils of human life, we will not get adjustment, but a niggling fear of the unusal and the excellent.

The Quality of Teachers

I do not wish to mince words. The educational and cultural level of the majority of American teachers is not impressive. On the whole they do not have a good grasp of the subject matter that they are teaching; courses on method will not replace the absent subject matter. In time and with teaching experience this deficiency is often remedied. But in so many cases there is no time: the turnover in the teaching profession as we all know is enormous; the median number of year of teaching before departure for marriage or motherhood is around three.

This leaves us with a small core of experienced teachers. Do we use them to teach the new teachers on the job? No. The organization of the school with respect to utilization of talent is something short of imaginative. It consists of a principal on top and a group of discrete teachers beneath her, and that is all. In large metropolitan high schools this is sometimes supplemented by having departments at the head of which is an experienced teacher. The communication that goes on between teachers is usually at a highly informal level and can scarcely be called comprehensive. It is usually about problem-children, not about social studies or mathematics or how to bring literature alive.

I would urge, and I believe that educators have taken steps in this direction, that we use our more experienced teachers for on-the-job training of less experienced, new teachers. I would also urge that there be established some means whereby the substantive topics taught in our elementary and high schools be included in some kind of special extension program provided by our eighteen hundred colleges and universities in the United States for the benefit of teachers. I am not speaking only of teachers colleges, but rather of all institutions of higher learning. Institutions of higher learning have a responsibility to the lower schools, and it can be exercised by arranging for continuous contact between those, for example, who teach history at the college level and those who are teaching history or social studies at the lower levels. And so, too, with literature or mathematics, or languages. To assume that somehow a teacher can be "prepared" simply by going through teacher training and then by taking courses on methods in summer school is, I think, fallacious. Often it is the case that the teacher, like her students, has not learned the material well enough to cross the barrier from learning to thinking.

III

It is quite plain, I think, that the task of improving the American Schools is not simply one of technique—however comforting it would be to some professional educators to think so. What is at issue, rather, is a deeper problem, one that is more philosophical than psychological or technological in scope. Let me put it in all innocence. What do we conceive to be the end product of our educational effort? I cannot help but feel that this rather overly simplified question has become obscured in cant. There is such an official din in support of the view that we are "training well-rounded human beings to be responsible citizens" that one hesitates to raise the question whether such an objective is a meaningful guide to what one does in classroom teaching. Surely the objective is worthy, and it has influenced the techniques of education in America, not always happily. For much of what we have called the embarrassment of passion can, I think, be traced to this objective, and so too the blandness of the social studies curriculum. The ideal, sadly, has also led to the standardization of mediocrity by a failure of the schools to challenge the full capacity of the talented student.

Since the war, there has been a perceptible shift in the problems being faced by schools and parents alike. It is the New Competition. Will Johnny and Sally be able to get into the college of their first choice or, indeed, into any college at all? The origins of the concern are obvious enough—the "baby bulge" has made itself felt. The results are not all bad, I would urge, or need not be. There are, to be sure, severe problems of overcrowding that exacerbate the difficulties already inherent in public education. And it is true that parental pressures for grades and production are increasing the proportion of children with "learning blocks" being referred to child guidance clinics.

But the pressures and the competition are also rekindling our awareness of excellence and how it may be nurtured. The shake-up of our smugness by the evident technical thrust of the Soviet Union has added to this awareness. Let me urge that it is this new awareness that requires shaping of expression in the form of a new set of ideals. Grades, admission to college, followed by admission to graduate school—these are surely not the ideals but, rather, the external signs.

Perhaps the fitting ideal is precisely as we have described it earlier in these pages, the active pragmatic ideal of leaping the barrier from learning into thinking. It matters not *what* we have learned. What we can *do* with what we have learned: this is the issue. The pragmatic argument has long been elaborated on extrinsic grounds, that the higher one has gone in the educational system the greater the economic gain. Indeed, at least one eminent economist has proposed that parents finance college education for their children by long-term loans to be repaid by the children on the almost certain knowledge that higher earning results from such education. All of this is the case, and it is indeed admirable that educational progress and economic success are so intimately linked in our society. I would only suggest that the pragmatic ideal be applied also to the intrinsic aspects of education. Let us not judge our students simply on *what* they know. That is the philosophy of the quiz program. Rather, let them be judged on what they can generate from what they know—how well they can leap the barrier from learning to thinking.

FOOTNOTE:

[1] Paper presented to Massachusetts Council on Teacher Education, February 13, 1958.

5   *Stability of Achievement and Recognition Seeking Behaviors from Early Childhood Through Adulthood*[*][1]

BY HOWARD A. MOSS AND JEROME KAGAN

EDITOR'S NOTE: Before you begin reading this article, speculate a little. You might even reflect a bit over your own life—particularly what you can remember about your early elementary school years. Do you see any relationships between your achievement strivings during the first four years of school and your subsequent achievement later on in school? What part did your mother play in your cognitive-intellectual development? Was it an active part? Passive? How do you suppose your mother's involvement or lack of involvement influenced the sort of learner you are today? You may find some interesting resemblances between your own life and the lives of the 71 subjects in this longitudinal study which deals with the long-term stability of achievement and recognition seeking behaviors over a fourteen-year period.

The supposition that selected adult response patterns are established at an early age is a primary assumption of developmental theory. Although literary documents and psychotherapy protocols have provided anecdotal support for this hypothesis, more objective validation has been difficult to obtain. The present paper is a second report that has emerged from a larger project on the stability of childhood behavior. The first paper indicated

* Reprinted from the *Journal of Abnormal and Social Psychology*, 1961, Vol. 62, by permission of the senior author and the American Psychological Association.

that dependent behavior in girls showed moderately high stability from the early school years through young adulthood (Kagan & Moss, 1960). The present report is concerned with the developmental consistency of two related behaviors: the tendency to strive for (a) mastery of selected skills (achievement behavior), and (b) social recognition through acquisition of specific goals or behaviors (recognition behavior).

The achievement variable emphasizes mastery of intellectual, athletic, mechanical, and artistic skills as well as competence in specialized crafts. Social recognition is obtained through acquisition of most of the above behaviors. For intellectual competence, athletic ability, acquisition of money, and positions of power in social groups are the primary methods of obtaining social recognition in the cultural milieu of our middle class population. Thus, the overt behaviors involved in achievement and recognition strivings overlap to some degree.

In an attempt to differentiate between these two variables, the investigators evaluated the degree to which the individual's mastery behavior was directed at satisfaction of an internal standard of excellence in order to gain self-approval (achievement motivation), in contrast to seeking approval from the social environment (recognition motivation). This is a difficult differentiation to make. The data to be presented reveal a high, positive correlation between ratings of these two behavioral variables. This interdependence suggests that it may be impossible to measure the "desire to improve at a skill" independent of the individual's "desire for social recognition" for this improvement.

METHOD

Subjects and General Procedure

The subjects were 36 males and 35 females from the Fels Research Institute's longitudinal population. They were enrolled in the project at birth, during the years 1929–1939. At the time of a recent adult assessment (1957–1959) they were between 20 and 29 years of age. The subjects came from predominantly middle class backgrounds, over half of the group were married; 70% had college degrees or were enrolled in a college, and the majority were living within a 30-mile radius of the institute. The adult group included 55 Protestants, 15 Catholics, and 1 Jew.

The heart of this study consists of correlations between the childhood information on these subjects and their adult behavior .The childhood data included (a) longitudinal observations of the child's behavior during the first 14 years of life in a variety of settings, (b) observations of the mother-child interaction during these years, (c) TAT protocols obtained in adolescence, and (d) annual Stanford-Benet intelligence test scores during the ages 5–11. Although the data collected during adulthood (age range

20–29) sampled a variety of techniques, this report utilizes only two sources of adult information, 5 hours of interview, and a TAT protocol.

Longitudinal Observations: Birth to Age 14

As a standard procedure of the Fels longitudinal program, psychologists or psychologically trained personnel summarized their observations of the child in the home, in the Fels nursery school and day camp, and in the subject's public school. The home reports were based on a visit to the home where mother and child were observed for half-day sessions. These home visits were generally made semiannually for the first 6 years of life and annually from 6 to 12. Most of the mothers were interviewed each year for the first 14 years of the child's life. The nursery school summaries were based on semiannual, free-play sessions from age 2.5 to 5. The sessions usually consisted of 15 consecutive half-day periods in groups of 10–12 children. Day camp typically consisted of an annual 2 week session of half-day periods during age 6–10 in which free and structured group activities were observed. Public school visits, made semiannually, consisted of a half-day observation of the child in his routine classroom activities. Finally, the subjects of age 6–14 were interviewed each year at the institute and a summary of the interview was prepared. All of the longitudinal reports for each subject were collated in chronological order and placed in the subject's individual file.

Scoring of longitudinal variables. A comprehensive list of rating scale variables (seven-point scale) was defined for the purpose of evaluating the narrative material just outlined. The material for each subject was divided into four age periods: 0–3, 3–6, 6–10, and 10–14. The senior author, who had no knowledge of the adult psychological status of the subjects, first read all the information for each subject for age 0–3 and made those ratings for which he had adequate information. Following a period of interpolated work, he studied each subject's material for age 3–6 and again made his ratings. This procedure was repeated for ages 6–10 and 10–14. A period of approximately 6 months intervened between the evaluation of the data for any one subject for each age period. This paper deals only with the stability of achievement and recognition behaviors and abridged definitions of these variables follow.

Childhood Variables

Achievement behavior: (Rated for ages 0–3, 3–6, and 6–10). This variable assessed the degree to which the subject tended to persist with challenging tasks, games, and problems, and his involvement in activities in which a standard of excellence was applicable. For 0–3, emphasis was given to persistence with perceptual-motor activities (e.g., making block towers, stringing beads, drawing, and coloring). For ages 3–6 and 6–10 the greatest weight was given to interest in and persistence with intellectual, mechanical, athletic, and fine motor activities.

For age 10–14 the general achievement variable defined above was differentiated into three variables dealing with different achievement areas (intellectual, mechanical, and athletic).

Intellectual achievement: (Rated for age 10–14). This variable assessed the degree to which the subject attempted to master language and numerical skills and showed involvement in the acquisition of knowledge.

Mechanical achievement: (Rated for age 10–14). This variable assessed the degree to which the subject attempted to master mechanical skills and manifested involvement in activities such as carpentry, construction of model vehicles, engines and motors, and craft work.

Athletic achievement: (Rated for age 10–14). This variable assessed the degree to which the subject attempted to master and showed involvement in athletic activities. These behaviors included swimming, hiking, baseball, football, basketball, tennis, acrobatics, and track events.

Recognition seeking behavior: (Rated for ages 6–10 and 10–14). This variable assessed the subject's striving to obtain goals that led to recognition from parents, teachers, and peers. The behaviors emphasized in the rating were (a) grades in school and school honors, (b) stated desire for status-laden vocations or ostentatious material goods, (c) striving for leadership in teams or clubs, (d) attempts to get recognition from farm activities (e.g., raise the best calf, the highest corn, etc.).

Maternal Variables

Maternal acceleration of developmental skills in child: (Rated for ages 0–3, 3–6, and 6–10). The home visits and maternal interviews yielded information on the mother's behavior and attitudes toward her child. The maternal variable that is directly relevant to the subject's achievement behavior was called *maternal acceleration*. It was defined in terms of the degree to which the mother showed concern over the subject's cognitive and motor development, and the degree to which she exhibited desires for precocious achievement in her child. The rating reflected the degree to which the mother "pushed" the subject's development beyond his abilities and her concern with his general achievement level.

Adult Interview

The junior author, who had no knowledge of the subject's childhood information, interviewed each subject and rated him (seven-point scale) on a variety of variables. The definitions of the variables related to achievement and recognition seeking behaviors follow.

Achievement behavior.   This variable evaluated the subject's behavioral attempts to master tasks for which "self-satisfaction" rather than social recognition was the *salient* goal. In achievement behavior, the subject was striving to attain a *self-imposed* standard of excellence. The rating was based on the subject's emphasis and concern with task mastery in his job and avocational pursuits.

Recognition seeking behavior.   This variable evaluated the subject's behavioral attempt to obtain symbols of status and social recognition. The rating was based on evidences of strivings for (*a*) vocational recognition, (*b*) academic awards and honors, (*c*) positions of leadership or recognition in community or vocational groups, (*d*) concern with conspicuous material display, (*e*) striving for upward mobility in social class position.

Concern with intellectual competence.   This variable assessed the value the subject placed upon intelligence, knowledge, academic achievement, and intellectual superiority regardless of whether the goal was to satisfy inner standards or to obtain social recognition.

Reliability of Longitudinal and Adult Interview Ratings

A random sample of 32 tape recorded adult interviews were independently studied and rated by a second judge to assess the reliability of the junior author's adult ratings. The reliabilities of the longitudinal variables were also assessed through independent ratings, by a second judge, of samples of 50–60 cases at each of the four age periods. The reliabilities of the adult and child ratings were determined by product-moment correlation coefficients. For the adult ratings of achievement behavior, recognition behavior, and intellectual concern the reliability coefficients were .84, .99, and .98, respectively. With the exception of one child behavior variable, the reliabilities of the longitudinal ratings ranged from .74 to .90 with a median coefficient of .81. The one low longitudinal reliability was for child's achievement for age 0–3 ($r = + .35$; $p < .01$; two-tailed).

TAT Achievement Fantasy: Adolescent and Adult Protocols

Early adolescent (median age of 14–6) protocols were available for 67 of the 71 subjects, and all 71 subjects were administered TAT stimuli following the adult interview. The adolescent protocol was based on seven cards from the Murray (1943) series (Cards 1, 5, 14, 17BM, 3BM, 6BM, and 3GF). The male adult protocol was based on 13 cards (4, 8BM, 7BM, 6BM, 12M, 17BM, 13MF, 14, 3BM, 5, 1, 3GF, and 18GF). The adult females were also administered 13 cards (4, 6GF, 12F, 2, 8GF, 17BM, 13MF, 14, 3BM, 5, 1, 3GF, and 18GF). For both the adolescent and adult protocols achievement themes were scored according to the scheme described by McClelland, Atkinson, Clark, and Lowell (1953). Since incidence of the subcategories of the McClelland scoring system were infrequent, only stories in which achievement behavior was the major aspect of the plot were considered. These are scored Ach Th in the McClelland scheme. For the adolescent protocol, there was a lack of comparability among the examiners with respect to the inquiry questions and only the spontaneous verbalization of the subject was scored. Agreement between two independent coders was 95%. The longitudinal and interview ratings of achievement and recognition behavior were made *without knowledge* of the subject's adolescent or adult TAT stories. Thus, the behavior and interview ratings were independent of each other and of the TAT thematic scores.

IQ Change

Each child was given the Stanford-Binet, Forms L and M alternately, annually from ages 5 through 11 by the same psychologist. The mean IQ for the entire Fels population is about 120 (SD of 15). For each subject, a smoothed plot of his IQ scores was obtained by averaging his three IQ scores around each age. For example, a child's smoothed or average IQ at age 6 was the result of averaging his IQ scores at ages 5, 6, and 7; his smoothed IQ at age 10 was the average of his IQs at ages 9, 10, and 11. This procedure tends to remove the chance variation associated with any one IQ score and has been used in other studies (Kagan, Sontag, Baker, & Nelson, 1958; Sontag, Baker, & Nelson, 1958). Each subject's smoothed IQ at age 6 was then subtracted from his smoothed IQ at age 10 and the resulting difference was used as a measure of IQ change. As with achievement themes, the child and adult achievement ratings were made without knowledge of the subject's IQ or his IQ change score.

In summary, four independent sources of data were analyzed; child and maternal behaviors for the first 14 years of life, adult behavior, adolescent and adult achievement themes, and childhood IQ change scores.

Statistical Analysis

Relationships among the following variables were evaluated: (a) childhood achievement and maternal acceleration ratings with the adult interview ratings, (b) adolescent achievement themes with adult achievement themes, (c) adolescent and adult achievement themes with the longitudinal and adult ratings, and (d) IQ change scores with the childhood and adult ratings. Product-moment correlations were used except when the TAT achievement score was involved. Since achievement themes were not normally distributed, contingency coefficients were used for all tests of association using this variable. Mechanical achievement for age 10–14 was the only variable for which there was a significant sex difference; the boys having a higher mean rating than the girls ($p < .05$; two-tailed).

RESULTS

Stability of Achievement and Recognition Behaviors

Table 1 presents the relationships between the child and adult ratings of achievement and recognition behavior, as well as the relation between maternal acceleration and the adult achievement variables. There are several important results in this table. The rating of achievement behavior for age 6–10 showed a significant, positive association with all three adult variables for both sexes. The rating of achievement for age 3–6 was predictive of adult behavior for the females but not for the males, a finding that suggests the earlier emergence of stable achievement strivings in girls' development than in boys. Of the three achievement behaviors rated for age 10–14, only intellectual mastery was predictive of adult achievement for both sexes. Involvement in mechanical activities was predictive of adult achievement for boys but not for girls. Athletic achievement showed no relationship to the rating of general adult achievement, and was negatively associated with intellectual concern for adult males ($p < .02$).

Recognition seeking behavior for age 6–10 was also predictive of adult achievement behavior. A few of the child variables were moderately intercorrelated and the three adult variables were highly intercorrelated (Tables 4, 5, and 6). This lack of independence makes some of the stability correlations between childhood and adulthood somewhat redundant.

Maternal Acceleration and Adult Behavior

Maternal concern with the child's developmental progress during the first 10 years of life showed low to moderate correlations with adult achievement behavior. The maternal rating for age 6–10 was not a better predictor of adult behavior than the maternal rating for the first 3 years of life. Moreover, the age 0–3 rating was associated with all three adult, achievement variables for girls, while it predicted only recognition behavior for adult males.

Stability of TAT Achievement Fantasy

Although different sets of TAT pictures were used in obtaining the adolescent and adult protocols, the three pictures that usually elicited achievement stories were presented at both administrations. Cards 1, 14, and 17BM, which elicited 77% of all the achievement themes, were common to both protocols. The strong tendency of these particular cards to elicit achievement themes has been noted in another study (Kagan & Moss, 1959). A typical achievement theme to Card 1 concerned a boy who wanted to master the violin and/or become a famous violinist. A typical achievement story to Card 17BM involved a person who was in a rope climbing contest and wanted to do his best to win. A common achievement story to Card 14 concerned an artist or student who had been working hard and was looking forward to fame and success as a result of his accomplishments.

The stability of the TAT achievement score between the adolescent and adult protocols was determined through the use of contingency coefficients. The stability coefficients were .34, .36, and .31 for boys, girls, and total group ($p < .10$, $< .05$, $< .02$; one-tailed). Thus, achievement themes also showed some degree of stability over this 10-year period. These data extend the findings of an earlier investigation (Kagan & Moss, 1959), in which the authors reported a 3 year stability coefficient of .32 ($p < .01$) for achievement themes obtained at median ages of 8–9 and 11–6. The stability coefficients between the adolescent and adult protocols are of the same magnitude as those found for the earlier age period.

Validity of Achievement Themes: Relations with Child and Adult Behavior

Contingency coefficients were computed relating the occurrence of adolescent and adult achievement themes with the longitudinal and adult achievement ratings. These results are presented in Table 2. The highest and most consistent relations were between the adult achievement themes and adult interview ratings. The only significant relation between adult themes and the childhood ratings held for mechanical achievement ($C = +.63$; $p < .001$ for boys, and $-.50$; $p < .02$ for girls).

The adolescent TAT was also more predictive of adult behavior than it was of the childhood ratings. Adolescent achievement themes predicted adult achievement behavior for women ($C = +.44$; $p < .01$) and intellectual concerns for men ($C = +.44$; $p < .01$). Adolescent achievement themes showed minimal association with the child's achievement behavior. The only significant positive association was with age 3–6 achievement for boys. Once again the rating of mechanical achievement for girls was negatively associated with achievement themes. This negative correlation may be due to the fact that this is the only variable for which markedly different behavioral referents were used in rating the two sexes. For boys, involvement in carpentry, engines, motors, and model airplanes was emphasized in the rating. These activities are sex-typed and girls

TABLE 1: *Relation between longitudinal ratings of childhood achievement and early maternal acceleration with adult achievement behavior (product-moment correlations)*

Childhood Variables	Age	Adult Variables					
		Achievement		Recognition		Intellectual Concerns	
		Males	Females	Males	Females	Males	Females
Recognition	6–10	.47***	.40**	.42**	.48***	.37**	.55****
	10–14	.25	.20	.36*	.39**	.24	.40**
Achievement	0–3	−.12	−.02	.01	−.22	−.08	−.02
	3–6	−.03	.45**	−.11	.49***	.13	.44**
	6–10	.46***	.38**	.57****	.51***	.69****	.49***
Achievement							
Intellectual	10–14	.40**	.42**	.60****	.56***	.66****	.49***
Mechanical	10–14	.20	.20	.46**	.02	.47**	.27
Athletic	10–14	−.18	.01	−.17	−.09	−.47**	.02
Material Acceleration	0–3	.22	.36*	.44*	.41*	.09	.36*
	3–6	.31	.09	.24	.12	.42**	.12
	6–10	.14	.33*	.16	.23	.32*	.43**

* *p* < .05; *one-tailed.*
** *p* < .02; *one-tailed.*
*** *p* < .01; *one-tailed.*
**** *p* < .001; *one-tailed.*

showed no interest in them. Participation in craft work (making jewelry, leather articles) and sewing was also used as evidence of involvement in mechanical activities and girls tended to choose these behaviors.

TABLE 2: *Relation between TAT achievement themes and child and adult achievement behavior (contingency coefficients)*

Longitudinal Variable	Age	Adolescent TAT (Median age 4–6)		Adult TAT (Median age 25)	
		Males	Females	Males	Females
Recognition	6–10	.21	.17	.26	.22
	10–14	−.20	−.18	−.31	.39
Achievement	0–3	−.15	−.25	−.20	.16
	3–6	.42*	.19	.19	.36
	6–10	.24	.15	.13	.30
Achievement					
Intellectual	10–14	.30	−.25	.26	.16
Mechanical	10–14	.31	−.62***	.63****	−.50**
Athletic	10–14	−.20	.12	.12	.17
Maternal Acceleration	0–3	.11	.51**	.25	−.08
	3–6	.37	.23	.27	.28
	6–10	.51***	.26	.24	.41*
Adult interview variables (median age 25)					
Recognition		.17	.26	.40**	.25****
Achievement		.19	.44***	.37*	.52****
Intellectual Concerns		.44***	.25	.31	.59****

  * *p < .05; one-tailed.*
 ** *p < .02; one-tailed.*
 *** *p < .01; one-tailed.*
**** *p < .001; one-tailed.*

Maternal acceleration during the first 10 years of life showed suggestive relationships with the adolescent achievement themes. For example, maternal acceleration for age 0–3 predicted achievement themes at adolescence for girls (C = + .51; $p < .02$), but not for boys. Maternal acceleration for age 6–10 predicted adolescent achievement themes for boys (C = + .51; $p < .01$) and adult achievement themes for girls (C = + .41; $p < .05$).

In summary, the adult and adolescent TAT stories showed moderate correlations with adult achievement but minimal association with the childhood achievement ratings. Maternal acceleration was associated, to some degree, with adolescent achievement themes.

IQ Increase and Achievement Behavior

The difference between the child's smoothed IQ at age 6 and 10 was used as a measure of IQ change. Earlier studies (Kagan *et al.*, 1958; Sontag *et al.*, 1958) have demonstrated that the amount of increase in IQ correlated both with independent behavioral indices of achievement strivings for age 6–10, and with early adolescent (age 10–14) achievement stories. These latter relations remain significant when the influence of the child's IQ at age 6 is statistically controlled. The present data allowed for a partial validation of these results and an extension of the Sontag et al. findings for adolescence and adulthood.

Table 3 presents the correlations between changes in IQ during age 6–10 and the longitudinal and adult behaviors. The amount of IQ increase was a fairly sensitive predictor of both intellectual achievement for age 10–14 ($r = .37$ and $.41$ for boys and girls; $p < .01$), and concern with intellectual competence in adulthood ($r = .49$ and $.42$; $p < .01$). These results support and extend the earlier studies and indicate that amount of IQ increase during the first 4 years of school is a moderately accurate index of the subject's motivation to master intellectual tasks during adolescence and early adulthood. It is important to note that IQ change showed no relation to mechanical or athletic strivings for boys, and was negatively

TABLE 3:   *Relation between IQ change and childhood and adult achievement variables (product-moment correlations)*

Longitudinal Variables	Age	Males	Females
Recognition	6–10	.24	.21
Recognition	10–14	.41**	.09
Achievement	0–3	.13	.04
Achievement	3–6	−.02	.24
Achievement	6–10	.39***	.47***
Achievement-intellectual	10–14	.37*	.41**
Achievement-mechanical	10–14	.15	.14
Achievement-athletic	10–14	−.16	−.46**
Maternal acceleration	0–3	−.06	.20
Maternal acceleration	3–6	−.03	−.12
Maternal aceleration	6–10	.10	.54***
Adult interview variables			
Recognition		.48***	.25
Achievement		.38***	.38**
Intellectual concern		.49***	.42***

  * $p < .05$; *one-tailed.*
 ** $p < .02$; *one-tailed.*
*** $p < .01$; *one-tailed.*

associated with athletic achievement for girls ($r = -.46$; $p < .02$). Thus, IQ increase is not a general measure of achievement strivings for all areas of task mastery. The IQ change measure predicts all three adult achievement ratings because the three adult variables are heavily weighted with concern over intellectual competence. Finally, the maternal acceleration rating for age 6–10 showed a positive relation with IQ change for girls ($r = +.54$; $p < .01$) but not for boys.

Intercorrelations among the Measures

There were, as might be anticipated, positive correlations among the achievement and recognition ratings. Tables 4, 5, and 6 present the intercorrelations among the variables that were rated for ages 6–10, 10–14, and

TABLE 4: *Intercorrelations among variables rated for age 6–10*

	Recognition	Achievement	Maternal Acceleration
Recognition	—	.77***	.57***
Achievement	.60***	—	.59***
Maternal acceleration	.39*	.44***	—

Note.—Data for males are in upper right; for females, in lower left.
* $p < 05$; two-tailed.
*** $p < .01$; two-tailed.

TABLE 5: *Intercorrelations among variables rated for age 10–14*

	Recognition	Intellectual Achievement	Mechanical Achievement	Athletic Achievement
Recognition	—	.74***	.23	.04
Intellectual achievement	.60***	—	.53***	−.11
Mechanical achievement	.17	.32	—	−.23
Athletic achievement	.24	.12	.07	—

Note.—Data for males are in upper right; for females in lower left.
*** $p < .01$; two-tailed.

adulthood. The correlations for the males are above and to the right of the diagonal; the female data are to the left and below the diagonal.

For all three age periods there were high, positive correlations among the achievement and the recognition variables. For age 10–14, recognition behavior was highly correlated with achievement strivings in the intellectual area, but only minimally related to mechanical or athletic achievement. This finding suggests that, for this middle class sample, mastery of intellectual skills is the primary method chosen to obtain social recognition. Perhaps for lower class samples this generalization might be less valid. The high correlations between recognition behavior and intellectual concern in adulthood, together with the fact that maternal acceleration predicted both variables, suggests that it is difficult to separate "recognition seeking behavior" from "attempts to improve intellectual competence."

TABLE 6: *Intercorrelations among adult interview variables*

	Achieve-ment	Recog-nition	Intellec-tual
Achievement	—	.72***	.73***
Recognition	.79***	—	.72***
Intellectual	.77***	.84***	—

Note.—Data for males are in upper right; for females, in lower left.
*** $p < .01$; two-tailed.

DISCUSSION

Stability of Achievement Strivings

The results indicate that strivings for intellectual mastery are moderately stable from the school years through early adulthood. This behavioral disposition emerges as a stable phenomenon at ages 3–6 for girls and 6–10 for boys. The stability of the behavior ratings is paralleled by the moderate stability of TAT achievement stories over a shorter age span. Moreover, achievement stories in adolescence and adulthood also predicted the adult behavior ratings. This consistent cluster of correlations adds construct validity to the TAT achievement variable and support to the conclusion that this class of behaviors is stable over time.

Involvement in athletics for age 10–14 showed no strong, positive relation to either IQ increase or adult achievement behavior and, in a few instances, negative relationships occurred. This was not because the interviewer failed to assess adult involvement in this particular activity. Rather, many of the adults who had been involved in athletics as early adolescents were not overly concerned with task mastery as adults and they tended to avoid intellectual activities.

The majority of the sample regarded positions of responsibility, intellectual challenge, and knowledge of the environment as highly desirable goals. If a subject had strong achievement motives he tended to gratify them through intellectually oriented endeavors. It is suggested that the mass media and social environment differentially emphasize the importance of different skills in accordance with the sex and age role characteristics of the individual. For adults, there tends to be an emphasis on intellectual competence and a de-emphasis on active mastery of athletic skills. Moreover, intellectual mastery is less involved in potential sex role conflict than mechanical or athletic behaviors. To excel at sports is one of the defining characteristics of masculinity. Some boys become involved in athletics in order to maintain their sex role identity and avoid peer rejection. An athletic girl will be subject to peer rejection for excessive participation in athletics. Thus, athletic mastery is under the control of motives and conflicts related to sex role identification in addition to needs for task mastery.

This latter point raises the question of the appropriate definition of achievement behavior and motivation. It is suggested that the concept of a general achievement motive is too broad a term, and it may be useful to replace this construct with a series of variables that relate to more specific behaviors. It seems more reasonable to talk about "desire to improve intellectual skills," or "desire to improve athletic skills" than to use the more global concept of need achievement. Individuals strive to perfect skills in different areas, and the motivations for these strivings are multiple. Prediction and comprehension of these phenomena might be facilitated if there was some differentiation among the behaviors and motives that are involved in task mastery.

The lack of predictive power of age 0–3 mastery behavior might have been due to the greater difficulty in rating this variable (the interrater reliability was .35). On the other hand, the behavioral referents for this rating differed from those used to assess mastery for the older age periods. Since 2-year-olds do not initiate intellectual or athletic mastery behavior, persistence with simple, perceptual-motor tasks (stringing beads, building towers) was the basis for this early rating. A high rating for 0–3 reflected a high threshold for satiation with simple, sensorimotor activities. At the older ages, the achievement rating was based on involvement with problem solving behaviors that were more similar in form to adult achievement behavior. The age 0–3 rating is dynamically different from the symbolic behaviors that characterize achievement during the preschool years.[1] This statement is supported by the fact that achievement for age 0–3 was negatively correlated with achievement for age 3–6 ($r = -.20$) and age 6–10 ($r = -.03$), and showed no relationship to achievement themes or IQ change. Persistence with simple sensorimotor tasks during the first 2 or 3 years of life is not an index of future intellectual, achievement strivings. The 2-year-old who will sit for 20 minutes trying to put a peg in a hole is not necessarily the ambitious scholar of the fifth grade.

Maternal Acceleration and Achievement

The ratings of maternal concern with the child's developmental skills were heavily weighted with encouragement of intellectual progress. The most consistent correlates of maternal acceleration were found with the ratings of adult concern with intellectual competence. Maternal acceleration for age 0–3 was slightly more predictive of adult behavior for girls than for boys. Similarly, maternal acceleration for age 6–10 was more predictive of IQ increase for daughters than for sons. The sex difference between these latter two correlations was significant at the .05 level. It is suggested that since the girl was more likely than the boy to identify with the mother, maternal encouragement of intellectual mastery should have had a greater effect on the development of the girl than on the boy.[2]

TAT Achievement Stories

Achievement themes on the TAT were moderately stable and were correlated with adult achievement behavior. The fact that the correlations were as high for females as for males, although the three critical cards illustrated male heroes, raises some question concerning the validity of the hero hypothesis. Since Cards 1, 14, and 17BM all picture a male in a potential achievement situation, one might expect that achievement themes for women would not be highly correlated with their achievement behavior. The present results indicate that the production of achievement themes may be more influenced by the subject's conception of what behaviors are appropriate for the hero, than by the degree of identification of storyteller with hero. Perhaps high achievement girls conceptualize the male role as being more associated with task mastery than do low achievement girls.

Atkinson (1957) has suggested that achievement themes have differential validity depending on whether or not the criterion task engages the subject's motivation. The achievement variables used in this study (ratings of overt behavior, IQ increase scores) measured "real life" behaviors that would be expected to engage the subject's motivation. The positive correlations obtained indicate that achievement themes are valid indices of intellective mastery when the conditions under which the behavioral samples are obtained are motive arousing.

Limitations on Generalizability

Although the stability correlations for achievement behavior are fairly high, the nature of this particular sample favored stability. The social milieu of these subjects remain constant throughout the first 17 years of their lives, and the parents and peers of these subjects retained their same values. The degree of stability obtained with this sample might not hold for populations that were more mobile, for different ethnic or social class groups, or for children subjected to major developmental traumata.

Social Reinforcement and Stability

The stability of achievement behavior is congruent with general reinforcement theory. Each time achievement strivings are rewarded through social approval or internal feelings of satisfaction, the strength of this behavioral tendency should be increased. If achievement strivings lead to failure, these behaviors should extinguish. The child who attains scholastic honors through effort is rewarded by the social environment, and this experience frequently leads to an expectancy of future success for similar behavior. This rewarding experience, coupled with the strong cultural approval for intellectual competence, increases the probability that the child will continue to engage in intellectual tasks. On the other hand, persistent failures in intellectually challenging situations are likely to lead to an expectancy of failure, and these expectancies can result in avoidance and/or withdrawal from involvement in intellectual behavior.

SUMMARY

This paper summarized results from a larger investigation on the stability of behavior from childhood through adulthood. This investigation dealt specifically with the long term stability of achievement and recognition seeking behaviors in subjects who were part of the Fels Research Institute's longitudinal population.

The subjects were 36 males and 35 females for whom extensive longitudinal information was available from birth through 14 years of age. One psychologist, who had no knowledge of the adult behavior of these subjects, studied narrative reports based on observations of the child in a variety of settings, and rated each child on achievement and recognition seeking behaviors for four age periods: 0–3, 3–6, 6–10, and 10–14. In addition, ratings were made for maternal acceleration of developmental skills for the first three age periods. A second psychologist, who had no knowledge of the childhood information, interviewed each subject in adulthood (age range 20–29) and rated him on three variables related to achievement and recognition seeking behavior in adulthood.

In addition, the following information was available for most subjects: (a) a 7 card TAT protocol administered during early adolescence (median age 14–6) and a 13 card TAT protocol following the adult interview, and (b) annual Stanford-Binet IQ tests from ages 5 through 11 which furnished an IQ change score over the years 6–10.

The major results were as follows:

1. Both achievement and recognition striving behaviors for age 6–10 showed significant positive correlations with similar behaviors during adulthood, the correlations ranged from .38 to .68 and all were significant at the .05 level or better.

2. Involvement in intellectual activities for age 10–14 showed high positive correlations with achievement behavior in adulthood while involvement in athletics during these years showed no positive relationship with adult achievement behavior. Involvement in mechanical tasks for age 10–14 showed positive correlations with adult achievement behavior for boys but not for girls.

3. Maternal acceleration of the child's developmental skills during the first 3 years of life predicted adult achievement behavior for women but not for men. Maternal acceleration of developmental skills during age 6–10 showed moderate correlations with adult concern with intellectual competence in both sexes.

4. Achievement stories told during adolescence and adulthood showed high positive correlations with adult achievement behavior. Maternal acceleration of developmental skills showed suggestive correlations with the occurrence of achievement stories in both adolescence and adulthood.

5. The amount of increase in IQ score during the years 6–10 showed high positive correlations with the ratings of achievement behavior during adulthood. In addition, increase in IQ showed positive correlations with age 6–10 achievement behavior, and with strivings for intellectual competence during age 10–14. Amount of IQ increase showed negative correlations with athletic achievement for age 10–14.

The results suggested that achievement strivings during the first 4 years of school are a moderately good index of future achievement behavior during adolescence and adulthood. There were high correlations between strivings for social recognition and intellectual achievement, and it was suggested that these variables are intimately related in a middle class population.

REFERENCES:

ATKINSON, J. W. Motivational determinants of risk-taking behavior. *Psychol. Rev.*, 1967, *64*, 359–372.

KAGAN, J., and MOSS, H. A. The stability and validity of achievement fantasy. *J. Abnorm. Soc. Psychol.*, 1959, *58*, 357–364.

KAGAN, J., and MOSS, H. A. The stability of passive and dependent behavior from childhood through adulthood. *Child Develpm.*, 1960, *31*, 577–591.

KAGAN, J., SONTAG, L. W., BAKER, C. T., and NELSON, VIRGINIA L. Personality and IQ change. *J. Abnorm. Soc., Psychol.*, 1958, *26*, 261–266.

MCCLELLAND, D. C., ATKINSON, J. W., CLARK, R. A., and LOWELL,E. L., *The Achievement Motive* (New York: Appleton-Century-Crofts, 1953).

MURRAY, H. A. *Thematic Apperception Test Manual* (Cambridge, Mass.: Harvard University Press, 1943).

PIAGET, J. *The Origins of Intelligence in Children* (New York: International Universities Press, 1952).

SONTAG, L. W., BAKER, C. T., and NELSON, VIRGINIA L. Mental growth and personality development. *Monogr. Soc. Res. Child Develpm.*, 1958, 23, No. 68.

FOOTNOTES:

[1] The differences in the content of mastery behaviors for ages 0–3 and 3–6 are analogous to Piaget's 1952 description of intellectual development. Piaget suggests that during the first 2 years the child is in the sensorimotor stage of intelligence in which simple perceptual-motor activity is salient. During the subsequent preschool years the child's intellectual activity becomes more symbolic and more comparable to adult problem-solving behavior.

[2] Research in progress at the institute, under the direction of Vaughn J. Crandall and Walter Katkovsky, is assessing the role of both mother and father in adoption of achievement motives and behaviors.

CHAPTER TWO

NATURE AND NURTURE OF MOTIVATION

6   *Motivation Reconsidered:*
     The Concept of Competence＊

BY ROBERT W. WHITE

EDITOR'S NOTE: Motivation is a complex phenomenon. There does not seem to be any one best better-than-all-others formula, or strategy which will motivate all students in the same way or to the same degree. What turns some students on is the very thing that may turn others off; what motivates John may discourage Bill; what excites Mary may bore Sally. In this paper, Dr. White skillfully weaves together the contributions of several areas of psychology which may help you to better understand the multiple dimensions of motivation and its relationship to the concept of competence.

When parallel trends can be observed in realms as far apart as animal behavior and psychoanalytic ego psychology, there is reason to suppose that we are witnessing a significant evolution of ideas. In these two realms, as in psychology as a whole, there is evidence of deepening discontent with theories of motivation based upon drives. Despite great differences in the language and concepts used to express this discontent, the theme is everywhere the same: Something important is left out when we make drives the operating forces in animal and human behavior.

The chief theories against which the discontent is directed are those of Hull and of Freud. In their respective realms, drive-reduction theory and psychoanalytic instinct theory, which are basically very much alike, have acquired a considerable air of orthodoxy. Both views have an appealing simplicity, and both have been argued long enough so that their main

＊ Reprinted from *Psychological Review,* 1959, Vol. 66, 297–333, by permission of the author and the American Psychological Association.

outlines are generally known. In decided contrast is the position of those who are not satisfied with drives and instincts. They are numerous, and they have developed many pointed criticisms, but what they have to say has not thus far lent itself to a clear and inclusive conceptualization. Apparently there is an enduring difficulty in making these contributions fall into shape.

In this paper I shall attempt a conceptualization which gathers up some of the important things left out by drive theory. To give the concept a name I have chosen the word *competence,* which is intended in a broad biological sense rather than in its narrow everyday meaning. As used here, competence will refer to an organism's capacity to interact effectively with its environment. In organisms capable of but little learning, this capacity might be considered an innate attribute, but in the mammals and especially man, with their highly plastic nervous systems, fitness to interact with the environment is slowly attained through prolonged feats of learning. In view of the directedness and persistence of the behavior that leads to these feats of learning, I consider it necessary to treat competence as having a motivational aspect, and my central argument will be that the motivation needed to attain competence cannot be wholly derived from sources of energy currently conceptualized as drives or instincts. We need a different kind of motivational idea to account fully for the fact that man and the higher mammals develop a competence in dealing with the environment which they certainly do not have at birth and certainly do not arrive at simply through maturation. Such an idea, I believe, is essential for any biologically sound view of human nature.

As a first step, I shall briefly examine the relevant trends of thought in several areas of psychology. From this it will become clear that the ideas advanced in this paper have already been stated, in one way or another, by workers in animal behavior, child development, cognitive psychology, psychoanalytic ego psychology, and the psychology of personality. If there is novelty in this essay, it lies in putting together pieces which are not in themselves new. They already lie before us on the table, and perhaps by looking once more we can see how to fit them into a larger conceptual picture.

THE TREND IN ANIMAL PSYCHOLOGY

One of the most obvious features of animal behavior is the tendency to explore the environment. Cats are reputedly killed by curiosity, dogs characteristically make a thorough search of their surroundings, and monkeys and chimpanzees have always impressed observers as being ceaseless investigators. Even Pavlov, whose theory of behavior was one of Spartan simplicity, could not do without an investigatory or orientating reflex. Early workers with the obstruction method, such as Dashiell (1925) and Nissen (1930), reported that rats would cross an electrified grid simply for the privilege of exploring new territory. Some theorists reasoned that activity of this kind was always in the service of hunger, thirst, sex, or some other organic need, but this view was at least shaken by the latent learning experiments, which showed that animals learned about their surroundings even when their major needs had been purposely sated. Shortly before 1950 there was a wave of renewed interest not only in exploratory behavior but also in the possibility that activity and manipulation might have to be assigned the status of independent motives.

Exploratory Behavior

In 1953 Butler reported an experiment in which monkeys learned a discrimination problem when the only reward was the opening of a window which permitted them to look out upon the normal comings and goings of the entrance room to the laboratory. The discriminations thus formed proved to be resistant to extinction. In a later study, Butler and Harlow (1957) showed that monkeys could build up a series of four different discriminations solely for the sake of inspecting the entrance room. Butler concluded that "monkeys—and presumably all primates—have a strong motive toward visual exploration of their environment and that learning may be established on the basis of this motive just as it may be established on the basis of any motive that regularly and reliably elicits responses." Montgomery, in 1954, reported a study with rats in which the animals, their major organic needs satiated, learned to avoid the short arm of a Y maze and to take the path which led them into additional maze territory suitable for exploration. Similar findings have been described by Myers and Miller (1954), whose rats learned to press a bar for the sake of poking their heads into a new compartment and sniffing around. Zimbardo and Miller (1958) enlarged upon this study by varying the amount of novelty in the two compartments. In their report "the hypothesis advanced is that opportunity to explore a 'novel' environment or to effect a stimulus change in the environment is the reinforcing agent."

These experiments make a strong case for an independent exploratory motive. The nature of this motive can be more fully discerned in situations in which the animals are allowed a varied repertory of behavior. In 1950 Berlyne published a searching paper on curiosity, a theme which he further developed in subsequent years (1955, 1957, 1958). The rats in his experiments were confronted with an unfamiliar space and later with various novel objects placed in it. Approaching, sniffing, and examining were readily elicited by each novelty, were fairly rapidly extinguished, but were restored nearly to original strength when a fresh novelty was added. Exploration on the part of chimpanzees has been studied by Welker (1956), who put various pairs of objects before the animals and observed the course of their interest. The objects were often first approached in a gingerly manner, with signs of uneasiness, then examined and handled quite fully, then discarded. Introducing a new pair of objects promptly reproduced the whole sequence, just as it did with the rats in Berlyne's experiments. Welker used pairs of objects to find out whether or not the chimpanzees would have common preferences. Bigness and brightness evoked more interest, and greater time was spent upon objects which could be moved, changed, or made to emit sounds and light.

Recent reviews by Butler (1958) and Cofer (1959) show that a great deal of similar work is going on in animal laboratories, generally with similar results.

Exploration as a Drive

The designers of these experiments have favored the idea that exploration should be listed as an independent primary drive. In all cases the experimental plan calls for the elimination of other primary drives by satiation. It is recognized, however, that a confirmed advocate of orthodoxy might bring up two objections to the proposed enlargement of the list of primary drives. He might claim that exploratory behavior could be explained as a consequence of secondary reinforcement, or he might contend that it is reinforced by reduction of anxiety.

The first argument meets an immediate difficulty in Butler's finding that discriminations learned on the basis of visual exploration are resistant to extinction. When reinforcement of primary drive never takes place in the experimental situation, it is to be expected that secondary reinforcement will not prevent extinction (Miller, 1951). But even in those cases where extinction is rapid, as it was with Berlyne's rats and Welker's chimpanzees, serious problems are raised by the quick recovery of exploratory behavior when a novel stimulus is introduced (Berlyne, 1950). In order to sustain the idea that secondary reinforcement accounts for this fact, we should have to suppose that primary rewards have often been connected with the exploration of novelties. It would have to be assumed, for instance, that the securing of food by young animals occurred with considerable frequency in connection with the investigation of novel objects. This image may seem to fit mature animals who search the environment for their food, but it certainly cannot apply to young mammals before they are weaned. Here the learning process can do virtually nothing to reinforce an interest in novelties. Gratification comes from following the same old cues to the same old consummatory responses, and the animal whose attention strays to some novel variation of the breast will only find himself frustrated. One can say that the whole mammalian pattern of infancy works in the opposite direction. The mother is more active than the young in providing gratifications, and the babies must be pursued and retrieved if they stray from the scene of her ministry. However one looks at it, the hypothesis of secondary reinforcement seems to me to demand improbable assumptions about the relationship in the lives of young animals between exploration and primary need gratification.

The hypothesis that exploratory behavior is related to fear and receives its reinforcement from the reduction of anxiety is at first glance considerably more plausible. It seems justified by the observation that Welker's chimpanzees showed uneasiness on first contact with novel objects, and it fits the behavior of rats in a new maze, as reported by Whiting and Mowrer (1943), where initial terror gave place to an exploration so feverish that the food reward was not eaten. Montgomery and Monkman (1955) have undertaken to challenge this hypothesis by a direct experimental attack. They showed that fear induced in rats before entering a novel situation did not increase exploratory behavior, and that fear induced within the novel situation decreased exploration to an extent correlated with the intensity of the fear. They find it more reasonable to suppose that fear and exploration are conflicting forms of behavior, and this view can also be defended on purely logical grounds. Fear shows itself in either freezing or avoidance, whereas exploration is clearly an instance of approach. There is hardly a more perfect example of conflict between incompatible responses than that of an animal hesitating between investigation and flight. It is clear that exploration can sometimes serve to reduce anxiety, but the proposition that it comes into existence only for this purpose cannot be so easily accepted.

What assumptions have to be made to support the thesis that exploration is motivated by anxiety reduction? It has to be assumed that certain characteristic stimuli arouse anxiety and that exploration of these stimuli is then found to reduce the anxiety. If the characteristics in question are those of novelty and unfamiliarity, we must heed Berlyne's reminder that for the infant all experience is novel and unfamiliar. Berlyne (1950) proposes that the exploratory reaction "may be one that *all* stimuli originally evoke, but which disappears (becomes habituated) as the organism becomes familiar with them." But if all stimuli at first arouse anxious tension, we would have to deduce that all response would consist of avoidance in the interest of reducing that tension. Approaching a stimulus and taking steps to increase its impact could not occur. An exploratory tendency must be there in the first place before it can achieve the function of reducing anxiety. As Woodworth (1958) expresses it, "if there were no exploratory drive to balance and overbalance the fear drive, an animal would be helpless in a novel situation." I find it hard to believe that creatures so liberally endowed with fear could ever achieve a working mastery of the environment if they were impelled toward it only by the pressure of organic needs.

Both hypotheses thus far examined—secondary reinforcement and anxiety reduction—require us to make improbable assumptions. There remains the possibility that exploration should simply be added to the list of primary drives and otherwise treated in orthodox fashion. Myers and

Miller (1954) suggest that this is the appropriate course, provided the new drive shows the same functional properties as those already known. "If an exploratory tendency can produce learning like other drives such as hunger, and also show a similar pattern of satiation and recovery, these functional parallels to already known drives would help to justify its classification in the same category." Logically the problem can be dealt with in this way, but we must consider very carefully what happens to the category of drive if we admit this new applicant to membership.

Using hunger as the chief model, the orthodox conception of drive involves the following characteristics: (a) there is a tissue need or deficit external to the nervous system which acts upon that system as a strong persisting stimulus; (b) this promotes activity which is terminated by a consummatory response with consequent reduction of need; (c) the reduction of need brings about the learning which gradually shapes behavior into an economical pursuit of suitable goal objects. In this scheme the tension of an aroused drive is interpreted as unpleasant, at least in the sense that the animal acts in such a way as to lower the drive and becomes quiescent when it is lowered. There are probably no living champions of so simple an orthodoxy, yet the scheme remains pervasive, and it is therefore worth while to observe that the proposed exploratory drive hardly fits it at all.

In the first place, the exploratory drive appears to bear no relation whatever to a tissue need or deficit external to the nervous system. It is, of course, clearly related to certain characteristics of stimulation from the external environment, a source of motivation which Harlow (1953) would like to see restored to a serious place in contemporary psychology; but it certainly cannot be correlated with a visceral need comparable to hunger, thirst, or sex. Considering the pattern of satiation and recovery shown by Welker's chimpanzees, Woodworth (1958) remarks that "what becomes satiated is not the exploratory tendency in general, but the exploring of a particular place or object." It is possible, as Hebb (1955) has pointed out, that the so-called "reticular activation system" in the brain stem creates a kind of general drive state, and this mechanism might indeed be flexibly responsive to changes in sensory stimulation. This interesting suggestion, however, is still a far cry from viscerogenic drives; it commits us instead to the novel idea of a neurogenic motive, one in which the state of the nervous system and the patterns of external stimulation conspire to produce motivated behavior. There is even a good deal of trouble in supposing that the adequate stimuli for exploration are either strong or persistent. Novelty certainly cannot be equated with strength or persistence, and animals seem readily able to disregard the stimuli to exploration when they are weary.

In the second place, exploratory behavior cannot be regarded as leading to any kind of consummatory response. It is usual for the animal's investigation to subside gradually. If the animal at some point turns away and leaves the once novel object we may say that its curiosity is "satisfied," but we do not mean by this that the equivalent of a consummatory response has just taken place. The sequence suggests rather that curiosity wears out and slowly falls to a level where it no longer guides behavior, at least until a fresh novelty comes into view.

Finally, in the case of exploratory behavior there is real difficulty in identifying reinforcement with need reduction. Montgomery (1954), describing the learning of the Y maze, points out that the short arm, essentially a dead end, would tend to reduce the exploratory drive, whereas the long arm, itself a complex maze, would increase it—but the long arm is chosen. If the long arm functions as a reinforcing agent, "the mechanism underlying this reinforcement is an *increase,* rather than a decrease, in the strength of the exploratory drive." In this experiment, as in their natural habitat, animals do not wait to have novelty thrust upon them, nor do they avoid situations in which novelty may be found. Such behavior can be most readily conceptualized by admitting that under certain circumstances reinforcement can be correlated with an increase in arousal or excitement rather than a decrease. A drive which has no consummatory climax seems almost to require this formulation. It is distinctly implausible to connect reinforcement with the waning of an agreeable interest in the environment or with a general progress from zestful alertness to boredom.

If we admit exploration to the category of drive we are thus committing ourselves to believe that drives need have no extraneural sources in tissue deficits or visceral tensions, that they are not necessarily activated by strong or persistent stimuli, that they do not require consummatory responses, and that drive increase can sometimes be a mechanism of reinforcement.

Activity and Manipulation

Exploration is not the only motive proposed by critics of drive orthodoxy, and novelty is not the only characteristic of the environment which appears to incite motivated behavior. Some workers have suggested a need for activity, which can be strengthened by depriving animals of their normal opportunities for movement. Kagan and Berkun (1954) used running in an activity wheel as the reward for learning and found it "an adequate reinforcement for the instrumental response of bar pressing." Hill (1956) showed that rats will run in an activity wheel to an extent that is correlated with their previous degree of confinement. It is certain that the activity wheel offers no novelty to the animals in these experiments. Nevertheless, they seem to want to run, and they continue to run for such long times that no part of the behavior can readily be singled out as a consummatory response. Perhaps an unpleasant internal state created by inactivity is gradually worked off, but this is certainly accomplished by a tremendous increase of kinaesthetic stimulation and muscular output which would seem to imply increased excitation in the system as a whole.

Harlow and his associates (Harlow, 1953; Harlow, Harlow, & Meyer, 1950) maintain that there is also a manipulative drive. It is aroused by certain patterns of external stimulation and reduced by actively changing the external pattern. The experiments were done with rhesus monkeys, and they involve the solving of a mechanical problem which, however, leads to no further consequences or rewards. The task might be, for instance, to raise a hasp which is kept in place by both a hook and a pin; all that can be accomplished is to raise the hasp, which opens nothing and leads to no fresh discoveries. When the hasp problem is simply installed in the living cages, the monkeys return to it and solve it as many as 7 or 8 times over several days. It seems unlikely that novelty can be postulated as the essential characteristic of the stimulus which evokes this repeated behavior. The simplest interpretation is rather that value lies for the animal in the opportunity, as Zimbardo and Miller (1958) express it, "to effect a stimulus change in the environment." This formulation suggests something like the propensities toward mastery or power that have often been mentioned in discussions of human motivation.

The addition of activity and manipulation to the list of primary drives can only make more serious the difficulties for the orthodox model that resulted from admitting exploration. But recent research with animals has put the orthodox model on the defensive even on its home grounds. It has become increasingly clear that hunger, thirst, and sex cannot be made to fit the simple pattern that seemed so helpful 40 years ago.

Changing Conceptions of Drive

In a brief historical statement, Morgan (1957) has pointed out that the conception of drive as a noxious stimulus began to lose its popularity among research workers shortly after 1940. "On the whole," he says, "the stimulus concept of drive owed more to wishful thinking than to experimental fact." When technical advances in biochemistry and brain physiology made it possible to bring in an array of new facts, there was a rapid shift toward the view that "drives arise largely through the internal environment acting on the central nervous system." One of the most influential discoveries was that animals have as many as a dozen specific hungers for particular kinds of food, instead of the single hunger demanded by Cannon's model of the hunger drive. If an animal's diet becomes deficient in some important element such as salt, sugar, or the vitamin-B complex, foods containing the missing element will be eagerly sought while other foods are passed by, a selectivity that obviously cannot be laid to contractions of the stomach. Similarly, a negative food preference can be produced by loading either the stomach or the blood stream with some single element of the normal diet. The early work of Beach (1942) of sexual behavior brought out similar complications in what had for a time been taken as a relatively simple drive. Hormone levels appeared to be considerably more important than peripheral stimulation in the arousal and maintenance of the sex drive. Further work led Beach (1951) to conclude that sexual behavior is "governed by a complex combination of processes." He points out that the patterns of control differ tremendously from one species to another and that within a single species the mechanisms may be quite different for males and females. Like hunger, the sex drive turns out to be no simple thing.

New methods of destroying and of stimulating brain centers in animals have had an equally disastrous effect on the orthodox drive model. The nervous system, and especially the hypothalamus, appears to be deeply implicated in the motivational process. Experimental findings on hypothalamic lesions in animals encourge stellar (1954) to believe that there are different centers "responsible for the control of different kinds of basic motivation," and that in each case "there is one main excitatory center and one inhibitory center which operates to depress the activity of the excitatory center." As research findings accumulate, this picture may seem to be too cleanly drawn. Concerning sexual behavior, for example, Rosvold (1959) concludes a recent review by rejecting the idea of a single center in the cerebrum; rather, the sex drive "probably has a wide neural representation with a complex interaction between old and new brain structures and between neural and humoral agents." Nevertheless, Miller's (1958) careful work seems to leave little doubt that motivated behavior in every way similar to normal hunger and normal pain-fear can be elicited by electrical stimulation of quite restricted areas of the hypothalamus. It is clear that we cannot regress to a model of drives that represents the energy as coming from outside the nervous system. Whatever the effects of peripheral stimulation may be, drives also involve neural centers and neural patterns as well as internal biochemical conditions.

What sort of model becomes necessary to entertain these newly discovered facts? In 1938 Lashley expressed the view that motivation should not be equated with disturbance of organic equilibrium but rather with "a partial excitation of a very specific sensorimotor mechanism irradiating to affect other systems of reaction." Beach (1942) postulated that there must be in the nervous system "a condition analogous to Sherrington's central excitatory state." Morgan, in 1943, undertook to capture the facts in a systematic theory which seems to have been well sustained by subsequent research (Morgan, 1957). He distinguished two types of process which he called *humoral motive factors* and *central motive states*. The humoral factors consist of chemical or hormonal constituents of the blood and lymph, and they are conceived to influence behavior chiefly by a direct sensitizing action on neural centers. The central motive states have several properties: They are partly self-maintaining through neural circuits, they tend to increase the organism's general activity, they evoke specific forms of behavior not strongly controlled by the environment, and they prime or prepare consummatory responses which will occur when adequate stimulation is found. This is a far cry from the orthodox model, but we must nowadays admit that the orthodox model is a far cry from the facts.

In view of this radical evolution of the concept of drive, it is not surprising to find the drive reduction hypothesis in serious difficulties. The earlier identification of reinforcement with drive reduction has been directly attacked in a series of experiments designed to show that learning takes place when drive reduction is ruled out.

In 1950 Sheffield and Roby showed that instrumental learning would take place in hungry rats when the reward consisted not of a nutritive substance but of sweet-tasting saccharine in the drinking water. This finding appeared to be "at variance with the molar principle of reinforcement used by Hull, which identifies primary reinforcement with 'need reduction.'" The authors naturally do not question the vital importance of need reduction, but they point out that need-reducing events may accomplish reinforcement through a mechanism more direct and speedy than the reduction of the need itself. They think that "stimulation and performance of a consummatory response appears to be more important to instrumental learning—in a primary, not acquired, way—than the drive satisfaction which the response normally achieves." Their findings are in line with an earlier experiment with chickens by Wolfe and Kaplon (1941), who used different sizes of food pellets so that the number of pecks and the amount of food received could be thrown out of their usual close connection. The chickens, we might say, would rather peck than eat; learning was more strongly reinforced when four pecks were necessary than when one peck was enough to take the same amount of food.

The substitution of the consummatory response for need reduction as the immediate reinforcing mechanism is a step in advance, but it soon turns out that another step is required. Can it be shown that an aroused need which does not reach consummation has a reinforcing effect? To test this possibility Sheffield, Wulff, and Backer (1951) provided male rats with the reward of copulating with a female, but not enough times to produce ejaculation. This reward was favorable to instrumental learning even though there was no need reduction and no performance of the final consummatory act. The results were supported by Kagan (1955), whose animals showed substantial learning under the same conditions, though learning was still faster when ejaculation was permitted. Sheffield, Roby, and Campbell (1954) have proposed a *drive-induction* theory according to which the property of reinforcement is assigned to the excitement of an aroused drive. We have already seen that some such assumption is essential if exploration is to be assigned the status of a drive. Here it can be added that the whole theory of pregenital sexuality involves motivation without consummatory acts and without any but the most gradual need reduction. And as a final blow to the orthodox hypothesis comes the finding by Olds and Milner (1954) that positive reinforcement can be brought about by direct electrical stimulation of certain areas of the brain. Once again we learn that neural centers are deeply implicated in the plot of motivation. The simple mechanics of need reduction cannot possibly serve as the basis for a theory of learning.

Twenty years of research have thus pretty much destroyed the orthodox drive model. It is no longer appropriate to consider that drives originate solely in tissue deficits external to the nervous system, that consummatory acts are a universal feature and goal of motivated behavior, or that the alleviation of tissue deficits is the necessary condition for instrumental learning. Instead we have a complex picture in which humoral factors and neural centers occupy a prominent position; in which, moreover, the concept of neurogenic motives without consummatory ends appears to be entirely legitimate. Do these changes remove the obstacles to placing exploration, activity, and manipulation in the category of drives?

Perhaps this is no more than a question of words, but I should prefer at this point to call it a problem in conceptual strategy. I shall propose that these three new "drives" have much in common and that it is useful to bring them under the single heading of competence. Even with the loosening and broadening of the concept of drive, they are still in important respects different from hunger, thirst, and sex. In hunger and thirst, tissue deficits, humoral factors, and consummatory responses retain an important position. The mature sex drive depends heavily on hormonal levels and is sharply oriented toward consummation. Tendencies like exploration do not share these characteristics, whatever else they have in common with the better known drives. It is in order to emphasize their intrinsic peculiarities, to get them considered in their own right without a cloud of surplus meanings, that I prefer in this essay to speak of the urge that makes for competence simply as motivation rather than as drive.

THE TREND IN PSYCHOANALYTIC EGO PSYCHOLOGY

Rather an abrupt change of climate may be experienced as we turn from the animal laboratory to the psychoanalytic treatment room, but the trends of thought in the two realms turn out to be remarkably alike. Here the orthodox view of motivation is to be found in Freud's theory of the instincts—they might be known to us as drives if an early translator had been more literal with the German *Trieb*.

Freud's Theories of Instinct and Ego

In his final work, Freud (1949) described instincts as "somatic demands upon mental life" and as "the ultimate cause of all activity." He wrote further:

> It is possible to distinguish an indeterminate number of instincts and in common practice this is in fact done. For us, however, the important

question arises whether we may not be able to derive all of these instincts from a few fundamental ones. . . . After long doubts and vacillations we have decided to assume the existence of only two basic instincts, *Eros* and the *destructive instinct* [Freud, 1949, p. 20].

The history of Freud's long doubts and vacillations has been lucidly related by Bibring (1941). Up to 1914 Freud used a two-fold classification of sexual instincts and ego instincts. The ego instincts made their appearance in his case histories in a somewhat moral character, being held responsible for the disastrous repression of sexual needs, but in systematic usage they were conceived as serving the goal of self-preservation, and hunger was generally taken as an appropriate model. In 1914, when he evolved the concept of narcissism and saw that it threatened to blur the line between sexual and ego tendencies, Freud (1925b) still expressed himself as unwilling to abandon an idea which followed the popular distinction of love and hunger and which reflected man's dual existence "as reproducer and as one who serves his own ends." Various facts, particularly those of sadism and masochism, served to overcome his reluctance, so that he finally united self-preservation and preservation of the species under the heading of Eros or life instincts, establishing destructiveness or the death instinct as the great antagonist in a profound biological sense (Freud, 1948). This highly speculative step proved to be too much for some of his otherwise loyal followers, and the earlier orthodoxy did not become entirely extinct.

It is easier to follow Freud's reasoning when we bear in mind the simultaneous development of his ideas about the mental apparatus. Bibring (1941) points out that even in his early thinking a sharp contrast was always drawn between instinct and mental apparatus. Instinct supplied the energy in the form of powerful, persisting internal stimuli; the apparatus guided it into channels which produced organized behavior and eventually put a stop to the persisting stimulation. In 1915 Freud wrote:

> The nervous system is an apparatus having the function of abolishing stimuli which reach it or of reducing excitation to the lowest possible level; an apparatus which would even, if this were feasible, maintain itself in an altogether unstimulated condition. . . . The task of the nervous system is—broadly speaking—*to master stimuli* [Freud, 1925c, p. 63].

During the next decade there was a considerable growth in his ideas about the mental apparatus, culminating in the well known division into id, ego, and superego. The activities of the ego now received much fuller recognition. Freud (1927) assigned to it "the task of self-preservation," which it accomplished through its several capacities of perception, memory, flight, defense, and adaptive action. One can see Freud's thought moving from a mechanical analogy—an engine and its fuel—toward a much more adaptational conception of the mental apparatus. Ego instincts did not wholly disappear, but the decline in their systematic importance was compensated by the insight that self-preservative tendencies were to some extent built into the whole living system. It is significant that as he took this course he came to question the earlier tension-reduction theory. In the last year of his life he declared it to be probable "that what is felt as pleasure or unpleasure is not the *absolute* degree of the tensions but something in the rhythm of their changes" (Freud, 1949).

Freud's tendency to revise his thinking makes it difficult to pin down an orthodox doctrine, but most workers will probably agree that his main emphasis was upon somatically based drives, a mental apparatus which received its power from the drives, and, of course, the multitude of ways in which the apparatus controlled, disguised, and transformed these energies. His treatment of the ego was far from complete, and it was not long before voices were raised against the conception that so vital and versatile a part of the personality could be developed solely by libidinal and aggressive energies.

An Instinct to Master

In 1942 Hendrick proposed that this difficulty be met by assuming the existence of an additional major instinct. "The development of ability to master a segment of the environment," he wrote, and the need to exercise such functions, can be conceptualized as an "instinct to master," further characterized as "an inborn drive to do and to learn how to do." The aim of this instinct is "pleasure in exercising a function successfully, regardless of its sensual value." The simpler manifestations are learning to suck, to manipulate, to walk, to speak, to comprehend and to reason; these functions and others eventually become integrated as the ego. "The central nervous system is more than a utility," Hendrick declared. The infant shows an immediate desire to use and perfect each function as it ripens, and the adult secures gratification from an executive function efficiently performed regardless of its service to other instincts.

Hendrick's procedure in this and two supporting papers (1943a, 1943b) is quite similar to that of the animal psychologists who propose listing exploration as an additional primary drive. The instinct to master has an aim—to exercise and develop the ego functions—and it follows hedonic principles by yielding "primary pleasure" when efficient action "enables the individual to control and alter his environment." It is to this extent analogous to the instincts assumed by Freud. But just as an exploratory drive seemed radically to alter the whole conception of drive, so the instinct to master implied a drastic change in the psychoanalytic idea of instinct. Critics were quick to point out that Freud had always conceived of instincts as having somatic sources external to the ego apparatus, a condition not met by the proposed instinct to master. There was nothing comparable to erogenous zones, to orgasm, or to the sequence of painful tension followed by pleasurable release. Mastery, the critics agreed, could not be an instinct, whatever else it might be.

It is of interest that Fenichel (1945), who definitely rejected Hendrick's proposal, gives us another close parallel to the animal work by attributing mastering behavior to anxiety-reduction. He argued that mastery is "a general aim of every organism but not of a specific instinct." He agreed that there is "a pleasure of enjoying one's abilities," but he related this pleasure to cessation of the anxiety connected with not being able to do things. "Functional pleasure," he wrote, "is pleasure in the fact that the exercise of a function is now possible without anxiety," and he contended that when anxiety is no longer present, when there is full confidence that a given situation can be met, then action is no longer accompanied by functional pleasure. We must certainly agree with Fenichel that anxiety *can* play the part he assigns it, but the proposal that all pleasure in ego functions comes from this source raises the same difficulties we have already considered in connection with exploratory behavior. That we exercise our capacities and explore our surroundings only to reduce our fear of the environment is not, as I have already argued, an assumption that enjoys high probability on biological grounds.

Hartmann on the Ego

A less radical change in the orthodox model is proposed by Hartmann, who, in a series of papers since 1939, often in conjunction with Kris and Loewenstein, has been refining and expanding Freud's views on the ego and the instincts. While the ego is conceived as a "substructure" of the personality, this term is somewhat metaphorical because in practice the ego has to be defined by its functions. The list of functions, which includes grasping, crawling, walking, perceiving, remembering, language, thinking, and intention, covers much the same ground that was indicated by Hendrick, but Hartmann does not attribute their growth to an instinct. On the other hand, Hartmann (1950) early came to the conclusion that development could not be explained, as Freud had seemed to conceive it, simply as a consequence of conflict between instinctual needs and frustrating realities. The instincts alone would never guarantee survival; they require mediation by the innate ego apparatus if they are to meet "the average expectable environmental conditions." He therefore proposed that we conceive of an autonomous factor in ego development, an independent maturation of functions taking place in a "conflict-free ego sphere." Functions such as locomotion ripen through maturation and through learning even when they are not caught up in struggles to obtain erotic and aggressive gratification or to avoid anxiety. As Anna Freud (1952) has pointed out, walking becomes independent of instinctual upheavals a few weeks after its beginning; thereafter, it serves the child impartially in situations of conflict and those that are free from conflict.

Hartmann's idea of autonomous ego development has of course been assumed all along by workers in child psychology, but it is an important step to relate it to Freud's disclosures concerning unconscious motivation.

In what now looks like an excess of enthusiasm for his own concepts, Freud (1925a) undertook to explain the outgrowing of the pleasure principle and the substituting of the reality principle as a simple and direct consequence of the frustration of instinctual needs. However, the reality principle contained the idea of postponing an immediate gratification in favor of a future one, and Hartmann (1956) properly notes that the capacities for postponement and anticipation cannot be conjured into existence simply by the collision of frustrating reality and ungratified need. Important as frustrations may be, these capacities must already be available, "some preparedness for dealing with reality" must already exist, before the frustration can produce its momentous educative effect. It can be seen from this example that Hartmann's analysis opens the way for profitable commerce between developmental psychologies inside and outside of psychoanalysis.

Hartmann's emphasis on adaptation permits him to perceive much more that is autonomous about the ego than was ever seriously included in Freud's systematic thought. He allows, for instance, that aims and interests which develop in the beginning as defenses against instincts may later become part of conflict-free spheres of activity—become interests in their own right—and thus achieve "secondary autonomy," a concept very close to Allport's (1937) functional autonomy of motives (Hartmann, 1950). He deals with the possibility that adaptive skills developing in the conflict-free sphere may have a decisive influence on the handling of conflicts. These skills have a history of their own, shaped jointly by the child's abilities and by the responses evoked from parents. As Monroe (1955) has expressed it, they have "a very important role in the development of the conscious and semiconscious psychological self." They may thus have a direct influence upon the outcome when a child becomes involved in conflict. Rapaport (1958) sees Hartmann's ideas on the autonomy of the ego as vital to the proper understanding not only of healthy development but also of psychopathology itself.

In explaining the autonomous growth of the ego, Hartmann makes generous use of the concept of maturation, but he naturally does not exclude learning. Hartmann (1950) entertains the possibility, mentioned casually from time to time by Freud (1916, 1949), that ego functions are supplied with their own sources of energy independent of instincts, and that there is pleasure connected with their mere exercise. However, he makes little systematic use of this idea, relying instead upon a concept more central in Freud's thinking, that of the neutralization of drive energies. Freud (1927) found that he could "make no headway" in accounting for the varied activities of the ego without assuming "a displaceable energy, which is in itself neutral, but is able to join forces either with an erotic or with a destructive impulse, differing qualitatively as they do, and augment its total cathexis." He speculated that the neutral energy came from Eros and could be conceived as desexualized libido. Hartmann, Kris, and

Loewenstein (1949) carried the idea forward a logical step by proposing that the energies of aggressive instincts could similarly be neutralized and placed at the disposal of the ego. Neutralized energy contributes to the development of the ego and makes possible a continuing interest in the objects of the environment regardless of their immediate relation to erotic or aggressive needs. Hartmann (1955) finds this concept particularly helpful in unscrambling the confusions that have arisen over the concept of sublimation.

The doctrine of neutralized instinctual energies is a curious one, and we should bear in mind the complex clinical findings that perhaps suggested it. Freud was an unquestioned genius in detecting the subtle operation of erotic urges and aggressive fantasies, along with elaborate mechanisms of defense, behind the seemingly objective or "neutral" activities of everyday life. Remarkable transformations of interest could sometimes be observed in the course of development. For example, a patient's childhood erotic rivalry and aggressive competition with his father might later disappear beneath a strong objective interest in running the family business; then suddenly, on the brink of success, this interest might come to a total halt, paralyzed by anxiety because the underlying instinctual goals came too close to symbolic fulfillment. The reappearance of instinctual preoccupations in such a case lends a certain color to the idea that they have somehow been driving the behavior all the time, even though the daily pursuit of business goals seems utterly remote from instinctual gratifications.

It is worth noticing that Freud's procedure in making the assumption of neutralized instinctual energy is similar to the one followed by orthodox behaviorists in connection with primary drives. These theorists started from the assumption that all behavior was powered by a limited number of organic drives, and then, in order to protect this assumption, they developed further hypotheses, such as secondary reinforcement, to account for motivated behavior that bore no obvious relation to primary goals. At the point where he could "make no headway" without postulating neutralization, Freud could conceivably have made a good deal of headway if he had been willing to assume that neutral energy, neither sexual nor aggressive, was available as a natural endowment in the first place. But he preferred to protect his assumption of two primary drives and to interpret other energies as transformations of these drives. Even so, the concept seems superfluous if we take Freud at his word about the nature of the life instincts. Freud (1949) made it clear that Eros included more than instincts having a sexual aim; its larger goal was "to establish even greater unities and to preserve them thus—in short, to bind together." Under this formula, it would seem possible to include energies inherently directed toward building up the integrated functions of the ego. But Freud did not exploit the full range of his theory of Eros and proposed only that neutral energies should be conceived as desexualized.

The concept of neutralization has in some respects had a good effect on psychoanalytic ego psychology. In Hartmann's writings, as we have seen, and in Rapaport's (1951, 1954) work on thinking, it has encouraged a strong interest in autonomous ego functions and a fresh analysis of their place in personality. Nevertheless, it seems to me an awkward conceptualization, one which in the end is likely to lead, as Colby (1955) has expressed it, to a "metapsychological snarl." The theory requires that instinctual energies can completely change their aims, which makes one wonder what purpose was served in the first place by defining them as having aims. It preserves an image of mobility of energies that seems much out of line with recent research on animal motivation, where energy is being conceived in a constantly closer relation to specific structures. To my mind it thus compares unfavorably with its quite straightforward alternative, which is that the alleged neutralized energies are there in the first place as part of the natural make-up of an adaptive organism. I shall later develop this possibility by means of the concept of competence in its motivational aspect, and I believe that this concept gains support from certain other lines of work in the psychoanalytic tradition.

Motility and a Sense of Industry

The trend away from instinct orthodoxy is illustrated by the work of Kardiner (1947) on what he calls "the development of the effective ego." Kardiner's reflections arose from his work on the traumatic neuroses of war. In these disorders the main threat is to self-preservation, and some of the most important symptoms, such as defensive rituals and paralyses, are lodged in the action systems that normally bring about successful adaptive behavior. It thus becomes pertinent to study the growth of action systems, to discover how they become integrated so as to maintain "controlled contact" with the environment and "controlled exploitation of objects in the outer world," and to work out the conditions which either favor or disrupt this acquired integration. Thinking along these lines, Kardiner is led to conclusions just about the opposite of Freud's: It is the successful and gratifying experiences, not the frustrations, that lead to increasingly integrated action and to the discrimination of self from outer world. Frustration produces chiefly disruptions and inhibitions which are unfavorable to the early growth of the ego. Children are gratified when they discover the connection between a movement executed and the accompanying and subsequent sensations. They are still more gratified when they carry out actions successfully; this "gives rise to the triumphant feeling of making an organ obedient to the will of the ego." Such experiences build up "a definite self- or body-consciousness which becomes the center and the point of reference of all purposeful and coördinated activity." Growth of the ego, in short, depends heavily upon action systems and the consequences of action. The course and vicissitudes of this development have to be studied in their own right, and they cannot be understood as side effects of the stages of libidinal development.

A similar theme is pursued to even more radical conclusions by Mittelmann (1954) in his paper on motility. Mittelmann regards motility, which manifests itself most typically in skilled motor actions such as posture, locomotion, and manipulation, as an "urge in its own right" in the same sense that one speaks of oral, excretory, or genital urges. From about 10 months of age it has a distinctly "driven" character, and there is restlessness and anger if it is blocked. During the second and third years the motor urge "dominates all other urges," so that it is proper to "consider this period the motor level of ego and libido development." The child makes tremendous efforts to learn to walk, and to walk well, and he exhibits joyous laughter as he attains these ends. Restrictions of motility may occur because the parents are anxious or because the child's assertiveness troubles them, and a lasting injury to the parent-child relationship may result. Clumsiness in motor or manipulative accomplishments may lead to self-hatred and dependence, for "the evolution of self-assertiveness and self-esteem is intimately connected with motor development." Motility is of central importance in many of the most characteristic functions of the ego. Partly by its means the infant differentiates himself from other objects, and the child's knowledge of objects depends on an extensive activity of manipulation and examination. "Thus motility becomes one of the most important aspects of reality testing." Because it is an element in all cognitive behavior, it can also be considered "the dominant integrative function." Mittelmann bases motor development, in short, on an independent urge, and he sees this urge as the really crucial motive behind the development of the ego.

Like Kardiner, Mittelmann does not attempt to formulate in detail the nature of the motility urge. It is likened not to an instinct but to a "partial instinct," and this seems to place it somewhere between Hendrick's instinct to master and Hartmann's dimly sketched independent energies of the ego. This indefiniteness may irk the systematic theorist, but Mittelmann's account of the part played by motility in ego development easily stands as a significant contribution. Even more influential in this respect is the work of Erikson (1953), who has given a highly detailed timetable of ego development. Erikson stays with the libido theory as far as it will go, but he passes beyond its reach in his account of the latency period and some of the later crises of growth. It is clear that something more than the orthodox instincts is involved in the "enormous value" with which the child in the second year "begins to endow his autonomous will." Something more would seem to be implied in the expanding imagination and initiative of the "phallic" child. Certainly more is involved during the school years, when children address themselves to motor, manual, and intellectual achievements and need "a sense of being able to make things and make them well and even perfectly: this is what I call the *sense of industry.*"

Erikson's (1950) theory of play is also influenced by the idea that learning to deal with the animate and inanimate worlds is an important preoccupation of childhood: "the playing child advances forward to new stages of real mastery." Action systems, motility, and a sense of industry all direct our attention to behavior which can scarcely be contained in the old bottle of instinct theory.

Glancing back over these trends in psychoanalytic ego psychology, we cannot fail to be impressed by striking similarities to the trend in animal work. Using Reik's familiar metaphor, we might say that those who listen with their two ears and those who listen with the third ear have apparently been hearing much the same sounds. In both realms there is discontent with drive orthodoxy. In both there is persistent pointing to kinds of behavior neglected or explained away by drive orthodoxy: exploration, activity, manipulation, and mastery. Similar theories have been proposed to account for the energies in such behavior: (a) they are derived or transformed in some way from the primary drives or instincts (secondary reinforcement, neutralization of drive energies); (b) they are powered by the need to reduce anxiety; (c) they can be accounted for only by postulating a new primary drive (exploratory drive, instinct to master). When these explanations are considered to have failed, the one remaining course is to work out a different idea of motivation. In his study of action systems, Kardiner prefers to leave the question of energy sources unanswered, but Erikson's sense of industry and Mittelmann's motility urge point to a motivational base which is only remotely analogous to primary drives or fundamental instincts. I believe that the difficulties in this undertaking can be greatly reduced by the concept of competence, to which we shall shortly turn.

RELATED DEVELOPMENTS IN
GENERAL PSYCHOLOGY

If a systematic survey were in order, it would be easy to show a parallel drift of opinion in other parts of the psychological realm. Among theorists of personality, for example, something like drive orthodoxy is to be found in the work of Dollard and Miller (1950), who have translated the main concepts of Freud's psychoanalysis, including processes such as repression and displacement, into the language of reinforcement theory. With them we might put Mowrer (1950), whose searching analysis of fear as an acquired drive has led him to postulate anxiety-reduction as the master motive behind the development of the ego. Discontent with drive orthodoxy has long been expressed by Allport (1937, 1946), who not only argues for a functional autonomy of motives from their infantile roots in primary drives but also seriously questions the law of effect, the very cornerstone of reinforcement theory. Little comfort for the orthodox can be found in Murray's (1938) detailed taxonomy of needs, especially when it comes to needs such as achievement and construction, which can be tied to primary drives only by conceptual acrobatics. Murray and Kluckhohn (1953), moreover, have made a case for pleasure in activity for its own sake, reviving the *Funktionslust* proposed many years ago by Karl Bühler (1924) and recently developed in some detail by French (1952). They also argue for instrinsic mental needs: "the infant's mind is not acting most of the time as the instrument of some urgent animal drive, but is preoccupied with *gratifying itself.*" Murphy (1947) takes the view that all tissues can become seats of tension and thus participants in drive; in addition to visceral drives, he postulates two independent forms, activity drives and sensory drives. Then there are workers such as Goldstein (1939) who approach the whole problem with a holistic philosophy which precludes the dictatorship of any isolated or partial drives. Goldstein (1940) assumes one master tendency, that toward self-actualization, of which the so-called visceral drives are but partial and not really isolated expressions, and which can find expression also in an urge toward perfection—toward completing what is incomplete, whether it be an outside task or the mastery of some function such as walking. It has been shown by the Ansbachers (1956) that Adler, never a friend of instinct orthodoxy, in his later years reached an idea very similar to the urge toward perfection. Maslow (1954, 1955), too, belongs with the heterodox. He insists that we should take account of growth motivation as well as the deficiency motivation implied in the visceral drives, and he offers the valuable idea of a hierarchy of motives, according to which the satisfaction of "lower" needs makes it possible for "higher" needs to emerge and become regnant in behavior.

Mention of these names must suffice here to show that the trends observed in animal psychology and psychoanalytic ego psychology are pervasive in contemporary psychological thought. Doubtless the same controversies and problems could be pointed out in child development, in cognitive psychology, and in other fields. But in order to advance to my main theme, I shall select only certain developments which bear directly on the concept of competence.

Needs for Excitement and Novelty

Human experience provides plentiful evidence of the importance of reducing excessive levels of tension. Men under wartime stress, men under pressure of pain and extreme deprivation, men with excessive work loads or too much exposure to confusing social interactions, all act as if their nervous systems craved that utterly unstimulated condition which Freud once sketched as the epitome of neural bliss. But if these same men be granted their Nirvana they soon become miserable and begin to look around for a little excitement. Human experience testifies that boredom is a bad state of affairs about which something must be done. Hebb (1949) has been particularly insistent in reminding us that many of our activities, such as reading detective stories, skin-diving, or driving cars at high speeds, give clear evidence of a need to raise the level of stimulation and excitement. Men and animals alike seem at times bent on increasing the impact of the environment and even on creating mild degrees of frustration and fear. Hebb and Thompson (1954) reflect upon this as follows:

> Such phenomena are, of course, well known in man: in the liking for dangerous sports or roller coasters, where fear is deliberately courted, and in the addiction to bridge or golf or solitaire, vices whose very existence depends upon the level of difficulty of the problems presented and an optimal level of frustration. Once more, when we find such attitudes toward fear and frustration in animals, we have a better basis for supposing that we are dealing with something fundamental if a man prefers skis to the less dangerous snowshoes, or when we observe an unashamed love of work (problem solving and frustration included) in the scientist, or in the business man who cannot retire. Such behavior in man is usually accounted for as a search for prestige, but the animal data make this untenable. It seems much more likely that solving problems and running mild risks are inherently rewarding, or, in more general terms, that the animal will always act so as to produce an optimal level of excitation [Hebb & Thompson, 1954, p. 551].

The concept of optimal stimulation has been developed by Leuba (1955), who sees it as helpful in resolving some of the problems of learning theory. Believing that most theorizing about motivation has been based upon "powerful biological or neurotic drives," Leuba bids us look at the much more common learning situations of nursery, playground, and school, where "actions which increase stimulation and produce excitement are strongly reinforced, sometimes to the dismay of parents and teachers." He proposes that there is an optimal level of stimulation, subject to variation at different times, and that learning is associated with movement toward this optimal level, downward when stimulation is too high and upward when it is too low. A similar idea is expressed by McReynolds (1956) concerning the more restricted concept of "rate of perceptualization." Monotonous conditions provide too low a rate, with boredom; excessive stimulation produces too high a rate, with disruptive excitement; the optimal rate yields the experience of pleasure. These ideas are now amply supported by recent experimental work on sensory deprivation (Lilly, 1956; Hebb, 1958).

In recent papers Young (1949, 1955) has argued for an hedonic theory of motivation, one in which affective processes "constitute a form of primary motivation." According to Young's theory, "an organism behaves so as to maximize positive affective arousal (delight, enjoyment) and to minimize negative arousal (distress)." McClelland (1953) has offered a version of hedonic theory which is of particular value in understanding the significance of novelty. Affective arousal occurs when a stimulus pattern produces a discrepancy from the existing adaptation level. Small discrepancies produce pleasant affect and a tendency to approach; large ones produce unpleasantness and a tendency toward avoidance. The child at play, like the young chimpanzee and the exploring rat, needs frequent novelty in the stimulus filed in order to keep up his interest—in order to maintain pleasant discrepancies from whatever adaptation level he has reached. Hebb's (1949) theory of the neurological correlates of learning also deals with novelty, though in a somewhat different way. He equates sustained interest with a state of neural affairs in which "phase sequences" are relatively complex and are growing, in the sense of establishing new internal relations. Such a state follows most readily from a stimulus field characterized by difference-in-sameness; that is, containing much that is familiar along with certain features that are novel. If the field is entirely familiar, phase sequences run off quickly, are short-circuited, and thus fail to produce sustained interest. Hebb's theory, which has the engaging quality of being able to explain why we enjoy reading a detective story once but not right over again, expresses in a neurological hypothesis the familiar fact that well-learned, habituated processes do not in themselves greatly interest us. Interest seems to require elements of unfamiliarity: of something still to be found out and of learning still to be done.

It seems to me that these contributions, though differing as to details, speak with unanimity on their central theme and would force us, if nothing else did, to reconsider seriously the whole problem of motivation. Boredom, the unpleasantness of monotony, the attraction of novelty, the tendency to vary behavior rather than repeating it rigidly, and the seeking of stimulation and mild excitement stand as inescapable facts of human experience and clearly have their parallels in animal behavior. We may seek rest and minimal stimulation at the end of the day, but that is not what we are looking for the next morning. Even when its primary needs are satisfied and its homeostatic chores are done, [an] organism is alive, active, and up to something.

Dealing with the Environment

If we consider things only from the viewpoint of affect, excitement, and novelty, we are apt to overlook another important aspect of behavior, its effect upon the environment. Moving in this direction, Diamond (1939) invites us to consider the motivational properties of the sensorineural system, the apparatus whereby higher animals "maintain their relations to the environment." He conceives of this system as demanding stimulation and as acting in such a manner as to "force the environment to stimulate it." Even if one thinks only of the infant's exploring eyes and hands, it is clear that the main direction of behavior is by no means always that of reducing the impact of stimulation. When the eyes follow a moving object, or when the hand grasps an object which it has touched, the result is to preserve the stimulus and to increase its effect. In more elaborate explorations the consequence of a series of actions may be to vary the manner in which a stimulus acts upon the sense organs. It is apparent that the exploring, manipulating child produces by his actions precisely what Hebb's theory demands as a basis for continuing interest: he produces differences-in-sameness in the stimulus field.

In a critical analysis of Freud's views on the reality principle, Charlotte Bühler (1954) makes a strong case for positive interests in the environment, citing as evidence the responsiveness and adaptiveness of the newborn baby as well as the exploratory tendencies of later months. The problem is worked out in more detail by Schachtel (1954) in a paper on focal attention. Acts of focal attention are characteristically directed at particular objects, and they consist of several sustained approaches "aimed at active mental grasp" while excluding the rest of the field. These qualities can be observed even in the infant's early attempts to follow a moving object with his eyes, and they show more clearly in his later endeavors to learn how objects are related both to himself and to one another. Such behavior bespeaks "a relatively autonomous capacity for object interest." Schachtel makes the proposal that this interest is pursued precisely at those times when major needs are in abeyance. High pressure of need or anxiety is the enemy of exploratory play and is a condition, as every scientist should know, under which we are unlikely to achieve an objective grasp of the environment. Low need pressure is requisite if we are to perceive objects as they are, in their constant character, apart from hopes and fears we may at other times attach to them. Schachtel doubts that "the wish for need-satisfaction alone would ever lead to object perception and to object-oriented thought." Hence an autonomous capacity to be interested in the environment has great value for the survival of a species.

Being interested in the environment implies having some kind of satisfactory interaction with it. Several workers call attention to the possibility that satisfaction might lie in having an effect upon the environment, in dealing with it, and changing it in various ways. Groos (1901), in his classical analysis of play, attached great importance to the child's "joy in being a cause," as shown in making a clatter, "hustling things about," and playing in puddles where large and dramatic effects can be produced. "We demand a knowledge of effects," he wrote, "and to be ourselves the producers of effects." Piaget (1952) remarks upon the child's special interest in objects that are affected by his own movements. This aspect of behavior occupies a central place in the work of Skinner (1953), who describes it as "operant" and who thus "emphasizes the fact that the behavior *operates* upon the environment to generate consequences." These consequences are fed back through the sense ograns and may serve to reinforce behavior even when no organic needs are involved. A rat will show an increased tendency to press a bar when this act produces a click or a buzz. A baby will continue to investigate when his efforts produce rattling or tinkling sounds or sparkling reflections from a shiny object. The young chimpanzees in Welker's experiment spent the longest time over objects which could be lighted or made to emit sounds. Skinner finds it "difficult, if not impossible, to trace these reinforcing effects to a history of conditioning." "We may plausibly argue," he continues, "that a capacity to be reinforced by any feedback from the environment would be biologically advantageous, since it would prepare the organism to manipulate the environment successfully before a given state of deprivation developed."

Woodworth's Behavior-Primacy Theory

The most far-reaching attempt to give these aspects of behavior a systematic place in the theory of motivation is contained in Woodworth's recent book, *Dynamics of Behavior* (1958). Woodworth takes his start from the idea that a great deal of human behavior appears to be directed toward producing effects upon the environment without immediate service to any aroused organic need. "Its incentives and rewards are in the field of behavior and not in the field of homeostasis." This is illustrated by exploratory behavior, which is directed outward toward the environment.

> Its long-range value as the means of making the child acquainted with the world he has to deal with later, and so equipping him through play for the serious business of life, can scarcely lie within the little child's horizon. His goals are more limited and direct: to see this or that object more closely, to find what is behind an obstacle, to hear the noise an object makes when it strikes the floor, to be told the name of a thing or person [Woodworth, 1958, p. 78].

More complex play, such as building with blocks, illustrates the same outgoing tendency and reveals more plainly the element of finding out what one can and cannot do with objects. Even social play falls into the pattern. Playmates do not chiefly supply affection or satisfy organic needs; rather, they "afford the opportunity to do something interesting in the environment."

Woodworth draws a contrast between *need-primacy* theories of motivation and the *behavior-primacy* theory. The latter holds that "all behavior is directed primarily toward dealing with the environment." It is to be noted that "dealing with the environment" means a good deal more than receiving stimuli and making responses. Stimuli must be taken as indicators of objects in space, and responses must be adapted to produce effects upon these objects. Even the so-called "mental" capacities, such as memory and ideational thinking, become in time high-level methods of dealing with the environment. Woodworth leaves no doubt as to what he considers basic in motivation. "We are making the claim that this direction of receptive and motor activity toward the environment is the fundamental tendency of animal and human behavior and that it is the all-pervasive primary motivation of behavior." Organic drives have to break into this constantly flowing stream of activity and turn it in a special direction. But the goals of drives cannot be achieved without effective action upon one's surroundings. The ever-present, ever-primary feature of motivation is the tendency to deal with the environment.

It may appear to some workers that Woodworth has overshot the mark by making primary what has commonly been regarded as secondary, and by reducing the familiar drives to what sounds a little like a subordinate station. Woodworth's theory, however, like Goldstein's concept of self-actualization, probably should be construed not as an attempt to down-grade the drives but rather as an insistence that they be kept in the context of a whole living organism which during its waking hours is more or less constantly active. Woodworth's emphasis on dealing with the environment makes his theory a point of culmination for many of those driftings away from drive orthodoxy which we have found to be persistent in so many different areas of psychology. It will soon appear that the concept of competence, to which I now turn, represents in many respects a similar way of thinking. It emphasizes dealing with the environment, and it belongs in the trend away from drive *orthodoxy*, but it is not intended to supplant, or even to subsume, such dynamic forces as hunger, sex, aggression, and fear, which everyone knows to be of huge importance in animal and human nature.

COMPETENCE AND THE PLAY OF CONTENTED CHILDREN

A backward glance at our survey shows considerable agreement about the kinds of behavior that are left out or handled poorly by theories of motivation based wholly on organic drives. Repeatedly we find reference to the familiar series of learned skills which starts with sucking, grasping, and visual exploration and continues with crawling and walking, acts of focal attention and perception, memory, language and thinking, anticipation, the exploring of novel places and objects, effecting stimulus changes in the environment, manipulating and exploiting the surroundings, and achieving higher levels of motor and mental coordination. These aspects of behavior have long been the province of child psychology, which has attempted to measure the slow course of their development and has shown how heavily their growth depends upon learning. Collectively they are sometimes referred to as adaptive mechanisms or as ego processes, but on the whole we are not accustomed to cast a single name over the diverse feats whereby we learn to deal with the environment.

I now propose that we gather the various kinds of behavior just mentioned, all of which have to do with effective interaction with the environment, under the general heading of competence. According to Webster, competence means fitness or ability, and the suggested synonyms include capability, capacity, efficiency, proficiency, and skill. It is therefore a suitable word to describe such things as grasping and exploring, crawling and walking, attention and perception, language and thinking, manipulating and changing the surroundings, all of which promote an effective—a competent—interaction with the environment. It is true, of course, that maturation plays a part in all these developments, but this part is heavily overshadowed by learning in all the more complex accomplishments like speech or skilled manipulation. I shall argue that it is necessary to make competence a motivational concept; there is a *competence motivation* as well as competence in its more familiar sense of achieved capacity. The behavior that leads to the building up of effective grasping, handling, and letting go of objects, to take one example, is not random behavior produced by a general overflow of energy. It is directed, selective, and persistent, and it is continued not because it serves primary drives, which indeed it cannot serve until it is almost perfected, but because it satisfies an intrinsic need to deal with the environment.

No doubt it will at first seem arbitrary to propose a single motivational conception in connection with so many and such diverse kinds of behavior. What do we gain by attributing motivational unity to such a large array of activities? We could, of course, say that each developmental sequence, such as learning to grasp or to walk, has its own built-in bit of motivation—its "ailment," as Piaget (1952) has expressed it. We could go further and say that each item of behavior has its intrinsic motive—but this makes the concept of motivation redundant. On the other hand, we might follow the lead of the animal psychologists and postulate a limited number of broader motives under such names as curiosity, manipulation, and mastery. I believe that the idea of a competence motivation is more adequate than any of these alternatives and that it points to very vital common properties which have been lost from view amidst the strongly analytical tendencies that go with detailed research.

In order to make this claim more plausible, I shall now introduce some specimens of playful exploration in early childhood. I hope that these images will serve to fix and dramatize the concept of competence in the same way that other images—the hungry animal solving problems, the child putting his finger in the candle flame, the infant at the breast, the child on the toilet, and the youthful Oedipus caught in a hopeless love triangle—have become memorable focal points for other concepts. For this purpose I turn to Piaget's (1952) studies of the growth of intelligence from its earliest manifestations in his own three children. The examples come from the first year of life, before language and verbal concepts begin to be important. They therefore represent a practical kind of intelligence which may be quite similar to what is developed by the higher animals.

As early as the fourth month, the play of the gifted Piaget children began to be "centered on a result produced in the external environment," and their behavior could be described as "rediscovering the movement which by chance exercised an advantageous action upon things" (1952, p. 151). Laurent, lying in his bassinet, learns to shake a suspended rattle by pulling a string that hangs from it. He discovers this result fortuitously before vision and prehension are fully coordinated. Let us now observe him a little later when he has reached the age of three months and ten days.

> I place the string, which is attached to the rattle, in his right hand, merely unrolling it a little so that he may grasp it better. For a moment nothing happens. But at the first shake due to chance movement of his hand, the reaction is immediate: Laurent starts when looking at the rattle and then violently strikes his right hand alone, as if he felt the resistance and the effect. The operation lasts fully a quarter of an hour, during which Laurent emits peals of laughter [Piaget, 1952, p. 162].

Three days later the following behavior is observed.

> Laurent, by chance, strikes the chain while sucking his fingers. He grasps it and slowly displaces it while looking at the rattles. He then begins to swing it very gently, which produces a slight movement of the hanging rattles and an as yet faint sound inside them. Laurent then definitely increases by degrees his own movements. He shakes the chain more and more vigorously and laughs uproariously at the result obtained [Piaget, 1952, p. 185].

Very soon it can be observed that procedures are used "to make interesting spectacles last." For instance, Laurent is shown a rubber monkey which he has not seen before. After a moment of surprise, and perhaps even fright, he calms down and makes movements of pulling the string, a procedure which has no effect in this case, but which previously has caused interesting things to happen. It is to be noticed that "interesting spectacles" consist of such things as new toys, a tin box upon which a drumming noise can be made, an unfolded newspaper, or sounds made by the observer such as snapping the fingers. Commonplace as they are to the adult mind, these spectacles enter the infant's experience as novel and apparently challenging events.

Moving ahead to the second half of the first year, we can observe behavior in which the child explores the properties of objects and tries out his repertory of actions upon them. This soon leads to active experimentation in which the child attempts to provoke new results. Again we look in upon Laurent, who has now reached the age of nine months. On different occasions he is shown a variety of new objects—for instance a notebook, a beaded purse, and a wooden parrot. His carefully observing father detects four stages of response: (*a*) visual exploration, passing the object from hand to hand, folding the purse, *etc.*; (*b*) tactile exploration, passing the hand all over the object, scratching, *etc.*; (*c*) slow moving of the object in space; (*d*) use of the repertory of action: shaking the object, striking it, swinging it, rubbing it against the side of the bassinet, sucking it, *etc.*, "each in turn with a sort of prudence as though studying the effect produced" (1952, p. 255).

Here the child can be described as applying familiar tactics to new situations, but in a short while he will advance to clear patterns of active experimentation. At 10 months and 10 days Laurent, who is unfamiliar with bread as a nutritive substance, is given a piece for examination. He manipulates it, drops it many times, breaks off fragments and lets them fall. He has often done this kind of thing before, but previously his attention has seemed to be centered on the act of letting go. Now "he watches with great interest the body in motion; in particular, he looks at it for a long time when it has fallen, and picks it up when he can." On the following day he resumes his research.

> He grasps in succession a celluloid swan, a box, and several other small objects, in each case stretching out his arm and letting them fall. Sometimes he stretches out his arm vertically, sometimes he holds it obliquely in front of or behind his eyes. When the object falls in a new position (for example on his pillow) he lets it fall two or three times more on the same place, as though to study the spatial relation; then he modifies the situation. At a certain moment the swan falls near his mouth; now he does not suck it (even though this object habitually serves this purpose), but drops it three times more while merely making the gesture of opening his mouth [Piaget, 1952, p. 269].

These specimens will furnish us with sufficient images of the infant's use of his spare time. Laurent, of course, was provided by his studious father with a decidedly enriched environment, but no observant parent will question the fact that babies often act this way during those periods of their waking life when hunger, erotic needs, distresses, and anxiety seem to be exerting no particular pressure. If we consider this behavior under the historic headings of psychology we shall see that few processes are missing. The child gives evidence of sensing, perceiving, attending, learning, recognizing, probably recalling, and perhaps thinking in a rudimentary way. Strong emotion is lacking, but the infant's smiles, gurgles, and occasional peals of laughter strongly suggest the presence of pleasant affect. Actions appear in an organized form, particularly in the specimens of active exploration and experimentation. Apparently the child is using with a certain coherence nearly the whole repertory of psychological processes except those that accompany stress. It would be arbitrary indeed to say that one was more important than another.

These specimens have a meaningful unity when seen as transactions between the child and his environment, the child having some influence upon the environment and the environment some influence upon the child. Laurent appears to be concerned about what he can do with the chain and rattles, what he can accomplish by his own effort to reproduce and to vary the entertaining sounds. If his father observed correctly, we must add that Laurent seems to have varied his actions systematically, as if testing the effect of different degrees of effort upon the bit of environment represented by the chain and rattles. Kittens make a similar study of parameters when delicately using their paws to push pencils and other objects ever nearer to the edge of one's desk. In all such examples it is clear that the child or animal is by no means at the mercy of transient stimulus fields. He selects for continuous treatment those aspects of his environment which he finds it possible to affect in some way. His behavior is selective, directed, persistent —in short, motivated.

Motivated toward what goal? In these terms, too, the behavior exhibits a little of everything. Laurent can be seen as appeasing a stimulus hunger, providing his sensorium with an agreeable level of stimulation by eliciting from the environment a series of interesting sounds, feels, and sights. On the other hand we might emphasize a need for activity and see him as trying to reach a pleasurable level of neuromuscular exercise. We can also see another possible goal in the behavior: the child is achieving knowledge, attaining a more differentiated cognitive map of his environment and thus satisfying an exploratory tendency or motive of curiosity. But it is equally possible to discern a theme of mastery, power, or control, perhaps even a bit of primitive self-assertion, in the child's concentration upon those aspects of the environment which respond in some way to his own activity. It looks as if we had found too many goals, and perhaps our first impulse is to search for some key to tell us which one is really important. But this, I think, is a mistake that would be fatal to understanding.

We cannot assign priority to any of these goals without pausing arbitrarily in the cycle of transaction between child and environment and saying, "This is the real point." I propose instead that the real point is the transactions as a whole. If the behavior gives satisfaction, this satisfaction is not associated with a particular moment in the cycle. It does not lie solely in sensory stimulation, in a bettering of the cognitive map, in coordinated action, in motor exercise, in a feeling of effort and of effects produced, or in the appreciation of change brought about in the sensory field. These are all simply aspects of a process which at this stage has to be conceived as a whole. The child appears to be occupied with the agreeable task of developing an effective familiarity with his environment. This involves discovering the effects he can have on the environment and the effects the environment will have on him. To the extent that these results are preserved by learning, they build up an increased competence in dealing with the environment. The child's play can thus be viewed as serious business, though to him it is merely something that is interesting and fun to do.

Bearing in mind these examples, as well as the dealings with environment pointed out by other workers, we must now attempt to describe more fully the possible nature of the motivational aspect of competence. It needs its own name, and in view of the foregoing analysis I propose that this name be *effectance*.

EFFECTANCE

The new freedom produced by two decades of research on animal drives is of great help in this undertaking. We are no longer obliged to look for a source of energy external to the nervous system, for a consummatory climax, or for a fixed connection between reinforcement and tension-reduction. Effectance motivation cannot, of course, be conceived as having a source in tissues external to the nervous system. It is in no sense a deficit motive. We must assume it to be neurogenic, its "energies" being simply those of the living cells that make up the nervous system. External stimuli play an important part, but in terms of "energy" this part is secondary, as one can see most clearly when environmental stimulation is actively sought. Putting it picturesquely, we might say that the effectance urge represents what the neuromuscular system wants to do when it is otherwise unoccupied or is gently stimulated by the environment. Obviously there are no consummatory acts; satisfaction would appear to lie in the arousal and maintaining of activity rather than in its slow decline toward bored passivity. The motive need not be conceived as intense and powerful in the sense that hunger, pain, or fear can be powerful when aroused to high pitch. There are plenty of instances in which children refuse to leave their absorbed play in order to eat or to visit the toilet. Strongly aroused drives, pain, and anxiety, however, can be conceived as overriding the effectance urge and capturing the energies of the neuromuscular system. But effectance motivation is persistent in the sense that it regularly occupies the spare waking time between episodes of homeostatic crisis.

In speculating upon this subject we must bear in mind the continuous nature of behavior. This is easier said than done; habitually we break things down in order to understand them, and such units as the reflex arc, the stimulus-response sequence, and the single transaction with the environment seem like inevitable steps toward clarity. Yet when we apply such an analysis to playful exploration we lose the most essential aspect of the behavior. It is constantly circling from stimulus to perception to action to effect to stimulus to perception, and so on around; or, more properly, these processes are all in continuous action and continuous change. Dealing with the environment means carrying on a continuing transaction which gradually changes one's relation to the environment. Because there is no consummatory climax, satisfaction has to be seen as lying in a considerable series of transactions, in a trend of behavior rather than a goal that is achieved. It is difficult to make the word "satisfaction" have this connotation, and we shall do well to replace it by [the] "feeling of efficacy" when attempting to indicate the subjective and affective side of effectance.

It is useful to recall the findings about novelty: the singular effectiveness of novelty in engaging interest and for a time supporting persistent behavior. We also need to consider the selective continuance of transactions in which the animal or child has a more or less pronounced effect upon the environment—in which something happens as a consequence of his activity. Interest is not aroused and sustained when the stimulus field is so familiar that it gives rise at most to reflex acts or automatized habits. It is not sustained when actions produce no effects or changes in the stimulus field. Our conception must therefore be that effectance motivation is aroused by stimulus conditions which offer, as Hebb (1949) puts it, difference-in-sameness. This leads to variability and novelty of response, and interest is best sustained when the resulting action affects the stimulus so as to produce further difference-in-sameness. Interest wanes when action begins to have less effect; effectance motivation subsides when a situation has been explored to the point that it no longer presents new possibilities.

We have to conceive further that the arousal of playful and exploratory interest means the appearance of organization involving both the cognitive and active aspects of behavior. Change in the stimulus field is not an end in itself, so to speak; it happens when one is passively moved about, and it may happen as a consequence of random movements without becoming focalized and instigating exploration. Similarly, action which has effects is not an end in itself, for if one unintentionally kicks away a branch while walking, or knocks something off a table, these effects by no means necessarily become involved in playful investigation. Schachtel's (1954) emphasis on focal attention becomes helpful at this point. The playful and exploratory behavior shown by Laurent is not random or casual. It involves focal *attention* to some object—the fixing of some aspect of the stimulus field so that it stays relatively constant—and it also involves the focalizing of *action* upon this object. As Diamond (1939) has expressed it, response under these conditions is "relevant to the stimulus," and it is change in the *focalized* stimulus that so strongly affects the level of interest. Dealing with the environment means directing focal attention to some part of it and organizing actions to have some effect on this part.

In our present state of relative ignorance about the workings of the nervous system it is impossible to form a satisfactory idea of the neural basis of effectance motivation, but it should at least be clear that the concept does not refer to any and every kind of neural action. It refers to a particular kind of activity, as inferred from particular kinds of behavior. We can say that it does not include reflexes and other kinds of automatic response. It does not include well-learned, automatized patterns, even those that are complex and highly organized. It does not include behavior in the service of effectively aroused drives. It does not even include activity that is highly random and discontinuous, though such behavior may be its most direct forerunner. The urge toward competence is inferred specifically from behavior that shows a lasting focalization and that has the characteristics of exploration and experimentation, a kind of variation within the focus. When this particular sort of activity is aroused in the nervous system, effectance motivation is being aroused, for it is characteristic of this particular sort of activity that it is selective, directed, and persistent, and that instrumental acts will be learned for the sole reward of engaging in it.

Some objection may be felt to my introducing the word *competence* in connection with behavior that is so often playful. Certainly the playing child is doing things for fun, not because of a desire to improve his competence in dealing with the stern hard world. In order to forestall misunderstanding, it should be pointed out that the usage here is parallel to what we do when we connect sex with its biological goal of reproduction. The sex drive aims for pleasure and gratification, and reproduction is a consequence that is presumably unforeseen by animals and by man at primitive levels of understanding. Effectance motivation similarly aims for the feeling of efficacy, not for the vitally important learnings that come as its consequence. If we consider the part played by competence motivation in adult human life we can observe the same parallel. Sex may now be completely and purposefully divorced from reproduction but nevertheless pursued for the pleasure it can yield. Similarly, effectance motivation may lead to continuing exploratory interests or active adventures when in fact there is no longer any gain in actual competence or any need for it in terms of survival. In both cases the motive is capable of yielding surplus satisfaction well beyond what is necessary to get the biological work done.

In infants and young children it seems to me sensible to conceive of effectance motivation as undifferentiated. Later in life it becomes profitable to distinguish various motives such as cognizance, construction, mastery, and achievement. It is my view that all such motives have a root in effectance motivation. They are differentiated from it through life experiences which emphasize one or another aspect of the cycle of transaction with environment. Of course, the motives of later childhood and of adult life are no longer simple and can almost never be referred to a single root. They can acquire loadings of anxiety, defense, and compensation, they can become fused with unconscious fantasies of a sexual, aggressive, or omnipotent character, and they can gain force because of their service in producing realistic results in the way of income and career. It is not my intention to cast effectance in the star part in adult motivation. The acquisition of motives is a complicated affair in which simple and sovereign theories grow daily more obsolete. Yet it may be that the satisfaction of effectance contributes significantly to those feelings of interest which often sustain us so well in day-to-day actions, particularly when the things we are doing have continuing elements of novelty.

THE BIOLOGICAL SIGNIFICANCE OF COMPETENCE

The conviction was expressed at the beginning of this paper that some such concept as competence, interpreted motivationally, was essential for any biologically sound view of human nature. This necessity emerges when we consider the nature of living systems, particularly when we take a longitudinal view. What an organism does at a given moment does not always give the right clue as to what it does over a period of time. Discussing this problem, Angyal (1941) has proposed that we should look for the general pattern followed by the total organismic process over the course of time. Obviously this makes it necessary to take account of growth. Angyal defines life as "a process of self-expansion"; the living system "expands at the expense of its surroundings," assimilating parts of the environment and transforming them into functioning parts of itself. Organisms differ from other things in nature in that they are "self-governing entities" which are to some extent "autonomous." Internal processes govern them as well as external "heteronomous" forces. In the course of life there is a relative increase in the preponderance of internal over external forces. The living system expands, assimilates more of the environment, transforms its surroundings so as to bring them under greater control. "We may say," Angyal writes, "that the general dynamic trend of the organism is toward an increase of autonomy. . . . The human being has a characteristic tendency toward self-determination, that is, a tendency to resist external influences and to subordinate the heteronomous forces of the physical and social environment to its own sphere of influence." The trend toward increased autonomy is characteristic so long as growth of any kind is going on, though in the end the living system is bound to succumb to the pressure of heteronomous forces.

Of all living creatures, it is man who takes the longest strides toward autonomy. This is not because of any unusual tendency toward bodily expansion at the expense of the environment. It is rather that man, with his mobile hands and abundantly developed brain, attains an extremely high level of competence in his transactions with his surroundings. The building of houses, roads and bridges, the making of tools and instruments, the domestication of plants and animals, all qualify as planful changes made in the environment so that it comes more or less under control and serves our purposes rather than intruding upon them. We meet the fluctuations of outdoor temperature, for example, not only with our bodily homeostatic mechanisms, which alone would be painfully unequal to the task, but also with clothing, buildings, controlled fires, and such complicated devices as self-regulating central heating and air conditioning. Man as a species has developed a tremendous power of bringing the environment into his service, and each individual member of the species must attain what is really quite an impressive level of competence if he is to take part in the life around him.

We are so accustomed to these human accomplishments that it is hard to realize how long an apprenticeship they require. At the outset the human infant is a slow learner in comparison with other animal forms. Hebb (1949) speaks of "the astonishing inefficiency of man's first learning, as far as immediate results are concerned," an inefficiency which he attributes to the large size of the association areas in the brain and the long time needed to bring them under sensory control. The human lack of precocity in learning shows itself even in comparison with one of the next of kin: as Hebb points out, "the human baby takes six months, the chimpanzee four months, before making a clear distinction between friend and enemy." Later in life the slow start will pay dividends. Once the fundamental perceptual elements, simple associations, and conceptual sequences have been established, later learning can proceed with ever increasing swiftness and complexity. In Hebb's words, "learning at maturity concerns patterns and events whose parts at least are familiar and which already have a number of other associations."

This general principle of cumulative learning, starting from slowly acquired rudiments and proceeding thence with increasing efficiency, can be illustrated by such processes as manipulation and locomotion, which may culminate in the acrobat devised new stunts or the dancer working out a new ballet. It is especially vivid in the case of language, where the early mastery of words and pronunciation seems such a far cry from spontaneous adult speech. A strong argument has been made by Hebb (1949) that the learning of visual forms proceeds over a similar course from slowly learned elements to rapidly combined patterns. Circles and squares, for example, cannot be discriminated at a glance without a slow apprenticeship involving eye movements, successive fixations, and recognition of angles. Hebb proposes that the recognition of visual patterns without eye movement "is possible only as the result of an intensive and prolonged visual training that goes on from the moment of birth, during every moment that the eyes are open, with an increase in skill evident over a period of 12 to 16 years at least."

On the motor side there is likewise a lot to be cumulatively learned. The playing, investigating child slowly finds out the relationships between what he does and what he experiences. He finds out, for instance, how hard he must push what in order to produce what effect. Here the S-R formula is particularly misleading. It would come nearer the truth to say that the child is busy learning R-S connections—the effects that are likely to follow upon his own behavior. But even in this reversed form the notion of bonds or connections would still misrepresent the situation, for it is only a rare specimen of behavior that can properly be conceived as determined by fixed neural channels and a fixed motor response. As Hebb has pointed

out, discussing the phenomenon of "motor equivalence" named by Lashley
(1942), a rat which has been trained to press a lever will press it with the
left forepaw, the right forepaw, by climbing upon it, or by biting it; a
monkey will open the lid of a food box with either hand, with a foot, or
even with a stick; and we might add that a good baseball player can catch a
fly ball while running in almost any direction and while in almost any
posture, including leaping in the air and plunging forward to the ground.
All of these feats are possible because of a history of learnings in which the
main lesson has been the effects of actions upon the stimulus fields that
represent the environment. What has been learned is not a fixed connection but a flexible relationship between stimulus fields and the effects that
can be produced in them by various kinds of action.

One additional example, drawn this time from Piaget (1952), is
particularly worth mentioning because of its importance in theories of
development. Piaget points out that a great deal of mental development
depends upon the idea that the world is made up of objects having substance and permanence. Without such an "object concept" it would be
impossible to build up the ideas of space and causality and to arrive at the
fundamental distinction between self and external world. Observation
shows that the object concept, "far from being innate or ready-made in
experience, is constructed little by little." Up to 7 and 8 months the Piaget
children searched for vanished objects only in the sense of trying to
continue the actions, such as sucking or grasping, in which the objects had
played a part. When an object was really out of sight or touch, even if only
because it was covered by a cloth, the infants undertook no further
exploration. Only gradually, after some study of the displacement of objects
by moving, swinging, and dropping them, does the child begin to make an
active search for a vanished object, and only still more gradually does he
learn, at 12 months or more, to make allowance for the object's sequential
displacements and thus to seek it where it has gone rather than where it
was last in sight. Thus it is only through cumulative learning that the child
arrives at the idea of permanent substantial objects.

The infant's play is indeed serious business. If he did not while away
his time pulling strings, shaking rattles, examining wooden parrots, dropping pieces of bread and celluloid swans, when would he learn to
discriminate visual patterns, to catch and throw, and to build up his
concept of the object? When would he acquire the many other foundation
stones necessary for cumulative learning? The more closely we analyze the
behavior of the human infant, the more clearly do we realize that infancy
is not simply a time when the nervous system matures and the muscles
grow stronger. It is a time of active and continuous learning, during which
the basis is laid for all those processes, cognitive and motor, whereby the
child becomes able to establish effective transactions with his environment
and move toward a greater degree of autonomy. Helpless as he may seem
until he begins to toddle, he has by that time already made substantial
gains in the achievement of competence.

Under primitive conditions survival must depend quite heavily upon achieved competence. We should expect to find things so arranged as to favor and maximize this achievement. Particularly in the case of man, where so little is provided innately and so much has to be learned through experience, we should expect to find highly advantageous arrangements for securing a steady cumulative learning about the properties of the environment and the extent of possible transactions. Under these circumstances we might expect to find a very powerful drive operating to insure progress toward competence, just as the vital goals of nutrition and reproduction are secured by powerful drives, and it might therefore seem paradoxical that the interests of competence should be so much entrusted to times of play and leisurely exploration. There is good reason to suppose, however, that a strong drive would be precisely the wrong arrangement to secure a flexible, knowledgeable power of transaction with the environment. Strong drives cause us to learn certain lessons well, but they do not create maximum familiarity with our surroundings.

This point was demonstrated half a century ago in some experiments by Yerkes and Dodson (1908). They showed that maximum motivation did not lead to the most rapid solving of problems, especially if the problems were complex. For each problem there was an optimum level of motivation, neither the highest nor the lowest, and the optimum was lower for more complex tasks. The same problem has been discussed more recently by Tolman (1948) in his paper on cognitive maps. A cognitive map can be narrow or broad, depending upon the range of cues picked up in the course of learning. Tolman suggests that one of the conditions which tend to narrow the range of cues is a high level of motivation. In everyday terms, a man hurrying to an important business conference is likely to perceive only the cues that help him to get there faster, whereas a man taking a stroll after lunch is likely to pick up a substantial amount of casual information about his environment. The latent learning experiments with animals, and experiments such as those of Johnson (1953) in which drive level has been systematically varied in a situation permitting incidental learning, give strong support to this general idea. In a recent contribution, Bruner, Matter, and Papanek (1955) make a strong case for the concept of breadth of learning and provide additional evidence that it is favored by moderate and hampered by strong motivation. The latter "has the effect of speeding up learning at the cost of narrowing it." Attention is concentrated upon the task at hand and little that is extraneous to this task is learned for future use.

These facts enable us to see the biological appropriateness of an arrangement which uses periods of less intense motivation for the development of competence. This is not to say that the narrower but efficient learnings that go with the reduction of strong drives make no contribution to general effectiveness. They are certainly an important element in capacity to deal with the environment, but a much greater effectiveness results from having this capacity fed also from learnings that take place in quieter times. It is then that the infant can attend to matters of lesser urgency, exploring the properties of things he does not fear and does not need to eat, learning to gauge the force of his string-pulling when the only penalty for failure is silence on the part of the attached rattles, and generally accumulating for himself a broad knowledge and a broad skill in dealing with his surroundings.

The concept of competence can be most easily discussed by choosing, as we have done, examples of interaction with the inanimate environment. It applies equally well, however, to transactions with animals and with other human beings, where the child has the same problem of finding out what effects he can have upon the environment and what effects it can have upon him. The earliest interactions with members of the family may involve needs so strong that they obscure the part played by effectance motivation, but perhaps the example of the well fed baby diligently exploring the several features of his mother's face will serve as a reminder that here, too, there are less urgent moments when learning for its own sake can be given free rein.

In this closing section I have brought together several ideas which bear on the evolutionary significance of competence and of its motivation. I have sought in this way to deepen the biological roots of the concept and thus help it to attain the stature in the theory of behavior which has not been reached by similar concepts in the past. To me it seems that the most important proving ground for this concept is the effect it may have on our understanding of the development of personality. Does it assist our grasp of early object relations, the reality principle, and the first steps in the development of the ego? Can it be of service in distinguishing the kinds of defense available at different ages and in providing clues to the replacement of primitive defenses by successful adaptive maneuvers? Can it help fill the yawning gap known as the latency period, a time when the mastery of school subjects and other accomplishments claim so large a share of time and energy? Does it bear upon the self and the vicissitudes of self-esteem, and can it enlighten the origins of psychological disorder? Can it make adult motives and interests more intelligible and enable us to rescue the concept of sublimation from the difficulties which even its best friends have recognized? I believe it can be shown that existing explanations of development are not satisfactory and that the addition of the concept of competence cuts certain knots in personality theory. But this is not the subject of the present communication, where the concept is offered much more on the strength of its logical and biological probability.

SUMMARY

The main theme of this paper is introduced by showing that there is widespread discontent with theories of motivation built upon primary drives. Signs of this discontent are found in realms as far apart as animal psychology and psychoanalytic ego psychology. In the former, the commonly recognized primary drives have proved to be inadequate in explaining exploratory behavior, manipulation, and general activity. In the latter, the theory of basic instincts has shown serious shortcomings when it is stretched to account for the development of the effective ego. Workers with animals have attempted to meet their problem by invoking secondary reinforcement and anxiety reduction, or by adding exploration and manipulation to the roster of primary drives. In parallel fashion, psychoanalytic workers have relied upon the concept of neutralization of instinctual energies, have seen anxiety reduction as the central motive in ego development, or have hypothesized new instincts such as mastery. It is argued here that these several explanations are not satisfactory and that a better conceptualization is possible, indeed that it has already been all but made.

In trying to form this conceptualization, it is first pointed out that many of the earlier tenets of primary drive theory have been discredited by recent experimental work. There is no longer any compelling reason to identify either pleasure or reinforcement with drive reduction, or to think of motivation as requiring a source of energy external to the nervous system. This opens the way for considering in their own right those aspects of animal and human behavior in which stimulation and contact with the environment seem to be sought and welcomed, in which raised tension and even mild excitement seem to be cherished, and in which novelty and variety seem to be enjoyed for their own sake. Several reports are cited which bear upon interest in the environment and the rewarding effects of environmental feedback. The latest contribution is that of Woodworth (1958), who makes dealing with the environment the most fundamental element in motivation.

The survey indicates a certain unanimity as to the kinds of behavior that cannot be successfully conceptualized in terms of primary drives. This behavior includes visual exploration, grasping, crawling and walking, attention and perception, language and thinking, exploring novel objects and places, manipulating the surroundings, and producing effective changes in the environment. The thesis is then proposed that all of these behaviors have a common biological significance: they all form part of the process whereby the animal or child learns to interact effectively with his environment. The word *competence* is chosen as suitable to indicate this common property. Further, it is maintained that competence cannot be fully acquired simply through behavior instigated by drives. It receives substantial contributions from activities which, though playful and exploratory in character, at the same time show direction, selectivity, and persistence in interacting with the environment. Such activities in the ultimate service of competence must therefore be conceived to be motivated in their own right. It is proposed to designate this motivation by the term effectance, and to characterize the experience produced as a *feeling of efficacy*.

In spite of its sober biological purpose, effectance motivation shows itself most unambiguously in the playful and investigatory behavior of young animals and children. Specimens of such behavior, drawn from Piaget (1952), are analyzed in order to demonstrate their constantly transactional nature. Typically they involve continuous chains of events which include stimulation, cognition, action, effect on the environment, new stimulation, etc. They are carried on with considerable persistence and with selective emphasis on parts of the environment which provide changing and interesting feedback in connection with effort expended. Their significance is destroyed if we try to break into the circle arbitrarily and declare that one part of it, such as cognition alone or active effort alone, is the real point, the goal, or the special seat of satisfaction. Effectance motivation must be conceived to involve satisfaction—a feeling of efficacy—in transactions in which behavior has an exploratory, varying, experimental character and produces changes in the stimulus field. Having this character, the behavior leads the organism to find out how the environment can be changed and what consequences flow from these changes.

In higher animals and especially in man, where so little is innately provided and so much has to be learned about dealing with the environment, effectance motivation independent of primary drives can be seen as an arrangement having high adaptive value. Considering the slow rate of learning in infancy and the vast amount that has to be learned before there can be an effective level of interaction with surroundings, young animals and children would simply not learn enough unless they worked pretty steadily at the crisis. The association of interest with this "work," making it play and fun, is thus somewhat comparable to the association of sexual pleasure with the biological goal of reproduction. Effectance motivation need not be conceived as strong in the sense that sex, hunger, and fear are strong when violently aroused. It is moderate but persistent, and in this, too, we can discern a feature that is favorable for adaptation. Strong motivation reinforces learning in a narrow sphere, whereas moderate motivation is more conducive to an exploratory and experimental attitude which leads to competent interactions in general, without reference to an immediate pressing need. Man's huge cortical association areas might have been a suicidal piece of specialization if they had come without a steady, persistent inclination toward interacting with the environment.

REFERENCES:

ALLPORT, G. W. *Personality: a Psychological Interpretation* (New York: Holt, 1937).

ALLPORT, G. W. Effect: a secondary principle of learning. *Psychol. Rev.*, 1946, 53, 335–347.

ANGYAL, A. *Foundations for a Science of Personality* (New York: Commonwealth Fund, 1941).

ANSBACHER, H. L., and ANSBACHER, ROWENA R. (Eds.), *The Individual Psychology of Alfred Adler* (New York: Basic Books, 1956).

BEACH, F. A. Analysis of factors involved in the arousal, maintenance and manifestation of sexual excitement in male animals. *Psychosom. Med.*, 1942, 4, 173–198.

BEACH, F. A. Instinctive behavior: reproductive activities. In S. S. Stevens (Ed.), *Handbook of Experimental Psychology* (New York: Wiley, 1951). Pp. 387–434.

BERLYNE, D. E. Novelty and curiosity as determinants of exploratory behavior. *Brit. J. Psychol.*, 1950, 41, 68–80.

BERLYNE, D. E. The arousal and satiation of perceptual curiosity in the rat. *J. Comp. Physiol. Psychol.*, 1955, 48, 238–246.

BERLYNE, D. E. Attention to change, conditioned inhibition (S^{I}R) and stimulus satiation. *Brit. J. Psychol.*, 1957, 48, 138–140.

BERLYNE, D. E. The present status of research on exploratory and related behavior. *J. Indiv. Psychol.*, 1958, 14, 121–126.

BIBRING, E. The development and problems of the theories of the instincts. *Int. J. Psychoanal.*, 1941, 22, 102–131.

BRUNER, J. S., MATTER, J., and PAPANEK, M. L. Breadth of learning as a function of drive level and mechanization. *Psychol. Rev.*, 1955, 62, 1–10.

BÜHLER, C. The reality principle. *Amer. J. Psychother.*, 1954, 8, 626–647.

BÜHLER, K. *Die geistige Entwicklung des Kindes* (4th ed.) (Jena: Gustav Fischer, 1924).

BUTLER, R. A. Discrimination learning by rhesus monkeys to visual-exploration motivation. *J. Comp. Physiol. Psychol.*, 1953, 46, 95–98.

BUTLER, R. A. Exploratory and related behavior: a new trend in animal research. *J. Indiv. Psychol.*, 1958, 14, 111–120.

BUTLER, R. A., and HARLOW, H. F. Discrimination learning and learning sets to visual exploration incentives. *J. Gen. Psychol.*, 1957, 57, 257–264.

COFER, C. N. Motivation. *Ann. Rev. Psychol.*, 1959, 10, 173–202.

COLBY, K. M. *Energy and Structure in Psychoanalysis* (New York: Ronald, 1955).

DASHIELL, J. F. A quantitative demonstration of animal drive. *J. Comp. Psychol.*, 1925, 5, 205–208.

DIAMOND, S. A neglected aspect of motivation. *Sociometry*, 1939, 2, 77–85.

DOLLARD, J., and MILLER, N. E. *Personality and Psychotherapy* (New York: McGraw-Hill, 1950).

ERIKSON, E. H. *Childhood and Society* (New York: Norton, 1950).

ERIKSON, E. H. Growth and crises of the healthy personality. In C. Kluckhohn, and H. A. Murray (Eds.), *Personality in Nature, Society, and Culture.* (2nd ed.) (New York: Knopf, 1953). Pp. 185–225.

FENICHEL, O. *The Psychoanalytic Theory of Neurosis* (New York: Norton: 1945).

FRENCH, T. M. *The Integration of Behavior.* Vol. 1. *Basic Postulates* (Chicago: Univer. Chicago Press, 1952).

FREUD, ANNA. The mutual influences in the development of ego and id: introduction to the discussion. In Ruth S. Eissler *et al.* (Eds.), *The Psychoanalytic Study of the Child.* Vol. 7. (New York: International Universities Press, 1952). Pp. 42–50.

FREUD, S. *Wit and its relation to the unconscious.* (New York: Moffat, Yard, 1961).

FREUD, S. Formulations regarding the two principles in mental functioning. In *Collected Papers.* Vol. 4 (London: Hogarth and Institute of Psycho-analysis, 1925). Pp. 13–21. (a)

FREUD, S. On narcissism: an introduction. In *Collected Papers.* Vol. 4 (London: Hogarth and Institute of Psycho-analysis, 1925). Pp. 30–59. (b)

FREUD, S. Instincts and their vicissitudes. In *Collected Papers.* Vol. 4 (London: Hogarth and Institute of Psycho-analysis, 1925). Pp. 60–83. (c)

FREUD, S. *The Ego and the Id.* (Trans. by J. Riviere.) (London: Hogarth, 1927).

FREUD, S. *Beyond the Pleasure Principle* (London: Hogarth, 1948).

FREUD, S. *An Outline of Psychoanalysis.* (Trans. by J. Strachey.) (New York: Norton, 1949).

GOLDSTEIN, K. *The Organism* (New York: American Book, 1939).

GOLDSTEIN, K. *Human Nature in the Light of Psychopathology* (Cambridge, Mass.: Harvard Univer. Press, 1940).

GROSS, K. *The Play of Man.* (Trans. by E. L. Baldwin.) (New York: Appleton, 1901).

HARLOW, H. F. Mice, monkeys, men, and motives. *Psychol. Rev.,* 1953, *60,* 23–32.

HARLOW, H. F., HARLOW, MARGARET K., and MEYER, D. R. Learning motivated by a manipulation drive. *J. Exp. Psychol.,* 1950, *40,* 228–234.

HARTMANN, H. Comments on the psychoanalytic theory of the ego. In Ruth S. Eissler *et al.* (Eds.), *The Psychoanalytic Study of the Child.* Vol. 5 (New York: International Universities Press, 1950). Pp. 74–95.

HARTMANN, H. Notes on the theory of sublimation. In Ruth S. Eissler *et al.* (Eds.), *The Psychoanalytic Study of the Child.* Vol. 10 (New York: International Universities Press, 1955). Pp. 9–29.

HARTMANN, H. Notes on the reality principle. In Ruth S. Eissler *et al.* (Eds.), *The Psychoanalytic Study of the Child.* Vol. 11 (New York: International Universities Press, 1956). Pp. 31–53.

HARTMANN, H. *Ego Psychology and the Problem of Adaptation.* (Trans. by D. Rapaport.) (New York: International Universities Press, 1958).

HARTMANN, H., KRIS, E., and LOEWENSTEIN, R. Notes on the theory of aggression. In Ruth S. Eissler et al. (Eds.), *The Psychoanalytic Study of the Child*. Vol. 3/4 (New York: International Universities Press, 1949). Pp. 9–36.

HEBB, D. O. *The Organization of Behavior* (New York: Wiley, 1949).

HEBB, D. O. Drives and the c.n.s. (conceptual nervous system). *Psychol. Rev.*, 1955, 62, 243–254.

HEBB, D. O. The motivating effects of exteroceptive stimulation. *Amer. Psychologist*, 1958, 13, 109–113.

HEBB, D. O., and THOMPSON, W. R. The social significance of animal studies. In G. Lindzey (Ed.), *Handbook of Social Psychology*. Vol. 1 (Reading, Mass.: Addison-Wesley, 1954). Pp. 532–561.

HENDRICK, I. Instinct and the ego during infancy. *Psychoanalyt. Quart.*, 1942, 11, 33–58.

HENDRICK, I. Work and the pleasure principle. *Psychoanalyt. Quart.*, 1943, 12, 311–329. (a).

HENDRICK, I. The discussion of the instinct to master. *Psychoanalyt. Quart.* 1943, 12, 561–565. (b)

HILL, W. F. Activity as an autonomous drive. *J. Comp. Physiol. Psychol.*, 1956, 49, 15–19.

JOHNSON, E. E. The role of motivational strength in latent learning. *J. Comp. Psychol.*, 1953, 45, 526–530.

KAGAN, J. Differential reward value of incomplete and complete sexual behavior. *J. Comp. Physiol. Psychol.*, 1955, 48, 59–64.

KAGAN, J., and BERKUN, M. The reward value of running activity. *J. Comp. Physiol. Psychol.*, 1954, 47, 108.

KARDINER, A., and SPIEGEL, H. *War Stress and Neurotic Illness* (New York: Hoeber, 1947).

LASHLEY, K. S. Experimental analysis of instinctive behavior. *Psychol. Rev.*, 1938, 45, 445–471.

LASHLEY, K. S. The problem of cerebral organization in vision. In H. Klüver, *Visual Mechanisms* (New York: Jacques Cattell, 1942). Pp. 301–322.

LEUBA, C. Toward some integration of learning theories: the concept of optimal stimulation. *Psychol. Rep.* 1955, 1, 27–33.

LILLY, J. C. Mental effects of reduction of ordinary levels of physical stimuli on intact, healthy persons. *Psychiat. Res. Rep.*, 1956, No. 5.

MASLOW, A. H. *Motivation and Personality* (New York: Harper, 1954).

MASLOW, A. H. Deficiency motivation and growth motivation. In M. R. Jones (Ed.), *Nebraska Symposium on Motivation 1955* (Lincoln, Neb.: Univer. Nebraska Press, 1955). Pp. 1–30.

MCCELLAND, D. C., ATKINSON, J. W., CLARK, R. A., and LOWELL, E. L. *The Achievement Motive* (New York: Appleton-Century-Crofts, 1953).

MCDOUGALL, W. *Introduction to Social Psychology* (16th ed.) (Boston: John Luce, 1923).

MCREYNOLDS, P. A. A restricted conceptualization of human anxiety and motivation. *Psychol. Rep.,* 1956, 2, 293–312. (Monogr. Suppl. 6.)

MILLER, N. E. Learnable drives and rewards. In S. S. Stevens (Ed.), *Handbook of Experimental Psychology* (New York: Wiley, 1951). Pp. 435–472.

MILLER, N. E. Central stimulation and other new approaches to motivation and reward. *Amer. Psychologist,* 1958, 13, 100–108.

MITTELMANN, B. Motility in infants, children, and adults. In Ruth S. Eissler *et al.* (Eds.), *The Psychoanalytic Study of the Child.* Vol. 9 (New York: International Universities Press, 1954). Pp. 142–177.

MONTGOMERY, K. C. The role of the exploratory drive in learning. *J. Comp. Physiol. Psychol.,* 1954, 47, 60–64.

MONTGOMERY, K. C., and MONKMAN, J. A. The relation between fear and exploratory behavior. *J. Comp. Physiol. Psychol.,* 1955, 48, 132–136.

MORGAN, C. T. *Physiological Psychology* (New York: McGraw-Hill, 1943).

MORGAN, C. T. Physiological mechanisms of motivation. In M. R. Jones (Ed.), *Nebraska Symposium on Motivation 1957* (Lincoln, Neb.: Univer. Nebraska Press, 1957). Pp. 1–35.

MOWRER, O. H. *Learning Theory and Personality Dynamics* (New York: Ronald, 1950).

MUNROE, R. *Schools of Psychoanalytical Thought* (New York: Dryden, 1955).

MURPHY, G. *Personality: a Biosocial Approach to Origins and Structure* (New York: Harper, 1947).

MURRAY, H. A. *Explorations in Personality* (New York and London: Oxford Univer. Press, 1938).

MURRAY, H. A., and KLUCKHOHN, C. Outline of a conception of personality. In C. Kluckhohn and H. A. Murray (Eds.), *Personality in Nature, Society, and Culture.* (2nd ed.) (New York: Knopf, 1953).

MYERS, A. K., and MILLER, N. E. Failure to find a learned drive based on hunger; evidence for learning motivated by "exploration." *J. Comp. Physiol. Psychol.,* 1954, 47, 428–436.

NISSEN, H. W. A study of exploratory behavior in the white rat by means of the obstruction method. *J. Genet. Psychol.,* 1930, 37, 361–376.

OLDS, J., and MILNER, P. Positive reinforcement produced by electrical stimulation of septal area and other regions of rat brain. *J. Comp. Physiol. Psychol.,* 1954, 47, 419–427.

PIAGET, J. *The Origins of Intelligence in Children.* (Trans. by M. Cook.) (New York: International Universities Press, 1952).

RAPAPORT, D. *Organization and Pathology of Thought* (New York: Columbia Univer. Press, 1951).

RAPAPORT, D. On the psychoanalytic theory of thinking. In R. P. Knight and C. R. Friedman (Eds.), *Psychoanalytic Psychiatry and Psychology* (New York: International Universities Press, 1954). Pp. 259–273.

RAPAPORT, D. The theory of ego autonomy: a generalization. *Bull. Menninger Clin.*, 1958, 22, 13–35.

ROSVOLD, H. E. Physiological psychology. *Ann. Rev. Psychol.*, 1959, 10, 415–454.

SCHACHTEL, E. G. The development of focal attention and the emergence of reality. *Psychiatry*, 1954, 17, 309–324.

SHEFFIELD, F. D., and ROBY, T. B. Reward value of a non-nutritive sweet taste. *J. Comp. Physiol. Psychol.*, 1950, 43, 471–481.

SHEFFIELD, F. D., ROBY, T. B., and CAMPBELL, B. A. Drive reduction vs. consummatory behavior as determinants of reinforcement. *J. Comp. Physiol. Psychol.*, 1954, 47, 349–354.

SHEFFIELD, F. D., WULFF, J. J., and BACKER, R. Reward value of copulation without sex drive reduction. *J. Comp. Physiol. Psychol.*, 1951, 44, 3–8.

SKINNER, B. F. *Science and Human Behavior.* (New York: Macmillan, 1953).

STELLER, E. The physiology of motivation. *Psychol. Rev.*, 1954, 61, 5–22.

TOLMAN, E. C. Cognitive maps in rats and men. *Psychol. Rev.*, 1948, 55, 189–208.

WELKER, W. L. Some determinants of play and exploration in chimpanzees. *J. Comp. Physiol. Psychol.*, 1956, 49, 84–89.

WHITING, J. W. M., and MOWRER, O. H. Habit progression and regression —a laboratory study of some factors relevant to human socialization. *J. Comp. Psychol.*, 1943, 36, 229–253.

WOLFE, J. B., and KAPLON, M. D. Effect of amount of reward and consummative activity on learning in chickens. *J. Comp. Psychol.*, 1941, 31, 353–361.

WOODWORTH, R. S. *Dynamics of Behavior* (New York: Holt, 1958).

YERKES, R. M., and DODSON, J. D. The relation of strength of stimulus to rapidity of habit-formation. *J. Comp. Neurol. Psychol.*, 1908, 18, 459–482.

YOUNG, P. T. Food-seeking drive, affective process, and learning. *Psychol. Rev.*, 1949, 56, 98–121.

YOUNG, P. T. The role of hedonic processes in motivation. In M. R. Jones (Ed.), *Nebraska Symposium on Motivation 1955* (Lincoln, Neb.: Univer. Nebraska Press, 1955). Pp. 193–238.

ZIMBARDO, P. G., and MILLER, N. E. Facilitation of exploration by hunger in rats. *J. Comp. Physiol. Psychol.*, 1958, 51, 43–46.

7   *Experience and the Development of Motivation:
      Some Reinterpretations*[*][1]

BY J. McV. HUNT

*EDITOR'S NOTE: In the previous article, Dr. White spoke of
the possible intrinsic motivational value which may be a part of
one's interaction with the environment. In a sense, this present
paper is an extension of some of the ideas and questions raised by
Dr. White. For example, Dr. Hunt raises the question of whether
or not all behavior is motivated. He goes a step further and
wonders whether or not it is true that "organisms become inactive
unless stimulated by homeostatic need or painful stimulation
. . . ." How about yourself? Are you ever "motivated" or inclined
to behave (work, solve problems, play) when, let's say, you are
homeostatically satisfied or comfortably warm? Do you ever do anything just for the sake of itself? Read this carefully and as you do
ask yourself, "What are the implications here for teachers? What
does it mean when translated into teacher/student behavior?"*

A recent issue of the *Saturday Evening Post* carried a cartoon that
some of you may have noted. It depicts a boy entering his house, perhaps
from school, where his father is sitting with his paper. The boy appears to
be fixing his father with an accusing glare. The punch-line reads, "Somebody goofed. I'm improperly motivated."

This cartoon depicts the vantage point from which I have been
examining what we think we know about the relation between experience
and motivation. When a child's behavior fails to fit the standards somebody
in our society holds for him, it is pretty well agreed among us who are

* Reprinted from *Child Development*, 1960, Vol. 31, 489–504, by permission
of the author and the Society for Research in Child Development, Inc.

supposed to be experts on human nature that "somebody goofed." And that somebody is usually considered to be a parent.

The question is: what is the proper formula? If one examines the accruing evidence relevant to what has been the dominant conception of the experiential sources of motivation, one can hardly escape the conclusion that this conceptual scheme needs some revisions. If we based our child-rearing entirely on our dominant theory of motivational development, we would probably goof as often and as badly as runof-the-mill parents.

Today I wish, first, to remind you of three of the most basic and general of the propositions in that theory of motivation which has been dominant for the past 30 to 40 years. These are propositions which, although stated in somewhat varied forms, have been shared by both psychoanalysts and academic behavior theorists. Secondly, I wish to cite evidence which calls these propositions into question, and thirdly, to suggest tentatively three new interpretative principles which appear to me to be congruent with a large number of facts and which have interesting implications.

Our conceptions of motivation have traditionally been concerned with three large questions. (a) Why does an organism or person become active? (b) Why does the organism or person act one way rather than another? and (c) How do you get the organism or person to change his behavior to something conceived to be more desirable or appropriate?

THE DOMINANT THEORY

Drive. According to our dominant theory, it is claimed, first of all, that "all behavior is motivated," and that the aim or function of every instinct, defense, action, or habit is to reduce or eliminate stimulation or excitation within the nervous system. It is not easy to state when this view was first presented. Signs of it appear in the seventh chapter of Freud's *Interpretation of Dreams* (15) in 1900, and the idea is full-blown in his paper entitled *Instincts and Their Vicissitudes* (17) in 1915. The idea also appears in Woodworth's *Dynamic Psychology* (68), published in 1918, where the term *drive* was first introduced into the glossary of American psychology. The idea was full-blown in Dashiell's *Fundamentals of Objective Psychology* (11) in 1928.

Although Freud (17) believed that the source of motivation lay outside the domain of psychology in physiology, American psychologists, untroubled by such limits to their domain, have gone on to answer the first question concerning what motivates organisms to become active by saying that they are *driven*. Organisms have been conceived to be driven, first, by those so-called primary, inner stimuli which arise from homeostatic in-balances or needs. With no shame whatsoever, psychologists have long cited the evidence from the work of such physiologists as Claude Bernard (5) and his successors, and especially of Walter B. Cannon (10), and also of the psychologist Curt Richter (59) to document this answer. Organisms are driven, second, by various forms of intense and painful external stimulation. It has been assumed that these two forms of stimulation arouse an inner state of excitement which has usually been called *drive*.

It is also assumed, as the proposition that "all behavior is motivated" implies, that the organism would be inactive unless driven by either inner or outer stimuli. Freud (17) has been highly explicit about this assumption, and the assumption lies implicitly behind the notion of conditioned or learned drive in behavior theory and behind the traumatic notion of anxiety in psychoanalysis. It is sometimes obvious, of course, that animals and people are sometimes active when it is hard to see how either homeostatic drive or painful external stimulation could be operative. It is then assumed that some of the weak, innocuous stimuli present must have been associated in the past with either painful stimuli or homeostatic needs. In such a way the weak stimuli which are present must have acquired the capacity to arouse the drive, often now called anxiety by psychologists as well as psychoanalysts, and it is such acquired or conditioned drive that is conceived to activate the organism.

Such conditioned drive or anxiety has been well demonstrated in the laboratory. Before World War II, Miller (45, 46) at Yale showed that rats which had been repeatedly shocked in a white box would, when later returned to the white box, make an effort to escape. Moreover, in the course of these efforts, they could be got to learn new skills such as that of turning a wheel to open a door. Rats which had not been shocked in the white box made no such efforts to escape. In another demonstration Solomon and Wynne (64) have shown that dogs which have experienced a tone or a buzzer paired a few times with a subtetanizing shock will run away from that tone or buzzer for hundreds of trials, with the average reaction time of starting continuing to decrease through 600 such trials. In my own work (31) rats fed irregularly in infancy ate more and sometimes (32) hoarded more than their litter-mate controls in adulthood after a period without food. Here, as I conceived it, the cues of hunger were conditioned to intense hunger excitement during the infantile experience. In adulthood the conditioned hunger drive facilitated the rate of eating and, sometimes, hoarding.

Such work has demonstrated that this notion of conditioned drive or anxiety, which goes back to the work of Bechterev (2) and Watson and Raynor (67), has a solid basis in reality. But in what has been the dominant theory of motivation, as epitomized by Freud's (18) later traumatic theory of anxiety and by the Hull (30) and Dollard-Miller (13, 47) theory of acquired drives, conditioning is conceived to be the only way in which an organism can become fearful of innocuous stimuli.

Habit.   Habit has been the answer to the second question concerned with why an animal or person acts one way rather than another. The organism is controlled by the habits which have served to reduce drive in the past when that organism was in the presence of the inner and outer drive stimuli and the cue stimuli impinging upon him at any given now. Under the term *habit,* I am including psychoanalytic modes, which have supposedly been fixated during infancy in the course of either too much gratification or too much frustration, and I am including also ego-defenses, or anxiety equivalents, and cathexes, as well as the instrumental responses and traits commonly investigated in psychological laboratories.

Changing behavior has been conceived to be a matter of motivating the organism with either punishment or homeostatic need to make the desired behavior which can then be reinforced by arranging for it to reduce the drive aroused by the punishment or the need. Although the conditions and conceptions of psychotherapy in the clinic differ considerably from the conditions and conceptions of the behavior theorist investigating learning in laboratory animals, in either case it is conceived that motivation is a necessity, and motivation means changing the emotional or drive conditions which are quite extrinsic to either the instrumental behavior or the cognitive, informational processes concerned.

This dominant theory has been a conceptual edifice of large dimensions and of considerable detail. It has provided a plausible account of both personality development and social motives. The experimental facts of homeostasis and of conditioned drive and fear are sound. Nevertheless, it has become more and more evident in the past 10 years that some of the basic assumptions of this dominant theoretical scheme and some of the explanatory extrapolations contradict facts and call for reinterpretation.

REINTERPRETATIONS

Is All Behavior Motivated?   The first of the assumptions to be called into question is the one that *all behavior is motivated* and that *organisms become inactive unless stimulated* by homeostatic need or painful stimulation or conditional stimuli for these. A large variety of observations contradict this assumption and imply spontaneous molar activity. Beach (1) has reviewed the observations of play in the young to show that playful activities are most likely to occur when either young animals or children are homeostatically satisfied and also comfortably warm. The very occurrence of either homeostatic need or strong external stimulation stops play and turns the young animal or child to activities calculated to relieve such stimulation. Berlyne (3, 4) has shown that well-fed and watered rats will explore areas new to them if given only the opportunity. Montgomery (49), moreover, has shown that hunger and thirst tend to limit the exploratory behavior of rats rather than facilitate it, and Montgomery and Monkman (50), as well as others, have shown that conditioned fear inhibits exploration. Harlow, Harlow, and Meyer (23) have demonstrated that well-fed monkeys will learn to unassemble a three-device puzzle with no other drive and "no other reward than the privilege of unassembling it." In another study Harlow (20) found two well-fed and well-watered monkeys worked repeatedly at unassembling a six-device puzzle for 10 continuous hours, and they were still showing what he characterized as enthusiasm for their work on the tenth hour of testing. From his observations of the human child, moreover, Piaget (55) remarks repeatedly on the enthusiastic and repeated performance of such emerging skills as the release of a toy, sitting up, standing, etc.

Such evidences of spontaneous behavior, which is unmotivated in the traditional sense, have led to the naming of such new motives as a curiosity drive by Berlyne (4), an exploratory drive by Montgomery (48), and exteroceptive and curiosity drives by Harlow (21). I would like to object that merely naming such drives explains nothing. If we continue, we shall be revisiting McDougall's (44) practice of postulating a separate drive for almost every variety of activities. Let us stop with noting that such observations do contradict our assumption that organisms will become inactive unless driven by homeostatic needs and painful stimuli and give up this ancient Greek notion that living matter is inert substance to which motion must be imparted by extrinsic forces. We can then embrace the thermodynamic conception of living things as open systems of energy exchange which exhibit activity intrinsically and upon which stimuli have a modulating effect, but not an initiating effect.

This notion of activity being intrinsic in living tissue is receiving support from studies of organ systems as well as studies of molar organisms. The EEG, for example, shows that brain cells are continuously active (33, 58). In sleep the slow waves of large amplitude are taken to imply that large numbers of cells are firing synchronously, and the effect of waking and stimulation and exciting the brain-stem-reticular formation is to asynchronize this firing which shows in rapid waves of low magnitude (42).

Granit (19) points out that the spontaneous firing of retinal cells increases with dark adaptation and thereby functions to prevent the deafferentization of visual contex with darkness. Twenty years ago, this spontaneous firing was considered, at worst, to be due to some failure of experimental control, or at best, noise in the channel of information. Recently, the Laceys (36) have found spontaneous fluctuations of sudomotor activity and cardiac activity which they also see as functioning in the control of the organism's relations with its environment. Especially intriguing is their notion that the carotid sinus mechanism functions as a feedback loop which participates in the directing of attention inward or outward by inhibiting or facilitating receptor inputs. But the point of mentioning these evidences of spontaneous activities of organ systems here is merely to help inter for good the notion that activity of living systems requires homeostatic need or painful external stimulation and to foster the idea that to live means to be active in some degree.

Reinforcement. This idea of activity being intrinsic in living organisms has implications for our conception of reinforcement. It makes it unnecessary to see all activity as a matter of either reducing or avoiding stimulation which is implied in the assumption that organisms become inactive unless stimulated. This is a second fundamental assumption of the dominant theory which has been shared by psychoanalysts and behavior theorists alike.

On the one hand, there is still a place for drive reduction. It is clear that under conditions of homeostatic need and painful stimulation, and perhaps under circumstances when the conditions of stimulation are changing with too great rapidity, both animals and persons learn techniques and strategies leading to gratification or reduction in external stimulation. The evidence that led Thorndike to formulate the "law of effect" is as convincing as ever. Moreover, in association with reductions of homeostatic need, animals and men may also learn cathexes or emotional attachments. The facts referred to are those highly familiar in secondary reinforcement (30, 54).

On the other hand, the facts implying that organisms show spontaneous molar activity also imply that, when animals and human beings have been living under conditions of low and unchanging stimulation for a time, increases of stimulation become reinforcing. Butler has shown that rhesus monkeys will learn quite complex discriminations with the only reward being a peek through a glass window (7) at the things in the next room or a few seconds of auditory experience (8). Berlyne (3) has shown that, the greater the variety of stimulation in an area which rats are permitted to explore, the longer they continue their explorations.

Especially important in this connection are the studies of human behavior under conditions of minimal variation in stimulation. I refer to the studies of perceptual isolation by Bexton, Heron, and Scott (6) at McGill and also the work of Lilly (41). At McGill, college students were paid 20 dollars a day to do nothing. They lay for 24 hours a day on a comfortable bed. The temperature was optimal and constant. Eyes, ears, and hands were shielded to minimize stimulus variation. Few subjects could endure more than two or three days of such conditions. They developed a desire for variation which was almost overwhelming.

While interpreting such facts in terms of a multiple set of drives for curiosity, exploration, or stimulation will get us only to a redescription of them, Hebb's (26) notion of an optimal level of activation—and I would like to add, stimulus variation below which *increases* are reinforcing and above which *decreases* are reinforcing—is an integrative conception of fair magnitude. Moreover, the drive-reduction principle of reinforcement may be seen to be but half of this more general curvilinear principle.

But this is probably not the whole story. It looks as if there were natively both positive and negative forms of exciting stimulation. Sheffield, Roby, and Campbell (61) have argued that the reinforcing effect of eating is not a matter of reduction of the hunger drive but rather a matter of the positive value of the consummatory act of eating. Moreover, Sheffield, Wulff, and Backer (62) have shown that male rats will learn mazes to get to females in heat even when they are allowed only intromission but not allowed to continue coitus to the point of drive-reducing ejaculation. From the fact that Davis (12) and his collaborators at Indiana have shown that showing pictures of nude women to college males increases excitement as shown by increased palmar conductance and the arrest of EEG-alpha, it is clear that such stimulation is exciting rather than excitement-reducing. Young (69) has long emphasized the importance of the hedonic quality of experience for reinforcement, and he has shown that speed of running in rat subjects increases with the concentration of sucrose in the incentive drink.

The suggestion that the two forms of excitation, one positive and one negative, are built into organisms comes also from the work of Olds and Milner (53). Electrical stimulation of the septal area is positively reinforcing, but electrical stimulation of the brain-stem reticular formation is negatively reinforcing. Perhaps, it is not without significance that the septal area is part of the old olfactory brain which has been considered to have an especially important part in the mediation of sexual and consummatory behavior in mammals. At any rate, it looks as though certain types of stimulation may be positively reinforcing even though they be intense and exciting. This may mean that the curvilinear principle may be limited in its domain to strong stimulation via the exteroceptors when homeostatic needs are minimized.

The suggestion of innate, positive, and negative exteroceptive stimulation comes secondly from recent work by Harlow (22). It has been customary to see an infant's cathexis or love for its mother developing as secondary renforcement largely out of its feeding experiences. Freud (16), of course, contended that the pleasure from stimulation of the oral erogenous zone furnished the experiential basis for both pleasure-sucking and maternal attachment, a contention which contradicted his most definitive formulations of drive theory (17). The fact that an infant must suck for its nourishment, according to libido theory (16, p. 587), merely guaranteed discovery of the pleasures of oral stimulation. Behavior theorists have seen both sucking and love of mother as forms of secondary reinforcement deriving from the fact that the child satisfies its hunger by means of sucking the mother's breasts (51, pp. 137 ff.). Harlow (22), however, has recently compared the degree of attachment of young monkeys to a wire mother-surrogate on which they nursed at a bottle with attachment to a padded and cloth-covered mother-surrogate on which they received nothing but the feel of the softness. In terms of the amount of time spent on each of the two mother-surrogates, the monkeys showed more than 10 times the attachment to the soft-padded surrogate as to the wire surrogate. When various fear-evoking stimuli were presented to the baby monkeys in their cages, it was to the padded and cloth-covered surrogate that the frightened, infant monkey turned, not to the wire surrogate on which it had been nursed. Harlow argues from these findings that it is the sensory quality of softness which gives the reinforcement. His study suggests, moreover, that it is important to investigate the capacity for various kinds of stimuli for positive and negative reinforcement in the very young. Pratt (57) cites a monograph by Canestrini (9) on the sensory life of the newborn for an observation that certain stimuli are associated with decreases in the rate of the heart beat, and are therefore pleasant, while others are associated with increases in heart rate and are unpleasant.[2] In view of the finding by Davis (12) and his collaborators that seeing a picture of a nude female results in reduction in the heart rate of male college students, it is possible that this physiological indicator may provide a technique for determining the direction of the reinforcing effect of stimuli in the newborn. At any rate, what is suggested is that McDougall's (44) old notion of natively positive and negative values for receptor inputs be re-examined.

Conditioned Fear and Anxiety. The third assumption that I wish to examine in the light of empirical evidence is the notion that fear and anxiety are *always* inculcated as a consequence of traumatic experiences of helplessness in the face of homeostatic need or painful external stimulation. Note that I am not denying that such conditioned fears do exist. I am only questioning the word *always* . . . are always inculcated as a consequence of traumatic experiences.

The first relevant studies go way back to the 1920's. Harold and Mary Cover Jones (34) attempted to test the claims of Watson (66) and Watson and Raynor (67), concerning conditioned fears. They exposed their subjects of various ages, ranging from early infancy to adult, to a large but sluggish and harmless bull-snake. Fear of the snake was exceedingly common among adults, teenagers, and latency-age children, but it was absent in children below three years of age. It began to appear among children older than three and was typical of children six and older. From the fact that the fear appeared at a younger age in those of higher intelligence than those of lower intelligence, the Joneses argued that fear of snakes is a response which comes automatically into the developing child's repertoire through maturation. This remains as an alternative hypothesis to that of conditioned fear.

A study by Frances Holmes (29), which is seldom cited, calls both of these interpretations into question. Holmes compared the fearfulness of the children of lower-class background, who were attending a day nursery, with the fearfulness of children of upper-class background, who were attending a private nursery school. She got her fear scores by indicating that the child could get some attractive toys with which to play by going into the dark room adjacent to the examining room, or by taking them off a chair situated beside that of a strange woman dressed in a large floppy black hat and a long gray coat, or by climbing along a plank some three feet off the floor. If the child started immediately for the toys, he got a score of one for that item. If he hesitated but ultimately went ahead on his own, he got a score of two. If he would go only if accompanied by the examiner, the score was three. If he refused to go at all, the score was four. There were seven such situations. The results show that the fear scores of the lower-class children averaged only about half the size of those for the upper-class children, and the fear scores for boys were lower than those for girls. Yet it would be the lower-class children who had experienced the more homeostatic need and painfully rough treatment than the upper-class children, and the boys had probably experienced more painful experiences than the little girls. That intelligence is not the factor is shown by the fact that the fear scores showed a correlation of only about $+.2$ with mental age, and the differences were still significant when intelligence was partialed out. Something besides either conditioned fear or the correlation between fear and intelligence is required to make these results comprehensible.

Recently evidence even more contradictory to the notion of conditioned fears has been coming from the work of Seymour Levine. Levine, Chevalier, and Korchin (40) have compared the adult behavior of rates shocked and rats petted daily from birth to their 20th day with the adult behavior of rats left continuously in their nests with their mothers. When he started this work, Levine expected to find that the shocked animals would show traumatic effects of their shock experiences in heightened emotionality, and damaged capacity to learn adaptive responses. On the contrary, the shocked animals, along with the handled animals, gained weight faster than those left in the nest (37, 38, 39, 40). Byron Lindholm, working with the writer, has repeated and confirmed this finding. Moreover, Levine's shocked and handled animals both showed less emotionality than those left continuously in the nest with their mothers, i.e., less emotionality in the sense that they defecated and urinated less frequently when placed in a strange situation. Finally, the shocked and handled animals, which have appeared alike in all of these experiments, learned an avoidance response more rapidly and drank more readily after 18 hours without water than did the rats left in the nest with their mother.

Clearly these results on both human children and rats imply that fear and anxiety must sometimes have some other basis than that of being associated with painful stimulation. As many of you know, Hebb (24, 25) has formulated a radically different explanation of fear which may be termed either an incongruity or a dissonance theory.

The facts which suggested Hebb's conception came largely from observing chimpanzees being raised under controlled conditions at the Yerkes Laboratory. Fear, defined as withdrawal behavior in response to the appearance of some object, does not appear in young chimpanzees until they are approximately four months old. Then, the objects feared are familiar objects in unfamiliar guise. Fear of strangers is an example. This appears spontaneously to the first stranger seen, so it cannot be based on associating strangers with painful stimulation. Fear of strangers does not appear in chimpanzees—or in children, I might add—who have always been exposed to a large number of persons. While the avoidance response is unlearned, the familiar, expected aspects of objects must be learned. The young animal must have established as residues of his experience cortical firing patterns (or cognitive structures—whichever term you like) from which new receptor inputs can be incongruous. Consider the kinds of objects regularly feared. They are, for instance, the familiar keeper or experimenter in strange clothes, the experimenter in a Hallowe'en mask, a plaster cast of a chimpanzee head (which lacks, of course, the familiarly attached body), an anesthetized chimpanzee infant (from which the familiar patterns of motion are absent). On the other hand, objects which have never entered into the young chimpanzee's life may be strange without evoking withdrawal. In other words, the feared object is one which excites receptors in a fashion which is incongruous with the central, sequential pattern of neural firing which has accrued as a residue of the chimpanzee or human infant's past experience. Until the central pattern has been learned, incongruous stimulation is possible.

Such a conception can well account for Holmes' findings that lower-class children are less fearful than higher-class children and that boys are less fearful than girls even though both lower-class children and boys of nursery school age are likely to have had the wider experience with the sorts of situations used by Holmes to evoke fear. It may well be that being shocked and handled provides a variety of experience which leaves the rat pups which have been subjected to it less disturbed by such things as open fields and 18 hours without water, but these effects may ultimately be found to be a matter of still another mechanism. It is too early to say.

Taking seriously this incongruity-dissonance conception of the genesis of fear leads to interesting reinterpretations of a great many of the motivational phenomena of child development. Consider these few. In considering separation anciety, the incongruity principle makes it unnecessary to puzzle about how the absence of mother could be the conditional stimulus for the traumatizing and helpless distress that has been supposed to have occurred in her absence. In considering fear of the dark, it also becomes unnecessary to puzzle about how the absence of light stimulation could so widely have been associated with painful stimulation. Multiple mothering need not be seen as a traumatizing experience in the light of this conception, but rather as an innoculation against social shyness and fear. The timidity of the over-protected child and the social shyness of the rural mountain people get an explanation which has been difficult in terms of the theory of conditioned fear.

MOTIVATION IN TERMS OF THE INCONGRUITY-DISSONANCE PRINCIPLE

This introduction of the incongruity-dissonance principle concludes the three reinterpretations I wish to present today, but I do wish to call your attention to the pervasive character of this incongruity-dissonance principle. It appears to have great explanation power which figures, in one guise or another, in several systematic theories, besides that of Hebb, all of which have been characterized as nondynamic.

Hebb's (25) theorizing is physiological, at least in a verbal sense, in that he conceives the residues of past inputs to be stored in semiautonomous, reverberating cerebral circuits which he terms *cell assemblies*. These cell assemblies are the neural analogue of concepts, and they get sequentially integrated into what he calls *phase sequences*. The sequential organization in time provides for the subjective phenomenon of expectation. When markedly incongruous receptor inputs disrupt this sequential organization, behavior is changed and the process is felt as unpleasant emotion. Slight degrees of incongruity, which can readily be accommodated, lend interest and may provide attractive problems, but the larger ones are repelling and perhaps even devastating.

Piaget (55, 56) utilizes very much the same incongruity notion to account for the development of intelligence and concepts in human children. In his system, the child comes at birth with certain sensory-motor coordinations which he terms schemata. Variation in stimulus situations calls for adaptive accommodations or changes in these schemata, which changes are assimilated or stored as residues. Piaget also finds limited incongruities between central schemata and receptor inputs to be interesting and facilitative of growth, but incongruities which extend beyond the child's capacity for accommodation instigate withdrawal or fear and even terror. In Piaget's theory the child's gestalt-like conceptions of reality (space, time, and number) are schemata which develop through a continuous process of accommodations and assimilations and become fixed or static only when the child's schemata come to correspond so well with reality that no further accommodations are required. Here agreement among people is dictated by reality.

Helson (27, 28) has called the residues of immediate past experience in the typical psychophysical experiment an adaptation level. Both he and McClelland (43) have seen affective arousal to be a matter of the size of the discrepancy between receptor inputs and the adaptation level. Small discrepancies may be attractively pleasant, large ones repellingly unpleasant. As an example, some of you will readily recall having experienced the affective startle that comes when you have been set to pick up what you thought was a full pail, only to find it empty.

Festinger (14) has recently written a book entitled *A Theory of Cognitive Dissonance* in which he shows that a discrepancy between belief about a situation and perception of that situation acts like a drive. The subject acts to reduce the *dissonance* by either withdrawing from the incredible situation or by changing his beliefs, and, not incidentally, he finds the dissonance highly unpleasant.

Rogers (60) has described the basis for anxiety as discrepancy between the "phenomenological field" and the perceived reality as represented by his two circles. Rogers' phenomenological field, however, is not the perceptually-given phenomenal field of such German phenomenologists as Delthei and Husserl. It is rather the inferred storehouse of past experience and represented in the present by expectations, aspirations, self-concept, and the like. Thus, his conceptual scheme appears to fall within the domain of the incongruity-dissonance principle.

Kelly's (35) *Psychology of Personal Constructs* also makes central use of this principle. The term *personal constructs* refers to the ways in which individuals construe and anticipate events. These each person derives from the way in which he has experienced such events in the past. When a person's constructions fail to predict events, this is disturbing, even anxiety-producing, and it motivates some kind of change, but the change may take place in defenses against such change of constructs or in avoiding such events, or in the constructs themselves.

Perhaps, it is worth noting in closing that this incongruity-dissonance principle makes both motivation and reinforcement intrinsic to the organism's relations with its environment, intrinsic, if you will, to the organism's information-processing. It is as if the organism operated like an error-actuated, feedback system where the error is derived from discrepancy between receptor-inputs of the present and the residues of past experience which serve as the basis for anticipating the future. The dominant view of the past half century has seen both motivation and reinforcement as extrinsic to the information-processing. This has put a tremendous burden of responsibility for the management of affective motivation on parents, teachers, and all those in positions of authority and control. Visions of man completely controlled, as exemplified by George Orwell's *1984*, are conceivable only by assuming that the extrinsic motivating forces of homeostatic need and painful stimulation are completely dominant. In this light the terror of the baby chimp at seeing his keeper in a Hallowe'en mask and the irritation of the believer when his beliefs are disconfirmed are perhaps symbols of hope. They may justify Abraham Lincoln's well-known dictum that "you can fool some of the people all the time, and all the people some of the time, but you cannot fool all the people all the time."

To return to the cartoon of the lad who was improperly motivated: Perhaps, the task of developing proper motivation is best seen, at least in nutshell form, as limiting the manipulation of extrinsic factors to that minimum of keeping homeostatic need and exteroceptive drive low, in favor of facilitating basic information-processing to maximize accurate anticipation of reality.

REFERENCES:

1. BEACH, F. A. Current concepts of play in animals. *Amer. Naturalist,* 1945, 79, 523–541.
2. BECHTEREV, V. M. *La Psychologie Objective.* (Translated by N. Kostyleff) (Paris: Alcan, 1913).
3. BERLYNE, D. E. Novelty and curiosity as determinants of exploratory behavior. *Brit. J. Psychol.,* 1950, 41, 68–80.
4. BERLYNE, D. E. The arousal and satiation of perceptual curiosity in the rat. *J. Comp. Physiol. Psychol,* 1955, 48, 238–246.
5. BERNARD, C. *Leçons sur les Propriétés Physiologiques et les Alterations Pathologiques des Liquides de l'Organisme* (Paris: Ballière, 1859). 2 vols.
6. BEXTON, W. H., HERON, W., and SCOTT, T. H. Effects of decreased variation in the sensory environment. *Canad. J. Psychol.,* 1954, 8, 70–76.
7. BUTLER, R. A. Discrimination learning by rhesus monkeys to visual-exploration motivation. *J. Comp. Physiol. Psychol.,* 1953, 46, 95–98.
8. BUTLER, R. A. Discrimination learning by rhesus monkeys to auditory incentives. *J. Comp. Physiol. Psychol.,* 1957, 50, 239–241.
9. CANESTRINI, S. Über das Sinnesleben des Neugebornen. [Alzheimer, A. and Lewandowsky, M. (Eds.)] *Monogr. Gesamt. Neurol. Psychiat.* (Heft 5.) (Berlin: Springer, 1913).
10. CANNON, W. B. *Bodily Changes in Pain, Hunger, Fear, and Rage* (New York: Appleton-Century, 1915).
11. DASHIELL, J. *Fundamentals of Objective Psychology* (Boston: Houghton Mifflin, 1928).
12. DAVIS, R. C., and BUCHWALD, A. M. An exploration of somatic response patterns: stimulus and sex differences. *J. Comp. Physiol. Psychol.,* 1957, 50, 44–52.
13. DOLLARD, J., and MILLER, N. E. *Personality and Psychotherapy* (New York: McGraw-Hill, 1950).
14. FESTINGER, L. *A Theory of Cognitive Dissonance* (Evanston, Ill.: Row, Peterson, 1957).
15. FREUD, S. The interpretation of dreams (1900). In *The Basic Writings of Sigmund Freud.* (Translated by A. A. Brill) (New York: Modern Library, 1938). Pp. 179–548.
16. FREUD, S. Three contributions to the theory of sex (1905). In *The Basic Writings of Sigmund Freud.* (Translated by A. A. Brill) (New York: Modern Library, 1938). Pp. 553–629.

17. FREUD, S. Instincts and their vicissitudes (1915). In *Collected Papers*, Vol. IV. (London: Hogarth, 1950). Pp. 60–83.
18. FREUD, S. *Inhibition, Symptom and Anxiety* (1926). (Translated by H. A. Bunker as *The Problem of Anxiety*.) (New York: Norton, 1936).
19. GRANIT, R. *Receptors and Sensory Perception* (New Haven: Yale Univer. Press, 1955).
20. HARLOW, H. F. Learning and satiation of response in intrinsically motivated complex puzzle performance by monkeys. *J. Comp. Physiol. Psychol.*, 1950, 43, 289–294.
21. HARLOW, H. F. Motivation as a factor in the acquisition of new responses. In *Current Theory and Research in Motivation: a Symposium* (Lincoln: Univer. of Nebraska Press, 1953). Pp. 24–49.
22. HARLOW, H. F. The nature of love. *Amer. Psychologist*, 1958, 13, 673–685.
23. HARLOW, H. F., HARLOW, M. K., and MEYER, D. R. Learning motivated by a manipulation drive. *J. Exp. Psychol.*, 1950, 40, 228–234.
24. HEBB, D. O. On the nature of fear. *Psychol. Rev.*, 1946, 53, 259–276.
25. HEBB, D. O. *The Organization of Behavior* (New York: Wiley, 1949).
26. HEBB, D. O. Drives and the c.n.s. (conceptual nervous system). *Psychol. Rev.*, 1955, 62, 243–254.
27. HELSON, H. Adaptation-level as frame of reference for prediction of psychophysical data. *Amer. J. Psychol.*, 1947, 60, 1–29.
28. HELSON, H. Adaptation-level as a basis for a quantitative theory of frames of reference. *Psychol. Rev.*, 1948, 55, 297–313.
29. HOLMES, FRANCES B. An experimental study of the fears of young children. In A. T. Jersild and Frances B. Holmes, Children's fears. *Child Develpm. Monogr.*, 1953, 20, 167–296.
30. HULL, C. L. *Principles of Behavior* (New York: Appleton-Century, 1943).
31. HUNT, J. MCV. The effects of infant feeding-frustration upon adult hoarding in the albino rat. *J. Abnorm. Soc. Psychol.*, 1941, 36, 338–360.
32. HUNT, J. MCV., SCHLOSBERG, H., SOLOMON, R. L., and STELLAR, E. Studies on the effects of infantile experience on adult behavior in rats. I. Effects of infantile feeding frustration on adult hoarding. *J. Comp. Physiol. Psychol.*, 1947, 40, 291–304.
33. JASPER, H. H. Electrical signs of cortical activity. *Psychol. Bull.*, 1937, 34, 411–481.
34. JONES, H. E., and JONES, MARY C. A study of fear. *Child Educ.*, 1928, 5, 136–143.

35. KELLY, G. A. *The Psychology of Personal Constructs* (New York: Norton, 1955).

36. LACEY, J. I., and LACEY, BEATRICE C. The relationship of resting automatic activity to motor impulsivity. In *The Brain and Human Behavior* (Baltimore: Williams and Wilkins, 1958). Pp. 144–209.

37. LEVINE, S. Infantile experience and consummatory behavior in adulthood. *J. Comp. Physiol. Psychol.*, 1957, 50, 609–612.

38. LEVINE, S. Infantile experience and resistance to physical stress. *Science*, 1957, 126, 405.

39. LEVINE, S. Noxious stimulation in infant and adult rats and consummatory behavior. *J. Comp. Physiol. Psychol.*, 1958, 51, 230–233.

40. LEVINE, S., CHEVALIER, J. A., and KORCHINE, S. J. The effects of shock and handling in infancy on later avoidance learning. *J. Pers.*, 1956, 24, 475–493.

41. LILLY, J. C. Mental effects of reduction of ordinary levels of physical stimuli on intact, healthy persons. *Psychiat. Res. Rep.*, 1956, No. 5, 1–9.

42. LINDSLEY, D. B. Psychophysiology and motivation. In M. R. Jones (Ed.), *Nebraska Symposium on Motivation* (Lincoln: Univer. of Nebraska Press, 1957). Pp. 44–105.

43. MCCLELLAND, D. C., ATKINSON, J. W., CLARK, R. A., and LOWELL, E. L. *The Achievement Motive* (New York: Appleton-Century-Crofts, 1953).

44. MCDOUGALL, W. *An Introduction to Social Psychology* (Boston: Luce, 1915).

45. MILLER, N. E. An experimental investigation of acquired drives. *Psychol. Bull.*, 1941, 38, 534–535.

46. MILLER, N. E. Studies of fear as an acquirable drive: 1. Fear as motivation and fear-reduction as reinforcement in the learning of new responses. *J. Exp. Psychol.*, 1948, 38, 89–101.

47. MILLER, N. E., and DOLLARD, J. *Social Learning and Imitation* (New Haven: Yale Univer. Press, 1941).

48. MONTGOMERY, K. C. The relation between exploratory behavior and spontaneous alternation in the white rat. *J. Comp. Physiol. Psychol.*, 1951, 44, 582–589.

49. MONTGOMERY, K. C. The effect of the hunger and thirst drives upon exploratory behavior. *J. Comp. Physiol. Psychol.*, 1953, 46, 315–319.

50. MONTGOMERY, K. C., and MONKMAN, J. A. The relation between fear and exploratory behavior. *J. Comp. Physiol. Psychol.*, 1955, 48, 132–136.

51. MUSSEN, P. H., and CONGER, J. J. *Child Development and Personality* (New York: Harper, 1956).

NATURE AND NURTURE OF MOTIVATION			107

52. OLDS, J. Physiological mechanisms of reward. In M. R. Jones (Ed.), *Nebraska Symposium on Motivation* (Lincoln: Univer. of Nebraska Press, 1955). Pp. 73–139.
53. OLDS, J., and MILNER, P. Positive reinforcement produced by electrical stimulation of septal area and other regions of the rat brain. *J. Comp. Physiol. Psychol.*, 1954, 47, 419–427.
54. PAVLOV, I. P. *Conditioned Reflexes.* (Translated by G. V. Anrep.) (Oxford: Oxford Univer. Press, 1927).
55. PIAGET, J. *The Origins of Intelligence in Children* (New York: International Universities Press, 1952).
56. PIAGET, J. *The Construction of Reality in the Child.* (Translated by Margaret Cook.) (New York: Basic Books, 1954).
57. PRATT, K. C. The neonate. In L. Carmichael (Ed.), *Manual of Child Psychology.* (2nd Ed.) (New York: Wiley, 1954). Pp. 215–291.
58. PROSSER, C. L. Action potentials in the nervous system of the crayfish: I. Spontaneous impulses. *J. Cell. Comp. Physiol.*, 1934, 4, 185–209.
59. RICHTER, C. P. Animal behavior and internal drives. *Quart. Rev. Biol.*, 1927, 2, 307–343.
60. ROGERS, C. R. *Client-Centered Therapy* (Boston: Houghton Mifflin, 1951).
61. SHEFFIELD, F. D., ROBY, T. B., and CAMPBELL, B. A. Drive reduction versus consummatory behavior as determinants of reinforcement. *J. Comp. Physiol. Psychol.*, 1954, 47, 349–355.
62. SHEFFIELD, F. D., WULFF, J. J., and BACKER, R. Reward value of copulation without sex drive reduction. *J. Comp. Physiol. Psychol.*, 1951, 44, 3–8.
63. SOLOMON, R. L., and BRUSH, ELINOR S. Experimentally derived conceptions of anxiety and aversion. In M. R. Jones (Ed.), *Nebraska Symposium on Motivation* (Lincoln: Univer. of Nebraska Press, 1956). Pp. 212–305.
64. SOLOMON, R. L., and WYNNE, L. C. Traumatic avoidance learning: acquisition in normal dogs. *Psychol. Monogr.*, 1953, 67, No. 4 (Whole No. 354).
65. THORNDIKE, E. L. *Educational Psychology.* Vol. I, *The Original Nature of Man;* Vol. II, *The Psychology of Learning.* (New York: Teachers Coll., 1913).
66. WATSON, J. B. *Psychological Care of the Infant and Child* (New York: Norton, 1928).
67. WATSON, J. B., and RAYNOR, ROSALIE. Conditional reactions. *J. Exp. Psychol.*, 1920, 3, 1–4.
68. WOODWORTH, R. S. *Dynamic Psychology* (New York: Columbia Univer. Press, 1918).
69. YOUNG, P. T. The role of hedonic processes in motivation. In M. R. Jones (Ed.), *Nebraska Symposium on Motivation* (Lincoln: Univer. of Nebraska Press, 1955). Pp. 193–237.

FOOTNOTES:

[1] Earlier versions of this paper were read at the Eleventh Annual Institute in Psychiatry and Neurology of the Veterans Administration Hospital at North Little Rock, Arkansas, 27 February 1959, and at colloquia of the Department of Psychology at Vanderbilt University and of the Department of Psychiatry at the Medical School of Colorado. The paper was prepared in connection with a survey of the implications of the work in behavioral science for childrearing which has been supported by the Russell Sage Foundation.

[2] An examination of Canestrini's (9) monograph shows that Pratt was mistaken in stating that Canestrini remarked upon decreases in heart rate being associated with pleasure but some of his published kymograph records do indicate decreases in heart rate. It may well be that heart rate could serve as an indicator of the emotional value of various sensory inputs, and these might be tested for their reinforcement values. I am indebted to Dr. William Gerler for reading this monograph carefully to check my own impressions of Canestrini's text.

8   *"Praise Reappraised"**

BY RICHARD E. FARSON

EDITOR'S NOTE: In both of the preceding articles, questions were raised about the motivational value and effectiveness of external reinforcement or recognition. This paper goes a step beyond the questions already posed and examines in detail a specific kind of reward. We not only use it frequently, but we are the receivers of it. Praise—what happens many times to people who get praised? More to the point, what is your usual reaction? Can you handle it comfortably or do you stand in red-skinned embarrassment? Have you ever thought about why it is that praise turns some on and other off? Consider the ideas here carefully. You may find yourself reconsidering what you think praise does to people and perhaps using it a bit more selectively. And maybe taking it better, too.

I am beginning to question the cherished idea that people enjoy being praised. I realize that I am in unfriendly territory because praise is perhaps the most widely used and thoroughly endorsed of all human relations techniques. Parents, businessmen, psychologists, teachers—everyone seems to believe in its value as a motivational tool, a reward, a way to establish good relationships.

But I wonder if praise accomplishes just what we think it does. Not that it does not have valuable functions (of which we are largely unaware), but I will bet our beliefs about its *value* are erroneous.

With considerable trepidation let me tentatively suggest:

* Reprinted from *Harvard Business Review*, September–October, 1963, by permission of the author and the publisher.

—Praise is not only of limited and questionable value as a motivator, but may in fact be experienced as threatening.

—Rather than functioning as a bridge between people, it may actually serve to establish distance between them.

—Instead of reassuring a person as to his worth, praise may be an unconscious means of establishing the superiority of the praiser.

—Praise may constrict creativity rather than free it.

—Rather than opening the way to further contact, praise may be a means of terminating it.

Although we may be fooling ourselves as to what praise accomplishes, some of its functions—such as maintaining distance, terminating contacts, establishing status or superiority—are in fact quite necessary and socially useful, even though we may prefer not to acknowledge these hidden benefits.

DEFINITION

What is praise? We are all quick to distinguish praise from flattery, which has connotations of insincerity and expediency. For my purpose here, praise is any statement that makes a *positive* evaluation of an object, person, act, or event, and that contains very little supplementary information—for instance:

"Nice work, you've done a fine job."
"You're a good boy."
"That painting of yours is excellent."

These are examples of praise—positive evaluations with little additional meaning.

On the other hand, a positive evaluation *plus* other information is not essentially, or merely, praise. A statement such as "The reason I think you've done such a good job . . ." or "How did you get that beautiful effect with ink alone?" invites a response and extends the encounter. Obviously such statements are more than praise and have different qualities and perhaps different results.

A simple definition or a simple analysis of praise is, of course, not possible. One must take into account the situation in which praise occurs, the history of the relationship one has with the other person, the attitudes that underlie the act of praise, and the motivations for it. Also, specific acts and techniques can never overcome the effects of one's basic attitudes toward others. Good relationships are dependent on good fundamental attitudes. And a good relationship can withstand many difficulties—even such difficulties as are brought on by praise.

NEGATIVE ASPECTS

What are the problems with praise?

First of all, the findings of scientific experiments on praise do not clearly demonstrate its value. Most of the studies done on this subject have compared praise with reproof or blame as motivational techniques. The results of these studies are mixed: in some cases praise was slightly more effective than reproof; in others, reproof was more effective than praise. In essence, all that can really be concluded from most research is that *some* response motivates people better than no response at all.

It has been demonstrated in psychological laboratories that we can shape human behavior by the use of rewards—symbols such as lights and bells which indicate that the subject is making correct responses or is gaining the approval of judges. But in the extremely complex situations of real life does praise work the same way? Does praise reward? After considerable observation I have come to the conclusion that it usually does not.

Watch people responding to praise. Don't they usually seem to be reacting with discomfort, uneasiness, and defensiveness? I have noticed that a very common response is a vague denial or derogation:

"I really can't take the credit for it."
"You're just saying that."
"Well, *we* like it."
"It was just luck."
"I like yours, too."
"Well, I do the best I can."

The one element these statements have in common is that they are all defensive reactions—efforts to cope with a difficult situation. Praise a house or garden and its owner hastens to point out its defects; praise an employee for a project and he is quick to play down his role in it. Under the stress of praise, some people often become uncomfortable, almost to the point of imitating the toe-digging reactions of small children. Apparently praise is something to be coped with, to be handled.

REASONS FOR DEFENSIVENESS

Why do people react to praise with defensiveness? Part of the reason may be that in praise there *is* threat—something one must defend against. After all, praise is an evaluation, and to be evaluated usually makes us uncomfortable. If we are weighed, we *may* be found wanting.

Most of us feel uncomfortable when we are negatively evaluated, so we tend to believe that positive evaluations should have the opposite effect, that they should be enhancing. Really, though, praise has many of the same basic problems and characteristics as do negative evaluations. Research indicates that *any* evaluation is likely to make people uncomfortable, defensive. Perhaps this is because, when you evaluate a person, you are often in some way trying to motivate him, to move him in a certain direction, to *change* him. Now while he himself may want to change, and while he may not like the person that he *is*, at the same time he is that person; his identity is very important, indeed essential, because it makes possible an answer to the question "Who am I?" Bad or good he must hold onto his identity. For this reason, the threat of change is one of the most fundamental and disquieting of psychological threats. So even though praise may only imply that one should change a bit in the direction one is already going, it *does* imply change, and therefore it may be almost as threatening as a negative evaluation.

Another reason why positive evaluation is discomforting lies in the fact that when a person praises us, it is clear that he is sitting in judgment. We become uneasy when we know someone is not only trying to change us but is continually judging us, grading us. In this situation, the absence of praise is especially threatening because we know that we are still being evaluated.

Often the change which praise asks one to make is not necessarily beneficial to the person being praised but will redound to the convenience, pleasure, or profit of the praiser. When we praise Tommy for making it to the bathroom in time, we are probably not so much delighted on Tommy's behalf as on our own; the change that complicated Tommy's life will make our own more convenient and pleasant. Much the same is true when we praise a salesman for neat call reports. Understandably, people feel threatened when they are being manipulated for another's benefit.

Our enthusiastic belief that praise is pleasing to people has resulted in its becoming a piece of psychological candy. We sugarcoat blame with praise, or use the "sandwich technique" whereby praise is followed by reproof, then again by praise. "I'm very pleased with your work, Fred," says the boss, "you're really getting the work out, *but* . . ." Fred then gets the unhappy part of the story, the reprimand. The boss finishes up with "Keep up the fine work," and Fred is shuttled out without quite knowing what hit him. This is also a favorite technique of parents and teachers. In fact, we have become so conditioned by its use from early childhood that when we are praised, we automatically get ready for the shock, the reproof.

Undoubtedly, the most threatening aspect of praise is the obligation it puts on us to be praiseworthy people. If we accept praise, if we really believe the best about ourselves, then we are under an obligation to behave accordingly. This is deeply frightening to us. For if we really believe it when we are told that we are competent, or intelligent, or beautiful, then we are continually on the spot to be competent, or intelligent, or beautiful, not only in the eyes of the person who praised us but, even worse, in our own eyes. The responsibility to be continually at our best, to live up to our talents and abilities, is perhaps our most difficult problem in living—and we naturally defend against it.

ISSUE OF CREDIBILITY

It may be that there simply is no effective response to praise given in a face-to-face situation. Even saying "thank you" is not entirely satisfactory—although it may be the least defensive way of coping with the behavioral impasse which praise uniformly produces. Perhaps this is one reason why written praise may be somewhat easier to accept. We can savor it without having to invent a modest response.

Of course, part of the problem hinges on the issue of credibility. Can we really believe what the praiser seems to want us to believe? Written praise may be more credible and therefore more rewarding to us. It most certainly is when we discover a praising remark about us written in a letter not intended for us to see. But part of credibility comes from within us. Are we psychologically prepared to accept the validity of comments which indicate our value? If you tell a person who strongly believes himself to be inadequate that he is in your opinion entirely adequate, then your statement is likely to be met with some resistance. The credibility of the praising remark has been determined by the person's internal needs to see himself in consistent ways.

POSITIVE FUNCTIONS

If praise is threatening to people for so many reasons, then why do we use it so often? Surely we do not want to retain in our repertoire responses that do not serve us in some functional way. What are the functions of praise? Why is it a conversational staple?

For one thing, people expect praise. We fish for compliments, subtly or openly. Why do we do this, if we don't really like praise? Probably because it is so important for each of us to feel valued by others. We hope that praise will make us feel that way. Sometimes it does. But because praise means so many things and exists in such complicated motivational contexts, its ability to reward us and indicate our value is questionable. Still, we invite it at the same time that we resist it. Perhaps in our other-directed society we have become so dependent on the approval of others that we must continually check just to make sure that we are not being devaluated.

For another thing, giving praise is easy to do. It makes conversation, and most of us have not enough energy, interest, or imagination to offer witty retorts, penetrating criticism, brilliant insights, or sensitive responses. We really do not want the burden of conversation to be that heavy anyway. Gross evaluations, like praise, are simpler and less demanding.

Then, too, praise, as we have seen, is a way of gaining status over another by establishing the fact that one is capable of sitting in judgment. Status is important to all of us, and though the person being evaluated may feel that the praise is threatening or diminishing, the praiser himself has increased his psychological size or, if he praises an inferior, has claimed or reinforced his status. It is interesting to note here that when the work of a high-status person is praised by a low-status person, this is often seen as presumptuous or even insulting. If a layman should tell Picasso, "You're a very good painter," he is not likely to be particularly well received. In order to be acceptable, he must give the praise in a way that respects the status difference.

Praise is also useful in maintaining the inter-personal distance. We talk a good deal about wanting to be close to people, but when you come right down to it, there really are very few people whom we want to be close to, or whom we admit to closeness with us. It is necessary to be able to maintain distance from people, to keep a little free space around ourselves—psychological elbowroom—especially in a society which fills our daily lives with so many contacts. In the search for techniques to establish distance between ourselves and others we find that praise is one of the most effective, simply because, when we evaluate people, we are not likely to gain emotional proximity to them. Compare the effects of praise with other behaviors—for instance, listening to another or revealing your feelings to another, and see for yourself if praise doesn't tend to hold off, to separate, while the other behaviors tend to include, to embrace.

CONTROL OF RELATIONSHIPS

Praise also helps to keep relatively stable patterns of relationship between people. If organizations are to function smoothly, it is probably quite important that certain hierarchies or structures be maintained.

How does praise work toward this end? Let's take as an example a problem-solving committee meeting that includes the executive vice president at one end of the hierarchy and a new junior assistant at the other:

If the assistant comes up with the brightest and most useful idea, some way must be found to accept it without lowering the status of the vice president in the eyes of the group, thereby disturbing the group's stability. Intuitively, the vice president may say to the young assistant, "That's a very good idea, young man." This not-so-simple act of praise has greased the whole situation. Status has been maintained (because as we remember, praise is a way of claiming status); the young man has been reminded of his place in the hierarchy; and the group is restored to comfortable equilibrium. Now the group can use the young man's idea without upsetting its psychological structure.

I am amazed to note how frequently we use praise as a sign that a conversation or interview is over. Listen and discover for yourself how many interpersonal transactions are ended with a positive evaluation. "It's good to talk with you" means "I've finished talking with you." And "You're doing fine; keep up the good work" communicates as well as any exit cue we have. For the busy parents to say to a child who has just offered her latest artistic creation, "Yes, Janie, that's a beautiful painting" may not better the relationship, but it will probably end the conversation. It is often tantamount to saying, "Go away; I'm busy right now." But of course we must have ways of doing just this, and praise is a very effective method.

So we see that by enabling us to terminate an encounter, by enabling us to keep a certain amount of psychological space between ourselves and others, by enabling us to maintain status—in short, to control our relationships—praise functions as one of the most important means by which we maintain consistent structure and equilibrium in any organization.

A HELPFUL ALTERNATIVE

It is when we want to develop initiative, creativity, judgment, and problem-solving ability in people that praise fails us most. To liberate these qualities in people we need to rely on internal motivation. We need to make people feel that they are free of our control. We *may* need to establish a more equalitarian atmosphere, and sometimes we need to create a closeness with superiors. But if praise produces status differences, not equality; if it creates distance, not closeness; if it is felt as a threat, not as a reassurance; then how do you establish a free, accepting, yet close relationship that will encourage independent judgment, effective decisions, and creative actions?

There is much that is unknown about this, but from a variety of settings including psychotherapy, education, and business we are learning that perhaps the most important aspects of a helpful relationship are a person's ability to be *honest* and to *listen*. This sounds simple enough, but these behaviors are very seldom displayed in our relations with others.

BEING HONEST

This does not mean being brutally frank; it means showing some of yourself to another person, transparently exhibiting some of your own feelings and attitudes. This is not easy because from early childhood we have learned to play roles which mask our feelings, as if being honest about them would only hurt others and destroy relationships. Actually, it is the other way around; we mask our feelings so that we will not have too many close—and possibly burdensome—relationships. The inevitable consequence of exposing and sharing feelings is emotional closeness. But closeness, as rewarding as it sometimes can be, is often uncomfortable, unpredictable. Masking our feelings may result in some alienation and anxiety but also in a lot of superficial psychological comfort.

Hiding our feelings and playing roles help to make situations predictable. We want to know what we and other people are going to do and say. We want behavior to be patterned and familiar, not continually spontaneous and varied. Maybe this is necessary in order to have a society at all. Perhaps there is a limit to the amount of spontaneity, emotionality, honesty, and variation that can be tolerated by any social system.

Curiously, we are no more honest about the positive, loving feelings we have than about our feelings of annoyance, mistrust, resentment, or boredom. As a matter of fact, negative feelings usually are less difficult to express honestly than are positive feelings. For some reason it is easier for most people to be honest about their feelings of anger than it is for them to be honest about their feelings of caring and love. In either case, the times when one can risk vulnerability are perhaps life's richest moments—but are not often psychologically comfortable moments.

EMPATHIC LISTENING

The other response which we find helpful in creating close relationships is to listen. This does not merely mean to wait for a person to finish talking, but to try to see how the world looks to this person and to communicate this understanding to him. This empathic non-evaluative listening responds to the person's feelings as well as to his words; that is, to the total meaning of what he is trying to say. It implies no evaluation, no judgment, no agreement (or disagreement). It simply conveys an understanding of what the person is feeling and attempting to communicate; and his feelings and ideas are accepted as being valid for him, if not for the listener.

One reason we do not listen more, of course, is because it is too difficult. To see how difficult it is, try establishing in any group discussion the ground rule that no one may present his own view until he has first satisfied the person who has just spoken that he fully comprehends what this person meant to communicate. That is, he must restate in his own words the total meaning of the message and obtain the person's agreement that this was indeed his message—that accurate listening did take place. In doing this we will find out that—

. . . it is extremely difficult to get one person to agree that he meant what another thought he meant;

. . . we usually fail in our attempts to understand;

. . . we typically spend our listening time preparing what we are going to say;

. . . when we do listen intently, we have a hard time remembering what it was that we were going to say, and when we do remember, we discover that it is a little off the subject;

. . . most argument and emotionality goes out of such a discussion;

. . . after a few minutes of this sort of "complete communication" we become rather weary.

It is also difficult to listen because if we allow ourselves to see the world through another's eyes and to fully understand his point of view, then we run the risk of changing ourselves, our own point of view. And, as previously indicated, change is something we try to avoid.

But at times when we *do* want to develop creativity and self-confidence in others, when we *do* want to establish a close relationship in which the other person feels free "to be himself," then expressing our own feelings honestly and listening sensitively may be far more helpful than offering praise.

TRY AN EXPERIMENT

If you doubt the effects of praise outlined here, you might experiment a bit with it. Check for yourself. The next time you praise someone, see what sort of reaction you get:

> Does he open up or does he become defensive, diffident, or uncomfortable?
> Does he appear to want to continue talking or to terminate the talk?
> Does he seem to be more motivated to work or does he seem less motivated?
> Then check yourself too:
> How do *you* feel when you receive praise?
> What do *you* do and say in response to it?
> How do *you* feel when you give praise?
> What are *you* trying to accomplish by it?

Another experiment, perhaps even more telling, is to accept the praise offered to you just as it seems to be intended. That is, the next time some praise comes your way indicating that the praiser wants you to believe that you are competent, or good, or smart, or attractive, show him that you accept this evaluation of you by saying something like, "I guess you think I'm very competent" or "You must think I'm a pretty good salesman." His reactions to this may indicate to you that his praise was intended to do much more than just convey that simple idea.

Let me sum up this way: It is questionable that praise is a fuel which motivates and stimulates people. On the other hand, praise is very useful indeed as a lubricant that keeps the wheels going around smoothly and predictably; we must have techniques like praise to keep our human relations in equilibrium.

Perhaps someday we will be able to look inward for evaluation rather than outward, to tolerate less order and equilibrium in our social organizations, and to enjoy increasing emotional closeness with greater numbers of people. But until that day praise will probably continue to serve us well in ways we seldom recognize.

CHAPTER THREE

DYNAMICS OF INTELLIGENCE AND CREATIVITY

9   *Intelligence from a*
*Perceptual Point of View**

BY ARTHUR W. COMBS

EDITOR'S NOTE: Debates about the nature of intelligence, what it is and what it consists of have echoed in research laboratories and halls of learning for years. What is your intelligence? More importantly, how did you get your intelligence? Inherited genes? Environmental opportunities? A bit of both? Dr. Combs explores a point of view which you may find intriguing as he suggests the possibility of intelligence being influenced, for better or for worse, by our perceptions. If there is merit to the notion that we learn, grow and behave in terms of the meaning we assign to events which happen to us rather than the externally observed nature of events, what implications does this have for how we view teaching? Or, to put it another way, do you behave in terms of how things seem to you or in terms of how they seem to someone else?

There is a growing trend in psychology toward viewing behavior as a function of perception. More and more we have come to understand that the individual's behavior is not so much a function of the physical stimulus as it is a function of his perceptions of the events to which he is exposed. It is the meaning of events to the individual rather than the externally observed nature of events which seems crucial in behavior. As a result, psychologists in increasing numbers are turning their attention to the

* Reprinted from the *Journal of Abnormal and Social Psychology*, 1952, Vol. XLVII, 662–673, by permission of the author and the American Psychological Association.

problems of human perception and are attempting to observe behavior, not from an external point of view, but from the point of view of the individual who is behaving. This paper is an attempt to relate this method of observation to the problem of intelligence. The question we wish to explore in this paper is: "What is the nature of intelligence viewed from a perceptual or phenomenological frame of reference?"

Intelligence as a Problem of Perception

By the term *intelligence* we ordinarily refer to the effectiveness of the individual's behavior. In a personal frame of reference the individual's behavior is described in terms of the perceptions that he can make in his own unique perceptive field. This perceptive field has been called by Snygg and Combs *The Phenomenal Field* and has been defined by them as "the universe of experience open to the individual at the moment of his behavior." In other words, the behavior of the individual will be dependent upon the perceptions that the individual makes in his phenomenal field at the moment of action. The effectiveness of his behavior will necessarily be a function of the adequacy of those perceptions.

If an entity in the perceptive field is vague and ill defined, the behavior of the individual will be correspondingly vague and lacking in precision. Until the child has clearly differentiated that 2 plus 2 equals 4, this function is comparatively meaningless and his behavior in arithmetic is correspondingly inaccurate and ineffective. Thus, the precision and effectiveness of the individual's behavior will be dependent upon the scope and clarity of his personal field of awareness. Intelligence, then, from a perceptual point of view becomes a function of the factors which limit the scope and clarity of an individual's phenomenal field.

The perceptions that could be made of any given situation, such as looking at a stone wall, for example, are, theoretically, practically infinite in number and quality. As a matter of fact, however, we are strictly limited in our perceptions of a stone wall to those which we, as human beings, can make. The perceptions possible to us are only those that people can make. We cannot, for instance, perceive the wall as it would appear to a man from Mars, or from the interior of an atom, or as it would appear to a centipede. What is more, we cannot even perceive it as it would appear to all people. Different people will perceive different aspects of the wall differently, even at the same instant. I can only perceive the wall, and hence behave toward it, in terms of the perceptions that I, as an individual, can make regarding it. I may, for instance, perceive it as a fine, sturdy fence enclosing my property, while a stone mason friend might perceive it as having been poorly designed or as having been built with too little cement in the mortar mixture. The perceptions open to my mason friend are the result of his unique experience. I, not having such experience, am incapable of those perceptions at this moment.

Potential and Functional Perceptions

Before proceeding further with our discussion of the limiting factors in perception, it is necessary for us to pause for a moment to distinguish between potential and functional perceptions. By potential perceptions I mean those perceptions that exist in the individual's unique field of awareness and that, given the right circumstances at any particular moment, *could* occur. The fact that a perception is potentially possible to any individual, by no means, however, means that it would occur at the moment of action. Even those perceptions that I can make potentially may not be active for me at any given moment. Potentially, I might be able, for instance, to perceive the wall that we have just been using as an example as a barrier to be gotten over, as an eyesore to be beautified, as composed of 687 bricks costing me $80.27, or as providing pleasant shade on a hot day. These are all potential perceptions I am capable of making about the wall. They will affect my behavior, however, only when they are active or functioning in my field of perceptions. When I am beating a hasty retreat pursued by a neighbor's angry dog, perceptions about the shade, beauty, or cost of the wall, though potential, are not functional in affecting my behavior. I behave only in terms of my functioning perception of the wall as something to get over—and quickly. The fact that particular perceptions may exist potentially in the phenomenal field of an individual is by no means a guarantee that they may exist functionally at the moment of action.

While the potential intelligence of the individual is of interest in judging his capacities, it is practically always a matter impossible to measure with any degree of accuracy. We can only sample those parts of a phenomenal field that *we* happen to feel are important. Obviously the measurement of a person's potential perceptions in these terms is open to extremely grave sampling error and improves in accuracy only as the individuals tested have common experience in the materials chosen for testing. It seems probable that an intelligence test cannot accurately measure the potential differentiations that the individual can make in his phenomenal field. Rather, what we usually measure are the subject's functional perceptions. That is, we measure what differentiations he can make when confronted with the necessity to do so for one reason or another. We may define these functional perceptions as: those perceptions in the field experienced by the individual at the moment of behaving.

From a perceptual viewpoint, if intelligence is the capacity for effective behavior, *the intelligence of an individual will be dependent upon the richness and variety of perceptions possible to him at a given moment.* To understand and effectively to foster intelligent behavior, it will be necessary for us to be concerned with the limiting factors upon the perceptions of an individual. We need to know not only what the individual *could* perceive, but what he *would* perceive at a given moment of behaving.

SOME LIMITING FACTORS UPON PERCEPTION

Physiologic Limitations on Perception

Certainly the physical limitations upon the organism affect the differentiations possible in the phenomenal field. Some forms of prenatal anomalies, like mongolism, microcephalia, and similar disorders, indubitably reduce the level of operation at which the individual can function and seriously impair the ability of the organism to make adequate perceptions. Similarly, there seems good reason to believe that some types of mechanical or disease injury to the central nervous system may result in impaired functioning, such as occurs in cerebral palsy, birth injuries, prefrontal lobotomy, the aftermath of such diseases as encephalitis or, even, in common childhood diseases accompanied by prolonged high fever. Various forms of endocrinopathies, particularly cretinism, also appear to have limiting effects upon differentiational capacity for some individuals. Such physical or biological limitations upon the organism have been widely studied but account for only a small proportion of those persons operating at impaired intelligence levels.

Other less dramatic forms of physical handicaps may also have important effects upon the perceptions possible to the individual, however. This is particularly true of individuals suffering impairment of various sense modalities which may inhibit the clarity or even the existence of some perceptions. We need to remind ourselves, however, that such persons may have as rich and varied a perceptive field within their own limitations as we have within ours. Testing persons living in one frame of reference with tests based on those of another can easily lead us astray, a fact well known to the makers of some tests for the handicapped. The limitations imposed upon perception by such physical handicaps as the loss or impairment of locomotion or the use of arms or hands are also important in limiting certain kinds of perceptions. These people experience different, but not necessarily fewer or poorer perceptions of events than so-called "normals."

Perhaps less well recognized in their effects upon perception are such factors as malnutrition, focal infections, and chronic fatigue, which may reduce both the need for and the ability to make adequate perceptions. It is well known in industrial psychology, for example, that fatigued workers are more likely to have accidents, perhaps because of failure to make the right differentiations at the right time. It is conceivable that persons suffering from chronic fatigue over long periods similarly fail to make differentiations useful to them on later occasions.

Certainly such physical factors as these have important effects upon the ability of the individual to make adequate differentiations in his perceptive field. The more dramatic of these have often been recognized and studied. Others, such as the effects of malnutrition, fatigue, and the like, have been less adequately explored. In spite of the lack of research in respect to some of the physical limitations upon intelligence, far more work has been done in this area, however, than in some of those to be discussed below.

Environment and Opportunity as a Limitation upon Perception

The differentiations in the phenomenal field that an individual can make will, of course, be affected by the opportunities for perception to which he has been exposed. To appear in the perceptive field an event must have been, in some manner, experienced by the person who perceives it. Environmental effects upon perception appear to be of two types, actual or concrete and symbolic or vicarious.

Exposure to actual environmental events. In the first place the perceptions possible to any individual will be limited, in part, by the actual environmental factors to which he has been exposed. Eskimos ordinarily do not comprehend bananas, nor African Bushmen snow, since neither has had the opportunity to experience these events in their respective environments. It is not necessary to go far afield for illustration, however. In our own country our experience with the testing of children in various parts of the nation has shown that perceptions are highly limited by the environmental conditions surrounding the individual. Mountain children, for example, often give bizarre responses on intelligence tests. Sherman and Henry found intelligence test results on such children arranged themselves in order of the opportunities provided by their environment.

There are differences also between the perceptions of rural and urban children, children from the North and children from the South, mountain and valley, seaboard and plains. Nor are such differences confined only to children. Adults, too, are limited in their perceptions by environmental factors. During the war I worked for a time in an induction station receiving men from thhe mountains of Kentucky, West Virginia, and southern Ohio. An intelligence test in use at this station was composed of a series of five pictures with instructions to the subject to cross out that one of each series of five objects that did not belong with the others. One set of five pictures showed four stringed instruments, a guitar, harp, violin, bass fiddle, and a trumpet. Large numbers of these back country men crossed out the harp because they had never seen one or because "all the others are things in our band." We cannot assume that these men were less able to make differentiations or had perceptive fields less rich than their examiner on the basis of these tests. We can only suggest that their perceptions are different from those who made the test. Presumably, had they made the test and administered it to the psychologist, the psychologist would have appeared rather dull!

Exposure to symbolic or vicarious events.   Differentiations may occur in the perceptive field upon a symbolic basis as well as from exposure to an actual event. That is, perceptions may occur in the individual's field through indirect exposure to experience as in reading, conversation, movies, and other means of communication. Although I cannot directly perceive that it is dangerous to expose myself to rays from an atomic pile, for example, I can differentiate this notion through what others whom I respect have told me. Ideas and concepts are largely differentiations of this sort and it is probable that many of our perceptions are acquired through a symbolic rather than an actual exposure. Certainly most of our formal schooling falls in this category which may explain, in part, why so little of it is effective in our behavior.

It will be recognized at once that exposure to events in no sense completely determines the perceptions that the individual will make. Exposure to events is only one of the factors involved in determining whether or not an event will be differentiated. Even with equivalent exposure, the perceptions we make are not alike. Perception is not an all or none proposition but a selective process. The same person in the same situation at different times may perceive quite different aspects of the situation and behave accordingly. The provision of opportunity to perceive is by no means a guarantee that a particular perception will occur, a phenomenon of which teachers are only too aware. The personal field of the individual is always organized and meaningful and, even with exposure to events, only those aspects that have meaning for the individual in his own unique economy will be differentiated with permanence.

The individual in a particular culture perceives those aspects of his environment that, from his point of view, he needs to perceive to maintain and enhance his self in the world in which he lives. This does not mean he makes fewer perceptions than an individual in another culture; he makes only *different* perceptions. Thus, intelligence tests made in one culture and applied in another do not measure the ability to differentiate, nor do they measure the richness of the individual's field. Perhaps what they really measure is no more than the difference between cultures. American-made intelligence tests applied to other cultures generally show the following arrangement of nationality groups in decreasing order: British Isles, Germany, France, Italy, the Balkans, Asiatic countries. It will be noted that these nationality groups are also roughly arranged in order of the degree of commonality with our own culture.

Time as a Limitation of Perception

Differentiation requires time. The richness of perception, therefore, will be in part a function of how long the individual has been in touch with experiences. While it is true that a perception is possible only when confronted by an experience, it is also true that this exposure must be long enough to make differentiation possible. This principle is familiar to anyone who has looked at a painting for a period of time. The perceptions which can be made are almost limitless if one looks long enough.

In thinking of the effect of time upon differentiation, it is necessary for us to keep in mind that we are speaking of the duration of the individual's experience with an event and not of the observer's experience. Thus, while it may appear to an outside observer that an individual is confronted by an experience, from the individual's own point of view, he may have no contact with it whatever. A child may sit in school all day, apparently exposed to the curriculum, but may actually be experiencing and perceiving quite different aspects of the situation. Perception is an internal, individual phenomenon and may be quite different from that of another person, even in the same situation.

Most perceptions that the individual makes are functions of previous differentiations he has made in his phenomenal field. For example, before one can perceive the mechanics of multiplication he must have perceived addition. In the same way, before he can perceive the function of a sand dome on top of the locomotive he must differentiate the fact that locomotive wheels sometimes slip. Clearly this process of differentiation takes time. It seems axiomatic that to make differentiations an individual must have lived long enough to do so, a fact we recognize in the construction of intelligence tests calibrated for various age levels, and which teachers recognize in the concept of readiness.

Differentiations in the phenomenal field seem to be occurring continuously as the organism seeks to satisfy its needs in the myriad situations of life. In this sense, intelligence never ceases to develop but is continuously increasing so long as the individual remains alive and operating. That intelligence seems to level off at age sixteen or later is probably a mere artifact of our method of observation. So long as the individual remains in school we have at least a modicum of comparable experience which can be tested in different persons. After the school years, when individuals are free to go their separate ways, this modicum of comparable experience rapidly disappears. The older one gets, the more diverse is his experience. Intelligence tests based upon comparability of experience may thus fail to evaluate properly the effectiveness of adults.

The Individual's Goals and Values as a Limiting Factor on Perception

Up to this point in our discussion we have been dealing with factors affecting perception that are widely discussed in the literature and for the most part are well understood. In the remainder of this paper let us turn our attention to several factors less well explored as they appear in a phenomenological setting. The first of these has to do with the effects of the individual's own goals and values as a limiting factor on perception.

From a phenomenological view the individual is forever engaged in a ceaseless attempt to achieve satisfaction of his need through the goals and values he has differentiated as leading to that end. These goals and values may be explicit or implicit, simple or complex, but they are always unique to the personality itself. The goals of an individual will vary in another respect as well. The individual's goals and values may be either positive or negative. That is, in the course of his experience, the person may differentiate some things as matters to be sought, while other things may be differentiated as matters to be avoided. What is more, although there is a considerable degree of stability in the major goals and values of a particular individual, there may be great fluctuations in how some goals are perceived from time to time, depending upon the total organization of the perceptual field at any moment.

The goals and values an individual seeks have a most important effect upon the perceptions he can make. Once goals have been established by the individual they continue to affect his every experience. Thus, the person who has differentiated good music as a goal to be sought, perceives music more frequently. His entire experience with music is likely to be affected. Certainly his experience will differ markedly from the person who has formulated a goal to avoid music at all costs. In the same way the experiences of children who perceive schooling as something to be sought are vastly different from those of children who try to avoid all aspects of schooling. If the fundamental thesis of this paper is accurate, that intelligence is a function of the variety and richness of the perceptive field, then the individual's goals must have a most important effect upon intelligence. A considerable body of research has been accumulating over the past several years, demonstrating this controlling effect of goals and values on the individual's perceptive experience. Such studies as those of J. M. Levine, R. Levine, Postman, and Bruner are fascinating cases in point.

This effect of goals on perception is by no means limited to the subject whose intelligence we wish to measure. It is equally true of the intelligence test constructor. It leads to the very confusing situation wherein the test constructor with one organization of goals perceives certain experiences to be marks of intelligence for another person who may or may not have similar goals. Indeed, the likelihood is that he, almost certainly, does not have similar goals. Intelligence tests thus become highly selected samplings of perception in terms of what the testers consider important. Low scores do not necessarily mean less rich and varied fields of perception; they may mean only fields of perception more widely divergent from those of the examiner. A young man whom the writer tested at an induction center during the war illustrates the point very well. This young man was a newsboy on the streets of a West Virginia city. Although he had failed repeatedly in grammar school and was generally regarded as "not bright," he appeared on a national radio hook-up as "The Human Adding Machine." He was a wizard at figures. He could multiply correctly such figures as 6235941×397 almost as fast as the problem could be written down. He astounded our induction center for half a day with his numerical feats. Yet, on the Binet Test given by the writer he achieved an IQ of less than 60! People in his home town, who bought his papers, amused themselves by giving him problems to figure constantly. When not so occupied this young man entertained himself by adding up the license numbers of cars that passed his corner. He was a specialist in numbers. Apparently as a result of some early success in this field, he had been led to practice numbers constantly, eventually to the exclusion of all else. This was one area in which a poor colored boy could succeed and he made the most of it. His number perceptions were certainly rich and varied but other things were not. Although he was capable of arithmetic feats not achieved by one in millions, he was classified as dull! I do not mean to argue that variety of perception is unimportant in effective behavior. I do mean to suggest the importance of goals in determining perception.

Cultural Effects on Goals and Perceptions

We have stated here that the richness of the individual's perceptive field is in part a function of the goals he has differentiated as important or threatening to him. But, clearly these goals are themselves the result of the individual's experience. The culture one grows up in deeply affects the goals one holds. Cultures both restrict and encourage, approve and disapprove the formulation of goals in the individual. This selective effect of the culture in large measure determines the goals sought and avoided by the individual. These goals in turn must exert important effects upon the perceptions that become part of the individual's perceptive field.

I remember the Kentucky moonshiner to whom I once administered the Wechsler-Bellevue. This man could not tell me "how many pints in a quart" although he had certainly been taught this fact in his early schooling. Knowing that my client did a considerable business in bootleg liquor, I framed the question differently and asked "Well, how do you sell your liquor?" He smiled tolerantly and replied, "Oh Boss, I just sell it by the jug full!" In his community to have done otherwise would have been to risk bankruptcy. In a culture where a jug is standard container for spirits, what need to know about quarts?

It is conceivable that low intelligence may be, at least in part, no more than a function of the goals an individual is striving to reach in achieving his need satisfaction. The well-known phenomenon in which intelligence tests give best results in the school years, when experience and goals have a degree of commonality, and break down badly following those years would seem to corroborate this point. Perhaps by concerning ourselves with human goals we can affect perception, and thus intelligence, much more than we believed possible. Can it be that the child of low apparent intelligence is not so much a problem of an unfortuante heredity as an unfortunate constellation of goals or values? We could do a great deal about intelligence if that were true.

The Self-Concept as a Factor Limiting Perception

We are just beginning to understand the tremendous effects of the individual's concept of self upon his perceptions and behavior. Lecky, for instance, reports the effect of a change in self-concept in improving the ability of children to spell. Other researchers have reported similar effects of the self-concept upon the perceptions which the individual may make. Clinical experience would tend to bear out such observations. Any clinician is familiar with numerous instances in which a child's conception of his abilities severely limited his achievement, even though his real abilities may have been superior to his perception of them. One needs but to go shopping with one's spouse to discover again how one's conception of himself as a male or female affects the things he sees and the things he hears.

Perception is a selective process and the conception one holds of himself is a vital factor in determining the richness and the variety of perception selected. It makes a great deal of difference, for example, how one perceives the president of our country if one conceives of himself as a democrat, a republican, or a communist. One needs but to observe a group of children to become aware that little boys perceive things quite differently from little girls. Professors do not perceive like truck drivers, although when I have had to ride with professor automobile-drivers, I have often wished they did. Thousands of people in our society avoid perceptions having to do with mathematical functions by their firm concept of themselves as people who "cannot do mathematics." The self-concepts we hold have a very vital effect in selecting the perceptions which become part of our perceptive fields. If the effectiveness of behavior is dependent on our perceptive fields, it follows that the self-concepts we hold must affect the "intelligence" of our behavior.

There is another factor in the effect of the self-concept upon perception that makes it even more important as a selector of experience. That factor is the circular effect of a given concept of self. Let us take, as an example, the child who has developed a concept of himself as "unable to read." Such a child is likely to avoid reading and thus the very experience which might change his concept of self is by-passed. Worse still, the child who believes himself unable to read, confronted with the necessity for reading, is more likely than not to do badly. The external evaluation of his teachers and fellow pupils, as well as his own observations of his performance, all provide proof to the child of how right he was in the first place! The possession of a particular concept of self tends to produce behavior that corroborates the self-concept with which the behavior originated.

Every clinician has had experience with children of ability who conceive of themselves as unable, unliked, unwanted, or unacceptable and perceive and behave in accordance with their perceptions. And this effect is not limited to children alone. It seems to me one of the great tragedies of our society that millions of people in our society perceiving themselves as able to produce only X amount, behave in these terms. Society, in turn, evaluates them in terms of this behavior and so lends proof to what is already conceived by the individual. Compared to this waste of human potential in our society, our losses in automobile accidents seem like a mere drop in the bucket. It is even conceivable in these terms that we create losses in intelligence. If, in our schools, we teach a child that he is unable and if he believes us and behaves in these terms, we need not be surprised when we test his intelligence to discover that he produces at the level at which we taught him!

It is conceivable that psychology has unwittingly contributed to this situation by the widespread publication of a static conception of intelligence and human capacities. The concept of severe limits upon the capacities of the organism simply corroborates the self-concept of the man in the street and decreases the likelihood of change in his concept of self. Even more important must be the effect upon our educational system. Teachers who believe in an unchanging character of child capacities provide the attitudes and experiences that produce and maintain a child's conception of self and his abilities. It is notorious that children's grades vary very little from year to year through the course of schooling. This continuous and little-changing evaluation must have important effects on the self-concept of the child. If the school system in which the child lives is thoroughly imbued with the notion that a child's capacities are comparatively fixed, it is even conceivable that the system may in large measure produce a child's intelligence level by the circular effect we have mentioned above.

Threat as a Factor in Perception

The last of the factors I should like to discuss as a possible factor in intelligence is the effect of threat upon the perceptive field. If our fundamental assumption that intelligence is a function of the richness and breadth of the phenomenal field is correct, the effect of threat on this field becomes a most important consideration. Although these effects have been so widely understood by the layman that they have been made a part of his everyday speech, it is interesting that until very recently the phenomenon has been given little attention by psychologists. The perception by the individual of threat to himself seems to have at least two major effects upon the perceptive field.

Restriction of the perceptive field under threat.   The first of these effects is the restrictive effect that the perception of threat to self seems to have on the individual's perception. When he feels himself threatened, there appears to be a narrowing of the perceptive field to the object of threat. This has often been described in the psychology of vision as "tunnel vision." The phenomenon is extremely common and almost everyone has experienced it at some moment of crisis in his lifetime. One hears it described in such comments as "All I could see was the truck coming at us," or, "I was so scared I couldn't think of a thing." There seems reason to believe that this effect is not limited to traumatic experiences alone, but exists in lesser degree in response to milder threats as well. Combs and Taylor, for example, have demonstrated the effect under extremely mild forms of threat.

Such limiting effects on perception must certainly have a bearing upon perceptions available to the individual in his phenomenal field. Subjects who have participated in food deprivation experiments report uniformly that when threatened by hunger, food becomes an obsession. Recently, at the dinner table, I asked my young daughter what she had learned at school that day. "Oh nothing," said she with much feeling, "But was our teacher mad! Wow!" It would appear from her remarks that, feeling threatened by an angry teacher, it was difficult for her to perceive much else. Her perceptions of the day were apparently entirely concerned with the nature of anger. No doubt these are valuable perceptions to possess, but I know of no intelligence test which measures them.

I recall, too, the behavior of two little girls whose mother was taken to a mental hospital at the beginning of the summer. The matter was kept a deep secret from these two children for fear they "would not understand." The children spent most of the summer with the writer's daughter in an incessant game of "hospital." From morning to night this game went on outside our living room window. Apparently, this preoccupation was the direct outcome of the threat they felt in the loss of their mother, for with the mother's return the game ceased as suddenly as it had begun. To the best of my knowledge it has not occurred since. Under threat there seem to be severe limits imposed upon the breadth and character of perception.

Defense of the perceptive field under threat. There is a second effect of threat upon the individual's perceptions. This effect has to do with the defense reactions induced in the individual on perceiving himself to be threatened. The perception of threat not only narrows the field and reduces the possibility of wide perceptions, but causes the individual to protect and cling to the perceptions he already holds. Thus, the possibility of perceptual changes is reduced and the opportunities for new perceptions or learning are decreased. Under threat, behavior becomes rigid. The fluidity and adaptation which we generally associate with intelligent behavior is vastly decreased. A number of interesting experiments in the past few years have demonstrated this phenomenon. Cowen, for example, illustrated this effect in problem solving.

Our own experiment previously mentioned also demonstrated this effect with even very mild forms of threat. This rigidity or resistance of perception to change under threat is well known to the layman and is well illustrated in some of the sayings of our culture. Such aphorisms as "Nobody ever wins an argument" or "You can lead a horse to water but you cannot make him drink" seem to be illustrations of a vague understanding of the phenomenon in the public mind. It is surprising that this principle has been so long overlooked.

I think it will be generally agreed that intelligence behavior is quite the antithesis of rigidity. In the terms we have used in this article, intelligent behavior is a function of the variety and richness of perception in the phenomenal field. Whatever produces narrowness and rigidity of perception becomes an important factor in limiting intelligence. If this reasoning is accurate, or even partly so, one is led to wonder about the effects of long-continued threat upon the development of intelligence. What of the child who has suffered serious threats to himself for long periods of his life, as in the case of the delinquent, for example? Or what of the child who has been seriously deprived of affection and warmth from those who surround him over a period of years? Is it possible that we have created low intelligence in such children? Axline has reported a number of cases in which intelligence scores improved considerably under therapy. We have observed similar changes in our own clinical practice.

It may be argued that, although threat seems to reduce perception, some people under threat apparently produce more effectively. I think, however, it is necessary for us to distinguish between "threat" and "challenge." In threat, the individual perceives himself in jeopardy and feels, in addition, a degree of inadequacy to deal effectively with the threat perceived. In challenge, the individual perceives himself threatened but feels at the same time a degree of adequacy to deal with the threat. It would appear that whether an event is perceived as threatening or challenging is a function of the individual's feeling of competence to deal with it. If this analysis is correct, it would explain why a situation that appears threatening to a person, from the viewpoint of an outside observer, might one time produce rigidity and another highly effective behavior. This description of events seems characteristic of the history of civilization as well as of individuals, if Toynbee's explanation can be given credence. He points out that the most productive (more intelligent?) societies are those in which the society faces some crisis within its capacities to cope with the situation (challenge), while societies without crisis or in which the crisis is overwhelming produce very little or collapse entirely.

SOME IMPLICATIONS OF THIS CONCEPTION OF INTELLIGENT BEHAVIOR

If the conception of intelligence we have been discussing in this paper should prove accurate, it seems to me to raise serious questions about some of our common assumptions with respect to intelligence and, at the same time, opens some exciting new possibilities for the treatment or education of persons we have often assumed to be beyond help. It implies that our conception of the limiting factors of intelligence may have been too narrow. It would suggest perhaps that our very point of view with respect to intelligence may have resulted in our own tunnel vision, such that we have not been able to perceive other factors given little attention to this point. Perhaps we have been too impressed with the limitations upon growth and development which we observe in physical maturation. We may, for instance, have jumped too quickly to the assumption that intelligent behavior was limited as severely as physical growth and that we have explored to exhaustion other factors that may limit intelligence.

I am not suggesting that physiologic limits do not exist in respect to intelligence. I am suggesting that we may have conceded too early that we have approached those limits. There is no doubt that we can demonstrate in some cases, such as mongolism, cretinism, and the like, that physical factors severely limit intelligence. But these cases are comparatively few compared to the so-called "familial" cases of low intelligence that we often assume are hereditary in origin. What evidence do we really possess that would lead us to the position that an individual of "normal" physical condition and vigor may be limited in his capacity for effective behavior by some physical condition? We assume there must be such factors operating because we canot explain his handicap otherwise. That biological science has not yet been able to demonstrate such physical bases has not deterred us in this. On the contrary, we have simply deplored the lack of sufficient advance in that discipline to demonstrate our conclusion! I should like to suggest that this may not be their failure but ours. Until it can be definitely established that limitations exist as biological functions, our task as psychologists is to assume that they may just as well be social or psychological in character and to work just as hard exploring the matter in our discipline as we expect the biologist to work in his.

Let us, for example, explore to the very fullest the possibility that in those cases where we cannot demonstrate biologic impairment, the limitations upon intelligence may be psychological. If it turns out not to be true, we shall find out in time. I do not believe we can afford to limit the places where we look by the pre-perceptions we have about the matter. Our responsibility here is too great. Education, to name but the most obvious of our social institutions, has in large measure predicated its goals and methods on a concept of humanity with certain static limitations on intelligence. If these limitations are not static, it is up to us as psychologists to find out. The task of the scientist is to question, not to be content with answers. We cannot afford to accept an undemonstrated point of view that prevents us from asking questions.

Some Implications for Intelligence Testing

If the concepts of intelligence we have been discussing prove accurate, another area of psychological thought toward which we must cast a quizzical eye is the area of intelligence testing. This is particularly important at a time when our culture has come to accept these instruments as trustingly as the family doctor's prescription. If our approach to intelligent behavior as a function of the variety and richness of the perceptual field is a valid consideration, we need to ask regarding these tests at least the following questions:

1. Is our sampling of the perceptive field truly adequate? If I lived for years in a prison cell, I presume I should become expert in perceptions about that cell. Unfortunately, they would be of little value outside the prison walls, but can it truthfully be said that my perceptions are less rich or varied, or only that they are less rich and varied about things I have not had opportunity to experience? Is the delinquent, with rich and varied perceptions on how to elude the police, less intelligent or has he simply not perceived things society wishes he had?

2. Since perceptions are always closely affected by need, by whose need shall we sample perceptions—yours, mine, society's, the subject's own? I suspect that in terms of his own needs and perceptions the subject might be deemed quite brilliant, though he might or might not appear so from the point of view of society. For the most part our tests are based on the assumption that academic, upper middle-class, intellectual perceptions are important. But are they? Can we assume that the expert machinist, who can perceive things "out of this world" for most of the rest of us about a piece of stock on his lathe, is less intelligent than a diplomat who perceives many things about foreign affairs? Can we be so sure of our values as to call one bright and the other dull? Can we blame the machinist for his lack of perception about foreign affairs without asking the diplomat to be equally skilled in the machinist's field of perceptions?

3. Finally, if perceptions are affected by the factors we have discussed in this paper, is it fair to sample intelligence irrespective of the control of such factors? Shall we, for example, examine the child who has lacked opportunity to perceive, has possessed a concept of self or been so threatened over a long period of time so as to have been unable to perceive what we wish to sample without consideration of those factors? Shall we overlook such factors and be satisfied that the perceptions important to us are not there, or shall we seek for ways to make it possible for the child to have them? Shall we assume that our failure to discover a particular perception present in the field is, *ipso facto*, evidence of lack of capacity; or seek to discover why it is not? On the positive side of the picture, if the concepts we have here been discussing are sound, there is reason to believe that intelligence may be far less immutable than we have thought. It may be that we can do far more than we have dreamed we could. Perhaps we may even be able to create intelligence!

Implications for Constructive Action

Who can say, for example, what results we might be able to achieve by a systematic effort to remove or decrease the effectiveness of the limitations on perception discussed in this paper? It is fascinating to speculate on the possibilities one might try in constructing a situation for a child, or adult, consciously designed to minimize the limitations imposed on perception by physical condition, environment, goals, and individual's self-concept, and the effects of perceived personal threat.

If the position we have taken is accurate, it would suggest that there is much we can do (*a*) to free individuals from the restraints upon perception and (*b*) to provide the opportunities for perception to occur.

1. First and most obviously, we should be able to discover and make available to far more people the means to achieve better physical condition. We have already done a good deal in this area but much needs yet to be done. Who can say, for instance, what completely adequate medical care for all our people might mean a generation hence?

2. If this discussion has merit, there lies the possibility of providing experiences for people that will make adequate perception possible. We have tried to do this in our schools, but have not always accomplished it. We have succeeded very well in gathering information and in making it available to students. We have not succeeded too well in making such information meaningful. Can it be that the decreases in school success with advance through the school years is more a function of lack of meaning for students than lack of intelligence? Is it enough to assume that experience provided by us to the student is truly provided when he is free to experience it? Has the child in school, who is so worried about his relationship with his peers that he cannot perceive what his book is saying, truly been provided opportunity to perceive?

In our training of children of "low intelligence," we often provide situations wherein they are carefully taught to perform repeatedly a simple act. Is it possible that in so doing we may be further narrowing their fields of perception and building self-concepts that produce even narrower perceptive fields?

What kinds of environments could we construct that might more effectively result in increased perception? Such experiments as Lippitt and White have carried on with democratic and autocratic environments suggest some possibilities, but we need to know much more. Perhaps we could learn to build such environments from observing with greater care and understanding the methods of good teachers.

3. Who can say what possible effects might occur from a systematic release of the individual's perceptions by the satisfaction of his most pressing needs or goals? We college professors insist we can produce more, which is another way of saying perceive more, when we have the leisure time to do so, when we are freed from the necessity of spending our time satisfying our needs for sheer existence. Can this be less true of others? It is possible that the child with needs of love, affection, status, prestige, or a girl friend might also be freed to perceive more widely and richly, if we could but find ways of helping him satisfy his needs. Ordinarily, we pay a good deal of attention to the physical needs of a child, understanding that with these needs unfulfilled, he makes a poor student. Is there any good

reason to suppose his psychological needs are less pressing or less important in freeing him to perceive widely and accurately? We spend much time and energy trying to find ways of "motivating" people or blaming them for not being motivated to do what we need them to do. We assume that if permitted to seek their own needs, people will not satisfy ours. Perhaps we should get further by helping them satisfy their needs; they might then be free to satisfy ours.

4. Most of our educational methods are directed at the provision of perceptions for the student. He is lectured, required, shown, exhorted, and coerced to perceive what someone thinks he should. It seems possible that with equal energy devoted to the matter of creating needs, goals, and values in students, rich and varied perceptions might be more efficiently produced.

What effects might we be able to produce by providing experiences that build adequate concepts of self in children and adults? What differences in the richness and variety of perception might result from a generation of people with "I can" rather than "I can't" conceptions of themselves? What possibilities of increased perceptions and hence of increased intelligence might accrue to such a program? Clinical experience has demonstrated frequently how a changed perception of self as a more adequate personality can free children for improved school performance, for example.

What would happen if we were consciously and carefully to set about the task of providing experiences that would lead people to conceptions of themselves as adequate, worthy, self-respecting people? If freedom to perceive is a function of adequate perceptions of self, it should not surprise us that the child who perceives himself as unwanted, unacceptable, unable, or unliked behaves in rigid fashion. It should be possible, too, to reverse this process and produce more adequate perceptions by systematic efforts at producing more adequate definitions of self. The possibilities seem tremendous but we have scarcely scratched the surface of this problem.

Finally, if threat to the individual has as important effects as seem indicated in this discussion, the removal of threat would seem a most important factor to consider in the release of the individual to perceive more adequately. The work of Rogers and his students in client centered therapy has already illustrated to some degree what possibilities freeing the individual to perceive more adequately may accomplish through the provision of a permissive nonthreatening relationship between counselor and client. We have already mentioned the effects Axline has reported following a permissive, nonthreatening form of play therapy.

Such effects do not seem limited to the therapeutic situation, however. A number of workers have applied this principle of permissiveness to the classroom situation with equally gratifying results. Experiments in student centered teaching at Syracuse have led many of us to believe in the tremendous educational possibilities in the removal of threat.

This paper has asked many questions. Indeed, it has asked far more questions than it has presumed to answer. That, it seems to me, is the function of theory. The picture of intelligence presented here as it seems from a phenomenological viewpoint may be accurate or false or, more likely, partly true and partly false. Only time and the industry of many observers can check its adequacy or inadequacy. It seems to me to pose problems that are both exciting and challenging. If it proves as stimulating to the reader as it has to the author, I shall rest content that a theory has achieved its purpose.

10 Intelligence at Adulthood: A Twenty-Five Year Follow-Up*

BY KATHERINE P. BRADWAY AND
CLARE W. THOMPSON

EDITOR'S NOTE: Whether you believe that intelligence is a function of perceptions, as suggested by Dr. Combs in the previous article, or a product of genetic determinants, or environmental factors, it still leaves open the question of intellectual growth over time. In reading number five, you found evidence linking early elementary school achievement and later adulthood achievement. Are there similar relationships between preschool IQ's and later adult IQ's? What are your hunches about the relative IQ gains of girls versus boys over a twenty-five year period? How about your own IQ at this point in your life? Do you think you're as "smart" as you will ever be or is there room for further mental growth? This article should help you to be clearer about these and related questions concerning intellectual growth.

Attempts to understand human intelligence were based initially on studies of children. In contrast, this paper deals with aspects of intelligence which cannot be studied adequately from data limited to childhood intelli-

* Reprinted from the *Journal of Educational Psychology*, 1962, Vol. 53, 1–14, by permission of the senior author and the American Psychological Association.

gence. Specifically, our approach has been to study as young adults a group of individuals previously tested during the preschool years and during adolescence.

Binet and Simon developed the original intelligence test to objectify the criteria which educators had been using for many years in assessing the capacities of children for purposes of school placement. The several early American adaptations of this test culminated in the 1916 Stanford-Binet, which provided indices of adult intelligence. The standardization group, however, consisted largely of children; adult indices were based on extrapolation.

The urgency of the needs for screening and assignment created by World War I led to the creation of truly adult intelligence tests but, consistent with these needs, these tests were for group rather than individual administration. Later revisions of individual intelligence tests (e.g., the 1937 and 1960 Stanford and the 1939 Kuhlmann) extended the upper limit by providing more difficult test items. Moreover, somewhat older subjects were included in the standardization groups, although the upper age levels of these groups did not go above the adolescent years into adulthood.

No adequate instrument existed by which the clinician could measure the intelligence of the individual adult until the publication of the Wechsler-Bellevue in 1939. Wechsler's large standardization sample started with children of 12 years and included older age groups up to 65 years. His emphasis on adult intelligence resulted in departure from the use of mental age, a concept which had contributed immeasurably to the interpretation of childhood intelligence, but which introduced confusion in the assessment of adult intelligence. His term "IQ" is not a continuation of Stern's quotient of mental age divided by chronological age; it is more comparable to a standard score. Unlike the revisions of the Binet, all of which had been based on the concept that intellectual abilities reach their peak at from 14 to 16 years of age, indices of intelligence for the first time took account of the continuation of intellectual growth into the adult years. This view of intellectual growth has been increasingly confirmed by more recent studies (Bayley, 1955; Bayley & Oden, 1955) including the present one. Although Wechsler calls his concept of intelligence global, the structure of the Wechsler-Bellevue (and its later revision, the WAIS) is such that several kinds of tasks are separately measured and separate indices of verbal and nonverbal abilities are provided.

The clinician trying to answer questions about the intelligence of an adult needs information about the unique growth rates of different kinds of abilities. No cross-sectional sampling can provide such information accurately. On the other hand, longitudinal studies pose problems of practice effects and of the attrition which inevitably occurs over a period of time. The clinician is also confronted with the problem of how most meaningfully to express the measured intelligence of any given adult. Should it be an index which compares him with his own age group? One which locates him on his own course of development and decline? Or several which represent an assessment of his various kinds of mental processes? Moreover, each of these requires that procedures for equating means and variability be worked out. Answers to many of these questions are necessary before valid predictions about adult intelligence can be made.

PROCEDURE AND SUBJECTS

Information for some of these answers is provided by the longitudinal study we have recently completed (Bradway & Robinson, 1961). A group of 111 adults aged 27 to 32 who had been tested 25 years earlier as part of the 1937 Stanford-Binet standardization sample of preschool children and again during their adolescent years was administered the Stanford-Binet and WAIS in 1956. The repetition of the Stanford-Binet permits analysis of improvement in the same tasks from adolescence to adulthood; the WAIS data permit comparison of child and adult measures of intelligence of the same individuals. Treatment of the data has included correlations between total scores, mental growth curves, an analysis of items for increase in per cent passing from adolescence to adulthood, and an analysis

TABLE 1:   *Correlations between test scores at the several administrations*

Test	1941 S-B (L)	1956 S-B (L)	1956 WAIS Full	1956 WAIS Verbal	1956 WAIS Performance
1931 S-B (L and M)	.65	.59	.64	.60	.54
1941 S-B (L)		.85	.80	.81	.51
1956 S-B (L)			.83	.89	.46
1956 WAIS Full				.87	.84
1956 WAIS Verbal					.59

of the predictive value of preschool items. This latter item analysis was based on: correlations between Stanford-Binet (Forms L and M) preschool items and both adolescent Stanford-Binet IQ and adult WAIS verbal and performance quotients, and comparisons between scores on special scales constructed from the several kinds of preschool items and later scores obtained on comparable adult WAIS scales. Because for one subject the WAIS was incomplete and educational attainment was not ascertained, and for another the 1931 Stanford-Binet IQ was invalid, the number of total subjects on which any one analysis is based varies from 109 to 111 depending upon which variables are involved in the analysis. No attempt was made in the two follow-ups to continue the procedure used in the initial examination of testing children within one month of a birthday; a larger deviation in the age distribution was a consequence.

RESULTS AND DISCUSSION

Constancy of the IQ

A finding of primary interest is that an individual's measured intelligence in relation to others of his same age is demonstrated to be more stable than previous studies suggest. These results are presented in Table 1. It will be noted that the correlation between preschool (1931) intelligence, and adult (1956) intelligence as measured by the full scale WAIS is .64. The measure of preschool intelligence was a combination of the two forms of the Stanford-Binet which became the 1937 Revision, and the measure of adult intelligence was a combination of the verbal and performance scales of the WAIS; thus the indices of intelligence at both ages were based on the most adequate measurements available when the data were collected. The reliability of each measurement was sufficiently high so that correcting for unreliability increases the correlation only slightly: from .64 to .69. The degree of correspondence over a 25-year period is not significantly different from the correlation of .65 (uncorrected) found between preschool and adolescent Stanford-Binet IQs after an interval of 10 years.

Also of note from Table 1 is the correlation of .80 between adolescent (1941) Stanford-Binet and adult (1956) WAIS. Although this is somewhat lower than the correlation of .85 between the adolescent and adult administrations of the Stanford-Binet, neither correlation is significantly different from the correlation of .83 between Stanford-Binet and WAIS administered to our subjects on the same day when they were adults. Apparently the Stanford-Binet measures at preschool and at adolescence is still being measured by the WAIS at adulthood.

A comparison of the columns of Table 1 shows a close similarity, both in absolute amount and in trend, between the 1956 verbal WAIS and the 1956 full scale WAIS when each is correlated with the Stanford-Binet administered at the three age levels. The performance WAIS correlations, on the other hand, are both lower in value and opposite in trend. The reason for this reversal in trend needs further study to determine whether the results reflect an increase in specialization of intelligence with age or are due to an increase in verbal content of the Stanford-Binet at the higher levels.

Growth and Decline of Intellectual Abilities

Our data contribute to the accumulating evidence that intellectual potential does not cease to increase at 16 years in contradiction to the conclusions of Terman and others. Table 2 summarizes our data for comparison of obtained IQs. In view of the conformance between the 1931 and 1941 Stanford-Binet IQs and between the standard deviations at the three ages, the fact that the 1956 Stanford-Binet IQ exceeds the 1941 Stanford-Binet IQ by a statistically significant amount is interpreted as a consequence of intellectual growth in these subjects beyond 16 years. The increase of 11 points in IQ corresponds to a gain in mental age score of 20 months beyond expectancy. The finding of a continuation of mental growth into adulthood is consistent with the findings of Bayley (1955) and others (Bayley & Oden, 1955). The implications of the difference between present and previously held conclusions regarding mental growth into adulthood deserve consideration. Bayley (1955, p. 817) suggests alternative explanations including the new generations' having more opportunity to develop their intellectual capacities than did their parents. Inhelder and Piaget (1958, p. 337) have pointed out the probability that Greek children were behind our own in growth of logical thinking and suggest that the age at which formal thinking begins "may be a product of progressive acceleration of individual development under the influence of education."

TABLE 2:   *Means and standard deviations of the two tests at the three administrations*

Test	1931		1941		1956	
	M	SD	M	SD	M	SD
Chronological age	4.0	1.1	13.6	1.4	29.5	1.5
S-B IQ	112.8[a]	15.9[a]	112.3[b]	16.4[b]	123.6[b]	15.0[b]
WAIS IQ						
Full					108.9	11.0
Verbal					110.4	13.3
Performance					105.0	11.5

[a] *Composite Form L and Form M.*
[b] *Form L.*

TABLE 3:   *Stanford-Binet scores for adults by year of age*

1956 Chronological age	N	S-B Mean 1956 IQ	S-B Mean 1956 MA
27.0–27.9	16	121.3	18.2
28.0–28.9	25	125.5	18.9
29.0–29.9	23	126.8	19.0
30.0–30.9	20	123.5	18.5
31.0–31.9	24	121.0	18.1

TABLE 4:   *WAIS scores for adults by year of age*

1956 Chronological age		Mean 1956 WAIS standard scores		
	N	Full	Verbal	Performance
27.0–27.9	16	119	67	51
28.0–28.9	24	127	72	56
29.0–29.9	23	129	73	55
30.0–30.9	20	126	72	54
31.0–31.9	24	119	70	50

The method of computing WAIS IQs assumes continuation of intellectual growth up to 34 years. The mean WAIS IQ of our group is lower in numerical value than expectancy based on the mean 1941 Stanford-Binet IQ. It will be noted, however, that the WAIS mean IQ is approximately one SD above 100, whereas the 1941 Stanford-Binet mean IQ is less than one SD above 100; so that in terms of relative deviations, the WAIS mean IQ is higher than the Stanford-Binet IQ, although not to a statistically significant degree. The verbal half of the WAIS approaches the 1941 Stanford-Binet results more closely than does the full scale, and the performance half less so.

The addition of the present data to those previously collected for this group of subjects gives us a third segment of the mental growth curve. Thus we can plot mental age against chronological age for the years 2 through 5, the years 11 through 15, and now the years 27 through 31. Two subjects were younger and one was older than these years and are omitted from this section. Table 3 summarizes the current data for the Stanford-Binet. . . .

Before we interpret what this lack of change during this 5-year period may mean, we must consider the possible ceiling effect. The 1937 Stanford-Binet has insufficient top for adults and therefore this flattening of the curve might be an artifact. To examine this possibility, a similar analysis was made of the results on the WAIS for these subjects, inasmuch as a low ceiling is not a limitation of that test. One of the subjects had a partial WAIS only and is omitted for this reason. . . . Table 4 summarizes the data for the WAIS. Analysis of variance for these three scores again shows the variation with chronological age not to approach significance. . . .

Further study to determine the role of ceiling effect was made by analyzing only those cases showing no or few passes at the Superior Adult III level of the Stanford-Binet. Also, because our group of subjects is somewhat above average, a separate study was made of those cases clustering around IQ 100. These additional studies, however, served only to substantiate the results just reported. The point at which mental growth as measured by these instruments terminates and at which the curve assumes a downward direction is not established by these data.

Sex Differences

Tests such as the Stanford-Binet are intentionally constructed to eliminate or to minimize sex differences. Consequently most investigators, including the present ones in earlier studies, have given little attention to this variable. It is in this area, however, that some of the most cogent findings of the present study emerge. As shown in Table 5, on all three administrations of the Stanford-Binet, female subjects achieved a higher mean score than did males. On the first two administrations, this difference was significant beyond the .01 level. On the 1956 testing, it did not reach significance. The males increased their scores from 1941 to 1956 to a greater extent than did the women. For the males, this increase was 13.7 and for the females it was 9.6; the difference of 4.1 is significant beyond the .01 level. Both females and males show a negative correlation between the 1941 Stanford-Binet IQ and the gain in IQ from 1941 to 1956, but the one for females is larger. For men this correlation is $-.23$ and for women $-.67$; the difference between these correlations is significant beyond the .01 level. Dividing the male and female groups according to whether they stopped their education at high school graduation or went beyond does not change the findings. . . . The decrease in standard deviation for females from 1941 to 1956 as shown in Table 5 reflects that these findings are due to the tendency of women with IQs which are high at adolescence not to increase their scores by adulthood as much as does the rest of the group.

A study of the individuals scoring high (from 130 to 150 IQ) on the 1956 Stanford-Binet yields further information. Females in this group had always scored high relative to the group: mean IQ of 125.9 in 1931, 127.8 in 1941, and 137.5 in 1956. For the males, however, becoming a member of this group represented a gain from an earlier lower point with most of the gain achieved by adolescence: mean IQ of 115.9 in 1931, 126.2 in 1941, and 140.7 in 1956. (It must be remembered that these 1956 Stanford-Binet IQs are, on the average, 11 points high, since they do not include a correction for the fact that there was a mean IQ increase of 11 points for the total sample.) Slightly but not significantly more women than men in this subgroup stopped education with high school graduation. Of those who started college, not a single man failed to finish, whereas one-third of the women dropped out before finishing. This leaves us with the familiar chicken-egg dilemma. Did the women drop out of college because their relative brightness as compared with men decreased—their promise not being realized in the same way as was that of the men? Or did the earlier termination of their academic education make the intelligence tests administered to them as adults relatively more difficult for them?

TABLE 5:   Sex differences on the Stanford-Binet

Test	Male	Female	Difference
1931 L-M			
N	51	59	
M	108.5	115.8	−7.3
SD	14.4	13.3	
CR*			2.79
1941 L			
N	52	59	
M	107.9	116.1	−8.2
SD	19.0	13.7	
CR*			2.58
1956 L			
N	52	59	
M	121.6	125.7	−4.1
SD	19.6	10.6	
CR*			1.36

* A value of 2.57 is significant beyond the .01 level and a value of 1.96 beyond the .05 level.

An analysis of the relation between IQ at adolescence and continuation of education for the total group was made. There is no significant difference for either sex between mean 1941 IQ of those who stopped their education with graduation from high school and the mean 1941 IQ of those who attended college but did not graduate (males: 100.7 and 102.5; females: 113.8 and 113.0). The mean 1941 IQ, however, of both the 17 males and the 14 females who graduated from college is significantly higher (124.6 and 125.0, respectively) than for those who did not graduate from college. Gain in IQ, on the other hand, is not consistently related to educational attainment. Mean IQ gains for males who did not go beyond high school graduation, who entered college but did not graduate, and who graduated from college were 14.7, 11.7, and 11.8, respectively. Corresponding mean gains for females were 8.2, 12.3, and 9.3, respectively. The differences between the mean gains for either sex are not large enough to be statistically significant with the small number of subjects involved (males: 22, 13, and 17 for successive educational attainments; females: 22, 22, and 14).

Because other investigators of adult intelligence have not reported sex differences of the nature found here, we cannot look beyond our own data for the answers to some of the questions which are posed. This seems to open up an area worthy of further study designed explicitly to explore this problem.

Increases in Abilities from Adolescence to Adulthood

With the establishment of the fact that there is increase in intelligence scores between adolescence and adulthood, one becomes interested in identifying the kinds of abilities which increase most. Within the range of abilities covered by the adult levels of the Stanford-Binet, it was possible to shed light on this question by comparing the proportion of our group passing each item as adolescents and as adults. The percentages of the present sample passing each item were calculated for the 1941 and 1956 results. Items occurring below a subject's basal age were assumed to have been passed; those occurring above a ceiling were assumed to have been failed. Since nearly all subjects passed in 1956 all those items through Level 14, it was possible to make meaningful comparisons for the four adult levels only. Table 6 lists each of the 26 items at these levels, arranged according to the magnitude of the increase in per cent passing over the 15-year period. The final column in the table classifies items by "type," following a system suggested by Davis (1941), into rote memory (M), reasoning (R), and vocabulary (V). The reasoning subscale has been further divided by Robinson into those items which appear to involve mental manipulation of practical, concrete concepts (RP) versus those dealing with more abstract concepts (RA). One might wonder whether those items having the lowest per cent passing in 1941 would by artifact show the most increase to 1956. The correlation between per cent passing in 1941 and increase from 1941 to 1956 was found, however, to be only .06.

Table 7 presents a comparison of the data which demonstrates the differential increases made by our subjects in the four classifications of items. Immediate rote memory items and those involving practical reasoning showed smaller increases than those involving abstract reasoning and vocabulary. This finding tends to confirm the conclusion of most investigators that growth of functions dependent on continued learning and on the building of concepts is more likely to continue into adulthood than is growth of memory or performance functions.

These data make it clear that one should not present conclusions about the growth of intelligence into the adult years without specifying what kinds of intelligence one means and how one is measuring these. If one

TABLE 6: *Items of Stanford-Binet (L) adult levels by magnitude of change in per cent passing from adolescence to adulthood*

Rank	Location	Item	Per cent Passing[a]		Increase	Chi square[b]	Type
			1941	1956			
1	AA-5	Proverbs I	22.5	81.1	58.6	76.26	RA
2	SAI-1	Vocabulary	35.1	92.8	57.7	80.07	V
3	SAII-1	Vocabulary	13.5	67.6	54.1	67.28	V
4	SAI-6	Essential Similarities	31.5	82.9	51.4	52.42	RA
5	SAI-5	Sentence Building	30.6	77.5	46.9	49.04	V
6.5	AA-6	Ingenuity	30.6	73.9	43.3	38.01	RP
6.5	SAIII-1	Vocabulary	1.8	45.0	43.2	52.84	V
8	AA-3	Difference between Abstract Words	49.5	91.9	42.4	48.05	V
9	SAIII-3	Opposite Analogies	8.1	48.7	40.6	44.89	V
10.5	AA-2	Codes	37.8	77.5	39.7	35.73	RP
10.5	SAII-5	Reconciliation of Opposites	29.7	69.4	39.7	34.89	RA
12	AA-1	Vocabulary	59.4	98.2	38.8	49.41	V
13	SAII-4	Proverbs II	6.3	44.1	37.8	42.81	RA
14	AA-7	Memory for Sentences V	36.9	72.1	35.2	27.63	M
15	SAII-2	Finding Reasons II	14.4	47.8	33.4	28.68	RA
16	AA-8	Reconciliation of Opposites	54.9	86.5	31.6	26.64	RA
17	AA-4	Arithmetic Reasoning	41.4	72.1	30.7	21.22	RP
18	SAIII-2	Orientation: Directions II	14.4	41.4	27.0	20.15	RP
19	SAI-3	Minkus Completion	24.3	50.5	26.2	16.18	V
20	SAI-4	Repeating 6 Digits Reversed	29.7	54.1	24.4	13.45	M
21	SAIII-5	Reasoning	3.6	24.3	20.7	19.82	RP
22	SAII-3	Repeating 8 Digits	17.1	35.1	18.0	9.34	M
23	SAIII-6	Repeating 9 Digits	3.6	16.2	12.6	9.89	M
24	SAIII-4	Paper Cutting II	11.7	22.5	10.8	3.57	RP
25	SAI-2	Enclosed Box Problem	50.4	55.9	5.5	0.62	RP
26	SAII-6	Repeating Thought of Passage	24.3	27.9	3.6	0.09	M

[a] $N = 111$.

[b] A chi-square of 10.83 is significant beyond the .001 level, 6.64 beyond the .01 level, and 3.84 at the .05 level. Hence all but

administered an intelligence test consisting solely of items measuring vocabulary and abstract reasoning, he would find more increase of "intelligence" into adulthood than if he used a test heavily weighted with memory and practical reasoning items. Thus one cannot realistically expect ever to describe the shape of *the* mental growth curve.

A finding in these data which has important implications when it comes to trying to predict amount of subsequent mental growth in an individual adolescent is the negative relationship between level of ability at adolescence and gain in mental age score from adolescense to adulthood. We have found, for example, that the higher the 1941 Stanford-Binet score, whether expressed as IQ or MA, the slightly lower the rate of increase (MA increase/CA increase) to 1956 for the group of 45 subjects who were 14 to 16 years of age in 1941. (For this analysis, subjects less than 14 years of age in 1941 were eliminated in order to minimize the operation of differential rates of mental growth in adolescence.) The correlations expressing this are not significantly different from zero. Comparable correlations for males and females considered separately are consistent with the findings on sex differences discussed earlier in that the females showed a significant negative relationship, whereas the males did not. . . .

Thus, although the adult scores on intelligence tests can be predicted with some accuracy from the score one obtains as an adolescent (as indicated by the correlations in Table 1), we have not isolated factors which permit us to predict the amount of mental age gain. The fact that adult intelligence can be predicted from adolescent intelligence with such a high degree of accuracy despite the lack of relation between adolescent intelligence and amount of gain to adulthood is, of course, due to the fact that the amount of gain at these levels represents such a relatively small proportion of the total "amount" of intelligence. We can anticipate that there will be an increase in mental age from adolescence to adulthood, but we cannot predict which subjects will gain most. We do know that amount

TABLE 7:   *Comparison of four subscales on increase from adolescence to adulthood*

	Number of items	Rank order among 26 items		Mean of increases in per cent passing
Scale		M	Mdn.	
Vocabulary	8	8.1	7.3	43.7
Reasoning				
Abstract	6	9.9	11.8	42.2
Practical	7	17.4	18.0	25.1
Memory	5	21.0	22.0	18.7

of gain is not dependent upon level of initial mental age, on the extent of education, or on the level of ancestral intelligence (Bradway & Robinson, 1961), in contrast to mental growth in the earlier years where these factors are important (Bradway, 1945a). Our only positive finding in this area is the one pointed out earlier, which is that adolescent girls with high IQs can be expected to increase less in mental age than will girls who test lower, or than males who test at any level.

Prediction of Adult Intelligence

The next questions which arise are those of how early can adult intelligence be predicted, and what are the best measures for predicting it. Or, what are the origins of adult verbal and nonverbal abilities?

An analysis of the predictive value of Stanford-Binet preschool items to adult WAIS scores can help answer these questions. At the time of the 1941 study, the principal investigator devised four subscales from the preschool Form I, and Form M Stanford-Binets and computed four subscale quotients for each subject (Bradway, 1945b). These were labeled "verbal quotient," "nonverbal quotient," "memory quotient," and "number concept quotient." Because the Stanford-Binet at the adolescent and adult levels is an almost wholly verbal instrument, it was not possible in that earlier study to determine whether or not one maintains his relative superiority and inferiority in these categories over any length of time. The administration of the Wechsler Adult Intelligence Scale in the present study, however, allows us to make such "profile" comparisons. Corresponding subscale indices were derived from the WAIS by using Comprehension, Similarities, Information, and Vocabulary for comparison with the 1931 verbal quotient; the Performance scale for comparison with the nonverbal quotient; Digit Span with the memory quotient; and Arithmetic with the number concept quotient. Inasmuch as the WAIS results are in standard scores, all that was necessary to obtain indices for these four WAIS categories which were comparable with each other was to divide the verbal total by four and the performance total by five. The mean of these four indices was then obtained for each subject, and his score for each category was expressed as a deviation from his own mean. A similar method was used for the 1931 scores, except that each of the four subscale scores had to be converted into standard scores before the individual profiles of deviation scores could be figured.

The stability of pattern over a period of 25 years was tested by the correlation between the deviation scores calculated as each individual's deviation from his own mean for the 1931 subscales, and the deviation scores also calculated as each individual's deviation from his own mean for the 1956 WAIS. Three of these four correlations are significant in the positive direction. For the verbal component, the Pearsonian r is .236

TABLE 8: Correlation of predictive preschool items of forms L and M of the Stanford-Binet with WAIS verbal quotients

Location	Item	r_{bis}[b]	Groups by years of age[a]	Type[b]
M II ½ 6[c]	Obeying Simple Commands	.93***	2½	V
L III 2[c]	Picture Vocabulary	.77**	2½	V
L III 4[c]	Picture Memories	.85***	2½	M
M III 3	Objects by Use	.66*	2½	V
M III 6	Repeating Three Digits	.67*	2½	M
L III ½ 2	Picture Vocabulary	.84**	4	V
L III ½ 5	Objects by Use	.98***	2½	V
L III ½ 6[c]	Comprehension I	.86**	4	V
M III ½ 6	Comprehension I	.74**	2½	V
L IV 1[c]	Picture Vocabulary	.85***	4	V
L IV 2[c]	Objects from Memory	.79**	4	M
L IV 4[c]	Pictorial Identification	.80**	4	V
L IV A[c]	Memory for Sentences I	.80**	4	M
M IV 6	Memory for Sentences I	.70*	2½	M
L IV ½ 6	Opposite Analogies I	.73**	4	V
M IV ½ 1	Animal Pictures	.64*	4	NV
M IV ½ 5	Materials	.74**	4	V
L V 5	Memory for Sentences II	.64*	4	M
M V 2	Number Concept of Three	.74**	4	NC
M V 3[c]	Pictorial Similarities and Differences	.61*	5½	V
L VI 4	Number Concepts	.71**	5½	NC
L VI 5	Pictorial Likenesses and Differences	.72***	5½	V
M VI 2	Copying Bead Chain	.55*	5½	NV
M VI 3[c]	Differences	.60*	5½	V
M VII 4[c]	Three Digits Reversed	.62*	5½	M

[a] There were 17 subjects in the 2½-year-old group, 16 in the 4-year-old, 17 in the 4½-year-old, and 21 in the 5½-year-old. The other groups (2-year-olds, 3-year-olds, 3½-year-olds, and 5-year-olds) were not large enough for valid calculations.

[b] These refer to the Bradway subscales described previously (Bradway, 1945b).

[c] Indicates used in 1960 L-M Revision of the Stanford-Binet.

* Significant beyond .05 level.   ** Significant beyond .02 level.   *** Significant beyond .01 level.

TABLE 9: *Correlations of predictive preschool items of forms L and M of the Stanford-Binet with WAIS performance quotients*

Location	Item	r bis	Groups by years of age[a]	Type[b]
M III 2[c]	Picture Vocabulary	.09***	2½	V
L III ½ 6[c]	Comprehension	.75*	4	V
L IV 1[c]	Picture Vocabulary	.75*	4	V
L IV 2[c]	Objects from Memory	.71*	4	M
L IV 4[c]	Pictorial Identification	.87***	4	V
L IV 5[c]	Discrimination of Forms	.71*	4	NV
M IV 3[c]	Opposite Analogies I	.70*	4	V
M IV 4[c]	Pictorial Identification	.70*	2½	V
M IV 6	Memory for Sentences I	.75*	4	M
L IV ½ 4	Materials	.68*	4½	V
L IV ½ A	Pictorial Identification	.71*	4	V
M IV ½ 1	Animal Pictures	.63*	4	NV
M IV ½ 3	Repeating Four Digits	.70*	2½	M
M IV ½ 5[c]	Materials	.69*	4	V
L V 4[c]	Copying a Square	.74*	4	NV
L V 6	Counting Four Objects	.62*	4½	NC
M V 2	Number Concept of Three	.75**	4	NC
M V 5	Comprehension II	.78***	5½	V
L VI 1	Vocabulary	.86***	5½	V
L VI 2	Bead Chain from Memory	.68*	4½	M
		.58*	5½	
L VI 3[c]	Mutilated Pictures	.82**	4½	NV
		.77***	5½	
L VI 5	Pictorial Likenessess and Differences	.53*	5½	V
M VI 2	Copying Bead Chain	.94***	5½	NV

TABLE 9 *continued*

Location	Item	r_{bis}	Groups by years of age[a]	Type[b]
M VI 5	Counting 13 Pennies	.67**	5½	NC
M VI 6	Opposite Analogies I	.73**	5½	V
L VII 1[c]	Picture Absurdities I	.61*	5½	V
M VII 4	Three Digits Reversed	.60*	5½	M

[a] There were 17 subjects in the 2½-year-old group, 16 in the 4-year-old, 17 in the 4½-year-old, and 21 in the 5½-year-old. The other groups (2-year-olds, 3-year-olds, 3½-year-olds, and 5-year-olds) were not large enough for valid calcualtions.

[b] These refer to the Bradway subscales described previously (Bradway, 1945b).

[c] Indicates used in 1960 L-M Revision of the Stanford-Binet.

* Significant beyond .05 level.

** Significant beyond .02 level.

*** Significant beyond .01 level.

significant at the .02 level; for the nonverbal component, .191 significant at the .05 level; and for the memory component, .301 significant at the .01 level. For the number concept component, (figured on 79 subjects rather than 110 because for 31 subjects no such ratio could be computed at the preschool ages) the correlation was only .089, not significant, suggesting that relative strength or weakness in this ability is not stable over a 25-year period. Inasmuch, however, as one's score on this scale contributes to his deviation scores on the other three, further analysis is necessary before drawing such a conclusion.

To study the predictive value of preschool items in more detail, biserial correlations of each Stanford-Binet preschool item to adult WAIS verbal quotient and adult WAIS performance quotient were calculated. This analysis is summarized in Tables 8 and 9 in which are listed those items whose biserial r's were significant beyond the .05 level for the indicated age groups.

The figures in the column headed "Groups by years of age" indicate the age group for which the corresponding biserial r was figured. Since there was no way of combining the age groups, biserial r's were figured for each 1931 age group for which an item was pertinent, which was defined for purposes of this analysis as each age group in which the number of subjects was 15 or more and for which the per cent passing the item was between 25 and 75. The distribution by type of the total 79 items for which biserial r's at one or more age levels were computed were as follows: 37 verbal, 24 nonverbal, 12 memory, and 6 number concept. The type designation follows that previously described by Bradway (1945b). Comparison of the frequency of each type found to have significant predictive value at one or more age levels and the total number of such items studied shows the following: of 37 verbal items, 14 (38%) predicted WAIS verbal IQ and 14 (38%) predicted WAIS performance IQ; of the 24 nonverbal items, 2 (8%) predicted WAIS verbal IQ and 5 (21%) predicted WAIS performance IQ; of the 12 memory items, 7 (59%) predicted WAIS verbal IQ and 5 (41%) predicted WAIS performance IQ; of the 6 number concept items, 2 (33%) predicted WAIS verbal IQ and 3 (50%) predicted WAIS performance IQ. This kind of analysis is only suggestive because the number of items is small, but it supplements in more detail the findings for the subscales reported above. In summary: verbal items predict both verbal and performance adult ability better than do nonverbal items; each kind of memory item (memory for digits forward and reversed, for sentences, for objects, for pictures, and for bead chain) predicts both WAIS verbal and performance ability; number concept items are inconsistent in their predictive value—the only significant negative correlation obtained being for a number concept item.

When one compares these results with those for the subscale deviation scores reported above, similarities are found. Both analyses suggest the greater value of verbal and memory items over nonverbal items in predicting adult abilities, and the unreliability of number concept items at the preschool level as predictors of adult abilities.

Measurement of Intelligence

After reviewing these data we are in a better position to approach the problems of what index or indices to use in expressing adult intelligence and how best to predict it. If the 1937 Stanford-Binet is used to measure adult intelligence, a use for which it was not specifically designed, it is apparent that a correctional factor of some kind must be applied to IQs obtained according to the published instructions. Merrill kindly applied the deviation scores provided in the 1960 Revision (Terman & Merrill, 1960) to our data. The resulting intelligence quotients are 109.3 in 1931, 109.4 in 1941, and 119.4 in 1956. These findings of identity between preschool and adolescence and a 10 point rise to adulthood indicate that the correction inherent in the 1960 deviation scores does not solve the problem. For our research purposes we rejected the use of a multiplicative factor because this would have changed the standard deviations, and used instead a subtractive factor which, since the standard deviations were nearly identical, was sufficient to equate the adult set of scores with the two previous ones. This, although a satisfactory solution for research purposes, may not be the optimal solution from the point of view of the clinician. Perhaps the possibility of revised deviation tables, accounting for greater increase into adulthood than do those published with the 1960 Revision, should be explored.

This problem is not encountered in measuring adult intelligence with the WAIS which was specifically designed for the measurement of adult intelligence. Moreover, our data demonstrate that there are different kinds of ability which have a degree of constancy throughout life. The structure of the WAIS is a recognition of this.

When new tests are constructed, those for adults would do well to provide valid measurements of different kinds of abilities, because the practicing clinician needs such information to evaluate selective impairment of intellectual functioning and for vocational guidance and occupational placement. In contrast, a preschool test heavily weighted with verbal items should be a more valid predictor of adult abilities, both verbal and nonverbal, than one utilizing many performance-type items. Moreover, the former would be consistent with the usual purpose for which preschool tests are used in that the prediction of school performance puts a heavy demand on verbal abilities.

The present data demonstrate that the defining of adult intelligence is complex. It is not expressed by a single index in terms of abilities, in terms of one's place relative to others of the same age group, or of one's location on a scale of development and decline. As Cameron and Magaret (1951, p. 158) have said in alluding to the use of tests in defining behavior, "Performance on test items alone can no more define biosocial immaturity than can a refractive index define the complex process of seeing."

SUMMARY

A group of 111 subjects who had been tested with the Stanford-Binet (S-B) at the preschool and adolescent levels were administered the S-B and WAIS at adulthood (25 years after initial testing). Correlations of preschool IQs with adult S-B and full WAIS IQs are .59 and .64. Correlations of adolescent IQs with adult S-B and full WAIS IQs are .85 and .80. The S-B IQ shows a mean increase of 11 points from adolescence to adulthood, which corresponds to a mental age gain of 20 months beyond what would be expected if mental growth ceases at 16 years. The data were analyzed in an attempt to determine the point at which mental growth, as measured by these tests, ceases, but it could not be determined.

The males show significantly more IQ gain from adolescence to adulthood than do the females ($p < .01$). Factors associated with amount of gain were not isolated except that girls with high IQs at adolescence increase less than do girls who initially test lower or than males who test at any level. There is no evidence that educational attainment is related to amount of gain.

Analysis of increases in per cent passing S-B items from adolescence to adulthood indicates that intellectual growth after adolescence is greater in abstract reasoning and vocabulary than in rote memory and practical reasoning.

Analysis of the value of S-B preschool items in predicting adult WAIS scores shows some stability of pattern of individual differences in verbal versus nonverbal versus memory superiority over the 25 years. It also shows the greater value of verbal and memory items over nonverbal items in predicting both verbal and performance adult IQs, and the unreliability of number concept items as predictors of adult abilities.

The data are interpreted as demonstrating that adult intelligence is complex and cannot be meaningfully expressed by a single index.

REFERENCES:

BAYLEY, NANCY. On the growth of intelligence. *Amer. Psychologist,* 1955, *10,* 805–818.

BAYLEY, NANCY, and ODEN, MELITA H. The maintenance of intellectual ability in gifted adults. *J. Gerontol.,* 1955, *10,* 91–107.

BRADWAY, KATHERINE P. An experimental study of factors associated with Stanford-Binet IQ changes from the preschool to the junior high school. *J. genet. Psychol.,* 1945, *66,* 107–128. (a)

BRADWAY, KATHERINE P. Predictive value of Stanford-Binet preschool items. *J. Educ. Psychol.*, 1945, 36, 1–16. (b)

BRADWAY, KATHERINE P., and ROBINSON, NANCY M. Significant IQ changes in twenty-five years: A follow-up. *J. Educ. Psychol.*, 1961, 52, 74–79. Mifflin, 1951).

CAMERON, N., and MAGARET, ANN. *Behavior Pathology.* (Boston: Houghton Mifflin, 1951).

DAVIS, F. B. The derivation of three subscores from the 1937 Revision of the Stanford-Binet Scales. *J. Consult. Psychol.*, 1941, 5, 287–291.

INHELDER, B., and PIAGET, J. *The Growth of Logical Thinking from Childhood to Adolescence* (New York: Basic Books, 1958).

TERMAN, L. M., and MERRILL, MAUD A. *Stanford-Binet Intelligence Scale* (Boston: Houghton Mifflin, 1960).

11 Factors that Aid and Hinder Creativity*

BY J. P. GUILFORD

EDITOR'S NOTE: It is one thing to be an "intelligent" person, but what do we mean when we say that one is "creative"? How about yourself, for example? From your point of view would you say that you're a creative person? Why? Or, for that matter, why not? What is the evidence for your conclusion? What hunches do you have regarding the relationship between creativity and IQ? Does having a high IQ mean having high creativity? Dr. Guilford discusses what he considers to be five major intellectual factors which influence the production of creative thinking. He also discusses some of the dominant psychological characteristics associated with creative people. Is it possible to help students be more creative, more divergent than convergent in their thinking? How? What can teachers do? What can you do?

In the part of our current *Zeitgeist* pertaining to psychology and education, no word has had a more dramatic rise in popularity than "creativity." After generally ignoring the subject, psychologists have come to realize their backwardness in knowledge of this subject. Employers have been asking for more inventive scientists, engineers, and managers. Special courses on how to think creatively have been springing up by the score. Special institutes are being held on the subject. Teachers and educators are asking how they can make courses more stimulating and how they can arouse more productive thinking on the part of students.

The interest is international, as well it might be. The whole world

*Reprinted from *Teachers College Record*, 1962, Vol. 63, 380–392, by permission of the author and the publisher.

faces two very critical problems—how to feed its exploding population and how to keep the peace. It has been estimated that in the next 20 years we shall need three times the number of scientists and engineers we now have, and they shall have to exercise all the ingenuity of which they are capable. We are reminded by the scriptures, however, that man does not live by bread alone. There is, I think, a very noticeable surgence of interest in the arts in all their forms. We wish to walk in beauty as well as in peace, freedom, and dignity. There is also good reason to desire increased creativity to achieve aesthetic goals,

Investigation of Creativity

My topic suggests that I give most consideration to the abilities and other traits of individuals that make some of them creative and some not. Knowing these traits should help us to recognize which persons are likely to have the potentialities of becoming creatively productive. The same knowledge should help us in taking steps that should increase creative output in ourselves and in others, and other steps that may remove obstacles in the way of creative productivity. Our primary concern, then, will be the basic facts concerning the nature of creative thinking and of the more creative persons, with reference to the application of this information.

Serious investigation of creativity by psychologists began only in recent years. For centuries the common idea had been that only the exceedingly rare person is genuinely creative and that creativity is a divine gift. As such, it was not to be investigated, or at best, there was little hope of understanding it. Even after Darwin came upon the scene, when creativity came to be regarded as some kind of rare, hereditary blessing, there was still little incentive to attempt to understand it because there was thought to be little that one could do about it. In addition to being very rare, the highly creative person's behavior is sometimes eccentric. This has sometimes branded him as being abnormal and even pathological. Mental pathology was similarly avoided as a subject of study by scientific investigators for a long time.

Creativity became an object of scientific study primarily because of the general interest in individual differences. This approach recognizes that individuals differ psychologically in traits or attributes that can be conceived as continua or dimensions—that there can be varying degrees of a quality possessed by different individuals. This concept was eventually applied to creativity, but in serious ways only about a dozen years ago. This new way of looking at the matter permitted us to think that not only a few peculiarly gifted persons but individuals in general possess some degree of the same creative trait or traits.

This conception has opened the door to many kinds of research. We need no longer study creativity by catching the rare persons who are recognized as having creativity to high degree; a multitude of subjects is now available to investigators. We can discover the various aspects of the phenomenon called "creativity." We can find out the conditions under which creative performance occurs or does not occur.

As in the case of all psychological characteristics that make up personality, we may be forced to recognize that heredity establishes limits of development for an individual. But there is considerable faith among educators that rarely does an individual realize full development in any respect and that there is generally considerable room for improvement. This faith should also be applied to the creative aspects of personality.

Basic Traits and Creativity

There are a number of approaches to the investigation of the traits or characteristics in which creative individuals are most likely to excel. Some investigators appear to regard the phenomenon of creativity as a single dimension of personality. It is my view that the creative disposition is made up of many components and that its composition depends upon where you fine it. Practically all investigators recognize that there are many potentially contributing conditions.

When the problem is approached from the standpoint of individual differences, the most natural scientific technique to apply is that of factor analysis. This is the approach that my associates and I have taken almost exclusively in the Aptitudes Project at the University of Southern California.

According to our original hypotheses (Guilford, 1950), we expected to find the more creative individuals to think with greater fluency, with more flexibility, and with greater originality. The tests designed to measure fluency present very simple tasks, and the quantity of output determines the scores. When told to produce a list of items of information of a certain kind, how many responses can the examinee give in a limited time? Quality does not count, but, of course, the responses must be appropriate.

Flexibility in thinking means a *change* of some kind—a change in the meaning, interpretation, or use of something, a change in understanding of the task, a change of strategy in doing the task, or a change in direction of thinking, which may mean a new interpretation of the goal.

There has been some debate concerning the meaning of "originality." In our research and in that of others, originality means the production of unusual, far-fetched, remote, or clever responses. But there are some who say that an idea is not original or novel unless no human being has ever thought of it earlier. This conception is worthless to the scientist because there is no way of knowing that an idea has never existed before. It is somewhat better to say that a novel idea is a new one so far as the particular individual who has it is concerned. But unless we know the individual's past history of thinking, we cannot be sure of meeting this criterion either.

Fortunately, we can resort to empirical signs of novelty in terms of the statistical infrequency of a response among members of a certain population that is culturally relatively homogeneous. This gives us some workable operations for applying the criterion of unusualness. The index of unusualness can therefore be purely objective. As for the far-fetched or remote associations and the clever responses, we have as yet no way to avoid some degree of subjectivity of judgment in assessing test performance to obtain an index of originality.

Another somewhat popular criterion of an original idea is that it is socially useful. Those who deal with practical affairs may be appropriately concerned about this aspect of produced ideas. But such a criterion involves us in values in a way that science cannot deal with directly; hence, the criterion of social usefulness can be quickly dismissed by the psychologist. This does not mean that as a person he is unconcerned about social usefulness. It does mean that as a scientist he cannot afford to be so concerned and so restricted.

Fluency Factors

We shall now give closer attention to the various factors of fluency, flexibility, and originality. It turns out that in verbal tests alone there are three differentiated fluency factors (Guilford and Christensen, 1957). Ideational fluency has to do with the rate of generation of a quantity of ideas. The idea produced may be as simple as a single word, as complex as the title for a picture or a story, or as phrases and short sentences that convey unitary thoughts. In a test, we may ask the examinee to list all the things he can think of that are solid, flexible, and colored. He may respond with *cloth, leaf, rose petal, hair, skin, leather,* and so on. Any response that fulfills the specifications accepted and counts toward the total score. In other tests, we may ask the examinee to list the consequences of a certain action or event, the various uses of an object, or some appropriate titles for a given story. In all such tests, there are strict time limits.

It is easy to see where an operation such as that in tests of ideational fluency fit into problem solving of many kinds. Perhaps a problem situation, when interpreted in a certain way, calls for an object with a certain set of specifications in order to solve it. Once these specifications are realized, the person who can list pertinent possibilities most rapidly could, other things being equal, solve the problem most quickly.

Many a problem calls for a running through of the likely possibilities during the earlier stage of interpreting or structuring it as well as during the stage of finding solutions. This process also probably depends in some degree upon ideational fluency. Of course it is not necessary to run through *all* the logical possibilities in solving a problem. One can ignore the less promising ones. This point will be touched upon later.

Another kind of fluency is called "associational fluency." It pertains to the completion of relationships, is distinction from the factor of ideational fluency, which involves giving ideas that fit a class. As a test of associational fluency, we may ask the examinee to list all the words he can think of that mean the opposite, or nearly the opposite, of the word "good." He may respond with *bad, poor, sinful, defective, awful, terrible,* and so on. This ability is most obviously of use to the creative writer, who wants to find quickly a variety of verbal expressions without having to resort to a thesaurus.

The factor of associational fluency may have more general utility—for example, whenever we apply thinking by analogy as our strategy in solving problems. Thinking of a correlate is the completion of an analogy. Many solutions to new problems are achieved by the practice of thinking by analogy. The success of certain kinds of engineers in their work has been predicted to a small extent by means of a test of associational fluency as found by Saunders (Taylor, 1956).

A third kind of fluency is called "expressional fluency." It has to do with the facile construction of sentences. We ask the examinee to write as many four-word sentences as he can, all different, with no word used more than once. We may give the initial letters of the four words, the same four being specified for each sentence—for example, "W—— c—— e—— n——." To this task, he may reply, "We can eat nuts." "Willie comes every night," "Wholesome carrots elevate nations," "Weary cats evade nothing," and so on. You will probably not be surprised when I tell you that in a ninth-grade sample, the girls obtained a higher mean score than the boys.

We do not know yet how much generality to attach to this factor, whether it is limited to tasks such as the writing of sentences or whether it is so broad as to pertain to organizing ideas into systems. If it is as broad as the latter suggestion, it should be of considerable consequence, perhaps in something as important as the trial-and-error development of a scientific theory. The factor has been found significantly related to ratings by psychologists of the creative performances of military officers.[1]

Flexibility Factors

One type of flexibility we first recognized as "spontaneous flexibility" because the tests that measure it do not even suggest that the examinee be flexible (Frick, *et al.,* 1959). Without his knowing it, he can make a good score if he varies his *kinds* of responses. If we tell the examinee to list all the uses he can think of for a common brick, the total number of uses listed is a good score for his status on the factor of ideational fluency. But we also score his performance in terms of the number of times he changes *category* of uses. For example, the person who responds with *build a house, build a school, build a factory,* etc., does not change his class of uses. Another person who responds with *make a paper weight, drive a nail, make baseball bases, throw at a cat, grind up for red powder, make a tombstone for a bird,* etc., changes class with each new response. He shows much more flexibility.

The person who makes a low spontaneous-flexibility score is rigid in the sense that he perseverates within one or a very few classes. As there are several kinds of flexibility in thinking, so there are several kinds of rigidity. When someone tells you that a certain person is rigid, beware of over-generalization of the term. We do not find in normal (nonpathological) people a very general trait of rigidity vs. flexibility. We find several. This does not say that there are no individuals who are rigid in just about every respect, but the general rule is that they may be rigid in some respects and not in others, at least so far as thinking is concerned.

A new hypothesis may be considered in connection with the factor of spontaneous flexibility. Some advisers on how to think creatively suggest that in starting to solve a new problem, we keep our thinking at a rather high level of abstraction. We think of it first in very general terms. Thus, the person who goes from class to class in the Brick Uses test is operating within the frame of reference of a much broader class within which there are subclasses. A higher level of abstraction may mean thinking in terms of broader classes. This has the effect of broadening the scope of the scanning process in searching for information. Going from one class to another in the Brick Uses test also means considering all the properties of a brick—its weight, its color, its texture, and so on. These are abstractions all lying within the class of the total nature of a brick. This is reminiscent of a stock method of practicing creative thinking, a method known as "attribute listing" and advocated by Crawford (1952).

A second kind of flexibility has been called *"adaptive* flexibility" for the reason that in tests in which it was first found, the examinee, to succeed, must make changes of some kind—changes in interpretation of the task, in approach or strategy, or in possible solutions. Our current interpretation of the factor of originality is that it is adaptive flexibility in dealing with verbal information.

We have a kind of test, called Plot Titles, in which the examinee is told a very short story and that he is to suggest as many appropriate titles for the story as he can. One of the stories is about a wife who is unable to speak until a specialist performs the appropriate surgery. Then her husband is driven to distraction by her incessant talking until another surgeon eliminates his hearing, when peace is restored in the family.

The number of commonplace titles given to the story may be used as a score for ideational fluency. Such titles include,

A man and his wife
Never satisfied
Medicine triumphs
A man's decisions
Talking and hearing

The number of responses rated as "clever" serves as a score for originality. Such titles are exemplified by

> The deaf man and the dumb woman
> Happiness through deafness
> Operation—peace of mind
> Yack, yack, hack

Several other types of tests serve to indicate individual differences in the factor of originality.

Elaboration

In the course of our investigations of abilities involved in planning (Berger, Guilford, and Christensen, 1957), we found another kind of ability we have called "elaboration." In one test, given the bare outlines of a plan, the examinee is asked to produce the detailed steps needed to make the plan work. The more details he adds, the better is his score. We believe that the unique feature of this ability is that in tests for it, one item of information leads to another as a kind of extension or completion. In more technical language, we say that the examinee is producing a *variety of implications*.

It was eventually recognized that the abilities of fluency, flexibility (including originality), and elaboration are similar in that the tests of them call for a variety of answers. There is no right or fully determined answer in connection with the information given in the item. There are now parallel tests in which each item *does* have one right answer because it is fully determined by the information given or because there is one conventionally accepted answer. A distinction has therefore been made between *divergent* thinking and *convergent* thinking to represent the two classes of abilities. The abilities of which I have been speaking thus far belong in the divergent-thinking category. Because the individual has to generate his answer or answers, starting from given information, in both categories of abilities, we speak of divergent-*production* factors vs. convergent-*production* factors, respectively.

Quantity vs. Quality

Several questions arise concerning the relationship of quantity and quality of production. One debated and investigated hypothesis is that "quantity breeds quality." This hypothesis holds that if a person produces a greater total number of ideas, he also produces a greater number of high-quality ideas in a limited time. Another view is that a mental set for quantity is inefficient because if a person spends his time producing a lot of low-quality responses, he cannot produce so many good ones.

There is another aspect of this controversy. When a person is set to give "good" answers, he is applying judgment or evaluation as he goes along. On the one hand, it is believed that an evaluative or critical attitude is generally inhibiting to the flow of ideas, good and poor alike. On the other hand, it is believed that the application of evaluation as one proceeds has a selective effect, holding back the low-quality responses and letting the high-quality responses come through.

The well-known brainstorming technique, attributed to Alex Osborn (1957) and employed by many others, conforms to the first of these two schools of thought. One of its chief claimed virtues is that the separation of production and evaluation—in other words, suspended judgment—is better procedure. As originally applied, of course, brainstorming has other features, which include thinking in small groups rather than thinking by individuals in seclusion.

The experimental results bearing upon the issue of suspended judgment are somewhat mixed. Meadow, Parnes, and Reese (1959) report that with suspended judgment, the production of "good" answers was a little more than doubled. The problems were to suggest unusual uses for a wire coat hanger and for a broom. The criteria for "good" responses were "unique" and "useful."

In our Aptitudes Project (Christensen, Guilford, and Wilson, 1957), we gave the Plot Titles test with and without the specific instruction to give clever titles. It was expected that the instruction for clever titles would entail more evaluation. The effects of this instruction were shown by a reduction in the number of low-quality responses, an increase in the number of high-quality responses, and a higher average rating of degree of cleverness.

Hyman (1960) found that his subjects generated 68% more responses under quantity instructions, but that this increase in "good" responses, where "good" meant uncommon and of "high quality," failed to keep pace with the total output. Hyman is probably right when he concludes that quantity may breed quality for some types of problems but not for others. It is also probably true that the *kind* of evaluative attitude applied by the thinker has much to do with the quantity and quality of responses he produces.

Divergent thinking is a matter of scanning one's stored information to find answers to satisfy a special search model. Evaluation comes into the picture in determining whether or not the produced information fits the search model. Relaxed evaluation would permit a broadening of the base of the search, whereas an evaluative attitude with some degree of strictness should narrow the search. In doing so, however, it may lead more efficiently to good answers. This should depend upon the clarity and accuracy of the search model. If the thinker has a good search model, the application of evaluation while he thinks should be helpful.

But if evaluation is of a more vague kind, such as that involving a fear of being unconventional, a fear of thinking socially unacceptable thoughts, or a fear of being wrong, it should be definitely better to suspend judgments based on such criteria. Evaluation incident to an overly strong desire for a quick solution would also be handicapping. But evaluation for the sake of efficient scanning, where there is good strategy in the scanning process, should be beneficial.

Hyman (1960) has found that a general critical attitude can have rather broad transfer effects in solving problems. A group of engineers, in Hyman's experiment, read some previously given solutions to a certain practical problem under the instruction to list all the good points that they could see in those solutions. A second group was instructed to list all the faults they could see in the same solutions. Later, in solving the same problem and in solving a new one, the uncritical readers suggested solutions of their own that were rated higher on the average than those of the critical group. Thus, very general critical attitudes must be taken into account.

Group vs. Individual Thinking

The question of group thinking vs. individual thinking has received a great deal of attention. The virtue claimed for group thinking in brainstorming is that one person stimulates another. In support of this hypothesis, Osborn (1961) reports that about a third of the ideas produced in group brainstorming are of the "hitchhiking" type. In such a case, one person's idea is based upon another person's idea.

There are results which do not support his hypothesis, however. Taylor, Berry, and Block (1958) found a larger number of unrepeated ideas produced by individuals working alone than by those working in groups, where both kinds of thinkers were working under the condition of suspended judgment. Taylor points out that the group condition may have the effect of channeling thinking in similar directions, reducing the variety and therefore the quantity of unrepeated ideas.

Perhaps neither the group nor the isolation condition is best under all circumstances or for all individuals. It is quite possible that both can be applied to advantage. The preference of the thinker should have something to do with the choice of condition. A great deal is made of the point that the highly creative person is an independent thinker and that his creation may be a highly personal thing. Torrance (Taylor, 1959) found that the more highly creative child (as indicated by his test scores) in a small group often works by himself or is somehow induced by the others to do so.

Whatever the outcome of brainstorming sessions in particular instances, experiments show that courses on creative thinking that are heavily weighted with brainstorming exercises seem to leave the students with beneficial results, and these results have some degree of permanence (Meadow and Parnes, 1959; Parnes and Meadow, 1960). How much of the improvement to attribute to the brainstorming technique and to which aspects of it the improvement should be attributed are open questions.

Context of Creation

From the discussion thus far, one may conclude that creative performances are to be identified psychologically as a small number of divergent-production operations. Two different qualifications must be introduced. One exception is that two of the factors that we in the Aptitudes Project regarded from the first as being pertinent to creative thinking fall outside the divergent-production group. The other exception is that I have not yet told the whole story regarding the divergent-production factors. I shall make good on the latter omission first.

I have repeatedly stated that the tests on the factors thus far described are *verbal* tests. They pertain to verbally stated information. There are other kinds of information, and the question comes up whether the same person is usually equally creative in handling different kinds of information, material, or content. From our analytical results, we can say that it can happen, but we should rarely expect the same person to be equally capable of creativity in science, in the arts, mathematics, administration, and musical composition. Highly creative individuals in many of these different areas may have outstanding qualities in common, but psychological study indicates that they also have some marked differences.

In the area of divergent-production abilities lone, we find that individuals may be uneven in handling verbal vs. concrete vs. symbolic material. Symbolic material is the kind with which the mathematician deals— numbers and letters. Fluency, flexibility, and elaboration in dealing with concrete (perceived) material are probably of greater importance to the inventor of gadgets, the painter, and the composer, whereas the same kinds of abilities for dealing with verbal material or content are more important for the creative writer and the scientist. In other words, there are parallel abilities for dealing with concrete (or figural) material, symbolic material, and verbally meaningful (or semantic) material.

One of our earlier hypotheses (Guilford, 1950) was that the unusually creative person has a high degree of sensitivity to problems. One person notices something wrong or in need of improvement, whereas another fails to observe defects, deficiencies, or errors. The observation of imperfections starts the creative person on his way to creative production. The observation of inadequacy of solutions also keeps the creative thinker at work on his problem (Merrifield, *et al.*, 1960).

Factor analysis has consistently upheld this hypothesis by finding an ability common to a variety of tests calling for the noticing of defects and deficiencies in such things as common household appliances, social customs, or in solutions to problems. Such an ability, however, seems to fit better in the general category of evaluative factors than it does in that of divergent production.

Not being satisfied with things as they are is a matter of evaluation. We hear a great deal about the "divine discontent" of the creative person.

It is said that Thomas A. Edison frequently admonished his workers with the comment, "There must be a better way. Go and find it." The uncreative, in contrast, are often willing to settle for half-way measures and tolerably successful solutions to problems.

Another of our initial hypotheses was that many an invention or new idea is the revision of something that is already known. But the revision is not an obvious one. It takes quite a change in the meaning, interpretation, or use of an object to achieve such an innovation. One of our tests, designed for such an ability, asks which of five objects or their parts could be most reasonably adapted to be used to start a fire when there are available the following items: a fountain pen, an onion, a pocket watch, a light bulb, and a bowling ball. The accepted answer is "pocket watch," since the cover of the watch face could be used as a condensing lens. Since this and other such tests call for one best answer, this factor falls logically in the convergent-production category. The feature that makes a contribution to creativity is that a *transformation* must occur; objects must be redefined. Individuals who are clever at improvising seem to show this kind of ability.

There are other abilities outside the divergent-production category that make some contribution to creative performances in their own ways. We have seen that one of the evaluative abilities—sensitivity to problems—has a function in getting the creative thinker started. Other evaluative abilities should have their uses, whether judgment is suspended or not, in determining whether the products of thinking are good, useful, suitable, adequate, or desirable. If the creator is to finish his job, he will eventually appraise his product, and he will revise it if he feels that revision is called for.

Cognition and Memory

Thus far I have spoken of three major categories of intellectual factors—abilities of divergent production, convergent production, and evaluation. There are two other major categories—cognitive abilities and memory abilities—all distinguished from those in the first-mentioned categories and from each other. Cognitive abilities have to do with discovery, recognition, or comprehension of information in various forms. Memory abilities have to do with storage or retention of information.

Many people, including some teachers, have for some reason disparaged memory and memory abilities. Some of them, who emphasize the importance of thinking, seem wrongly to believe that good thinking and good memory are incompatible qualities, perhaps even negatively correlated. Actually, good memory contributes to good thinking.

It is not a good, well-stocked memory, as such, that is bad, for even the most creative people have given due credit to stored information. It is the way in which storage is achieved and organized that makes the difference between the graduate who is sometimes described as "merely a walking encyclopedia" and the graduate who has a usable and fruitful fund of information. Memory abilities thus make their indirect but important contribution to creative performance.

The question often arises concerning the relation of creativity to intelligence. In connection with this question, the usual conception of "intelligence" is that which is measured by such tests as the Stanford-Binet, the Wechsler scales, or the California Test of Mental Maturity.

In discussing abilities related to creativity, I have referred to them as intellectual factors. It is very doubtful whether these abilities, particularly those in the divergent-production category, are represented to any appreciable degree in standard IQ tests. IQ tests were designed to predict success in school learning, particularly in reading, arithmetic, and the subject-matter or informational courses. But we now know that there are many other kinds of intellectual abilities.

Studies of groups of research scientists and engineers (Taylor, 1960) show that such groups have high average scores on IQ tests. They would need to have higher-than-average IQs to have passed all their academic hurdles, most of them including the PhD. But only a fraction of these are outstanding for creative performance. But within groups of scientists and engineers, the correlation found between IQ-test scores and creative performance is usually rather low. This is due in part to the restriction of range of IQ within such groups. The evidence seems to indicate that although the qualities in traditional IQ intelligence may be of some help to the creative scientist or engineer, they are by no means sufficient.

The low correlation between creativity and IQ is also found at younger age groups. In high school students, Getzels and Jackson (Taylor, 1959) found that if the highest 20% of the subjects on IQ were selected as "gifted," 70% of those who stood in the highest 20% in terms of divergent-thinking tests would have been missed. Torrance (Taylor, 1959) has reported a similar finding in the elementary grades. In both instances, it was reported that the teachers knew their high-IQ students better and liked them better. The high-creative without high IQs were often regarded as nuisances, and they were somewhat estranged from other students. Those with both high IQ *and* high creativity were recognized as having unusual but sound ideas, to be good in planning and improvising, and effective in getting attention.[2]

Non-aptitude Traits

The assessment of traits of temperament, interest, and attitude in connection with creativity has been approached in various ways. One approach has been to find the most outstandingly creative individuals in different professional groups, such as architects, writers, and scientists, and to assess them quite thoroughly by methods that are available. If a creative group differs systematically from the general population or, better, some group outside the profession but matched with it for age, sex, and educational level, it is concluded that this creative group stands apart or is distinguished by the personality trait or traits in question.

There are obvious dangers in drawing conclusions from studies of this kind, unless an appropriate control group has been used. When it is found that creative architects, scientists, mathematicians, and writers alike tend to score highest on theoretical and esthetic interest on the Allport-Vernon-Lindzey *Study of Values*, this may occur just because any high-IQ group would do the same (MacKinnon, 1960). When it is found that the creative males tend to score relatively in the direction of femininity on the masculinity-femininity scale of the *Minnesota Multiphasic Personality Inventory* scale, we remember that Terman and Miles (1936) found that as members of the two sexes are more intelligent and better educated, they respond more alike to test items on masculinity vs. femininity. Nor should it be surprising that the creative groups just mentioned should tend to score high on the Strong *Vocational Interest Blank* scales for architect, psychologist, and author-journalist.

A somewhat better approach is to obtain two samples from the same profession, composed of highly creative and less creative individuals, respectively. The groups can then be compared with respect to various assessed qualities. Sometimes the groups are distinguished on the basis of judgments by their teachers (Drevdahl, 1956; Hammer, 1961). In still other studies, subjects of mixed occupations but similar in IQ and educational level have been tested with measures of creative aptitude and of non-aptitude traits (Guilford, et al., 1957).

Non-aptitude Differences

We have had to recognize that creative occupational groups share parallel but different exceptional abilities. We should expect the various groups to show some non-aptitude qualities in common and also to show some differences. One difference, for example, has been noted between creative students of art and of science. The more creative art student has been reported to be more of an observer than a participant in what is going on (Hammer, 1961). The more creative science student is reported to be more of a participant than the less creative student (Garwood, 1961). Such observations should prevent our generalizing conclusions obtained from one creative group to all other creative groups.

There are many ways in which creative people of many groups are alike, however. There is general agreement that the highly creative person, particularly the original person, is self-confident. Which comes first, originality or self-confidence? It is a little like the old hen-and-the-egg problem. Probably, it works both ways: Originality yields success and hence self-confidence, and self-confidence leads the individual to attempt to solve problems where others would give up. In some instances, self-confidence goes over into conceit, as we have all been aware. Sometimes this is fed by the adulations of admirers. Sometimes it may suggest an underlying hypersensitivity to criticism.

Along with self-confidence, there is usually self-assurance or social boldness. The creative person is especially confident about his own judgment and his own evaluations of his work. He is often described as an independent thinker, which includes having an independent set of values. If he thinks his product is good, he discounts the criticisms of others and may disparage their judgments.

Not only is he more or less independent of other people's judgments, he may be self-sufficient in that he can take people or he can let them alone. He is likely to find ideas more important than people, though he is not necessarily a social recluse. These qualities do not add to his popularity with others, so he is in danger of becoming estranged from his parents, his teachers, and his peers. Contributing to this state of affairs also is a lack of mutual understanding. The creative child and his associates may need special counseling to help smooth over some roughness in interpersonal relationships. This can be done without curbing development along creative lines.

We have found that young men who stand high in one or more kinds of fluency are likely to be somewhat impulsive, cheerful, and relaxed. Those who score high in tests of originality tend to have strong esthetic interests, and they like to indulge in divergent thinking. They do not feel much need for meticulousness or for discipline. Somewhat surprisingly, they show no particular dislike for conventional or socially approved behavior, nor do they show signs of neuroticism.

One of the striking traits found by Getzels and Jackson (Taylor, 1959) among high school students who stand high in divergent-thinking tests is a strong sense of humor. This is shown particularly in the kinds of stories they tell in response to pictures. For example, one picture showed a young man working at his desk at six-thirty in the morning. A bright but less creative student wrote the following kind of story: "This young man is very ambitious to get ahead. He comes early every morning to impress his boss so he will be promoted." A more creative student told the following kind of story: "This picture is the office of a firm that manufactures breakfast cereals. It has just found a formula to produce a new kind of cereal that will bend, sag, and sway. The man is a private eye employed by a rival firm to obtain the formula. He thinks he has found it and copies it. It turns out to be the wrong formula, and the competitor's factory blows up."

Such stories usually involve some novel twist or transformation, such as the expression regarding the cereal that will "bend, sag, and sway." Many stories derive their humor from such a source. The person who makes up such stories is exhibiting verbal or semantic transformations, which is a sign that he has a fair degree of the factor of originality. Since this is a semantic ability, and since Getzels and Jackson's tests were verbal, we may well question whether the affiliation of humor and the ability to produce transformations extends to other kinds of content, figural or symbolic. It is probably true, however, that creative painters, composers, and mathematicians also experience a certain amount of enjoyment, if not amusement, in playfulness with their own kinds of materials.

Final Suggestions

Although the temperament and motivational qualities can help us somewhat in identifying potentially creative people, no one of them is a dependable sign, nor would all of them collectively be sufficient. Neither do these qualities help us very much in understanding the nature of the creative processes. On the whole, we have less chance of changing individuals with respect to these qualities in order to increase their creativity, except for changing certain attitudes.

Our chief hope, then, of either identifying the more creative persons or enhancing their creative performances lies with the aptitude factors. If we regard the intellectual factors as distinct but somewhat generalized thinking skills, this statement seems more reasonable. We develop skills by practicing them. The question, then, is one of what kinds of practice can best be applied and under what conditions.

An understanding of the nature of the skills is one of the most important steps either for the teacher or the student. When we know what kind of skill is to be developed, we have a more clearly defined goal toward which to work. Torrance (Taylor, 1959) reports that even after 20 minutes of instruction on the nature of divergent-thinking processes, gradeschool children showed a clearly observable improvement in performing tasks of this type.

Although special courses on creative thinking have proved beneficial, our whole educational system can be of greater help by giving more attention to this subject. There is abundant opportunity to teach almost any subject in ways that call for productive thinking rather than rote memory. Even the multiplication tables can be taught in ways that give the pupil insight into properties of the number system.

In some experimental courses at the University of Illinois in which mathematics is taught from the lower grades on by what is called a "discovery" method, instead of telling the child the axioms and other principles of mathematics, the teacher lets him discover tham for himself by exposing him to appropriate examples. Also at the University of Illinois, science is being taught to children by a discovery method. Some natural phenomenon is demonstrated without explanations to the class, perhaps in motion-picture form. From then on, it is a matter of the students' asking questions, with minimum information being given by the teacher, until the student develops his own satisfactory hypothesis.

Education in this country has unfortunately been too much dominated by the learning theory based upon the stimulus-response model of Thorndike, Hull, and Skinner. People, after all, are not rats (with a few exceptions), and they are not pigeons (with similar exceptions). Let us make full use of the human brains that have been granted to us. Let us apply a psychology that recognizes the full range of human intellectual qualities. We must make more complete use of our most precious national resource— the intellectual abilities of our people, including their creative potentialities.

REFERENCES:

BERGER, R. M., GUILFORD, J. P., and CHRISTENSEN, P. R. A factor-analytic study of planning abilities, Psychological Monographs, 1957, 71, Whole No. 435.

CHRISTENSEN, P. R., GUILFORD, J. P., and WILSON, R. C. Relations of creative responses to working time and instructions, Journal of Experimental Psychology, 1957, 53, 82–88.

CRAWFORD, R. P. Techniques of Creative Thinking (New York: Hawthorn Books, 1952).

DREVDAHL, J. E. Factors of importance for creativity, Journal of Clinical Psychology, 1956, 12, 21–26.

FRICK, J. W., et al. A factor-analysis study of flexibility in thinking, Educational and Psychological Measurement, 1959, 19, 469–496.

GARWOOD, D. S. Some Personality Factors Related to Creativity in Young Scientists, Unpublished doctoral dissertation, Claremont (California) Graduate School, 1961.

GUILFORD, J. P. Creativity, American Psychologist, 1950, 5, 444–454.

GUILFORD, J. P., et al. The Relations of Creative-Thinking Aptitudes to Non-aptitude Personality Traits, Report of University of Southern California Psychological Laboratory, No. 20, 1957.

GUILFORD, J. P. Three faces of intellect, American Psychologist, 1959, 14, 469–479.

GUILFORD, J. P., and CHRISTENSEN, P. R. A Factor-Analytic Study of Verbal Fluency, Report of University of Southern California Psychological Laboratory, No. 17, 1957.

GUILFORD, J. P., and MERRIFIELD, P. R. The Structure of Intellect Model: Its Uses and Implications, Report of University of Southern California Psychological Laboratory, No. 24, 1960.

HAMMER, E. F. Creativity (New York: Random House, 1961).

HYMAN, H. H. Some Experiments in Creativity (Schenectady: General Electric Company, 1960).

MACKINNON, D. What do we mean by talent, and how do we use it?, In The Search for Talent, College Entrance Examination Board, 1960.

MEADOW, A., PARNES, S. J., and REESE, H. Influence of brainstorming instructions and problem sequence on a creative problem solving test, *Journal of Applied Psychology*, 1959, 43, 413–416.

MEADOW, A., and PARNES, S. J. Evaluation of training in creative problem solving, *Journal of Applied Psychology*, 1959, 43, 189–194.

MERRIFIELD, P. R., *et al*. A factor-analytical of problem-solving abilities, Report of University of Southern California Psychological Laboratory, No. 22, 1960.

OSBORN, A. F. *Applied Imagination* (New York: Charles Scribner's Sons, 1957).

OSBORN, A. F. *Development of Creative Education* (Buffalo: Creative Education Foundation, 1961).

PARNES, S. J., and MEADOW, A. Evaluation of persistence of effects produced by a creative problem solving course, *Psychological Reports*, 1960, 7, 357–361.

TAYLOR, C. W. (Ed.) *Research Conference on the Identification of Creative Scientific Talent* (Salt Lake City: University of Utah Press, 1956, 1958, 1959).

TAYLOR, D. W., BERRY, P. C., and BLOCK, C. H. Does group participation when using brainstorming facilitate or inhibit creative thinking?, *Administrative Science Quarterly*, 1958, 3, 23–47.

TAYLOR, D. W. Thinking and creativity, *Annals of the New York Academy of Sciences*, 1960, 91, 108–127.

TERMAN, L. M., and MILES, C. C. *Sex and Personality* (New York: McGraw-Hill, 1936).

FOOTNOTES:

[1] From an unpublished study conducted jointly by the Aptitudes Project at the University of Southern California and the Institute for Personality Assessment and Research, University of California, Berkeley.

[2] For systematic treatments of a unified theory of intelligence see (Guilford, 1959; Guilford and Merrifield, 1960).

12   Self-Actualization and Beyond*

BY A. H. MASLOW

EDITOR'S NOTE: At first glance this paper may not seem to fit here. At least this was my first impression when considering where to use it in the book. But the more I thought about it, the more it did fit—particularly in this section dealing with intelligence and creativity. Think about it—what does it really mean to be "intelligent" or "creative"? Does it mean to be closed to one's self and one's experiences, or does it imply a certain openness to one's best hunches and deepest feelings? Although Dr. Maslow is talking to counselors in this paper, the ideas seem to have a universal quality which goes beyond just the counselor's role. After all, what does a counselor or therapist do? He releases people, he helps open people to be themselves so they can use their intellectual and creative potential in more productive ways. Isn't this what a good teacher does? A good parent? A good husband or wife? A good friend, even? Self-actualization—an ideal or is it really possible? What do you think?

What I plan to discuss today are ideas that are in midstream rather than ready for formulation into a final version. I find that with my students, and with other people with whom I share these ideas, the notion of self-actualization gets to be almost like a Rorschach ink blot: it frequently tells me more about the person using it than about reality. What I would like to do today is explore some of the nature of self-actualization,

* Reprinted by permission of the author. Address delivered at the Workshop on the Training of Adult Counselors in Chatham, Mass., in May, 1965.

not as a grand abstraction, but in terms of the operational meaning of the self-actualizing process. What does self-actualization mean in moment to moment terms? What does it mean on Tuesday at four o'clock?

My investigations on self-actualization (to my horror, dismay, shock, and surprise—the only ones in existence) were not planned to be research and did not start out as research. They started out as the effort of a young intellectual in his twenties to try to understand two of his teachers whom he loved, adored, and admired, and who were very very wonderful people. It was a kind of high IQ devotion. I could not be content simply to adore, but sought to understand why these two people were so different from the run-of-the-mill of people in the world. These two people were Ruth Benedict and Max Wertheimer. They were my teachers after I came with a Ph.D. from the West to New York City, and here were these most remarkable human beings. My training in psychology equipped me not at all for understanding them. It was as if they were not quite people but something more than people. My own investigation began as a pre-scientific thing. I made descriptions and notes on Max Wertheimer, and I made notes on Ruth Benedict, and when I tried to understand, write about, and think about my own journal and my own notes, I realized in one wonderful moment that their two patterns could be generalized. I was talking about a kind of person, not about two non-comparable individuals. There was wonderful excitement in that. I tried to look to see if this pattern could be found elsewhere, and I did find it elsewhere, in one person after another.

By ordinary standards of laboratory research, of rigorous and controlled research, this simply was not research at all. My generalizations grew out of *my* selection of certain kinds of people. Obviously, other judges are needed. So far, one man has selected perhaps two dozen people whom he liked, or admired very much, and thought were wonderful people and then tried to figure them out and found that he was able to describe a syndrome—the kind of pattern that seemed to fit all of them. These were people only from Western cultures, people selected with all kinds of built-in biases. But unreliable as it is, that was the only operational definition of self-actualizing people as I described them in my first publication on the subject. After I published the results of my investigations there appeared perhaps six, eight, or ten other lines of evidence that supported the findings, not by replication but by an approach from a different angle. Carl Rogers' findings and those of his students add up to corroboration for the whole syndrome. The new work with LSD, all the studies on the effects of therapy, (good therapy that is), some test results—in fact everything I know adds up to corroborated support, though not replicated support, for that study. I personally feel very confident about its major conclusions. I cannot conceive of any research that would make major changes in the pattern, though I am sure there will be minor changes. I have made some of those myself. But my confidence in my rightness is not a scientific datum. If you question the kind of data I have from my researches with monkeys and dogs, you are bringing my competence into doubt or calling me a liar, and I have a right to object. If you question my findings on self-actualizing people, you may do so because you don't know very much about the man who selected the people on whom all the conclusions are based. The conclusions are in the realm of pre-science, the realm of affirmations that are set forth in a form that can be put to test. In that sense, they are scientific.

The people I selected for my investigation were older people, people who had lived much of their lives out and were visibly successful. We do not yet know about the applicability of the findings to young people. We do not know what self-actualization means in other cultures, though a study of self-actualization in China is now in process, as well as one in India. We do not know what the findings of these new studies will be but of one thing I have no doubt: when you select out for careful study very fine people, strong people, creative people, saintly people, sagacious people —in fact, exactly the kind of people that I picked out, then you get a different view of mankind. You are asking how tall people can grow, what can a human being perhaps become? And these are the Olympic gold medal winners—the best we have got. Now the fact that somebody can run a hundred yards in less than ten seconds means that in potentiality any baby that is born into the world is, in theory, capable of doing so too. In that sense, any baby that is born into the world can in principle reach the heights that actually exist and can be described. When you look at mankind this way, your thinking about psychology and psychiatry changes radically. For example, 99 per cent of what has been written on so-called learning theory is simply irrelevant to a grown human being. Learning theory does not apply to a human being growing as tall as he can. Most of the literature on learning theory deals with what I call "extrinsic learning" to distinguish it from "intrinsic learning." Extrinsic learning means collecting acquisitions to yourself like keys in your pocket or coins that you pick up. Extrinsic learning is adding another association or adding another craft. The process of learning to be the best human being you can be is another business altogether. The far goals for adult education, and for any other education, are the processes, the ways in which we can help people to become all they are capable of becoming. This I call intrinsic learning and I am confining my remarks today entirely to it. That is the way self-actualizing people learn. To help the client achieve such intrinsic learning is the far goal of counseling.

These things I *know* with certainty. There are other things that I feel very confident about—"my smell tells me" so to speak. Yet I have even fewer objective data on these points than I had on those above. Self-actualization is hard enough to define. How much harder it is to ask the question, "Beyond self-actualization, what?" Or, if you will, "Beyond authenticity, what?" Just being honest is, after all, not sufficient in all this. What else can we say of self-actualizing people?

Self-actualizing people are, without one single exception, involved in a cause outside their own skin, in something outside of themselves. They are devoted, working at something, something which is very precious to them—some calling or vocation in the old sense, the priestly sense. They are working at something which fate has called them to somehow and which they work at and which they love, so that the work-joy dichotomy there disappears. One devoted his life to the law, another to justice, another to beauty or truth. All, in one way or another, devote their lives to the search for what I have called the "Being" values, (B for short), the ultimate values which are intrinsic, which cannot be reduced to anything more ultimate. There are about fourteen of these "B" values including truth and beauty and goodness of the ancients, and perfection, simplicity, comprehensiveness, and several more. These "B" values are described in the appendix to my book, "Religions, Values, and Peak Experiences," which came out about six months ago. They are the values of being. The existence of these "B" values adds a whole set of complications to the structure of self-actualization. These "B" values behave like needs. I have called them *meta-needs*. Deprivation of them breeds certain kinds of pathologies which have not yet been described. I call them *"meta-pathologies"*—the sickness of the soul which comes, e.g., from living among liars all the time and not trusting anyone. And just as we need counselors to help people with the simpler problems of unmet needs, so we may need *meta-counselors* to help the soul-sickness that grows from the unfulfilled *meta-needs*. In certain definable and empirical ways, it is necessary for man to live in beauty rather than ugliness, as it is necessary for him to have food for an aching belly or rest for a weary body. In fact, I would go so far as to claim that these "B" values are the meaning of life for most people, but many people don't even recognize that they have these meta-needs. Part of our job as counselors may be to make them aware of these needs in themselves, just as the classical psychoanalyst has made his patients aware of their instinctoid basic needs. Ultimately, perhaps, we will come to think of ourselves as philosophical or religious counselors.

We try to help our students move and grow toward self-actualization. These youngsters are all wrapped up in value problems. These youngsters are, *in principle,* very wonderful people, though in actuality they often seem to be little more than snotty kids, but I assume (in the face of all behavioral evidence sometimes) that they are in the classical grand sense, idealistic. I assume that they are looking for values and that they would love to have something to devote themselves to, to be patriotic about, to worship, adore, love. These youngsters are making choices from moment to moment of going forward or retrogressing, moving backward or moving toward self-actualization. As a counselor, or a meta-counselor, what can you tell them about becoming more fully themselves? What do you do when you self-actualize? Do you grit your teeth and squeeze? What does self-actualization mean in terms of actual behavior, actual procedure?

First of all, self-actualization means experiencing fully, vividly, selflessly, with full concentration and total absorption. It means experiencing without the self-consciousness of the adolescent. At this moment of experiencing, the person is wholly and fully human. This is a self-actualization moment. This is a moment when the self is actualizing itself. As individuals, we all experience such moments occasionally. As counselors, you can help clients to experience them more often. You can encourage them to become totally absorbed in something and to forget their poses and their defenses and their shyness—to go at it whole hog. From the outside, we can see that this can be a very sweet moment. In these youngsters who are trying to be very tough and cynical and sophisticated, we can see the recovery of some of the guilelessness of childhood, some of the innocence and sweetness of the face can come back as they devote themselves fully to a moment and throw themselves fully into the experiencing of it. The key word for this is "selflessly," and our youngsters suffer from too little selflessness, too much self-consciousness, self-awareness.

Second, let us think of life as a process of choices, one after another at various choice points. At each point there is a progression choice and a regression choice. There may be a movement toward defense, toward safety, toward being afraid, but over on the other side is the growth choice. To make the growth choice instead of the fear choice a dozen times a day is to move a dozen times a day toward self-actualization. Self-actualization is an on-going process; it means making each of the many single choices about whether to lie or be honest, whether to steal or not steal at a particular point, to make each of these choices as a growth choice. This is movement toward self-actualization.

Third, to talk of self-actualization implies that there is a self to be actualized. A human being is not a *tabula rasa*, not a lump of clay or plastocene, but a something which is already there, at least a cartilaginous structure of some kind. A human being is at minimum, his temperament, his biochemical balances, and so on. There is a self, and what I have sometimes referred to as "listening to the impulse voices" means letting the self emerge. Most of us, most of the time (and especially does this apply to children, young people), listen not to ourselves but to Mommy's voice being introjected or Daddy's voice, or to the voice of the Establishment of the Elders, of authority or tradition. As a simple first step toward self-actualization, I sometimes suggest to my students that when they are given a glass of wine and asked how they like it, they don't look at the label on the bottle in order to get the cue about whether or not they should like it, but that instead they close their eyes if possible, and they make a hush, and they look within themselves and try to shut out the noise of the world and then to savor it on their tongues and look to the Supreme Court inside there and then come out and say, "I like it" or "I don't like it." That statement is different from the usual kind of phoniness that we all indulge in. At a party recently, I caught myself looking at the label on a bottle and assuring my hostess that she had indeed selected a very good Scotch. But then I caught myself—what was I saying? I knew little about Scotches. I had no idea whether this was good or not, but this kind of thing we all do. Refusing to do it is part of the on-going process of actualizing yourself. Does *your* belly hurt? Or does it feel good? Does this taste good on *your* tongue? Do *you* like lettuce?

Fourth, when in doubt, be honest rather than not. I am covered by that phrase "when in doubt . . ." so that we need not argue too much about diplomacy. Frequently, when we are in doubt we are not honest. Our college students are not honest much of the time. They are playing games and posing. The boys swagger around trying to look like something out of a movie, and the girls are trying to appear glamorous. They do not take easily to the suggestion to be honest. But looking within one's self for many of the answers implies taking responsibility. That is in itself a great step toward actualization. This matter of responsibility has been little studied. It is not a part of the American Psychological Association's psychology. It doesn't turn up in our textbooks, for who can investigate responsibility in white rats? It is an almost tangible part of psychotherapy. In psychoanalysis you can see it, you can feel it, you know this moment of responsibility. You know what it feels like. This is one of the great steps. Each time one takes responsibility, this is an actualizing of the self.

Fifth, we have talked so far of experiencing without self-awareness, of making the growth choice rather than the fear choice, of listening to the impulse voices and of being honest and taking responsibility. All these things are steps toward self-actualization and all of them guarantee better life choices. Do each of these little things each time the choice point comes and they will add up to better choices about what is constitutionally right for you, what your destiny is, who your wife or husband will be, what your mission in life will be. You cannot choose wisely for a life unless you dare to listen to yourself, *yourself*, at each moment in life, and to say calmly, "No, I don't like such and such."

The art world, in my opinion, has been captured by a small group of opinion and taste makers, whom I feel suspicious about. That is an *ad hominem* judgment, but it seems fair enough for people who set themselves up as able to say, "You like what I like or else you are a fool." We must teach people to listen to their own tastes. Most people don't do it. You rarely hear before a puzzling painting, "That is a puzzling painting." We had a dance program at Brandeis a few nights ago—a weird thing altogether, with electronic music, tapes, and people doing surrealistic and dada things—and when the lights went up everybody looked stunned and nobody knew what to say. In that kind of situation most people will make some smart chatter instead of saying, "I would like to think about this." Making an honest statement involves daring to be different, unpopular, non-conformist. If we cannot teach our students, young or old, about being prepared to be unpopular, we might just as well give up right now at anything. To be courageous rather than afraid is another version of the same thing.

Sixth, self-actualization is not only an end state but it is also the process of actualizing your potentialities at any time, in any amount. It is a matter of becoming smarter by studying if you are an intelligent person, as our college students are. Self-actualization means using your IQ, using your intelligence. It does not mean doing some far-out thing necessarily, but it may mean going up to your dormitory room and sweating, studying, getting the mathematics or physics. Self-actualization can consist of finger exercises at a piano keyboard. Self-actualization means working to do well the thing that you want to do. To become a second-grade physician is not a good path to self-actualization. You want to be first-rate, or as good as you can be.

Seventh, peak experiences are transient moments of self-actualization. They are moments of ecstasy which you cannot buy, cannot guarantee, cannot even seek. You must be as C. S. Lewis wrote, "surprised by joy." But you can set up the conditions so that peak-experiences are more likely, or you can perversely set up the conditions so that they are less likely. You can reassure young people about discovering things they do not like to do. Some of our youngsters at Brandeis have come in prepared to be astronauts, and they take physics and math and find out that it's not what they thought. Breaking up an illusion, getting rid of a false notion, learning what they are not good at, learning what their potentialities are *not*—this is also part of discovering what yourself is in fact.

Practically everyone does have peak experiences, only not everyone knows it. Some people wave these small mystical experiences aside. Helping people to recognize these little moments of ecstasy when they happen is one of the jobs of the counselor—or meta-counselor. But, how does one's psyche, with nothing external in the world to point at—there is no blackboard there—look into another person's secret psyche and then try to communicate? You have to work out a new way of communication. I have tried one. It is described in another appendix in that same book, under the title, "Rhapsodic Communications." I think that kind of communication may be more of a model for teaching, counseling, for helping adults to become as fully developed as they can be than the kind we are used to when we see teachers writing on the board. If I love Beethoven, and I hear something in a quartet that you don't, how do I teach you to hear? The noises are there, obviously. But I hear something very, very beautiful and you look blank. You hear the sounds. How do I get you to hear the beauty? That is more our problem of teaching than teaching the A, B, C's, or demonstrating arithmetic on the board, or pointing to a dissection of the frog. These things are external to both people, and one has a pointer and you can both look at the same time. This kind of teaching is easy, the other one much harder, but it is part of our job as counselors. It is meta-counseling.

Eighth, finding out who you are, what you are, what you like, what you don't like, what is good for you and what is bad, where you are going and what your mission is—opening yourself up to yourself, means the exposure of psycho-pathology. It means identifying defenses, and after defenses have been identified, it means encouraging people to give them up. And this is painful, for defenses are against something which is unpleasant, but it is worth while. If the psycho-analytic literature has taught us nothing else, it has taught us that repression is not a good way of solving problems. Let me talk about one defense mechanism that is not mentioned in the psychology textbooks, though it is a very important defense mechanism to the snotty and yet idealistic youngster of today. It is the defense mechanism of *de-sacralizing*. These youngsters mistrust the possibility of values and virtues. They feel themselves swindled or thwarted in their lives. Most of them have, in fact, dopey parents whom they don't respect very much, parents who are quite confused about values themselves, and who frequently are simply terrified of their children and who never punish them or stop them from doing things that are wrong. So you have a situation where the youngsters simply despise their elders— often for good and sufficient reason. And the youngsters have learned to make a big generalization and they won't listen to anybody who is grown up, especially if the grownup uses the same words which they've heard from the hypocritical mouth. They have heard their fathers talk about being honest or being brave or being bold and seen their fathers being the opposite of all these things. The youngsters have learned to reduce the person to the concrete object, and to refuse to see what he might be, or refuse to see him in symbolic values, or refuse to see him or her eternally. Our kids have de-sacralized sex, for example. Sex is nothing, it is a natural thing and they have made it so natural that it has lost its poetic qualities in many instances, which means that it has lost practically everything. Self-actualization means giving up this defense mechanism and learning, or being taught, to re-sacralize. (I have had to make up these words because the English language is rotten for good people. It has no decent vocabulary for the virtues. Even the nice words get all smeared up. Love, for instance.)

Re-sacralizing means being willing, once again, to see a person "under the aspect of eternity," as Spinoza says, or to see him in the medieval Christian unitive perception, that is, being able to see the sacred, the eternal, the symbolic. It is to see Woman with a capital W and everything that that implies even when one looks at a particular woman. Another example: you go to medical school and dissect a brain. Certainly something is lost if you don't get awed, but see the brain only as one concrete thing without the unitive perception. Open to re-sacralization, you see it as a sacred object also, see its symbolic value, see it as a figure of speech, see it, so to speak, in its poetic aspects.

Re-sacralization often means an awful lot of corny talk—"very square," the kids would say. But for the counselor, especially for the counselor of older people, where these philosophical questions about religion and the meaning of life come up, this is a most important way of helping the person to move toward self-actualization. The youngsters may say that it is square, the logical positivists may say that it is meaningless, but for the person who seeks your help in this process it is obviously very meaningful and very important and you'd better answer him or you're not doing what it is your job to do.

Put all of these points together and we see that self-actualization is not a matter of one great moment. It is not true that on Thursday at four o'clock the trumpet blows and one steps into the Pantheon forever and altogether. Self-actualization is a matter of degree, of little accessions accumulated one by one. Our students are inclined to wait for some kind of inspiration to strike and then to say that, "At 3:23 on this Thursday I became self-actualized!" People who can be selected as self-actualizing subjects, people who fit the criteria, go about it in these little ways: they listen to their own voices, they take responsibility, they are honest, and they work. They find out who they are and what they are in terms not only of their mission in life but of the way their feet hurt when they wear such and such shoes and whether they do or do not like eggplant or stay up all night if they drink too much beer. All this is what the real self means. They find their own biological natures, their congenital natures which are irreversible or difficult to change.

These are the things people do as they move toward self-actualization. Who, then, is a counselor? And how can he help the people who come to him to make this movement in the direction of growth?

Counseling is not concerned with training nor with molding, nor with teaching in the ordinary sense of telling people what to do and how to do it. It is not concerned with propaganda. It is a Taoistic uncovering. Taoistic means the non-interfering, the "let be." Taoism is not a *laissez-faire* philosophy nor a philosophy of neglect nor of refusal to help or care. As a kind of model of this process we might think of a therapist who, if he is a decent therapist and also a decent human being, would never dream of imposing himself upon his patients or propagandizing in any way, or trying to make the patient into an imitation, or to use himself as a model. What he does, the good clinical therapist, is to help his particular client to unfold, to break through the defenses against his self-knowledge, to recover himself and get to know himself. Ideally, the therapist's rather abstract frame of reference, the textbooks he has read, the schools that he has gone to, his beliefs about the world—these should never be perceptible to the patient. Respectful of the inner nature, the being, the essence of this "younger brother," he would recognize that the best way for him to lead a good life is to be more fully himself. The people we call sick are the people who are not themselves, the people who have built up all sorts of neurotic defenses against being human. And just as it makes no difference to the rosebush whether the gardener is Italian or French or Swedish, so it should make no difference to the younger brother how his helper learned to be a helper. What the helper has to give are certain services that are independent of his being Swedish or Catholic or Mohammedan or Freudian or whatever he is.

These basic concepts include, imply, and are completely in accord with the basic concepts of Freudian psycho-dynamics. It is a Freudian principle that unconscious aspects of the self are repressed and that the finding of the true self requires the uncovering of these unconscious aspects. Implicit is a belief that truth heals much. Learning to break through one's repressions, to know one's self, to hear the impulse voices, to uncover the triumphant nature, to reach knowledge, insight, and the truth—these are the requirements.

A ten-year-old paper by Lawrence Kubie, "The Forgotten Man in Education," originally published in the Harvard Education Review, made long ago the point that one ultimate goal of education is to help the person become a human being, as fully human as he can possibly be. If you do not accept the importance of the unconscious and work to do away with repression and defenses, then education is missing its ultimate goal.

I have used the words "therapy," "psychotherapy," and "patient." Actually, I hate all those words and I hate the medical model that they imply because the medical model suggests that the person who comes to the counselor is a sick person, beset by disease, by illness, seeking a cure, whereas, actually, of course, we hope that the counselor will be the person who helps to foster the self-actualization of people rather than helping to cure a disease.

The helping model has to give way, too; it just doesn't fit. It makes us think of the counselor as the person or the professional who knows, reaching down from his privileged position above to the poor jerks below who don't know and have to be helped in some way, the poor cripples who don't talk back much. Nor is the counselor to be a teacher, in the usual sense, because what teachers have specialized in and gotten to be very good at, is what I have called "extrinsic learning," whereas the process of growing into the best human being you can be is, instead, intrinsic learning.

The existential therapists have wrestled with this question of models, and I can recommend to you James Bugental's book, *Beyond Authenticity, What?*, for a discussion of the matter. Jim Bugental suggests that we call counseling or therapy "ontogogy" which means trying to help people to grow to their fullest possible height. Perhaps that's a better word than the one I once suggested, a word derived from a German author, *"psychogogy,"* which means the education of the psyche. Whatever the word we use, I think that the concept we will eventually have to come to is one that Alfred Adler suggested a long, long time ago when he spoke of the "older brother." The older brother is the loving person who takes responsibility, just as you do for your young kid brother. Of course you know more, you've lived longer, but you are not qualitatively different, you are not in another realm of discourse, and you help him in particular ways. Earlier I used the word "horticultural." I hope you caught the reference there, the idea of helping onions to grow to be onions and not trying to change them over into turnips. Let me give you another example of the kind of thing I am talking about:

If a young man wants to be a professional prizefighter, he goes to some professional gymnasium, offers himself to the manager, and says, "I would like to be a boxer." And then the manager, characteristically, I'm told (I don't know, I've never tried this myself), will get one of his experienced fighters and say, "Take him into the ring and try him out." The instructions are always "stretch him." That is, let him go as far as he can, see how hard he can hit, find out the hardest he can possibly hit, find out how much he can take, see how fast he is, see how good his reflexes are—stretch him to his fullest capacity and get some notion there of the real self—the intrinsic self I was talking about before. This is the job of finding capacity, of determining whether this young man does seem to have promise (and that itself is an instinctoid statement). Now suppose he's good, he's fast, he's strong, he's powerful, and so on. If he looks good, do you think that the manager gives him a manual to read and tells him, "Now you forget everything you know and you start at Point 1 and you go on to Points 2 and 3 and 4? No. He takes this young man and tries to train him to be the best possible kind of fighter that he already is. He tries to improve him and he tries to make him better than he is, *in his own style*. See how different this is from the "teaching somebody who doesn't know nothin'," model! A child comes along, one who doesn't know any French at all. You pour it into him. You start from scratch. But especially with adults we are not in that position. We already have a start, we already have capacities, talents, directions, missions, callings, and then the job is, if we are to take this model seriously, to help them to be more perfectly what they already are, to be more full, more actualizing, more realizing in fact what they are in potentiality.

PART TWO

Toward Understanding the Nature of Instruction

"A teacher who can arouse a feeling for one single good action, for one single good poem, accomplishes more than he who fills our memory with rows of neutral objects, classified with name and form." Goethe (1749-1832)

Teaching is more than the simple presentation of facts and information. It is that, of course, but more. It is a relationship between an instructor and his students which, for better or for worse, either enhances or interferes with what students learn and how long it lasts if they do learn. Part II will acquaint you with the psychology of group behavior, the psychology of teacher behavior, recent innovations in instruction, and some of the major issues and concerns related to testing and grading.

The four articles in Chapter Four will give you a sampling of the broad spectrum of research related to classroom dynamics and teaching processes. *Can* we tell good teachers from poor teachers? Article 13 suggests that we can, indeed, and points to a substantial body of research to justify this conclusion. Dr. McKeachie speaks to the importance of understanding the psychology of group behavior and how it is related to teaching methods. Dr. Rogers presents, perhaps, the most controversial paper of all in Article 16 in which he asserts that ". . . *anything that can be taught to another is relatively inconsequential, and has little or no significant influence on behavior.*" Could this be true? Maybe. Maybe not. You are invited only to keep an open mind as you read these and other related ideas in this chapter

Chapter Five confronts you with four major issues when it comes to considering recent innovations in instruction. Dr. Skinner believes we need teaching machines and presents a sound case for why we do. Dr. Fitzgerald is not so sure about this and raises important questions as to the ultimate worth of teaching machines. Educational television, team teaching, and nongraded programs all have their place in the scheme of contemporary innovations and each is explored in this chapter.

The problems tackled in Chapter Six are as old as education itself. Sooner or later every teacher, whether in kindergarten or graduate school, has to test students and grade them. In Article 22, Dr. Ebel begins with the assertion that the measurement of educational achievement is essential to effective education. The subsequent three articles were deliberately chosen to raise a series of questions rather than to cite a list of answers to the problem of testing and grading. *Are* teacher grades valid? *Is* testing a menace to education? Should, for that matter, grades be abandoned altogether? These are not easy questions to answer, but they are, nonetheless, questions which every concerned person must come to grips with sooner or later. Hopefully, this chapter will stimulate you to probe even deeper into your private philosophy of testing and grading.

CHAPTER FOUR

CLASSROOM DYNAMICS AND TEACHING PROCESSES

13   *What Research Tells Us About the Characteristics of "Good" and "Bad" Teachers**

BY DON E. HAMACHEK

EDITOR'S NOTE: Anyone with any experience in school at all has had exposures to "good" and "bad" teachers. Although what constitutes a good or bad teacher depends partly on one's values and point of view, there nonetheless is a substantial body of research which has attempted to point out the differences. This article is an effort to synthesize and integrate what research has to say. What are your ideas about the differences between good and bad teachers?

It is, I think, a sad commentary about our educational system when it keeps announcing both publicly and privately that "good" and "bad" teachers cannot be distinguished from each other. Probably no area in education has been so voluminously researched as has teacher effectiveness and considerations which enhance or constrict this effectiveness. As Gage (1960) has noted, not only is the literature on teacher competence overwhelming but even the bibliographies on the subject are becoming unmanageable. Nonetheless, we are still told that we cannot tell the good guys from the bad guys. For example, Biddle and Ellena in their book, *Contemporary Research on Teacher Effectiveness* (1964), begin by saying that ". . . the problem of teacher effectiveness is so complex that no one today knows what *The Competent Teacher* is" (p. 2). I think we *do* know what the competent, or effective, or successful, or whatever you care to call him, teacher is, and in the remainder of this paper I will be as specific as possible in citing *why* I think we know and some implications for teacher-training programs.

*Prepared especially for this volume.

WHAT THE RESEARCH SAYS

Perhaps the best place to begin is with the facts, the evidence, if you will, gathered by various researchers investigating so-called "good" and "bad" teachers. Because of the reality of space limitations, this is by no means an exhaustive review of all the research related to the problem at hand, but it is, I think, representative of the kind and variety of research findings linked to questions of teacher effectiveness. By and large, each investigation has attempted to probe one or more of the following dimensions of teacher personality and behavior: (1) Personal Characteristics; (2) Instructional Procedures and Interaction Styles; (3) Perceptions of Self; (4) Perceptions of Others. So with these four categories serving as a guide, let us begin a four-dimensional tour through the land of research to see if we can, indeed, sort out the "good guys" from the "bad guys" and thereby spell out the differences between them.

(1) *Personal Characteristics of Good versus Poor Teachers.* I think we would all agree that it is quite possible to have two teachers of equal intelligence, training, and grasp of subject matter but who, at the same time, differ considerably in influence and in the results they achieve with students. Part of the difference can be accounted for by the effect of a teacher's personality on the learners.

One of the most interesting investigations was conducted by Hart (1934) which was based upon the opinions of 3,725 high school seniors concerning best-liked and least-liked teachers. A total of 43 different reasons were listed for "Liking Teacher A Best" and 30 different reasons for "Liking Teacher Z Least." It is interesting to examine the first four most frequently cited reasons in each category.

Four Most Frequently Mentioned Reasons for Liking
"Teacher A" Best Reported by 3,725 High School Seniors

1. Is helpful in schoolwork, explains lessons and assignments clearly and thoroughly and uses examples in teaching.   51%
2. Cheerful, happy, good-natured, jolly, has sense of humor and can take a joke.   40%
3. Human, friendly, companionable, "one of us."   30%
4. Interested in and understands pupils.   26%

Four Most Frequently Mentioned Reasons for Liking
"Teacher Z" Least Reported by 3,725 High School Seniors

1. Too cross, crabby, grouchy, never smiles, nagging, sarcastic, loses temper, "flies off the handle."   50%

2. Not helpful with schoolwork, does not explain lessons and assignments, not clear, work not planned.   30%
3. Partial, has "pets" or favored students, and "picks on certain pupils."   20%
4. Superior, aloof, haughty, "snooty," overbearing, does not know you out of class.   20%

You will note that personality traits monopolize the top rankings after the first items which deals with teaching technique as it immediately affects students. Interestingly enough, mastery of subject matter, which is vital but badly overemphasized by specialists, ranks sixteenth on both lists.

Hart's general findings have been corroborated time and again by later studies. For example, Witty (1947), in connection with the "Quiz Kids" program, received 12,000 letters on the theme, "The Teacher Who Helped Me Most." An analysis of those letters revealed that the top ranking traits were the following:

(1) Cooperative, democratic attitudes; (2) kindliness and consideration for the individual; (3) patience; (4) wide interests; (5) personal appearance and pleasant manner; (6) fairness and impartiality; (7) sense of humor; (8) good disposition and consistent behavior; (9) interest in pupils' problems; (10) flexibility; (11) use of recognition and praise; (12) unusual proficiency in teaching a particular subject.

Even at the college level (Bousfield, 1940) there is evidence to suggest that students still rank first the professor's interest in his students and their problems and his willingness to give attention to them.

So far, we have been examining desirable personal characteristics of teachers as these characteristics are identified by students. For the most part, these characteristics group themselves under the general heading of capacity for warmth, patience, tolerance, and interest in students. What happens when these personal qualities are related to the more rigid test of whether having them or not makes any difference in the actual performance of students?

Sears (1963), for example, found that there are positive correlations between the extent to which a teacher reflects a personal interest in and willingness to listen to students' ideas and the creativity shown by students. As a further example, Cogan (1958) found that warm and considerate teachers got an unusual amount of original poetry and art from their high school students. Reed (1962) found that teachers higher in a capacity for warmth favorably affected their pupils' interests in science.

Heil, Powell, and Feifer (1960) went a step further and related student achievement to interaction between differential teacher and student personalities. They compared the various teacher-pupil personality combinations in terms of pupil achievement, teacher knowledge, and classroom settings. Using scores from achievement tests as their criterion measure, they found that the well-integrated (healthy, well-rounded, flexible) teachers were most effective with *all* types of students. Two other identified teacher personality "types" (fearful and turbulent) were successful with only certain types of students.

And then, of course, there is the autocratic-democratic continuum of teacher behavior. The research devoted to investigating this continuum is long and impressive (Lewin, *et al.,* 1939; Tiedeman, 1942; Anderson, 1946; to name a few). Without exception, research in this area all points to a rather significant dislike for and antagonism toward the autocratic, domineering type of teacher. Indeed, Lewin and his associates found that students not only *preferred* the more democratic teacher, but they also *accomplished* more with the help of cooperative, thoughtful teachers, both in subject-matter learning and in the development of personal-social moral traits.

Teacher personality and behavior does seem to have a kind of contagion potential in the sense that students can be influenced for better or for worse by a teacher's personal characteristics. For example, Sears (1963) found that teachers who like pupils tend to have pupils who like each other. Spaulding (1963) found that the self-concepts of elementary school children were apt to be higher and more positive in classrooms in which the teacher was "socially integrative" and "learner supportive." What this and other research cited here seems to suggest is that through the psychological principles of imitation and identification the teacher becomes a model for appropriate behavior and that students take on, assume, and ultimately reflect (probably unconsciously) those personal characteristics most dominant in the teacher.

In essence, I think the evidence is quite clear when it comes to sorting out good or effective from bad or ineffective teachers on the basis of personal characteristics. Effective teachers appear to be those who are, shall we say, "human" in the fullest sense of the word. They have a sense of humor, are fair, empathetic, more democratic than autocratic, and apparently are more able to relate easily and naturally to students on either a one-to-one or group basis. Their classrooms seem to reflect miniature enterprise operations in the sense that they are more open, spontaneous, and adaptable to change. Ineffective teachers apparently lack a sense of humor, grow impatient easily, use cutting, reducing comments in class, are less well-integrated, inclined to be somewhat authoritarian and are generally less sensitive to the needs of their students. As suggested by the studies on the authoritarian personality by Adorno, *et al.* (1950), one has to wonder whether the bureaucratic conduct and tone of the ineffective teacher's classroom is not merely a desperate measure to support the weak pillars of his own personal superstructure.

(2) *Instructional Procedures and Interaction Patterns of Good versus Poor Teachers.* If there really are such polar extremes as "good" or "poor" teachers, then we could reasonably assume that they might differ not only as far as personal characteristics are concerned but also in the way they conduct themselves in a classroom.

One of the most recent and complete investigations related to this problem was carried out by Flanders (1960) who studied teacher influence styles, pupil attitudes, and resulting achievement in seventh grade social studies and eighth grade mathematics. He uncovered four essential elements of teacher influence in the classrooms in which achievement and attitudes were superior. (1) The teacher was capable of providing a range of roles, spontaneously, that varied from fairly active, dominative supervision on the one hand, to a more reflective, discriminating support on the other hand. Mirrored here is the kind of teacher who is not only able to achieve a measure of student compliance but who is also able to support student initiative. (2) The teacher was able to control his own spontaneous behavior so that he could switch from one role to another at will; in other words, a teacher who did not blindly pursue a single behavioral-instructional path to the exclusion of other possibilities. (3) The teacher had enough understanding of the principles of teacher influence to make possible a bridge between his diagnosis of a situation and the course of action he could take. (4) The teacher was able to combine sensitivity and criticalness so that, as the classroom's master observer, he was able to make reasonable diagnoses of current conditions. We should keep in mind, too, that these skills, which characterized successful teachers, were superimposed upon a firm grasp of the subject matter being taught.

Interestingly, those teachers who were *not* successful were the very ones who were inclined to use the same instructional procedures and methodology in a more or less rigid fashion. That is, there seemed to be little variation from one classroom situation to the next. In particular, unsuccessful teachers seemed to lack the ability to expand or restrict the freedom of action of the students through the use of their own verbal influence.

In general, the Flanders study suggests that teachers who were able to provide flexible influence styles, by shifting from the direct to the indirect depending on the situation, were better able to create climates in which students learned more. The students of teachers who were unable to do this learned less.

An earlier effort to investigate the differences in the use of instructional procedures and teaching styles between good and poor teachers was conducted by Barr (1929). Detailed stenographic records, observation charts, and various time charts were kept on 47 teachers of social studies in high school deemed to be superior and 47 deemed well below average in teaching skills. Practically every conceivable act and every expression of teacher and pupil interaction was considered, about 37 factors in all. The following are fragmentary samples of behaviors which distinguished good from poor teachers.

Characteristic Comments Made by Poor But Not by Good Teachers

Are you working hard? . . . Aren't you ever going to learn that word? . . . Everyone sit up straight, please. . . . I'm afraid you're confused. . . . No, that's wrong. . . . Oh dear, don't you know that? . . . Oh, sit down. . . . Say something. . . . and so on, through nearly one hundred different expressions. Note the overtones of frustration, futility and impatience which leak through most.

Characteristic Comments Made by Good But Not by Poor Teachers

Aha, that's a new idea. . . . Are you going to accept that as an answer? I should like more proof. . . . Do you suppose you could supply a better word? . . . Can you prove your statement? . . . Don't you really think you could? . . . I'm not quite clear on that—think a moment. . . . Let's stick to the question. . . . Probably my last question wasn't a good one. . . . and so on, through a long list. Note here the emphasis on challenging the student, on pushing and encouraging him to go beyond where he may be at the moment.

This study also demonstrated that not only did poor teachers give more assignments than good teachers but, almost without exception, they also gave some sort of textbook assignment as a part of their daily procedure. In contrast, the majority of good teachers used something other than textbook assignments. They used outside books, problem-project assignments, and when the text was assigned good teachers were more likely to supplement it with topics, questions, or other references. Poor teachers usually gave far more assignments, but they took less time in giving them. The better teachers, however, were more likely to give fewer assignments, each one covering a topic or unit of respectable size and taking some time to develop.

The teacher's responsibility for maintaining discipline in a classroom is another area in which research has demonstrated where there are differences in teacher-student interaction patterns. For example, in a study by Kounin and Gump (1961), three pairs of punitive versus non-punitive first grade teachers were selected from three elementary schools. Each of the 174 children in these teachers' classrooms was individually interviewed about what he thought was "the worst thing to do in school" and was asked for his explanations of why these behaviors were bad. Regarding their responses as expressions of their preoccupations, it was concluded that children who have punitive teachers, as against those with nonpunitive teachers, manifest more overt aggression; are more unsettled about misbehavior in school; *are less concerned with learning and school-related values* (italics mine); and show some, but not consistent, indication of a reduction in rationality pertaining to school misconduct. This certainly is not all-inclusive evidence, but it is, I think, another indication of how the way a teacher interacts with students influences both cognitive and affective student behavior. Although there probably isn't a teacher alive who has not been punitive at one time or other, it would not seem unreasonable to suggest that good teachers are inclined to be less punitive than poor teachers.

There is also evidence to suggest that when a teacher is able to personalize his teaching he is apt to be more successful, particularly when it comes to motivating students to do better work. For example, Page (1958) conducted an experiment with high school and junior high school students and teachers in which the teachers graded objective tests of their pupils and then randomly assigned each paper to one of three groups. The group-one student was given back his paper with no comment except a mark. Each group-two student was given a stereotyped, standard comment from "excellent" if his score was high to "let's raise this grade." Every C student, for example, received his mark with the notation, "perhaps try to do still better." For those in group three, the teacher wrote a personal comment on every paper saying whatever he thought might encourage that particular student. On the next objective test, groups two and three outperformed group one. This suggests that the personalized comments had a greater effect than standardized comments and that even a very short standard comment written on the paper produced measurable achievement gains. The greatest improvement was made by the failing students in group three who received encouraging personal notes on their papers. This study points up the motivational implications of evaluative practices that go far beyond the simple indication of right or wrong answers. It certainly does seem to be true that teachers who reflect an active personal interest in their students' progress and who show it are more likely to be successful than teachers who are more distant and impersonal.

How about teaching styles as they are related to either "learner-centered" or "teacher-centered" approaches? In an investigation by Flanders (1951), experimentally produced climates simulating the two approaches mentioned above were designed. In the learner-centered climate the teacher was acceptant and supportive of the student and problem-centered in approach; in the teacher-centered climate the teacher was directive and demanding, often deprecating in his behavior toward students. The major conclusions reached were: (1) The "teacher-centered" behavior of directing, demanding, and using private criteria in deprecating a student leads to hostility to the self or teacher, aggressiveness, or sometimes withdrawal, apathy, and even emotional disintegration; (2) The learner-centered behavior of accepting the student, being evaluative or critical only by public criteria, and being usually supportive, elicited problem-orientation, decreased personal anxiety, and led to emotionally readjusting and integrative behavior. Again, evidence to suggest that teachers are likely to be more successful with learner-centered democratic approaches.

Stern (1963) reviewed 34 studies (largely college classes) comparing nondirective with directive instruction in influencing two types of learning outcomes: (a) gain in cognitive knowledge and understanding, and (b) attitude change toward self and others. In regard to cognitive gains, he concludes: "In general, it would appear that the amount of cognitive gain is largely unaffected by the autocratic or democratic tendencies of the instructor" (p. 427). However, when he summarizes the findings related to attitude change toward the self and others, the conclusion is somewhat different: "Regardless of whether the investigator was concerned with attitudes toward the cultural outgroup, toward other participants in the class, or toward the self, and the results generally have indicated that nondirective instruction facilitates a shift in a more favorable, acceptant direction" (p. 427). Once more we find evidence to support the notion that, at least as far as affective variables are concerned, a more nondirective, democratic teaching style is likely to be associated with positive changes in student behavior. As a further example of this, Tiedeman (1942) found that the teacher who was disliked most by students was a domineering, authoritarian person. As a matter of fact, the older the student (hence the greater the need for autonomy?), the more intense the dislike.

We must remember that with comprehensive studies such as those cited in this section, there is much overlap between the classroom behaviors of good and bad teachers. None of the studies cited here demonstrated that there were classroom practices which appeared exclusively with either good or poor teachers. Nevertheless, there are characteristics which seem to appear more consistently with one group than the other. For example, when it comes to classroom behavior, interaction patterns, and teaching styles, good or effective teachers seem to be superior in the following ways:

1. Willingness to be flexible, to be direct or indirect as situation demands
2. Capacity to perceive world from student's point of view
3. Ability to "personalize" their teaching
4. Willingness to experiment, try out new things
5. Skill in asking questions (as opposed to seeing self as a kind of answering service)
6. Knowledge of subject matter and related areas
7. Skill in establishing definite examination procedures
8. Willingness to provide definite study helps
9. Capacity to reflect an appreciative attitude (evidenced by nods, comments, smiles, etc.)
10. Conversational manner in teaching—informal, easy style

(3) *Self-Perceptions of Good versus Poor Teachers.* This is, perhaps, one of the most significant differences between good and poor teachers. We do not have to go any further than our own personal experiences to know that the way we see, regard, and feel about ourselves has enormous impact on both our private and public lives. How about good versus poor teachers? How do they see themselves?

Ryans (1960a and b), in a monumental teachers' characteristics study involving some 6000 teachers in 1700 schools and 450 school systems, found that there were, indeed, differences between the self-related expressions of high emotional stability teachers versus low emotional stability teachers. For example, the more emotionally stable teachers were more apt to have the following kinds of self-reports: (1) frequently named self-confidence and cheerfulness as dominant traits in themselves; (2) said they liked active contact with other people; (3) expressed interests in hobbies and handicrafts; (4) reported their childhoods to be happy experiences.

On the other hand, teachers with lower emotional maturity scores (1) had unhappy memories of childhood; (2) seemed *not* to prefer contact with others; (3) were more directive and authoritarian; (4) expressed less self-confidence.

We can be even more specific. For example, Arthur Combs (1965) in his book, *The Professional Education of Teachers,* cites several studies which reached similar conclusions about the way good teachers typically see themselves (pp. 70–71).

1. Good teachers see themselves as identified with people rather than withdrawn, removed, apart from, or alienated from others.
2. Good teachers feel basically adequate rather than inadequate. They do not see themselves as generally unable to cope with problems.
3. Good teachers feel trustworthy rather than untrustworthy. They see themselves as reliable, dependable individuals with the potential for coping with events as they happen.
4. Good teachers see themselves as wanted rather than unwanted. They see themselves as likable and attractive (in personal, not physical sense) as opposed to feeling ignored and rejected.
5. Good teachers see themselves as worthy rather than unworthy. They see themselves as people of consequence, dignity, and integrity as opposed to feeling they matter little, can be overlooked and discounted.

In the broadest sense of the word, good teachers see themselves as good people. Their self-perceptions are, for the most part, positive, tinged with an air of optimism and colored with tones of healthy self-acceptance. I dare say that self-perceptions of good teachers are not unlike the self-perceptions of any basically healthy person, whether he be a good brick-layer, a good manager, a good doctor, a good lawyer, a good experimental psychologist, or you name it. Clinical evidence has told us time and again that *any* person is apt to be happier, more productive, and more effective when he is able to see himself as fundamentally and basically "enough." (Readers who may want to follow this self-perception idea further will find the following references useful as basic sources: Combs and Snygg, 1959; Hamachek, 1965; Jersild, 1955; Jourard, 1963; Maslow, 1954; Rogers, 1961.)

(4) *Perceptions of Others by Good versus Poor Teachers.* Research is showing us that not only do good and poor teachers view themselves differently, but they also have some characteristic differences in the way they perceive others. For example, Ryan (1964) reported several studies which have produced findings that are quite similar and in agreement when it comes to sorting out the differences between how good and poor teachers view others. He found, among other things, that outstandingly "good" teachers rated significantly higher than notably "poor" teachers in at least five different ways with respect to how they viewed others. The good teachers had (1) more favorable opinions of students; (2) more favorable opinions of democratic classroom behavior; (3) more favorable opinions of administrators and colleagues; (4) a greater expressed liking for personal contacts with other people; (5) more favorable estimates of other people generally. That is, they expressed belief that very few students are difficult behavior problems, that very few people are influenced in their opinions and attitudes toward others by feelings of jealousy, and that most teachers are willing to assume their full share of extra duties outside of school.

Interestingly, the characteristics that distinguished the "lowly assessed" teacher group suggested that the relatively "ineffective" teacher is self-centered, anxious, and restricted. One is left with the distinct impression that poor or ineffective teachers have more than the usual number of paranoid-like defenses. For example, turning to Ryan (1964) again, we find that he reports that his "ineffective teachers believe a substantial portion of parents' visits to school are made to criticize the teacher or the school and that a fairly large portion of people (40–60 percent) are influenced in their opinions and attitudes toward others by feelings of jealousy" (p. 89).

It might be well, at this point, for us to bear in mind Ryan's cautionary note:

> Certainly the research (referring to his own) has not settled the question, who is the good teacher? However, there are some interesting suggestions here—some clues that may help to identify "good" and "poor" teachers if one is willing to accept the kind of definition employed in this research. Such a definition indicates that teachers are "good" if

they rank very high among their colleagues with respect to such observable classroom behaviors as warmth and kindliness, systematic and businesslike manner, and stimulating and original teacher behavior (p. 90).

Combs (1965) has investigated the perceptual differences between good and poor teachers, and he suggests that good teachers can be clearly distinguished from poor ones with respect to the following perceptions about people (p. 55):

1. The good teacher is more likely to have an internal rather than external frame of reference. That is, he seeks to understand how things seem to others and then uses this as a guide for his own behavior.
2. The good teacher is more concerned with people and their reactions than with things and events.
3. The good teacher is more concerned with the subjective-perceptual experience of people than with objective events. He is, again, more concerned with how things seem to people than just the so-called or alleged "facts."
4. The good teacher seeks to understand the causes of people's behavior in terms of their *current* thinking, feeling, beliefs, and understandings rather than in terms of forces exerted on them now or in the past.
5. The good teacher generally trusts other people and perceives them as having the capacity to solve their own problems.
6. The good teacher sees others as being friendly and enhancing rather than hostile or threatening.
7. The good teacher tends to see other people as being of worth rather than unworthy. That is, he sees all people as possessing a certain dignity and integrity.
8. The good teacher sees people and their behavior as essentially developing from within rather than as a product of external events to be molded or directed. In other words, he sees people as creative and dynamic rather than passive or inert.

I am sure it comes as no surprise to any of us that how we perceive others is highly dependent on how we perceive ourselves. If a potential teacher (or anyone else for that matter) likes himself, trusts himself, and his confidence in himself, he will likely see others in this same light. Research is beginning to tell us what common sense has always told us, namely, people grow, flourish, and develop much more easily when in relationship with someone who projects an inherent trust and belief in their capacity to become what they have the potential to become.

It is one thing to say that good teachers have a generally more positive veiw of others, but does this have anything to do with how students achieve and behave? There is evidence to suggest that it does. For example, Davidson and Lang (1960) found that among the boys and girls in grades 4–6, those children with the more favorable self-images were those who more likely than not perceived their teacher's feelings toward them more favorably. They also found that the more positive the perception of their teacher's feelings, the better was their academic achievement, and the more desirable their classroom behavior as rated by teachers.

It seems to me that we can sketch at least five interrelated generalizations from what research is telling us about how good teachers differ from poor teachers when it comes to perceptions of others. In relation to this, good teachers can be characterized in the following ways:

1. They seem to have generally more positive views of others—students, colleagues, and administrators.
2. They do not seem to be as prone to view others as critical, attacking people with ulterior motives, but rather see them as potentially friendly and worthy in their own right.
3. They have a more favorable view of democratic classroom procedures.
4. They seem to have the ability and capacity to see things as they seem to others—i.e., the ability to see things from the other person's point of view.
5. They do not seem to see students as persons "you do things to" but rather as individuals capable of doing for themselves once they feel trusted, respected, and valued.

WHAT, THEN, IS A GOOD TEACHER?

(1) A Good Teacher Is a Good Person: Simple as it sounds, a good teacher does, indeed, seem to be, first and foremost, a good person. He rather likes life, is reasonably at peace with himself, has a sense of humor, and enjoys other people. If I interpret the research correctly, what it seems to be saying is that there is no one best better-than-all-others type teacher. Nonetheless, there are clearly distinguishable "good" and "bad" teachers. As a general statement, a good teacher is good because he does not seem to be dominated by a narcissistic self which demands a spotlight, or a neurotic need for power and authority, or a host of unconscious fears and tremblings which demote him from the master of his class to its mechanic.

(2) The Good Teacher Is Flexible: By far, the single most repeated adjective used to describe good teachers is "flexibility." Either implicitly or, most often, explicitly this characteristic emerges time and again over all others when good teaching is discussed in the research. In other words, the good teacher does not seem to be overwhelmed by a single point of view or

approach to the extreme of being afflicted by a kind of intellectual myopia. A good teacher knows that he cannot be just one sort of person and use just one kind of approach if he intends to meet the multiple needs of his students. Good teachers are, in a sense, "total" teachers. That is, they seem able to be what they have to be to meet the demands of the moment. They seem able to move with the shifting tides of their own needs, the student's, and do what has to be done to handle the situation. A total teacher can be firm when necessary (say "No!" and mean it) or permissive (say "Do it your way!" and mean that, too) when appropriate. It depends on many things and good teachers seem to know when and how to move with the tides of shifting classroom circumstances.

THE NEED FOR FLEXIBLE "TOTAL" TEACHERS

There probably is not an educational psychology course taught which does not, in some way, deal with the highly complex area of individual differences. Even the most unsophisticated undergraduate is aware that people differ in readiness and capacity to handle academic learning. For the most part, our educational technology (audio-visual aids, programmed texts, teaching machines, etc.) is making significant advances designed to assist teachers in coping with the intellectual differences among students. We have been making strides in the direction of offering flexible programs and curriculums, but we are somewhat remiss when it comes to preparing flexible, "total" teachers. Just as there are intellectual differences among students, there are also personality differences which can have just as much impact on achievement. If this is true, then perhaps we need to do more about preparing teachers who are sensitive to the nature of these differences and who are able to take them into account as they plan for their classes.

Do personality differences among students really exist? Apparently they do. For example, Wispe (1951), Smith, et al. (1956), and Mc-Keachie (1958) have reported experiments which demonstrate that teaching methods do, indeed, interact with student personality characteristics. In all these experiments some students were placed in discussion or lecture sections where expectations were clearly defined, while other students were placed in more open-ended sections where they were free to establish objectives and course procedures. In the Smith, et al., experiment, the more highly structured sections were taught in a cold, impersonal, even punitive manner, while the unstructured sections were conducted with a warm, supportive, and permissive hand. In all three instances, a certain kind of student emerged who appeared to demand a high degree of structure to make optimum progress. Wispe describes these students as personally insecure and dependent and goes on to say:

Being intensely frustrated and lacking the personal security to make the best of a bad situation, this student becomes rigid, intropunitive, and vindictive in his evaluation of sections and instructors. To this student the permissive section meetings are "absolutely worthless," a place where intellectual confusion is heaped upon personal anxiety (pp. 176–177).

On the other hand, there were also the more personally secure students who found the permissive, open-ended class very much to their liking and who flourished under those conditions. In any case, whether a student is secure or insecure, dependent or independent, these personality dimensions do make a difference when it comes to determining whether one teaching method or another will be successful.

Compulsivity and anxiety are two other personality characteristics which apparently interact with teaching method. For example, Grimes and Allinsmith (1961) examined the effects of personality variables with teaching method held constant and discovered that under structured teaching compulsive children do substantially better than less compulsive children but compulsivity makes no difference in unstructured settings. On the other hand, highly anxious children do poorly in unstructured classrooms. Children who are both highly anxious and highly compulsive do their best work in structured classes, and those who are highly anxious but *low* in compulsivity do poorly in unstructured classes.

Other evidence also points to individual differences in non-intellectual factors. Della Piana and Gage (1955), for example, found that some pupils are more concerned about feelings and personal relationships, while others are mainly achievement-oriented. Classes made up mostly of students of the first type tend to accept the teacher whom they like and reject the teacher whom they dislike on personal grounds. Classes composed of students of the second type pay less attention to teacher warmth in estimating their acceptance or rejection of certain teachers.

The point I have tried to make here is that what is important for one student is not important to another and that this is one reason why cookbook formulas for good teachers are of so little value and why teaching is inevitably something of an art. The choice of instructional methods makes a big difference for certain kinds of pupils, and a search for the "best" way to teach can succeed only when learners' intellectual *and* personality differences are taken into account. Hence, the evidence does not support the belief that successful teaching is possible only through the use of some specific methodology. A reasonable inference from existing data is that methods which provide for adaptation to individual differences, encourage student initiative, and stimulate individual and group participation are superior to methods which do not. In order for the former methods to come about, perhaps what we need first of all are flexible, "total" teachers who are as capable of planning around people as they are around ideas.

IN CONCLUSION

This paper has attempted to point out that even though there is no single best or worst kind of teacher, there are clearly distinguishable characteristics associated with "good" and "bad" teachers. There is no one *best* kind of teaching because their is no *one kind* of student. Nonetheless, there seems to be enough evidence to suggest that whether the criteria for good teaching is on the basis of student and/or peer evaluations or in terms of student achievement gains, there are characteristics of both which consistently overlap. That is, the good teacher is able to influence both student feeling and achievement in positive ways.

Who are *good* teachers? Generally speaking, they are persons who know their material and who are basically warm, responsive, flexible individuals who seem as sensitive to relationship variables as they are to cognitive variables. Second, they seem to view teaching as more than an objective presentation of facts—they also see it as a subjective, existential process of guiding a student to the threshold of his own potential for understanding.

REFERENCES:

ADORNO, T. W., E. FRENKEL-BRUNSWIK, D. J. LEVINSON, and R. N. SANFORD. *The Authoritarian Personality* (New York: Harper, 1950).

ANDERSON, H., and J. E. BREWER. *Studies of Teachers' Classroom Personalities II*, "Effects of Teachers' Dominative and Integrative Contacts on Children's Classroom Behavior," *Applied Psychological Monograph No. 8*, American Psychological Association (Stanford: Stanford University Press, June, 1946).

BARR, A. S. *Characteristic Differences in the Teaching Performance of Good and Poor Teachers of the Social Studies* (Bloomington, Ill.: Public School Publishing Co., 1929).

BIDDLE, B. J., and W. J. ELLENA, *Contemporary Research on Teacher Effectiveness* (New York: Holt, Rinehart and Winston, 1964).

BOUSEFIELD, W. A. "Student's Rating on Qualities Considered Desirable in College Professors," *School and Society*, February 24, 1940, pp. 253–256.

COGAN, M. L. "The Behavior of Teachers and the Productive Behavior of Their Pupils," *Journal of Experimental Education*, XXVII, December, 1958, pp. 89–124.

COMBS, A. W., and D. SNYGG. *Individual Behavior*, 2nd edition (New York: Harper, 1959).

COMBS, A. W. *The Professional Education of Teachers* (Boston: Allyn and Bacon, 1965).

DAVIDSON, H. H., and G. LANG. "Children's Perceptions of Their Teachers' Feelings Toward Them Related to Self-Perception, School Achievement, and Behavior," *Journal of Experimental Education*, 29, 1960, pp. 107–118.

DELLA PIANA, D. M., and N. L. GAGE. "Pupils' Values and the Validity of the Minnesota Teacher Attitude Inventory," *Journal of Educational Psychology*, XLVI, March, 1955, pp. 167–168.

FLANDERS, N. A. "Personal-Social Anxiety as a Factor in Experimental Learning Situations," *Journal of Educational Research*, XLV, October, 1951, pp. 100–110.

FLANDERS, N. A. *Teacher Influence, Pupil Attitudes and Achievement: Studies in Interaction Analysis*. Final Report, Cooperative Research Project No. 397, University of Minnesota, Minneapolis, 1960.

GAGE, N. C. Address appearing in "Proceedings," *Research Resume*, 16, California Teachers Association, Burlingame, California, 1960.

GRIMES, J. W., and W. ALLINSMITH. "Compulsivity, Anxiety, and School Achievement," *Merrill-Palmer Quarterly*, 7, 1961, pp. 247–271.

HAMACHEK, D. E. (Ed.), *The Self in Growth, Teaching, and Learning* (Englewood Cliffs, N.J.: Prentice-Hall, 1965).

HART, F. W. *Teachers and Teaching* (New York: Macmillan, 1934), pp. 131–132, 250–251.

HEIL, L. M., M. POWELL, and I. FEIFER. *Characteristics of Teacher Behavior Related to the Achievement of Children in Several Elementary Grades*, Office of Education, Cooperative Research Branch, U.S. Department of Health, Education, and Welfare, Washington, D.C., 1960.

JERSILD, A. T. *When Teachers Face Themselves*, Bureau of Publications, Teachers College, Columbia University, 1955.

JOURARD, S. M. *Personal Adjustment*, 2nd edition (New York: Macmillan, 1963).

KOUNIN, J. S., and P. V. GUMP. "The Comparative Influence of Punitive and Nonpunitive Teachers Upon Children's Concepts of School Misconduct," *Journal of Educational Psychology*, LII, February, 1961, pp. 44–49.

LEWIN, K., R. LIPPITT, and R. K. WHITE, "Patterns of Aggressive Behavior in Experimentally Created Social Climates," *Journal of Social Psychology*, Vol. 10, May, 1939, pp. 271–299.

MCKEACHIE, W. J. "Students, Groups, and Teaching Methods," *American Psychologist*, 13, 1958, pp. 580–584.

MASLOW, A. H. *Motivation and Personality* (New York: Harper, 1954).

MORSE, W. C. "Training Teachers in Life-Space-Interviewing," *American Journal of Orthopsychiatry*, 33, 1963, pp. 727–730.

PAGE, E. P. "Teacher Comments and Student Performance," *Journal of Educational Psychology*, XLIX, 1958, pp. 173–181.

REED, H. B. "Implications for Science Education of a Teacher Competence Research," *Science Education,* XLVI, December, 1962, pp. 473–486.

ROGERS, C. R. *On Becoming a Person* (Boston: Houghton-Mifflin, 1961).

RYANS, D. G. *Characteristics of Teachers: Their Description, Comparison, and Appraisal,* American Council on Education, Washington, D.C., 1960a.

RYANS, D. G. "Prediction of Teacher Effectiveness," *Encyclopedia of Educational Research,* 3rd edition (New York: Macmillan, 1960), pp. 1486–1490.

RYANS, D. G. "Research on Teacher Behavior in the Context of the Teacher Characteristics Study," in *Contemporary Research on Teacher Effectiveness,* edited by Biddle, B. J., and W. J. Ellena (New York: Holt, Rinehart and Winston, 1964), pp. 87–90.

SEARS, P. S. "The Effect of Classroom Conditions on Strength of Achievement Motive and Work Output of Elementary School Children." In press.

SIMON, D., and D. SARKOTICH. "Sensitivity Training in the Classroom," *NEA Journal,* January, 1967, pp. 12–13.

SMITH, D. E. P., R. L. WOOD, J. W. DOWNER, and A. L. RAYGOR. "Reading Improvement as a Function of Student Personality and Teaching Method," *Journal of Educational Psychology,* 47, 1956, pp. 47–59.

SMITH, H. C. *Sensitivity to People* (New York: McGraw-Hill, 1966).

SPAULDING, R. "Achievement, Creativity, and Self-Concept Correlates of Teacher-Pupil Transactions in Elementary Schools," University of Illinois, Urbana, Illinois, U.S. Office of Education Cooperative Research Project No. 1352, 1963.

STERN, G. C., "Measuring Non-Cognitive Variables in Research on Teaching," in *Handbook of Research on Teaching,* edited by N. L. Gage (Chicago: Rand McNally, 1963), p. 427.

TIEDEMAN, S. C., "A Study of Pupil-Teachers Relationships," *Journal of Educational Research,* May, 1942, pp. 657–664.

WINGO, G. MAX. "Methods of Teaching," *Encyclopedia of Educational Research,* 3rd edition, edited by Chester W. Harris (New York: Macmillan, 1960).

WISPE, L. G. "Evaluating Section Teaching Methods in the Introductory Course," *Journal of Educational Research,* 45, 1951, pp. 161–186.

WITTY, P. "An Analysis of the Personality Traits of the Effective Teacher," *Journal of Educational Research,* May, 1947, pp. 662–671.

14   Psychology and the Teaching Art*

by William James

EDITOR'S NOTE: *If you read carefully the second paragraph of this article, you will quickly see that William James (1842–1910) was a psychologist both of and beyond his time. Just as it is true that knowing about history, algebra, English, or social studies, or whatever, does not necessarily mean that you can teach these subjects, so, too, is it true that simply knowing about psychology does not guarantee that you will be a good teacher. (Or, for that matter, a good psychologist.) Professor James speaks eloquently to this point.*

As regards this subject of psychology, now, I wish at the very threshold to do what I can to dispel the mystification. So I say at once that in my humble opinion there *is* no 'new psychology' worthy of the name. There is nothing but the old psychology which began in Locke's time, plus a little physiology of the brain and senses and theory of evolution, and a few refinements of introspective detail, for the most part without adaptation to the teacher's use. It is only the fundamental conceptions of psychology which are of real value to the teacher; and they, apart from the aforesaid theory of evolution, are very far from being new.—I trust that you will see better what I mean by this at the end of all these talks.

I say moreover that you make a great, a very great mistake, if you think that psychology, being the science of the mind's laws, is something from which you can deduce definite programmes and schemes and methods of instruction for immediate schoolroom use. Psychology is a science, and teaching is an art; and sciences never generate arts directly out of themselves. An intermediary inventive mind must make the application, by using its originality.

The science of logic never made a man reason rightly, and the science of ethics (if there be such a thing) never made a man behave rightly. The most such sciences can do is to help us to catch ourselves up and check ourselves, if we start to reason or to behave wrongly; and to criticise ourselves more articulately after we have made mistakes. A science only lays down lines within which the rules of the art must fall, laws which the follower of the art must not transgress; but what particular thing he shall positively do within those lines is left exclusively to his own genius. One genius will do his work well and succeed in one way, while another succeeds as well quite differently; yet neither will transgress the lines.

The art of teaching grew up in the schoolroom, out of inventiveness and sympathetic concrete observation. Even where (as in the case of Herbart) the advancer of the art was also a psychologist, the pedagogics and the psychology ran side by side, and the former was not derived in any sense from the latter. The two were congruent, but neither was subordinate. And so everywhere the teaching must *agree* with the psychology, but need not necessarily be the only kind of teaching that would so agree; for many diverse methods of teaching may equally well agree with psychological laws.

To know psychology, therefore, is absolutely no guarantee that we shall be good teachers. To advance to that result, we must have an additional endowment altogether, a happy tact and ingenuity to tell us what definite things to say and do when the pupil is before us. That ingenuity in meeting and pursuing the pupil, that tact for the concrete situation, though they are the alpha and omega of the teacher's art, are things to which psychology cannot help us in the least.

The science of psychology, and whatever science of general pedagogics may be based on it, are in fact much like the science of war. Nothing is simpler or more definite than the principles of either. In war, all you have to do is to work your enemy into a position from which the natural obstacles prevent him from escaping if he tries to; then to fall on him in numbers superior to his own, at a moment when you have led him to think you far away; and so, with a minimum of exposure of your own troops, to hack his force to pieces, and take the remainder prisoners. Just so, in teaching, you must simply work your pupil into such a state of interest in what you are going to teach him that every other object of attention is banished from his mind; then reveal it to him so impressively that he will remember the occasion to his dying day; and finally fill him with devouring curiosity to know what the next steps in connection with the subject are. The principles being so plain, there would be nothing but victories for the masters of the science, either on the battlefield or in the schoolroom, if they did not both have to make their application to an incalculable quantity in the shape of the mind of their opponent. The mind of your own enemy, the pupil, is working away from you as keenly and eagerly as is the mind of the commander on the other side from the scientific general. Just what the respective enemies want and think, and what they know and do not know, are as hard things for the teacher as for the general to find out. Divination and perception, not psychological pedagogics or theoretic strategy, are the only helpers here.

But, if the use of psychological principles thus be negative rather than positive, it does not follow that it may not be a great use, all the same. It certainly narrows the path for experiments and trials. We know in advance, if we are psychologists, that certain methods will be wrong, so our psychology saves us from mistakes. It makes us, moreover, more clear as to what we are about. We gain confidence in respect to any method which we are using as soon as we believe that it has theory as well as practice at its back. Most of all, it fructifies our independence, and it reanimates our interest, to see our subject at two different angles,—to get a stereoscopic view, so to speak, of the youthful organism who is our enemy, and, while handling him with all our concrete tact and divination, to be able, at the same time, to represent to ourselves the curious inner elements of his mental machine. Such a complete knowledge as this of the pupil, at once intuitive and analytic, is surely the knowledge at which every teacher ought to aim.

15   Students, Groups, and Teaching Methods*

BY WILBERT J. MCKEACHIE

EDITOR'S NOTE: This paper examines in detail the intra- and interpersonal variables influencing student performance and group behavior. Do not be deluded into believing that because the research reported here has been done with college students, it bears little relevancy to high school and elementary teaching and learning. As you read, keep the following questions in mind: What kind of student is most likely to succeed in "group-centered" classes? How is anxiety related to how a student achieves in a course? If you reduce anxiety, does this insure higher performance? Is it possible to motivate students too much? How would you describe your own motivational level and anxiety? How are these related to your own performance as a student?

One of the most exciting, and frustrating, areas of applied research is research on college teaching—and particularly on the teaching of psychology.

The general psychology course at the University of Michigan is not required, but it is elected by over 90% of the undergraduates. At present the course enrolls approximately 2,700 students a year who are taught in some 55 sections varying in size from 10 to 30. Some of these sections are combined into groups of 50 to 250 for two of the four meetings a week. About 30 graduate students and faculty members are engaged in teaching in the course, and five graduate assistants are employed. This staff meets

---

*Reprinted from *The American Psychologist*, 1958, Vol. 13, No. 10, 580–584, by permission of the author and the American Psychological Association.

twice weekly in a seminar and usually develops a strong interest in teaching problems and in experimental treatment of these problems (12). An excellent research situation is thus available. With a relatively large number of sections and teachers involved, teacher and group differences can be randomized more effectively than in most educational research, and the general interest in research on the part of the teaching staff permits a high degree of control over experimental manipulations. Our research projects have thus involved a number of people. Some of the research has been carried out for doctoral dissertations, while other programs have involved several generations of graduate assistants and teaching fellows, beginning sometimes with a small-scale trial in a single section and developing into a controlled experiment involving several hundred students.

RESEARCH ON TEACHING METHODS

In 1946 the best summary of research on the teaching of psychology was that of Wolfle (19). He summarized it by quoting Longstaff's statement of 1932:

> . . . the experimental evidence submitted to the present time tends to support the general conclusion that there is little difference in student achievement in large and small classes and, also, that it makes little difference as to what method of presentation of the materials of the course is used (9, p. 33).

Our group of teaching fellows did not accept this conclusion. Strongly influenced by the research of Lewin and his colleagues, we argued a good deal about the merits of discussion teaching. Pressed by our leaders, Harold Guetzkow and Lowell Kelly, we agreed that the only way to settle our arguments was to attempt to devise measures of outcomes by which we could compare the discussion method with other methods of teaching.

Following the model of Lewin, Lippitt, and White's study of authoritarian, democratic, and laissez faire group climates (8), we set up three styles of teaching: recitation, discussion, and group tutorial. As we have previously reported, the results of that experiment did not fit our preconceptions. As compared to discussion and tutorial methods, the more autocratic recitation method proved not only to produce superior performance on the final examination, but also to produce greater interest in psychology, as measured by the election of advanced courses in psychology (7). Furthermore, students liked it better than the other methods.

During the ensuing years, we were attempting further manipulations of teaching methods, and we continued to be concerned with social psychological variables. We were particularly interested in the *power* of the group to determine its own fate and the degree of interaction between group members. Thus, in our next experiment (1, 2, 11, 13) we compared classes which differed in two major respects. One of these was in the degree of power given to the class in making group decisions about assignments, class activities, etc. The other difference was in the degree to which student-to-student interaction was encouraged. In our experimental classes the group made many group decisions, and the students were encouraged to direct their comments to each other rather than to the teacher. Decisions made by the group in the experimental classes were imposed by the instructor on the control classes. Student participation in class discussion was also encouraged in the control groups, but all interaction was mediated through the instructor. He asked questions, answered student questions, and was the focus of class activities.

As compared with our earlier experiment this experiment was more radical both in the freedom given the experimental groups and in the fact that it involved all of the students' hours in class. However, we tried to do a better job of taking into account students' need for achievement by giving them frequent checks on their progress through summaries and evaluations given in the concluding minutes of class periods.

The results of this experiment were more encouraging for advocates of group-centered methods. This time there was *no* significant difference between the two types of classes on their final examination scores, but one unique bit of qualitative evidence supported our feelings that teaching makes a difference in learning. We recorded class discussions following the showing of the film "Feeling of Rejection." The instructor took no part in these discussions. The transcripts of the discussion were evaluated by two clinical psychologists who knew nothing about the experiment. Both psychologists agreed that the group-centered class showed much more insight into the dynamics of the case and was less frightened and defensive than the instructor-centered class. The instructor-centered class tended to label the behavior of the heroine without apparent understanding of her difficulties (3).

Our conclusion that group-centered teaching tended to promote greater insight was supported by the finding of Gibb and Gibb (5) that their "participative action" method produced greater self-insight and role-flexibility than conventional teaching methods did. Like us, the instructor in the Gibb experiment gave a good deal of initial direction but gradually relinquished control.

WHAT TYPE OF PERSONALITY SUCCEEDS IN GROUP-CENTERED CLASSES?

Despite these glimmerings of encouragement, it was evident that the conglomeration of variables included under the title group-centered teaching has no great, uniform effect upon student learning. We saw two possible paths of further research. One of these was to attempt to determine more precisely the important group variables involved in group-centered teaching. The second was to investigate what student characteristics made a difference in responses to group-centered teaching. In his doctoral dissertation Joseph Patton, of our group, made a two-pronged attack upon these problems (16).

Patton felt that an important variable in group-centered classes was the students' acceptance of responsibility for learning. In his experiment he compared traditional classes to two classes in which there were no examinations, no lectures, and no assigned readings. Students in the experimental classes decided what reading they would do, what class procedures would be used, what they would hand in, and how they would be graded, so that they had even more power than had our previous experimental groups. At the end of the course, these classes, as compared to the control group, (a) felt that the course was more valuable; (b) showed greater interest in psychology; (c) tended to give more dynamic, motivational analyses of a problem of behavior.

Patton also obtained individual measures of acceptance of responsibility within the experimental classes and found that the degree to which the student accepted responsibility was positively correlated with gain in psychological knowledge, gain in ability to apply psychology, rating of the value of the course and interest in psychology. Thus the effect of giving students additional responsibility seemed to depend upon the student's readiness to accept responsibility.

But what sort of student will accept responsibility in such a course? Patton's research also investigated this question. He found that the students who liked the experimental class and assumed responsibility were likely to be independent of traditional authority figures and high in need for achievement.

ANXIETY AND TEST PERFORMANCE

In thinking about student reactions to teaching methods it was inevitable that we should be concerned about the relationship between students and faculty. Perhaps because we were young and inexperienced, we all wanted very much to be liked by our students, and we were well liked—most of the time. I say "most of the time" because all of us dreaded giving and returning tests. No matter how carefully our tests were constructed, they elicited bitter, aggressive reactions from our students. Perhaps the very fact that our students felt accepted by us enabled them to attack our tests more freely than they would have dared to in more authoritarian classes; and, because our tests tried to go beyond straight memory for facts, we probably aroused more anxiety than other examiners did.

One of our teaching fellows, Louis Berman, suggested that some of the aggression might be dissipated by permitting students to write comments on tests. So we tried this experimentally: giving half of the students answer sheets with spaces for comments; and half, standard answer sheets. Our measures of students' feelings about the tests failed to show any difference between the two groups; but, much to our surprise, the students who had the opportunity to write comments made higher scores on the test (18).

We have described elsewhere the series of experiments which followed this finding (14). The important thing was that our results held up in a series of experiments, and these experiments gave us some new ideas about student motivation in a classroom situation.

Up until this point we had thought that our big problem was to increase student motivation. Now it appeared that some of our students were already too highly motivated—at least for performance on tests. We interpreted our findings as indicating that student anxiety during classroom examinations builds up to such a point that it interferes with memory and problem solving. Reducing the stress of the examination by permitting students to write comments thus resulted in improved performance.

Just as our research on teaching methods had directed our attention to the interaction between situational variables and individual differences in motivation, here, too, we became interested in the individual differences in students' reactions to more and less stressful test situations.

In his doctoral dissertation Neil Carrier (4) investigated the manner in which individual differences in four personality variables affected performance in more and less stressful testing situations. In his "low stress" condition students had answer sheets with spaces for comments, and the test was administered in a friendly, relaxed fashion. In the "high stress" condition, the test was taken in a strange room, was administered by an austere stranger who announced that he would answer no questions during the test, and students were told that a point would be deducted for every wrong answer but that they must answer every question. In the students' words this was a "real, rugged situation."

The techniques used to increase stress were chosen with an eye on the personality dimensions Carrier intended to study. One of his variables was *need for achievement*, and the announcement of the penalty for wrong answers was specifically aimed at the person whose need for achievement is characterized by a strong fear of failure. Similarly he presumed that the person with a strong *need for affiliation* would be affected by the austere, unfriendly attitude of the proctor. Donald Smith's *permeability* dimension (17) was chosen because it is thought to involve the extent to which an individual is influenced by changes in the external situation, and the highly permeable individual is thought to be dependent upon others in decision making situations. Similarly Smith's *stability* dimension is presumed to indicate the individual's general level of anxiety, and we would expect that highly anxious individuals would be likely to "crack up" under additional stress.

As usual Carrier's results gave us some surprises. The first was that one of the most important variables determining reaction to stress in his experiment was *sex*. Women were hit much harder than men by his stress situation. Once we had Carrier's result, we could think of all sorts of reasons why it should be so—the findings of McClelland, Atkinson, and their associates on sex differences in achievement imagery (10), Guetzkow's findings of sex differences in rigidity (6), and Margaret Mead's descriptions of women's achievement conflicts (15)—but we had just never thought seriously of a sex difference before.

But the tests of the original hypothesis were also interesting. In general, *need for achievement* and *need for affiliation* failed to predict reactions to our stress situation. However, the *permeable* students were detrimentally affected by stress.

Carrier's results encouraged us to investigate other measures of fear of failure and anxiety and their relationship to performance in more and less stressful testing situations. In our next experiment half of a group of 350 students taking a test received conventional IBM answer sheets; half received answer sheets with space for comments. In addition, half of the students had received one of the tranquilizing drugs, meprobamate ("Miltown"), from a physician associated with the Institute of Mental Health Research, while the other half had received a placebo. All of the students had taken a number of tests of anxiety and of need of achievement a week prior to the examination. Thus we were able to investigate a number of relationships. One of the simplest of these was the effect of meprobamate on performance. If most students are too anxious, such a drug should improve test scores. Our results did not confirm this hypothesis. Students who actually had the Miltown reported experiencing less anxiety during the examination than did the placebo group, but they did not make better scores.

The really interesting results of the experiment were the interactions. The sex-drug interaction was significant both in its effect on performance and on anxiety, with women benefiting from the drug more than men. So once again sex turns out to be an important variable.

DISCUSSION

Motivation. At present I begin my consideration of student behavior in terms of motives. Achievement motivation would seem to be a particularly important motive for determining classroom behavior, but our results indicate that it alone is not a good predictor of achievement in our classes. It seems to me now that this is because a lot of motives are directed toward grades. Not that all students are working for *A*s—far from it. But whether a student is trying to maintain a straight A average or simply to keep eligible for the football team, grades are such universal student incentives that general motivation measures are not powerful predictors of achievement in a single, typical, college class.

Complicating our problem is the curvilinear effect of motivation on performance. As we saw in our studies of testing situations, it appears that we can push motivation too high. Up to a point, increasing motivation improves performance; but, if we try to scare some of our poorly motivated students into doing better, we may be pushing some of our more anxious students over the brink into disorganization.

Instrumental Behavior.   Since motivational measures are not sufficient to give us a complete understanding of student behavior, we must turn to a second intervening variable, which I term instrumental behavior or habit. Our students have been in school for 12 to 15 years. It is not surprising that they have developed rather strong expectations about the instrumental behaviors necessary for them to attain their desired grades. They expect the teacher's behavior and his requirements of them to fit into a particular pattern; and, when this pattern is altered, they are likely to be disturbed unless the instructor clearly indicates the instrumental behaviors now required for them to satisfy their motives.

Situational Factors.   In varying our teaching methods we are varying cues to student motives, but more important we are affecting the student's perception of the instrumental behaviors necessary if he is to satisfy his motives. In our initial Lewin-Lippitt-White-type experiment, students did well in the recitation class and liked it because the instrumental behaviors required were ones which almost all students have learned in their earlier schooling.

The importance of the power of the group in our later experiments was that it gave the students some control over the situation. Because the instrumental behaviors were chosen by the group, they were less ambiguous than in a nondirective situation and we would also expect the group to select behaviors which were within the repertoire of most members of the group.

Student-to-student interaction is important, we feel, because of its relation to interpersonal liking. By increasing liking for other group members, we counteract the threat caused by the reduced ability of students to depend upon the teacher. We suspect that this is particularly important for the more dependent students.

Thus, once again we see the importance of situational factors in affecting students' perceptions of the probability that certain instrumental behaviors will be successful.

It is in this area of expectations that differences between colleges are important. For example, students at Brooklyn College rate large classes as favorably as small classes, while students at Grinnell College rate instructors less favorably in classes over 30. I would interpret this as being due to differences in student expectations. Students in different colleges may differ greatly in the degree to which their motivation is bound up in grades, but I suspect that there is even more difference between colleges in student expectations about classroom situations.

It is not surprising that we find that sex is an important variable, since biological and cultural factors interact in differentiating men from women in consistent ways. Like other researchers, we find that women are more highly motivated, achieve more nearly up to their abilities, and are more greatly affected by changes in the classroom situation than are men.

REFERENCES:

1. BOVARD, E. W., JR. The experimental production of interpersonal affect. *J. Abnorm. Soc. Psychol.*, 1951, 46, 521–528.
2. BOVARD, E. W., JR. The psychology of classroom interaction. *J. Educ. Res.*, 1951, 45, 215–224.
3. BOVARD, E. W., JR. Clinical insight as a function of group process. *J. Abnorm. Soc. Psychol.*, 1952, 47, 534–539.
4. CARRIER, N. A. *Stress, Personality, and Performance on Course Examinations.* Unpublished doctoral thesis, University of Michigan, 1956.
5. GIBB, L. M., and GIBB, J. R. The effects of the use of "participative action" groups in a course in general psychology. *Amer. Psychologist*, 1952, 7, 247. (Abstract)
6. GUETZKOW, H. *An Analysis of the Operation of Set in Problem-Solving Behavior.* Unpublished doctoral thesis, University of Michigan, 1948.
7. GUETZKOW, H., KEELY, E. L., and MCKEACHIE, W. J. An experimental comparison of recitation, discussion, and tutorial methods in college teaching. *J. Educ. Psychol.*, 1954, 45, 193–207.
8. LIPPETT, R., and WHITE, R. K. The "social climate" of children's groups. In R. G. Barker, J. S. Kounin, and H. F. Wright, *Child Behavior and Development* (New York: McGraw-Hill, 1943). Pp. 485–508.
9. LONGSTAFF, H. P. Analysis of some factors conditioning learning in general psychology. Part I. *J. Appl. Psychol.*, 1932, 16, 9–48.
10. MCCLELLAND, D. C., ATKINSON, J. W., CLARK, R. A., and LOWELL, E. L. *The Achievement Motive* (New York: Appleton-Century-Crofts, 1953).
11. MCKEACHIE, W. J. Anxiety in the college classroom. *J. Educ. Res.*, 1951, 45, 153–160.
12. MCKEACHIE, W. J. A program for training teachers of psychology. *Amer. Psychologist*, 1951, 6, 119–121.

13. MCKEACHIE, W. J. Individual conformity to attitudes of classroom groups. *J. Abnorm. Soc. Psychol.*, 1954, 49, 282–289.
14. MCKEACHIE, W. J., POLLIE, D., and SPEISMAN, J. Relieving anxiety in classroom examinations. *J. Abnorm. Soc. Psychol.* 1955, 50, 93–98.
15. MEAD, M. *Male and Female* (New York: Mentor, 1955).
16. PATTON, J. A. *A Study of the Effects of Student Acceptance of Responsibility and Motivation on Course Behavior.* Unpublished doctoral thesis, University of Michigan, 1955.
17. SMITH, D. E. P., WOOD, R. L., DOWNER, J. W., and RAYGOR, A. L. Reading improvement as a function of students' personality and teaching methods. *J. Educ. Psychol.*, 1956, 47, 47–59.
18. TEEVAN, R., and MCKEACHIE, W. Effects on performance of different instructions in multiple-choice examinations. *Mich. Acad. Sci., Arts, Letters*, 1954, 39, 467–475.
19. WOLFLE, D. L. The first course in psychology. *Psychol. Bull.*, 1942, 39, 685–712.

16   *Personal Thoughts on Teaching and Learning**

BY CARL ROGERS

EDITOR'S NOTE: The three preceding articles have been reviews and syntheses of research related to teaching processes and classroom group behavior. None have suggested that teaching does not or cannot go on, which is in striking contrast to what you are about to read. Dr. Rogers is an eminent psychologist who has been a major force on the psychological scene for over thirty years. From his own personal experience and research he has advanced a widely accepted theory of counseling called "client-centered counseling." Whether you agree with his ideas or not, you will find it difficult to shrug this article aside. Could it be true that ". . . anything that can be taught to another person is relatively inconsequential. . . ."? Maybe. Maybe not. What do you think?

I wish to present some very brief remarks, in the hope that if they bring forth any reaction from you, I may get some new light on my own ideas.

I find it a very troubling thing to *think*, particularly when I think about my own experiences and try to extract from those experiences the meaning that seems genuinely inherent in them. At first such thinking is very satisfying, because it seems to discover sense and pattern in a whole host of discrete events. But then it very often becomes dismaying, because I

---

* From *On Becoming a Person* (Boston: Houghton Mifflin Company, 1961), Chapter 13, 275–278. Copyright ©, 1961 by Carl Rogers. Reprinted by permission of the author and the publishers.

realize how ridiculous these thoughts, which have much value to me, would seem to most people. My impression is that if I try to find the meaning of my own experience it leads me, nearly always, in directions regarded as absurd.

So in the next three or four minutes, I will try to digest some of the meanings which have come to me from my classroom experience and the experience I have had in individual and group therapy. They are in no way intended as conclusions for some one else, or a guide to what others should do or be. They are the very tentative meanings, as of April 1952, which my experience has had for me, and some of the bothersome questions which their absurdity raises. I will put each idea or meaning in a separate lettered paragraph, not because they are in any particular logical order, but because each meaning is separately important to me.

a. I may as well start with this one in view of the purposes of this conference. *My experience has been that I cannot teach another person how to teach.* To attempt it is for me, in the long run, futile.

b. *It seems to me that anything that can be taught to another is relatively inconsequential, and has little or no significant influence on behavior.* That sounds so ridiculous I can't help but question it at the same time that I present it.

c. *I realize increasingly that I am only interested in learnings which significantly influence behavior.* Quite possibly this is simply a personal idiosyncrasy.

d. *I have come to feel that the only learning which significantly influences behavior is self-discovered, self-appropriated learning.*

e. *Such self-discovered learning, truth that has been personally appropriated and assimilated in experience, cannot be directly communicated to another.* As soon as an individual tries to communicate such experience directly, often with a quite natural enthusiasm, it becomes teaching, and its results are inconsequential. It was some relief recently to discover that Søren Kierkegaard, the Danish philosopher, had found this too, in his own experience, and stated it very clearly a century ago. It made it seem less absurd.

f. As a consequence of the above, *I realize that I have lost interest in being a teacher.*

g. When I try to teach, as I do sometimes, I am appalled by the results, which seem a little more than inconsequential, because sometimes the teaching appears to succeed. When this happens I find that the results are damaging. It seems to cause the individual to distrust his own experience, and to stifle significant learning. *Hence I have come to feel that the outcomes of teaching are either unimportant or hurtful.*

h. When I look back at the results of my past teaching, the real results seem the same—either damage was done, or nothing significant occurred. This is frankly troubling.

i. As a consequence, *I realize that I am only interested in being a learner, preferably learning things that matter, that have some significant influence on my own behavior.*

j. *I find it very rewarding to learn,* in groups, in relationships with one person as in therapy, or by myself.

k. *I find that one of the best, but most difficult ways for me to learn is to drop my own defensiveness, at least temporarily, and to try to understand the way in which his experience seems and feels to the other person.*

l. *I find that another way of learning for me is to state my own uncertainties, to try to clarify my puzzlements, and thus get closer to the meaning that my experience actually seems to have.*

m. This whole train of experiencing, and the meanings that I have thus far discovered in it, seem to have launched me on a process which is both fascinating and at times a little frightening. *It seems to mean letting my experience carry me on, in a direction which appears to be forward, toward goals that I can but dimly define, as I try to understand at least the current meaning of that experience.* The sensation is that of floating with a complex stream of experience, with the fascinating possibility of trying to comprehend its ever changing complexity.

I am almost afraid I may seem to have gotten away from any discussion of learning, as well as teaching. Let me again introduce a practical note by saying that by themselves these interpretations of my own experience may sound queer and aberrant, but not particularly shocking. It is when I realize the *implications* that I shudder a bit at the distance I have come from the commonsense world that everyone knows is right. I can best illustrate that by saying that if the experiences of others had been the same as mine, and if they had discovered similar meanings in it, many consequences would be implied.

a. Such experience would imply that we would do away with teaching. People would get together if they wished to learn.

b. We would do away with examinations. They measure only the inconsequential type of learning.

c. The implication would be that we would do away with grades and credits for the same reason.

d. We would do away with degrees as a measure of competence partly for the same reason. Another reason is that a degree marks an end or a conclusion of something, and a learner is only interested in the continuing process of learning.

e. It would imply doing away with the exposition of conclusions, for we would realize that no one learns significantly from conclusions.

I thing I had better stop there. I do not want to become too fantastic. I want to know primarily whether anything in my inward thinking as I have tried to describe it, speaks to anything in your experience of the classroom as you have lived it, and if so, what the meanings are that exist for you in *your* experience.

CHAPTER FIVE

INNOVATIONS IN INSTRUCTION

17   *Why We Need Teaching Machines**

BY B. F. SKINNER

EDITOR'S NOTE: Technological advances in education have made revolutionary inroads in recent years and among the most dramatic of these is the teaching machine. Some teachers view it as a threat, others as a godsend. Is it really possible for a machine to teach? Do students really learn? Is a teaching machine really more efficient than a live teacher? Or does it depend? If so, on what? This article by Dr. Skinner presents a strong case for why we do, indeed, need machines. Do you agree? Be sure to read the article following this for the other side of the coin.

Current suggestions for improving education are familiar to everyone. We need more and better schools and colleges. We must pay salaries which will attract and hold good teachers. We should group students according to ability. We must bring textbooks and other materials up to date, particularly in science and mathematics. And so on. It is significant that all this can be done without knowing much about teaching or learning. Those who are most actively concerned with improving education seldom discuss what is happening when a student reads a book, writes a paper, listens to a lecture, or solves a problem, and their proposals are only indirectly designed to make these activities more productive. In short, there is a general neglect of education method. (Television is no exception, for it is only a way of amplifying and extending *old* methods, together with their shortcomings.)

It is true that the psychology of learning has so far not been very helpful in education. Its learning curves and its theories of learning have not yielded greatly improved classroom practices. But it is too early to

* Reprinted from *Harvard Educational Review*, Fall, 1961, Vol. 31, 377–398, by permission of the author and the publisher.

conclude that nothing useful is to be learned about the behavior of teacher and student. No enterprise can improve itself very effectively without examining its basic processes. Fortunately, recent advances in the experimental analysis of behavior suggest that a true technology of education is feasible. Improved techniques are available to carry out the two basic assignments of education: constructing extensive repertoires of verbal and nonverbal behavior and generating that high probability of action which is said to show interest, enthusiasm, or a strong "desire to learn."

The processes clarified by an experimental analysis of behavior have, of course, always played a part in education, but they have been used with little understanding of their effects, wanted or unwanted. Whether by intention or necessity, teachers have been less given to teaching than to holding students responsible for learning. Methods are still basically aversive. The student looks, listens, and answers questions (and, incidentally, sometimes learns) as a gesture of avoidance or escape. A good teacher can cite exceptions, but it is a mistake to call them typical. The birch rod and cane are gone, but their place has been taken by equally effective punishments (criticism, possibly ridicule, failure) used in the same way: the student must learn, or else!

By-products of aversive control in education range from truancy, early dropouts, and school-vandalism to inattention, "mental fatigue," forgetting, and apathy. It does not take a scientific analysis to trace these to their sources in educational practice. But more acceptable techniques have been hard to find. Erasmus tells of an English gentleman who tried to teach his son Greek and Latin without punishment. He taught the boy to use a bow and arrow and set up targets in the shape of Greek and Latin letters, rewarding each hit with a cherry. He also fed the boy letters cut from delicious biscuits. As a result, we may assume that the boy salivated slightly upon seeing a Greek or Latin text and that he was probably a better archer; but any effect on his knowledge of Greek and Latin is doubtful.

Current efforts to use rewards in education show the same indirection. Texts garnished with pictures in four colors, exciting episodes in a scientific film, interesting classroom activities—these will make a school interesting and even attractive (just as the boy probably liked his study of Greek and Latin), but to generate specific forms of behavior these things must be related to the student's behavior in special ways. Only then will they be truly rewarding or, technically speaking, "reinforcing."

We make a reinforcing event contingent on behavior when, for example, we design a piece of equipment in which a hungry rat or monkey or chimpanzee may press a lever and immediately obtain a bit of food. Such a piece of equipment gives us a powerful control over behavior. By scheduling reinforcements, we may maintain the behavior of pressing the lever in any given strength for long periods of time. By reinforcing special kinds of responses to the lever—for example, very light or very heavy presses or those made with one hand or the other—we "shape" different forms or topographies of behavior. By reinforcing only when particular stimuli or classes of stimuli are present, we bring the behavior under the control of the environment. All these processes have been throughly investigated, and they have already yielded standard laboratory practices in manipulating complex forms of behavior for experimental purposes. They are obviously appropriate to educational design.

In approaching the problem of the educator we may begin by surveying available reinforcers. What positive reasons can we give the student for studying? We can point to the ultimate advantages of an education—to the ways of life which are open only to educated men—and the student himself may cite these to explain why he wants an education, but ultimate advantages are not contingent on behavior in ways which generate action. Many a student can testify to the result. No matter how much he may *want* to become a doctor or an engineer, say, he cannot force himself to read and remember the page of text in front of him at the moment. All notions of ultimate utility (as, for example, in economics) suffer from the same shortcoming: they do not specify effective contingencies of reinforcement.

The gap between behavior and a distant consequence is sometimes bridged by a series of "conditioned reinforcers." In the laboratory experiment just described a delay of even a fraction of a second between the response to the lever and the appearance of food may reduce the effectiveness of the food by a measurable amount. It is standard practice to let the movement of a lever produce some visual stimulus, such as a change in the illumination in the apparatus, which is then followed by food. In this way the change in illumination becomes a conditioned reinforcer which can be made immediately contingent on the response. The marks, grades, and diplomas of education are conditioned reinforcers designed to bring ultimate consequences closer to the behavior reinforced. Like prizes and medals, they represent the approval of teachers, parents, and others, and they show competitive superiority, but they are mainly effective because they signalize progress through the system—toward some ultimate advantage of, or at least freedom from, education. To this extent they bridge the gap between behavior and its remote consequences; but they are still not contingent on behavior in a very effective way.

Progressive education tried to replace the birch rod, and at the same time avoid the artificiality of grades and prizes, by bringing the reinforcers of everyday life into the schools. Such natural contingencies have a kind of guaranteed effectiveness. But a school is only a small part of the student's world, and no matter how real it may seem, it cannot provide natural reinforcing consequences for all the kinds of behavior which education is to set up. The goals of progressive education were shifted to conform to this limitation, and many worthwhile assignments were simply abandoned.

Fortunately, we can solve the problem of education without discovering or inventing additional reinforcers. We merely need to make better use of those we have. Human behavior is distinguished by the fact that it is affected by small consequences. Describing something with the right word is often reinforcing. So is the clarification of a temporary puzzlement, or the solution of a complex problem, or simply the opportunity to move forward after completing one stage of an activity. We need not stop to explain *why* these things are reinforcing. It is enough that, when properly contingent upon behavior, they provide the control we need for successful educational design. Proper contingencies of reinforcement, however, are not always easily arranged. A modern laboratory for the study of behavior contains elaborate equipment designed to control the environment of individual organisms during many hours or days of continuous study. The required conditions and changes in conditions cannot be arranged by hand, not only because the experimenter does not have the time and energy, but because many contingencies are too subtle and precise to be arranged without instrumental help. The same problem arises in education.

Consider, for example, the temporal patterning of behavior called "rhythm." Behavior is often effective only if properly timed. Individual differences in timing, ranging from the most awkward to the most skillful performances, affect choice of career and of artistic interests and participation in sports and crafts. Presumably a "sense of rhythm" is worth teaching, yet practically nothing is now done to arrange the necessary contingencies of reinforcement. The skilled typist, tennis player, lathe operator, or musician is, of course, under the influence of reinforcing mechanisms which generate subtle timing, but many people never reach the point at which these natural contingencies can take over.

A relatively simple device supplies the necessary contingencies. The student taps a rhythmic pattern in unison with the device. "Unison" is specified very loosely at first (the student can be a little early or late at each tap) but the specifications are slowly sharpened. The process is repeated for various speeds and patterns. In another arrangement, the student echoes rhythmic patterns sounded by the machine, though not in unison, and again the specifications for an accurate reproduction are progressively sharpened. Rhythmic patterns can also be brought under the control of a printed score.

Another kind of teaching machine generates sensitivity to properties of the environment. We call an effective person "discriminating." He can tell the difference between the colors, shapes, and sizes of objects, he can identify three-dimensional forms seen from different aspects, he can find patterns concealed in other patterns, he can identify pitches, intervals, and musical themes and distinguish between different tempos and rhythms— and all of this in an almost infinite variety. Subtle discriminations of this sort are as important in science and industry and in everyday life as in identifying the school of a painter or the period of a composer.

The ability to make a given kind of discrimination can be taught. A pigeon, for example, can be *made* sensitive to the color, shape, and size of objects, to pitches, and rhythms, and so on—simply by reinforcing it when it responds in some arbitrary way to one set of stimuli and extinguishing responses to all others. The same kinds of contingencies of reinforcement are responsible for human discriminative behavior. *The remarkable fact is that they are quite rare in the environment of the average child.* True, children are encouraged to play with objects of different sizes, shapes, and colors, and are given a passing acquaintance with musical patterns; but they are seldom exposed to the precise contingencies needed to build subtle discriminations. It is not surprising that most of them move into adulthood with largely undeveloped "abilities."

The number of reinforcements required to build discriminative behavior in the population as a whole is far beyond the capacity of teachers. Too many teachers would be needed, and many contingencies are too subtle to be mediated by even the most skillful. *Yet relatively simple machines will suffice.* [One such apparatus] is adapted from research on lower organisms. It teaches an organism to discriminate selected properties of stimuli while "matching to sample." Pictures or words are projected on translucent windows which respond to a touch by closing circuits. A child can be made to "look at the sample" by reinforcing him for pressing the top window. An adequate reinforcement for this response is simply the appearance of material in the lower windows, from which a choice is to be made.

The child identifies the material which corresponds to the sample in some prescribed way by pressing one of the lower windows, and he is then reinforced again—possibly simply because a new set of materials now appears on the windows. If he presses the wrong window, all three choices disappear until the top window has been pressed again—which means until he has again looked at the sample. Many other arrangements of responses and reinforcements are, of course, possible. In an auditory version, the child listens to a sample pattern of tones and then explores other samples to find a match.

If devices similar to these were generally available in our nursery schools and kindergartens, our children would be far more skillful in dealing with their environments. They would be more productive in their work, more sensitive to art and music, better at sports, and so on. They would lead more effective lives. We cannot assert all this with complete confidence on the present evidence, but there is no doubt whatsoever *that the conditions needed to produce such a state of affairs are now lacking.* In the light of what we know about differential contingencies of reinforcement, the world of the young child is shamefully impoverished. And only machines will remedy this, for the required frequency and subtlety of reinforcement cannot otherwise be arranged.

The teacher is, of course, at a disadvantage in teaching skilled and discriminative behavior because such instruction is largely nonverbal. It may be that the methods of the classroom, in which the teacher is said to "communicate" with the student, to "impart information," and to build "verbal abilities," are better adapted to standard subject matters, the learning of which is usually regarded as more than the acquisition of forms of behavior or of environmental control. Yet a second look may be worthwhile. Traditional characterizations of verbal behavior raise almost insuperable problems for the teacher, and a more rigorous analysis suggests another possibility. We can define terms like "information," "knowledge," and "verbal ability" by reference to the behavior from which we infer their presence. *We may then teach the behavior directly.* Instead of "transmitting information to the student" we may simply set up the behavior which is taken as a sign that he possesses information. Instead of teaching a "knowledge of French" we may teach the behavior from which we infer such knowledge. Instead of teaching "an ability to read" we may set up the behavioral repertoire which distinguishes the child who knows how to read from one who does not.

To take the last example, a child reads or "shows that he knows how to read" by exhibiting a behavioral repertoire of great complexity. He finds a letter or word in a list on demand; he reads aloud; he finds or identifies objects described in a text; he rephrases sentences; he obeys written instructions; he behaves appropriately to described situations; he reacts emotionally to described events; and so on, in a long list. He does none of this before learning to read and all of it afterwards. To bring about such a change is an extensive assignment, and it is tempting to try to circumvent it by teaching something called "an ability to read" from which all these specific behaviors will flow. But this has never actually been done. "Teaching reading" is always directed toward setting up specific items in such a repertoire.

It is true that parts of the repertoire are not independent. A student may acquire some kinds of responses more readily for having acquired others, and he may for a time use some in place of others (for example, he may follow written directions not by responding directly to a text but by following his own spoken instructions as he reads the text aloud). In the long run all parts of the repertoire tend to be filled in, not because the student is rounding out an ability to read, but simply because all parts are in their several ways useful. They all continue to be reinforced by the world at large after the explicit teaching of reading has ceased.

Viewed in this way, reading can also be most effectively taught with instrumental help. A pupil can learn to distinguish among letters and groups of letters in an alphabet simply as visual patterns in using the device and procedures just described. He can be taught to identify arbitrary correspondences (for example, between capitals and lower-case letters, or between handwritten and printed letters) in a more complex type of stimulus control which is within reach of the same device. With a phonographic attachment, correspondences between printed letters and sounds, between sounds and letters, between words and sounds, between sounds and printed words, and so on, can be set up. (The student could be taught all of this without pronouncing a word, and it is possible that he would learn good pronunciation more quickly if he had first done so.)

The same device can teach correspondences between words and the properties of objects. The pupil selects a printed or spoken word which corresponds in the language to, say, a pictured object or another printed or spoken word. These semantic correspondences differ in important respects from formal matches, but the same processes of programming and rein-forcement can—indeed, must—be used. Traditional ways of teaching reading establish all these repertoires, but they do so indirectly and, alas, inefficiently. In "building a child's need to read," in motivating "his mental readiness," in "sharing information," and so on, the teacher arranges, sometimes almost surreptitiously, many of the contingencies just listed, and these are responsible for whatever is learned. An explicit treatment clarifies the program, suggests effective procedures, and guarantees a coverage which is often lacking with traditional methods. Much of what is called reading has not been covered, of course, but it may not need to be taught, for once these basic repertoires have been established, the child begins to receive automatic reinforcement in responding to textual material.

The same need for a behavioral definition arises in teaching other verbal skills (for example, a second language) as well as the traditional subjects of education. In advancing to that level, however, we must transcend a limitation of the device [described]. The student can *select* a response without being able to speak or write, but we want him to learn to *emit* the response, since this is the kind of behavior which he will later find most useful. The emission of verbal behavior is taught by another kind of machine. A frame of textual material appearing in the square opening is incomplete: in place of certain letters or figures there are holes. Letters or figures can be made to appear in these holes by moving sliders (a keyboard would be an obvious improvement). When the material has been completed, the student checks his response by turning a crank. The machine senses the settings of the sliders and, if they are correct, moves a new frame of material into place, the sliders returning to their home position. If the response is wrong, the sliders return home, and a second setting must be made.

The machine can tell the student he is wrong without telling him what is right. This is an advantage, but it is relatively costly. Moreover, correct behavior is rather rigidly specified. Such a machine is probably suitable only for the lower grades. A simpler and cheaper procedure, with greater flexibility, is to allow the student to compare his written response with a revealed text. [A device using this principle exists.] It is suitable for verbal instruction beyond the lower primary grades—that is, through junior high school, high school, and college, and in industrial and profes-sional education. Programmed material is stored on fan-folded paper tapes. One frame of material, the size of which may be varied with the nature of the material, is exposed at a time. The student writes on a separate paper strip. He cannot look at unauthorized parts of the material without recording the fact that he has done so, because when the machine has been loaded and closed, it can be opened only by punching the strip of paper.

The student sees printed material in the large window at the left. This may be a sentence to be completed, a question to be answered, or a problem to be solved. He writes his response in an uncovered portion of a paper strip at the right. He then moves a slider which covers the response he has written with a transparent mask and uncovers additional material in the larger opening. This may tell him that his response is wrong without telling him what is right. For example, it may list a few of the commonest errors. If the response he wrote is among them, he can try again on a newly uncovered portion of the paper strip. A further operation of the machine covers his second attempt and uncovers the correct response. The student records a wrong response by punching a hole alongside it, leaving a record for the instructor who may wish to review a student's performance, and operating a counter which becomes visible at the end of the set. Then the student records the number of mistakes he has made and may compare it with a par score for the set.

Exploratory research in schools and colleges indicates that what is now taught by teacher, textbook, lecture, or film can be taught in half the time with half the effort by a machine of this general type.[1] One has only to see students at work to understand why this is a conservative estimate. The student remains active. If he stops, the program stops (in marked contrast with classroom practice and educational television); but there is no compulsion for he is not inclined to stop. Immediate and frequent reinforcement sustains a lively interest. (The interest, incidentally, outlasts any effect of novelty. Novelty may be relevant to interest, but the material in the machine is always novel.) Where current instructional procedures are highly efficient, the gain may not be so great. In one experiment[2] involving industrial education there was approximately a 25% saving in the time required for instruction, something of the order of a 10% increase in retention, and about 90% of the students preferred to study by machine. In general, the student generally likes what he is doing; he makes no effort to escape—for example, by letting his attention wander. He need not force himself to work and is usually free of the feeling of effort generated by aversive control. He has no reason to be anxious about impending examinations, for none are required. Both he and his instructor know where he stands at all times.

No less important in explaining the success of teaching machines is the fact that each student is free to proceed at his own rate. Holding students together for instructional purposes in a class is probably the greatest source of inefficiency in education. Some efforts to mechanize instruction have missed this point. A language laboratory controlled from a central console presupposes a group of students advancing at about the same rate, even though some choice of material is permitted. Television in education has made the same mistake on a colossal scale. A class of twenty or thirty students moving at the same pace is inefficient enough, but what must we say of all the students in half a dozen states marching in a similar lock step?

In trying to teach more than one student at once we harm both fast and slow learners. The plight of the good student has been recognized, but the slow learner suffers more disastrous consequences. The effect of pressure to move beyond one's natural speed is cumulative. The student who has not fully mastered a first lesson is less able to master a second. His ultimate failure may greatly exaggerate his shortcoming; a small difference in speed has grown to an immense difference in comprehension. Some of those most active in improving education have been tempted to dismiss slow students impatiently as a waste of time, but it is quite possible that many of them are capable of substantial, even extraordinary, achievements if permitted to move at their own pace. Many distinguished scientists, for example, have appeared to think slowly.

One advantage of individual instruction is that the student is able to follow a program without breaks or omissions. A member of a class moving at approximately the same rate cannot always make up for absences, and limitations of contact time between student and teacher make it necessary to abbreviate material to the point at which substantial gaps are inevitable. Working on a machine, the student can always take up where he left off or, if he wishes, review earlier work after a longer absence. The coherence of the program helps to maximize the student's success, for by thoroughly mastering one step he is optimally prepared for the next. Many years ago, in their *Elementary Principles of Education*,[3] Thorndike and Gates considered the possibility of a book "so arranged that only to him who had done what was directed on page one would page two become visible, and so on." With such a book, they felt, "much that now requires personal instruction could be managed by print." The teaching machine is, of course, such a book.

In summary, then, machine teaching is unusually efficient because (1) the student is frequently and immediately reinforced, (2) he is free to move at his natural rate, and (3) he follows a coherent sequence. These are the more obvious advantages, and they may well explain current successes. But there are more promising possibilities: the conditions arranged by a good teaching machine make it possible to apply to education what we have learned from laboratory research and to extend our knowledge through rigorous experiments in schools and colleges.

The conceptions of the learning process which underlie classroom practices have long been out of date. For example, teachers and textbooks are said to "impart information." They expose the student to verbal and nonverbal material and call attention to particular features of it, and in so doing they are said to "tell the student something." In spite of discouraging evidence to the contrary, it is still supposed that if you tell a student something, he then knows it. In this scheme, teaching is the transmission of information, a notion which, through a false analogy, has acquired undue prestige from communication engineering. Something is undoubtedly transmitted by teacher to student, for if communication is interrupted, instruction ceases; but the teacher is not merely a source from which knowledge flows into the student. We cannot necessarily improve instruction by altering the conditions of transmission—as, for example, by changing to a different sensory modality. This is a mistake made by some so-called teaching machines which, accepting our failure to teach reading, have tried to restore communication by using recorded speech. The student no longer pores over a book, as in the traditional portrait; he stares into space with earphones on his head. For the same reasons improvements in the coding of information may not be immediately relevant.

The student is more than a receiver of information. He must take some kind of action. The traditional view is that he must "associate." The stream of information flowing from teacher to student contains pairs of items which, being close together or otherwise related, become connected in the student's mind. This is the old doctrine of the association of ideas, now strengthened by a scientific, if uncritical, appeal to conditioned reflexes; two things occurring together in experience somehow become connected so that one of them later reminds the student of the other. The teacher has little control over the process except to make sure that things occur together often and that the student pays attention to them—for example, by making the experiences vivid or, as we say, memorable. Some devices called teaching machines are simply ways of presenting things together in ways which attract attention. The student listens to recorded speech, for example, while looking at pictures. The theory is that he will associate these auditory and visual presentations.

But the action demanded of the student is not some sort of mental association of contiguous experiences. It is more objective and, fortunately, more controllable than that. To acquire behavior, *the student must engage in behavior*. This has long been known. The principle is implied in any philosophy of "learning by doing." But it is not enough simply to acknowledge its validity. Teaching machines provide the conditions needed to apply the principle effectively.

Only in the early stages of education are we mainly interested in establishing *forms* of behavior. In the verbal field, for example, we teach a child to speak, eventually with acceptable accent and pronunciation, and later to write and spell. After that, topography of behavior is assumed; the student can speak and write and must now learn to do so appropriately— that is, he must speak or write in given ways under given circumstances. How he comes to do so is widely misunderstood. Education usually begins by establishing so-called formal repertoires. The young child is taught to "echo" verbal behavior in the sense of repeating verbal stimuli with reasonable accuracy. A little later he is taught to read—to emit verbal behavior under the control of textual stimuli. These and other formal repertoires are used in later stages of instruction to evoke new responses without "shaping" them.

In an important case of what we call instruction, control is simply transferred from so-called formal to thematic stimuli. When a student learns to memorize a poem, for example, it is clearly inadequate to say that by reading the poem he presents to himself its various parts contiguously and then associates them. He does not simply read the poem again and again until he knows it. (It is possible that he could never learn the peom in that way.) Something else must be done, as anyone knows who has memorized a poem from the text. The student must make tentative responses while looking away from the text. He must glance at the text from time to time to provide fragmentary help in emitting a partially learned response. If a recalled passage makes sense, it may provide its own automatic confirmation, but if the passage is fragmentary or obscure, the student must confirm the correctness of an emitted response by referring to the text after he has emitted it.

A teaching machine facilitates this process. It presents the poem line by line and asks the student to read it. The text is then "vanished"—that is, it becomes less and less clear or less and less complete in subsequent presentations. Other stimuli (arising from the student's own behavior in this case) take over. In one procedure a few unimportant letters are omitted in the first presentation. The student reads the line without their help and indicates his success by writing down the omitted letters, which are confirmed by the machine. More of the line is missing when it again appears, but because he has recently responded to a fuller text, the student can nevertheless read it correctly. Eventually, no textual stimulus remains, and he can "recite" the poem.

(If the reader wishes to try this method on a friend or member of his family without a machine, he may do so by writing the poem on a chalk board in a clear hand, omitting a few unimportant letters. He should ask his subject to read the poem aloud but to make no effort to memorize it. He should then erase another selection of letters. He will have to guess at how far he can go without interfering with his subject's success on the next reading, but under controlled conditions this could be determined for the average student quite accurately. Again the subject reads the poem aloud, making no effort to memorize, though he may have to make some effort to recall. Other letters are then erased and the process repeated. For a dozen lines of average material, four or five readings should suffice to eliminate the text altogether. The poem can still be "read.")

Memorized verbal behavior is a valuable form of knowledge which has played an important role in classical education. There are other, and generally more useful, forms in which the same processes are involved. Consider, for example, a labeled picture. To say that such an instructional

device "tells the student the name of the pictured object" is highly ellipti-
cal—and dangerous if we are trying to understand the processes involved.
Simply showing a student a labeled picture is no more effective than
letting him read a poem. He must take some sort of action. As a formal
stimulus, the label evokes a verbal response, not in this case in the presence
of other verbal behavior on the part of the student, but in the presence of
the picture. The control of the response is to pass from the label to the
picture; the student is to give the name of the pictured object without
reading it.

The steps taken in teaching with labeled pictures can also be arranged
particularly well with a machine. Suppose we are teaching medical-school
anatomy at the textbook level. Certain labeled charts represent what is to
be learned in the sense that the student will eventually (1) give the names
of indicated parts and describe relations among them and (2) be able to
point to, draw, or construct models of parts, or relations among them, given
their names. To teach the first of these, we induce the student to describe
relations among the parts shown on a fully labeled chart. One effect of
this is that he executes the verbal behavior at issue—he writes the names of
the parts. More important, he does this while, or just after, looking at
corresponding pictured details. He will be able to write the names again
while looking at a chart which shows only incomplete names, possibly only
initial letters. Finally, he will be able to supply the complete names of parts
identified only by number on still another chart. His verbal responses have
passed from the control of textual stimuli to that of pictured anatomical
details. Eventually, as he studies a cadaver, the control will pass to the
actual anatomy of the human body. In this sense he then "knows the
names of the parts of the body and can describe relations among them."

([A device may be] designed to skip one or two steps in "vanishing"
textual stimuli. A fully labeled chart may be followed by a merely
numbered one. The student writes the name corresponding to a number in
the first space. If he cannot do this, he operates the machine to uncover,
not merely some indication that he is right or wrong, but additional help—
say, a few letters of the correct response.)

Learning a poem or the names of pictured objects is a relatively
straight-forward task. More complex forms of knowledge require other
procedures. At an early point, the main problem becomes that of analyzing
knowledge. Traditionally, for example, something called "a knowledge of
French" is said to permit the student who possesses it to do many things.
One who possesses it can (1) repeat a French phrase with a good accent,
(2) read a French text in all the senses of reading listed above, (3) take
dictation in French, (4) find a word spoken in French on a printed list,
(5) obey instructions spoken in French, (6) comment in French upon
objects or events, (7) give orders in French, and so on. If he also "knows
English," he can give the English equivalents of French words or phrases
or the French equivalents of English words or phrases.

The concept of "a knowledge of French" offers very little help to the would-be teacher. As in the case of reading, we must turn to the behavioral repertoires themselves, for these are all that have ever been taught when education has been effective. The definition of a subject matter in such terms may be extraordinarily difficult. Students who are "competent in first-year college physics," for example, obviously differ from those who are not—but in what way? Even a tentative answer to that question should clarify the problem of teaching physics. It may well do more. In the not-too-distant future much more general issues in epistemology may be approached from the same direction. It is possible that we shall fully understand the nature of knowledge only after having solved the practical problems of imparting it.

Until we can define subject matters more accurately and until we have improved our techniques of building verbal repertoires, writing programs for teaching machines will remain something of an art. This is not wholly satisfactory, but there is some consolation in the fact that an impeccable authority on the excellence of a program is available. The student himself can tell the programmer where he has failed. By analyzing the errors made by even a small number of students in a pilot study, it is usually possible to work a great improvement in an early version of a program. ([A machine may be] designed to supply the necessary feedback to the programmer in a convenient form. When a student punches an error, he marks the back of the printed material, which eventually carries an item-by-item record of the success or failure of the programmer. This is obviously valuable during the experimental stages of programming, but it will also be desirable when machines are widely used in schools and colleges, since publishers can then periodically call in programs to be studied and improved by their authors. The information supplied might be compared to a record showing the percentage of students who have misunderstood each sentence in a text.)

The teaching machine [described above] falls far short of the "electronic classrooms" often visualized for the schools and colleges of the future. Many of these, often incorporating small computers, are based on misunderstandings of the learning process. They are designed to duplicate current classroom conditions. When instruction is badly programmed, a student often goes astray, and a teacher must come to his rescue. His mistakes must be analyzed and corrected. This may give the impression that instruction is largely a matter of correcting errors. If this were the case, an effective machine would, indeed, have to follow the student into many unprofitable paths and take remedial action. But under proper programming nothing of this sort is required. It is true that a relatively important function of the teacher will be to follow the progress of each student and to suggest collateral material which may be of interest, as well as to outline further studies, to recommend changes to programs of different levels of difficulty, and so on, and to this extent a student's course of study will show "branching." But changes in level of difficulty or in the character of the subject need not be frequent and can be made as the student moves from one set of material to another.

Teaching machines based on the principle of "multiple choice" also often show a misunderstanding of the learning process. When multiple-choice apparatuses were first used, the organism was left to proceed by "trial and error." The term does not refer to a behavioral process but simply to the fact that contingencies of reinforcement were left to chance: some responses happened to be successful and others not. Learning was not facilitated or accelerated by procedures which increased the probability of successful responses. The results, like those of much classroom instruction, suggested that errors were essential to the learning process. But when material is carefully programmed, both subhuman and human subjects can learn while making few errors or even none at all. Recent research by Herbert S. Terrace,[4] for example, has shown that a pigeon can learn to discriminate colors practically without making mistakes. The control exerted by color may be passed, *via* a vanishing technique, to more difficult properties of stimuli—again without error. Of course we learn something from our mistakes—for one thing, we learn not to make them again—but we *acquire* behavior in other ways.

The teaching machines of S. J. Pressey,[5] the first psychologist to see the "coming industrial revolution in education," were mechanical versions of self-scoring test forms, which Pressey and his students also pioneered. They were not designed for programmed instruction in the present sense. The student was presumed to have studied a subject before coming to the machine. By testing himself, he consolidated what he had already partially learned. For this purpose a device which evaluated the student's selection from an array of multiple-choice items was appropriate. For the same purpose multiple-choice material can, of course, be used in all the machines described above. But several advantages of programmed instruction are lost when such material is used in straightforward instruction.

In the first place, the student should *construct* rather than *select* a response, since this is the behavior he will later find useful. Secondly, he should advance to the level of being able to emit a response rather than merely recognize a given response as correct. This represents a much more considerable achievement, as the difference between the sizes of reading and writing vocabularies in a foreign language demonstrates. Thirdly, and more important, multiple-choice material violates a basic principle of good programming by inducing the student to engage in erroneous behavior. Those who have written multiple-choice tests know how much time, energy, and ingenuity are needed to construct plausible wrong answers. (They must be plausible or the test will be of little value.) In a multiple-choice *test,* they may do no harm, since a student who has already learned the right answer may reject wrong answers with ease and possibly with no undesirable side-effects. The student who is *learning,* however, can scarcely avoid trouble. Traces of erroneous responses survive in spite of the correction of errors or the confirmation of a right answer. In multiple-choice material designed to teach "literary appreciation," for example, the student is asked to consider three or four plausible paraphrases of a passage in a poem and to identify the most acceptable. But as the student reads and considers inacceptable paraphrases, the very processes which the poet himself used in making his poem effective are at work to destroy it. Neither the vigorous correction of wrong choices nor the confirmation of a right choice will free the student of the verbal and nonverbal associations thus generated.

Scientific subjects offer more specific examples. Consider an item such as the following, which might be part of a course in high school physics:

> As the pressure of a gas increases, volume decreases. This is because:
> (a) the space between the molecules grows smaller
> (b) the molecules are flattened
> (c) etc. . . .

Unless the student is as industrious and as ingenious as the multiple-choice programmer, it will probably not have occurred to him that molecules may be flattened as a gas is compressed (within the limits under consideration). If he chooses item (b) and is corrected by the machine, we may say that he "has learned that it is wrong," but this does not mean that the sentence will never occur to him again. And if he is unlucky enough to select the right answer first, his reading of the plausible but erroneous answer will be corrected only "by implication"—an equally vague and presumably less effective process. In either case, he may later find himself recalling that "somewhere he has read that molecules are flattened when a gas is compressed." And, of course, somewhere he has.

Multiple-choice techniques are appropriate when the student is to learn to compare and choose. In forming a discrimination . . . an organism must be exposed to at least two stimuli, one of which may be said to be wrong. Similarly, in learning to "troubleshoot" equipment there may be several almost equally plausible ways of correcting a malfunction. Games offer other examples. A given hand at bridge may justify several bids or plays, no one of which is wholly right and all the others wrong. In such cases, the student is to learn the most expedient course to be taken among a natural array of possibilities. This is not true in the simple acquisition of knowledge—particularly verbal knowledge—where the task is only rarely to discriminate among responses in array. In solving an equation, reporting a fact of history, restating the meaning of a sentence, or engaging in almost any of the other behavior which is the main concern of education, the student is to *generate* responses. He may generate and reject, but only rarely will he generate a set of responses from which he must then make a choice.

It may be argued that machines which provide for branching and decision-making are designed to teach more than verbal repertoires—in particular, that they will teach thinking. There are strategies in choosing from an array, for example, which require kinds of behavior beyond the mere emission of correct responses. We may agree to this without questioning the value of knowledge in the sense of a verbal repertoire. (The distinction is not between rote and insightful learning, for programmed instruction is especially free of rote memorizing in the etymological sense of wearing down a path through repetition.) If an "idea" or "proposition" is defined as something which can be expressed in many ways, then it may be taught by teaching many of these "ways." What is learned is more likely to generalize to comparable situations than a single syntactical form, and generalization is what distinguishes so-called deeper understanding.

But not all thinking is verbal. There are, first of all, alternative, parallel nonverbal repertoires. The mathematician begins with a verbal problem and ends with a verbal solution, but much of his intervening behavior may be of a different nature. The student who learns to follow or construct a proof entirely by manipulating symbols may not engage in this kind of thinking. Similarly, a merely verbal knowledge of physics, as often seen in the student who has "memorized the text," is of little interest to the serious educator. Laboratories and demonstrations sometimes supply contingencies which build some nonverbal knowledge of physics. Special kinds of teaching machines could help, for machines are not only not confined to verbal instruction, they may well make it possible to reduce the emphasis on verbal communication between teacher and student.

A more clear-cut example of the distinction between verbal and nonverbal thinking is musical composition. The composer who "thinks musically" does more than perform on an instrument or enjoy music. He also does more than use musical notation. In some sense he "thinks" pitches, intervals, melodies, harmonic progressions, and so on. It should not surprise us that individuals differ greatly in their "abilities" to do this, since the necessary contingencies are in very short supply. One might attack the problem by setting up an explicit kinesthetic repertoire in which "thinking a pitch" takes the form of identifying a position on a keyboard. A device which arranges the necessary contingencies is under development. With its help we may discover the extent to which students can in general learn (and at what ages they can learn most effectively) to strike a key which produces a tone which has just been heard. Similar devices might generate important forms of nonverbal mathematical behavior or the behavior exhibited, say, by an inventor conceiving of a device in three dimensions, as well as creative repertoires in other forms of art. Here is an extraordinary challenge to the technology of instrumentation.

There is another sense in which the student must learn to think. Verbal and nonverbal repertoires may prepare him to behave in effective ways, but he will inevitably face novel situations in which he cannot at first respond appropriately. He may solve such problems, not by exercising some mental ability, but by altering either the external situation or the relative probabilities of parts of his own repertoire. In this way he may increase the probability of an adequate response.

In this sense, thinking consists of a special repertoire which we may call self-management. For example, the student may alter the extent to which the environment affects him by "attending" to it in different ways. As one step in teaching thinking we must teach effective attending. The phrase "Pay attention!" is as common on the lips of teachers as "Open, please" on those of dentists—and for much the same reason: both phrases set up working conditions. The student may pay attention to avoid punishment and in doing so may learn to pay attention, but where aversive sanctions have been given up, teachers have resorted to attracting and holding attention. The techniques of the publication and entertainment industries are extensively invoked. Primers are usually decorated with colored pictures, and high school textbooks are sometimes designed to resemble picture magazines. Films dramatize subject matters in competition with noneducational films and television.

Attention which is captured by attractive stimuli must be distinguished from attention which is "paid." Only the latter must be learned. Looking and listening are forms of behavior, and they are strengthened by reinforcement. A pigeon can learn to match colors, for example, only if it "pays attention to them." The experimenter makes sure that it does so, not by attracting its attention, but by reinforcing it for looking. Similarly, a well-taught student pays attention to sentences, diagrams, samples of recorded speech and music, and so on, not because they are attractive but because something interesting occasionally happens *after* he has paid attention.

Most audio-visual devices fail to teach attention because they stimulate the student *before* he looks or listens closely. No matter how well a four-colored text or a dramatically filmed experiment in physics attracts attention, it prepares the student only for comics, advertising, picture magazines, television programs, and other material which is *interesting on its face*. What is wanted is an adult who, upon seeing a page of black-and-white text, will read it because it may *prove* interesting. Unfortunately, the techniques associated with captured and paid attention are incompatible. Whenever a teacher attracts the attention of a student, he deprives him of an opportunity to learn to pay attention. Teaching machines, with their control over the consequences of action, can make sure that paying attention will be effectively reinforced.

Another activity associated with thinking is studying—not merely looking at a text and reading it but looking and reading *for the sake of future action*. Suppose we show a child a picture and later, in the absence of the picture, reinforce him generously for correct answers to questions about it. If he has done nothing like this before, he will probably not be very successful. If we then show him another picture, he may begin to behave in a different way: he may engage in behavior which will increase the probability that he will later answer questions correctly. It will be to his advantage (and to ours as educators) if this kind of behavior is taught rather than left to chance. We teach a student "how to study" when we teach him to take notes, to rehearse his own behavior, to test himself, to organize, outline, and analyze, to look for or construct mnemonic patterns, and so on. Some of these behaviors are obvious, but others are of more subtle dimensions and admittedly hard to teach. Machines have an advantage in maintaining the contingencies required for indirect or mediated reinforcement.

Other aspects of thinking, including the solution of personal problems, can also be analyzed and directly programmed. This is not current practice, however. Students are most often "taught to think" simply by thrusting them into situations in which already established repertoires are inadequate. Some of them modify their behavior or the situation effectively and come up with solutions. They may have learned, but they have not necessarily been taught, how to think.

Logicians, mathematicians, and scientists have often tried to record and understand their own thinking processes, but we are still far from a satisfactory formulation of all relevant behaviors. Much remains to be learned about how a skillful thinker examines a situation, alters it, samples his own responses with respect to it, carries out specific verbal manipulations appropriate to it, and so on. It is quite possible that we cannot teach thinking adequately until all this has been analyzed. Once we have specified the behavior, however, we have no reason to suppose that it will then be any less adaptable to programmed instruction than simple verbal repertoires.

Teaching machines and the associated practices of programmed instruction will have proved too successful if their practical consequences are allowed to overshadow their promise for the future. We need teaching machines to help solve a very pressing problem, but we also need them to utilize our basic knowledge of human behavior in the design of entirely new educational practices.

Teaching machines are an example of the technological application of basic science. It is true that current machines might have been designed in the light of classroom experience and common sense, and that explanations of why they are effective can be paraphrased in traditional terms. The fact remains that more than half a century of the self-conscious examination of instructional processes had worked only moderate changes in educational practices. The laboratory study of learning provided the confidence, if not all the knowledge, needed for a successful instrumental attack on the *status quo*. Traditional views may not have been actually wrong, but they were vague and were not entertained with sufficient commitment to work substantial technological changes.

As a technology, however, education is still immature as we may see from the fact that it defines its goals in terms of traditional achievements. Teachers are usually concerned with reproducing the characteristics and achievements of already educated men. When the nature of the human organism is better understood, we may begin to consider not only what man has already shown himself to be, but what he may become under carefully designed conditions. The goal of education should be nothing short of the fullest possible development of the human organism. An experimental analysis of behavior, carried out under the advantageous conditions of the laboratory, will contribute to progress toward the goal. So will practical experiments conducted in schools and colleges with the help of adequate instrumentation.

FOOTNOTES:

[1] Under the direction of Allen Calvin of Hollands College, an 8th grade class in the Roanoke School System completed all the work of a 9th grade class in algebra in one term. Test scores were comparable with a normal 9th grade performance, and a test nine months later showed a retention of at least 90% of the material learned.

[2] More recent results with the same material improved in the light of the earlier experiment were reported by J. L. Hughes and W. J. McNamara at the Annual Meeting of the American Psychological Association in New York, September, 1961. Their work concerned the use of programmed texts in industrial education.

[3] Thorndike, Edward, and Gates, Arthur. Elementary Principles of Education. (New York: B. Macmillan Co., 1929).

[4] Terrace, Herbert S. Discrimination Learning With and Without Errors (unpublished Ph.D. Dissertation, Department of Psychology, Harvard University, 1961).

[5] Pressey, S. J. A simple apparatus which gives tests and scores—and teaches. School and Society, 1926, 23, 373–376. This article and other articles concerning teaching machines by S. J. Pressey are included in Lumsdaine, A. A., and Glaser, Robert (eds.), Teaching Machines and Programmed Learning: A Source Book (Washington, D.C.: National Education Association, 1960).

18   Teaching Machines: A Demurrer*

BY H. T. FITZGERALD

EDITOR'S NOTE: The preceding article gave you one point of view about teaching machines. Dr. Skinner maintains that "we need teaching machines to help solve a very pressing problem." A quite different point of view is taken in this paper and Mr. Fitzgerald is frank to admit that he finds "the thought of millions of children spending hours each day with millions of machines in millions of separate cubicles an appalling prospect." As with all things which influence human behavior in one way or another, whether teaching machines are feasible or not may depend less on what the evidence is and more on what our values are. What are your values regarding teaching machines?

There is a new force in American education, coming up fast and strong: teaching machines. A number of educators have already claimed that this innovation shows great promise in helping to solve the current national "crisis" in education. By now, most people have heard about teaching machines (programmed instruction), but there has been remarkably little public discussion about the issues involved in their use or, from what one can learn from talking to people, little private thinking.

For those who have not had any contact with one, a teaching machine is any one of a rapidly increasing variety of desk-sized devices that presents a student, first, with a printed item of information, a statement, or a fact (a "prompt") and then with a question about that information. The student

---

* Reprinted from School Review, Vol. 70 (Autumn, 1962), 247–256, by permission of The University of Chicago Press. Copyright 1962 by the University of Chicago.

answers the question by writing a word or a group of words in a space on the blank or by selecting one of a series of multiple-choice answers or by punching a key. He then presses a button or a slide to reveal the correct answer to the question and compares it with his own. If his response is the same as that revealed by the machine, he presses another button for the next prompt and question. If his answer is incorrect, he goes back to review previous steps or to a branch that tells him why his choice was incorrect. A series of several hundred to several thousand closely graduated, interlocking question-and-answer frames are required to cover a particular subject, such as elementary principles of logic or basic inorganic chemistry. The student works at his own pace but cannot proceed to a new frame until he has successfully answered the question in the preceding frame. The machine may also be equipped to time the student, to score his errors, and to compute his standing in relation to other students. The student also may simultaneously listen over earphones to recorded instructions. After he has completed the program, a new roll of paper, filmstrip, tape, or set of cards is installed in the machine for the next sequence, and the student goes on to more data, more questions, and more answers.

With various mechanical and electronic elaborations, these machines are based on a well-known principle of learning first demonstrated with laboratory animals: the conditioning of behavior through reinforcement and repetition. But instead of the rat and pigeon psychologist's pellet of food or negative electric shock, praise and the satisfaction of getting correct answers provide reinforcement for human students. Also, humans are capable of learning their way through much more complicated mazes and of memorizing an incredibly greater number of correct responses than laboratory animals are. Therefore, learning a subject like fundamentals of electricity is largely a matter of learning (or giving) a large number of correct responses to logically related sequences of questions that constitute the subject. Or, to put it in another way, once a subject has been carefully divided ("programmed") into a series of many small bits of information ("steps"), a student has only to learn by repetition and reward ("rapid and frequent reinforcement") the correct answers to a series of questions about the small bits of information. Instrumentation of the sort described here makes it possible to shape a wide variety of verbal and non-verbal behaviors of students. In short, since this is a behaviorist view, learning is conditioning, learning is behavior. Even thinking is a behavior that can be analyzed and produced to specification.

All this may sound rather surprising, presented as it is here so baldly, but it represents the learning theory of the psychologists who have developed programmed instruction. However, the companies that are now hard at work building, improving, and marketing teaching machines will not stress the conditioning aspect because of its uninspiring connotations. Rather, public school boards and educational administrators are being presented with a long list of advantages that these machines offer.

First, they will save money and help solve the teacher shortage. Even though a single machine costs several hundred dollars and hundreds of machines will be required to program a school, they will save on teachers' salaries in the long run, since one classroom teacher can supervise many more students. Students work (study) in separate booths, so that problems of discipline and cheating are greatly reduced. A missed lesson can easily be made up, and even slow learners eventually complete the course.

Advantages are also seen in the impersonal nature of machine learning, especially for the hard core who have the wrong attitudes toward schooling and the conventional classroom situation. Machines are patient; they do not shame or disparage as human teachers might do, or be perceived to do. Skinner of Harvard University, a pioneer and the most important single figure in the field, argues that "aversive" practices (failing, punishing) are one of the worst features of conventional teaching, while programmed learning is always affectively positive, since machine instruction insures mastery at every stage. Solving problems successfully encourages even poor students, and the gadgetry involved in operating the machine is said to be intrinsically interesting. When mass production reduces the cost, families of school-age children will be able to afford a teaching machine to provide an opportunity for self-instruction in the home.

A student learns more rapidly and more thoroughly from programmed courses because he is forced to concentrate on the material before him and because he gets immediate feedback on his progress. The quality of education in the schools will improve because students will be exposed to programs that reflect the methods of the nation's best teachers, rather than suffering under the possibly mediocre teachers of their own community. The time saved by both teacher and superior pupil can be used for individual counseling and creative work. The uniformity of instruction and the elimination of the factor of subjectivity in grading are also held to be advantages. Finally, in return for his greater productivity, the teacher can ask society to improve his economic position.

Like much earnest, unreflective salesmanship, some of this scarcely merits argument. Besides, with all this consensus and cheering, one feels reluctant to criticize, especially before the system has been given a fair chance to demonstrate its merits in actual operation. So let us be satisfied here with raising a few skeptical questions on the possibility of disadvantages.

Take, for example, the problem of rigidity, or lack of flexibility. Programmed learning by its nature requires plodding, step by minute step, across the expanse of a subject or sub-subject. The machines do not readily lend themselves to skimming for an over-all view, to dipping into a future chapter to anticipate development or returning to an earlier chapter to check points already made to weigh and compare information. Programmed learning also resists changes and growth of subject matter. A great deal of effort must be spent in developing any single program, and the result is a logically integrated unity. It reminds one of a piece of close hand knitting that cannot be altered anywhere once it is completed, without unraveling the whole garment. Knowledge, however, and our approach to it are dynamic and change slowly or rapidly. A live instructor can supplement his syllabus with references to recent research, critical reviews or articles, and related information from other fields. Styles change, too. Those who have worked with educational films know how quickly they become dated and how distracting this aging is to content. But because of the investment by producers and film libraries, prints are often not revised or withdrawn from circulation until they become antiquated.

Yet perhaps the worst rigidity of programmed learning is its natural tendency to infallibility. Despite all the assurances of the authors, their stance of pious open-mindedness, their denial of dogmatism, we can expect that in a short time, when the machines get out into boroughs and parishes, we will repeat the experience we have had with intelligence, aptitude, personality, and scholarship testing. When there is a choice between "A, B, C, D, or E (none of these)" and the manual says that "C" is the correct answer, there is no appeal. You may write to the organization that publishes the test, but your protest will be lost in the endless baffles of educational bureaucracy. The most you can hope for is a note expressing an "appreciation of your interest" and a promise of possible revision "at some future date, pending further research in this and related areas." Meanwhile, the machines go blindly on, scoring "C" as correct and deducting fractional points for answers marked "A, B, D, or E (none of these)."

In attempting to apply the principles of animal learning to human learning, the programmers have made a false analogy, a technical error. A word rarely has the semantic specificity of reference and effect to persons that a grain of corn or a flashing light has to laboratory animals. Yet even if the answers were completely free of error and the wording devised so as to be unambiguous and capable of only one interpretation, the single-answer approach to education remains objectionable in principle. This approach assumes that our knowledge of the world is a fixed and orderly body of facts and conclusions. It implies a concept of reality wrapped up in separate little packages and tied with string, stacked neatly on the shelves of a vast warehouse. But the task of intelligence is more than that of a warehouse employee picking stock down the aisles, more than that of a novitiate reciting a long catechism of correct answers. Education is also inquiry, insight, emergence, the development of a critical faculty and an intuition of the web of interdependent hypotheses and inferences, the structure of abstractions about the seen and the unseen that comprises our understanding of the physical world. Learning is also exploring, conceptualizing, experimenting, interacting, valuing. Reality is also process, flow, a great running together, a barely intelligible, absurd, endless poem, a brilliant light at the entrance to our cave.

Perhaps all this sounds like rhetorical arm-waving, but even on a flatly pragmatic basis the problem of content must be faced. A number of companies are now manufacturing teaching machines and are beginning to compete with one another in the same way that the textbook and audio-visual people compete. High-volume sales are important to reduce cost; and in cultivating as wide a market as possible, there will be a tendency to oversimplify subjects, to eliminate anything extraneous (and therefore connected with other subjects), to boil the day's lesson down to a few definite points that we can trust the student to carry away with him. This approach is what makes the package programs frequently used in conference training programs in industry so dull. Each problem selected is neatly resolved by a school solution. Similarly, the play for markets and the fear of offending anyone—no controversy—is what makes many textbooks and commercial educational films mediocre, infrequently stimulating.

Admittedly, the best people are now pioneering in the field of programmed learning, and they are laboring with the best of intentions. As the field grows, however, they will be supplemented by the hacks and hawkers whom we have already met in the testing companies whose sales representatives gladly offer a whole series of superficial personality traits to schools and employers so that they may determine who is introverted or extroverted, socially mature and adjusted. (Do you drive a car rather fast? Do you have a low-pitched voice? Were you bashful when you were a child? Do you like fishing?)

Moreover, in making a choice between the Apex programmed course in basic economics and the Zenith programmed course in basic economics—both of which claim to be rigorously, systematically correct—someone or some group in the local school system will have to work through the content of each to decide which is more correct. Such a comparison, interesting as it may be, will be unavailable to individual students or teachers, who can now review various available textbooks. The child will get either economics by Apex or economics by Zenith; but, because his learning is based on conditioning, he will not be able to benefit from both. And if the student does not agree with one or more of the machine's positions, it is just too bad: he cannot argue with the machine, ask it questions, or request further clarification. He will have to accept and give back the wanted answer, or it will not let him proceed with the remainder of the course. But if the child has started his education on the machines in the primary grades (as is also proposed), by the time he gets to economics he will not be in the habit of asking questions. "I'm really awfully glad I'm a Beta because . . ."

In spite of these demurrers, one can expect that teaching machines will achieve a fair amount of currency in the coming years. The cold war has enlisted education as part of our national policy (for example, the National Defense Education Act) and has provided new money along with new pressures. In this country, a typical political response to any given problem is to spend more money to solve it. But money will not increase the supply of people with good minds, at least not in the short run; and money cannot guarantee to eliminate the ambiguities, the random undependability of people. Jones, with a wide grasp of his subject matter, may not give so good a lecture as Brown, and even Brown's performance may vary in quality from day to day. Even deciding whether Brown is better than Jones requires study and the exercise of personal values and judgment, something that has not been too popular since the advent of the tenure system. Small wonder, then, that spending money for hardware—new buildings, equipment, gadgets—provides an appealing solution to the public demand for more education, while allowing the administrator to feel that he has left no stone unturned in providing the most up-to-date, the best facilities.

Efficiency and the solution of immediate, practical problems are difficult to argue against, especially in public forums. A prominent example is the gradual spread over the years of government control and surveillance in many phases of what was once considered the private life of private citizens. Each legislative act, each administrative interpretation, has been justified at the time of its inception by expediency, by the need for the efficient solution of specific problems. And by these imperceptible steps, personal freedom has been constricted. It would be no surprise, as the next possibility, during a really serious military crisis, to see the introduction of a national system of identification cards. Many salient reasons would be advanced for their need; they would greatly simplify the work of government agencies, the police, the tax people, insurance companies, and banks. Almost everyone would benefit, and what really good arguments could be offered in opposition?

In the same way, teaching machines have the magical attraction of efficiency, of solving one of the country's pressing problems, and in their own small way, they lead to the slow spread of—if not authoritarianism as such—authoritarian thinking. We are certainly a long way from state control of education, as in the USSR, but we already show tendencies toward centralization and away from pluralism, especially as we become a mass society and the problem of order, of dealing with sheer numbers of people, becomes acute.

Programmed instruction may turn out to be only a passing fad, but we have seen other movements that did not pass away. The problem of scholarship and college-entrance testing, for example, has already been largely turned over to the IBM scoring machines. Teaching machines are admittedly based on the theory of reinforcement, of rote learning, of stimulus-response, of a mechanical one question—one answer. This is an intrinsically undemocratic—worse, an anti-intellectual—theory of learning. The next step should be to strengthen "rapid and frequent reinforcement" by, let us say, a mild electric shock for incorrect answers. To this, of course, the student would voluntarily submit because he has been convinced of its efficiency, just as wholly innocent people submit to polygraph tests to most efficiently prove their innocence.

Finally, there are some of us who will find a deeper, more personal distaste for learning from a machine, from interacting with it. This is a rather quaint, almost archaically humanistic idea, but it is there, nevertheless. We spend entirely too much time with machines these days. The most prominent example is watching television as a passive substitute for an active, emotional life with real people, but other examples come to mind. The difficulty is that, taken one at a time, all our interactions with machines have some value (television is educational), but the total effect in our lives is more than the sum of its parts. Interaction with is not the same as using a machine, such as an electric drill or a vacuum cleaner, but involves being somehow part of the machine or being subjected to it. A year or so ago I attended a twenty-four-hour reading improvement course that was built around the use of an automatic projector that flashed on a screen words and sentences of varying lengths at varying speeds. When the machine is in operation, one is paced by it, with the sense of being harnessed to it. I did best when I achieved the proper mental set, by turning off conscious thinking and allowing the images direct access to a sort of blank mind.

There are many, I know, who do not experience any distaste in living among and through machines, just as there are many who feel perfectly at home with plastic furniture, synthetic flavored food, and tranquilized affect; and to such as those, of course, these remarks will have little relevance, except as an opportunity for an ascription of questionable motives. Such is the temper of the times! Nevertheless, I find the thought of millions of children spending hours each day with millions of machines in millions of separate cubicles an appalling prospect.

Perhaps an analogy will explain. One may compare the merits of paper roses with real roses, but all the good arguments, all the advantages —economy, durability, accuracy, availability, habituation, and relativity of taste—are on the side of paper roses. There's not much one can say in favor of a live rose, except to assert lamely, naively, that it is true, that it does not betray. And any good dialectician has a ready answer for that kind of romantic subjectivity. There is not much one can say for learning from a live teacher either, considering all his imperfections, or for learning in the company of other live students, considering the distractions of their greater imperfections. One can merely suggest, hope for the occasional nuances, the sparks, the candor, the possibility of sharing perceptions and intelligence and experience, the possibility of learning humanity from humans. Teaching machines only teach (condition) machines.

19   Educational Television*

BY WALTER A. WITTICH

EDITOR'S NOTE: Like teaching machines, educational television is making a significant impact in the educational enterprise. The breadth of this impact is discussed by Dr. Wittich in terms of the instructional possibilities of television, its recent educational programs, and its significance and implications for teachers. Educational television is no panacea, but when viewed as a teacher's aid and not as a teacher's replacement, it can be a useful supplementary tool.

Educational Television officially made its appearance in 1952. Since the first channel for educational broadcast purposes was assigned to Houston, Texas, public schools ten years ago, 70 educational television stations have gone on the air and others are being planned. This growth parallels the rapid increase in general television use in the United States from fewer than 5,000,000 sets in use according to the 1950 census, to 65,000,000 sets in 51,000,000 household units, as shown in the 1960 census.

THE INSTRUCTIONAL ROLE OF TV

The mention of educational television can be counted upon to start a lively discussion. At one extreme are those who say educational television can do anything better. Those who are opposed minimize or deny its

* Reprinted from *Educational Perspectives*, 1962, Vol. 1, 11–13, by permission of the author and the publisher.

usefulness. The truth of the matter is being revealed by hundreds of research studies concerned with the classroom use of educational television. Since 1955, over 400 formal and informal investigations have been made of the role and the efficiency of educational television. These studies have investigated the use of television as a master teaching device, as a means of carrying a large group instruction to hundreds or thousands of students, as a means of permitting the gifted learner to carry on independent study at his own pace and to the limits of his capacity to learn during sustained study periods. Investigations have measured educational television efficiency at the primary grade, high school, college, and adult levels, and in virtually all subject areas of the curriculum. Research results are summarized in Table 1.

This research supports several important generalizations:

1. Educational television makes it possible for large groups of students to learn as efficiently from television lessons as they can from face-to-face instruction. The comparison here is usually made between television instruction to groups as large as tens of thousands of pupils and the instructional outcomes which usually result when one teacher teaches a group of from 20 to 30 pupils. The implications of such large group instruction efficiency demand the study and attention of both professional educators and lay people.

2. Gifted pupils can learn more through television than through typical classroom instruction, and at accelerated rates, limited only by the individual's capacity and endurance.

3. Educational television makes it possible for a level of preplanning, rehearsal, and arrangement of teaching materials that is seldom possible in typical teaching situations. There are television teachers currently at work whose assignment is limited to one half-hour television lesson per day. However, a 12- to 14-hour day is barely enough time to permit the kind of endless planning, rehearsing, revising, and perfecting which typically precedes the best of educational television currently in use. With such concentrated effort, learning experiences of high quality can be provided through educational television.

The last five years have witnessed an exciting beginning of educational television research. No longer need it be argued that educational television can or cannot improve instruction. Today, rather, the basic problem is the manner in which subject areas, which lend themselves to television instruction, can best be served by television.

CURRENT EDUCATIONAL TELEVISION PROGRAMS

Under the direction of Superintendent Brish at Hagerstown, Maryland, one may witness one of the "oldest" research projects in this new medium. Begun six years ago, the Hagerstown television research was

TABLE I. *The Effectiveness of Instructional Television*

Level		Math.	Science	Social Studies	Humanities History Lit., Arts	Language Skills	Health Safety	Total	
3rd–6th Grades	+TV	14	8	12	0	14	2	50	+TV
	n.s.d.	21	14	11	0	36	4	86	n.s.d.
	–TV	3	1	1	0	10	1	16	–TV
7th–9th Grades	+TV	4	9	0	2	0	3	18	+TV
	n.s.d.	11	8	1	7	0	1	28	n.s.d.
	–TV	2	3	0	0	0	0	5	–TV
10th–12th Grades	+TV	0	3	3	4	1	1	12	+TV
	n.s.d.	10	7	17	17	6	0	57	n.s.d.
	–TV	5	3	0	9	4	0	21	–TV
College	+TV	0	1	1	0	0	1	3	+TV
	n.s.d.	4	26	24	11	12	7	84	n.s.d.
	–TV	0	1	4	3	1	4	13	–TV
Total	+TV	18	21	16	6	15	7	83	+TV
	n.s.d.	46	55	53	35	54	12	255	n.s.d.
	–TV	10	8	5	12	15	5	55	–TV
								Total 393	

Based on a recent analysis by Wilbur Schramm, "What We Know About Learning from Instructional Television," Institute for Communication Research, Stanford University, 1961. The table shows out of a total of 393 TV research projects, 83 established television as a superior technique, 255 reported no significant difference existing between television instruction and face-to-face or traditional instruction, and 55 reported a significant difference for traditional types of instruction.

247

developed on a countywide basis in which outlying schools (some of them 40 miles away from Hagerstown) were interconnected by coaxial cables. At Hagerstown, a central television control center, surrounded by several rehearsal classrooms, went into operation with 22 television teachers involved in the demanding task of originating television instruction for use by classroom teachers. The television teachers at Hagerstown were chosen because of their interest in the medium and their background and ability in teaching. As each was confronted with the task of arranging for television teaching, he became involved in planning for the use of many audio-visual materials, as he sought to portray, through demonstration and the use of film clips, slides, models, charts, and graphics, the highest quality of learning experience. Needless to say, when one stands before one's colleagues, he is very much "on the spot," and what ordinarily would pass as good instruction in the day-to-day environment of a classroom no longer can be depended upon to meet the exacting standards of television instruction, which, among other things, attempts to compress a maximum amount of communication into a minimum amount of time.

Following years of planning, evaluating, and replanning, the Hagerstown television experiment now closely coordinates the planning of the classroom teachers with that of the television group. Representatives of the two groups have met in conferences to coordinate better the kind of teaching purposes envisioned by the classroom teacher with the unique strengths of the television teacher to supply learning experiences which ordinarily would lie beyond the time, budget, and mechanical opportunities of the classroom teacher to create. The classroom teacher does best what can be accomplished through discussion, interchange of ideas, question and answer, and reference and resource work, whereas the television teacher assumes the responsibility for the gathering together of fugitive visual materials which will enhance the learning experiences broadcast into the classroom. The result is an improved quality of day-to-day teaching which is possible only under such an arrangement: an "electronic" kind of team teaching is going on.

Another application of educational television is to be found in the program of the Midwest Program on Airborne Television Instruction, usually referred to as MPATI. After three years of preparation and with a budget of over $10,000,000 provided by business and foundations, including the Ford Foundation, MPATI began on September 11, 1961, a program of television broadcasts to an audience of an estimated 2,000,000 pupils and their teachers. By means of two television stations built into the fuselage of the aircraft, videotaped lessons are beamed to receiving sets in schools in six states.

Each day, Monday through Thursday throughout this school year, the "flying classroom" circles for five or six hours above the little town of Montpelier, Indiana. The airborne television impulses radiate more than 200 miles in all directions from a 24-foot sending antenna projecting vertically from the belly of the aircraft. The flying station broadcasts to schools in Illinois, Indiana, Kentucky, Michigan, Ohio, and Wisconsin. The MPATI curriculum includes a trial series of 16 courses of instruction, ranging from elementary school through college subjects: music, foreign languages, arithmetic—including a special course for gifted children, science, and history. College students have classes in algebra, chemistry, and Russian. Eventually these taped courses may be available to Hawaii.

In broad terms, the purposes of MPATI are similar to those sought at Hagerstown, namely, to apply more careful planning to difficult portions of the curriculum, and thus to make possible learning experiences heretofore denied to the individual classroom. Through the screen of a television set, located in the independent classroom which may be hundreds of miles from the broadcast source, it is today possible to bring the advantages of modern communication tools into the most remote learning environment.

Another important kind of educational television involves the concept of total instruction. This refers to a process whereby an entire lesson is recorded on television film or video tape and becomes the major learning experience available to the student. This preplanned and recorded learning experience is supplemented by textbooks, study manuals, and an opportunity for feedback through means of interchange of written lessons. The key stimulus, however, is provided through recorded television teaching. When such learning is participated in by gifted students working individually or in small groups, remarkable outcomes have been recorded.

At the City Junior College in Chicago, it is currently possible to receive two years of junior college instruction entirely via television. The method of preparation of the learning materials is similar to those used in Hagerstown and MPATI. However, the student, seated as a remote classroom learner, is able to receive instruction through a television screen or in some cases, from a motion picture projector which projects the kinescope recording. He is thus able to proceed as rapidly as the broadcast schedule permits or as rapidly as he can witness and react to the film record of such broadcasts. In the City Junior College, 32 tests of television instruction have been undertaken in the fields of English, social studies, science, psychology, and the humanities. The data reveal that in 17 cases television instruction had as good results as face-to-face instruction and in eleven cases was superior. In two cases, classroom instruction was superior. Such research points to the possibility that large areas of traditionally taught subject content can be taught more efficiently through educational television.

A very special kind of television instruction is currently being broadcast from the College of Education of the University of Hawaii to teachers enrolled on Oahu and the neighbor islands. Through this 42-lesson televised course in methods of improving classroom instruction through the use of new communication media, a team of teachers is brought into the students' own local school room through television.

Thus Hawaii is involved in finding out whether or not television instruction can overcome the barriers of remoteness, distance, and accessibility to traditional teacher education facilities. The time can be envisioned when, in addition to residence instruction, large portions of the curriculum can be offered through television broadcast, through the relayed use of video tapes, or more important, through the independent learner's reacting privately to kinescopes of entire courses.

Instruction by television has been advanced markedly by the development of video tapes, a technique by which a program can be recorded on a wide ribbon of magnetic tape. The use of the kinescope makes it possible to transfer or to record a television program on a reel of 16mm sound motion picture film. The result can then be used much as a motion picture is used, either for classroom group instruction or for independent study. Other contemporary techniques include telefilm recording, video tape broadcast, and kinescope film broadcast. The latter two are coordinated with feedback techniques which involve individual long-distance telephone hookups, or signaling devices which are a part of the television broadcast network itself. In such ways the viewer can immediately record by electronic means his reactions to questions which flash instantaneously on the screen or to verbal questions by the television teacher. The results of such feedback can be made immediately available to the instructor to guide him in his explanations or to suggest a change of pace in his presentation.

THE TEACHER AND ETV

Teachers are likely to become deeply involved in educational television in the future. Therefore, some of the broad claims which can be made for television in classroom instruction or in professional education are here set forth.

1. Television is a remarkable, efficient technique for using cross-media communication tools. That is, television is the efficient carrier for all the modern communication devices—films, slides, tapes, opaque, vugraph, demonstrations, charts, specimens, models. As a master teacher or lecturer-demonstrator uses these techniques, television makes it possible for the individual viewer, even though he may be miles distant, to see the best of learning materials available for educational use.

2. Student teachers of tomorrow will have the opportunity of viewing through closed-circuit or broadcast, the various aspects of pupil-teacher relationships which occur in the privacy of the classroom. All of a large group can see the same teacher with his class and thus have a common experience for later discussion and evaluation. At the same time, this use of television insures the privacy and the candidness of a learning situation which is usually altered when visitors walk into a classroom.

3. Educational television is a challenge to any teacher who is interested in seeing models of instructional technique which employ the so-

called cross-media approach to learning. The best examples of educati. television teaching employ a wide variety of modern teaching tools, e.g. 16mm sound motion picture films, slides, charts, tapes, models, specimens. Those who have had the opportunity of watching Professor Harvey White, as he has taught the continental classroom course in modern physics, or Dr. Peter H. Odegard as he conducted the recent NBC course entitled "The Structure and Functions of American Government," have seen outstanding teachers who employ, when they feel it desirable, the most appropriate learning tool during the learning process. Television thus can become a challenging experience for the teacher who would compare his own teaching techniques to those employed by television instructors who have at their command all of the resources of the modern communication world. Again and again, teachers who have observed educational television have reported that they were as interested in the teaching techniques as in the content presented.

The teacher is and must always be the judge of the usefulness of educational television as it can be used in his own classroom. Television must be judged, therefore, in much the same manner as are films, filmstrips, models, and other modern teaching tools.

Educational television, to paraphrase Charles Dickens, can be the best of things or it can be the worst of things. Television, when defined from the standpoint of its electronic characteristics, is but a carrier wave. As a carrier wave, it can communicate ideas; hence, what is carried is everything. Thus, it can be concluded that the output of television can be no more than its input.

What we put into educational television, for example, may be a demonstration of a teaching technique. If this is arranged by a poor teacher, who merely verbalizes before a background of gray drapes, the input which is caught by the television camera and broadcast is almost certain to be poor. However, a vastly different kind of output is possible when an excellent teacher goes through all the necessary stages to present an effective demonstration. The stages include careful preplanning, arranging for necessary materials, and rehearsing before a psychologist interested in laws of learning, an audio-visual communications expert, and an experienced educational television director.

Effective educational television, difficult as it may be to achieve, is surely the goal for all who work with this medium. The progress made in the ten-year history of educational television is enormous and yet the future seems unlimited.

20   Team Teaching: An Assessment*

BY HAROLD D. DRUMMOND

EDITOR'S NOTE: Team teaching is another of the important innovations in instruction during recent years. Most innovations spur discussions regarding their value, and in this article Dr. Drummond cites nine "advantages" consistently associated with the team teaching concept in terms of an explicit set of assumptions. As with any idea which involves one person working with one or more other people, what may make the difference, so far as success is concerned, is not so much whether the idea is good, but whether the relationship between the people involved is. How about yourself? What do you think would make the difference as to whether or not you could work in a team-teaching situation?

Interest in team teaching has grown rapidly since 1958. In that year the National Association of Secondary-School Principals devoted the January issue of *The Bulletin* to the work of its Commission on the Experimental Study of the Staff in the Secondary School (NASSP, 1958). In the two-year period preceding that issue (1955–57), not a single article on the subject of team teaching was listed in the *Education Index*. In the following two-year period, by contrast, the *Index* listed eight articles. Between July 1959 and June 1960, 35 articles appeared in published

---

* Harold D. Drummond, "Team Teaching: An Assessment," *Educational Leadership,* 19: 160–165, December, 1961. Reprinted with permission of the Association for Supervision and Curriculum Development and Harold D. Drummond. Copyright © by the Association for Supervision and Curriculum Development.

journals and, through June 1961, an additional 19 entries had been listed. No doubt the output will continue to mount, for everyone seems to want to jump on the bandwagon of "team teaching" (Bush).

At the moment, it appears likely that in hundreds of secondary schools and in many elementary schools the instructional staffs are doing something which they call team teaching. What types of team teaching are reported by school systems? What are characteristics of present developments? What advantages are claimed for team teaching, and what problems are inherent in the structures already adopted?

TYPES OF TEAM TEACHING

The education profession has suffered for years because it has lacked precise terminology. Team teaching is another example—the term already has almost as many meanings as there are school systems doing something with it. At present, there appear to be at least the following five types of team teaching in various stages of development and/or experimentation. Variations from these types are, of course, myriad.

1. *A hierarchy of teaching assignments.* Several school systems (see Anderson, Johnson, Stone) have attempted to develop instructional teams which are based upon a specified hierarchy of teaching assignments. At the top of the hierarchy is a team leader who is a person with superior educational preparation, several years of teaching experience, and leadership qualities. The team leader often is given a lighter teaching load and a salary commensurate with the leadership responsibilities he is asked to assume. The team, in school systems developing hierarchal assignments, usually also consists of senior teachers (who receive extra pay, but not as much as that received by the team leader), regular teachers (often those without previous experience or those new to the system), part-time teaching assistants, and clerical aides. In order to cover the costs of the increased salaries for leadership and for clerical help, additional pupils are assigned to the team—usually at least one extra class section for three or four certified teachers.

2. *Coordinate- or co-teaching.* In school systems using this approach, teachers are assigned to a large group of pupils (usually a multiple of the number the teachers would have under more traditional assignments; e.g., two teachers to 60 youngsters, three teachers to 90) and they plan together *as peers* how best to provide for the pupils for whom they are responsible. As in the previously described "hierarchy" plan, sometimes instruction is provided to the entire group by one teacher. Sometimes one teacher works with most of the youngsters in the group while the other works with a

small group of the gifted or with those needing remedial instruction. Sometimes each of the teachers has a "normal-sized" group of about 30 pupils each. Attempts are made in the planning to utilize to the fullest extent the strengths of each teacher. Such plans usually have been described as existing within established departments at secondary school levels or at grade levels in elementary schools.

3. *Team teaching across departmental lines.*   In several junior and senior high schools attempts have been made to improve the program, and hopefully to improve learning, by devising schedules for instructional teams which provide a two- or three-period block of related content (e.g., American history, American literature). Students have, normally, one period with the social studies teacher, followed by one period with the English teacher (or the reverse). Often, when desirable, the two groups are combined for the double period—as for a field trip, orientation to a new unit, lecture by an outstanding resource person, visual aids, and the like. The teachers have at least one free period at the same hour so that joint planning is possible.

4. *Part- or full-time helpers.*   Many descriptions of team teaching indicate a fairly standard teaching role for the regularly certificated teacher, but seek to improve his teaching effectiveness by providing additional help of various kinds, including instructional secretaries, theme or paper correctors, laboratory assistants, learning materials coordinators, and audio-visual experts. To employ the additional personnel without substantial increases in instructional costs, teachers usually are asked to accept responsibility for a larger number of learners than normal (usually 35 to 40). The teacher retains active control of the planning and most instructional phases of teaching, utilizing the helpers on the team for particular tasks of a more routine nature.

5. *Trading groups.*   In an informal way this method of capitalizing on the particular strengths of teachers has been utilized for years by elementary school teachers. The teachers have said, in essence, "If you'll take my art—you're good in it and I'm not—I'll take your music," or "If you take my science, I'll take your social studies." Until recently, such "trading" was rare at the secondary school level, but it may be growing now as a result of the staff utilization studies.

Several reports indicate that two or three teachers of a particular subject, such as general science, plan their work so that they trade groups for particular units of content. The trading is done, ostensibly, to make certain that the groups receive instruction from the best-qualified teacher of the team, and also to ensure that the teachers have an opportunity to provide instruction geared to their own interests and competencies.

AN ASSESSMENT

Any attempt at assessment of educational practices is, of necessity, made from a value base. In most previously published reports, an attempt has been made to assess practices in team teaching by utilizing three types of data: achievement as measured by standardized or by locally-constructed tests, teacher opinions (sometimes buttressed by student and parent opinions), and per-pupil costs. The data collected and reported generally indicate: (a) Students do as well or perhaps a little better on standardized tests when taught by teaching teams of the various types described. Usually the obtained differences are not significant when fairly sophisticated statistical measures are employed to analyze the data. (b) Teachers, generally, are willing to continue the team approach, although there are numerous indications that not all teachers make good team members. Increasingly, reports indicate that differences among teachers need to be recognized equally as much as do variations among learners (see Hanvey and Tenenberg, Weiss). The reports seem to show a feeling of, "We are working on the frontier—trying to find a better way of proceeding," which undoubtedly has positive value for heightened morale. The increased workloads (meetings, meetings, meetings!) seem to have been shouldered with enthusiasm by the participants. In the long pull, better ways of equalizing instructional loads probably will need to be developed or morale may slip. (c) Students and their parents generally favor what has been tried. Many learners are at first skeptical or negative, but as teachers gain confidence and competence in their changed roles, reports from them indicate positive support for the team approach. (d) Costs rise slightly. The extent of the increased costs usually is not specifically reported. Three ways of bearing the increased costs have been utilized: increased local appropriations, employing fewer qualified teachers and increasing the pupil-teacher ratio, and support from foundations. Many of the additional costs have been the result of improved instructional resources—books, films, overhead projectors, and the like.

While these criteria of achievement, opinion, and cost are measurable, to some extent at least, they do not necessarily provide good bases for assessment unless one subscribes to the following premises: (a) that education is best which results in highest achievement as measured by tests, standardized or otherwise; (b) that education is best which results in expressed teacher satisfaction with administrative practices (and perhaps student and parent approval also); (c) that education is best which increases present per-pupil costs only slightly and may in time tend to lower costs. These premises seem to be questionable as criteria for a profession to use in assessing the worth of an innovation.

The assessment which follows, also made from a value base, is developed to the extent possible on the following assumptions: (a) learning of high quality requires interaction between the teacher and the learner and between the learner and other learners; (b) learning of high quality is more likely to occur when teachers are patient, understanding, intellectually alert, and free to make decisions based upon their best professional judgment; (c) what is learned must be used (more functionally than on an examination) or before long it will not be known.

These assumptions obviously eliminate cost as a function of quality (although most administrators at present must consider the cost-quality factor) because the writer assumes that this nation *can* afford instruction of high quality for its children and youth. The assumptions also eliminate teacher opinions as expressed on questionnaires or verbally to members of the administrative and supervisory staffs. What is essential for effective learning is not necessarily highly correlated with what teachers prefer. To state the assumption another way, what teachers consider to be good teaching may not result in the most effective learning. The spotlight should be focused on the *learning process* rather than on teaching.

These assumptions also eliminate achievement as measured by tests. Teachers know what most achievement tests contain or are likely to contain. Using almost any organizational structure, they can, therefore, make sure that the learners make about average gains in achievement. Obviously, any structure which results in *marked* improvement on standardized tests should be seriously considered. Whether the instructional technique or structure should be adopted widely, even if better test results are obtained, is another matter—a matter for professional judgment. Students who score higher on standardized tests, in other words, are not necessarily better educated.

What assessment can be made of the various types of team teaching using the value assumption that good learning results from the interaction of learner and learners with patient, understanding, intellectually alert, free teachers who see that what is learned is used? Nine "advantages" consistently reported for team teaching are given in italics below. In each instance, some comments based upon the value orientation of the writer follow in regular type.

Few pupils are limited to the instructional competence of a single teacher at a grade level or in a department at the secondary level. As a result, few teachers in this arrangement get to know individual pupils as well as in traditional arrangements. Interaction between the superior teachers and the learners (especially in the hierarchal plan) is minimal. Personal contacts of learners with teachers tend to be limited to teachers of lesser competence and experience.

Persons most highly qualified provide instruction to large groups, thus saving much time for the total staff which can be used for more effective planning and for instruction in smaller-than-average groups. Questions learners have during the lecture must be deferred until a later time.

Moreover, what the teacher wants to teach is not necessarily what the pupil needs or wants to learn. The learner may, in fact, already know what is being presented to a large group. The same problem exists, of course, when teachers lecture to normal-sized groups. May there not be a better way to teach?

In presentations to large groups, better use is made of visual aids because more time can be devoted to the preparation of needed materials by specially-qualified team members. Substituting a picture of a magnet on an overhead projector as a lecturer explains how it works (as was shown recently in the television report, "The Influential Americans") may result in undesirable verbalization not sufficiently based on real, firsthand experiences by the learners themselves. Skillful presentations do not necessarily result in effective learning experiences.

Most uniformity in instruction is achieved because all students are taught, both in the large groups and the small, by the same teachers. Sections pupils are assigned to thus make less difference than in traditionally organized schools. Uniformity in instruction is not necessarily desirable. The degree of desirability depends largely upon how much flexibility is provided for the very bright students and the slow learners. Individualization of instruction, whether in traditional or team approaches to teaching, is a valid and desirable goal. To the degree that attention to individual differences is provided (this varies in different team teaching plans), the learning is likely to be effective.

Less repetition is required of teachers, especially at the secondary level where several sections of the same class have been traditionally assigned. Repeating a lecture to several sections of the same class probably *is* wasteful—but getting to know the pupil is *essential* for interaction. Almost all reports indicate that less discussion occurs as team teaching is undertaken. Perhaps more "ground" can be covered, but that is no guarantee that more learning has taken place.

Teacher competencies are better utilized. Instruction tends to become more formal, less spontaneous. In the hierarchal plan, young, inexperienced teachers undoubtedly have more opportunity to learn from team leaders, but the conception is supported that superior teachers lecture to large groups while teachers drawing lower salaries and with less teaching experience work with smaller groups. Learners, as a result, get individual help from teachers who probably are least qualified to give it. These weaknesses, it should be noted, are not apparent in the coordinate and interdepartmental plans where teachers operate as peers.

Better provisions are made for helpers—librarians, audio-visual experts, clerks, and the like—to do routine tasks. A definite boon to the profession! The only problem which should be noted: effective coordination of such helpers takes time. In the opinion of this analyst, such help should and could be provided regardless of the structure for teaching developed by the school system.

Group size is clearly related to function. Large groups are formed for activities which are effective with large groups, and vice versa. This concept makes sense. In the judgment of this assessor, the "coordinate" and the "across departmental lines" teams have the greatest possibility of built-in flexibility at this point. The "hierarchal plan," because of the specified roles, probably has the least likelihood of achieving flexibility in grouping.

Of necessity, students assume more responsibility for their own learning. As more and more instruction is provided in large groups, a greater share of the school day is given to independent study on the part of learners. If education is effective, the more mature the learner, the more able to guide and direct his own learning endeavors he should be. Generally, then, this claimed advantage of team teaching is desirable. Perhaps even a greater measure of independence could be achieved other ways, however.

A FINAL WORD

The worth of attempts at team teaching are not proven to date. The main value of the attempts which have been made thus far undoubtedly lies in the staff growth which has occurred as a result of the experimentation.

Experimentation should be continued. Much more sophisticated research designs should be used, so that variables in the situations can be more carefully controlled. While team teaching is being tested more carefully, some school systems (perhaps the same ones) should also be testing other approaches to improvement of learning, such as: assigning not more than 20 pupils to a teacher, shortening the teacher-directed part of the school day and lengthening the pupil-directed portions of the day, utilizing more programmed materials as these become available, basing more instruction on the "workshop way of learning," orienting in-service education programs for teachers more toward intellectual growth, providing better learning materials centers and instructional secretaries in every school, and lengthening the school year for a larger number of teachers so that more time for planning and preparation is available.

REFERENCES:

ANDERSON, R. H. Team teaching in action. *Nation's Schools,* May 1960, 65, 62–65.

ANDERSON, R. H. Team teaching. *NEA J.,* March 1961, 50, 52–54.

ANDERSON, R. H., HAGSTROM, E. A., and ROBINSON, W. M. Team teaching in elementary school. *Sch. Rev.,* Spring 1960, 68 (1), 71–84.

BRUNTZ, G. G. Team approach to social science teaching. *High Sch. J.,* April 1960, 43, 370–374.

BUSH, R. N. Editorial: The team teaching bandwagon. *Calif. J. Secondary Educ.*, April 1960, 35, 207–208. (This issue and the February 1960 issue of the same publication contain a number of articles on team teaching most of which are not listed individually because of space.)

FORD, P. M. Different day for the English teacher. *Eng. J.*, May 1961, 50, 334–337.

HANVEY, R., and TENENBERG, M. S. University of Chicago Laboratory School, Chicago, Illinois, evaluates team teaching. *The Bull.*, National Association of Secondary School Principals, January 1961, 45, No. 261, 189–197.

JOHNSON, R. H., and LOBB, M. D. The transformation of the sacred secondary school schedule. *Calif. J. Secondary Educ.*, February 1960, 35, 96–105.

MAHONEY, W. M. Try coordinate teaching. *Amer. Sch. Board J.*, November 1959, 139, 13–14.

National Association of Secondary-School Principals. *The Bull.* Complete issues devoted to staff utilization studies include: January 1958, 42, No. 234; January 1959, 43, No. 243; January 1960, 44, No. 252; January 1961, 45, No. 261. (These bulletins comprise the most extensive reporting available—each issue containing reports from systems undertaking experimentation under the Commission on the Experimental Study of the Utilization of the Staff in the Secondary School. Most individual reports are not listed herein, to conserve space.)

SMITH, V. H. Team teaching has its advantages. *Eng. J.*, April 1960, 49, 242–244.

STETSON, G. A., and HARRISON, J. P. Junior high school designed for team teaching. *Amer. Sch. Board J.*, May 1960, 140, 38–42.

STONE, W. J. New designs for secondary school scheduling. *Calif. J. Secondary Educ.*, February 1960, 35, 126–130.

WARD, J. O. Another plan for coordinate teaching. *Amer. Sch. Board J.*, February 1960, 140, 10.

WEISS, T. M., and MORRIS, MARY SCOTT. Critique of the team approach. *Educ. Forum*, January 1960, 24, 207–208.

21 Nongraded Programs: What Progress*

BY HUGH V. PERKINS

EDITOR'S NOTE: *Increasingly, nongraded programs are growing in stature and acceptance—particularly at the elementary school level. Dr. Perkins addresses himself to the major educational and philosophical arguments behind the nongraded plan which have prompted many lay persons and educators to adopt the idea. As you consider the possible merits of nongraded programs, you might also want to consider two basic questions: (1) Would you want to teach in a nongraded school? (2) Would you want your own children to attend a nongraded school? Why? Or, for that matter, why not?*

Among the most perplexing realities which continuously recur in the life of every teacher are the marked differences in achievement, intelligence, motivation, cultural and experiential background, and physical and social maturity which exist within any group of learners. For decades educators have given lip service to the need for teaching children as individuals and for providing more adequately for individual differences. They have conducted extensive research in child development over nearly a half-century, have studied insights gained by teachers during two decades of participation in child study programs, and have noted the continuing research in perception, learning and personality. All these have demonstrated that learning is most effective when it is meaningful and is related

---

* Hugh V. Perkins, "Nongraded Programs: What Progress," *Educational Leadership*, 19: 166–169, December, 1961. Reprinted with permission of the Association for Supervision and Curriculum Development and Hugh V. Perkins. Copyright © by the Association for Supervision and Curriculum Development.

to the individual needs, perceptions and interests of the learner, when it begins where the learner is, and when it is perceived by the learner as enhancing his own self-concept.

Yet, in spite of these influences, until recently no break-through has been achieved toward fully implementing the principles of individual differences. The critical reexamination of American education which has been carried on by educators and lay groups since 1957 has resulted in the development of fresh new approaches to age-old problems in education. During this period also, novel but promising approaches toward solution of an educational problem which heretofore has gone largely unnoticed, have suddenly come under closer scrutiny and have become the focal point for intensive study and experimentation.

One such approach and type of organization is the nongraded school. This arrangement provides a flexible grouping and organization of curriculum content that enables children of varying abilities and rates of maturing to experience continuous progress in learning. Although the specific details of nongraded organization vary in different school systems where it is being used, certain general characteristics may be noted.[1] In most of these schools the nongraded organization functions only during the primary years, but often is linked with the kindergarten program. A few schools are experimenting with this type of organization in the intermediate years.

The nongraded type of organization appears to have had the greatest influence on the program and pattern of grouping in reading. Characteristically, the reading experiences of the primary years are organized into eight to ten sequential steps or levels through which each child moves at his own rate. Probably its most unique feature is the flexibility possible in moving a child from group to group or from one classroom to another at any time his growth warrants such a change.

In an effort to assess the present status of nongraded programs, this writer analyzed questionnaire responses from 14 representative systems, many of which have used some type of nongraded pattern of organization for three years or more.[2]

IMPETUS FOR INITIATING PROGRAM

The most frequently mentioned reason for adopting a nongraded type of organization was a growing dissatisfaction which teachers and administrators expressed regarding promotional policies they had been using. In many cases this dissatisfaction was echoed also by parents. Several respondents felt that the nongraded program might give them a longer period of time for studying the progress of individual pupils before making a decision on retention. It was hoped, too, that such a plan might result in larger numbers of children completing the primary program in the normal period of time. Many respondents mentioned their desire to eliminate the feeling of frustration children have as the result of failure.

An important impetus in the initiation of these programs was the strong conviction held by key administrators and teachers that educational practice should be more consistent with what is known concerning individual differences. The nongraded types of organization seemed to hold promise of fuller realization of development and learning for all children. Other educators were dissatisfied with the achievement of their students in reading and language arts. They believed that reading performance would improve in a nongraded program in which children move to successive levels only when they are ready for that level.

What were the educational and philosophical considerations which prompted these respondents to change their attitude toward a nongraded program?

The administrators and faculty members believed that: (a) learning should be continuous; (b) children grow and learn at different rates and each should have the opportunity to achieve at his own rate; (c) the school program should be flexible so as to meet varying developmental needs and growth patterns of individual children; and (d) greater achievement will result when children experience success in school.

Nearly all respondents indicated that an initial and continuing orientation is used to acquaint teaching staff and parents with the objectives and operation of the nongraded program. Typically, a study by the faculty has preceded its introduction. In some schools parents have participated with teachers in the preparation of orientation materials and in the development of a new report card. It seems clear that the general acceptance of the nongraded program by communities using it is due in no small measure to the careful and continuing orientation of both staff and parents.

Respondents report that the chief advantages of the nongraded pattern of organization are these: fewer children are retained, children's progress in learning is greater and more continuous, flexibility in grouping has succeeded in fitting the educational program more closely to the needs and maturity of the individual child, and pressures for achievement and maintaining standards have been eliminated or markedly reduced. In addition, some nongraded schools report: an improvement in teacher-parent rapport; slower children are identified earlier; higher teacher and pupil morale; and increased teamwork among teachers and between teachers and parents. Moreover, when learning experiences are tailored to the needs of the individual, curriculum takes on new meaning. The flexibility inherent in the nongraded program permits the use of team teaching approaches and allows teachers to work with the same group more than one year.

Disadvantages noted were that some teachers and parents find absence of specific grade standards difficult to accept. Teaching a nongraded group requires more work of the teacher, but it also is apparently more satisfying. Several respondents mentioned the increased time and effort required in keeping records. Another mentioned the problem of articulating the "levels" program with other subject areas such as arithmetic and social studies. Finally, several report problems relating to the orientation and adjustment of new teachers to the nongraded program. One reports difficulty in finding teachers who are willing to work with the less mature or the slow learner. Another holds that a few teachers may use absence of grade levels as an excuse for their own indifferent performance.

MORE EVALUATION NEEDED

Much of the evaluation of nongraded programs has been informal and has consisted of questionnaire reactions of parents and teachers, observed behavioral changes in individual children, and comparisons of achievement test scores. Collectively, these evaluations show that children are making significantly greater progress in reading achievement than are matched children in traditional classrooms, and that the reactions of parents and teachers are in general favorable. (1) The nongraded pattern appears to be especially facilitative in enabling the more capable children to achieve advanced reading skills and to proceed toward independent reading much sooner than previously.

Shapski found that children in a nongraded program scored significantly higher than did matched controls in traditional graded schools. She also found that children at all ability levels benefited from the individualized flexible program, with those of superior intelligence making the greatest gains of all. In addition, Shapski found that under the nongraded plan less than half as many children of average or low average intelligence spend four years in the primary program as would occur if the decision on promotion was rendered at the end of their first year of school.(2)

The marked increase in interest shown and the adoption of some kind of nongraded organization by hundreds of schools each year indicate clearly the need for more controlled and definitive studies of nongraded programs. What are the effects of this type of experience on other areas of children's learning and development? We need to learn much more concerning the effects of these programs through carefully controlled studies which assess the changes in children's self concepts, levels of anxiety, levels of aspiration and feelings of self-esteem, increase in peer status, and changes in other skill and subject areas. Only then can the effectiveness of these programs be ascertained, the findings used to make needed improvements, and the knowledge gained for adapting and modifying a general structure to fit the specific needs of a particular school and community. Some of these studies are already under way, but many more are needed.

A LOOK TO THE FUTURE

The mounting widespread interest in and acceptance of the nongraded program mark this movement as one which is likely to have a strong influence on future educational programs and organization. It is evident that this arrangement implements in educational practice much that we now know about individual differences. Too, in the freedom given the learner to proceed at his own pace, in the lessening of pressures, and in opportunities given each child to experience success, the nongraded program brings to fuller realization the qualities of a favorable climate for learning.

On the other hand, some rather obvious limitations and pitfalls have been noted in nongraded patterns of organization. First, in most nongraded schools the individualization of instruction has been confined to reading. While reading is a skill of central importance, it is apparent that individualization and pacing of instruction leading to increased achievement in other areas also are long overdue. Secondly, there is danger that without a strong commitment to a program based on the individual rates of maturing and needs of children, the sequence of stepwise levels may result in the replacing of grade standards by another set of standards different in name only.

Finally, with the nongraded pattern having proved successful in many schools which planned carefully in orienting teachers and parents prior to its introduction, there is great danger that other school systems will jump on a nongraded bandwagon without an adequate preparation of staff and community. Experience suggests that schools should prepare carefully and begin slowly so that the nongraded program which emerges is one that is tailored to particular children of a particular school and community. Planning for children's development should not result in a mad dash for the new look merely so that educators and parents may feel that they are educationally outfitted in the latest style!

Much of the potential of the nongraded patterns is as yet untapped. Thus far, it has been used primarily as an organizational device for grouping pupils, yet it has the potential for becoming much more than this. This more valid view of children and their development calls for new approaches to the curriculum. The exploding increase in knowledge emphasizes the need for sequential organization of content so that individualization and pacing of instruction can be carried out in all fields. In truth, our lives are far too short and our needs are too great for us to afford the luxury of children's being bound to rigid standards and inflexible segments of content organized as grades through which students pass in lock-step fashion.

The nongraded pattern of organization, together with the body of philosophical and psychological principles which give it meaning, has the opportunity for influencing profoundly the pattern and organization of elementary education in America and possibly secondary and higher education as well. The extent to which this influence results in educational change will depend upon those of us who use and develop its pattern and philosophy.

A look into the future might hopefully reveal innumerable varieties and types of individualized, self-paced patterns of instruction, each developed as a result of thoughtful planning and continuous evaluation in relation to the unique needs of students and community. In a broader context, one might hope that the knowledge gained in the development of this and other instructional patterns might lead to a more comprehensive and functional understanding of how human beings learn and develop. The extent to which these hopes are realized depends upon the wisdom and commitment of those of us who labor in these vineyards.

REFERENCES:

1. INGRAM, VIVIEN, "Flint Evaluates Its Primary Cycle," *Elementary Sch. J.*, November, 1960, *81*, 76–80.
2. SHAPSKI, MARY K., "Ungraded Primary Reading Programs An Objective Evaluation," *Elementary Sch. J.*, October, 1960, *61*, 41–45.

FOOTNOTES:

[1] For a comprehensive discussion of the nongraded school, see John I. Goodland and Robert H. Anderson, *The Nongraded Elementary School*, New York: Harcourt, Brace and Co., 1959. Also see various articles appearing in educational journals.

[2] The writer is indebted to the following school systems which responded to this survey: Corona and Torrance, California; Pocatello, Idaho; Moline and Park Forest, Illinois; Baltimore and Germantown, Maryland; Marblehead, Massachusetts; Dearborn, Michigan; Reno, Nevada; Dayton and Youngstown, Ohio; Savannah, Georgia; and Milwaukee, Wisconsin.

CHAPTER SIX

Issues and Concerns About Testing and Grading

22   *Measurement and the Teacher**

by Robert L. Ebel

EDITOR'S NOTE: Whether one believes that testing is a good idea or not, the fact remains that teachers do have to assess, in one way or another, students' achievement. Dr. Ebel has had vast experience as both a high school and college teacher and has confronted both the theory and practice of measuring educational achievement. What follows, then, is a sampling "of the important things classroom teachers need to know about educational measurement" as seen through the eyes of an expert in educational measurement. This article will help set the tone for those to follow in this chapter.

The principles of measurement of educational achievement presented in this article are based on the experience and research of a great many people who have been working to improve classroom testing. The particular principles discussed here were selected on the basis of their relevance to the questions and problems which arise most often when tests of educational achievement are being considered, prepared and used. While some of the principles may seem open to question, we believe a case can be made in support of each one.

1. *The measurement of educational achievement is essential to effective education.* Learning is a natural, inevitable result of human living. Some learning would occur even if no special provision were made for it in schools, or no special effort were taken to facilitate it. Yet efficient learning

* Robert L. Ebel, "Measurement and the Teacher," *Educational Leadership,* 20: 20–24, October, 1962. Reprinted with permission of the Association for Supervision and Curriculum Development and Robert L. Ebel. Copyright © 1962 by the Association for Supervision and Curriculum Development.

of complex achievements, such as reading, understanding of science, or literary appreciation, requires special motivation, guidance and assistance. Efforts must be directed toward the attainment of specific goals. Students, teachers and others involved in the process of education must know to what degree the goals have been achieved. The measurement of educational achievement can contribute to these activities.

It is occasionally suggested that schools could get along without tests, or indeed that they might even do a better job if testing were prohibited. It is seldom if ever suggested, though, that education can be carried on effectively by teachers and students who have no particular goals in view, or who do not care what or how much is being learned. If tests are outlawed, some other means of assessing educational achievement would have to be used in their place.

2. *An educational test is no more or less than a device for facilitating, extending and refining a teacher's observations of student achievement.* In spite of the Biblical injunction, most of us find ourselves quite often passing judgments on our fellow men. Is candidate A more deserving of our vote than candidate B? Is C a better physician than D? Is employee E entitled to a raise or a promotion on his merits? Should student F be given a failing mark? Should student L be selected in preference to student M for the leading role in the class play?

Those charged with making such judgments often feel they must do so on the basis of quite inadequate evidence. The characteristics on which the decision should be based may not have been clearly defined. The performances of the various candidates may not have been observed extensively, or under comparable conditions. Instead of recorded data, the judge may have to trust his fallible memory, supplemented with hearsay evidence.

Somewhat similar problems are faced by teachers, as they attempt to assess the achievements of their students. In an effort to solve these problems, tests have been developed. Oral examinations and objective examinations are means for making it easier for the teacher to observe a more extensive sample of student behavior under more carefully controlled conditions.

The price that must be paid for a test's advantages of efficiency and control in the observation of student achievements is some loss in the naturalness of the behavior involved. In tests which attempt to measure the student's typical behavior, especially those aspects of behavior which depend heavily on his interests, attitudes, values or emotional reactions, the artificiality of the test situation may seriously distort the measurements obtained. But this problem is much less serious in tests intended to measure how much the student knows, and what he can do with his knowledge. What is gained in efficiency and precision of measurement usually far outweighs what may be lost due to artificiality of the situation in which the student's behavior is observed.

3. *Every important outcome of education can be measured.* In order for an outcome of education to be important, it must make a difference. The behavior of a person who has more of a particular outcome must be observably different from that of a person who has less. Perhaps one can imagine some result of education which is so deeply personal that it does not ever affect in any way what he says or does, or how he spends his time. But it is difficult to find any grounds for arguing that such a well concealed achievement is important.

If the achievement does make a difference in what a person can do or does do, then it is measurable. For the most elementary type of measurement requires nothing more than the possibility of making a verifiable observation that person or object X has more of some defined characteristic than person or object Y.

To say that any important educational outcome is measurable is not to say that satisfactory methods of measurement now exist. Certainly it is not to say that every important educational outcome can be measured by means of a paper and pencil test. But it is to reject the claim that some important educational outcomes are too complex or too intangible to be measured. Importance and measurability are logically inseparable.

4. *The most important educational achievement is command of useful knowledge.* If the importance of an educational outcome may be judged on the basis of what teachers and students spend most of their time doing, it is obvious that acquisition of a command of useful knowledge is a highly important outcome. Or if one asks how the other objectives are to be attained—objectives of self-realization, of human relationship, of economic efficiency, of civic responsibility—it is obvious again that command of useful knowledge is the principal means.

How effectively a person can think about a problem depends largely on how effectively he can command the knowledge that is relevant to the problem. Command of knowledge does not guarantee success, or happiness, or righteousness, but it is difficult to think of anything else a school can attempt to develop which is half as likely to lead to these objectives.

If we give students command of knowledge, if we develop their ability to think, we make them intellectually free and independent. This does not assure us that they will work hard to maintain the status quo, that they will adopt all of our beliefs and accept all of our values. Yet it can make them free men and women in the area in which freedom is most important. We should be wary of an educational program which seeks to change or control student behavior on any other basis than rational self-determination, the basis that command of knowledge provides.

5. *Written tests are well suited to measure the student's command of useful knowledge.* All knowledge can be expressed in propositions. Propositions are statements that can be judged to be true or false. Scholars, scientists, research workers—all those concerned with adding to our store of

knowledge, spend most of their time formulating and verifying propositions.

Implicit in every true-false or multiple-choice test item is a proposition, or several propositions. Essay tests also require a student to demonstrate his command of knowledge.

Some elements of novelty are essential in any question intended to test a student's command of knowledge. He should not be allowed to respond successfully on the basis of rote learning or verbal association. He should not be asked a stereotyped question to which a pat answer probably has been committed to memory.

6. *The classroom teacher should prepare most of the tests used to measure educational achievement in the classroom.* Many published tests are available for classroom use in measuring educational aptitude or achievement in broad areas of knowledge. But there are very few which are specifically appropriate for measuring the achievement of the objectives of a particular unit of work or of a particular period of instruction. Publishers of textbooks sometimes supply booklets of test questions to accompany their texts. These can be useful, although all too often the test questions supplied are of inferior quality—hastily written, unreviewed, untested, and subject to correct response on the basis of rote learning as well as on the basis of understanding.

Even if good ready-made tests were generally available, a case could still be made for teacher-prepared tests; the chief reason being that the process of test development can help the teacher define his objectives. This process can result in tests that are more highly relevant than any external tests are likely to be. It can make the process of measuring educational achievement an integral part of the whole process of instruction, as it should be.

7. *To measure achievement effectively the classroom teacher must be (a) a master of the knowledge or skill to be tested, and (b) a master of the practical arts of testing.* No courses in educational measurement, no books or articles on the improvement of classroom tests, are likely to enable a poor teacher to make good tests. A teacher's command of the knowledge he is trying to teach, his understanding of common misconceptions regarding this content, his ability to invent novel questions and problems, and his ability to express these clearly and concisely; all these are crucial to his success in test construction. It is unfortunately true that some people who have certificates to teach lack one or more of these prerequisites to good teaching and good testing.

However, there are also some tricks of the trade of test construction. A course in educational measurement, or a book or article on classroom testing can teach these things. Such a course may also serve to shake a teacher's faith—constructively and wholesomely—in some of the popular misconceptions about the processes of testing educational achievement.

Among these misconceptions are the belief that only essay tests are useful for measuring the development of a student's higher mental processes; that a test score should indicate what proportion a student does know of what he ought to know; that mistakes in scoring are the main source of error in test scores.

8. *The quality of a classroom test depends on the relevance of the tasks included in it, on the representativeness of its sampling of all aspects of instruction, and on the reliability of the scores it yields.* If a test question presents a problem like those the student may expect to encounter in his later life outside the classroom, and if the course in which his achievement is being tested did in fact try to teach him how to deal with such problems, then the question is relevant. If the test questions involve, in proportion to their importance, all aspects of achievement the course undertakes to develop, it samples representatively. If the scores students receive on a test agree closely with those they would receive on an independent, equivalent test, then the test yields reliable scores.

Relevance, representativeness and reliability are all matters of degree. Procedures and formulas for calculating estimates of test reliability are well developed, and are described in most books on educational measurement. Estimates of representativeness and relevance are more subjective, less quantitative. Yet this does not mean that relevance and representativeness are any less important than reliability. The more a test has of each the better. While it is possible to have an irrelevant and unrepresentative but highly reliable test, it is seldom necessary and never desirable, to sacrifice any one of the three for the others.

Either essay or objective test forms can be used to present relevant tasks to the examinees. Ordinarily, the greater the novelty of a test question, that is, the smaller the probability that the student has encountered the same question before, or been taught a pat answer to it, the greater its relevance. Because of the greater number of questions involved, it is sometimes easier to include a representative sample of tasks in an objective than in an essay test. For the same reason, and also because of greater uniformity in scoring, objective tests are likely to yield somewhat more reliable scores than are essay tests.

9. *The more variable the scores from a test designed to have a certain maximum possible score, the higher the expected reliability of those scores.* Reliability is sometimes defined as the proportion of the total variability among the test scores which is not attributable to errors of measurement. The size of the errors of measurement depends on the nature of the test—the kind and the number of items in it. Hence for a particular test, any increase in the total variability of the scores is likely to increase the proportion which is not due to errors of measurement, and hence to increase the reliability of the test.

Figure 1 shows some hypothetical score distributions for three tests. The essay test consists of 10 questions worth 10 points each, scored by a

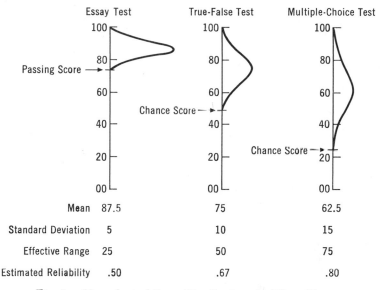

	Essay Test	True-False Test	Multiple-Choice Test
Mean	87.5	75	62.5
Standard Deviation	5	10	15
Effective Range	25	50	75
Estimated Reliability	.50	.67	.80

Fig. 1.   *Hypothetical Score Distributions for Three Tests.*

teacher who regards 75 as a passing score on such a test. The true-false test consists of 100 items, each of which is worth one point if correctly answered, with no subtraction for wrong answers. The multiple-choice test also includes 100 items, each of which offers four alternative answer options. It, too, is scored only for the number of correct answers given, with no "correction for guessing."

Note, in the data at the bottom of Figure 1, the differences among the tests in average score (mean), in variability (standard deviation), in effective range and in estimated reliability. While these are hypothetical data, derived from calculations based on certain assumptions, they are probably reasonably representative of the results most teachers achieve in using tests of these types.

It is possible to obtain scores whose reliability is above .90 using 100 multiple-choice items, but it is not easy to do, and classroom teachers seldom do it in the tests they construct. It is also possible to handle 100-point essay tests and 100-item true-false tests so that their reliability will equal that of a 100-item multiple-choice test. But again, it is not easy to do and classroom teachers seldom succeed in doing it.

10. *The reliability of a test can be increased by increasing the number of questions (or independent points to be scored) and by sharpening the power of individual questions to discriminate between students of high and low achievement.* Figure 2 illustrates the increases of test reliability which can be expected as a result of increasing the number of items (or

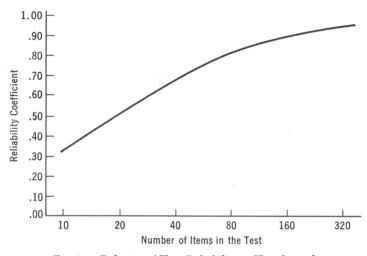

Fig. 2.   Relation of Test Reliability to Test Length.

independent points to be scored) in a test. Doubling the length of a 10-item test whose reliability coefficient is .33 increases the reliability to .50. Doubling again brings it up to .67, and so on. These estimates are based on the Spearman-Brown formula for predicting the reliability of a lengthened test. While the formula requires assumptions which may not be justified in all cases, its predictions are usually quite accurate.

Figure 3 shows how the maximum discriminating power of an item is related to its level of difficulty. These discrimination indices are simply differences between the proportions of correct response from good and poor students. Good students are those whose total test scores fall among the top 27 percent of the students tested. Poor students are those whose scores make up the bottom 27 percent. An item of 50 percent difficulty does not necessarily have (and usually will not have) an index of discrimination of 1.00. Its discriminating power may be zero, or even negative. But items of middle difficulty have higher ceilings on their discriminating power. What is more important, they not only can have, but usually do have, greater discriminating power than very easy or very difficult items. An item that no one answers correctly, or that everyone answers correctly, cannot discriminate at all. Such an item adds nothing to the reliability of a test.

In summary, the 10 principles stated and discussed in this article represent only a sample of the important things classroom teachers need to know about educational measurement. These principles, and the brief discussion of each presented here, may serve to call into question some common practices in classroom testing, or to suggest some ways in which

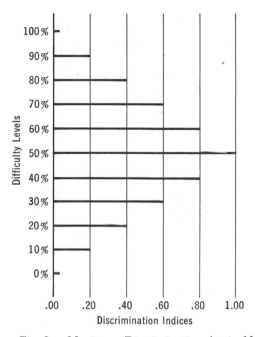

Fig. 3.   *Maximum Discrimination Attainable*
with Items at Different Levels of Difficulty.

classroom tests might be improved. They are not likely, and are not intended, to say all that needs to be said or do all that needs to be done to improve educational measurement in the classroom. It is our sincere belief, however, that a teacher whose classroom testing reflects an understanding of these principles will do a better than average job of measuring student achievement.

23   How Invalid Are Marks Assigned by Teachers?*

BY ROBERT SCRIVEN CARTER

EDITOR'S NOTE: *Have you ever thought about the factors which enter into a teacher's interpretation of test results and distribution of grades? (Like, maybe, your grade?) We frequently hear that girls get better grades than boys, particularly in elementary and high school. Why? Are girls smarter? Don't boys work as hard? In the preceding article, Dr. Ebel asserted that "Every important outcome of education can be measured." This may be true, but according to this eye-opening study, it can also be measured erroneously if we are not careful. Read on and as you do, keep a sensitive eye to the implications here for your own grading practices.*

With the rapid development of objective testing procedures in the United States, it was to be expected that there would be numerous investigations concerning teachers' marks. Mathematics, traditionally a subject which lends itself to objective measurement, has come in for its share of these investigations. There is a scarcity of investigations of the validity of teachers' marks in beginning algebra. Most studies devoted to the question of teachers' marks have been carried out with respect to elementary school arithmetic or with plane geometry. The latter, usually an elective subject, is not necessarily subject to the same factors in teachers' assignment of marks. Of the research in the elementary school field, a great portion is

* Reprinted and abridged from the *Journal of Educational Psychology*, 1962, Vol. 43, 218–228, by permission of the author and the American Psychological Association.

274

devoted to a discussion of sundry philosophical aspects of the question or an evaluation of the theoretical implications of marks in general.

THE PROBLEM

The investigation was designed to determine whether or not teachers tend to favor one sex and whether the sex favored tends to be determined by the sex of the teacher. The study sought an answer to the problem: With intelligence held constant, what is the relationship between the sex of the student and the sex of the teacher in the assignment of marks in beginning algebra? . . .

MATERIALS AND SUBJECTS

Results of an investigation of this type are of most value when they can be used for evaluation and interpretation over a wide area, or by a large number of individuals. With this in mind the investigation was undertaken in a city in western Pennsylvania. Two hundred sixty pupils took part in the testing program from which the basic data for this study were obtained. This investigation is based on two hundred thirty-five pupils taking high-school algebra for the first time. In all, nine classes were used, four classes being taught by women and five classes being taught by men. Of the students, one hundred thirty-five were boys and one hundred were girls. Since students are assigned to classes alphabetically, no known selective factors operate which would give a biased sample.

In the school in which the investigation was made, there are six teachers, three men and three women, teaching beginning algebra. The six teachers all hold valid Permanent High School Certificates issued by the Pennsylvania Department of Public Instruction. None of the teachers have had less than fifteen years of experience. The training of the three men and the three women used in this study was almost identical. Whatever effect factors of age, training, and experience may have on assigned marks was minimized.

During the last week of the first semester, the investigator administered the Otis Quick-Scoring Mental Ability Test, Beta Test, Form A, and the Colvin-Schrammel Algebra Test. Test I, Form A, to all students enrolled in the course in beginning algebra in the public school of a western Pennsylvania city. One week following the end of the first semester the examiner inspected the permanent record cards for the subjects used in the investigation. These cards were inspected in the office of the principal. From the cards, the examiner secured the necessary information concerning the marks assigned by individual teachers to each student as an indication of his level of achievement for the semester.

TABLE 1. *Differences and Critical Ratios Between Scores Made by Boys and Girls on the Otis Quick Scoring Mental Ability Tests, Beta Test*

N	Sex	Mean	SD	SE_M	Diff. (M_1-M_2)	SE_D	CR
	Taught by Men						
75	Boys	107.28	11.59	1.36			
58	Girls	108.90	8.84	1.16			
					1.62	1.79	.91
	Taught by Women						
60	Boys	107.60	8.15	1.05			
42	Girls	107.38	9.14	1.41			
					.22	1.76	.13
	Boys (Taught by)						
75	Men	107.28	11.59	1.36			
60	Women	107.60	8.15	1.05			
					−.32	1.72	−.19
	Girls (Taught by)						
58	Men	108.90	8.84	1.16			
42	Women	107.38	9.14	1.41			
					1.52	1.83	.83
	Totals (Taught by)						
133	Men	107.97	10.64	.92			
102	Women	107.51	8.57	.85			
					.46	1.25	.37
	Totals						
135	All Boys	107.42	10.34	.89			
100	All Girls	108.25	8.99	.90			
					−.83	1.26	−.66

RESULTS OF THE TESTING PROGRAM

For the purpose of this investigation, the sample is divided into four groups: 1) Boys taught by men teachers. 2) Girls taught by men teachers. 3) Boys taught by women teachers. 4) Girls taught by women teachers.

In the presentation of the data which follow, the results of the testing program are presented so as to reflect these categories.

A) Intelligence test results

In Table I are shown the critical ratios of the differences of the various groups with respect to mental ability as measured by the Otis Test. The differences for the various groups (range 1.62 to −.83), when treated statistically, give critical ratios that range from .91 to .13. The largest

TABLE II. *Mean Differences and Critical Ratios Between Scores Made by Boys and Girls on the Colvin-Schrammel Algebra Achievement Test, Form A*

N	Sex	Mean	SD	SE_M	Diff. (M_1-M_2)	SE_D	CR
	Taught by Men						
75	Boys	30.84	9.32	1.08			
58	Girls	29.15	7.74	1.02			
					1.69	1.49	1.13
	Taught by Women						
60	Boys	29.51	8.42	1.09			
42	Girls	30.52	7.19	1.11			
					−1.01	1.56	−.65
	Boys (Taught by)						
75	Men	30.84	9.32	1.08			
60	Women	29.51	8.42	1.09			
					1.33	1.54	.86
	Girls (Taught by)						
58	Men	29.15	7.74	1.02			
42	Women	30.52	7.19	1.11			
					−1.37	1.51	−.91
	Totals (Taught by)						
133	Men	30.10	8.70	.75			
102	Women	29.93	6.77	.67			
					.17	1.00	.17
	Totals						
135	All Boys	30.25	8.18	.70			
100	All Girls	29.73	7.54	.75			
					.52	1.02	.51

difference shown, that between boys and girls taught by men (1.62), gives a critical ratio of only .91. Differences as large as 1.62 might be expected by chance one out of five times. It is important to realize, therefore, that with respect to intelligence, as measured by the Otis Quick-Scoring Mental Ability Test, there are no statistically significant differences between the groups in the present investigation.

B) Algebra achievement test scores

The critical ratios of the differences between the means of the various groups based on the results of the Colvin-Schrammel Algebra Test are found in Table II. Differences range from 1.69 (the difference in mean scores for boys and girls taught by men) to .17 (the difference between groups taught by men and by women). It is to be noted that the average boy makes a better score on this test than does the average girl. The mean score for boys taught by men is higher than the mean score for girls taught by men. On the other hand the average score for girls taught by women exceeds the average score for the boys. The student whose sex is the same as that of the teacher makes higher mean scores than do the students whose sex is opposite to that of the teacher.

With respect to average achievement in algebra, as measured by the Colvin-Schrammel Test, the differences among the various groups in this investigation are not significant. The largest critical ratio, the critical ratio between the mean score for boys and girls taught by men, 1.13, indicates that differences as large as 1.69 could be expected by chance thirteen times out of one hundred. It must be concluded, then, that the small differences among the various groups could happen by chance, and, as far as ability in algebra is concerned, boys and girls, whether the teacher is a man or a woman, show equal algebra achievement within the limits of the present data.

C) Marks assigned by teachers

The critical ratios of the differences between the mean grades assigned to boys and girls by teachers of beginning algebra are found in Table III. Although it has been shown that no significant differences exist among the various groups in either intelligence or algebra achievement, significant differences are found in the marks assigned by teachers of beginning algebra.

The average mark assigned by men is 6.44 points lower than the average mark assigned by women. This difference is nearly six times the standard error of the difference. This cannot be attributed to chance factors. In all instances the girls receive higher average marks than do the boys. In the present investigation, the difference in marks assigned by men and women teachers indicates that men assign lower marks to boys and to girls.

More specifically, the data show that boys are given lower average marks than are girls, regardless of the sex of the teacher assigning the marks; but, marks assigned by men are lower than those assigned by women. Consequently, boys get the lowest average marks when those marks are assigned by men. Girls, on the other hand, get the highest marks when those marks are assigned by women teachers. . . .

SUMMARY

With respect to intelligence, no significant differences existed among any of the groups. In the results of the algebra achievement scores, small and, on the whole, insignificant differences favored the group whose sex was the same as the sex of the teacher. The differences in achievement

TABLE III.   *Differences and Critical Ratios Between Marks Assigned to Boys and to Girls by Teachers of Beginning Algebra*

N	Sex	Mean	SD	SE_M	Diff. (M_1-M_2)	SE_D	CR
	Taught by Men						
75	Boys	76.61	8.19	.95			
58	Girls	79.50	6.60	.87			
					−2.89	1.29	−2.24
	Taught by Women						
60	Boys	82.63	9.08	1.17			
42	Girls	86.71	8.67	1.34			
					−4.08	1.78	−2.29
	Boys (Taught by)						
75	Men	76.61	8.19	.95			
60	Women	82.63	9.08	1.16			
					−6.02	1.50	−4.01
	Girls (Taught by)						
58	Men	79.50	6.60	.87			
42	Women	86.71	8.67	1.34			
					−7.21	1.60	−4.51
	Totals (Taught by)						
133	Men	77.87	7.67	.67			
102	Women	84.31	9.15	.91			
					−6.44	1.13	−5.70
	Totals						
135	All Boys	79.29	9.10	.78			
100	All Girls	82.53	8.34	.83			
					−3.24	1.14	−2.84

were not significant at the one per cent level of confidence, indicating that the small differences which were present could have been accounted for by chance.

When the teachers' marks in beginning algebra were investigated, significant differences were observed. Girls made significantly higher marks than did the boys. Women teachers tended to give higher marks than did the men teachers. Specifically, when marks were assigned, boys were given lower marks than were the girls, regardless of whether the teacher was a man or a woman; but, marks assigned by men teachers were lower than marks assigned by women teachers.

CONCLUSIONS

1) It was evident from the data, although no significant differences could be found in intelligence or in algebra achievement, that significant

differences existed in the marks assigned by teachers, differences clearly not attributable to chance. The differences, generally, gave the advantage to the girls. It was made clear that the girls were no smarter, did not know any more algebra, but they did receive higher marks.

2) There were definite indications that intelligence was a factor in the assignment of marks. The correlation coefficient between teachers' marks and algebra achievement gave some indication that, theoretically, at least, they represent measurement of the same variable.

3) When intelligence was partialled out, and thus held constant, the relationship between teachers' marks and achievement declined. This indicated that the teachers' marks not only reflected achievement but also intelligence. Since the relationship was far from perfect, some other factors entered into the assignment of marks by teachers of beginning algebra.

4) It must be concluded that teachers' marks represent more than chance estimates of the pupils' achievement. The findings in the present investigation indicate that teachers' marks represent achievement, but, and this is important, they give evidence of the effects of intelligence upon the teacher.

5) It must also be concluded in the light of the data in the present investigation that the sex of the teacher was not so important in the investigation of marks as was the sex of the student. Regardless of whether the teacher was a man or a woman, boys were penalized in the assignment of marks. The penalty was not so great, at least so far as these data were concerned, if the teacher was a man. There was higher correlation between achievement and teachers' marks when the teacher was a man.

6) The data indicated a definite necessity for the refining of marks, if these marks are to reflect true achievement. The data used in this investigation proved that there is a slight overrating of girls generally and an underrating of boys, especially by women teachers. . . .

24   Nine Common Misconceptions About Tests and Test Results*

BY HENRY L. DYER

EDITOR'S NOTE: Testing, no matter what form it takes, is usually not a topic which most people can discuss unemotionally. Indeed, our very emotional involvement may stand in the way of a more objective look at what tests and test results are really all about. In this article, Dr. Dyer points to the major misconceptions which may get in the way of a better understanding and more appropriate use of intelligence, personality, achievement, and aptitude tests. Since misconceptions are built on false assumptions, it might prove interesting for you to examine your assumptions as you read this paper.

In his recent book called *The Schools,* Martin Mayer speaks of testing as a "necessary evil." I disagree. It is not *necessarily* evil. Tests *could* be a blessing to education if only teachers and counselors and educational administrators would divest themselves of a number of misconceptions about what tests can and cannot do and would learn to use test results more cautiously and creatively in the educational process.

There are nine principal misconceptions that seem to stand in the way of the appropriate use of tests.

The *first* misconception is the notion that aptitude or intelligence tests measure something called "native ability," something fixed and immutable within the person that determines his level of expectation for all time. I am

---

* Reprinted and abridged from *New York State Education,* October, 1961, Vol. 49, 16–19, by permission of the New York State Teachers Association. (This article was originally titled, "Is Testing a Menace to Education?")

not prepared to say such an inherent entity does not exist. The chances are it does. Studies in genetics certainly support the idea, and so do many psychological studies. But intelligence or aptitude tests do not *measure* such an entity—at least not directly, and certainly not in any interpretable manner.

What intelligence tests do measure is the individual's performance on certain types of mental tasks . . . a long time after the child has first entered the world. The kinds of mental tasks that appear in any intelligence or aptitude test are clearly the kinds that a student *learns* to perform from his experiences in the world around him. The amount of learning based on such experiences may depend on many things that can vary enormously from one child to another—the number and quality of books available in his home, the kind of talk he hears, the richness and variety of his surroundings, the vividness and emotional quality of the thousands of happenings in his life from day to day. It is absurd to suppose that a child's score on an intelligence test by-passes all these factors, to suppose that such a score gets directly at the brains he was born with.

I prefer to think of an intelligence test as essentially indistinguishable from an achievement test—that is, as a measure of how well, at a given point of time, a student can perform certain well-defined tasks. The main difference between the tasks in a so-called achievement test and those in a so-called intelligence test is, generally speaking, that the tasks in an achievement test are usually learned over a relatively short time and those in an intelligence test are learned over a relatively long time.

The consequences of thinking of an aptitude test as measuring some immutable determiner of student performance can be pretty serious. First, such thinking encourages the dangerous idea that one can, from an aptitude score, decide once and for all at a fairly early age what kind and level of educational or vocational activity a student is fitted for. It nurtures that hardy perennial, for instance, that if a student has an IQ of 115 or better he ought to prepare for college, and if his IQ is below 115 he ought to make other plans—this, despite all the studies which have shown that an IQ may be highly variable for a given student, that colleges vary enormously in the quality of students they enroll, and that some low scorers succeed in college while some high scorers fail. I have often wondered how many educational crimes are annually committed on the strength of the theory that intelligence tests measure something they cannot possibly measure.

A second consequence, almost as serious, is the conception that a student with a high aptitude score and low achievement scores (or low grades in school) is an "under-achiever"—another hardy perennial. It was exploded 30 years ago, but it is back and can lead to some rather distressing treatment of individual pupils. The diagnosis goes that a student with a high aptitude score and low achievement scores is "unmotivated" or "lazy" or suffering from some sort of emotional disturbance. Granted there may be some grounds for such diagnoses, nevertheless they are scarcely inferable from the discrepancy in scores alone. And some new and possibly more useful insights about such students might be forthcoming if one frankly regarded the discrepancies simply as differences in performance on one kind of achievement test as compared to another.

Finally, the idea that aptitude tests are supposed to measure native ability leads to the persistent and embarrassing demand that they should be "culture free"; that if they are, as they must be, affected by the student's background of experience in school and at home, then *ipso facto,* they are "unfair" to the underprivileged. I wish we could get it *out* of people's heads that tests are unfair to the underprivileged and get it *into* their heads that it is the hard facts of social circumstance and inadequate education that are unfair to them. If educational opportunities are unequal, the test results will also be unequal.

A *second* misconception about tests is the notion that a prediction made from a test score, or from a series of test scores, or from test scores plus other quantifiable data, are, or should be, perfectly accurate, and that if they are not, the tests must be regarded as no good. This fallacy arises from a confused conception of what constitutes prediction. There are some people—maybe most people—who think of prediction as simply an all-or-none, right-or-wrong business. If a test score predicts that Johnny will get B in American history, the score is right if he actually gets a B; it is wrong if he gets a B— or a C. I suppose this is a legitimate way of thinking about prediction in certain circumstances, but it is scarcely fair to the test and it may well be unfair to Johnny. A more meaningful and useful way of thinking about a prediction is to regard it as a statement of the odds: A given test score might predict that Johnny has 8 chances in 10 of getting a grade of B or better in American history, and 3 chances in a hundred of flunking. This approach recognizes that in forecasting future events, especially human events, we never have sufficient information to be sure of being right every time, but we do have information, in the form of test scores and other data, which, if appropriately organized, can help us make better decisions than would be possible without them.

The *third* misconception is that standardized test scores are infallible or perfectly reliable. Reliability, I remind you, has to do with the degree to which the score of an individual stands still on successive testings. It rarely occurs to the uninitiated that a test can never be more than a *sample* of a student's performance and that, in consequence, the score on any test is afflicted with sampling error. To the man-in-the-street, to many teachers, school administrators and parents, who have never reflected on the problem, a score is a score is a score, and they are shocked to find that when a student takes one test today and an alternate form of the same test tomorrow, his score can change. Anyone who deals with a test score must always be conscious that such a score, like any sort of measurement whatever, is clouded with uncertainty, that it is never more than an estimate of the truth.

A *fourth* misconception is the assumption that an achievement test measures all there is to measure in any given subject matter area—that an achievement test in history, for example, measures everything a high school student should know about the facts of history and how to deal with them. It never seems to occur to some people that the content of a standardized achievement test in any particular subject matter area may be only partially related to what a specific course of study in that area may call for.

If people will only take the trouble to look critically at the insides of achievement tests and not just at their covers, they will almost certainly find that even the test best suited to their purposes still fails to sample *all* the types of learning that are sought in a given subject, or even all the most important types of learning. And it may also often include matters that the student is not expected to know. The consequence is, of course, that on a particular standardized achievement test a student may look considerably better or considerably worse than he really is, and decisions based on his score may miss the boat by a considerable margin.

A *fifth* misconception is that an achievement test can measure only a pupil's memory for facts. This used to be true. But a good modern achievement test gets at far more than a command of facts alone; it usually measures in addition the pupil's skill in reasoning with the facts he remembers and also his skill in reasoning with facts newly presented to him. It is this introduction into achievement tests of the requirement to reason, to cope with problems, to think clearly, critically and even creatively that helps to blur the distinction between aptitude and achievement tests. The modern achievement test recognizes that as students come up through the grades they are, or ought to be, learning to think as well as to know. It recognizes also that there may be many different kinds of thinking to measure, depending upon the subject matter in which the thinking is required. The result is that a well-conceived battery of achievement tests gives the same sort of information one would get from a general intelligence test plus a good deal more.

A *sixth* misconception has to do with profiles of achievement or aptitude scores, that a profile of scores summarizes clearly and efficiently a considerable amount of reliable information about the relative strengths and weaknesses of an individual. Test technicians have inveighed repeatedly against the use of profile charts on the grounds that they are often grossly misleading, that the differences they depict—even when they appear large—may be, and usually are, unreliable differences, that the score scales used for the several tests in the profile may not be comparable, that the several measures which show on the profile may have the appearance of being highly independent measures when, in fact, many of them may be highly correlated—in short, that the apparent clarity and efficiency of a test score profile is really an illusion covering up all sorts of traps and pitfalls in score interpretation which even the most wary can scarcely avoid. Yet the profile chart is still in much demand and in wide use, primarily, I suppose, because it is extraordinarily convenient. Mere administrative convenience is hardly sufficient justification for hiding confusion under a false coat of simplicity. Good test interpretation takes mental effort, a bit of imagination and some willingness to cope with complexity.

A *seventh* misconception is that interest inventories measure some kind of basic orientation of a student irrespective of the kinds of experiences to which he has been or will be exposed. Let me cite just one example. A presumably well-trained guidance counselor in a high school where the large majority of students go on to college was confronted by a girl with top-notch scholastic standing in all of the college preparatory subjects. Her parents were college-trained people, had always expected their daughter would go to a liberal arts college; the daughter had always enthusiastically entertained the same idea. The counselor, however, was apparently bewitched by one of the girl's scores on an interest inventory which indicated her major interest was in clerical work. Disregarding all the other evidence, the counselor insisted that the girl was unfitted for the work of a liberal arts college and would be happy only in a secretarial school. Tears on the part of the child, anger on the part of the parents and hell-to-pay all around. Certainly interest test scores are useful in promoting thought and self-analysis, but certainly also the tests are scarcely capable of probing deeply enough into an individual's past and future to warrant anything approaching the dogmatism which characterized this counselor.

The *eighth* misconception is that on a personality test an individual reveals deep and permanent temperamental characteristics of which he himself may be unaware. I suppose there is nothing about the whole testing business that frightens me more than this. Anyone close to the research in personality testing who has any critical sense at all knows that we have still barely scratched the surface of a field whose dimensions are still far from defined. To put it perhaps a little too strongly, personality tests—the inventories, the projective tests, all of them—are scarcely beyond the tea-leaf-reading stage. To be sure, there is some interesting—even exciting—research going on in the area, but none of it yet adds up to tests that can be trusted as evidence leading to important decisions about children.

There are four major weaknesses in personality tests. First, they purport to measure traits such as introversion-extroversion, neurotic tendency, gregariousness, tolerance for ambiguity, and the like—all of which are highly fuzzy concepts, to say the least, and for none of which there are any agreed-upon definitions. There is not even any general agreement on what we mean by the word "personality" itself. How can you describe or classify a person meaningfully with a test whose scores do not themselves have any clear or rigorous meaning?

Secondly, it is characteristic of current personality tests that the behavior they sample is essentially superficial nonsignificant behavior. By this I mean when a subject answers such a question as "Do you often daydream?" his response of "Yes" or "No" may well be nothing more than a purely random phenomenon quite unconnected with any of his habitual behavior tendencies. The whole essence of the measurement problem is to secure reliable samples of human behavior under standardized conditions which will have strong correlates with the universe of behavior an individual habitually exhibits in his waking life. The personality tests currently available have yet to demonstrate that they can provide such samples.

Thirdly, even if we were able to establish some meaningful personality traits, we still know little or nothing about their stability. We still don't know whether an introvert at age 15 may not turn into an extrovert by the time he is 22.

Finally, of course, practically all personality tests can be faked. I proved to my own satisfaction how fakable such tests are when I gave one to a class I was once teaching. I asked the students to take a personality inventory twice—once to prove that they were thoroughly well adjusted people and once to prove that they were ready for a mental institution. The first set of scores showed that the whole class was a bunch of apple-cheeked extroverts; the second set showed that they were all nuts.

Please do not misunderstand me. I take a very dim view of current personality tests, and I think the general public is being much too frequently taken in by the mumbo-jumbo that goes with them. On the other hand, I am very much in favor of as much solid research as we can possibly get into the fundamental dynamics of human behavior, for we shall never be in full command of the educational process until we have far more understanding than we now have of what makes children tick. There are glimmerings of hope, but we are not out of the woods yet, and who can tell when we will be? In the meantime, let's not kid ourselves by putting our trust in gimmicks.

The *ninth* and final misconception is this: that a battery of tests can tell all one needs to know in making a judgment about a student's competence, present and potential, and about his effectiveness as a human being. The fact is that no test or series of tests now available is capable of giving the total picture of any child. Tests can illuminate many areas of his development, suggest something about his strengths and weaknesses, show in certain respects how he stands among his peers. But there are still many important aspects of learning and human development where we must still rely upon the observation and judgment of teachers if we are to get something that approaches a complete description of the child as a functioning individual. There are subtle but supremely important human elements in the teaching-learning situation that no combination of tests yet devised is able to capture. Such elements are elusive, but if ever we lose sight of them, the educational process in all its ramifications will become something less than the exciting human enterprise it should always be.

These are the nine misconceptions which I think most frequently lead to wide misuse of tests and test results. Some of our brasher critics have argued that, since tests are so widely misused, they do constitute a menace to sound education and therefore should be abolished. This argument is specious. It is the same as saying that automobiles should be abolished because they are a menace to human life when reckless drivers are at the wheel. Or it is the same as saying that teachers should be abolished because too many of them make psychometric hash out of marks and test scores.

In any case, I think it is highly unlikely that tests will be abolished any more than that textbooks will be abolished. Too many schools have discovered that, menace or not, they cannot operate effectively without them. The problem is not one of doing away with tests and testing but of getting people to use tests intelligently. When this happens testing will cease to be a mere administrative convenience or, worse still, a burden on the souls of teachers and pupils; it will become an effective instrument for vitalizing the total educational process and for helping to insure that in these days of skyrocketing enrollments the individual pupil will not be lost in the shuffle.

25   The Continuing Debate: To Mark or Not To Mark?*

BY ROBERT L. EBEL AND JOHN H. SUEHR

EDITOR'S NOTE: The three preceeding articles have exposed you to some of the basic principles of measurement, some of the possible reasons behind invalid grades, and some of the common misconceptions which interfere with a more appropriate use of tests and test results. We are at that point now which every teacher must face sooner or later: "To mark or not to mark?" It is one thing to talk about measuring achievement—few would disagree that this is important. The controversy is over how one assesses and reports this achievement. Grades? Parent-teacher conferences? Written evaluations? No grades at all? Dr. Ebel thinks grades are important and cites why he thinks so. Dr. Suehr thinks they are bad and minces no words in describing why. Now, then, what's your stance on the grading issue?

SHOULD SCHOOL MARKS BE ABOLISHED?

DR. EBEL

School marks of some kind are a significant element in almost all formal programs of education. Yet there are few educational practices that

* Reprinted from the *Michigan Journal of Secondary Education*, Fall, 1964, Vol. 6, No. 1, 12–30, by permission of the authors and the publisher. (Originally titled "Should School Marks Be Abolished?" by Robert L. Ebel; and "Marking and Reporting That is Meaningful, Accurate, and Human" by John H. Suehr.)

have been attacked more persistently, or for which a wider variety of remedies have been proposed. Clearly, the problem of marking is one that merits careful consideration, not only by school administrators but also by teachers, students, and all others concerned with the processes of education.

What Is a School Mark?

For the purposes of this discussion it may be helpful to define the term "school mark" rather specifically. *A school mark is a number or a letter that is used to express the level of a student's achievement in some subject of study.* At the beginning of this century numerical marks were prevalent. Usually the numbers purported to express the percent a student had learned of what he was expected to learn. Often a mark somewhere in the vicinity of 70 was regarded as the minimum passing mark.

Somewhat later, letter marks began to replace numerical marks in many schools and colleges. The system that became most popular made use of five letters, defined approximately in these terms:

A—excellent
B—good
C—average
D—poor
F—failing

This system, or some variant of it, is prevalent today.

The Need for Periodic Reports

The case for school marks, as here defined, rests primarily on the validity of two propositions. Here is the first.

It is educationally useful to determine, and to report periodically, the level of a student's achievement in each of the major subjects he is studying.

This proposition simply asserts that some kind of a determination of educational achievement should be made from time to time, and reported in some fashion to those who need to know it. It implies that if superior educational achievements are desired they must be defined, identified, and rewarded. The proposition suggests that those concerned with the processes of education ought to pay attention, systematically, to the results they are getting.

This seems to be a reasonable suggestion. Formal education is a purposeful activity. It is directed toward the attainment of certain goals. It requires the skillful management of complex processes. Things can go wrong, so that students sometimes fall far short of the desired levels of achievement. If these deficiencies are to be corrected, the first requirement is that they be clearly recognized. Periodic reports of levels of student achievement permit this recognition.

Formal education is an important activity. Communities go to a great deal of trouble to establish and maintain schools. Laws are passed, taxes are assessed, buildings are built, teachers are employed, courses are planned and taught, all for the purpose of promoting student learning. Is it reasonable to provide excellent facilities for learning without making some effort to assess what is being learned? Reports of student achievement provide one basis for this assessment.

Formal education is a cooperative activity. It requires the coordinated efforts, not only of students and teachers but also of school administrators and parents. All of them have a legitimate interest in the outcome of their efforts. They have a real need to know to what extent educational goals are being achieved, for if those goals are being attained badly they may need to change the nature and magnitude of their efforts. Reports on levels of student achievement can help to provide them with this knowledge.

Some Apparent Exceptions

Can not education occur in the absence of periodic evaluations? Indeed it can. A great deal of a person's education is gained informally or incidentally, not as a result of purposefully planned and carefully organized educational programs. While the extent and quality of a person's informal education will affect his success in formal schooling, it is not feasible or necessary to assess informal educational attainments separately and directly. The situations in which periodic determinations and reports of levels of achievement are most useful are those in which the educational experiences are planned and organized most purposefully to help students attain definite goals.

There are a few notable examples of educational programs, such as Sunday School programs, and certain educational-recreational programs for adults, in which formal efforts to evaluate student achievement are rare or absent altogether. In some of these no very definite goals for attainment are set. Continued attendance and participation is valued more highly than the achievement of any particular kinds or levels of competence. Learning unquestionably goes on, and in some instances it may go on very well. In other instances it appears to go very badly. Specific data on average levels of achievement are necessarily lacking. If no attempt is made to assess levels of achievement precisely and formally, no very specific or dependable data are likely to exist to show how good or poor the average level of achievement may be.

Some Logical Dilemmas

Those who claim that learning proceeds better in the absence than in the presence of systematic determinations of achievement encounter an interesting logical problem. They cannot provide evidence to support the claim without doing what they say ought not to be done. They must measure achievement to prove that learning is facilitated by not measuring achievement. It is impossible in principle to show that more will be learned when no attempt is made to determine how much has been learned. And there is something patently absurd in the assertion that the best progress will be made when no attention is paid to progress. It is like suggesting that a business will prosper best if it keeps no financial accounts, or that a driver will reach his destination most certainly if he drives with his eyes closed.

Somewhat the same logic applies to the suggestion that informal procedures for assessing and reporting student achievement provide better information than formal procedures. The only difference between the two is that the formal procedures are planned more carefully and purposefully, and executed more systematically. Surely careless, incidental, unsystematic determinations and reports cannot in the long run provide more useful information than can be obtained from purposeful, painstaking procedures. In almost all human activities, painstaking effort is a better recipe for success than casual indifference.

School Marks and Pupil Adjustment

Thus far in this discussion our attention has been directed toward educational achievement, toward cultivation of the student's knowledge and development of his abilities. But what of his feelings? What of his adjustment? Is there no danger that our periodic reports of levels of achievement may have the effect of destroying self-confidence and discouraging educational efforts?

There is indeed, and recognition of this danger has been largely responsible for suggestions that precise, systematic reports on achievement ought to be abolished, or at least de-emphasized. But the suggestions are unsound. If adopted they tend to impair achievement without contributing much to improved adjustment. Let us explain.

A rational person living in a real world is bound to experience failure as well as success. What he regards as success, and what as failure depends largely on his own self concept, and his own level of aspiration. If that level is much too high, he may experience failure rather consistently. But if he has come to terms with himself, and with the demands of the world, most of his days will seem to be reasonably satisfactory. The occasional stunning defeats will be balanced by about an equal number of glorious successes.

Anyone who expects his own performances to be consistently above average *for him* is expecting the impossible. Anyone who expects to excel others in all lines of endeavor is expecting the improbable. Most of us manage to find a few things we can do a little better than most other people, and we concentrate on doing those things. We settle for near average performance in most other activities.

These considerations are relevant to educational programs too. A school that strives to avoid experiences of failure is not helping students to come to terms with themselves or with life. A school that tries to shield a student from knowledge that he does some things better than others, and that some others can do many things better than he can, is not contributing much to his adjustment either. On the other hand, a school whose programs offer nothing but a high probability of failure to some of its students in anything they attempt to learn can hardly qualify as a good school. But in such cases it is the school's program, not the reports of achievement that should be blamed and corrected. The reports did not create the failure, and the failures would still be there, whether reported or not. In fact, systematic reports of student achievement can contribute to the solution of problems like this, by calling attention to their existence.

Thus even when the primary goal is adjustment rather than achievement, a good case can be made for periodic reports of student levels of achievement. To ignore differences in attainments, or to withhold information about them from those most concerned, the students and their parents, really solves no problems and helps no one in the long run. Ignorance is a poor ally to education, and the encouragement of ignorance has no place in the process of education. We need to know, and periodic determination and reporting of achievements help us to know, how well our efforts are succeeding and in what ways they need to be redirected.

The Case for Symbolic Marks

The second major proposition supporting the case for school marks is this.

A standard set of symbols, such as conventional letter or numerical marks, can provide a satisfactory means for reporting levels of student achievement.

Symbols such as these have the useful virtues of simplicity, conciseness, and convenience. If properly used they can have the essential virtue of unequivocal meaningfulness. Of course they cannot communicate all that might be useful about a student's strong and weak points, or the reasons for his successes or deficiencies. They provide only a single over-all index of the general level of achievement. But this is by all odds the most important thing to communicate in the first instance. It provides an excellent starting point and stimulus for more detailed investigations of attainments, deficiencies, and possible corrective actions.

The two chief rivals of symbolic marks are individually written descriptive reports and oral interviews. Both of these are much more time consuming than symbolic marks to prepare or conduct. While they permit communication of many more different items of information, each of these items tends to be less specifically stated, and to be less well supported by specific evidence. In these reports and interviews teachers try to say mainly pleasing, general things, in the interests of good interpersonal relations. Many of the same things can be said, without serious falsification, of almost all their students. Hence it is not surprising that teachers sometimes report difficulty in finding different ways to express the same impressions they have about many of their pupils.

The time required to write reports and conduct interviews raises other serious questions. It may impose an extra burden on the teachers. In some schools classes are dismissed for half a day over a two week period to allow the teacher time to interview the parents of each child separately. Whether a child's educational development is promoted enough, as a result of one half-hour interview, to make up for the loss of ten half-days of school work may be open to question.

The Meaningfulness of Marks

But, actually, how much meaning does a symbolic mark have? What does an A in first year French, or a D in beginning algebra, really signify?

To begin with, such marks have very little to say directly about how much French or how little chemistry the student knows. What they can say is that the student who got the A in French showed outstanding achievement, in comparison with his peers, all of whom were presumably seeking to attain the same goals. The D in chemistry reflects below average achievement. On the assumption that a reasonably good course was fairly well taught to moderately capable students, a well informed educator can make some pretty good guesses as to how much French or chemistry has been mastered in each case. But the meaning of the mark is essentially relative meaning, expressing the achievement of one student in relation to that of his classmates.

This is clearly limited meaning, but it is far from meaninglessness. It is about all the meaning one can reasonably ask of a standard set of symbols applied to all kinds of course content. Somewhat surprisingly, it may signify more with respect to actual content mastery than can be gleaned from the typical written report or oral interview.

To make a quantitative measure of achievement (i.e. a mark) *completely* meaningful with respect to content mastered, one would need a *complete* inventory of that content and all of its possible applications. This is a task so great as to be practically impossible of completion. The best one can hope for, ordinarily, is to approximate such an inventory with a sample of the items of knowledge and ability it ought to include. A good objective achievement test may provide such a sample. If one has a copy of the test before him, and knows what score a particular student made on it, he can form a reasonably accurate impression of what the student can or cannot do in that area of achievement.

The achievements of a group can often be reported meaningfully by indicating what proportion of its members can successfully complete each of a small number of representative tasks. During World War II, Admiral Nimitz used this technique effectively to report on the mathematical competence (or lack of it) of naval recruits. He presented a list of sixteen problems requiring fundamental arithmetical operations with whole numbers, common fractions and decimals, and reported that the average recruit could solve less than half of those problems correctly.

Limitations of Marks

The second proposition said that symbolic marks *can* be satisfactory. Often, it must be admitted, they are not. In some cases the school faculty has not taken the trouble to define the marks clearly, and to supervise the use of the marking system so as to maintain the defined meanings. In other cases, and for various reasons, teachers do not secure enough reliable data on levels of student achievement to make the marks they issue reasonably accurate. But the logical remedy for these deficiencies is to correct them, not to abolish marks.

School marks have a limited but an important function. They sometimes need to be supplemented by written reports and oral interviews. On the grounds of convenience and meaningfulness, however, they have definite advantages over other forms of periodic reports. They merit the widespread use that is currently made of them in an overwhelming majority of schools and colleges.

MARKING AND REPORTING THAT IS MEANINGFUL, ACCURATE, AND HUMAN

DR. SUEHR

Few practices of secondary schools are more criticized yet more universally practiced than that of evaluating student progress with letter symbols. An innovation in secondary school marking and reporting is needed that will in fact be in keeping with present knowledge of individual differences in abilities, interests, and personalities, as well as the process of learning.

In America, such ideals as life, liberty, the pursuit of happiness have become significant among our reasons for being. The nature of our objectives suggests that their accomplishment—our success as a nation—depends upon EACH of our people experiencing in significant ways the above mentioned ideals.

The MISSION of a secondary school is to assist EVERY student to develop real strengths—knowledge, understanding, attitudes, skills, and habits of life—to sustain him in a manner of living that is personally rewarding and socially beneficial.

A, B, C, D, and F marks are the most common symbols used to report educational achievement and progress in schools.

Traditional marks attempt to combine into a single letter mark levels of academic proficiency, improvement, rate of change, teacher judgment of student character as manifest through study habits, neatness, perseverance, effort, and many other factors. When a wide variety of different items are being compared by means of a single symbol, the evaluation is valid only when the same symbol applies to all facets.

The marks of evaluation given are accepted by the student as evaluations of himself. They become a part of his self-concept.

Many factors influence self-concept, but the judgment of teachers is highly important in the eyes of the student and his peers. The feeling of successful accomplishment is essential in building wholesome attitudes. The marks of evaluation should assist the student to develop a self-concept that is oriented in success– not in failure. Repeated studies of drop-outs show that the statement, "School is not for me," is supported by reference to grade cards. Therapists and sensitive counselors are well acquainted with such self-derogatory remarks as, "I'm just dumb!"

A more scientific approach toward educational problems is developing; marking and reporting practices which evolved during less enlightened times must also be changed. A new philosophy of reporting and marking should be developed for secondary schools based upon a recognition of individual differences in place of arbitrary standards for all. Evaluation should be more strongly focused on the school and less on the individual student.

Parents often consider marks as evaluations of the worth of the child and of their success or failure as parents. They, therefore, become important far beyond the importance which they merit. Parents learn to distrust and teach their children to distrust and question the motives and honesty of teachers and schools.

Very often the parent asks, "What have I done? I can't get my son interested in school. How have I failed?" While this may be a culturally accepted way of accusing the teacher of failing, it points to the fact that parents take personally marks given to their children. Low marks result in emotional outbursts at home. Parents force children to study. In some cases they withdraw children and place them in jobs, kick them out of the homes, or send them to boarding schools. Thus do parents reject and expel an unacceptable concept to themselves.

When parents do not reject the child, they may turn on the school and encourage the child to act out the family anger against teacher, principal and building.

Because of damage done to self-concepts by the traditional marking system, many students defensively resort to asocial and disapproved behavior. This leads to kick-outs, delinquency, and emotional handicaps.

Over ninety per cent of the children committed to correctional institutions have regularly experienced school failure. There is an increase in reckless driving, fist fights, and vandalism following the issuance of grade cards. Aggressive behavior by boys is an attempt to compensate for feelings of inferiority resulting from low marks. Girls experiencing difficulty in school are most often those who attempt to remake their faces and to gain approval through coy, brazen, and seductive behavior.

The pounding effect of repeated low marks emotionally handicaps students by making it more difficult for them to persist in studying and by reinforcing constrictive or "freeze-up" reactions during examinations. The fear of the anticipated failure-punishment overwhelms the student. Miraculous it is that so many students keep coming to schools as long as they do when the schools keep impressing them of their inferiority.

Marks are commonly used to maintain discipline, to coerce, and to punish. This is referred to as "Motivation."

Although teachers and principals are almost unanimous in their assertion that they disapprove using marks to punish, their expressed philosophies are incongruous with their actions.

Marks are sometimes inappropriately used to reward.

As often as they are used to punish, marks are used to reward. Attendance, punctuality, persistence, conscientiousness, spelling, grammar, a cleverly turned phrase and all of the little personality traits which fit the teacher's value system reflect in improved grades. Many an adult remarks with a grin, "When I was in school I studied the teacher more than the subject." What is this if not a tacit acknowledgment that blandishments, flattery and shrewd attention to the ego-involvement of the teacher are more rewarding than attention to subjects and texts?

Because of the lack of validity and rationale, the mental health of teachers is strained at each grading period.

Teachers develop philosophies of marking in keeping with their own personality structures. This is necessary because they must supply what rationale they can to the irrational tool they are obliged to use.

Some mark low at the first grading period and gradually raise the marks as the year passes. Sometimes the intent is to encourage after showing the students what they don't know. Sometimes it has the purpose of stimulating parents to call on the teacher so that she may, by implication and innuendo, point out what a poor job the teacher of the grade, year, subject, or level just below her does. Later she will demonstrate her capabilities by raising the marks. Some mark high because they feel this will encourage. Then they "bite their nails" over those who feel they are doing so well they need not work. Some try to grade ability and effort, ignoring achievement; others try to grade achievement and ignore ability and effort. The conscientious teacher worries about the marks she gives, and she should.

Educators have long been dissatisfied with the present system of grading. They have not discarded it because suggested "improvements" were almost always more of the same. Teachers, parents, and administrators meet time and again to study and revise report cards. They usually send to other schools for samples of what they are doing. This leads to few new ideas since there has been no attack on the basic underlying principles.

An adequate change requires a careful study of the purposes for having secondary schools. Basically, high schools instruct in five areas: Skills, Information, Art-Appreciation-Emotion, Problem-Solving, and Character Traits.

Most skills can be objectively measured, compared, and reported. Such evaluation will be in the nature of speculation.

How many more words per minute could I have typed had I practiced more? What is wrong with my typing rhythm? Is my time better spent working on something else? Push-ups or pull-ups in physical education may be reported and compared. Since evaluations are always personal, they should be treated in this manner.

Helping students acquire information and knowledge is a second important goal of education. Facts learned are memory items and memory can be checked through objective tests of recognition and recall.

Information is drawn from a vast ocean of facts, literature, and ideas so great that no class can do more than sample it. Learnings of this type may be objectively measured but comparisons are difficult. An objective measurement may be valid, but when it cannot be compared it lacks reliability. Even though the scores of two people may not legitimately be compared, the student can measure his own learning through a test-retest procedure. Teacher and tester skills have not developed sufficiently to make possible the measurement of all knowledge absorbed by students. Nonetheless skills have been developed which permit sampling measurements. Many nationally standardized tests are available and should be used both as guides and as ways of reporting scores.

Helping students learn ways to express their emotions and to interpret the emotions of others is a third charge of education.

The goals of education include knowledge of self, understanding one's own characteristics and motivations, and the appropriate development of individual abilities and interests. They include the understanding of man and society, and the development of a determination to strive for the welfare of all people. They involve effectiveness in communicating ideas and feelings, and in overcoming barriers to communication. Present tests do not touch the major personal elements and must remain subjective.

Teacher judgments relating to appreciation, art, and emotional expression should be descriptive. Where evaluations are made, they should be personal—teacher to parents, teacher to student, or student to student. Some tests of musical, artistic, and dramatic ability are available, but validity is low and in terms of employment or education. Such tests do not measure the personal aspect which is most important to the student. The student's declaration of his enjoyment of the class should be considered, with his family inspired attitudes, when judging the effectiveness of the class.

Evaluation in this field is a highly personal matter both for the evaluator and the evaluated. The teacher may evaluate this behavior according to the way she perceives conformity, initiative, creativeness, or resistance, but it must be an evaluation from the teacher's point of view. Worth remembering is that the more important and far-reaching a behavioral change is, the more difficult it is to measure. Secondary schools have not yet begun to recognize that feelings are facts.

The application of skills, knowledge, and appreciation in a problem-solving situation is one of the most vital aspects of education.

While a few tests have been developed to measure certain aspects of problem-solving ability, this must eventually be determined pragmatically, and any prior valuation must be subjective. Teachers may ingeniously devise problems to test a student's problem-solving ability. They never know, however, what fraction of the solution was derived from memory and mimicry, and what resulted from a flexible arrangement of previous learning into new and original concepts.

Judgments relating to problem-solving ability should be descriptive and in terms of challenges met or failed. Such judgments cannot be communicated in single words or letters. Conferences are most appropriate. Diary type statements maintain some aspects for later reference. Teacher, parent and student should listen to one another concerning this aspect of development. All comments should be directed toward helping the student to learn to use his abilities to solve the problem which he will face.

Finally, educational efforts are directed toward helping students develop habits and attitudes which assist them to fill their roles as citizens.

There are many habits, traits, and attitudes which are essential to successful living in a complex society. The list is almost inexhaustible, and success must be subjectively evaluated. The very listing of examples shows that they must be dealt with from the perceptions of the recorder. Marks such as Satisfactory, Unsatisfactory, and Needs Improvement are meaningless. This kind of evaluation is subject to the question, "Was this a wise way to approach this?" "Do you now see a way to improve in the future?" "What may have influenced your actions?" Judgment of personal characteristics reflects the teacher's value system. Reports must be descriptive so that students, teachers, and parents can accept and plan for improvement.

Several secondary school principals have read this article prior to publication. They have unanimously agreed with the content, but all have asked, "How would you make the change?" The asking of this question has significant meaning for preparation and in-service training programs of school administrators. One might begin by reading for understanding a book such as THE PLANNING OF CHANGE by Benne, Bennis, and Chinn, published by Holt, Rinehart, and Winston, 1962.

A RESPONSE TO DR. SUEHR ON MARKING

Dr. Ebel

Much of what Dr. Suehr has said seems true and reasonable to me. It *is* the mission of the school to educate every pupil as well as possible. The achievements which constitute that education *are* varied, complex, and not the same for all students. The teacher's aim *should be* to promote success rather than to detect failure. His evaluation of a pupil's achievement *is not* a simple task. Sometimes he does it rather badly. The reports he gives of those evaluations *are not* always received by pupils and parents with delight, or even with composure. Avenues of communication between teachers, pupils and parents other than the report card *are* always useful and sometimes essential. Schools need to be evaluated as well as (but not instead of!) pupils. On all these points and others we are in full agreement.

But on some important points we differ. I see systematic reporting, and the use of letter grades as aids rather than as obstacles to optimum educational achievement. I do not believe that the informal, ad hoc, subjective, descriptive, discursive, or self-evaluations that Dr. Suehr recommends, useful as they may be on occasion as supplements, can adequately replace periodic, systematic, concise, formal, objective reports from teachers on the educational achievements of their pupils. And I believe that symbolic letter grades, carefully assigned in conformity with the clearly specified principles of a coherent grading system, can communicate efficiently and meaningfully the central facts about levels of educational achievement.

A letter mark is clearly limited in meaning, but it need not be, and seldom *is* meaningless. It describes succinctly and specifically the over-all level of achievement. It surely does not tell all that could be told about that achievement. It often does not even begin to tell all the pupil or parent needs to know in order to act wisely to improve learning. But it provides an excellent starting point. In at least nine cases out of ten it tells as much as anyone wants to know or is likely to use effectively. Definiteness, conciseness and efficiency are some of the major virtues of a letter mark.

Part of the apparent difference of opinion between Dr. Suehr and me may be due to our focus of attention on different aspects of the total educational process. Dr. Suehr is interested in student development, and in doing things constructively to solve the educational problems that arise in the course of that development. It does not seem to him that conventional marking systems do much to foster that development or to solve those problems. If anything, he feels, marks create additional problems.

My interest is also in student development and the solution of educational problems. But a problem must be recognized and reported to those concerned before it can be effectively solved. And the educational enterprise must have immediate, tangible goals of achievement if it is to function effectively. Periodic, systematic reports of achievement, it seems to me, serve both of these purposes quite effectively.

Dr. Suehr obviously believes that some type of evaluation is essential in education, but he is appalled by the emotional damage and by the behavioral excesses that result from letter grading in general and from low letter grades in particular. He paints a much blacker picture of child rejection, vandalism and delinquency as consequences of grading than seems realistic to me. His position seems unrealistic to me, too, in appearing to claim for students all of the pleasures of success without any of the pains of failure. I do not believe this is possible. Pain is part of the price we pay for being alive, and grief part of the price for being human. Success is not a meaningful concept unless failure is possible and sometimes experienced. If evaluations of achievement are to have any significance they can not always be laudatory and comfortable. Sometimes they must hurt.

What bothers Dr. Suehr is that letter grades, in his judgment, hurt pupils and parents much more often and much more badly than they ought to be hurt. Again, I must say that I think he overstates the case, but his point is not without some foundation. If the pupil or his parents or his teachers are very foolish they may do things and think things and say things about school grades that do in fact contribute to dropouts, delinquency and emotional maladjustments. But most pupils, parents, and teachers are not that foolish. Certainly they don't need to be. And if they are, what is to blame? Is it the grading system or the foolishness?

One final point. I think Dr. Suehr is attacking the wrong enemy. It is educational failures, not the grades reporting them, that do the damage. In some cases the failures may be due to inappropriate educational programs, unrealistic aspirations or inadequate guidance. If so, these ought to be corrected. But it is not the fault of the steam gauge that a boiler explodes, and explosions can't be prevented by getting rid of the indicators. Quite the reverse! Educational deficiencies need to be corrected. I don't believe we can do it by refusing to look for them or to report them. And I don't believe Dr. Suehr does either.

A RESPONSE TO DR. EBEL ON MARKING

Dr. Suehr

Participating in an exercise of this nature makes vivid the advantage of two-way communication: Dr. Ebel and I have had the opportunity to check clarification of meaning; the reader should be so fortunate.

I would first like to mention some points where I feel agreement between us.

All constituents of the educational process should be concerned with evaluation of student achievement.

At this time, the emphasis is too strongly placed on the teacher. Involve the student, parent, and others in this process. Schools have yet to realize the help available, for student learning of many kinds, in the students themselves. A few schools have uniquely and profitably involved parents.

Formal, systematic evaluation of student achievement should be made by every school.

The difficulty of the task can create apathy on the part of many, but more refined methods will become available through continued attack on the problem.

Schools should be periodically evaluated, and student achievement should be one basis for this evaluation.

A more careful evaluation of the society in which we live, and the school's role in producing this society, would be welcome. If a small segment of the effort presently spent on evaluation of individuals in our society were used to evaluate the larger systems, a great benefit could be reaped. Evaluation of the individual might be lessened, and goal setting could become a common practice for the larger system.

As I see it, areas of disagreement between Dr. Ebel and me of some degree and kind are:

The purpose of schools in American Society.

One can define a limited goal for an educational activity and proceed with some objectivity to report progress toward its realization. This is today the common practice, while the broader, more desired and more difficult to evaluate goals are being ignored. In time, the historians of education will be amazed at present day lack of practice of knowledge in the behavioral sciences. Marking and reporting practices will be pointed to as one outstanding example.

The degree to which informal education should be considered when assessing progress in formal education.

An educator can close his mind to past and present outside the classroom experiences of students but the effect will still be there and evaluation processes should consider it. There are cultural differences in the same neighborhood.

The effect of present marking and reporting practices on students' self-concept.

The many factors forming one's self-concept are beyond known knowledge, but there should be little doubt that many failures are in fact created by marks. A greater emphasis must be placed on learning as a need in and of itself; presently much formal student activity is to pass the exam, to get the "A," the credit, the rank in class, the diploma, etc. Given the proper climate, no one is more interested in learning and wants more to succeed than the individual student himself. Much evaluation can and should be placed on him. In a few far-sighted secondary schools and classrooms in America, students are becoming responsible for their own learning and exams are taken by student request.

The usefulness of letter or numerical symbols for reporting student achievement.

Dr. Ebel seems more optimistic about the ability of symbols to accurately and adequately communicate a considerable body of knowledge. He probably considers the detailed plan I proposed as too ambitious and burdensome. Actually, it would be less of a chore and would eliminate many problems presently faced by teachers, administrators, law enforcement officials, and society in general. Grades are reported as first used at Oxford University; it's interesting to note that Oxford no longer uses letter grades and there is reason to hope that other institutions will follow.

What an "A" or a "D" in a Course Really Means

People in college admission offices throughout the country are perplexed by this problem. Even considering the assumptions stated by Dr. Ebel, I would strongly question the argument. I hope Admiral Nimitz didn't make the recruits feel too badly because those failing his little test might make the better sailors.

The Usefulness of Parent-Teacher Conferences

There is a trend in American schools toward fewer marking and reporting periods, and more parent-teacher conferences. The climate, as noted by Dr. Ebel, in which parent-teacher conferences are often held is in fact a criticism of present educational practice. The more personal the grading process becomes the more insecure the teacher is about her judgment. In one secondary school where the students started carrying their report cards to class and receiving their grades in individual conferences with their teacher, the GPA made a significant rise. The problem created by feelings of both parents and teachers is further indication of how educational institutions ignore feelings and the trouble people in general have in dealing with their feelings.

PART THREE

Toward Understanding Forces Which
Influence Growth and Development

"What could be more charming than a boy before he has begun to cultivate his intellect? He is beautiful to look at; he gives himself no airs; he understands the meaning of art and literature instinctively; he goes about enjoying his life and makes other people enjoy theirs." Virginia Woolf

Growth processes are as universal as they are individual. At the moment of birth, any two babies are as much alike as they will ever be, but from that time on they will grow increasingly *unlike* each other. Indeed, even though each growing child may share in common certain physical, or emotional, or intellectual, similarities, each, nonetheless, will develop that particular combination of characteristics which will enable him to be quite unlike any other person in the entire world.

The eleven readings in Chapters Seven and Eight are devoted to examining both the internal and external forces which contribute to the differential growth processes and developmental consequences of each growing child and adolescent.

The first reading in this section will introduce you to eight basic stages in the growth cycle of man which are closely linked to the expectations society makes on all of us as we move up the ladder of development. From here you will move into the secret world of the pre-adolescent as Dr. Redl addresses himself to the question of "What makes them tick?" We will then examine some fundamental techniques for building secure children in our schools as Dr. Stendler suggests positive ways in which teachers may contribute to the adjustment of children. What are some relationships between physical growth and personality development? In reading number 29, Dr. McCandless presents research evidence linking these two phenomena which may cause you to speculate about the relationships between your own physical development and the kind of person you see yourself as being. And how about adolescents? Are they as bad as we read about them to be—as parents (yours, maybe) say they are? The last two readings in Chapter Seven will confront you with two quite different points of view about this. Is it true, as Dr. Hurlock suggests, that many adolescents ". . . are turning into second-rate students, second-rate workers, and second-rate citizens." Or, is it true, as Dr. Keller suggests, that "Youth . . . have been getting better instead of worse." Whatever the answer, it is a matter for question and debate, and these two readings invite you to do just that.

The question of child-rearing practices and their consequences is explored at many levels in Chapter Eight. The question of child-rearing practices and their consequences is explored at many levels in Chapter Eighth. Dr. Bronfenbrenner suggests that child-rearing practices have changed drastically over the past 25 years and speculates about the influence this has had (and is having) on growing children. If you have ever wondered about the relationships between maternal behavior (like your mother's, say) and the subsequent behavior of children (like your own behavior, for example), selection 33 will help you to a clearer understanding of those relationships.

An extraordinarily sensitive discussion by Dr. Fromm has something to say to practically anyone interested in helping children love life and reach their full potential. Finally, the last two readings in Chapter Eight present you with two clashing diametrically opposed points of view about how to raise children. Do you want to raise children in a manner deliberately planned to achieve certain ends? Or, would you prefer to guide children so that each grows according to his own nature? If you have not thought about it, these two readings will encourage you to do so. In the continuing dialogue between what you already know and what you will discover, the readings in Part III may help you to be clearer about the issues related to child-rearing and other forces which influence growth and development.

CHAPTER SEVEN

GROWTH PROCESSES AND DEVELOPMENTAL CONSEQUENCES

26   *Youth and the Life Cycle**

BY ERIK H. ERIKSON

EDITOR'S NOTE: This reading is included here to serve as a backdrop for subsequent readings in this chapter dealing with growth processes. In the following interview article, Dr. Erikson identifies what he considers to be eight critical stages in man's psychosocial development, and the special crisis they bring. As you read this article, you might reflect over your own growth and development. The experience you had during each of the psychosocial stages you have gone through may have had a lot to do with the kind of person you are, and Dr. Erikson's growth framework described here will assist you to better understand the psychological undercurrents involved in growing up.

Question: Are there any points about your concepts of psychosocial development which you would now like to stress in the light of what you have heard about how they have been interpreted during the past decade in the training of professional persons and through them of parents and future parents?

Yes, I am grateful for the opportunity of making a few observations on the reception of these concepts. You emphasize their influence on teaching in various fields; let me pick out a few misunderstandings.

I should confess to you here how it all started. It was on a drive in the

* Reprinted from *Children*, March-April, 1960, Vol. 7, No. 2, by permission of the author and the Children's Bureau, Social Security Administration, U.S. Department of Health, Education, and Welfare.

countryside with Mrs. Erikson that I became a bit expansive, telling her about a kind of ground plan in the human life cycle, which I seemed to discern in life histories. After a while she began to write, urging me just to go on; she had found my "plan" immediately convincing. Afterward, a number of audiences of different professional backgrounds had that same sense of conviction—so much so that I (and others) became somewhat uneasy: after all, these psychosocial signposts are hardly *concepts* yet, even if the whole plan represents a valid *conception,* one which suggests a great deal of work.

What Mrs. Erikson and I subsequently offered to the White House Conference of 1950 was a kind of worksheet, which has, indeed, been used by others as well as myself in scientific investigation, and well integrated in a few textbooks. But its "convincingness" has also led to oversimplifications. Let me tell you about a few.

There has been a tendency here and there to turn the eight stages into a sort of rosary of achievement, a device for counting the fruits of each stage—trust, autonomy, initiative, and so forth—as though each were achieved as a permanent trait. People of this bent are apt to leave out the negative counterparts of each stage, as if the healthy personality had permanently conquered these hazards. The fact is that the healthy personality must reconquer them continuously in the same way that the body's metabolism resists decay. All that we learn are certain fundamental means and mechanisms for retaining and regaining mastery. Life is a sequence not only of developmental but also of accidental crises. It is hardest to take when both types of crisis coincide.

THE EIGHT STAGES IN THE LIFE CYCLE OF MAN

"Personality," Erikson has written, "can be said to develop according to steps predetermined in the human organism's readiness to be driven toward, to be aware of, and to interact with a widening social radius, beginning with a dim image of a mother and ending with an image of mankind. . . ." Following are the steps he has identified in man's psychosocial development, and the special crises they bring. In presenting them, he has emphasized that while the struggle between the negatives and positives in each crisis must be fought through successfully if the next developmental stage is to be reached, no victory is completely or forever won.

1. Infancy: Trust versus Mistrust

The first "task" of the infant is to develop "the cornerstone of a healthy personality," a basic sense of trust—in himself and in his environment. This comes from a feeling of inner goodness derived from "the mutual regulation of his receptive capacities with the maternal techniques of provision"[1]—a quality of care that transmits a sense of trustworthiness and meaning. The danger, most acute in the second half of the first year, is that discontinuities in care may increase a natural sense of loss, as the child gradually recognizes his separateness from his mother, to a basic sense of mistrust that may last through life.

II. Early Childhood: Autonomy versus Shame and Doubt

With muscular maturation the child experiments with holding on and letting go and begins to attach enormous value to his autonomous will. The danger here is the development of a deep sense of shame and doubt if he is deprived of the opportunity to learn to develop his will as he learns his "duty," and therefore learns to expect defeat in any battle of wills with those who are bigger and stronger.

III. Play Age: Initiative versus Guilt

In this stage the child's imagination is greatly expanded because of his increased ability to move around freely and to communicate. It is an age of intrusive activity, avid curiosity, and consuming fantasies which lead to feelings of guilt and anxiety. It is also the stage of the establish ment of conscience. If this tendency to feel guilty is "over-burdened by all-too-eager adults" the child may develop a deep-seated conviction that he is essentially bad, with a resultant stifling of initiative or a conversion of his moralism to vindictiveness.

IV. School Age: Industry versus Inferiority

The long period of sexual latency before puberty is the age when the child wants to learn how to do and make things with others. In learning to accept instruction and to win recognition by producing "things" he opens the way for the capacity of work enjoyment. The danger in this period is the development of a sense of inadequacy and inferiority in a child who does not receive recognition for his efforts.

V. Adolescence: Identity versus Identity Diffusion

The physiological revolution that comes with puberty—rapid body growth and sexual maturity—forces the young person to question "all sameness and continuities relied on earlier" and to "refight many of the earlier battles." The developmental task is to integrate childhood identifi-cations "with the basic biological drives, native endowment, and the opportunities offered in social roles." The danger is that identity diffu-sion, temporarily unavoidable in this period of physical and psychological upheaval, may result in a permanent inability to "take hold" or, because of youth's tendency to total commitment, in the fixation in the young person of a negative identity, a devoted attempt to become what parents, class, or community do not want him to be.

VI. *Young Adulthood: Intimacy versus Isolation*

Only as a young person begins to feel more secure in his identity is he able to establish intimacy with himself (with his inner life) and with others, both in friendships and eventually in a love-based mutually satisfying sexual relationship with a member of the opposite sex. A person who cannot enter wholly into an intimate relationship because of the fear of losing his identity may develop a deep sense of isolation.

VII. *Adulthood: Generativity versus Self-Absorption*

Out of the intimacies of adulthood grows generativity—the mature person's interest in establishing and guiding the next generation. The lack of this results in self-absorption and frequently in a "pervading sense of stagnation and interpersonal impoverishment."

VIII. *Senescence: Integrity versus Disgust*

The person who has achieved a satisfying intimacy with other human beings and who has adapted to the triumphs and disappointments of his generative activities as parent and coworker reaches the end of life with a certain ego integrity—an acceptance of his own responsibility for what his life is and was and of its place in the flow of history. . . .

In each crisis, under favorable conditions, the positive is likely to outbalance the negative, and each reintegration builds strength for the next crisis. But the negative is always with us to some degree in the form of a measure of infantile anxiety, fear of abandonment—a residue of immaturity carried throughout life, which is perhaps the price man has to pay for a childhood long enough to permit him to be the learning and the teaching animal, and thus to achieve his particular mastery of reality.

You may be interested to know that further clinical research has indicated that our dream life often depicts a recovery of mastery along the lines of these stages. Moreover, nurses have observed that any adult who undergoes serious surgery has to repeat the battle with these nemeses in the process of recovery. A person moves up and down the scale of maturity, but if his ego has gained a positive balance during his developmental crises, the downward movements will be less devastating than if the balance, at one stage or another, was in the negative.

Of all the positive aspects mentioned, trust seems to have been the most convincing—so convincing, in fact, that some discussions never reach a consideration of the other stages. I don't mean to detract from the obvious importance of trust as the foundation of the development of a healthy personality. A basic sense of trust in living as such, developed in infancy through the reciprocal relationship of child and mother, is essential to winning the positive fruits of all the succeeding crises in the life cycle:

maybe this is what Christmas, with its Madonna images, conveys to us. Yet, it is the nature of human life that each succeeding crisis takes place within a widened social radius where an ever-larger number of significant persons have a bearing on the outcome. There is in childhood, first, the maternal person, then the parental combination, then the basic family and other instructing adults. Youth demands "confirmation" from strangers who hold to a design of life; and later, the adult needs challenges from mates and partners, and even from his growing children and expanding works, in order to continue to grow himself, And all of these relationships must be imbedded in an "ethos," a cultural order, to guide the individual's course.

In our one-family culture (supported by pediatricians and psychiatrists who exclusively emphasize the mother-child relationship) we tend to lose sight of the fact that other people besides parents are important to youth. Too often we ask only where a given youth came from and what he once was, and not also where he was going, and who was ready to receive him and his intentions and his specific gifts. Thus we have movements to punish parents for the transgressions of their children, ignoring all the other persons and environmental factors that entered into the production of a young person's unacceptable behavior and failed to offer support to his positive search.

Another way in which the life cycle theory has been oversimplified is in the omission of stages which do not fit into the preconceived ideas of the person who is adopting or adapting the theory. Thus a large organization devoted to parenthood distributed a list of the stages but omitted *integrity versus despair*—the problem of senescence. This is too easy a way to dispose of grandparents; it robs life of an inescapable final step; and, of course, it defeats this whole conception of an intrinsic order in the life cycle.

This kind of omission ignores the "cogwheeling" of infantile and adult stages—the fact that each further stage of growth in a given individual is not only dependent upon the relatively successful completion of his own previous stages, but also on the completion of the subsequent stages in those other individuals with whom he interacts and whom he accepts as models.

Finally, I should point to the fact that what my psychoanalytic colleagues warned me of most energetically has, on occasion, come to pass: even sincere workers have chosen to ignore my emphasis on the intrinsic relation of the psychosocial to the psychosexual stages which form the basis of much of Freud's work.

All of these misuses, however, may be to a large extent the fault of my choice of words. The use of simple, familiar words like "trust" and "mistrust" apparently leads people to assume that they know "by feel" what the theory is all about. Perhaps this semantic problem would have been avoided if I had used Latin terms, which call for definitions.

I may point out, however, that I originally suggested my terms as a basis for discussions—discussions led by people who have an idea of the interrelatedness of all aspects of human development. For the eight stages of psychosocial development are, in fact, inextricably entwined in and derived from the various stages of psychosexual development that were described by Freud, as well as from the child's stages of physical, motor, and cognitive development. Each type of development affects the other and is affected by it. Thus, I feel that discussants would do well to study each key word in its origins, in its usages in various periods and regions, and in other languages. Simple words that touch upon universal human values have their counterpart in every living language, and can become vehicles of understanding at international conferences.

Incidentally, I made up one new word because I thought it was needed. To me, "generativity" described the chief characteristic of the mature adult. It was turned into a comfortable, if inaccurate, homespun word before it ever left the Fact-Finding Committee of 1950. I had deliberately chosen "generativity" rather than "parenthood," or "creativity," because these narrowed the matter down to a biological and an artistic issue instead of describing the deep absorption in guiding the young or in helping to create a new world for the young, which is a mark of maturity in parents and nonparents, working people and "creative" people alike.

Enough of this faultfinding! But it *is* interesting to see what can happen to new ideas; and you *did* ask me.

Question: *During the past 10 years you have been treating and studying mentally ill young people at a public clinic in a low-income area in Pittsburgh and at a private, comparatively expensive, mental hospital in the Berkshires. Have you found any common denominator in the disturbances of these patients—from such opposite walks of life—that would seem to point to any special difficulty harassing the young people of our land today?*

Since 1950, I have concentrated on the life histories of sick young people in late adolescence and early adulthood primarily in order to study one of the crises magnified, as it were, with the clinical microscope. I think that our initial formulations of the identity crisis have been clinically validated and much refined.

Many of these sick young people in their late teens and early twenties had failed during their adolescence to win out in the struggle against identity confusion. They were suffering so seriously from a feeling of being (or, indeed, wanting to be) "nobody" that they were withdrawing from reality, and in some cases even attempting to withdraw from life itself: in other words, they were regressing to a position where trust had to be reinstated. Their malaise proved to be related to the same sense of diffuseness which drives other young adults to incessant and sometimes delinquent activity—an effort to show the world, including themselves, that they are "somebody" even if deep down they do not believe it.

In the meantime, of course, the identity issue has been taken up by many writers and by some magazines, almost in the form of a slogan. We are prone to think that we have cornered an issue when we have found a name for it, and to have resolved it when we have found something to blame. So now we blame "the changing world."

Actually, there is no reason why youth should not participate with enthusiasm in radical change; young people are freer for change than we are. The bewildering thing for them must be that we now complain about change, having eagerly caused it ourselves with inventions and discoveries; that we seem to have played at change rather than to have planned it. If we had the courage of our inventions, if we would grow into the world we have helped to create, and would give youth coresponsibility in it, I think that all the potential power of the identity crisis would serve a better world than we can now envisage.

Let me say a word about identity, or rather about what it is not. The young person seeking an identity does not go around saying, even to himself, "Who am I?" as an editorial in a national magazine suggested last year's college graduates were doing on their way home. Nor does the person with a secure sense of identity usually stop to think or to brag about the fact that he has this priceless possession, and of what it consists. He simply feels and acts predominantly in tune with himself, his capacities, and his opportunities; and he has the inner means and finds the outer ways to recover from experiences which impair this feeling. He knows where he fits (or knowingly prefers not to fit) into present conditions. . . .

This sense of a coincidence between inner resources, traditional values, and opportunities of action is derived from a fusion of slowly grown, unconscious personality processes—and contemporary social forces. It has its earliest beginnings in the infant's first feelings of affirmation by maternal recognition and is nurtured on the quality and consistency of the parental style of upbringing. Thus identity is in a sense an outgrowth of all the earlier stages; but the crucial period for its development to maturity comes with the adolescent crisis.

Every adolescent is apt to go through some serious struggle at one time or another. The crises of earlier stages may return in some form as he seeks to free himself from the alignments of childhood because of both his own eagerness for adulthood and the pressures of society. For a while he may distrust what he once trusted implicitly; may be ashamed of his body, and doubtful of his future. He experiments, looking for affirmation and recognition from his friends and from the adults who mean most to him. Unconsciously, he revamps his repertory of childhood identifications, reviving some and repudiating others. He goes in for extremes—total commitments and total repudiation. His struggle is to make sense out of what has gone before in relation to what he now perceives the world to be, in an effort to find a persistent sameness in himself and a persistent sharing of some kind of essential character with others.

Far from considering this process to be a kind of maturational malaise, a morbid egocentricity of which adolescents must be "cured," we must recognize in it the search for new values, the willingness to serve loyalties which prove to be "true" (in any number of spiritual, scientific, technical, political, philosophical, and personal meanings of "truth") and thus a prime force in cultural rejuvenation.

The strengths a young person finds in adults at this time—their willingness to let him experiment, their eagerness to confirm him at his best, their consistency in correcting his excesses, and the guidance they give him—will codetermine whether or not he eventually makes order out of necessary inner confusion and applies himself to the correction of disordered conditions. He needs freedom to choose, but not so much freedom that he cannot, in fact, make a choice.

In some adolescents, in some cultures, in some historical epochs this crisis is minimal; in others it holds real perils for both the individual and society. Some individuals, particularly those with a weak preparation in their preceding developmental crises, succumb to it with the formation of neuroses and psychoses. Others try to resolve it through adherence—often temporary—to radical kinds of religious, political, artistic, or criminal ideologies.

A few fight the battle alone and, after a prolonged period of agony characterized by erratic mood swings and unpredictable and apparently dangerous behavior, become the spokesmen of new directions. Their sense of impending danger forces them to mobilize their capacities to new ways of thinking and doing which have meaning, at the same time, for themselves and their times. In my book *Young Man Luther* I have tried to show how identity is related to ideology and how the identity struggle of one intense young genius produced a new person, a new faith, a new kind of man, and a new era.

I think I chose to write about Luther and his time because there are many analogies between our time and his, although today the problems which beset all historical crises are global and, as it were, semifinal in character. Today, throughout the world, the increasing pace of technological change has encroached upon traditional group solidarities and on their ability to transmit a sense of cosmic wholeness and technological planfulness to the young.

To me one of the most disturbing aspects of our technological culture is the imbalance between passive stimulation and active outlet in the pleasures that are sanctioned for young people. With the passing of the western frontier and the accelerated appearance of automatic gadgets, young people have become increasingly occupied with passive pursuits which require little participation of mind or body—being conveyed rapidly through space by machines and watching violent fantasies at the movies or on television—without the possibility of matching the passive experience with active pursuits. When an adolescent substitutes passivity for the adventure and activity which his muscular development and sexual drives require, there is always the danger of explosion—and I think that this accounts for much of the explosive, unexpected, and delinquent acts on the part of even our "nice" young people.

This is probably why "Westerns," always on the borderline of the criminal and the lawful, capture the passive imagination of a youth which has traditionally substituted identification with the rugged individualist— the pioneer who ventures into the unknown—for commitment to a political ideology; and which now finds itself confronted with increasing demands for standardization, uniformity, and conformity to the rituals of a status-convention. While the national prototype has historically been based on readiness for change, the range of possibilities of what one might choose to be and of opportunities to make a change [has] narrowed. To this has been added most recently the rude shaking of the once "eternal" image of our Nation's superiority in productivity and technical ingenuity through the appearance of Sputnik and its successors.

Thus one might say the complexity of the adolescent state and the confusion of the times meet head on.

However, I believe that the "confusion" derives from a hypocritical denial of our true position, both in regard to obvious dangers and true resources. When youth is permitted to see its place in a crisis, it will, out of its very inner dangers, gain the strength to meet the demands of the time.

Clinical experience with young people has, it is true, verified that combination of inner and outer dangers which explains aggravated identity crises. On the other hand, it has convinced me and my colleagues, even in hospital work, of the surprising resources which young people can muster if their social responsibilities are called upon in a total environment of psychological understanding.

Question: *Does this kind of confusion have anything to do with juvenile delinquency?*

I would not want to add here to the many claims concerning distinct and isolated causes of juvenile delinquency. But I would like to stress one contributing factor: the confused attitudes of adults—both laymen and professionals—toward the young people whom we, with a mixture of condescension and fear, call teenagers.

Except perhaps in some rare instances of congenital defects resulting in a low capacity to comprehend values, juvenile delinquents are made, not born; and we adults make them. Here, I am not referring to their parents exclusively. True, many parents, because of their own personalities and backgrounds, are not able to give their children a chance for a favorable resolution of the identity crisis. Nor am I referring to the failure of society at large to correct those blights on the social scene—such as overcrowded slums and inequality of opportunities for minority groups—which make it impossible for tens of thousands of young people to envisage an identity in line with the prevailing success-and-status ideology.

Rather I am referring to the attitudes of adults—in the press, in court, and in some professional and social institutions—which push the delinquent young person into a "negative identity," a prideful and stubborn acceptance of himself as a juvenile delinquent—and this at a time when his experimentation with available roles will make him exquisitely vulnerable (although he may not admit or even know it) to the opinions of the representatives of society. When a young person is adjudicated as a potential criminal because he has taken a girl for a ride in somebody else's car (which he intended to abandon, not to appropriate), he may well decide, half consciously, of course, but none the less with finality, that to have any real identity at all he must be what he obviously *can* be—a delinquent. The scolding of young people in public for the indiscretions they have committed, with the expectation that they show remorse, often ignores all the factors in their histories that force them into a delinquent kind of experimentation. It is certainly no help toward a positive identity formation.

In his insistence on holding on to an active identity, even if it is temporarily a "negative" one from the point of view of society, the delinquent is sometimes potentially healthier than the young person who withdraws into a neurotic or a psychotic state. Some delinquents, perhaps, in their determination to be themselves at all costs and under terrible conditions have more strength and a greater potential for contributing to the richness of the national life than do many excessively conforming or neurotically defeatist members of their generation, who have given up youth's prerogatives to dream and to dare. We must study this problem until we can overcome the kind of outraged bewilderment which makes the adult world seem untrustworthy to youth and hence may seem to justify the choice of a delinquent identity.

Actually, transitory delinquency, as well as other forms of antisocial or asocial behavior, often may be what I have called a *psychosocial moratorium*—a period of delay in the assumption of adult commitment. Some youths need a period of relaxed expectations, of guidance to the various possibilities for positive identification through opportunities to participate in adult work, or even of introspection and experimentation—none of which can be replaced by either moralistic punishment or condescending forgiveness.

Question: *The theme of the 1960 White House Conference on Children and Youth charges the Conference with studying and understanding "the values and ideals of our society" in its efforts "to promote opportunities for children and youth to realize their full potential for a creative life in freedom and dignity." On the basis of the scheme which you presented to us in 1950, could you add a word about how these values, once identified, can be transmitted in a way that will insure their incorporation into the value systems of the young?*

Like every other aspect of maturity the virtues which we expect in a civilized human being grow in stages as the child develops from an infant to an adult. What is expected of a child at any time must be related to his total maturation and level of egostrength, which are related to his motor, cognitive, psychosexual, and psychosocial stages. You can't expect total obedience from a two-year-old who must test a growing sense of autonomy, nor total truth from a four-year-old involved in the creative but often guilt-ridden fantasies of the oedipal stage.

It would be in line with the course of other historical crises if in our nation today a certain sense of moral weakness were producing a kind of frantic wish to enforce moral strength in our youth with punitive or purely exhortative measures.

Today, a sense of crisis has been aggravated by the long cold war and the sudden revelation of the technical strength of a supposedly "backward" rival. We are wondering whether we have made our children strong enough for living in such an unpredictably dangerous world. Some people, who suddenly realize that they have not been responsible guardians of all the nation's young, now wonder whether they should have beaten moral strength into them or preached certain absolute values more adamantly.

No period, however, can afford to go back on its advances in values and in knowledge, and I trust that the 1960 White House Conference will find a way to integrate our knowledge of personality development with our national values, necessities, and resources. What we need is not a plan whereby relatively irrresponsible adults can enforce morality in their children, but rather national insistence on a more *responsible* morality on the part of adults, paired with an *informal* attitude toward the *development* of moral values in children. Values can only be fostered gradually by adults who have a clear conception of what to expect and what not to expect of the child as, at each stage, he comes to understand new segmentts of reality and of himself, and who are firm about what they are sure they *may* expect.

It must be admitted that psychiatry has added relatively little to the understanding of morality, except perhaps by delineating the great dangers of moralistic attitudes and measures which convince the child only of the adult's greater executive power, not of his actual moral power or true superiority. To this whole question, I can, on the basis of my own work, only indicate that the psychosocial stages discussed in 1950 seem to open up the possibility of studying the way in which in each stage of growth the healthy child's developmental drives dispose him toward a certain set of qualities which are the necessary fundaments of a responsible character: in *infancy,* hope and drive; in *early childhood,* will and control; in the *play age* purpose and direction; in the *school age,* skill and method; and in *adolescence,* devotion and fidelity. The development of these basic qualities in children, however, depends on the corresponding development in adults of qualities related to: in *young adulthood,* love, work, and affiliation; in *adulthood,* care, parenthood, and production; and in *old age,* "wisdom" and responsible renunciation.

Now I have given you another set of nice words, throwing to the winds my own warning regarding the way they can be misunderstood and misused. Let me point out, therefore, that I consider these basic virtues in line with our advancing psychoanalytic ego-psychology, on the one hand, and without advancing knowledge of psychosocial evolution, on the other, and that the conception behind this list can only be studied in the context of advancing science. I will discuss this further in a forthcoming publication, but I mention it now because I thought I owed you a reference to the way in which my contribution of 1950 has gradually led me in the direction of the great problem of the anchoring of virtue in human nature as it has evolved in our universe.

We ought to regard the breaking of a child's spirit—by cruel punishment, by senseless spoiling, by persistent hypocrisy—as a sin against humanity. Yet today we have back-to-the-woodshed movements. Last year in the legislature of one of our greatest states a bill was introduced to allow corporal punishment in the public schools and was lauded by part of the press. This gave the Soviets a chance to declare publicly against corporal punishment, implying that they are not sufficiently scared by their own youth to go back on certain considered principles in the rearing of the young. Actually, I think that we stand with the rest of the civilized world on the principle that if adult man reconsiders his moral position in the light of historical fact, and in the light of his most advanced knowledge of human nature, he can afford, in relation to his children, to rely on a forbearance which step by step will bring the best *out* of them. . . .

FOOTNOTE:

[1] Erik H. Erikson, "Growth and Crises of the 'Healthy Personality,'" Symposium on the Healthy Personality (New York: Josiah Macy, Jr., Foundation, 1950).

27   Pre-adolescents—What Makes Them Tick?*

BY FRITZ REDL

EDITOR'S NOTE: In this very readable article, Dr. Redl describes some of the wild and unpredictable antics associated with children going through that little-known growth stage called pre-adolescence. Two possible explanations for pre-adolescent behavior are offered along with some suggestions as to how parents (teachers, too) can survive this crucial period of developmental metamorphosis. We sometimes forget that growth involves not just physical changes but psychological changes as well. This paper should help you focus more clearly on the psychological aspects of growth during pre-adolescence.

The period of pre-adolescence is a stretch of no-man's land in child study work. By pre-adolescence I mean the phase when the nicest children begin to behave in a most awful way. This definition cannot exactly be called scientific, but those who have to live with children of that age will immediately recognize whom I am talking about. This also happens to be the age about which we know least. Most of our books are written either about Children or about Adolescents. The phase I am talking about lies somewhere between the two—crudely speaking, between about nine and thirteen, in terms of chronological age, or between the fifth and eighth grade in terms of school classification.

It is surprising that we know so little about this age, but there certainly is no doubt that it is one of the most baffling phases of all. Most referrals to child guidance clinics occur around this age, and if you look for

* Reprinted from *Child Study*, 1944, Vol. XXI, 44–48, 58–59, by permission of the author and the Child Study Association of America, Inc.

volunteers to work on programs in recreation or child care, you will make this peculiar discovery: you will have no trouble finding people who just love to bathe little babies until they smell good and shine. You will have a little more, but not too much, trouble finding people who are just waiting for a chance to "understand" adolescents who "have problems" and long for a shoulder on which to cry. But the pre-adolescent youngster offers neither of these satisfactions. You won't find many people who will be very happy working with him.

Are they children? No. Of course, they still look like young children. Practically no visible change has as yet taken place in their sex development. The voice is about as shrill and penetrating as it ever was, the personal picture which they represent is still highly reminiscent of a child—of about the worst child you have met, however, definitely not of the child they themselves were just a short time ago.

Are they adolescent? No. While filled with a collector's curiosity for odd elements of information about human sex life at its worst, they are not as yet really maturing sexually. While they occasionally like to brag about precocity in their sex attitude, "the boy" or "the girl" of the other sex is still something they really don't know what to do with if left alone with it for any length of time. While impertinent in their wish to penetrate the secrets of adult life, they have no concepts about the future, little worry about what is going to happen to them, nothing they would like to "talk over with you."

The reason why we know so little about this phase of development is simple but significant: it is a phase which is especially disappointing for the adult, and especially so for the adult who loves youth and is interested in it. These youngsters are hard to live with even where there is the most ideal child-parent relationship. They are not as much fun to love as when they were younger, for they don't seem to appreciate what they get at all. And they certainly aren't much to brag about, academically or otherwise. You can't play the "friendly helper" toward them either—they think you are plain dumb if you try it; nor can you play the role of the proud shaper of youthful wax—they stick to your fingers like putty and things become messier and messier the more you try to "shape" that age. Nor can you play the role of the proud and sacerdotal warden of the values of society to be pointed out to eager youth. They think you are plain funny in that role.

So the parent is at a loss and ready for a desperate escape into either of two bad mistakes—defeatism or tough-guy-stubbornness. The teacher shrugs her shoulders and blames most of this pre-adolescent spook on the teacher the youngster had before her, or on lack of parental cooperation, and hopes that somehow or other these children will "snap out of it." Even the psychiatrist, otherwise so triumphantly cynical about other people's trouble with children, is in a fix. For with these children you can't use "play techniques" any longer. They giggle themselves to death about the mere idea of sitting in one room with an adult and playing a table game while that adult desperately pretends that this is all there is to it. And one can't use the usual "interview technique" either.

They find it funny that they should talk about themselves and their life, that they should consider as a "problem" what has "just happened," that they should try and remember how they felt about things, and that they are constantly expected to have "worries" or "fears"—two emotions which they are most skillful at hiding from their own self-perception, even if they do occur. Most of these youngsters seriously think the adult himself is crazy if he introduces such talk, and they naïvely enjoy the troubles they make, rather than those they have, and would much rather bear the consequences of their troubles than talk about them, even though those consequences include frustration or a beating or two.

Research, too, with very few exceptions, has skipped this period. If you study adolescence, you certainly can have graphs and charts on the rate at which the growth of pubic hair increases, the timing between that and the change of voice, and the irrelevance of both in terms of psychosexual development. Unfortunately, at the age we are talking about little of all this seems to take place. No drastic body changes occur, and whatever may happen within the glands is certainly not dramatic enough to explain the undoubtedly dramatic behavior of that phase. For a while some Yale biologists tried to discover an increase in hormone production around the age of eight, long before there is any visible sex maturation. However, they had trouble in making their research results useful for practical purposes. It took them weeks for one specimen of urine to be boiled in the right way as to show up the existence or non-existence of these hormones, and in the meantime Johnny would probably have been kicked out of five more schools anyway. In short, research has discreetly left this phase alone, and has retired from it, as it always does from things which are either too hard to demonstrate by statistical methods, or too hot to talk about after they have been discovered.

Thus, the practitioner—the parent, the teacher, counsellor or group worker—is left to his own devices. Fortunately, most of the things which are characteristic symptoms of this phase are known to us all.

PRE-ADOLESCENT BEHAVIOR—BAD AND IMPROPER

Here are some of the most frequent complaints adults raise in connection with their attempts to handle pre-adolescents: Outwardly, the most striking thing about them is their extreme physical restlessness. They can hardly stand still, running is more natural to them than walking, the word sitting is a euphemism if applied to what they do with a table and a chair. Their hands seem to need constant occupational therapy—they will turn up the edges of any book they handle, will have to manipulate pencils, any objects near them, or any one of the dozen-odd things they carry in their pockets, or even parts of their own body, whether it be nose and ears, scratching their hair, or parts of the anatomy usually taboo in terms of infantile upbringing. The return to other infantile habits is surprisingly intensive in many areas: even otherwise well-drilled and very housebroken youngsters may again show symptoms like bed-wetting, soiling, nail-biting, or its substitutes, like skin-chewing, finger-drumming, etc. Funny gestures and antics seem to turn up overnight with little or no reason—such things as facial tics, odd gestures and jerky movements, long-outgrown speech disorders, and the like.

In other areas these youngsters do not return to exactly the same habits of their infancy, but they go back to typical problem areas of younger childhood and start again where they had left off. Thus their search for the facts of life which had temporarily subsided under the impact of partial parental explanations will be resumed with vehemence, and with the impudence and insistence of a news correspondent rather than with the credulity of an obedient young child. It is the oddity, the wild fantastic story and the gory detail which fascinate them more than parental attempts at well-organized explanations of propagation, which they find rather boring.

Their old interpretation of the difference of sexes is revived, too. Girls seem obviously inferior to boys, who again interpret the difference in sex as that of a minus versus plus rather than of a difference in anatomical function. Thus girls are no good unless they are nearly like boys; and where the direct pride in masculine sexuality is subdued, indirect bragging about the size and strength of the biceps takes its place and becomes and sets the evaluation of anybody's worth. The girls go through somewhat the same phase, accept the interpretation of the boys all too eagerly and often wander through a period of frantic imitation of boyish behavior and negation of their female role. What sex manipulation does occur at this age usually happens in terms of experimentation and is on a highly organic level and very different from the masturbation of later adolescent years.

The fantasy life of youngsters of this age is something to look into, too. Wild day-dreams of the comic strip type of adventure, on the one hand, long stages of staring into empty space with nothing going on in their conscious mind on the other, are the two poles between which their fantasy life moves rapidly back and forth. Often manipulative play with a piece of string or the appearance of listening to the radio cover long stretches of quickly changing flights of ideas, and youngsters who reply "nothing," when you ask them what they were thinking about, do not necessarily lie. This description really fits the content as far as it could possibly be stated in any acceptable logical order and grammatical form.

The most peculiar phenomena, though, are found in the area of adult-child relationships. Even youngsters who obviously love their parents and have reason to do so, will develop stretches of surprising irritability, distrust, and suspicion. Easily offended and constantly ready with accusations that adults don't understand them and treat them wrongly, they are yet very reckless and inconsiderate of other people's feelings and are quite surprised if people get hurt because of the way they behave. The concept of gratitude seems to be something stricken from the inventory of their emotions. The worst meal at the neighbors', at which they weren't even welcome, may be described more glowingly in its glory than the best-planned feast that you arranged for their birthday. The silliest antics, the most irrelevant possessions or skills of neighbors will be admired 'way beyond any well-rooted qualities and superior achievements of father and mother.

Daily life with Junior becomes a chain of little irritations about little things. The fight against the demands of obeying the rules of time and space is staged as vehemently as if the children were one or two years old again. Keeping appointed meal times, coming home, going to bed at a prearranged hour, starting work, stopping play when promised—all these demands seem to be as hard to get across and as badly resented, no matter how reasonable the parents try to be about them, as if they were the cruel and senseless torments of tyranny.

Lack of submission to parent-accepted manners becomes another source of conflict. If these youngsters would listen as attentively to what Webster has to say as they do the language of the worst ragamuffin on the street corner, their grades in English would be tops. Dressing properly, washing, keeping clean are demands which meet with obvious indignation or distrust. In a way, they seem to have lost all sense of shame and decency. Previously clean-minded youngsters will not mind telling the dirtiest jokes if they can get hold of them, and the most charming angels of last year can spend an hour giggling over the acrobatics which a youngster performs with his stomach gas and consider it the greatest joke.

And yet, while unashamed in so many ways, there are other areas of life where they become more sensitive rather than more crude: the idea of being undressed or bathed by their own parent may all of a sudden release vehement feelings of shame hitherto unknown to their elders, and the open display of affection before others makes them blush as though they had committed a crime. The idea of being called a sissy by somebody one's own age is the top of shamefulness and nearly intolerable because of the pain it involves.

One of the most interesting attitude changes during this period is that in boy-girl relationships. The boy has not only theoretical contempt for the girl but he has no place for her socially. Social parties which adults push so often because they find the clumsiness of their youngsters so cute, and because it is so safe to have boys and girls together at that age, such social dances are a pain in the neck to youngsters, who would obviously much rather have a good free-for-all or chase each other all over the place. The girls have little place in their lives for the same-age boys either. It is true that with them the transition through this pre-adolescent period usually is shorter than with the boys. But for a time their actual need for boy company is nil. The picture is different, though, if you watch the children within their own sex gangs. Then, all of a sudden, in talks under safe seclusion with their buddies, the boys or girls will display a trumped-up interest in the other sex, will brag about their sexual knowledge or precocity or about their success in dating. All this bragging, however, though it is about sex, is on an entirely unerotic level; the partner of the other sex only figures in it as the fish in the fisherman's story. The opposite sex, like the fish, serves only an indirect means for self-glorification.

WHAT MAKES THEM TICK?

The explanation of this peculiar phenomenon of human growth must, I think, move along two lines. One is of an *individualistic* nature, the second is a chapter in *group psychology*.

Explanation No. I: During pre-adolescence the well-knit pattern of a child's personality is broken up or loosened, so that adolescent changes can be built into it and so that it can be modified into the personality of an adult

Thus, the purpose of this developmental phase is not *improvement* but *disorganization;* not a permanent disorganization, of course, but a dis-organization for future growth. This disorganization must occur, or else the higher organization cannot be achieved. In short, a child does not become an adult by becoming bigger and better. Simple "improvement" of a child's personality into that of an adult would only produce an over-sized child, an infantile adult. "Growing" into an adult means leaving behind, or destroy-ing some of what the child has been, and becoming something else in many ways.

The real growth occurs during adolescence: pre-adolescence is the period of preliminary loosening up of the personality pattern in order that the change may take place. It is comparable to soaking the beans before you cook them. If this explanation is true, then we can understand the following manifestations:

1. During this "breaking-up-of-child-personality" period, old, *long-forgotten or repressed* impulses of earlier childhood will come afloat again, for awhile, before they are discarded for good. This would explain all that we have described about the return to infantile habits, silly antics, irritating behavior, recurring naughty habits, etc.

2. During this period of the breaking up of an established pattern, we also find that *already developed standards and values* lose their power and become ineffectual. Therefore the surprising lack of self-control, the high degree of disorganization, the great trouble those youngsters have in keeping themselves in shape and continuing to live up to at least some of

the expectations they had no difficulty living up to a short time ago. The individual conscience of the child seems to lose its power, and even the force of his intelligence and insight into his own impulses is obviously weakened. This would explain all we have said about their unreliability, the lowering of these standards of behavior, the disappearance of some of the barriers of shame and disgust they had established and their surprising immunity to guilt feelings in many areas of life.

3. During a period of loosening up of personality texture, we would expect that the whole individual will be full of conflict, and that the *natural accompaniments* of conflict will appear again, namely, *anxieties and fears*, on the one hand, and *compulsive mechanisms of symbolic reassurance*, on the other. This is why so many of these youngsters really show fears or compulsive tics which otherwise only neurotic children would show. Yet this behavior is perfectly normal and will be only temporary. This would explain the frequent occurrence of fantastic fears in the dark, of ghosts and burglars, and it would also explain the intensity with which some of these youngsters cling to protective mechanisms, like the possession of a flashlight or gun as a symbol of protection, or the display of nervous tics and peculiar antics which usually include magic tricks to fool destiny and assure protection from danger or guilt.

For a long time I thought that all this about finishes the picture of pre-adolescent development, until a closer observation of the group life of pre-adolescents showed me that such a theory leaves much unexplained. It seems to me that there is still another explanation for a host of pre-adolescent symptoms.

Explanation No. II: During pre-adolescence it is normal for youngsters to drop their identification with adult society and establish a strong identification with a group of their peers

This part of pre-adolescent development is of a group psychological nature, and is as important to the child's later functioning as a citizen in society as the first principle is for his personal mental and emotional health. This group phenomenon is surprisingly universal and explains much of the trouble we adults have with children of pre-adolescent age. To be sure that I am rightly understood, I want to emphasize that what happens during this age goes way beyond the personal relationship between Johnny and his father. Johnny's father now becomes for him more than his father: he becomes, all of a sudden, a representative of the value system of adult society versus the child, at least in certain moments of his life. The same is true the other way around. Johnny becomes more to his father than his child: at certain moments he isn't Johnny any more but the typical representative of Youth versus Adult. A great many of the "educational" things adults do to children, as well as many of the rebellious acts of children toward adults, are not meant toward the other fellow at all; they are meant toward the general group of "Adults" or "Youth" which this other person represents. To disentangle personal involvement from this group psychological meaning of behavior is perhaps the most vital and so far least attempted problem of education in adolescence.

If this explanation is true, then it seems to me that the following phenomena of pre-adolescent behavior will be well understood:

1. In no other age do youngsters show such a deep need for *clique and gang formation* among themselves as in this one. From the adult angle this is usually met with much suspicion. Of course, it is true that youngsters will tend to choose their companions from among those who are rejected, rather than approved of, by their parents. Perhaps we can understand why the more unacceptable a youngster is on the basis of our adult behavior code, the more highly acceptable he will be in the society of his own peers. The clique formation of youngsters among themselves usually has some form of definitely "gang" character: that means it is more thoroughly enjoyed by being somewhat "subversive" in terms of adult standards. Remember how youngsters often are magically fascinated by certain types of ring-leaders, even though this ring-leadership may involve rather harmless though irritating activities—such as smoking, special clothes, late hours, gang language, etc.

From the angle of the adult and his anxieties, much of this seems highly objectionable. From the angle of the youngster and his normal development, most of it is highly important. For it is vital that he satisfy the wish for identification with his pals even though or just because such identification is sometimes frowned upon by the powers that be. The courage to stick to his pal against you, no matter how much he loves you and otherwise admires your advice is an important step forward in the youngster's social growth.

2. In all groups something like an *unspoken behavior code* develops, and it is this unwritten code on which the difference between "good" and "bad" depends. Up to now the youngster has lived within the psychological confines of the adult's own value system. Good and bad were defined entirely on the basis of adult tastes. Now he enters the magical ring of peer-codes. And the code of his friends differs essentially from that of adult society. In some items the two are diametrically opposed. In terms of the adult code, for instance, it is good if children bring home high grades, take pride in being much better than the neighbor's children, in being better liked by the teacher, and more submissive to the whims of the teaching adult than are other people's children. In terms of peer-standards things are directly reversed. Studying too much exposes you to the suspicion of being a sissy, aggressive pride against other children is suspiciously close to teacher-pet roles, and obedience to the adult in power often comes close to being a fifth columnist in terms of "the gang."

Some of the typically adult-fashioned values are clearly rejected by peer standards; others are potentially compatible at times, while conflicting at other times; some of them can be shared in common. Thus, a not too delinquent "gang" to which your youngster is proud to belong may be characterized by the following code-range: it is all right in this gang to study and work reasonably well in school. It is essential, though, that you dare to smoke, lie, even against your own father, if it means the protection of a pal in your gang, that you bear the brunt of scenes at home if really important gang activities are in question. At the same time this gang would not want you to steal, would be horrified if your sex activity went beyond the telling of dirty stories, and would oust you tacitly because they would think you too sophisticated for them. The actual group of pre-adolescents moves between hundreds of different shades of such gang-codes, and the degree to which we adults have omitted opening our eyes to this vital phase of child development is astounding.

3. The change from *adult-code* to *peer-code* is not an easy process for a youngster but full of conflict and often painful. For, while he would like to be admired by his pals on a peer-code basis, he still loves his parents personally and hates to see them misunderstand him or have them get unhappy about what he does. And, while he would love to please his family and be again accepted by them and have them proud of him, he simply couldn't face being called a sissy or be suspected of being a coward or a teacher's pet by his friends. In most of those cases where we find a serious conflict between the two sets of standards, we will find the phenomenon of *social hysteria*. This applies to youngsters who so overdo their loyalty to either one of the two behavior standards that they then have to go far beyond a reasonable limit. Thus, you find youngsters so scared of being thought bad by their parents that they don't dare to mix happily with children of their own age; and you find others so keen to achieve peer status with friends of their own age that they begin to reject parental advice, every finer feeling of loyalty to the home, and accept all and any lure of gang prestige even if it involves delinquent and criminal activity. It is obvious that a clear analysis by the adult and the avoidance of counter-hysteria can do much to improve things.

HOW TO SURVIVE LIFE WITH JUNIOR

If any of the above is true, then it should have an enormous impact on education. For then most of this pre-adolescent spook isn't merely a problem of things that shouldn't happen and ought to be squelched, but of things that should happen, but need to be regulated and channelized. Of course, you can't possibly just let Junior be as pre-adolescent as he would like without going crazy yourself, and you definitely shouldn't think of self-defense only and thus squelch the emotional and social development of your offspring. How to do both—survive and also channelize normal but tough growth periods without damage to later development—is too long a story to complete in a short article. But here are a few general hints:

1. Avoid Counter-Hysterics

It seems to me that ninety per cent of the more serious problems between children and parents or teachers on which I have ever been consulted could have been easily avoided. They were not inherent in the actual problems of growth. They were produced by the hysterical way in which the adults reacted to them. Most growth problems—even the more serious ones—can be outgrown eventually, though this may be a painful process—provided the adults don't use them as a springboard for their own over-emotional reactions. This does not mean that I advocate that you give up and let everything take its course. I do suggest you study the situation and decide where to allow things and where to interfere. The problem is: whichever you decide to do—the *way* you do it should be realistic, free from hysteric over-emotionalism. With this policy in mind you can enjoy all the fun of having problems with your child without producing a problem child.

2. Don't Fight Windmills

Let's not forget that pre-adolescents are much more expert in handling us than we ever can be in handling them. Their skill in sizing us up and using our emotions and weaknesses for their own ends has reached a peak at this age. It took them eight to ten years to learn, but they have learned by thorough observation. While we were worrying about them, they were not worried about us, and they had ample time and leisure to study psychology. This means that if they now go out on the venture of proving to themselves how emancipated they are, they will choose exactly the trick which will irritate us most. They will develop pre-adolescent symptoms in accordance with their understanding of our psychology. Thus, some of them will smoke, curse, talk about sex, or stay out late. Some will stop being interested in their grades, get kicked out of school, or threaten to become the type of person who will never be acceptable in good society. Others again will develop vocational interests which we look down on, will choose the company we dread, talk language which makes us jump, or may even run away at intervals.

But whatever surface behavior they display—don't fall for it. Don't fight the behavior. Interpret the cause of it first, then judge how much and in what way you should interfere. Thus, Johnny's smoking may really mean he is sore that his father never takes him to a football match, or it may mean he thinks you don't appreciate how adult he already is, or it may mean he has become dependent on his class-clown. Mary's insistence upon late hours may mean she doesn't know how to control herself, or it may mean she is sore because her school pals think you are social snobs who live a life different from theirs, or it may mean she is so scared that her sex ignorance will be discovered that she has to run around with a crowd more sophisticated about staying up late, so as to hide her lack of sophistication in another respect.

In any case, all these things are not so hard to figure out. Instead of getting excited and disapproving of the strange behavior, just open your eyes for a while and keep them open without blinking.

3. Provide a Frame of Life Adequate for Growth

No matter how much you dislike it, every pre-adolescent youngster needs the chance to have some of his wild behavior come out in some place or other. It will make a lot of difference whether or not he has a frame of life adequate for such growth. For example: Johnny needs the experience of running up against some kind of adventurous situation where he can prove he is a regular guy and not just mother's boy. Cut him off from all life situations containing elements of unpredictability and he may have to go stealing from the grocery store to prove his point. Give him a free and experimental camp setting to be adventurous in and he will be happily pre-adolescent without getting himself or anybody else in trouble. All youngsters need some place where pre-adolescent traits can be exercised and even tolerated. It is your duty to plan for such places in their life as skillfully as you select their school or vocational opportunities.

4. Watch Out for Pre-adolescent Corns

Most people don't mind their toes being stepped on occasionally. But if there is a corn there, that is a different matter. Well, all pre-adolescents have certain corns, places where they are hypersensitive. Avoid these as much as possible. One of the most important to avoid is harking back to their early childhood years. The one thing they don't want to be reminded of is of themselves as small children, yourself as the mother or father of the younger child. If you punish—don't repeat ways you used when they were little. If you praise—don't use arguments that would please a three-year-old but make a thirteen-year-old red with shame or fury. Whether you promise or reward, threaten or blackmail, appeal to their sense, morals, or anything else, always avoid doing it in the same way you used to do when they were little.

I have seen many pre-adolescents reject what their parents wanted, not because they felt that it was unreasonable or unjustified, but on account of the way in which the parents put the issue. There is something like a developmental level of parental control as well as developmental levels of child behavior. The two have to be matched or there will be fireworks.

5. If in Doubt, Make a Diagnostic Check-up

Not all the behavior forms we described above are always merely "pre-adolescent." Some of them are more than that. After all, there are such things as juvenile delinquents and psycho-neurotics, and we shouldn't pretend that everything is bound to come out in the wash.

Usually you can get a good hunch about dangerous areas if you check on these points: How deep is the pre-adolescent trait a youngster shows? If it is too vehement and impulsive, too unapproachable by even the most reasonable techniques, then the chances are that Johnny's antics are symptoms not only of growth but also of something being wrong somewhere and needing repair. Often this may be the case: Five of Johnny's antics are just pre-adolescent, pure and simple, and should not be interfered with too much. However, these five are tied up with five others which are definitely serious, hang-overs from old, never really solved problems, results of wrong handling, wrong environmental situations, or other causes. It will do no good to brush off the whole matter by calling it pre-adolescent. In that case the first five items need your protection and the other five need a repair job done. Whenever you are very much in doubt, it is wise to consult expert help for the checkup—just as you would in order to decide whether a heart murmur is due to too fast growth or to an organic disturbance.

28   Building Secure Children in Our Schools*

BY CELIA BURNS STENDLER

EDITOR'S NOTE: *Unfortunately, classroom practice does not always keep pace with theories and facts related to growth and development. Dr. Stendler suggests that some of our notions of how children develop are based on poor mental hygiene and contribute negatively to a student's total adjustment in school. Before reading this article, answer "true" or "false" to the following statements: (1) If a child does a thing once, chances are he'll continue doing it; (2) If a child will simply try hard enough, he can do almost anything; (3) Once a child knows he's good, there's a tendency for him to let up on trying to learn; (4) If a child is having fun, chances are he isn't learning; (5) Everyone fails sometime and he might as well experience failure early. How did you do? Read on and find out.*

In 1942, a study was published which had important bearings for classroom teachers in America. This was a study of the emotional adjustment of children in three large public schools of a midwestern city. On the basis of the evidence which Rogers presents, the average classroom teacher can expect that twelve per cent of the pupils in her classroom will have seriously maladjusted personalities and that as high as thirty per cent will show evidence of being poorly adjusted to some degree.

* "Building Secure Children in Our Schools," by Celia Burns Stendler. From *Childhood Education*, January, 1949, Vol. 25, No. 5. Reprinted by permission of the author and the Association for Childhood Education International, 3615 Wisconsin Avenue, N.W., Washington, D.C., 20016.

Those who are raising eyebrows at these figures and questioning whether the situation with regard to mental health is as serious as Rogers pictures it may be interested to know that the judgment of other experts supports Rogers' estimates. Indeed, one mental hygienist has estimated that out of one hundred children in school, one or two will spend part of their lives in jail, eight or ten will be committed to mental institutions, and thirty to fifty will be maladjusted to a lesser degree.

Sociologists, too, are pointing out that the kind of social order in which we live is creating serious personality disturbances. James West argues that " 'rugged individualism' exacts a heavy toll in the security of the individual by compelling him to maintain defensive hostilities to all around him outside the family unit and even within it." A social order which fosters extreme competitiveness, hostility, and envy is not conducive to the best mental health.

Many teachers will support Mr. Rogers and the other authors quoted who share his point of view. Indeed, some teachers feel that the number of maladjusted children may be increasing. There are primary teachers who report that they are dealing with more children in their classes who are emotionally disturbed than ever before. There are junior high and senior high school teachers who are disturbed by the increasing number of difficult pupils with whom they come in contact.

Even if many teachers feel that predictions of the number of individuals who will have personality disturbances are exaggerated and that the situation is not as dark as has been pictured, nevertheless most of us will probably agree that many of the pupils with whom we are dealing have some peculiar quirks which keep them from functioning as efficiently as they might otherwise. Unfortunately, we teachers frequently adopt a procedure for dealing with these quirks which only serves to make them worse. Yet schools *can* promote better adjustment, can help to build secure children. It will be the task of this article to point out first steps in the process.

One of the first steps we shall need to take in building secure children in our classrooms is to examine our theories of child development. Whether we are a teacher of forty first graders or a science teacher in a junior high, whether we are a graduate of a two-year normal school or have a master's degree from a college of education, whether we have ever taken any work in the field of child development or not, we teach and treat children according to our ideas of how children grow and develop.

Most of these ideas are part of our culture and we learn them just as we learn habits of speech and attitudes toward other people. Perhaps because these ideas are learned so painlessly, we rarely question their origin or their validity. We may be surprised when we do so to find that recent research has proved some of our theories wrong and that we may be operating on a principle which stands in the way of doing an effective job in promoting the good adjustment of pupils. Indeed, some of us may actually be adding to the burden of troubled youngsters.

Let us examine some of our notions of how children develop to see which ones are based upon poor mental hygiene and which ones contribute positively to the adjustment of children.

IF HE DOES IT ONCE

One of the most common misconceptions of how children grow and develop is the notion that if a child does a thing once, chances are he'll be doing it that way for the rest of his life. Therefore, in order to build correct habits, we must correct a child the first time he does something wrong. We don't want him to build up wrong ways of behaving or develop the notion that he can get away with something. Here are a few examples of how this principle looks in operation:

> If a five-year-old has trouble with the letter "r" we must correct him every time he mispronounces a word so he won't be doing it that way forever.
> If we find a thirteen-year-old smoking cigarettes, we should punish him severely so he won't learn the habit at that age.
> If we tell John to remain at three o'clock to finish his work and he slips out to play baseball, we should call his home and have him return to school so he won't learn the habit of evading responsibility.

This notion undoubtedly represents a popularization of Watsonian behaviorism in its attempts to explain all actions in terms of the conditioned reflex. John would learn he could slip out after school if he did it once because the connection would have been made in his nervous system between (a) neglecting work and (b) having a good time after school. Similarly, the more a pupil says the "r" sound wrong, the stronger the improper connection becomes and the less likelihood is there of changing to the correct sound. But what John B. Watson left out of the picture were the two following principles:

> As the child moves from one phase of development to another, he will revise many of the habits which have prevailed for a time. The nine-year-old who delights in blood-and-thunder radio serials may completely reject these same programs when he is thirteen. The pre-school child who says "I don't got any" will slough off such speech patterns of his own accord as he takes on the speech patterns of his social group. The dirty, unkempt preadolescent roughneck changes into a dandified gentleman when he first sees a girl as a girl. In other words, some of the traits which we see in children may be attributed to a particular phase of development and will disappear with age.
> All behavior is caused, and in many cases the explanation may lie deep in the emotions. Bill may continue to be dirty and rough and unkempt even when the rest of his gang has dolled up and is dating the girls. But the reason he continues in his preadolescent behavior may not

be because he was not corrected when he first began but because he may have grown up with the idea that he doesn't amount to much. He may feel so inadequate, have such a poor opinion of himself that he can't bring himself to revise his old habits. An overly-simple, superficial explanation of Bill's behavior in terms of habit-formation may stand in the way of planning a program for the boy which will really help him.

IF HE TRIES HARD ENOUGH

A second misconception which bears examination is the belief that if a child will simply try hard enough, he can do anything. "He could be an A student if he'd only try hard enough." "Johnny can do his arithmetic when he puts his mind to it." "If he'd make more of an effort, he could learn to read."

Many of us make statements similar to these about some of our students. Such notions about how children grow and develop undoubtedly had their origins in theories of the will—that man can, by the use of his will-power, develop his capacities to the fullest extent. But let us see how this works out with children.

In the first place, we grossly misjudge the intelligence of children in our classrooms. One writer shows that teachers may err in estimating intelligence quotients of pupils even to the extent of classifying as geniuses some children with intelligence quotients well below 90.

In Lewis Terman's famous *Genetic Studies of Genius* he reports that if one is allowed only one method of locating the highest IQ in a classroom, the chances of getting the right child are better if one picks the youngest child in the room rather than if one trusts a teacher's judgment. In other words, unless we have some objective evidence, we may be wrong when we assume that a child *has* the ability to do better work.

In the second place, a child may not be able to produce to the best of his ability not because he doesn't want to hard enough but because of an emotional barrier. A third grade pupil may not be able to learn to read because he's been told in not too subtle a fashion that reading is something he's no good at; he may have repeated the first grade because he couldn't learn to read and so he may look upon it as something he can't do.

A sounder approach to child growth would include recognition of the fact that feelings sometimes get in the way of a child's doing his best work academically. Notice the word *academically*. This means that a student may actually be doing his best in other fields. A high school English pupil may not be doing well in class but it may be because he is putting so much time and energy into learning how to get along with the other sex. This latter job, and very important one, he does very well but receives no credit for it on his report card. Indeed, as Havighurst has pointed out, unless the high school student sees the relationship between the academic task and his developmental task, the academic task will have to be policed.

IF HE KNOWS HE'S GOOD

Another misconception of child behavior which many teachers harbor is that we must never let the child know how good he is; we must always hold up higher standards than he can possibly meet. Too many of us operate on the notion that once a child knows he's good, he will immediately stop trying to learn. Therefore, a child is never good; he is only better than he was and on his way to becoming still better.

John has written a number of excellent compositions in the Fall but when report card time comes we give him a B so that he'll have the higher goal of A to shoot at in the next report. Giving him an A may keep him from trying to improve.

Mary comes up to show her booklet. "It's nice," we say unenthusiastically, "but let's see what we can suggest to make it better."

There is no quarrel with the notion that most of us may be capable of doing better work more efficiently than we are now doing, but there is argument against the theory that the way to get a child to raise his level of aspiration is to tell him continually he isn't good enough the way he is. Actually the task of helping a child choose a goal of a higher degree of difficulty is not so simple.

However, we do know that praise facilitates the rise of the level of aspiration. An experiment with young children shows that when they are praised for what they have done, they tend to choose a task of a relatively higher degree of difficulty the next time. We also know that it may be necessary for a child to feel that he *can* lower his level of aspiration.

Experiments by C. Anderson would seem to indicate that if the choice of a goal with a lesser degree of difficulty is made impossible, regression of the maturity of aspiration can be observed. In other words, if a child is made to feel he *cannot* lower his level of aspiration, he may act in a manner characteristic of a younger age level.

Not only do we block progress by withholding praise but we are frequently unrealistic in setting goals in terms of a child's ability. As has been pointed out above, we frequently misjudge an individual pupil's ability. Furthermore, we are inclined to encourage children to overshoot the mark rather than to choose a level of aspiration they are capable of attaining.

IF HE IS HAVING FUN

A fourth fallacy in our thinking about how children grow and develop is the notion that if a child is having fun, he isn't learning; learning is a painful experience.

Witness the kindergarten teacher who stops her class after fifteen minutes of "work period" where the children have been busy learning social skills in the doll corner, with the blocks, at the easel, at the workbench—the teacher who stops all this and calls her class together to start on a directed activity so that the children may begin to learn to work together.

Or the high school English teacher whose class is engaged in a gripe session on certain school regulations before the period officially begins. When the bell rings, the teacher briskly calls the class to order and organizes a group discussion so that the class may have practice in discussion skills.

The plain fact of the matter is that we don't always recognize learning when we see it; we are too prone to think children can only learn when they are working directly with the teacher at tasks which are either tedious or difficult. While we may enjoy seeing children have fun, there is a bit of the Puritan in many of us and we feel strongly that children must not enjoy themselves too much when they are supposed to be working.

HE'S GOING TO FAIL SOMETIME

Closely related to the fallacy discussed above is a fifth one: children must experience hardship, frustration, and failure. It is good for them not only because it prepares them for failure later on in life but also because it teaches them to take the consequences of their behavior. A child who doesn't learn to read in the first grade must repeat the grade so that he won't learn "he can get away with anything," and since he is going to fail at something later in life he might as well learn now.

Aside from the obvious criticisms of such a position in the light of what we know about how and when children learn to read, there is also the question one might raise regarding the advisability of experiencing failure. Does experiencing continual failure or failure in an area deemed very important really teach a child a constructive lesson? Does it inspire a teacher to do better work to have a superintendent tell her she is a poor teacher and that she compares most unfavorably with other teachers? Is a housewife a better housewife because her husband continually reminds her that the house is untidy, that his shirts are not properly ironed, that she is too extravagant, and that she is also a failure as a mother?

The process of growing up inevitably brings many frustrations. Rather than deliberately setting the same standards for all children which automatically condemns some to failure, the teacher who is interested in building secure children helps them to set a goal which they can attain and gives them a pat on the back on their way to attaining it. Having many opportunities to achieve success builds up in a child the feeling of power, that he can do things, that he amounts to something. When he feels good about himself, he is better able to take the inevitable frustrations he will meet in life.

There are doubtlessly many other stereotyped notions which we have about how children grow and develop. The list presented here is not meant to be exhaustive. It is hoped that it may be a starting point for us to examine our ideas about children, to accept those that stand up under critical examination, and to reject those that stand in the way of building secure children.

29   Physical Factors and Personality*

BY BOYD R. MCCANDLESS

EDITOR'S NOTE: How we have grown in a physical sense cannot be easily separated from how we grow in a psychological sense. Drawing from a substantial body of research Dr. McCandless suggests that "the human body, the way it is handled, and general physical appearance are fundamentally linked to social living, self-concepts, and very possibly choice of vocation." What are the developmental consequences for girls and boys who are early- or late-maturers? Are the consequences different for boys and girls? Consider your own physical growth. Do you see ways in which it has contributed to the kind of person you are today? This very excellent article will help you to understand better the relationships that can exist between physical growth and personality development.

Every facet of social and personal development is affected by the body. The first, although by no means the most profound or important, impression a person makes on others in ordinary social living is likely to be based on his physiognomy and on his body and the way he handles it. Typically, one's first comments in attempting to describe a stranger concern his physical characteristics and his age: the dimensions most commonly used in such descriptions are height, weight, general body build, coloring, and attractiveness. Unusual and striking attributes of grace or awkwardness, thinness or obesity, apparent strength or weakness, and voice pitch are also likely to be mentioned.

* Reprinted and abridged from *Children and Adolescents*, by Boyd R. Mc-Candless, copyright © 1961 by Holt, Rinehart and Winston, Inc. Used by permission of the author and publisher.

An individual's conception of his body appears to be closely related to his self-concept. If he thinks well of himself, he is likely to be tolerant and accepting of his body; if he is self-rejecting, he rejects his body image (Laverne C. Johnson, 1956; Secord and Jourard, 1953). Self-rejection has been found to be associated with perceived parental rejection. This perceived rejection includes notions of being regarded as unattractive, or weak, or sickly by one's parents.

The nature of one's body and its functioning probably has much significance in the development of a pattern of interests, and possibly in selecting a vocation, although there is no conclusive evidence about this relationship. It is obvious that the weak and awkward boy will not, for example, become a professional athlete. His stuurdy and graceful age-mate has before him a wider range of available interests, hobbies, and occupations. Bodies and faces that are markedly unattractive by cultural standards handicap their possessor in his social and heterosexual life, and create additional problems to be solved in an existence that, for most people, is already sufficiently complex.

For many years there has persisted in the United States the stereotyped notion that one type of growth or development occurs at the expense of other types. Commonplace are the cliches; "all brawn and no brain"; "beautiful but dumb"; "the mad genius"; and their like.

Much research has been done on the relation of physical growth to other variables. The conclusions are not particularly helpful for guiding a particular child, although the generalization that "all good things cluster together" has been generally borne out. A large group of children selected because they are far above average in intelligence, and compared with another large group of the same age and sex distribution selected because they are far below average in intelligence, will be found to be heavier, handsomer, healthier, stronger, and better coordinated. However, many of these relations are the result, not of intelligence, but of social status. The bright children come from wealthier homes, which provide them with better nutrition, better schooling, and more chances for constructive physical exercise. Although height and weight may correlate better than .60 with intelligence, intelligence and motor coordination are unlikely to show a correlation higher than the low .20's. . . .

PHYSICAL FACTORS AND PERSONALITY

It has already been mentioned that between the ages of 11 and 13 girls are, on the average, taller and heavier than boys. Also, most girls reach physical maturity, although not necessarily "official" pubescence, earlier than most boys by about two years. The problems associated with this differential rate of maturity are obvious to anyone who visits a sixth-, seventh-, eighth-, or ninth-grade classroom, or who knows children in this age range. Whereas many of the girls are interested in dating and dancing, their male peers are frequently a head shorter than they, physically immature, and markedly uninterested in things heterosexual. The girl is thus reduced to going out with boys who chronologically are considerably older than she; or the boy is forced into the company of someone larger and more mature than he. This maturational difference has occasioned some to propose that girls should start school earlier than boys. Although there is merit to this suggestion, it is impractical for obvious reasons.

The Effect of Early Physical Maturity on Boys

Research workers at the University of California (e.g., Mary Cover Jones and Bayley, 1950; Mussen and Jones, 1957; and Mary Cover Jones, 1957) have investigated the consequences of early and late physical maturing for boys, and H. E. Jones (1949) and Mary Cover Jones and Mussen (1958) have reported results for early- and late-maturing girls. These workers report on data from a longitudinal study of California children, some of whom are still participating in their middle thirties.

The Jones and Bayley study (1950) uses skeletal age, as judged from x-rays of the long bones of the hand and the knee, as its criterion of physical maturity. From a group of 90 boys who were studied for an average of about four and a half years, the 16 most consistently accelerated and the 16 most consistently retarded were studied intensively by means of observations and ratings both by professional adults and by the boys' buddies.

At the age of 14, ratings of physical maturity made from nude photographs showed almost no overlap between the two groups. The physically accelerated boys were taller, heavier, showed more advanced pubic hair, and had larger genitals. From 13 to 15 years of age the physically retarded boys tended to be long-legged, of slender build, and relatively weak during the period when they lagged most markedly behind in size. The retarded boys were rated by adults as lower in physical attractiveness, less masculine, less well groomed, and more animated and eager ("childish"). They sought attention more, were more affected and less matter-of-fact, and were tenser. However, they did not differ from the more advanced group in ratings of popularity, leadership, prestige, poise, assurance, cheerfulness, or social effect on the group. They were considered to be less mature in a heterosexual social situation.

When rated by their buddies, the physically retarded boys showed up about the same as when rated by adults, but the differences between them and the physically advanced group were less marked. Buddies estimated the physically retarded to be more restless, talkative, and bossy. They believed that they were more attention-seeking and less inclined to have assurance in class. Their buddies regarded them as less popular, and as less likely to be leaders. They were also rated as less likely to have older friends, as being

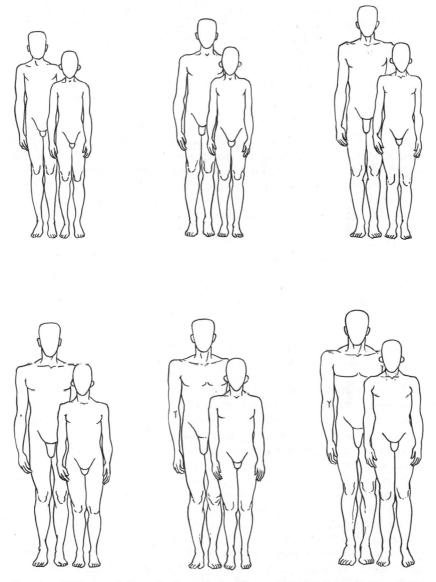

Fig. 1.   *Differential Growth of an Early Maturing and a Late Maturing Boy. Drawings represent the Boys' Statuses at Yearly Intervals from 11½ to 16½ Years of Age. (Adapted from Shuttleworth, 1949.)*

shorter on a sense of humor about themselves, and as having a less attractive general appearance.

The Mussen and Jones study (1957) uses data taken from the Thematic Apperception Test, given to 17 late-maturers and 16 early-maturers when they were 17 years of age. In this test, the subject is shown a series of pictures and is asked to tell a story about each one: who the characters are, what has happened, and how it comes out. From the story he tells, a number of judgments (sometimes of dubious validity) can be made. As has been mentioned in Chapter 6, psychologists assume that the story-teller—the subject—projects his own needs and ideas onto the central character of the story he tells (the hero). This hero's actions, then, are assumed to be those that the story-teller sees as reasonable or desirable for himself. The hero's motives and needs are assumed to be those of the subject of the investigation. The TAT is one of the most useful measures of personality—Lindzey and co-workers (1952, 1955, 1956, and 1958), for example, have contributed evidence to show that it is, within broad limits, valid—although care should be taken not to overgeneralize from it.

In the Mussen and Jones study, it was found that more of the late- than of the early-maturers used TAT themes such as the following: the hero (with whom the boy presumably identified) was described in negative terms (for instance, as being an imbecile, a weakling, or a fanatic); the hero is rejected, scorned, or disapproved of by parents or by the authorities; the hero leaves home and/or defies his parents; the hero falls in love, or has a romance; the hero is helped, encouraged, or given something by someone other than his parents. One other theme came close to distinguishing significantly between the two groups: More of the late-maturers described the hero as feeling helpless and seeking aid or sympathy.

These patterns cluster sensibly together, and allow us to make tentative inferences about certain tendencies of this group of physically retarded boys. They are more likely than physically advanced boys to possess negative or derogatory self-concepts; they seem to blame their parents for their status, although perhaps not consciously; and they feel relatively weak, alone, and helpless. Hence, they seek assistance and affiliation.

The physically advanced group more frequently than the retarded group told stories in which the hero was aggressive in a physical and asocial fashion. They also tended somewhat more frequently to say that the picture elicited in them no thoughts or feelings. Here, perhaps, is an indication of self-confidence—an assurance that they can get away with aggressive behavior if they feel that way; and a tendency to be rather matter-of-fact, or unimaginative, as was observed by the raters in the Jones and Bayley study discussed above.

There were no differences between the two groups of boys in the number who told stories in which the hero is prevented by his parents from doing something he wants to; in which he establishes good relations with his parents; attempts to gain a high goal or do something creditable; or seeks fame and/or high prestige status. In other words, we can infer, very tentatively, that although the physically retarded boys bear somewhat more hostility toward their parents, they have, when compared with the physically advanced boys, an equal amount of positive feeling; and that the two groups subscribe equally to the cultural notion of the successful, occupationally climbing, bold man.

Mary Cover Jones (1957) has reported on two groups of 20 males (although at one point in her article she talks of 43 subjects), one early-, the other a late-maturing group. Average physical differences between the groups at age 14 were enormous: for example, the average height of the early-maturers was 5 feet 8 inches; that of the late-maturers only 5 feet even. Their respective average weights were approximately 127 pounds and 93 pounds. Ratings of body build showed the early-maturers to be more "mesomorphic"—i.e., with rugged bone and muscular structure.

However, at the time of Jones's follow-up, when the boys had become men averaging 33 years of age, physical differences had partially disappeared. The early-maturers averaged 5 feet 10 inches in height and 172 pounds in weight. The average figures for the late-maturers were 5 feet 9½ inches and 165 pounds. Although the early-maturers still appeared to conform more closely to the cultural notion of a "good build," differences between the groups were slight.

A number of questionnaires and tests were administered to these men, and significant differences were found on several measuress (more than would be predicted by chance). These differences are quite harmonious with those obtained from an analysis of the TAT stories used by Jones and Mussen. The men who were early-maturing as boys scored higher than those who were late-maturing on measures of "good impression" and dominance; the late-maturers averaged higher scores on a test where high scores are said to refer to rebelliousness, touchiness, impulsivity, self-indulgence, assertiveness, and insightful self-preoccupation. Late-maturers scored significantly higher on a test of "succorance"—the tendency to look for help and support from others. There was a significant tendency for early-maturers to be less impulsive and more responsible.

Ames (1957) also studied this same group of 40 men from the California Growth Study, concentrating on different aspects of their behavior. Ames' findings are dramatic. An index of skeletal age, which he used as his criterion of maturity, predicted social behavior at the age of 33 better than *any* social measure obtained for the subjects during the time they were being studied (when they were from about 11 to about 18 years old). Some of Ames' correlations are worth listing and discussing here. His information about the men's adult status came from interviews with them. As has been pointed out before, the interview method has real weaknesses, but frequently (as in this case) it is the only method of study available.

Ames judged the men's occupational status, and found a correlation between skeletal maturation rate and status of .47, a highly significant figure, which means that the early-maturers were more successful occupationally than the late-maturers. Hypothetically, the boys did not differ originally in social class. When the degree of the men's informal social participation (their tendency to go out and have a good time) was rated, it was found to correlate .48 with skeletal maturation rate. Formal social participation (lodges, clubs, church affairs, and the like) correlated .44 with maturation rate. The relation of skeletal maturation rate to occupational social participation (business socialization) was a lower but still significant .35.

Fifteen of these 40 young men held positions in which they supervised or directed the work of subordinates. Of this group, only 3 were late-maturers. Eight of the men held some type of office in a club, lodge, or civic group. Of this number, none was a late-maturer.

The best single prediction of adult social behavior resulting from *social behavior data gathered when these men were boys* was obtained from a measure of clubhouse popularity, based on watching the boys in a number of social situations during which they were interacting with both boys and girls. This measure correlated .39 with adult informal social participation and was the only significant correlation found between adolescent social measures andd adult status and social behavior, although even it reached significance at only the .05 level.

Kinsey, Pomeroy, and Martin (1949) used as their criterion of physical maturity the age at which their subjects reported first ejaculation. Boys and men reporting early sexual maturity are considered by Kinsey and his colleagues as "the more alert, energetic, vivacious, spontaneous, physically active, socially extrovert, and/or aggressive individuals in the population." (p. 325) Late-maturers were more frequently described as "slow, quiet, mild in manner, without force, reserved, timid, taciturn, introvert, and/or socially inept." (pp. 325–326) Early sexual maturity is associated with the almost immediate adoption of a pattern of regular consummatory sexual activity. Late-maturers delay adopting such a pattern. Early-maturers report consistently higher levels of sexual activity from adolescence on until their fifties, although the differences between them and late-maturers become less extreme with age. But, over the years, early-maturers average about one fifth more sexual outlets than late maturers.

Implications of Physical Maturation and Personality Studies

Such data as those reported in the preceding section are impressive. It seems as though one of the most important things that could happen to a boy to assure his future good adjustment and success would be to mature early physically.

However, these findings, although dramatic and important, need to be considered thoughtfully. First, it should be noted that although some of the correlations (particularly from the Ames study) are high, even for the highest (between informal social participation and skeletal rate of maturation, .48), less than 25 percent of the variance of one variable is accounted for by the other. In other words, knowing a boy's skeletal maturation rate improves the accuracy of prediction about his social life in his thirties, but still leaves 75 percent of the variables that make him a "social drip" or "the life of the party" unknown.

Second, the samples used by Ames and Mary Cover Jones were small and highly selected. Also, as in any longitudinal study, two factors operate to make the sample of adults very different from the sample that was originally obtained. First, there are many dropouts. These may leave the study for a number of reasons: lack of interest in research, lack of time to co-operate as subjects, departure from the area, and so on. Lower-class subjects are more likely to drop out than middle-class subjects. Other subjects may not get along with the investigator. We do not know what the characteristics are of those who drop out, but there are many questions that should be asked, both about those who remain and those who leave a longitudinal study. Second, the long-time study of parents and their children may actually change the family relations.

We know from the Mary Cover Jones and Bayley study (1950) that the adult raters regarded the physically precocious youngsters as the more attractive. Might this fact have resulted in friendship bonds between the research workers and the more stable and mature of the early-maturers, so that in their thirties they were willing, for friendship's sake, to cooperate in the study, whereas the less stable and emotionally mature members of the advanced group dropped out? It is also apparent that the late-maturers were more in need of help and support, and perhaps more dependent on adults. It is possible that an active sympathy in the research worker was aroused by these relatively immature and dependent youngsters, so that considerable warmth and security was given them? As adults, then, when asked to return to the study, may not the most immature and dependent of the late-maturers have agreed to cooperate, perhaps hoping in some way to re-establish the pleasant bonds that had existed in their teens? We do not know the answers to these questions, but the factors implied by them may have affected the results reported by Jones and Ames, and should at least be considered in evaluating these studies.

In any longitudinal study, the investigators have an unknown influence on the populations studied. Could these influences have been positive for early-maturing, independent youngsters and negative for late-maturing and dependent boys? The California Growth Study was well enough designed, and its staff members sufficiently skilled, to make such an interaction unlikely, but at the same time its possibility must be considered.

Whatever questions we may ask about design and sample in these studies, we cannot overlook the implications of their findings. It is probable that the differences in adjustment and social behavior noted between groups of early- and late-maturing boys are socially mediated—that is, are a function of the way society reacts to the mature and the immature fourteen-year-old, rather than of the physiological or biochemical factors making for maturity or immaturity.

Body Build and Personality in Boys and Men

For thousands of years, philosophers and physicians and, more recently, anthropologists and other scientists have speculated (and done research) on relations between body build, function, constitution, and temperament. Efforts to classify body type apparently date back at least to Hippocrates (460?–377? B.C.). Tucker and Lessa (1940) state: "It is a curious and perhaps significant fact that 2500 years ago Hippocrates said that there are two roots of human beings, the long thins and the short thicks. Almost all simple classifications of type since that time have nearly the same basis, despite variety of nomenclature and detail of description." (p. 419) Kretschmer (1925) used a somewhat similar classification of body type in his controversial but influential hypotheses about the relations of body build to temperament and mental illness (for example, that long lean people, if they succumb to mental disease, will become schizophrenics; short blocky people manic-depressives).

In their scholarly review, Tucker and Lessa include a bibliography of 334 items, a large number of which refer to body build or constitution and temperament.

Sheldon has received much attention for his work in the area of body build and temperament. He and his colleagues (1940, 1942) have interested themselves in methods of characterizing body build and relating it to personality. One of his works (1949) takes an extreme position, and is endorsed by few; and the statistical assumptions of his whole technique of classifying or describing body build have been strongly and tellingly criticized (e.g., Hammond, 1957; Humphreys, 1957; Meredith, 1940). However, his work has had so much impact that this text would not be complete without a brief description of it.

Sheldon has worked mostly with college-age students—that is, people in late adolescence. His data are ordinarily nude front, side, and back photographs, and he has worked more with male than with female subjects. Each photograph is rated from 1 (having very little of) to 7 (having very much of) on three dimensions: endomorphy, mesomorphy, and ectomorphy. The barrel-chested, big-bellied individual would receive a high *endomorph* rating; the muscular, broad-shouldered, narrow-hipped, rather big-boned individual would be rated high on *mesomorphy*; the lean and skinny individual, whose external body surface is large in relation to his weight, would obtain a high rating on *ectomorphy*. Figure 2 consists of line drawings illustrating these patterns at 11½ years and Figure 3 shows the same boys three and a half years later.

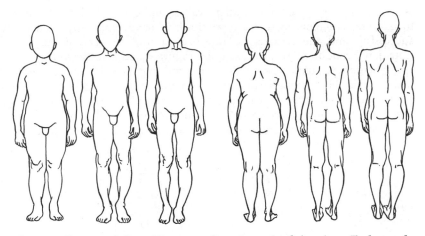

Fig. 2.   Front and Rear Views, reading from the left, of an Endomorph, a Mesomorph, and an Ectomorph Boy, aged about 11½ Years. (Adapted from Shuttleworth, 1949.)

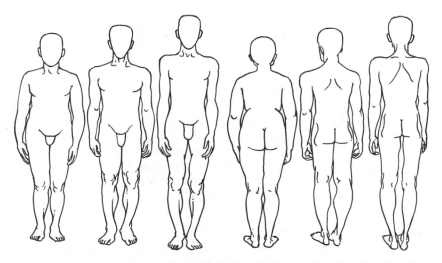

Fig. 3.   The Three Boys Shown in Fig. 2, in the Same Order from left to right, at 15 Years of Age. (Adapted from Shuttleworth, 1949.)

Each photograph is given three ratings: a 7-1-1 would describe an almost impossibly pure case of endomorphy; a 1-1-7 an equally improbable example of ectomorphy. Sheldon also rates on *dysplasia* (bodily disharmony), *gynandromorphy* (bisexuality), *texture*, and *hirsutism* (hairiness). However, these are subsidiary values and of relatively little interest to us here. Attempts to somatotype children have been only moderately successful, and the somatotype has been found to vary sharply with nutritional condition (see, for example, Figure 4 and Shuttleworth, 1949).

Sheldon postulates personality patterns that go with these different body builds. He maintains that the individual high in endomorphy will have a personality type that he names "viscerotonia"; the personality type accompanying high mesomorphy is "somatotonia" and ectomorphs are "cerebrotonic." The viscerotonic is generally relaxed, sociable, loves food

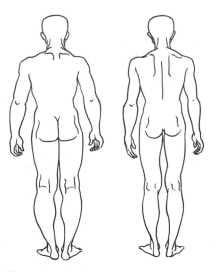

Fig. 4. A Demonstration of the Changes Occurring as a Result of Near Starvation of the Body Build of a Pronounced Mesomorph. The Somatotype Rating Changes Sharply in the Direction of Ectomorphy.

and comfort, and has an affectionate attitude toward people. The somatotonic is muscularly active, bodily assertive, and has great personal vigor. The cerebrotonic is restrained, inhibited, and shrinks from social obligations.

Should Sheldon be proved correct in his belief that there is an immutable, biological link between body build and temperament, the hope of improving society through education and social welfare would be sharply curtailed. The evidence in support of Sheldon's theory is very weak, although not entirely negative (see, for example, Child, 1950; and

Janoff *et al.*, 1950). However, even if linkages between body build and personality (or between time of physical maturity and personality) should be found, it is not necessary to go to genetics to account for them. If a certain type of body build or quality arouses characteristic and consistent negative or positive social reactions, then, according to social-learning theory, predictable and differential types of personality development will occur.

One ingenious study (Brodsky, 1954) suggests that there *are* differential social reactions to characteristic body builds. Brodsky prepared five 15-inch silhouettes of males, representing: (1) extreme endomorph; (2) endomesomorph; (3) mesomorph; (4) ectomesomorph; and (5) ectomorph. He also constructed a questionnaire containing such items as the following: Which one of this group of five men is most aggressive? Which one of this group of five men is least aggressive?

To secure divergent research populations, Brodsky recruited 75 male medical and dental college students from Howard University, all or almost all of whom would be expected to be Negro; and 50 male college students from George Washington University, all presumably white. The questionnaire was given to the men in groups numbering no more than 5. There were no important differences in the way the two samples of respondents answered, so Brodsky pooled his groups. This homogeneity in opinion of superficially quite different groups of men lends weight to the notion of a "cultural stereotype," or characteristic way of regarding body build.

The various traits were usually assigned by the respondents to the "pure" silhouettes—the endomorph, mesomorph, and ectomorph. Those assigned to the given silhouette by a third or more of the respondents are listed below:

More than one third of the respondents labeled the *endomorph* silhouette as representing the man who eats the most, eats the most often, will make the worst soldier, will make the poorest athlete, will be the poorest professor of philosophy, can endure pain the least well, will make the least successful military leader, will be least likely to be chosen leader, will make the poorest university president, will be the least aggressive, will drink the most, will be least preferred as a personal friend (but, ironically, would have many friends), will make the poorest doctor, and will put his own interests before those of others.

This picture is an almost consistently negative one. If there is any truth to the notion that a person behaves as he is expected to behave, a dismal picture of the direction of personality growth of the endomorph is presented by this study.

The *mesomorph* fares as favorably as the endomorph does unfavorably: the respondents said that he would make the best athlete, the most successful military leader, and the best soldier. They chose him as the man who would assume leadership, as well as the man who would be elected as leader. He was judged not to smoke at all, and to be self-sufficient, in the sense of needing friends the least. However, he was most preferred as a friend, and was judged to have many friends. Respondents also said that he would be the most aggressive, would endure pain the best, would never have a nervous breakdown, and would drink the least.

The stereotype of the *ectomorph* is far less socially desirable than that of the mesomorph, but in general more favorable than that of the endomorph. The ectomorph was judged to be the most likely to have a nervous breakdown before the age of 30, to eat the least, and the least often, to smoke three packs of cigarettes a day, to be least self-sufficient, in the sense of needing friends the most (but, unfortunately, was judged to have the fewest friends), to hold his liquor the worst, to make a poor father, and, as a military leader, to be likely to sacrifice his men with the greatest emotional distress.

This study illustrates that there may be certain characteristic ways of reacting to different types of male physique, and that the pattern of reaction is such as to favor the mesomorph. In this context, it should be mentioned that Jones's early-maturers, best adjusted according to her criteria, were more mesomorphic in average body build than her late-maturers.

These relationships remain only suggestions until more research has been done, but *provocative* suggestions they are.

The Advantages to the Male of Early Physical Maturation and Strong Body Build

It has already been noted (Mary Cover Jones and Bayley, 1950) that adult raters give more favorable ratings to early- than to late-maturing boys, and that their peers esteem early-maturers somewhat more highly (although other research does not give strong support to this conclusion). It is not unlikely that positions of leadership are allocated earlier by adults to such boys. Hence, if expectations in any way govern development, the boys will develop into more responsible and mature people, more socially self-confident than late-maturers.

Certainly, there is a period of years during junior high school when the early-maturers excel at athletics because of their superior height, weight, and strength. Athletic prowess, for boys, is a matter of tremendous prestige. At maturity they do not, as a group, lose their status as far as height, weight, and musculature are concerned, and may as individuals remain burlier than average- and late-maturers (although within the group their adult height is distributed much like that of the male population as a whole).

It must be remembered that the vital capacity of these boys—the amount of oxygen per unit of time that the body can utilize—lags behind their more obvious physical capacity. In other words, although they may appear very grown-up, they have not reached adult stamina, nor will they do so for two or three years after they have achieved maximal height and adult weight. Stolz and Stolz (1951), in this connection, cite the case history of Ben, a boy tall and rugged for his years, who was placed early in competitive athletics but was not able to perform, and consequently lost much prestige. This failure appeared to be due to his lag in vital capacity— he simply could not gulp in and utilize the large amounts of air needed for persistence in hard physical activity.

Early-maturing boys possess a clear heterosexual advantage for a period of several years, maturing as they do at about the same time as the girls in their classes. Consequently, their drives and interests are relatively well matched with those of their feminine age-mates, and they are able to take out their girls without the embarrassment of being the shorter and slighter member of the pair.

Late-maturing boys, on the other hand, although for the most part they catch up in height and weight with their early-maturing peers, undergo a long period of social disadvantage during an important formative period of their lives. During this time, they are likely to be perceived and treated as relatively immature and irresponsible, are at a disadvantage in athletics, and are biologically unready for, and hopelessly outclassed in, courtship competition. As Kinsey has pointed out, early-maturing boys not only precede late-maturers as far as initial sexual experience is concerned, but they establish a regular pattern for sexual satisfaction much earlier and, for many years, retain a higher rate of sexual output than late-maturers. This pattern may produce considerable conflict for early-maturers during adolescence (before sexual activity is condoned), but its net effects should be positive, including as they do an important and enduring source of satisfaction and a contribution to a self-concept of sexual adequacy and virility. Such a self-concept should also favor satisfactory and appropriate sex-role identification.

Physical Maturation, Body Build, and Adjustment in Girls and Women

Fewer data exist for girls than for boys concerning the relationship between body build and temperament, and between time of sexual maturity and later personality. H. E. Jones (1949) has made many provocative suggestions concerning these relationships. He has suggested, for example, that for girls in our society, early development is disadvantageous, late physical maturing advantageous—a pattern opposite to that for boys, but resulting from similar general social principles. There is some tendency for early-maturing girls to be stockier, later in their development, than their late-maturing sisters. In our culture, the stocky figure is not the fashionable one. The social gap between the early-maturing girl and the boys in her class is of course striking—a span of important years goes by before there is any boy of her age who is tall enough so that she can appear in

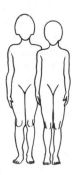
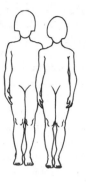
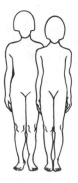
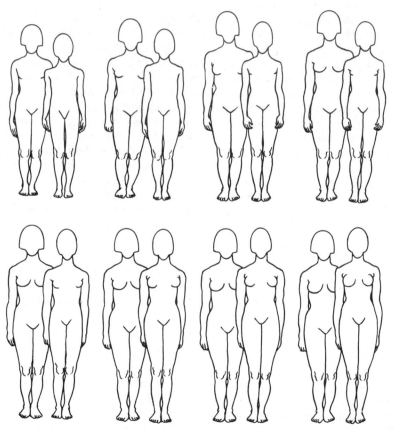

Fig. 5.   *Differential Growth of an Early and a Late Maturing Girl. The First Four Pairings are Drawn at Yearly Birthdays from 8 through 11 Years. Other Pairings are at Half-Year Intervals from 11½ Years through 14½ Years of Age. (Adapted from Shuttleworth, 1949.)*

public with him without feeling conspicuous. Sexual maturity attained while psychologically immature may engender confusion, conflict, and uncertainty. The early-maturing girl may be driven beyond her depth in courtship, dating boys substantially older and more sophisticated than she, with attendant social-sexual complications. H. E. Jones (1949) has reported that late-maturing girls were judged by adult observers to have attained higher prestige, and to show more leadership, than early-maturers. They were also rated as having greater social-stimulus value. In summarizing a study in press at the time of this writing, Mary Cover Jones and Mussen (1958) state that, over a three-year period of time, late-maturing girls were more frequently mentioned in the high-school paper, and were elected to more offices in extracurricular activities. However, an analysis of TAT stories told by these girls at the age of 17 revealed few differences between early- and late-maturers (only 2 out of 20 differences were statistically significant). If anything, on this measure of "fantasy," the early-maturers showed more characteristics believed to be favorable than the late-maturing group.

Trait Status and Personal Concern

Earlier in this chapter mention was made of the intimate relation between self-concept and attitude toward one's own body. It was also pointed out that a healthy, well-proportioned, strong, and graceful body undoubtedly aids, although it does not necessarily accompany, good emotional development and adjustment, whereas graceless and unattractive bodies often make personal adjustment more difficult.

The advantages, particularly to boys, of early physical maturity have been discussed. It has been pointed out that, by men at least, mesomorphic body build is more favorably regarded than endo- or ectomorphic structure.

It is probable that most children, particularly before and during adolescence, worry considerably about the development of their primary and secondary sex characteristics. Schonfeld (1950) for example, believes that inadequate masculine physique (including delay of puberty, small sex organs, or deficiency in secondary sex characteristics) can be a matter of considerable concern to boys and result in serious personality conflicts or psychosomatic complaints (physical ailments often considered to be psychological in their origin). His report is based on a population of 256 boys seen by him, who had expressed concern over their physical development, or whose parents had been worried about it. Most of these boys, he found, were normal in the sense that their development fell within the limits of normal variability.

Schonfeld has reported very good success in treating these boys. Thirty-five percent of them were adequately taken care of simply by reassurance, and the majority of the rest profited from re-education, psychotherapy, and, in some cases, hormonal treatment.

Angelino and Mech (1955) report that girls, too, worry about their physical development. Most of their worries center on the possibility that deviant height and weight development will interfere with, or complicate, their social and emotional life.

There is no question that children should receive more information than most of them are now given about the ways their bodies grow and are likely to grow. Few youngsters (or, for that matter, their parents) understand the wide variability in physical growth and the onset of pubescence. One boy, known to the author, began at 14 to have nightmares and to lose weight. He became moody and depressed, was insolent to his parents whereas previously he had been a model boy, withdrew from his former circle of school friends, and showed deterioration of a previously highly superior academic performance. This boy was a somewhat late-maturing youngster who was, in addition, one year advanced academically, so that at 14 he was in a grade where he was the youngest by almost a year, and where some boys were almost 17 years of age.

On the basis of professional advice, his parents decided to leave, where he could find it, a little volume prepared by Shuttleworth (1949), which, by means of pictures and easily understandable text, portrays the great variability in reaching pubescence. The boy's natural curiosity led him into the volume, and, almost as if by magic, his symptoms of conflict disappeared. A few months later he talked with his parents about his earlier conflicts and worries, and told them how obtaining factual information on the basis of which he could peg his own physical development, compare it with that of his older friends, and predict its course, had alleviated his concerns. Not all adolescent worries, of course, can be so easily dissipated.

Many adolescent worries are quite unrealistic, as, to some degree, were this boy's. Although objectively inadequate physical development can lead to conflict and disturbance, conflict and disturbance can also be tied, in symptomatic fashion, to perfectly adequate and normal physical development. A well-developed but insecure girl can (and many have been known to) blame her lack of social success on the fact that she is "too fat" or "too busty," when in reality she has excellent proportions. A normally sturdy, muscular boy can, in an almost neurotic fashion, think of himself as skinny, or an attractive but stocky boy believe that he is fat.

SUMMARY

The human body, the way it is handled, and general physical appearance are fundamentally linked to social living, self-concepts, and very possibly choice of vocation. Charting how the body grows and develops is an important task assumed by scholars in child development and physical anthropology. One major goal of such scholars is to describe and establish the norms, or general characteristics, of physical growth and body build and function. These norms do not *explain*, but they assist in establishing a range of acceptable variation, which is useful both psychologically and physically.

A second task assumed by research workers in the field of physical growth is to uncover general principles of development. To date, the cephalocaudal (head to tail) and proximodistal (center axis to periphery) principles of development hold up well for both physical growth and motor development. The third principle is that of development from general to specific action patterns. This principle has aroused considerable argument; the best conclusion that can be drawn is that, whereas the most conspicuous development is from the general to the specific, development in the other direction also occurs: the processes are complementary.

Different parts of the body grow according to different patterns. The *neural* pattern is one of rapid increase during infancy and slow gains during later childhood and adolescence; the *sexual* pattern is one of little change (long latency) up to somewhat before the time of adolescence (12 or 13 years for boys, 11 or 12 for girls). At this time the primary and secondary sex characteristics "mushroom," usually reaching mature development in five or six years. The *somatic pattern* (including changes in height and weight) is one of rapid growth in infancy, moderately rapid growth in childhood, a spurt preceding pubescence, and a tapering off from the middle to the late teens.

Other scientific goals in the study of physical growth include determining the factors that modify physical growth, and their relation to growth, health, stamina, and so on at all age levels. For example, how does growth vary from season to season, or from one climate to another? Does excessively rapid growth in infancy exert a positive or deleterious effect on the health of adolescents and adults—and so on. Another goal is to determine the relation between physical growth and other aspects of development: How are patterns of growth related to strength and speed, or to intelligence?

Physical growth, by definition, involves change. The seven varieties of anatomical change that have been most studied are the following:

1. Changes in kind (the zygote is very different in kind from the sperm and egg that make it up; pubic hair is very different from childhood down).

2. Changes in number (at 5, the child has 48 to 52 teeth in one stage of development or another; by adolescence, 20 deciduous—baby—teeth have been lost; by late adolescence one or more third molars—the wisdom teeth—have often been lost; and by old age it is common to have lost all of one's teeth).

3. Changes in size (the child steadily increases in height, for example, to 18 years or so, but in middle and old age height actually decreases; the primary sex characteristics develop very slowly during childhood, but increase dramatically in size before, during, and for a time after puberty).

4. Changes in shape (the proportions of the adolescent are very different from those of the baby; the chest becomes broader and flatter during childhood, more circular again after middle age).

5. Changes in position (elbows and knees at first project outward from the sides of the body—later the knees rotate toward the front, the elbows toward the back; feet move from paralleling the axis of the lower leg toward the perpendicular).

6. Changes in pigmentation (hair usually grows darker during childhood and ordinarily grays in middle and old age; skins darkens in middle age).

7. Changes in texture (muscles harden, particularly for males during and after adolescence; in middle and old age, bones become brittle and skin loses its elasticity).

Changes in function also occur. The mouth becomes less an instrument of sucking, more an instrument of biting, chewing, and vocalizing; the sphincters come under voluntary control; legs are used for walking. The penis acquires the function of ejaculation.

Babies seem to be divided about evenly as far as "natural" hand preference is concerned, but by about their second year, 90 percent or more of them have chosen or been trained to right-handedness. When it is possible to develop a right-handed preference without undue pressure on the infant, this should be done; our culture is *dextral*, and it is obviously more convenient to be right-handed.

Sexual behavior varies greatly according to social class, and men seem to indulge more in sex, including its fantasy aspects, than women. Overt sexual behavior seems to be more "social" among those with less education (i.e., they tend more to *mutual* sex behavior, less to such solitary sex behavior as masturbation). Almost all boys and men have masturbated to orgasm, and most have experienced intercourse, before marriage; whereas about 50 percent of women enter marriage as virgins, and only about one fourth of them have masturbated. Women's sex desires reach their maximum later than those of men, and these trends may produce complications in the relations between the sexes.

Attainment of physical maturity is an important landmark in our culture. It comes at a time when the child is changing in many ways—indeed, social change for young people in their early teens is as dramatic as physical change, and the two are closely linked in their dynamics and their results.

For boys, almost all the consequences of early physical maturity—immediately and for fifteen or more years thereafter—appear to be fortunate. Early exposure to opportunities for leadership, the prestige they enjoy in athletics during this important and formative period, the closing of the social gap between them and girls of their own age—all seem to give them a "start" that is better than that enjoyed by the late-maturing boy.

For girls, the evidence concerning the effects of differential physical maturity is unclear. Temporarily, early maturity may be to their advantage, but long-lasting positive correlates of early maturity have not been revealed.

There is no convincing evidence that body build is associated with personality, although one interesting study indicates that if there are correlations between personality and body build, social mediation could account for them. In United States culture, the mesomorphic (muscular) body build is regarded far more favorably than the ectomorphic (long and lean), which in turn meets with more approval than the endomorphic (stocky). If social expectancies have an influence on personality, the positive expectancies held for the mesomorph should influence him favorably, whereas the negative expectancies for the mesomorph may have deleterious effects.

REFERENCES:

AMES, R. "Physical Maturing Among Boys as Related to Adult Social Behavior: A Longitudinal Study," *California Journal of Educational Research*, 8: 69–1957.

ANGELINO, H., and E. V. MECH. "Fears and Worries Concerning Physical Changes: A Preliminary Survey of 32 Females," *Journal of Psychology*, 39: 195–198, 1955.

BRODSKY, C. M. *A Study of Norms for Body Form—Behavior Relationships* (Washington, D.C.: Catholic University of America Press, 1954).

CHILD, I. L. "The Relation of Somatotype to Self-Ratings on Sheldon's Temperamental Traits," *Journal of Personality*, 18: 440–53, 1950.

HAMMOND, W. H. "The Status of Physical Types," *Humanistic Biology*, 29: 223–41, 1957.

HUMPHREYS, L. G. "Characteristics of Type Concepts with Special Reference to Sheldon's Typology," *Psychological Bulletin*, 54: 218–28, 1957.

JANOFF, IRMA Z., L. H. BECK, and I. L. CHILD. "The Relation of Somatotype to Reaction Time, Resistance to Pain, and Expressive Movement," *Journal of Personality*, 18: 454–460, 1950.

JOHNSON, LAVERNE C. "Body Cathexis as a Factor in Somatic Complaints," *Journal of Consulting Psychology*, 20: 145–49, 1956.

JONES, H. E. "Adolescence in Our Society," in *The Family in a Democratic Society*, anniversary papers of the Community Service Society of New York (New York: Columbia University Press, 1949), pp. 70–82.

JONES, MARY C. "The Later Careers of Boys Who Were Early- or Late-Maturing," *Child Development*, 28: 113–28, 1957.

JONES, MARY C., and NANCY BAYLEY. "Physical Maturing Among Boys as Related to Behavior," *Journal of Educational Psychology*, 41: 129–148, 1950.

JONES, M. C., and P. H. MUSSEN. "Self-Conceptions, Motivations, and Interpersonal Attitudes of Early- and Late-Maturing Girls," *Child Development*, 29: 491–501, 1958.

KINSEY, A. C., W. B. POMEROY, and C. E. MARTIN, *Sexual Behavior in the Human Male* (Philadelphia: W. B. Saunders Company, 1948).

KRETSCHMER, E. "Körperbau und character," 2nd revised edition, translated by W. J. H. Sprott as *Physique and Character* (London: Kegan Paul, Trench, Trubner and Company, 1925).

LINDZEY, G., CHARLOTTE TEJESSY, and H. S. ZAMANSKY. "Thematic Apperception Test: An Empirical Examination of Some Indices of Homosexuality," *Journal of Abnormal Social Psychology*, 57: 67–75, 1958.

LINDZEY, G., and CHARLOTTE TEJESSY. "Thematic Apperception Test: Indices of Aggression in Relation to Measures of Overt and Covert Behavior," *American Journal of Orthopsychiatry*, 26: 567, 576, 1956.

LINDZEY, G., and D. KALNINS. "Thematic Apperception Test: Some Evidence Bearing on the 'Hero Assumption,'" *Journal of Abnormal Social Psychology*, 57: 76–83, 1958.

LINDZEY, G., and P. S. HERMAN. "Thematic Apperception Test: A Note on Reliability and Situational Validity," *Journal of Professional Technique*, 19: 36–42, 1955.

LINDZEY, G. "Thematic Apperception Test: Interpretative Assumptions and Related Empirical Evidence," *Psychological Bulletin*, 49: 1–25, 1952.

MEREDETH, H. V. "Comments on 'The Varieties of Human Physique,'" *Child Development*, 11: 301–309, 1940.

MUSSEN, P. H., and MARY C. JONES. "Self-Conceptions, Motivations, and Interpersonal Attitudes of Late- and Early-Maturing Boys," *Child Development*, 28: 242–256, 1957.

SCHONFELD, W. A. "Inadequate Masculine Physique as a Factor in Personality Development of Adolescent Boys," *Psychomatic Medicine*, 12: 49–54, 1950.

SECORD, P. F., and S. M. JOURARD. "The Appraisal of Body-Cathexis: Body Cathexis and the Self," *Journal of Consulting Psychology*, 1953, 17: 343–347.

SHELDON, W. H. *The Varieties of Human Physique* (New York: Harper and Brothers, 1940).

SHELDON, W. H. *The Varieties of Temperament* (New York: Harper and Brothers, 1942).

SHELDON, W. H., E. M. HARTT, and E. MCDERMOTT. *Varieties of Delinquent Youth* (New York: Harper and Brothers, 1949).

SHUTTLEWORTH, F. K. "The Adolescent Period: A Pictorial Atlas," *Monogr. Soc. Res. Child Develpm.*, 14, 1949.

STOLZ, H. R., and LOIS M. STOLZ. *Somatic Development of Adolescent Boys* (New York: The Macmillan Company, 1951).

30   American Adolescents of Today—A New Species*

BY ELISABETH B. HURLOCK

EDITOR'S NOTE: *This and the article immediately following reflect diametrically opposing viewpoints about the nature of the American adolescent. Are today's adolescents conformers who follow the
herd? Are they preoccupied with status symbols? Are they irresponsible? Are they anti-intellectual? Are they impossible to control? Consider the arguments here carefully, and then to balance the picture,
read Dr. Kelley's views in the next reading.*

American adolescents of today are different from adolescents of past
generations and from adolescents in many other cultures throughout the
world. This is not due to mutation in their hereditary endowment but to
cultural factors which did not exist in past generations.

Because adolescents of today are so different in so many different ways
from their parents' and even more so from their grandparents' generation,
the gap between the generations grows progressively wider. Adolescents
complain that their parents "don't understand them" while parents and
teachers of their parents' generation frankly admit that this is true.

Newness does not necessarily mean improvement. Today's adolescents
may have more knowledge, more sophistication, and many cultural advantages which, in past generations, were limited to a few, but that does
not make them "better" as potential adult citizens in a democracy.

In fact, the behavior of some of today's adolescents and the social

* Reprinted from *Adolescence*, 1966, Vol. 1, No. 1, 7–21, by permission of the
author and Libra Publishers, Inc.

problems they create make many members of the older generation question whether the "old-fashioned" adolescent was not superior to the new species. From a source as high as the Vatican, Pope Paul warned the young people of Italy recently to "avoid the fashionable weakness for skepticism and decadence of certain young people." (23)

What Is Responsible for the "New Species"?

The finger of blame has, to date, been pointed in every conceivable direction. Some maintain that growing up in the suburbs, with the feeedom of the "wide open spaces," does not instill in children the desire to conform to social expectations as was true when people lived mainly in cities and had to learn at an early age to behave in a civilized way. Others claim that the break-down in family solidarity, with divorce, remarriage, social mobility, and the break-up of the elongated family system are at the basis of the trouble. Still others claim that the trend toward teenage marriages and teenage parenthood is indeed a case of the "blind leading the blind." The immaturity of the parents makes them incapable of bringing up their children to be law-abiding, socially conforming young people.

The most commonly accepted explanation is the radical change that has taken place in our child-rearing attitudes in the last generation— especially among parents of today's adolescents who went to college and who learned the evils to come from frustration and the advantages from self-expression. As a result, ever since their children were born, they shied away from "thwarting" them. If, as a small child, the adolescent of today wanted to explore, he was permitted to do so regardless of whether or not he broke some of his parents' choicest possessions or turned the parents' hair prematurely gray for fear that he would hurt or kill himself. He was permitted to say what popped into his mind, regardless of whether what he said hurt peoples' feelings or deflated their egos. Permissiveness, once established, is hard to change, especially if parents believe it is "good for the child" even though hard for them to take.

Many schools in recent years have adopted the policy of permissive- ness—the "progressive education movement"—where pupils literally run the schools and where teachers and school authorities cater to their wishes and whims. Even worse, law-enforcing officers in recent years have been imbued with the philosophy of permissiveness, accepting pranks serious enough to justify arrest for juvenile delinquency on the grounds that "kids will be kids." A reputable lawyer had the gall, recently, to go to the parents of a girl who had been raped by a boy from a socially prominent and well- to-do family to ask them not to press charges against the boy on the grounds that "boys will be boys." And this occurred in a state where rape by boys eighteen years of age or older carries the death penalty while those younger—as this boy was—faced imprisonment of fifteen years for the crime. (24)

Why, one may justifiably ask, has this philosophy of child-rearing gained such widespread acceptance when any mature adult, with even the fundamental knowledge of how to bring up children, should know that no child is capable of knowing what society will tolerate and what it will not unless his parents and teachers guide him? There is no one answer. Some attribute it to parental revolt against their own strict upbringing. As children, they vowed that when they became parents they would not thwart their children as their parents had thwarted them. Others attribute it to the experiences of many fathers of today's adolescents in World War II. As a revolt against the regimentation of their lives in the armed services, they went to the extreme of wearing and doing what they pleased when they returned to the college campuses to complete their education. And, later, when they became parents, they carried over this attitude of permissiveness into their parental roles.

The more widely accepted reason for permissiveness is to point the finger of blame at Freud and the psychoanalytic school. Although it is true that the Freudian doctrine blames the thwarting of strong innate drives—such as the sex drive—for many cases of adult maladjustment, there is nothing in it that could be possibly interpreted to mean that it advocates permissive upbringing of children. (10) However, misinterpretations of Freudian doctrines by laymen have been used to justify their own permissiveness.

It is a well-known fact that young people tend, on the whole, to be more lax and more permissive than older people. This stems, in part, from feelings of insecurity about what they should do and, in part, from a desire to have fun while they are still young enough to enjoy themselves. While there are no statistics available at the present time to show whether problem adolescents are more likely to have parents below the age norm for law-abiding adolescents, there is a widespread opinion among those who deal with juvenile delinquents that their parents are younger, less serious about their parental responsibilities, and less sure of how to cope with any trouble that might arise than are parents of non-troublesome adolescents. (12, 14)

The affluence of the American society of today which has permeated every social class means that adolescents' earnings from after-school or vacation jobs are not needed to supplement the family income and that, in many cases, it is not even necessary for them to work. The family provides them with generous enough allowances to "live up to the Joneses." Affluence means independence and free time to get into mischief. Put in another way, today's adolescent can literally thumb his nose at his parents and do as he pleases. If his parents become too demanding, the adolescent has a powerful weapon to silence them—he will threaten to leave home and get a job. Knowing that his parents want him to "better himself" and knowing that the stepping stone to rising in the social ladder is education, today's adolescent is fully aware that his parents will back down and let him do as he pleases.

Another explanation for the new species of adolescents in America today is the tendency to model their behavior, their clothes, their speech, and most important of all, their values, along the lines of the new American heroes and heroines—people from the world of sports and of entertainment. In the past, the heroes were the people who made contributions to the greatness of our country—soldiers, statesmen, writers, scientists, or just good citizens. Today's adolescent puts on a pedestal people who make money overnight, who live a glamorous life rivaling the luxuries of ancient Rome, and whose methods of rise to the top may not always be in keeping with the American tradition. While many people who are in the limelight of popular attention are law-abiding citizens, worthy of being imitated, far more are not. If the adolescent is dazzled by their quick and apparently easy success, it is not surprising that he puts them on a pedestal to serve as models for his life instead of some sturdy plodder who lacks glamour. (1) (7)

The final explanation often given for our new species of American adolescent is the education emphasis placed on democracy. From the moment the American child steps on the doorstep of first grade until he graduates from high school, college, or graduate school, he is exposed to teaching which lauds the advantages of a democracy and stresses the evils of an autocracy. He is not only permitted to think independently and to express these thoughts freely, but is encouraged to do so. To parents of adolescents who were brought up to "respect their elders," this comes as a shock and often causes a real trauma.

From the above outline it should be apparent that no one aspect of American culture is responsible but rather the total American culture. And, because of the economic and military power of the United States in the eyes of the world, it is not surprising that young people in the less prosperous and less successful nations would want to model themselves on the American adolescent as he is depicted in the mass media. Because adolescents in these cultures are dissatisfied with existing conditions and feel that there is little hope for improvement, it is only logical that they would want to model themselves on the American adolescent, believing that by doing so they too will improve their lot in life.

Characteristics of the New Species of American Adolescent

1. *Peer conformity.*   While adolescents in all cultures tend to want to be alike, because being different is interpreted by them to mean being "inferior," today's adolescents seem to be driven by a compulsion to follow the herd, whether for good or for bad. They are afraid that any indication of originality, in thought, in action, or in appearance, will make them into "squares." The herd they follow is their own peer group—the group within the adolescent culture with which they have achieved acceptance and identity. When there is a conflict between peer-group values and adult values, they will accept the former and reject the latter. If, for example, it

is the thing to do among their friends to cheat, they will cheat; if it is not the thing to be a virgin, they will quickly give up their virginity.

Naturally, not all American adolescents are driven by an equally strong compulsion to follow the herd but few escape it. The ones most affected are those whose status within the group is somewhat precarious or those who want to improve the status they already have. The only adolescents who seem to be able to retain their individuality are those whose status is so secure that nothing can shake it—the adolescent the sociologist calls the "star," those whose status is so hopeless that nothing they can say or do will lead to their acceptance by the peer group, and those who are not interested enough in peer activities to care whether they are acceptable to the group or not. Few fall in any one of these three categories.

There are two major reasons for the adolescent's willingness to relinquish his individuality in favor of peer conformity. The first is that our status-seeking, "live-up-to-the-Joneses" culture provided the adolescent with a model of conformity since he has left his crib. Everywhere he goes, he is confronted with conformists, whether in the home, in the neighborhood, in the school, in the community, or in the mass media. It is not surprising, under such conditions, that he grows up with the idea that a non-conformist is a "square" and that he will never be able to make a success of life.

The second reason for obsessive conformity is the high value placed on popularity. If it is essential to follow the crowd to gain acceptance by the crowd, he will pay the price. If, on the other hand, being an individual means loneliness and, even worse, a derogatory attitude from members of the peer group, he will do all within his power to avoid having this happen to him.

2. *Preoccupation with status symbols.* In our social-class-conscious culture of today, it would be surprising if the American adolescent of today were not anxious to be identified in the minds of the peer group members with the leading crowds. He knows that the way to make this identification possible is to have status symbols that create the impression that he is one of the crowd. That is why clothes that equal or surpass in quality and quantity those of his classmates, a car of his own, money for dates and good times, trips to Florida or Bermuda at Easter and to Europe in the summer, are so important to him. The less secure he is in his status, the more preoccupied he becomes with status symbols which, he hopes, will make his status more secure.

That status symbols are important to an adolescent becomes apparent when one examines the juvenile delinquency statistics and discovers that the major crime is theft—clothes and costume jewelry among girls and cars among boys. Another line of evidence of the importance status symbols play in the adolescent's life comes from studies of school and college dropouts. While it is true that some dropouts are academic failures, most are social failures. Boys and girls who cannot have the status symbols their classmates have are not socially acceptable to them. As a result, school and college lose their appeal and the boys and girls drop out, get jobs, and hope to improve their social status by earning money to buy the status symbols they believe are essential to this.

3. *Irresponsibility.*   Today's adolescents tend to follow the philosophy of "let John do it." "John" may be their parents, their teachers, or even "Uncle Sam." "John" is rarely the adolescent himself. They may be meticulous about their appearance, but their school assignments are thrown together, home chores are either neglected completely or done so badly that someone has to do them over, they are constantly late for appointments with only the flimsiest excuses, they do not bother to answer party invitations but appear anyway, they raid the refrigerator without a thought as to whether the food was meant for the next meal, they ask a girl to "go steady" and then drop her if they find someone else who strikes their fancy, they appear late for part-time jobs and often drop them without notice, and, worst of all, they rush into marriage because they are "fed up with the family" but with no thought as to how they are going to support the marriage.

The finger of blame can be pointed only in one direction—to parents and teachers who have tolerated such behavior since the adolescents were young children. The philosophy of life that fosters such behavior is that of the "happy, carefree childhood." Parents and teachers who believe that lack of responsibility will lead to happiness, bend over backwards to assume the responsibilities the adolescent should have been assuming. By the time he reaches adolescence, he expects things to be handed to him on a silver platter, and if he does not get what he expects, he complains that his parents and teachers are "mean." The more parents and teachers try to instill in the young people a sense of responsibility, the more they are accused of "yakity-yaking."

4. *Anti-work attitude.*   Closely related to the lack of responsibility that characterizes far too many of our American adolescents of today is their unfavorable attitude toward work. Having been waited on hand and foot, and having had everything made easy for them in the hopes that this will make them happy, they develop the habit of putting forth as little effort as possible. Even worse, they look upon work as an evil that should be avoided at any cost. If they can get reasonably good grades by cheating, why study? If they can hold down a job by turning out some work, why "kill oneself for a slavedriver"? If they can get the prestige of being on a committee, why not let the person who is chairman of the committee do the work? If they can get the gist of a classic by reading a "true comic" or by seeing a movie based on the book, why bother to wade through the book itself? Even more important is the grumbling he hears from mother about

how tired she is after a day of housework or from father about his exhausting day in the office. How could an adolescent look upon work other than unfavorably with such models before him and how could he be expected to do anything but develop the attitude that he wasn't going to "kill himself" with work?

5. *Anti-intellectualism.* In spite of the fact that more and more adolescents are finishing high school, going on to college and even to graduate school than ever before, this is definitely not evidence of intellectual curiosity or interests. Instead, it is a way to "better themselves"—to climb the ladder by getting a better job which, in turn, will enable them to live better and be associated with the "right people." Even more so than in the past, a person with intellectual interests is an "egghead," a "square" in a population where the important holes are for "rounds."

To achieve the goal of getting ahead, good grades are essential but cheating makes this possible. At the same time, it gives more time to have fun—to participate in extracurricular activities. Thus, they can literally kill two birds with one stone—they can have good grades and they can have their fun. Not all students, of course, suffer from the prevailing anti-intellectualism. But they are in such a small minority that they must literally hide their brains to avoid the stigma of being labelled a "brain." If they must make a choice between intellectual and non-intellectual interests, it is generally not in favor of the former. That is why our underachievers among the bright students—students who in the past would have been our real intellectuals because they wanted knowledge for knowledge's sake, not for grades—are growing at such an alarming rate.

6. *New values.* When adolescents complain that members of the older generation "don't understand" them, they are speaking the truth. Some of the cherished American values that have come down from our founding fathers have literally been dumped in favor of new values which members of the older generation · cannot understand or accept. A few examples, form the superficial to the more serious, will serve to illustrate what a revolution there has been in the past generation. Having manners has always been a value in the American culture, as it is in every civilized culture. Today's adolescents do not agree. To them, these are only superficialities that are too trivial to bother with. Dressing up and being well groomed had always been an accepted part of the party pattern until today's adolescents put their stamp of disapproval on such "non-essentials." Having a "nest egg" for the proverbial rainy day is a value preached to people throughout the world but the American adolescent of today rejects it on the grounds that one should "eat, drink and be merry today" and let the future take care of itself or let Uncle Sam take care of you. Virginity at the time of marriage is a value that every civilized culture has accepted but today's adolescents reject it as "mid-Victorian."

Where, one may justifiably ask, do these new values come from? Not from one source alone but from several, the most important of which are the new types of individuals adolescents choose as their heroes and ideals, mass media that glamourize extravagance and paint thrift as dowdy or imply that virginity belongs to another era, and from the adolescent's lack of sense of social responsibility which is part of his general irresponsibility. Some of these new values unquestionably arise within the peer group itself. If the group as a whole gives its stamp of approval to behavior that is expedient, though not in accordance with the standards of the larger social group, it is accepted as "right" by the adolescent. When, for example, it is important to get high grades but this might make having fun difficult, the adolescent will cheat and justify his doing so by claiming that "everyone does it" and, therefore, it is all right. Similarly, if it is important to be popular and if popularity with members of the other sex can be guaranteed by saying "Yes" rather than "No," a girl will engage in premarital sex behavior and then justify her doing so on the grounds that it is quite all right, so long as you love the boy—at least at the time.

7. *Disrespect for older generations.*   With values of their own which are often so different from those of their parents and grandparents, it is not surprising that today's adolescents feel that all members of the older generations are out of step with the times. This, in turn, is interpreted by them to mean that the young generation, if it wants to get along in today's world, must reject the influence of the older generations. In doing so, they develop a derogatory attitude not only toward their relatives but toward all people over thirty.

This unfavorable attitude toward older people is reinforced by what they see or hear around them. Father complains about the "old dodos who run our country," mother shows obvious annoyance at the thought of the inconvenience she will experience when elderly relatives come to visit or become permanent members of the household, older workers are replaced by young ones in jobs, and the mass media are constantly emphasizing the "plight of the elderly." Lack of respect and esteem for age and experience are so much a part of the American culture of today that it would be unrealistic to expect today's adolescents to have attitudes that are other than unfavorable.

There are two important consequences of these unfavorable attitudes. The first is that it deprives adolescents of the guidance of anyone old enough and experienced enough to offer it. Since adolescents reject the values and attitudes of older people on general principles, it is not surprising that they would consider any advice from older people so out of step with modern times that it would not fit into their problems or help them to solve them.

Equally as serious is the second consequence: the constant friction that it engenders in the home. While expecting parents to pay their bills and assume many responsibilities for their daily living, they literally say

"Hands off" when it comes to doing what their parents advise and expect from them. Furthermore, their derogatory attitude can do nothing but infuriate parents. While family friction has always existed in homes where there are adolescents striving to gain their independence, the derogatory attitude toward the very people adolescents expect to do so much for them is a bitter pill for parents to swallow. In time, it weakens family solidarity and leads to a break-up of the family loyalty which has always characterized the American family.

8. *Criticism and reform.* Adolescents have always had a critical attitude toward their elders, whether parents or teachers, and have always vowed that, when they grew up, they would do things differently. However, it would have been unthinkable for them to verbalize their criticisms to their elders and even more unthinkable for them to tell their elders how they should do things. For many American adolescents of today, one of the favorite indoor sports is debunking those in authority, and this they do directly not indirectly. An adolescent daughter will tell her mother, to her face, that she is "too fat," that her dress is "too long," that she is "inefficient" in her running of the home, and that she is "allowing her mind to go to seed" by not keeping up-to-date on the latest music, popular books, and movies. Father is not spared a similar critical analysis by his adolescent son. While the parent of the same sex is usually the target of critical attacks, parents of the opposite sex come in for their share.

Nor are teachers and school authorities spared in the adolescent's zeal to reform. He does not hesitate to tell his teacher, to her face, that the assignments are too long, that the grade he received was "unfair," that she treats the class like a "lot of kids," and that she has "old-fashioned ideas," if they differ from his. Many times he will even go to the extreme of telling the teacher how she should run the class, what assignments she should give, and how she should deal with troublesome students.

When school authorities impose rules the students think are unfair, they send a delegation to the principal to tell him what the students will tolerate and what they won't. If he is unwilling to reform to meet their demands, they may picket the school, go on a sit-down strike and refuse to study, or absent themselves from school until their "wrongs" have been righted. Older adolescents, on college campuses, protest the dismissal or lack of promotion of a teacher they like and literally demand that the college reverse its stand. If they are forbidden by the college authorities to talk about any subject they wish on the campus, they will picket the administration building and, when told to disperse, will start a riot. (30)

All of this, it should be very evident, is a case of the effects of overly permissive child-training come home to roost. If the adolescent has been permitted, from his earliest childhood, to say what he thinks, regardless of how it might affect others, and if he has been given little or no training in learning the manners that govern the lives of all civilized peoples, it would be surprising if he turned into a tactful, respectful person. No adult would want adolescents not to make their contribution to progress. If they can see flaws in the ways their parents and teachers are doing things, and can offer practical, constructive suggestions for improvement, few adults would object to having this new and fresh perspective. However, it is not the criticism and suggestion for reform *per se* that angers adults: it is the excessively rude and derogatory manner that is used to present them. It becomes a case where the adolescent sits in judgment on his parents and teachers, rather than a co-operative working together for the improvement of the home or school.

9. *Disregard for rules and laws.* Every generation of adolescents has, to some extent, felt that the rules and laws that govern society were too strict, but today's adolescents seem, in far too large numbers, to feel that they are to be disregarded or broken. Parents of today complain that their adolescent sons and daughters are impossible to control—that they do just as they please, go where they please, and return home when they please. In today's schools, most teachers spend more time on maintaining order in the classrooms than on actual teaching of subject matter. In many communities, the police are busier with the antics of teenage gangs than with adult criminality. The rise in juvenile delinquency, especially among the "affluent" members of society, is one of the shocking facts of American life of today.

To members of the older generation who believe that the only way to bring up children is by authoritarian control and that to "spare the rod means to spoil the child," the ready explanation is the laxity of our child-training methods. This is too pat an explanation to be tenable, though in part it is unquestionably true. Not, of course, because corporal punishment is the only way to make a child into a law-abiding citizen but rather because parents who spare the rod also spare the child of any necessity of toeing the mark. It is the general laxity of their training that has resulted in the child's belief that he can be a law unto himself that has resulted in the child's disregard for rules. By the time he reaches adolescence, the belief is so firmly fixed in his mind that he disregards the laws of the land just as he earlier learned to disregard family rules.

Added to this explanation is that of lack of responsibility. The adolescent who finds it easier to "let John do it" than to assume responsibility for his own affairs except when it suits his convenience to do so, has little motivation to think of the good of the social group.

10. *Unrealistic levels of aspiration.* Adolescence is always a period of dreaming, of making plans for the future that will lead to a better life. Today's American adolescents share that dreaming with adolescents of the past and of other cultures but they go much further. Their dreams are not only far more unrealistic but they are convinced that they will reach the

rainbow at the end of their dreams with minimum effort. When their unrealistic aspirations are not realized, it is always someone else's fault, never theirs. If they aspire unrealistically high in their academic goals, for example, they seek a ready scapegoat to blame. It may be their parents who made them do home chores or take part-time jobs, thus giving them too little time to study; it may be their teachers who had a "grudge against them"; or it may be the "curve-raisers" in the class who make it "tough" for the other students.

What is responsible for this new trend toward unrealistic thinking and planning? And it is new because in past generations an adolescent who engaged in it would be told that he was getting "too big for his britches" and quickly brought down to reality. Parents, unquestionably, are the biggest offenders. Far too many believe that the reason they did not get further ahead in life than they did was that they never had the opportunities. To see to it that their children are not handicapped in the same way, they give them every possible opportunity, even at great personal sacrifice. And, because today's adolescents are growing up in a period of affluence where every social class is sharing the rewards, and in a culture that has eliminated any barriers to opportunity for any groups, parents believe that their children have as good a chance to get ahead as anyone else. This belief they foster in their children so that, by the time their children reach adolescence, it is not surprising that they believe the sky is the limit.

Teachers are not completely blameless in fostering unrealistic thinking on the part of adolescents. Many a teacher who finds a student doing well in one subject tells him he can do equally well in other subjects if he will only study harder. This, of course, is not necessarily true. Abilities of unequal levels of excellence are far more common than of equal levels. Nor is it necessarily true that if a student will study harder he can do better. Some students are doing the best they can with what ability they have. Studying harder may result in higher grades, based more on effort than on achievement but, when these students must compete with other students of greater ability and when they are judged on the basis of achievement only—as in the case of the College Entrance Examinations—they will be forced to recognize that their achievements are inferior.

Is the "New Species" Superior?

From the brief survey of some of the outstanding characteristics of American adolescents of today, there can be no question about the fact that they are a "new species." However, newness is not synonymous with superiority. Unquestionably, in some respects the American adolescent of today is superior to the adolescent of past generations. Certainly he has had more advantages, socially, culturally, and educationally, than the majority of adolescents in the past. As a result, he has more knowledge and sophistication about the world in which he lives than adolescents of past generations. But this does not mean that he is superior as a person, or that when he reaches adulthood he will be prepared to help our nation become a stronger and better place in which to live than it is today. Some adolescents of course will, but they are not typical of the "new species."

On the other hand, there is ample evidence that far too many American adolescents of today whose hereditary endowments and cultural advantages would normally lead to high achievements are turning into second-rate students, second-rate workers, and second-rate citizens. The increase in underachievement among our most able high-school and college students and in dropouts testifies to this as does the attitude of their employers toward the slipshod quality of work they do and their preoccupation with coffee-breaks and clock-watching. The shocking rise in juvenile delinquency among the affluent, not among the "slum kids" alone, is further evidence that today's adolescent is not superior to adolescents of past generations.

Another important criterion is that of happiness. Today's adolescents are not happy. Instead, they are bored, jaded, and disillusioned to the point where they turn to drink and narcotics to "drown their sorrows" and give them a stimulant that will make them feel more adequate and self-important. Even without going to the extreme of using stimulants to bolster their egos, there are far too many who suffer from feelings of inadequacy and failure to the point where they question their own worth, who wonder if life is worth living, and who talk glibly about committing suicide.

To be happy, a person must not only have a feeling of confidence that he can achieve success within his capacities but he must retain a sense of individuality and identity. Today's adolescents do not have this. Even before they leave the high school and college campuses, they have become the adult men and women in the "gray flannel suits." Even worse, they are so imbued with the fear that they will be regarded as "squares" if they discard the gray flannel suits for garb more to their liking that they are headed for a life where conformity to the herd will rule their every thought and action. This is not a good prognostication for happiness ahead.

REFERENCES:

1. BERGER, B. M. Teen-agers Are an American Invention. *The New York Times,* July 13, 1965.
2. BERNARD, H. W. *Human Development in Western Culture* (Boston: Allyn & Bacon, 1962).
3. COLE, L., and I. N. HALL. *Psychology of Adolescence,* 6th ed. (New York: Holt, Rinehart, and Winston, 1964).

4. COLEMAN, J. S. *The Adolescent Society* (New York: The Free Press of Glencoe, 1961).
5. CONANT, J. B. *The American High School Today* (New York: McGraw-Hill, 1959).
6. CROW, L. D., and A. CROW. *Adolescent Development and Adjustment,* 2d ed. (New York: McGraw-Hill, 1965).
7. Esquire Magazine. Special Edition: Teen Time. *Esquire,* July, 1965.
8. FRANK, L. K., and M. H. FRANK. *Your Adolescent, at Home and in School* (New York: Viking, 1956).
9. FRIEDENBERG, E. Z. *The Vanishing Adolescent* (Boston: Beacon Press, 1959).
10. FREUD, S. *The Standard Edition of the Complete Psychological Works of Sigmund Freud* (London: Hogarth, 1953–1962).
11. GALLUP, G., and E. HILL. Youth: the Cool Generation. *Saturday Evening Post,* December, 1961.
12. GLUECK, S., and E. T. GLUECK. *Family Environment and Delinquency* (Boston: Houghton Mifflin, 1962).
13. GOTTLIEB, D., and C. RAMSEY. *The American Adolescent* (Homewood, Ill.: Dorsey Press, 1963).
14. HECHINGER, F. M. Affluent Delinquency. *The New York Times,* September 5, 1963.
15. HECHINGER, G., and F. M. HECHINGER. *Teen-Age Tyranny* (New York: Morrow, 1963).
16. HECHINGER, G., and F. M. HECHINGER. College Morals Mirror Our Society. *The New York Times,* April 14, 1963.
17. HORROCKS, J. E. *Psychology of Adolescence,* 2d ed. (Boston: Houghton Mifflin, 1962).
18. JERSILD, A. T. *The Psychology of Adolescence,* 2d ed. (New York: Macmillan, 1963).
19. Journal of Marriage and the Family. American Adolescents in the Mid-sixties. *Journal of Marriage and the Family,* 1965, 27, No. 2.
20. KELLEY, E. C. *In Defense of Youth* (Englewood Cliffs, N.J.: Prentice-Hall, 1962.)
21. MOHR, G. J., and M. A. DESPRES. *The Stormy Decade: Adolescence* (New York: Random House, 1958).
22. MUUS, R. E. *Theories of Adolescence* (New York: Random House, 1962).
23. New York Times Report: Pope warns youth on wild outbursts over entertainment. *The New York Times,* July 5, 1965.
24. New York Times Report: Raped girl's family says father sought exoneration of son. *The New York Times,* July 10, 1965.
25. PACKARD, V. *The Status Seekers* (New York: Pocket Books, 1961).
26. REMMERS, H. H., and D. H. RADLER. *The American Teenager* (New York: Bobbs Merrill, 1957).
27. STRANG, R. *The Adolescent Views Himself* (New York: McGraw-Hill, 1957).

28. U.S. News and World Report. Changes in Today's College Students. *U.S. News & World Report,* February 17, 1964.
29. U.S. News and World Report: Why Young People "go bad." *U.S. News & World Report,* April 26, 1965.
30. U.S. News and World Report: A Cure for Campus Riots. *U.S. News & World Report,* May 17, 1965.

31   Many Hold False Ideas About Youth*

BY EARL C. KELLEY

EDITOR'S NOTE: *The preceding article presented you with one point of view about the American adolescent. This is another point of view. Weigh both articles carefully. Consider not only their evidence and ideas but your own experience and ideas as well. What is your stand regarding the nature of the American adolescent?*

I have wanted to say that the general public does not understand youth, but this is too mild. Not only do we not understand them, we hold false notions about them. These ideas do not result merely in our being puzzled about young people; they cause us to take action in the wrong direction. These ideas and their results have not only been disproved by research but have failed us again and again through the ages. To cling to them is to fall back far beyond the age of science and reason to the pre-scientific days of witchcraft and even back to voodooism. Some of these false ideas are listed below.

1) *Many believe that children are born bad and have to be coerced into being good.* This accounts for many acts of aggression committed by adults on babies even in the cradle. These acts are sometimes perpetrated on infants so young that they have not yet even gained their eyesight or their sense of hearing. What such an infant can feel about this is that he has been born into a hostile world. The idea that children are born bad accounts for the "training" concept which rightly belongs to the rearing of animals, such as horses and dogs, but is never successful with humans. This

* Earl C. Kelley, *In Defense of Youth,* © 1962. Reprinted by permission of Prentice-Hall, Inc., Englewood Cliffs, New Jersey.

is the opposite of the concept of growth and education. While training seeks to close the mind so that only one response will be available, education in its true sense is designed to open the mind, to reveal the wide world, and to make an infinite number of responses possible. Modern science has shown that children are born neither good nor bad. "Goodness" and "badness" are adult concepts, and they are learned. They are products of the lives people lead from birth on. They depend upon the quality of living available to the young over which the young have no control.

2) *Many believe that youth has gone to the dogs.* This is an idea which seems to be firmly implanted in the minds of most adults. One is tempted to attribute it to the changed conditions under which we live. But when we realize that this complaint is in the literature almost as far back as written language goes, we see that we would still have this complaint even if we had not changed the conditions under which we live. The citation of these complaints could fill a large book and would become extremely tiresome. Perhaps it will suffice to quote Socrates, who lived four hundred years before Christ, and to add that this sentiment has been repeated *ad nauseam* ever since, reaching new depths in the last year or two. Twenty-five hundred years ago Socrates is quoted as having said:

> Children now love luxury. They have bad manners, contempt for authority. They show disrespect for elders, and love chatter in place of exercise. Children are now tyrants, not the servants of their households.

It seems odd, but the very people who complain about modern youth often like to tell in glowing terms of their own depredations when they were boys. Of course, a story is always improved in the telling, but even after discounting for this, some of the reminiscent confessions are amply horrifying. It is true that more of the shortcomings of youth come to our attention because we live closer together than we did formerly, because we have invented probation officers and juvenile courts, and because people dearly love to read about delinquency. Since we live closer together and there are more of us, there is doubtless more anti-social behavior among some young people.

The over-all evidence, however, is that youth as a whole behave better than they ever did. Careful research has shown that they read better, spell better, and cipher better than they ever did. Not only that, but school discipline and behavior are better than ever before. It is now unheard of for a school to be closed because the students are out of control. But in 1837, one hundred and fifty schools in Massachusetts alone were closed for this reason. In Boston in 1850, it took sixty-five beatings a day to keep a school of four hundred going. About 1875, an uncle of mine decided on teaching as a career and started with a country one-room school. His professional career ended when the pupils tipped the outhouse over, door down, with him in it. I never heard how he got out, but by the time I knew him he was an aging farmer.

Indeed, in my time, the idea that the function of the pupils was to throw out the teacher was not yet dead. The first teaching I did was in a one-room, eight-grade country school where my predecessor had been vanquished. It was a peculiar school in that, though public, it had only boys in it. I learned that nobody would send a girl to the school because it was considered too tough. I have always wondered about it because, although I was only eighteen years old and weighed less than 130 pounds dripping wet (I went into teaching instead of farming because I wasn't very good at farm work) nobody bothered me at all. No pupil ever laid a hand on me, or I on him. The only brush with destiny I had was when one of the fathers came in after school when I was alone and told me that he was going to "thrash me within an inch of my life." This seemed odd, because I thought I was getting along fine with his boy. Since he had stated his errand, however, I picked up the stove poker and said that then was the best time to try. He retreated through the open door, and I never saw him again.

I tell this to make the point that the only trouble I had was with an adult and that I cannot conceive how the former teacher got himself ejected unless he subjected these pupils to extreme aggravation. My success must have come from what I did not do rather than what I did. I did not know any child psychology and my confidence was only exceeded by my ignorance.

Youth, it seems to me, have been getting better instead of worse in spite of living under more difficult circumstances than was formerly the case.

3) *It is often said that parents do not love their young these days.* Many people believe that parents have become irresponsible and that they no longer care what happens to their young. If parents really cared about their young, they would see to it that their youth did not bother you and me as they now do.

It is true, of course, that some parents care more than others. This has, however, probably always been the case, since people are unique in every way. In the farm community where I grew up, before the automobile had become a factor in our lives, there were parents who seemed to take less care of their young than others. I expect this will always be true.

But in all studies of the nature of the human organism, or of the animals less than human, there is nothing to indicate that parental love has lessened. Parental love for the young is deep-seated and persistent. It can be observed in many of the lower animals. It has had survival value throughout the long history of mankind. How this powerful force, working through the ages, could lessen or disappear in one generation is impossible to explain.

Parents do have to rear their young under more difficult circumstances than they did before America became so heavily industrialized. I shall have more to say about this shortly. There is no reason to believe that they care less; on the contrary, because it is more difficult, they probably are more concerned than ever before. On account of these difficulties they are entitled to our sympathy and understanding, rather than our blame and scorn.

4) *Many believe that violence will cure any youth of anything.* The same people who believe that parents no longer care about their young accuse them of being over-indulgent. This must mean that parents love their children too much. These people often aver that there is nothing the matter with our youth that a good licking wouldn't cure. They want parents to substitute the knout for love. This belief in the value of violence is so common in our culture that it is frightening. It would seem that the evils of violence would be so apparent, after millenniums of its use, that we would at last be ready to at least try something else. These words may never be finished because we, through our age-long pursuit of violence as a cure for everything, may render this beautiful earth a dead planet, not only devoid of human life but also of blameless, peace-loving animals and the plants on which they depend. Yet many still cry "Hit him!" "Beat him!" "Jail him!"

These people get their impulses from far in the past, in the pre-scientific days when man was far more naïve than he is now supposed to be. These impulses or beliefs come from the days of the iron maiden and the whipping post. Those were the days when elderly helpless women were thrown into a river. If they floated, they were witches and were taken out, dried off, and burned. If they sank, they were not witches and died an honorable, though watery, death. In those days, the mentally ill were often beaten to drive out the evil spirits.

Although the return of the whipping post is often advocated in the public press (not editorially, so far as I know), the laws of our nation have gradually become more enlightened. Our jails are often degrading and our chain gangs are utterly inhuman, but we no longer beat people in public, and many states in the Union have accepted the futility of capital punishment as a control over behavior.

It seems to me that the biggest lesson the human race could learn, while it can still learn, is that violence never gained anything in the long history of man. "A good beating" never made youth better, even though it might appear to have done so. It never served any purpose except to make youth more fearful, more hostile, more secretive, and more aggressive. It never drew parent and child closer together, but always pushed them farther apart. I would go so far as to say that, unless the youth has been too badly damaged, there is nothing a good loving will not cure. This, of course, applies to our relationships with each other as well as with youth, and if it could spread all over the world, it would be the way to peace. We cannot be at war with our youth and at peace with those more remote from us.

CHAPTER EIGHT

CHILD-REARING: STRATEGIES, CONFLICTS AND OUTCOMES

32   The Changing American Child: A Speculative Analysis*[1]

BY URIE BRONFENBRENNER

EDITOR'S NOTE: In this selection, Dr. Bronfenbrenner analyzes the changing styles of child-rearing during the past 25 years. If child-rearing practices are changing, then this would suggest that not only is the family structure changing but that disciplinary methods and socialization techniques are changing, too. The author asserts that ". . . the democratic family . . . tends to produce young people who do not take initiative, looks to others for direction and decision, and cannot be counted on to fulfill obligations." Why does this happen? What are the consequences of fathers becoming more affectionate and less authoritarian and mothers assuming more and more of the disciplinary role? These and related questions are discussed in this provocative article.

A QUESTION OF MOMENT

It is now a matter of scientific record that patterns of child rearing in the United States have changed appreciably over the past twenty-five years (Bronfenbrenner, 1958). Middle class parents especially have moved away from the more rigid and strict styles of care and discipline advocated in the early Twenties and Thirties toward modes of response involving greater tolerance of the child's impulses and desires, freer expression of affection, and increased reliance on "psychological" methods of discipline, such as

* Reprinted from The Journal of Social Issues, 1961, Vol. 17, pp. 6–18, by permission of the author and the publisher.

reasoning and appeals to guilt, as distinguished from more direct techniques like physical punishment. At the same time, the gap between the social classes in their goals and methods of child rearing appears to be narrowing, with working class parents beginning to adopt both the values and techniques of the middle class. Finally, there is dramatic correspondence between these observed shifts in parental values and behavior and the changing character of the attitudes and practices advocated in successive editions of such widely read manuals as the Children's Bureau bulletin on *Infant Care* and Spock's *Baby and Child Care*. Such correspondence should not be taken to mean that the expert has now become the principal instigator and instrument of social change, since the ideas of scientists and professional workers themselves reflect in part the operation of deep-rooted cultural processes. Nevertheless, the fact remains that changes in values and practices advocated by prestigeful professional figures can be substantially accelerated by rapid and widespread dissemination through the press, mass media of communication, and public discussion.

Given these facts, it becomes especially important to gauge the effect of the changes that are advocated and adopted. Nowhere is this issue more significant, both scientifically and socially, than in the sphere of familial values and behavior. It is certainly no trivial matter to ask whether the changes that have occurred in the attitudes and actions of parents over the past twenty-five years have been such as to affect the personality development of their children, so that the boys and girls of today are somewhat different in character structure from those of a decade or more ago. Or, to put the question more succinctly: has the changing American parent produced a changing American child?

A STRATEGY OF INFERENCE

Do we have any basis for answering this intriguing question? To begin with, do we have any evidence of changes in the behavior of children in successive decades analogous to those we have already been able to find for parents? If so, we could take an important first step toward a solution of the problem. Unfortunately, in contrast to his gratifying experience in seeking and finding appropriate data on parents, the present writer has, to date, been unable to locate enough instances in which comparable methods of behavioral assessment have been employed with different groups of children of similar ages over an extended period of time. Although the absence of such material precludes any direct and unequivocal approach to the question at hand, it is nevertheless possible, through a series of inferences from facts already known, to arrive at some estimate of what the answer might be. Specifically, although as yet we have no comparable data on the relation between parental and child behavior for different families at successive points in time, we do have facts on the influence of parental treatment on child behavior at a given point in time; that is, we know that certain variations in parental behavior tend to be accompanied by systematic differences in the personality characteristics of children. If we are willing to assume that these same relationships obtained not only at a given moment but across different points in time, we are in a position to infer the possible effects on children of changing patterns of child rearing over the years. It is this strategy that we propose to follow.

THE CHANGING AMERICAN PARENT

We have already noted the major changes in parental behavior discerned in a recent analysis of data reported over a twenty-five year period. These secular trends may be summarized as follows:

1. *Greater permissiveness towards the child's spontaneous desires*
2. *Freer expression of affection*
3. *Increased reliance on indirect "psychological" techniques of discipline (such as reasoning or appeals to guilt) vs. direct methods (like physical punishment, scolding, or threats)*
4. *In consequence of the above shifts in the direction of what are predominantly middle class values and techniques, a narrowing of the gap between social classes in their patterns of child rearing.*

Since the above analysis was published, a new study has documented an additional trend. Bronson, Katten, and Livson (1959) have compared patterns of paternal and maternal authority and affection in two generations of families from the California Guidance Study. Unfortunately, the time span surveyed overlaps only partially with the twenty-five year period covered in our own analysis, the first California generation having been raised in the early 1900's and the second in the late '20's and early '30's. Accordingly, if we are to consider the California results along with the others cited above, we must make the somewhat risky assumption that a trend discerned in the first three decades of the century has continued in the same direction through the early 1950's. With this important qualification, an examination of the data cited by Bronson, Katten, and Livson (1959) points to still another, secular trend—a shift over the years in the pattern of parental role differentiation within the family. Specifically:

5. *In succeeding generations the relative position of the father vis-à-vis the mother is shifting with the former becoming increasingly more affectionate and less authoritarian, and the latter becoming relatively more important as the agent of discipline, especially for boys.*

"PSYCHOLOGICAL" TECHNIQUES OF DISCIPLINE AND THEIR EFFECTS

In pursuing our analytic strategy, we next seek evidence of the effects on the behavior of children of variations in parental treatment of the type noted in our inventory. We may begin by noting that the variables involved in the first three secular trends constitute a complex that has received considerable attention in recent research in parent-child relationships. Within the last three years, two sets of investigators, working independently, have called attention to the greater efficacy of "love-oriented" or "psychological" techniques in bringing about desired behavior in the child (Sears, Maccoby, and Levin, 1957; Miller and Swanson, 1958, 1960). The present writer, noting that such methods are especially favored by middle class parents, offered the following analysis of the nature of these techniques and the reasons for their effectiveness.

Such parents are, in the first place, more likely to overlook offenses, and when they do punish, they are less likely to ridicule or inflict physical pain. Instead, they reason with the youngster, isolate him, appeal to guilt, show disappointment—in short, convey in a variety of ways, on the one hand, the kind of behavior that is expected of the child; on the other, the realization that transgression means the interruption of a mutually valued relationship. . . .

These findings [of greater efficacy] mean that middle class parents, though in one sense more lenient in their discipline techniques, are using methods that are actually more compelling. Moreover, the compelling power of these practices is probably enhanced by the more permissive treatment accorded to middle class children in the early years of life. The successful use of withdrawal of love as a discipline technique implies the prior existence of a gratifying relationship; the more love present in the first instance, the greater the threat implied in its withdrawal (Bronfenbrenner, 1958).

It is now a well established fact that children from middle class families tend to excel those from lower class in many characteristics ordinarily regarded as desirable, such as self-control, achievement, responsibility, leadership, popularity, and adjustment in general.[2] If, as seems plausible, such differences in behavior are attributable at least in part to class-linked variations in parental treatment, the strategy of inference we have adopted would appear on first blush to lead to a rather optimistic conclusion. Since, over the years, increasing numbers of parents have been adopting the more effective socialization techniques typically employed by the middle class, does it not follow that successive generations of children should show gains in the development of effective behavior and desirable personality characteristics?

Unfortunately, this welcome conclusion, however logical, is premature, for it fails to take into account all of the available facts.

SEX, SOCIALIZATION, AND SOCIAL CLASS

To begin with, the parental behaviors we have been discussing are differentially distributed not only by socio-economic status but also by sex. As we have pointed out elsewhere (Bronfenbrenner, 1961), girls are exposed to more affection and less punishment than boys, but at the same time are more likely to be subjected to "love-oriented" discipline of the type which encourages the development of internalized controls. And, consistent with our line of reasoning, girls are found repeatedly to be "more obedient, cooperative, and in general better socialized than boys at comparable age levels." But this is not the whole story.

. . . At the same time, the research results indicate that girls tend to be more anxious, timid, dependent, and sensitive to rejection. If these differences are a function of differential treatment by parents, then it would seem that the more "efficient" methods of child rearing employed with girls involve some risk of what might be called "over-socialization" (Bronfenbrenner, 1961).

One could argue, of course, that the contrasting behaviors of boys and girls have less to do with differential parental treatment than with genetically-based maturational influences. Nevertheless, two independent lines of evidence suggest that socialization techniques do contribute to individual differences, *within the same sex,* precisely in the types of personality characteristics noted above. In the first place, variations in child behavior and parental treatment strikingly similar to those we have cited for the two sexes are reported in a recent comprehensive study of differences between first and later born children (Schachter, 1959). Like girls, first children receive more attention, are more likely to be exposed to "psychological" discipline, and end up more anxious and dependent, whereas later children, like boys, are more aggressive and self-confident.

A second line of evidence comes from our own current research. We have been concerned with the role of parents in the development of such "constructive" personality characteristics as responsibility and leadership among adolescent boys and girls. Our findings reveal not only the usual differences in adolescents' and parents' behaviors associated with the sex of the child, but also a striking contrast in the relationship between parental and child behaviors for the two sexes. To start on firm and familiar ground, girls are rated by their teachers as more responsible than boys, whereas the latter obtain higher scores on leadership. Expected differences similarly appear in the realm of parental behavior: girls receive more affection, praise, and companionship; boys are subjected to more physical punishment and achievement demands. Quite unanticipated, however, at least by us, was the finding that both parental affection and discipline appeared to facilitate effective psychological functioning in boys, but to impede the development of such constructive behavior in girls. Closer examination of our data indicated that both extremes of either affection or discipline were deleterious for all children, but that the process of socialization entailed somewhat different risks for the two sexes. Girls were especially susceptible to the detrimental influence of over-protection; boys to the ill effects of insufficient parental discipline and support. Or, to put it in more colloquial terms: boys suffered more often from too little taming, girls from too much.

In an attempt to account for this contrasting pattern of relationships, we proposed the notion of differential optimal levels of affection and authority for the two sexes.

The qualities of independence, initiative, and self-sufficiency, which are especially valued for boys in our culture, apparently require for their development a somewhat different balance of authority and affection than is found in the "love-oriented" strategy characteristically applied with girls. While an affectional context is important for the socialization of boys, it must evidently be accompanied by and be compatible with a strong component of parental discipline. Otherwise, the boy finds himself in the same situation as the girl, who, having received greater affection, is more sensitive to its withdrawal, with the result that a little discipline goes a long way and strong authority is constricting rather than constructive (Bronfenbrenner, 1958).

What is more, available data suggest that this very process may already be operating for boys from upper middle class homes. To begin with, differential treatment of the sexes is at a minimum for these families. Contrasting parental attitudes and behaviors toward boys and girls are pronounced only at lower class levels, and decrease as one moves up the socioeconomic scale (Kohn, 1959; Bronfenbrenner, 1958). Thus our own results show that it is primarily at lower middle class levels that boys get more punishment than girls, and the latter receive greater warmth and attention. With an increase in the family's social position, direct discipline drops off, especially for boys, and indulgence and protectiveness decrease for girls. As a result, patterns of parental treatment for the two sexes begin to converge. In like manner, we find that the differential effects of parental behavior on the two sexes are marked only in the lower middle class. It is here that girls especially risk being overprotected and boys not receiving sufficient discipline and support. In upper middle class the picture changes. Girls are not as readily debilitated by parental affection and power; nor is parental discipline as effective in fostering the development of responsibility and leadership in boys.

All these trends point to the conclusion that the "risks" experienced by each sex during the process of socialization tend to be somewhat different at different social class levels. Thus the danger of overprotection for girls is especially great in lower class families, but lower in upper middle class because of the decreased likelihood of overprotection. Analogously, boys are in greater danger of suffering from inadequate discipline and support in lower middle than in upper middle class. But the upper middle class boy, unlike the girl, exchanges one hazard for another. Since at this upper level the more potent "psychological" techniques of discipline are likely to be employed with both sexes, the boy presumably now too runs the risk of being "oversocialized," of losing some of his capacity for independent aggressive accomplishment.

Accordingly, if our line of reasoning is correct, we should expect a changing pattern of sex differences at successive socio-economic levels. Specifically, aspects of effective psychological functioning favoring girls should be most pronounced in the upper middle class; those favoring boys in the lower middle. A recent analysis of some of our data bears out this expectation. Girls excel boys on such variables as *responsibility* and *social acceptance* primarily at the higher socio-economic levels. In contrast, boys surpass girls on such traits as *leadership, level of aspiration,* and *competitiveness* almost exclusively in lower middle class. Indeed, with a rise in a family's social position, the differences tend to reverse themselves with girls now excelling boys.[3]

TRENDS IN PERSONALITY DEVELOPMENT: A FIRST APPROXIMATION

The implications for our original line of inquiry are clear. We are suggesting that the "love-oriented" socialization techniques, which over the past twenty-five years have been employed in increasing degree by American middle class families, may have negative as well as constructive aspects. While fostering the internalization of adult standards and the development of socialized behavior, they may also have the effect of undermining capacities for initiative and independence, particularly in boys. Males exposed to this "modern" pattern of child rearing might be expected to differ from their counterparts of a quarter century ago in being somewhat more conforming and anxious, less enterprising and self-sufficient, and, in general, possessing more of the virtues and liabilities commonly associated with feminine character structure.[4]

At long last, then, our strategy of inference has led us to a first major conclusion. The term "major" is appropriate since the conclusion takes as its points of departure and return four of the secular trends which served as the impetus for our inquiry. Specifically, through a series of empirical links and theoretical extrapolations, we have arrived at an estimate of the effects on children of the tendency of successive generations of parents to become progressively more permissive, to express affection more freely, to utilize "psychological" techniques of discipline, and, by moving in these directions to narrow the gap between the social classes in their patterns of child rearing.

FAMILY STRUCTURE AND PERSONALITY DEVELOPMENT

But one other secular trend remains to be considered: what of the changing pattern of parental role differentiation during the first three decades of the century? If our extrapolation is correct, the balance of power within the family has continued to shift with fathers yielding parental authority to mothers and taking on some of the nurturant and affectional functions traditionally associated with the maternal role. Again we have no direct evidence of the effects of such secular changes on successive generations of children, and must look for leads to analogous data on contemporaneous relationships.

We may begin by considering the contribution of each parent to the socialization processes we have examined thus far. Our data indicate that it is primarily mothers who tend to employ "love-oriented" techniques of discipline and fathers who rely on more direct methods like physical punishment. The above statement must be qualified, however, by reference to the sex of the child, for it is only in relation to boys that fathers use direct punishment more than mothers. More generally, . . . the results reveal a tendency for each parent to be somewhat more active, firm, and demanding with a child of the same sex, more lenient and indulgent with a child of the opposite sex. . . . The reversal is most complete with respect to discipline, with fathers being stricter with boys, mothers with girls. In the spheres of affection and protectiveness, there is no actual shift in preference, but the tendency to be especially warm and solicitous with girls is much more pronounced among fathers than among mothers. In fact, generally speaking, it is the father who is more likely to treat children of the two sexes differently (Bronfenbrenner, 1958).

Consistent with this pattern of results, it is primarily the behavior of fathers that accounts for the differential effects of parental behavior on the two sexes and for the individual differences within each sex. In other words, it is paternal authority and affection that tend especially to be salutary for sons but determinental for daughters. But as might be antici-pated from what we already know, these trends are pronounced only in the lower middle class; with a rise in the family's social status, both parents tend to have similar effects on their children, both within and across sexes. Such a trend is entirely to be expected since parental role differentiation tends to decrease markedly as one ascends the socio-economic ladder. It is almost exclusively in lower middle class homes that fathers are more strict with boys and mothers with girls. To the extent that direct discipline is employed in upper middle class families, it tends to be exercised by both parents equally. Here again we see a parallelism between shifts in parental behavior across time and social class in the direction of forms (in this instance of family structure) favored by the upper middle class group.

What kinds of children, then, can we expect to develop in families in which the father plays a predominantly affectionate role, and a relatively low level of discipline is exercised equally by both parents? A tentative answer to this question is supplied by a preliminary analysis of our data in which the relation between parental role structure and adolescent behavior was examined with controls for the family's social class position. The results of this analysis are summarized as follows: . . . Both responsibility and leadership are fostered by the relatively greater salience of the parent of the same sex. . . . Boys tend to be more responsible when the father rather than the mother is the principal disciplinarian; girls are more dependable when the mother is the major authority figure. . . . In short, boys thrive in a patriarchal context, girls in a matriarchal. . . . The most dependent and least dependable adolescents describe family arrangements that are neither patriarchal nor matriarchal, but equalitarian. To state the issue in more provocative form, our data suggest that the democratic family, which for so many years has been held up and aspired to as a model by professionals and enlightened laymen, tends to produce young people who "do not take initiative," "look to others for direction and decision," and "cannot be counted on to fulfill obligations" (Bronfenbrenner, 1958).

In the wake of so sweeping a conclusion, it is important to call attention to the tentative, if not tenuous character of our findings. The results were based on a single study employing crude questionnaire methods and rating scales. Also, our interpretation is limited by the somewhat "attenuated" character of most of the families classified as patriarchal or matriarchal in our sample. Extreme concentrations of power in one or another parent were comparatively rare. Had they been more frequent, we suspect the data would have shown that such extreme asymmetrical patterns of authority were detrimental rather than salutary for effective psychological development, perhaps even more disorganizing than equalitarian forms.

Nevertheless, our findings do find some peripheral support in the work of others. A number of investigations, for example, point to the special importance of the father in the socialization of boys (Bandura and Walters, 1959; Mussen and Distler, 1959). Further corroborative evidence appears in the growing series of studies of effects of paternal absence (Bach, 1946; Sears, Pintler and Sears, 1946; Lynn and Sawrey, 1959; Tiller, 1958). The absence of the father apparently not only affects the behavior of the child directly but also influences the mother in the direction of greater over-protectiveness. The effect of both these tendencies is especially critical for male children; boys from father-absent homes tend to be markedly more submissive and dependent. Studies dealing explicitly with the influence of parental role structure in intact families are few and far between. Papanek (1957), in an unpublished doctoral dissertation, reports greater sex-role differentiation among children from homes in which the parental roles were differentiated. And in a carefully controlled study, Kohn and Clausen (1956) find that "schizophrenic patients more frequently than normal persons report that their mothers played a very strong authority role and the father a very weak authority role." Finally, what might best be called complementary evidence for our inferences regarding trends in family structure and their effects comes from the work of Miller, Swanson, and their associates (1958; 1960) on the differing patterns of behavior exhibited by families from *bureaucratic* and *entrepreneurial* work settings. These investigators argue that the entrepreneurial-bureaucratic dichotomy represents a new cleavage in American social structure that cuts across and overrides social class influences and carries with it its own characteristic patterns of family structure and socialization. Thus one investigation (Gold and Slater, 1958) contrasts the exercise of power in families of husbands employed in two kinds of job situations: (a) those working in large organizations with three or more levels of supervision; (b) those self-employed or working in small organizations with few levels of supervision. With appropriate controls for social class, equalitarian families were found more frequently in the bureaucratic groups; patriarchal and, to a lesser extent, matriarchal in the entrepreneurial setting. Another study (Miller and Swanson, 1958) shows that, in line with Miller and Swanson's hypotheses, parents from these same two groups tend to favor rather different ends and means of socialization, with entrepreneurial families putting considerably more emphasis on the development of independence and mastery and on the use of "psychological" techniques of discipline. These differences appear at both upper and lower middle class levels but are less pronounced in higher socio-economic strata. It is Miller and Swanson's belief, however, that the trend is toward the bureaucratic way of life, with its less structured patterns of family organization and child rearing. The evidence we have cited on secular changes in family structure and the inferences we have drawn regarding their possible effects on personality development are on the whole consistent with their views.

LOOKING FORWARD

If Miller and Swanson are correct in the prediction that America is moving toward a bureaucratic society that emphasizes, to put it colloquially, "getting along" rather than "getting ahead," then presumably we can look forward to ever increasing numbers of equalitarian families who, in turn, will produce successive generations of ever more adaptable but unaggressive "organization men." But recent signs do not all point in this direction. In our review of secular trends in child rearing practices we detected in the data from the more recent studies a slowing up in the headlong rush toward greater permissiveness and toward reliance on indirect methods of discipline. We pointed out also that if the most recent editions of well-thumbed guidebooks on child care are as reliable harbingers of the future as they have been in the past, we can anticipate something of a return to the more explicit discipline techniques of an earlier era. Perhaps the most important forces, however, acting to redirect both the aims and methods of child rearing in America emanate from behind the Iron Curtain. With the firing of the first Sputnik, Achievement began to replace Adjustment as the highest goal of the American way of life. We have become concerned—perhaps even obsessed—with "education for excellence" and the maximal utilization of our intellectual resources. Already, ability grouping, and the guidance counsellor who is its prophet, have moved down from the junior high to the elementary school, and parents can be counted on to do their part in preparing their youngsters for survival in the new competitive world of applications and achievement tests.

But if a new trend in parental behavior is to develop, it must do so in the context of changes already under way. And if the focus of parental authority is shifting from husband to wife, then perhaps we should anticipate that pressures for achievement will be imposed primarily by mothers rather than fathers. Moreover, the mother's continuing strong emotional investment in the child should provide her with a powerful lever for evoking desired performance. It is noteworthy in this connection that recent studies of the familial origins of need-achievement point to the matriarchy as the optimal context for development of the motive to excel (Strodtbeck, 1958; Rosen and D'Andrade, 1959).

The prospect of a society in which socialization techniques are directed toward maximizing achievement drive is not altogether a pleasant one. As a number of investigators have shown (Baldwin, Kalhorn and Breese, 1945; Baldwin, 1948; Haggard, 1957; Winterbottom, 1958; Rosen and D'Andrade, 1959), high achievement motivation appears to flourish in a family atmosphere of "cold democracy" in which initial high levels of maternal involvement are followed by pressures for independence and accomplishment.[5] Nor does the product of this process give ground for reassurance. True, children from achievement-oriented homes excel in planfulness and performance, but they are also more aggressive, tense, domineering, and cruel (Baldwin, Kalhorn and Breese, 1945; Baldwin, 1948; Haggard, 1957). It would appear that education for excellence if pursued single-mindedly may entail some sobering social costs.

But by now we are in danger of having stretched our chain of inference beyond the strength of its weakest link. Our speculative analysis has become far more speculative than analytic and to pursue it further would bring us past the bounds of science into the realms of science fiction. In concluding our discussion, we would re-emphasize that speculations should, by their very nature, be held suspect. It is for good reason that, like "damn Yankees" they too carry their almost inseparable sobriquets: speculations are either "idle" or "wild." Given the scientific and social importance of the issues we have raised, we would dismiss the first of these labels out of hand, but the second cannot be disposed of so easily. Like the impetuous child, the "wild" speculation responds best to the sobering influence of friendly but firm discipline, in this instance from the hand of the behavioral scientist. As we look ahead to the next twenty-five years of human socialization, let us hope that the "optimal levels" of involvement and discipline can be achieved not only by the parent who is unavoidably engaged in the process, but also by the scientist who attempts to understand its working, and who—also unavoidably—contributes to shaping its course.

REFERENCES:

ACKERMAN, W. I. "Teacher Competence and Pupil Change," *Harvard Educational Review*, 24: 273–89, 1954.

BACH, G. R. "Father-Fantasies and Father-Typing on Father-Separated Children," *Child Development*, 17: 63–79, 1946.

BALDWIN, A. L., J. KALHORN, and F. H. BREESE. "The Appraisal of Parent Behavior," *Psychological Monographs*, 48: 3, 1945.

BALDWIN, A. L. "Socialization and the Parent-Child Relationship," *Child Development*, 19: 127–36, 1948.

BRONFENBRENNER, U. "Socialization and Social Class Through Time and Space," in E. Maccoby, T. M. Newcomb, and E. L. Hartley (Eds.), *Readings in Social Psychology* (New York: Holt, Rinehart and Winston, 1958), pp. 400–425.

BRONFENBRENNER, U. "Some Familial Antecedents of Responsibility and Leadership in Adolescents," in L. Petrullo and B. M. Bass (Eds.), *Leadership and Interpersonal Behavior* (New York: Holt, Rinehart and Winston, 1961), pp. 239–71.

BRONSON, W. C., E. S. KATTEN, and N. LIUSON. "Patterns of Authority and Affection in Two Generations," *Journal of Abnormal and Social Psychology*, 58: 143–152, 1959.

GOLD, M., and C. SLATER. "Office, Factory, Store, and Family: A Study of Integration Setting," *American Sociological Review*, 23: 64–74, 1948.

HAGGARD, E. A. "Socialization, Personality, and Academic Achievement in Gifted Children," *School Review*, 65: 388–414.

KOHN, M. L. and J. A. CLAUSEN. "Parental Authority, Behavior and Schizophrenia," *American Journal of Orthopsychiatry*, 26: 299–313, 1956.

KOHN, M. L. "Social Class and Parental Values," *American Journal of Sociology*, 44: 337–351, 1959.

LYNN, D. B., and W. L. SAWREY. "The Effects of Father-Absence on Norwegian Boys and Girls," *Journal of Abnormal and Social Psychology*, 59: 258–262, 1959.

MILLER, D. R., and G. E. SWANSON. *The Changing American Parent* (New York: John Wiley and Sons, 1958).

MILLER, D. R., and G. E. SWANSON. *Inner Conflict and Defense* (New York: Holt, Rinehart and Winston, 1960).

PAPANEK, M. *Authority and Interpersonal Relations in the Family.* Unpublished doctorial dissertation, Radcliffe College.

ROSEN, B. L., *and* R. D'ANDRADE. "The Psychosocial Origins of Achievement Motivation," *Sociometry*, 22: 185–217, 1959.

SCHACHTER, S. *The Psychology of Affiliation* (Stanford: Stanford University Press, 1959).

SEARS, R. R., E. MACCOBY, and M. LEVIN. *Patterns of Child Rearing* (New York: Harper and Row, 1957).

SEARS, R. R., M. H. PINTLER, and P. S. SEARS. "Effects of Father-Separation on Preschool Children's Doll Play Aggression," *Child Development*, 17: 219–43, 1946.

STRODTBECK, F. L. "Family Interaction, Values, and Achievement," in D. G. McClelland, et al. (Eds.), *Talent and Society* (Princeton, N. J.: VanNostrand, 1958), pp. 135–94.

TILLER, P. O. "Father-Absence and Personality of Children of Sailor Families," *Nordisk Psykologis Monograph Series*, 9: 1958.

WINTERBOTTOM, M. R. "The Relation of Need Achievement to Learning Experiences in Independence and Mastery," in J. W. Atkinson (Ed.), *Motives in Fantasy, Action and Society* (Princeton, N.J.: VanNostrand, 1958), pp. 453–94.

FOOTNOTES:

[1] This paper draws heavily on results from a program of research being conducted by the author in collaboration with Edward C. Devereux and George J. Suci. The contribution of these colleagues to facts and ideas presented in this paper is gratefully acknowledged. The research program is supported in part with grants from the National Science Foundation and the National Institutes of Health.

[2] For a summary of findings on social class differences in children's behavior and personality characteristics, see Mussen and Conger (1956).

[3] These shifts in sex difference with a rise in class status are significant at the 5% level of confidence (one-tailed test).

[4] Strikingly similar conclusions were reached . . . in a provocative essay by Green (1946). With little to go on beyond scattered clinical observations and impressions, Green was able to detect many of the same trends which we have begun to discern in more recent systematic empirical data.

[5] Cold democracy under female administration appears to foster the development of achievement not only in the home but in the classroom as well. In a review of research on teaching effectiveness, Ackerman reports that teachers most successful in bringing about gains in achievement score for their pupils were judged "least considerate," while those thought friendly and congenial were least effective. (Ackerman, 1954).

33 Maternal Behavior, Child Behavior, and Their Intercorrelations from Infancy Through Adolescence*

BY EARL S. SCHAEFER AND NANCY BAYLEY

EDITOR'S NOTE: In selection number 32, Dr. Bronfenbrenner argued that mothers are assuming a more dominant role in child-rearing practices. If this is true (and it seems to be), what are some of the relationships between maternal behavior and child behavior? If mothers are playing a more important part in discipline and upbringing of children, how do they affect emotional-social adjustment and academic achievement? Does the impact of a mother's early relationships with her children last through adolescence? Indeed, in what ways has your relationship with your mother influenced your behavior?

INTRODUCTION

The major goal of this research is to achieve further understanding of the relation of maternal behavior to the social and emotional development of the child through utilization of long-term growth records. Mother-child relationships are analyzed from observations of maternal behavior during infancy, interviews with mothers at preadolescence, and ratings of child behavior from infancy through adolescence. Perhaps the major contribu-

* Reprinted from *Monographs of the Society for Research in Child Development*, 1963, Vol. 28, Ser. No. 87, 9–11, 91–96, by permission of the senior author and the Society for Research in Child Development.

tion of the study is an investigation of the predictability of subsequent behavior of the child from early observations of maternal behavior. Many of the results supplement the findings of cross-sectional studies of mother-child interaction while others serve as a check on conclusions derived from retrospective studies.

Extensive analyses of maternal behavior, which provide a basis for our analysis of mother-child relationships, have already been reported in a series of publications. The first of these describes a set of rating scales for maternal behavior, based on concepts derived from both previous research and clinical investigations (11). A conceptual model for maternal behavior was developed from empirical organizations of the intercorrelations of the ratings (8). Additional studies have described the relations of maternal behavior to socioeconomic status (2) and the consistency of maternal behavior from infancy to preadolescence (10). Because of the complexity of the mother-child intercorrelations, a section on maternal behavior which summarizes and also supplements these earlier reports is included here to facilitate cross-references between maternal and child behaviors.

Ratings of the children's behavior from infancy through adolescence are also analyzed to determine their organization and consistency over time. The child behavior ratings are described, reliability estimates are given, and intercorrelations, both within age levels and across age levels, are reported. Variables for each age level are organized within a reference framework provided by a conceptual model for social and emotional behavior. Predictability of later behavior from early behavior is investigated. The behavior ratings are also correlated with socioeconomic variables.

Sample

The subjects of this investigation are the mothers and children included in the Berkeley Growth Study who have been observed at the University of California Institute of Human Development at frequent intervals from the time they were born in 1928 and 1929 (1, 6). The criteria for inclusion in the study were that the infant be full-term and of white, English-speaking parents who were willing and able to cooperate in the planned series of tests and measurements. The babies, who were born in two Berkeley, California, hospitals, were first seen by the pediatrician in the study at about 3 days of age. Within a six-month period 61 babies (31 boys and 30 girls) were registered in the study. A few of these dropped out and a few replacements were made. The data analyzed in this monograph are on 27 boys and 27 girls for whom relatively complete records on maternal behavior and child behavior are available for the first few years of life. The samples are smaller at later ages but never less than 13 subjects of either sex.

Data

The main emphasis of the Berkeley Growth Study was upon mental, motor, and physical development. Data on socioeconomic status had been assumed to be relevant and were collected by a home visitor at the beginning of the study and again when the children were 10 years old. It was also recognized that the emotional environment of the child as revealed by mother-child interactions might be of importance to development. Notes on maternal behavior were recorded by an observer of the test situation during the children's first three years. Further data on maternal behavior were obtained in home interviews between the child's age of 9 to 14 years. During the frequent testing sessions at the institute, ratings were made and notes were written on the social, emotional, and task-oriented behavior of the child. Other data were collected with personality inventories, interest inventories, and projective techniques but these records are not analyzed here.

All of the data on maternal and child behavior that are analyzed in this monograph were derived from observations of overt behavior of the subjects. The observations of the researchers were recorded either in the form of ratings or in the form of extensive notes immediately after the testing sessions. The descriptive notes were subsequently rated by persons who did not know the subjects. None of these data are from self-reports, such as personality inventories or attitude scales, or from indirect inferences or interpretations, as from projective techniques. The data do not include time samples of behavior or codings of discrete behaviors but are based upon molar perceptions of total testing or interview sessions. These analyses of overt behavior in the testing situation do not exclude the possibility of different types of reactions in different settings, with different persons, or at other levels, for example, the fantasy level, of response (7).

Organization of Data. The large amount of material collected over a period of 18 years made it necessary to combine many of the discrete items into a smaller number of molar concepts. Maternal behavior variables are composites of several behavior ratings that are related to the same general concept. Highly correlated child behavior ratings for an age level were combined into a single score. The adolescent behavior variables were derived by combining two to eight interrelated adjective rating scales. These groupings of data give more reliable estimates of the molar concepts and also permit more economical data analysis.

Data for adjacent ages were also combined to increase the stability of scores for an age level. Thus the child behavior ratings between 10 and 36 months are a combination of ratings from three adjacent testing sessions. The child behavior ratings between 27 and 96 months combine data from two testing sessions, and those between 9 and 12 years are summations of data from three testing sessions. The early maternal behavior ratings were made from notes on observations of approximately 20 testing sessions during the first three years of the child's life and the later ratings of maternal behavior were made from notes on from one to three interviews between 9 and 14 years (mostly at 12 and 13 years).

SUMMARY, DISCUSSION, AND INTERPRETATION

The discussion of the major findings given here supplements the summaries of the analyses of maternal behavior, child behavior, and their intercorrelations that have been given in the preceding chapters. The earlier descriptions of the sample, data, and statistical analysis have provided a basis for the critical evaluation of these findings. Such a critical evaluation suggests that many of the findings on the consistency of maternal behavior and child behavior and on mother-child intercorrelations should be regarded as hypotheses for further investigation rather than as definite conclusions. However, the circumplex models for maternal behavior and for child behavior have been replicated by organizations of data reported by other investigators. Since the correlations between the circumplex-ordered sets of data on maternal behavior and child behavior reveal clear patterns, the conclusions are not based upon isolated correlations but upon patterns of high correlations. The patterns of intercorrelation that are revealed by the tables and figures increase the probability that these findings could be replicated in future research.

*Development of Conceptual Models for Maternal Behavior
and for Child Behavior*

A continuous chain of related maternal behaviors was developed by placing variables that had high intercorrelations adjacent to one another. Factor analyses of the correlation matrices for both the observations during infancy and the interviews at preadolescence revealed two rotated factors that were labelled love versus hostility and autonomy versus control. A generalization of these empirical organizations led to a conceptual model for maternal behavior that included many of the molar concepts that have been developed in social psychological studies of parent-child interaction. Organizations of other sets of empirical data on maternal behavior, and equivalent conceptual models independently developed by other researchers, have confirmed the generality of this conceptual model for maternal behavior.

The sequential ordering of the focal but overlapping maternal behavior variables clarified the conceptual structure and facilitated the integration of the findings into meaningful patterns. The data also led to a systematic ordering of maternal behavior variables at three levels of abstraction or generality. Maternal behavior concepts at an intermediate level of abstraction, such as Expression of Affection, were defined by a set of specific behaviors at a lower level of abstraction. The factor analysis and circumplex ordering suggested dimensions of love versus hostility and autonomy versus control at a higher level of abstraction.

The success of this attempt to develop a systematic ordering of concepts at the same level of abstraction and to distinguish levels of abstraction suggests the feasibility of developing a taxonomy of maternal behavior. The conceptual model presented here might be considered an initial approach to such a taxonomy. The model recognizes the equivalence of many existing concepts, provides a sequential ordering of focal but overlapping concepts, and clarifies the relation between concepts at different levels of abstraction. The model might be used as a conceptual framework for the integration of existing research and for planning future research on parent-child relationships.

Circumplex organizations of the data on the social and emotional behavior of the children also reveal sequential orderings within a two-dimensional space. A conceptual model that includes two major dimensions (extraversion versus introversion and love versus hostility) and four combinations of these basic dimensions (friendliness, conformity, withdrawal, and aggressiveness) was used as a reference framework for the organizations. The child behavior ratings at each age level were well ordered within the two-dimensional space of this model.

The clear patterns of neighboring variables of this study support the generality of the conceptual model and suggest that other data on social and emotional behavior could also be organized with this model. The model could also be used as the basis for a taxonomy of social and emotional behavior in the same manner as suggested for the maternal behavior model. If data on maternal behavior and data on social and emotional behavior of children were well ordered with these two models, the models would provide a conceptual structure for the integration of the many existing studies of parent-child interaction. If an ordered set of parent behaviors were systematically related to an ordered set of child behaviors, clear patterns of parent-child relationships would be revealed.

Consistency and Correlates of the Maternal Behavior Dimensions

The observations of maternal behavior during infancy and the maternal interviews at preadolescence permitted a test of the consistency of maternal behavior across this time interval. Relatively high consistency was found for the dimension of love versus hostility and relatively low consistency for the dimension of autonomy versus control. This appears reasonable, since the child's need for a positive relationship remains constant but his need for autonomy varies from birth to maturity. Therefore, more change in maternal behavior might be expected on the autonomy dimension than on the love dimension. However, another explanation should be considered, the mother's greater ability to change in one kind of behavior than in another. Studies in child guidance clinics have shown that mothers who reject their children are resistant to treatment and that significant changes in attitude are rare. Although the consistency of maternal hostility or rejection may be partially determined by the personality structure of the mother, it may also be to some extent independent of her behavior with other persons. The data reported here indicate that accompanying the mother's feeling for the child is related perception of the child. Hostile mothers perceive more faults in the child while loving mothers perceive positive characteristics of the child. Heider's (5) discussion of interpersonal perception indicates that ambiguous behavior will be assimilated and integrated with an observer's prior perceptions of a person. Therefore, the mother's negative feelings and negative perception of the child would tend to maintain themselves through time. For this reason, it would appear that efforts to facilitate the development of positive relationships between mothers and children might be more successful than efforts to change negative relationships.

The data were also analyzed to determine those characteristics of the mother and of her situation that are related to her behavior with her child. For boys, and to some extent for girls, low socioeconomic status, financial stress, and poor physical health of the mother are correlated with maternal hostility. For both sexes, maternal hostility between 9 and 14 years is correlated with low marital happiness. Rejection of the homemaking role, negative emotional states, and mood swings have high positive correlations, and cooperativeness with the examiners and interviewer have high negative correlations with maternal hostility. These data suggest that maternal hostility toward the child is highly related to the woman's emotional maladjustment, to poor relationships both with husband and others, and to environmental stresses and frustration.

Consistency of the Child Behavior Dimensions

A conceptual analysis of the ratings for the four age levels, infancy, early childhood, late childhood and adolescence, suggested that the two major dimensions of extraversion versus introversion and love versus hostility, or positive versus negative social responses, are to some extent sampled at each age level. The data were analyzed to determine the consistency of these dimensions through time. The early infancy ratings of activity and rapidity, which were interpreted as relating to the dimension of extraversion, have the highest correlations with behavior at subsequent age levels. Activity and rapidity are significantly negatively correlated with ratings of positive task-oriented behavior of boys through the age of 12 years. For girls, activity and rapidity during infancy are negatively correlated with task-oriented behaviors throughout childhood and are positively correlated with extraverted aggressive behaviors at adolescence. Although the early ratings of activity and rapidity are positively correlated with maternal hostility for boys, they are relatively independent of maternal behavior for girls. Apparently maternal hostility is not a necessary condition for the development of high activity in infants. These findings suggest that high motility may be an innate rather than an acquired characteristic and that high motility during infancy may be predictive of subsequent behavior. The findings agree with the researches of Fries (4) and Escalona and Heider (3) in suggesting the salience and consistency of activity level in the process of development. More systematic study of activity level from birth onward might be a profitable extension of this research. Further research might reveal antecedents, perhaps genetic, or prenatal, as well as additional behavioral correlates of activity level.

Positive versus negative social adjustment during the first two years of life shows very little correlation with later behavior for either sex. More enduring patterns of adjustment develop at later ages since both social and task-oriented behaviors are relatively consistent for both boys and girls from about 4 to 12 years. However, consistency is lower for girls than for boys during the latter part of this period. Specifically, correlations between ratings at 9 to 10 years and at 10½ to 12 years are extremely high for boys and relatively low for girls. In contrast, high correlations are found for social behaviors between the 9- to 12-year ratings and the adolescent ratings (12–18 years) for girls with lower correlations for boys. These high consistency correlations—despite the interval between ratings, the different rating methods, and the different raters—suggest that behavior of girls in the testing situation is relatively consistent from early adolescence forward. The lower consistency of boys' behavior across the latter time interval indicates that adolescence is a period of change for boys as well as girls, although these changes begin later for boys.

Evidence was found for both consistency and change in overt behavior. Perhaps the most striking finding was the pervasive and relatively high correlations of early activity and rapidity with subsequent behavior, particularly for girls. The evidence does not support a hypothesis that patterns of positive versus negative social behavior are fixed during infancy, but it does support a hypothesis that more enduring behavioral traits are developed during the latency period. Social and emotional development during childhood appears similar to intellectual development in that stability increases with age. Unlike intellectual development, social and emotional behaviors show relatively rapid change at adolescence, with these changes beginning earlier for girls than for boys.

Correlation of Maternal Behavior with Child Behavior

The love-hostility dimension of maternal behavior frequently showed high correlations with child adjustment variables. Maternal love versus hostility during the first three years is significantly correlated with happy, calm, and positive behaviors of both sons and daughters during that period. Similar relations are found with the positive social and positive task-oriented behaviors of daughters through 4 years and with positive task-oriented behaviors of sons through 12 years. Although early maternal love is significantly correlated with sons' early positive social and emotional responses in the test situation, these correlations decrease at later ages, while the correlations with positive task-oriented behaviors remain significant. Perhaps the quality of the early mother-son relationship is more highly correlated with sons' attitude toward achievement or toward intellectual performance than with social behavior at later ages.

An interpretation of these correlations as revealing maternal influence upon the behavior of the child is supported by the high consistency of the love-hostility dimension of maternal behavior as contrasted to the relatively low consistency of child behavior across this time span. A finding that maternal behavior during the first three years has a high correlation with sons' behavior at 6 through 9 years of age than it does with sons' current behavior may reveal the cumulative effect of consistent parent behaviors upon child behavior.

More significant correlations of maternal behavior with sons' behavior than with daughters' behavior have been found in this study. Maternal behavior has shown significant correlations only with current behavior of daughters, but with prior, current, and subsequent behavior of sons. For example, maternal love-hostility during the first three years is significantly correlated with sons' behavior through 12 years but with daughters' behavior only through 4 years. Maternal behavior between 9 and 14 years is significantly correlated with sons' behavior at all of the ages studied but with daughters' behavior only at adolescence. One interpretation of these data is that girls' adjustment reflects more their current interpersonal situation while the adjustments of boys reflect more stable structures which have developed through their entire history of interpersonal relationships.

These findings strongly suggest that the relations of maternal behavior to child behavior vary with sex and age of the child. Since the relations of maternal behavior to child behavior differ for boys and girls, it is recommended that in all future studies the correlations of maternal behavior and paternal behavior with the behavior of boys and of girls be studied separately. Since both parental behavior and child behavior change through time, studies should be done at a number of homogeneous age levels. Systematic increases and decreases of parent-child correlations through time suggest a need for longitudinal studies of the antecedents of the child's social and emotional behavior. Also, paternal behavior as well as maternal behavior should be investigated to obtain information on the interaction of sex of child and sex of parent as they relate to parent-child correlations.

The data reported here, if interpreted from the viewpoint of social psychological theory, support hypotheses about maternal influence upon the development of the child. An analysis of progressive changes in parent-child correlations suggests that the child's social, emotional, and task-oriented behaviors are, to some extent, a reaction to the parental behaviors he has received throughout the period of childhood. Despite this conclusion, the consistency of a dimension of activity-passivity, and its relative independence of parent-child relationships, also supports hypotheses that the human infant is not completely plastic but responds to his environment in accordance with his innate tendencies.

REFERENCES:

1. BAYLEY, N. "Mental Growth During the First Three Years: A Developmental Study of 61 Children by Repeated Tests," *Genet. Psychol. Monogr., 14,* 1933, pp. 1–92.
2. BAYLEY, N., and SCHAEFER, E. S. "Relationships between Socioeconomic Variables and the Behavior of Mothers Toward Young Children," *J. Genet. Psychol., 96,* 1960, pp. 61–77.
3. ESCALONA, S. K., and HEIDER, G. M. *Prediction and Outcome, Basic Books,* 1959.
4. FRIES, M. E., and WOOLF, P. J. "Some Hypotheses on the Role of the Congenital Activity Type in Personality Development," *Psychoanal. Stud. Child., 8,* 1954, pp. 48–62.
5. HEIDER, F. *The Psychology of Interpersonal Relations,* Wiley, 1958.
6. JONES, H. E., and BAYLEY, N. "The Berkeley Growth Study," *Child Develpm., 12,* 1941, pp. 167–173.
7. LEARY, T. F. *Interpersonal Diagnosis of Personality,* Ronald Press, 1957.
8. SCHAEFER, E. S. "A Circumplex Model for Maternal Behavior," *J. Abnorm. Soc. Psychol., 59,* 1959, 226–235.
9. SCHAEFER, E. S., and BAYLEY, N. "Consistency of Maternal Behavior from Infancy to Preadolescence," *J. Abnorm. Soc. Psychol., 61,* 1960, pp. 1–6.
10. SCHAEFER, E. S., BELL, R. Q., and BAYLEY, N. "Development of a Maternal Behavior Research Instrument," *J. Genet. Psychol., 95,* 1959, 83–104.
11. WHITING, J. W. M., and CHILD, I. L. *Child Training and Personality,* Yale University Press, 1953.

34   On Bringing Up Children Who Love Life*

BY ERICH FROMM AS INTERVIEWED
BY RICHARD HEFFNER

EDITOR'S NOTE: Dr. Fromm is a psychoanalyst and social psychologist who has spent his professional life studying human behavior in relation to the social-political-religious-sexual parameters of our culture. Up to this point in Chapter Eight, you have been exposed to three articles which speak directly to the various kinds of child-rearing styles and practices. If you have read those articles, you have some ideas about how to encourage (or discourage) achievement-motivation, personal autonomy, self-esteem, etc. But how do we bring up children who love life, who have a sense of zest, curiosity, and enthusiasm for living? Dr. Fromm ranges over many ideas in this selection, but basically it is a discussion about two kinds of people —those who love life in the sense of loving all that is alive, whether it is a child or a tree or a flower or a thought, and those who love death, who love all that is decaying, dirty, not alive. If we really want children to appreciate the idea of being alive, then there are implications for all of us about how to encourage a "love of life" concept.

Interviewer: Why do you think so many of our young people are cynical today?

Fromm: Because they feel that between 1914 and today there have been many good ideas, many good intentions, yet the world gets worse and

* Reprinted from *McCalls,* October, 1965, 132–133, 213–219, by permission of Dr. Erich Fromm, the interviewer, Mr. Richard D. Heffner, and the publisher. (This article was originally titled, "An Interview With Erich Fromm.")

worse. I'm convinced that good intentions are dangerous, because they often befog the issues and make one feel sufficiently good to go on with bad acts.

Interviewer: In my radio and TV programs, I find almost invariably a tendency on the part of the speaker to be overly optimistic. Is this dangerous?

Fromm: Very dangerous. I usually try to impress on my students, without too much success, I gather, that there is nothing more dangerous to a patient than to be encouraging. If a person wants to change, wants to get well, he needs to mobilize all his vital energies, and he can mobilize them *only* if he sees how serious the situation is. If, on the other hand, I try to be "encouraging" and to make him feel "Well, things aren't so bad, and everything will be all right," and so on, I paralyze him; I take away from him the most important thing he has, and that is the ability to act in an emergency situation. When people see the situation is clearly one of emergency, they have energies they never dreamed they had, because it's finally clear to them what's at stake. But to most people, it's not clear what's at stake in their personal life at any given moment. I'm afraid that holds true for political life, too.

We always say, "Things are not so bad," "Things are all right," "Things can get better," until the moment when we find ourselves, as people say these days, "involved"—as if it had nothing to do with our own decision.

Interviewer: But don't people believe that fear immobilizes?

Fromm: Well, fear as such might immobilize; but if it is not fear that is engendered but a clear recognition—"This is the fork of the road," "These are my two alternatives," "I walk either here or there"—then, indeed, I think it is part of human nature to try to save life, one's own life; to try that which either physically or mentally preserves life. Otherwise, there would be no hope for any kind of therapy or for positive action or for any change. Most people fail in life because they never see where or when they have to make a decision; they *think* only when it's too late.

Interviewer: You say "fail in life." You mean in the larger sense?

Fromm: Yes, indeed. I don't mean in a job. I mean on the *most* important thing or the *only* important thing in which one can fail, and that is in living. I really believe the air of life is freedom. Now, I don't like the word "freedom" any more, because it has been so misused these days. We call "free" any nation that is politically allied with us. That seems to be the only criterion, so I would rather use the word "independence," and would mean by independence, the capacity of a person to owe his existence to himself, to think himself, to feel himself, authentically, genuinely, and not to *think* feelings without *having* feelings—in all fields of life, in love, in art, in everything.

Interviewer: What do you mean, "think feelings"?

Fromm: Well, what I mean is this. You find, let us say, a person who is indoctrinated to believe that modern art or modern music is beautiful. Now, I am not a specialist in these fields, so I'm not saying they aren't— they just don't happen to be for me. But you do find very often people who are brainwashed, indoctrinated, so they see a piece of abstract art and think it is very impressive, or very beautiful, or heaven knows what. While actually if you could find out what they *really* feel—they feel nothing, but they *think* they feel something.

Now, the same thing holds true, let us say, in marriages. People are indoctrinated to think that if two people are married, have children, don't quarrel, the man isn't unfaithful—which these days seems to be a rather rare phenomenon—they love each other, because they have been told that, provided all these things are present, it is love. What you might find in reality is that they feel nothing. They have a kind of friendly feeling you might have toward a stranger. This has been shown in some psychological experiments.

I think it is very important to differentiate between what is an authentic feeling and what is a *thought* about a feeling, and there are an awful lot of people today who think they feel something but don't feel anything.

Interviewer: A couple of times you have said "now" and "today." Do you think we more frequently think feelings today than we did before?

Fromm: Yes, I do. It's hard to prove, of course, and I'm not claiming that this is a new phenomenon; but it is quite clear that today there is more indoctrination culturally, there are more books and more lectures that tell you what you *ought* to feel than in the past, and therefore people know better what they're *supposed* to feel. If you took a still relatively simple peasant community which doesn't have so much access to all our media of communication, you would find that people are less indoctrinated as to what they are supposed to feel, and therefore many of their feelings are more genuine.

Interviewer: But there isn't any way out of this, is there? Isn't this a phenomenon that will just increase in intensity?

Fromm: Well, look, if this increases in intensity, we will end up in a madhouse. We are already at the point where most people don't know what they feel, and that means they don't know who they are.

Interviewer: Do you see any possibility that this trend can be reversed?

Fromm: Yes, I do. I very definitely do, and I have faith in it. People are getting tired of the sense of meaninglessness of life; of the sense that they are little automatons; of the sense that they have really nothing to say about their own lives; of trying to save time and then kill it; of trying to be a success and, when reaching what they want—with the very few exceptions of creative people—of feeling "So what? What has been the meaning?" I should like to quote the Old Testament, which says, "They have lacked in joy in the midst of plenty." And I think that is what could be said about ourselves. I personally believe this is sin.

Now, how can it be reversed? In the first place, people will react to it. The human individual, the human society, reacts to things that are bad. Just as a body, in fact, reacts against poisons or stuff that damages it. Somebody has to be very sick if his body doesn't react any more. Then it's hopeless.

And maybe we are hopeless. But I don't think so, because I see, on the other hand, signs of great vitality in our society, especially in the United States. We see a great deal of spontaneity, of searching, of freedom, of lack of intimidation; we see a young generation searching for things, being anxious to have answers that are not traditional answers.

Interviewer: Obviously, though, the change must take place on the individual level.

Fromm: I think so. The individual must consider living more important than anything else. But most people wouldn't even know what I'm talking about when I talk of living. Of *being*.

Interviewer: They would interpret it in terms of success. In terms of material things.

Fromm: Exactly. It is an interesting thing, you know, that in the use of the verbs "to have" and "to be," people talk in terms of "I have." For instance, people say, "I have insomnia," instead of saying, "I cannot sleep." "I have a problem," instead of saying, "I am unhappy." And they have, of course, a car and children and a house and a psychoanalyst; but everything is expressed in terms of "I have" connected with a noun, and not in terms of "to be" connected with a verb.

You can find a tremendous shift in our language from the emphasis on verbs to the emphasis on nouns in terms of "I have." This is an example of alienation. There is no such thing as a problem or a neurosis or freedom. I suffer, I have difficulties in living—well, you couldn't even say I am free, but I am freeing myself. I am liberating myself, because this is a process. But to talk about nations that *have* freedom, people who *have* freedom is just like talking about people who have cars. "To have" makes sense in terms of things, but it doesn't make sense in terms of people. In terms of people, the question is "to be," and to experience life, there is being. Now, people today don't experience life as *being* but as *having* something, because our whole system is centering around what one can buy and what one has.

Interviewer: How does one help a young person, a child, experience life as "being" rather than "having"?

Fromm: In the first place, of course, by example. Now, what do I mean by example? What can a mother do? Not being phony. Being realistic. Being honest. Not expressing feelings that are not authentic. Not gushing, "Isn't that wonderful?" Not listening to some nonsense or to some triviality and saying, "Isn't that fine?"—which teaches the child, from the very beginning, that really one can or one should indulge in these phony feelings. Being oneself. Not smiling when one doesn't feel like smiling. Not expressing admiration for this, that or the other when one doesn't feel like it.

In fact, I should like to say one thing: Most children are born with faith. The faith that Mother will nurse them when they are thirsty, that Mother will cover them when they are cold, that Mother will comfort them when they have pain. This is the original faith. I am not so convinced of original sin, but I *am* convinced of original *faith,* because otherwise a child could not live. If mothers nursed their children only when they were good, most children would die.

Now comes a peculiar period in the life of a child—and it's not only one event—namely, that which you might call the shattering of faith. The child discovers for the first time that Mother *lies*. Mother lies not only with words but also with her face. The child sees Mother greet Mrs. So-and-So and smile all over and gush all over her, and then Mrs. So-and-So goes, and Mother says something very nasty about her. Now, we adults more or less take lying for granted; but we don't appreciate enough what a shattering experience it is for the child—what a discovery it is for the child—when for the first time he hears people lie.

Then comes the question: How does the child react to this shattering of the original faith? Let us say the positive reaction is if the child than becomes more critical and yet keeps his faith in a critical way. Now, this faith can be expressed in religious terms, in human terms. But some children never recover, because they get one blow after the other. They eventually end in complete hopelessness or in complete cynicism. The hopelessness sometimes is covered up by phony hope, phony optimism. And sometimes it is plain cynicism. That is what we see in many of the young generation, in many of our beatniks, in many of our delinquents. They are frankly cynical.

Now, what a mother can do is to be very aware of this problem—of the original faith of the child—and try to act so as not to create in the child a feeling that nothing can be relied on.

Interviewer: The child is going to meet lies, whether at the breast of the mother or far from it. How does one prepare a child for the rest of the world?

Fromm: Well, that is a crucial question, and it would take probably several volumes to answer it. In the first place, it is a question of how much faith the mother and the father have themselves. Faith, I believe, is a character trait. Let me explain what I mean. I have asked many people, "Do you know any people you would be absolutely sure couldn't do certain things? Let us say, they couldn't harm a person in any serious way for the sake of a material advantage. Do you know anyone you would be absolutely certain wouldn't do that?"

Many people say, "Well, I cannot be *absolutely* certain. Ninety-nine per cent—it's very unlikely, but how can I ever be certain about it?" These are people without faith, because if one really has understood the essence of another person, then there are always some people of whom one could be absolutely certain, as certain as one is of anything that obeys the law of nature.

Now, that I call faith. On what is love based except on faith? How can you love a person unless you are certain this is he or she? How can you love unless you are certain of yourself? There is a very pertinent sentence of Nietzsche's I think touches on this problem. Nietzsche once defined man as the animal who can make promises. What does it mean to make a promise? I am certain of myself. I know that five years from now I shall be the same person I am now. Naturally, we all change and we all develop, and yet there are certain things that remain permanent.

Interviewer: You said that having faith is a matter of character. What gives one person that character? Why does one person have faith and another person not?

Fromm: Well, it may have something to do with constitutional elements, like everything else.

Interviewer: What do you mean by constitutional elements?

Fromm: Constitutional elements are what we call temperaments— habitual moods of a person which are characteristic for him and are constitutionally given, with which he is born.

Interviewer: Have you always felt as firmly as you do now about the constitutional elements?

Fromm: No, I haven't. Actually, I must say about thirty years ago, if I had listened to myself talking now, I would have labeled myself as a real reactionary to put so much attention on constitution, because I would have thought, "Well, that means he doesn't really believe in the possibility of improvement of the human race." But I have changed my view in various aspects.

In my analytical work, I have convinced myself that people are different not only because of their experiences in life or their environment. I believe that environment, especially the experience in the early years, makes a great deal of difference; but, nevertheless, I think it is dishonest if I claim that two people, one of whom is very sick and one of whom is relatively normal, are the way they are because of their environment only.

Interviewer: I wonder, as a father, do I want my sons to be trustful, then be hurt? To create this new person who will, we hope, be more trustful, less cynical, more hopeful, to what extent does a parent prepare a child for what he will find?

Fromm: Well, I would say we are talking here about a basic decision, what one would call a religious decision—namely, the choice between God and Caesar. Now, I don't belong to any religion, and I am a nonbeliever in any theological sense. However, I find myself very often in a profound understanding with liberal Jesuit priests, because we share a common concern that what matters is man's soul and that if he loses his soul, no riches he gains will serve him.

I think modern parents often don't make up their minds, and of course not only modern parents. Parents have failed to all the time. Otherwise, we would live in a different world. The really important thing in life is to sacrifice certain, or to risk certain, worldly goods, to risk certain worldly advantages, in order to be fully alive, to be fully developed. What matters is to *be* much and not to *have* much.

I would like my children, in the first place, to have the deepest insight, the greatest courage, as much love as anyone could have, and to be able to risk that they might, in the worldly sense, not fare so well. I talk often with students, young people, and they say, well, that's all very nice, but if we acted that way, we would starve.

And I usually answer that I think this is a great underestimation of the United States. We may come to that point, which is the point of a dictatorship; but I hope we don't. Somebody could write a very interesting doctoral thesis with the title: "How and to what extent and in what places can honest men succeed in the United States in 1965?" And I am not joking.

Interviewer: Suppose I were writing my doctoral dissertation on the subject you suggest. In what areas do you think one would find the greatest capacity for an honest man to be happy?

Fromm: Well, I could say in what areas one wouldn't, and there I would talk about some very sensitive points. As, for instance, the areas of the communications industry, of the entertainment industry, which showed themselves to be very easily frightened in the McCarthy times. I would say, on the other hand, the skilled worker, the good professional—whether he is a surgeon or any other professional—anyone who offers services that are useful and necessary has an opportunity to be honest and happy. In services that are easily expendable and are controlled by people who are interested only in their profit the opportunity is less, naturally.

The tendency toward development of big corporations makes my positive view a little less promising. Last year, I gave a seminar for middle executives of some big corporations, and I asked them, "How much freedom do you really have?" And most of them said, "Oh, all the freedom. Of course, we wouldn't say things that are unpleasant, or this, that, or the other, but we have all the freedom." After the seminar—it was before the election—one of the executives came to me and opened his coat and showed me inside his coat a Johnson button.

Interviewer: Inside his coat.

Fromm: Yes, inside his coat. He said, "Well, I just wanted to show you what degree of freedom I have in my corporation." Now, these people are not aware that they don't have enough, that they don't have much freedom, and I don't know, frankly, whether there is a terrific amount of difference between being an engineer in a Russian state-owned factory or in one of our big corporations, with regard to how much they permit themselves to think and feel things they're not supposed to.

Some people, for instance, if they are serious about their independence, and at the same time not wanting to starve, may think of becoming artisans, of doing any number of things in which they are not controlled by an opinion climate that tells them what to say, what not to say. It's true that the areas in which people can express their individuality and can be nonconformist and yet not suffer are narrowing down. Now, here I come to a point that refers to a question you asked before—what can we do?

I think we can try to create sufficient public opinion against the idea that people have to conform in their dress and and their hats and their opinions in order to make a good car or a good computer. This is simply not so. We should wake up to the fact that one can produce very successfully even if people don't conform. But all this depends on one thing, whether we really mean what we talk about all the time. We talk about freedom. We talk about individualism. We talk about the values of the Western tradition. Now we must challenge ourselves and ask: Is all this really important to us? If so, then let's do something about it, and if it's not, let's stop talking about it.

Interviewer: This, I would presume, is what the parent can do with the child—to give an example of self-examination, to ask himself, at least within the bosom of his family, if he really means what he says.

Fromm: Exactly. For instance, one of the most important things is whether the child believes the parent means what he says. There are some parents who carry inner authority. You immediately notice or sense that they mean what they say. What they say comes from within. Then you have other people who talk from the head. They talk *words*.

Now, children have a much more acute feeling for that than adults have, and I have seen parents, with inner authority, whose children are well-disciplined and well-behaved without their ever raising their voices or any spanking or any punishment, because their children know what they want and that they mean what they say.

I am afraid most parents don't know what they want and don't mean what they say, because they have no convictions. In fact, many parents in America today try to learn from their children what's right and wrong because it's the latest. Now, I think here begins a very important thing. What authenticity, what genuineness does a child experience in his environment?

Let me mention a study that has been made in which parents and their schizophrenic children were assembled. The parents were asked to do nothing but talk. Well, these parents talked, and what became apparent was the mood of complete emptiness. I don't mean small talk, which is, you might say, a matter of civilized life, of having some human contact that is not heavily weighted.

But what you find is that many people—well, I have seen many couples who have talked, who have really talked to each other for the first time *only* when they talk divorce. Then they were, for the first time, real—while until then, for twenty years, let us say, they avoided intimacy. People *think* they want intimacy; but actually they avoid it all the time, because in order to confront another person with intimacy, you have to be willing to show *yourself* and to be yourself, to shed that image you like to protect.

It requires a certain readiness to see oneself as one is and to see another person. It requires even a certain sense, I would say, of humanity, to let a person be and to let oneself be, without being indignant or overtolerant.

Interviewer: Do you think our inability to say, "This is me and this is you" is partially the reason for the high divorce rate in the United States?

Fromm: I think it is. I think people avoid each other in the first place.

Interviewer: Avoid?

Fromm: Avoid each other. Look. What happens is, I think, if two people fall in love, that's a wonderful, very exhilarating experience, because two strangers suddenly become intimate. But they become intimate only from being strangers to *not* being strangers. Once they have ceased to be strangers, they are strangers again.

At first, it's physical intimacy, which is very exhilarating, but has its limits as something that makes people intimate. There is nothing more deceptive than physical, sexual intimacy. It's notorious that many people, men and women, can have sex relationships with many other people and never be intimate with anyone. It's a momentary breaking down of barriers, but not necessarily depth of contact. I think that leads to many divorces, because people believe they haven't found the right person, rather than seeing it is a failure in their *way* of communicating with the person. They will *never* find the right person.

I think it has also to do, actually, with our consumption society. You buy a new car every second year, and you get yourself a new wife or husband every fifth year, always thinking the new model is better. Well, that is the logic of a consumer industry, in which you want to have something new because you are not really related to anything or anybody.

Interviewer: You started by talking about falling in love. Does this phrase have any meaning?

Fromm: Well, it's an unfortunate phrase, in a way, because even falling in love is characteristic for this whole mood. Falling is not standing, and if you take our American phrase "he falls" or "she falls" for someone, what a fantastic phrase this is, to fall for someone. It is the abandonment of judgment, of realism, for an illusion. It's a particular kind of idolatry, where you suddenly build a picture of something wonderful. Only when you come to your senses, you see this was all not so. Then you start talking to the lawyers. But it may take some time—one year, two years, three years, five years.

Now, I am not talking against divorce. I think if two people cannot live happily together, they'd better separate, and especially it's better for the children. I have seen many people who have the idea they cannot separate because of the children. Now, that is usually an excuse for reasons of their own why they can't separate. I remember one man who said he just couldn't destroy his ten-year-old boy's belief in his happy marriage, and that's why he couldn't divorce, although he and his wife were fighting every day, wildly. Finally, the boy said to him, "You know, Dad, I don't know how you can stand to live with that woman. I would have left her long ago." Well, that shattered *that* reason for not getting a divorce. Divorce is very often as much of an illusion as marriage is—namely, it's the illusion that it is the wrong partner, when actually it's the wrong attitude of both people, who avoid intimacy, who cannot experience intimacy, and who then think another object will do.

Interviewer: Do you think it is possible to love someone without having spent considerable time, perhaps even years, with that person?

Fromm: It depends on the depth with which one person experiences another person. This is in itself a very interesting psychological phenomenon—what one person experiences of another person. Let us take one extreme. A man looks at a girl who looks like the latest Hollywood model, and he is mostly impressed by her legs or something else or by her figure. This is the girl every man would like to have, and so he feels very attracted. She may be dumb, she may be vicious, she may be anything, or she may be very nice; but he is not interested in all that, because his attention is drawn to only one sector, if I may say so, of—

Interviewer: The public sector.

Fromm: Of this girl. That is an extreme case. Let us say he could see the same girl, and while she has all these qualities, he could see she is really a terribly boring girl, and after six months, he cannot stand her; or he could see she's a very sad girl. This is only one example of what I mean. If we really ask how do we experience each other, then we have thousands of layers of depth of experience.

Interviewer: To get back to this question of loving is related to marriage. I have felt so often that in your books you seem to be saying that loving is not related to marriage; it is something else. And I wonder whether it even makes very much sense, in your thinking, to talk about love and marriage in the same breath.

Fromm: Well, there is certainly a fact that many marriages are not based on love.

Interviewer: You say many. Do you mean most or a few or—

Fromm: Well, I'm afraid I would have to say *most*. There are no statistics, but I think most so-called good marriages, those that avoid the divorce courts, are marriages in which two people have found a common interest, don't dislike each other, are decent to each other, and have a common interest in their children, but no very intense or deep feeling. The question here really is how deeply and intensely a person feels things that have nothing to do with business.

That leads me back to what I was talking about: how one experiences other people. Does one see only the first layer, the most superficial layer? Does one see another layer—a little deeper? How far does one go? What does one see? Or does one see the person essentially as being nice because he doesn't dislike me? Or as being nice because he is successful? Or as being wonderful if he's very successful? What of the other human being do we really perceive and what of ourselves do we really perceive? There are many degrees to which we become aware of what is real in ourselves.

Perhaps I should say a word about the whole concept of what is psychoanalysis. There is no such thing as the unconscious. That's a sheer abstraction. I may have a cellar in my house, but I don't have an unconscious. What it really means to be aware of the unconscious is to see the full reality of another person and of myself. That is to say, *to see that which is hidden.* Knowledge is nothing but seeing. Most people have an idea that knowledge is information. If I go to the university, if I go to lectures, if I read things, then I have knowledge. That's not knowledge. Knowledge is what I acquire by penetrating actively through a surface and seeing something to which I was blind before, which I didn't see before.

That's why the artist has such an important function in human society. He helps us see a reality, a deep reality within a person, which, with the superficial eye of common sense, we wouldn't otherwise see.

Interviewer: Doctor Fromm, from time to time you have made what might be interpreted as hostile, unfriendly, cutting remarks about psychoanalysis. I'm a little bit surprised. I wonder if you would elaborate.

Fromm: Well, yes. I'm a little embarrassed, really, because it sounds rather nasty, being a psychoanalyst, making these cutting remarks about psychoanalysis. Analysis is one of the greatest discoveries for the understanding of man. However, under the impact of its success—namely, of being a new, you might say, substitute for religion—it's becoming a fashion.

I'm afraid many psychoanalysts have failed to live up to the seriousness and to the challenge of their task, and I speak sometimes cuttingly of psychoanalysis, as one might speak cuttingly of that which one loves very much, because I am sensitive to the misuses of analysis.

Interviewer: What kind of misuses?

Fromm: Well, people who think that if they talk long enough they will be happy, that one can get happy by talking for five years. Nobody gets happy by talking. One gets happy only—if one gets happy at all, and that's difficult enough—by making a tremendous effort. Analysis has very often, in the urban population, become a substitute for religious interest, philosophical interest, political interest. The analyst replaces the priest. Here you have a man who listens if you pay him for it. One feels less lonely.

But there is a legitimate analysis, which helps one find who one is; discover what is real in oneself and in others; see where one has been blind; enlarge one's sensitivity; relieve a wrong sense of guilt, which is often nothing but fear; and maybe evoke a greater sense of one's responsibility.

Interviewer: Could you define your idea of a "responsible" person?

Fromm: A responsible person is a person who *responds,* who responds as a human being, as a full-fledged human being, to what he is confronted with. Let us say a mother responds to the needs of her child. That's not difficult, because it is partly in the nature of the mother. Most mothers are responsible mothers, because they respond. With a teacher, it's more difficult, because very often he does not respond to the needs of his students, because he only does his duty, and that is to teach them certain things the administrators said he should teach them.

As citizens, we should respond to the political situation or the social situation. I often think in terms of sentences you find in the Prophets: "The lion hath roared, who will not fear? The Lord God hath spoken, who can but prophesy?" This is response. Fear is a response to danger. Responsibility is not to force a person. Responsibility is not false encouragement. Responsibility is to respond spontaneously to the situation, truthfully, realistically, to say what one thinks, what one feels, and then to leave the other person free, free even to do what's bad for him.

Interviewer: How do you teach your students the ability, shall we say, to respond?

Fromm: I usually say to my students, "If you really learn to concentrate on what the patient says and learn to respond, this is one of the most exciting professions one can have. But if you don't learn that, you will be so bored to death that you will regret for the rest of your lives that you have ever taken this profession."

Interviewer: By responding, do you mean by being directional?

Fromm: No, no, no, not at all. I mean getting wet by what the patient says, by understanding it fully, by listening with such concentration that you don't just think, you feel in yourself, you experience in yourself, every situation the patient describes, and then you respond with your skill. By responding, I don't mean you tell him what to do. You tell him what you hear. You tell him, "So this is you."

Interviewer: How much have you changed your mind about Freud's theories?

Fromm: Early in my practice, I found that certain things in Freudian theory—especially the libido theory—really were not right. But there is only one thing about which I believe Freud was completely wrong, and that is the psychology of women.

Interviewer: How was he wrong?

Fromm: Well, because he had the fantastic idea that libido was masculine, that women were castrated men.

He had no concept of the polarity between male and female, because he was such a convinced patriarchal man that he couldn't imagine the equality between male and female, and really his whole theory about women—that all they want is to be men, and that they are afraid of castration, and all that—is just an example of what I would call the war propaganda of the ruling masculine sex.

The war between the sexes has been going on for several thousand years, and men's propaganda about it is just as silly as war propaganda. Men say women are less courageous; it's notorious that they are *more* courageous. That they are less realistic; it's notorious that they are *more* realistic. Women are more concerned with the question of war and peace than men are.

Interviewer: Apparently you believe there are very basic differences between men and women besides the obvious physical ones.

Fromm: Well, I think there are characterological differences, thank God, and personality differences between men and women, because if they were not there, where would Eros be? Then the difference would amount only to an anatomical and physiological difference, which I guess is, to a large extent, all the difference we find today in the United States. Not only in the United States. In modern industrial society, there is a tremendous neutralization of Eros—that is to say, of the passion to unite the two poles—and what we find instead is the substitution of sheer sexuality for Eros.

Interviewer: Will you elaborate on that?

Fromm: Well, what I mean is that the basic polarity, the most fundamental polarity, in life is the polarity between male and female, whether in flowers or in animals or in man. That's just how nature is.

Now, there is always the problem of how polarity is met, and I think there are only three possibilities. First, the two poles unite, and in this union they become one, at least for the moment. They resolve their polarity in the act of union—that's what I call Eros. Or, second, the two poles cannot unite. They still want each other, but they are too afraid or too hostile to unite, and then you have all the many forms of hate and fear that exist between the two sexes.

What we find in modern industrial culture is the third possibility— the two poles tend to neutralize each other. The characterological differ- ence between the male and female personalities is reduced as much as possible, so that the only difference is the obvious physiological, anatomical difference. Thus men and women relate to each other only sexually, and I think this is one reason sex has become so central.

Interviewer: You mean because it's the only level on which we can relate?

Fromm: Yes, and also by which the male-female differences can be expressed.

Interviewer: When you speak of the characterological difference, what do you mean?

Fromm: Obviously, we all feel that there is a difference. We could say the woman normally has a receiving quality, a mother quality, a quality of being, let us say, more natural, and the man has more of a penetrating, aggressive quality.

I have written an article that deals with some of the characterological differences between men and women, based on their anatomical and physiological differences—for instance, the physiological difference of the sexual act. The man has to "perform," and the woman doesn't—this can create in the man a greater insecurity, a vague fear of failure, and a greater sensitivity to ridicule.

The woman never has to prove anything, except in very primitive countries, where she has to prove something by having children. So in a more primitive country, a childless woman is like an impotent man in our society. But sexually the woman doesn't have to prove anything. The man has to. It's a clear-cut question—it's what the Spaniards call the moment of truth—whether he is or isn't potent.

With a woman, there is no such clear-cut truth. I think that makes a great deal of difference for the constant self-concern of the man—the need to prove himself. Women are by nature much less vain than men are. Women have to be concerned with presenting themselves well, because they are still the defeated sex, and therefore they have to win the men. But actually, from what I have seen, men are more vain, because men basically want to prove something all the time. Now, whether that is so or not is a matter of research, which hasn't been done. But from what I have seen, men are basically more vain or more narcissistic. Freud's notion that women are more narcissistic is deceptive.

Interviewer: Is this the area in which you think Freud was most mistaken?

Fromm: Yes.

Interviewer: What do you see happening in the relationships of the sexes, in terms of what you were saying before? You say a leveling off—

Fromm: I think a leveling off. It has to do with the basic experience that is happening to people—an increasing strangeness, alienation, lack of intimacy, fear of intimacy. Feelings are suspect, strong feelings are suspect of being sentimental, old-fashioned.

Actually, we live in a schizoid culture, in which the style and the feeling are very matter-of-fact, very detached, in which you find what is characteristic of real schizophrenia—namely, a good deal of separation between affect and thought.

I should like to give an example. Take a book like Herman Kahn's on atomic war, and other fairly common statements made in discussions about war. They say, "Well, sixty million dead in the first day of nuclear war is acceptable; a hundred million dead would not be acceptable." Now, a man can make such a statement only if the thought is separated from the affect, because the thought itself is so horrible one could not talk so—I won't say glibly, but so quietly about it if one really *felt* what this means. That's what I call schizoid.

We are all matter-of-fact. We think we are terribly intelligent; we observe, but we don't feel much, and I think that's the style of our culture. It's dangerous.

Interviewer: Could we turn for a moment to what you think is valid in Freud?

Fromm: I think that all great discoveries of Freud are valid, only they are somewhat too narrow. They need to be freed from the narrow mechanistic, materialistic concept of the libido theory and be translated into a view that takes in account the whole existence of man.

Freud has seen one of the most important phenomena of life in general and in neurosis specifically—the tremendous importance of the tie to the mother. But I think this tie is *not* primarily a sexual tie. Instead, I see it as a pregenital tie. That is to say, it is a purely affective, emotional tie. Mother represents for the little child security, certainty, help, admiration. She is all-enveloping, which makes a little child feel "I am here, I am loved, I am protected, I am admired, life has no problems." Life has indeed no problems for the little boy who is loved by his mother.

Now, Freud assumes that this is essentially a sexual tie and that it is particularly strong in the life of the little boy, let us say, at the age of five or six. In the first place, I don't believe it's a sexual tie, for one reason: There is nothing more fickle than sexual attachment. But *emotional* ties are more difficult to dissolve. Sometimes you find conflict between the fickleness of sexual attraction and the firmness of emotional and human attraction. Besides that, there is another element. Freud and Freudians often think that the later life is only a repetition of childhood, and they forget that in many respects the adult needs Mother just as much as a little child does.

The life of the adult is more insecure, because he is more aware of it. He has to make decisions; he is more uncertain; he is more helpless. In many ways, he is a child; in some ways, he isn't. In other words, the adult, *too*, is afraid of freedom; the adult, too, wants certainty; the adult, too, wants somebody who loves him unconditionally; the adult, too, really wants to get away from the risks of freedom, from the risks of life, and therefore he very easily retains a deep longing for somebody who promises certainty, love, admiration, who doesn't make conditions.

Now, that can be a woman, that can be the church, that can be the state, that can be anything, an idea. All I'm saying is that this intense attachment to Mother which Freud discovered is not primarily a sexual attachment, but follows from the conditions of human existence—that is, from the deep longing for a source of certainty and protection and admiration, which solves the basic human problem, the problem of uncertainty, the fear of freedom, the fear of independence, the fear of being left alone.

Man is the only case in nature where life becomes aware of itself. He must make choices, make decisions, risk failure. He is aware of all that threatens him and eventually of the ultimate reality and certainty that is death.

What can man do to give an answer to this situation? There are only a certain number of ascertainable ways in which man can solve the problem of existence. As an animal, man wants to live; but as a human, he wants to find unity. He wants to overcome a sense of complete separation. He wants to be one with something.

He can do that in two ways—the regressive way or the progressive way. What I call the regressive way is to try to obliterate that which is specifically human, and that is awareness. Mankind has tried that for many hundreds of thousands of years by the obliteration of reason with drugs, alcohol, sexual orgies, and—

Interviewer: The church?

Fromm: No, I don't mean through the church. I think the church has sometimes turned into a new form of idolatry. All religions have. But basically if you take all primitive religions, you find an attempt to solve the problem of human existence by getting rid of that uniquely specific human quality—awareness—and therefore being rid of the conflict that one is *in* nature and yet *outside* nature.

Interviewer: This is the regressive way.

Fromm: Yes. The progressive way appeared in the history of mankind at a peculiar point all over the world, between 1500 B.C. and 500 B.C., where you find in China, in India, in Egypt, in Palestine and in Greece a new concept, that man could find full unity with the world not by reducing awareness, but by developing his reason and his love to such a point that he could attain a sense of solidarity, of oneness, of harmony with the world.

This aim—to find unity, to overcome separateness by full development of all the human qualities—has been given different names. In China, it has been called Tao. In India, it has been called Nirvana, or enlightenment. The Hebrews called it God; the Greeks have given it a different name, the "unmoved mover." Actually, these are different conceptualizations of the same basic aim—a new harmony.

Interviewer: How optimistic are you about the ability of the human race to survive in the nuclear age?

Fromm: I am very cheered up by the active interest of many students and many people in foreign policy. But I am not optimistic. But look here. I don't think it is a question of optimism or pessimism.

If one is very sick and the doctor says there's only a five-per-cent chance to live, one does everything under the sun to make use of this five-per-cent chance. And that is my feeling. I am not optimistic at all; but I am alive, and as long as I am alive and I see life around me, I shall not lose my faith that life will prevail and that man can prevail. That doesn't mean I am optimistic. Statistically speaking, I am pessimistic; but I don't think one can approach human affairs with statistical concepts.

Interviewer: Our children today are surrounded by violence on every side. Do you feel that violence is a larger ingredient in our lives now than it was half a century ago, a century ago?

Fromm: Well, it's awfully hard to say. We bring up our children under a lot of violence. I find the violence we see in the movies or on television just disgusting. No pornographic film could possibly be as harmful as the films that portray violence and sadism and that our children look at five, or six hours a day. But it all depends on the social class. In many ways, life has become for some people more comfortable today and less violent.

Interviewer: Less brutal.

Fromm: Less brutal. It's hard to compare without really studying this very carefully. But take television. Now, if I had children, I would not permit them to look at most of what television offers. I might not even have a television set. I would consider it like a vice, like eating pounds of candy, which I wouldn't permit, either. I would, however, try to give the children enough stimulation so they wouldn't have any urge to look at that fool thing.

Interviewer: You talked of the fickleness of sexual ties. What implication does that have for the potential of maintaining the traditional marriage relationship? Does this mean that infidelity, which seems to be an increasingly dominant factor in American life, will increase, and perhaps should increase, in recognition of what you consider to be the basic biological fickleness of sexual ties? Are we, in recognition of this basic fickleness, hypocritical? You were talking about the damage done to the child by the parents' hypocrisy. Isn't the element of the marriage relationship that insists on fidelity—isn't that an example of hypocrisy?

Fromm: Well, it could be. It all depends on how serious, how close, how strong the real emotional, affective tie is between the two people.

Interviewer: But you distinguished between those ties, those emotional ties, those ties of genuine feeling, and the sexual ties. Now we have traditionally, moralistically attempted to join these, not with the result that our marriages have maintained themselves or that our wives and our husbands have been faithful, but possibly with just the opposite result. So the question I ask you is whether a parent who is trying *not* to present himself or herself as hypocritical should perhaps inform a child or stress that physical ties, contrary to our traditional moral precepts, are not bound by the same rules that emotional ties—

Fromm: Well, there are several problems. In the first place, I think— and I implied that before—sexuality as such is not a harmful thing. It's an expression of life. So we should not teach our children to be afraid of original sin and especially of sexual expressions, as if they were a sin. Sexual expressions usually—unless they are very perverted in a sadistic way, or so on—express life, and I would say that all that expresses life is of primary value. I could not look from a Victorian, moralistic standpoint at sex as being something sinful or bad.

However, I have my doubts, grave doubts, whether it is a particularly good situation when married people change their sexual partners, for the simple reason that I think this is possible only at the expense of sacrificing a great deal of intimacy. People are not that secure; people are in need of believing in the real interest and love of another person, and I think—I may be old-fashioned—that all the various, all the sexual changes of partner actually prevent depth of feeling and confidence between people.

Few men are really untouched by the fact that their wives sleep with someone else, and few women are untouched by it—there is, in many cases, a lack of sincerity. In many cases, the whole relationship becomes that of a nice friendship, in which also sex loses its intensity, because, all right, so there is a certain amount of sexual pleasure people find with somebody else; but neither is this relationship particularly deep, nor is the relationship with their wives or husbands particularly deep.

Now, in the upbringing of children, I would certainly not be in favor of telling children that sex is bad and sinful; but I would try to teach them that they might experience something of the depth and intensity of a human relation, of a relationship to one other person, without illusions. But I do believe that from a certain age on, when people are married, the enjoyment of the sexual relationship with other people stands in the way of the full development of intimacy between the two people who are married. Now, you see, one might say there isn't too much emotional intimacy in the first place, and there should be no objection to their having sexual affairs. I don't think there *is* an objection. I do think, however, that it replaces quality by quantity. That is to say, instead of trying to work out a human relationship, with all its complications and all its depth, and to arrive at a solution, which is a terribly difficult thing, as we all know, one avoids that task by having many pleasant relationships, sexual relationships, and thereby being freed from the task of really solving the very difficult problem of two human beings.

Interviewer: Now let's go back again to the youngsters.

Fromm: Well, with the youngsters—the youngsters should learn very well what is a deep, intense relationship between a man and a woman and what is a superficial relationship. I could imagine a girl who wants to have several sexual affairs without being deeply involved in them, because she wants to know something about this aspect of life and wants to know men. Yet she should know that this is different from what could happen between a man and a woman if they try to develop a very deep, intimate, lasting relationship. Now, you might say theoretically, yes, we could develop that, and still one sleeps with one and one sleeps with the other. But I'm afraid this is very rare in practice.

Interviewer: Would you urge youngsters to have sexual activities before marriage?

Fromm: I would not urge them, because I think that's kind of funny, to urge them. Nature urges them enough. You see, this all is connected with a basic question—the love of life and the love of death. My own definition of good and evil would be: Good is all that serves life and enhances life, and evil is all that strangles life and tries to corrupt it or to kill it. The average person loves life to a certain extent—at least, he loves to be alive, and to some extent he loves life. But some people love life more than others, and I don't mean loving life in the sense of not wanting to die, but loving life in the sense of loving all that is alive, whether it is a child or a tree or a flower or a thought.

In contrast to that, there are the people who are fascinated by death, by all that is *not* alive, by all that is decaying, all that is dead, all that is dirty, all that is unalive—and, I would add, all that is only mechanical. You find people who come to life only when they talk about death and illness.

You find mothers who are interested in their children only when the children are sick. You find people who are most interested in burials or most interested, when they read the newspaper, in reading the death notices. You find that in dreams, their dreams of feces, of destruction, of blood, of dismembered bodies, and, in fact, people in whom that is very marked are severely sick people.

I believe that the normal instinct is the attraction toward life and to life. But many people—I don't know how many; my private guess is about twenty per cent—are attracted by all that is decayed, by all that is illness, by all that is not alive, by all that is purely mechanical. There was a cartoon in the *New Yorker* some years ago in which a girl asks for a perfume and the salesgirl tells her, "This is very attractive. It smells like a new sports car," the point being that today many men are more interested in sports cars than they are in women. Now, I believe that's profoundly immoral.

Interviewer: Is there some way in which one can foster and encourage the love of life?

Fromm: Yes, by one's own love of life. If a child lives in a family where people really love life, where there is interest in life and not interest in death and decay and in the mechanical, where one can get excited about something that is alive, this will foster the constitutional ability of that child to love life, and I think the ability is there in most children.

35   Walden Two*

BY B. F. SKINNER

EDITOR'S NOTE: The subject of control and freedom has come up repeatedly in the articles in this chapter. This selection and the one immediately following by A. S. Neill will place in sharp contrast the larger implications and overtones of those two concepts. Walden Two is a utopia. It is a fictional novel of a society deliberately planned to achieve certain ends. Children are not left to "grow according to nature," but, rather, their entire growth is carefully regulated according to basic principles of "human engineering." The basic notion is that a good man does not just happen. He is produced by certain conditions, and these conditions must be specified and controlled precisely. Consider the arguments carefully and then read selection number 36 for the other point of view.

The quarters for children from one to three consisted of several small playrooms with Lilliputian furniture, a child's lavatory, and a dressing and locker room. Several small sleeping rooms were operated on the same principle as the baby-cubicles. The temperature and the humidity were controlled so that clothes or bedclothing were not needed. The cots were double-decker arrangements of the plastic mattresses we have seen in the cubicles. The children slept unclothed, except for diapers. There were more beds than necessary, so that the children could be grouped according to developmental age or exposure to contagious diseases or need for supervision, or for educational purposes.

We followed Mrs. Nash to a large screened porch on the south side of the building, where several children were playing in sandboxes and on swings and climbing apparatuses. A few wore "training pants"; the rest were naked. Beyond the porch was a grassy play yard enclosed by closely trimmed hedges, where other children, similarly undressed, were at play. Some kind of marching game was in progress.

As we returned, we met two women carrying food hampers. They spoke to Mrs. Nash and followed her to the porch. In a moment five or six children came running into the playrooms and were soon using the lavatory and dressing themselves. Mrs. Nash explained that they were being taken on a picnic.

"What about the children who don't go?" said Castle. "What do you do about the green-eyed monster?"

Mrs. Nash was puzzled.

"Jealousy. Envy," Castle elaborated. "Don't the children who stay home ever feel unhappy about it?"

"I don't understand," said Mrs. Nash.

"And I hope you won't try," said Frazier, with a smile. "I'm afraid we must be moving along."

We said good-bye, and I made an effort to thank Mrs. Nash, but she seemed to be puzzled by that too, and Frazier frowned as if I had committed some breach of good taste.

"I think Mrs. Nash's puzzlement," said Frazier, as we left the building, "is proof enough that our children are seldom envious or jealous. Mrs. Nash was twelve years old when Walden Two was founded. It was a little late to undo her early training, but I think we were successful. She's a good example of the Walden Two product. She could probably recall the experience of jealousy, but it's not part of her present life."

"Surely that's going too far!" said Castle. "You can't be so godlike as all that! You must be assailed by emotions just as much as the rest of us!"

"We can discuss the question of godlikeness later, if you wish," replied Frazier. "As to emotions—we aren't free of them all, nor should we like to be. But the meaner and more annoying—the emotions which breed unhappiness—are almost unknown here, like unhappiness itself. We don't need them any longer in our struggle for existence, and it's easier on our circulatory system, and certainly pleasanter, to dispense with them."

"If you've discovered how to do that, you are indeed a genius," said Castle. He seemed almost stunned as Frazier nodded assent. "We all know that emotions are useless and bad for our peace of mind and our blood pressure," he went on. "But how arrange things otherwise?"

"We arrange them otherwise here," said Frazier. He was showing a mildness of manner which I was coming to recognize as a sign of confidence.

"But emotions are—fun!" said Barbara. "Life wouldn't be worth living without them."

"Some of them, yes," said Frazier. "The productive and strengthening emotions—joy and love. But sorrow and hate—and the high-voltage excitements of anger, fear, and rage—are out of proportion with the needs of modern life, and they're wasteful and dangerous. Mr. Castle has mentioned jealousy—a minor form of anger, I think we may call it. Naturally we avoid it. It has served its purpose in the evolution of man; we've no further use for it. If we allowed it to persist, it would only sap the life out of us. In a cooperative society there's no jealousy because there's no need for jealousy."

"That implies that you all get everything you want," said Castle. "But what about social possessions? Last night you mentioned the young man who chose a particular girl or profession. There's still a chance for jealousy there, isn't there?"

"It doesn't imply that we get everything we want," said Frazier. "Of course we don't. But jealousy wouldn't help. In a competitive world there's some point to it. It energizes one to attack a frustrating condition. The impulse and the added energy are an advantage. Indeed, in a competitive world emotions work all too well. Look at the singular lack of success of the complacent man. He enjoys a more serene life, but it's less likely to be a fruitful one. The world isn't ready for simple pacifism or Christian humility, to cite two cases in point. Before you can safely train out the destructive and wasteful emotions, you must make sure they're no longer needed."

"How do you make sure that jealousy isn't needed in Walden Two?" I said.

"In Walden Two problems can't be solved by attacking others," said Frazier. . . .

"That's not the same as eliminating jealousy, though," I said.

"Of course it's not. But when a particular emotion is no longer a useful part of a behavioral repertoire, we proceed to eliminate it."

"Yes, but how?"

"It's simply a matter of behavioral engineering," said Frazier.

"Behavioral engineering?"

"You're baiting me, Burris. You know perfectly well what I mean. The techniques have been available for centuries. We use them in education and in the psychological management of the community. . . ."

"Each of us," Frazier began, "is engaged in a pitched battle with the rest of mankind."

"A curious premise for a Utopia," said Castle. "Even a pessimist like myself takes a more hopeful view than that."

"You do, you do," said Frazier. "But let's be realistic. Each of us has interests which conflict with the interests of everybody else. That's our original sin, and it can't be helped. Now, 'everybody else' we call 'society.' It's a powerful opponent, and it always wins. Oh, here and there an individual prevails for a while and gets what he wants. Sometimes he storms the culture of a society and changes it slightly to his own advantage. But society wins in the long run, for it has the advantage of numbers and of age. Many prevail against one, and men against a baby. Society attacks early, when the individual is helpless. It enslaves him almost before he has tasted freedom. The 'ologies' will tell you how it's done. Theology calls it building a conscience or developing a spirit of selflessness. Psychology calls it the growth of the super-ego.

"Considering how long society has been at it, you'd expect a better job. But the campaigns have been badly planned and the victory has never been secure. The behavior of the individual has been shaped according to revelations of 'good conduct,' never as the result of experimental study. But why not experiment? The questions are simply enough. What's the best behavior for the individual so far as the group is concerned? And how can the individual be induced to behave in that way? Why not explore these questions in a scientific spirit?

"We could do just that in Walden Two. We had already worked out a code of conduct—subject, of course, to experimental modification. The code would keep things running smoothly if everybody lived up to it. Our job was to see that everybody did. Now, you can't get people to follow a useful code by making them into so many jacks-in-the-box. You can't foresee all future circumstances, and you can't specify adequate future conduct. You don't know what will be required. Instead you have to set up certain behavioral processes which will lead the individual to design his own 'good' conduct when the time comes. We call that sort of thing 'self-control.' But don't be misled, the control always rests in the last analysis in the hands of society.

"One of our Planners, a young man named Simmons, worked with me. It was the first time in history that the matter was approached in an experimental way. . . . Simmons and I began by studying the great works on morals and ethics—Plato, Aristotle, Confucius, the New Testament, the Puritan divines, Machiavelli, Chesterfield, Freud—there were scores of them. We were looking for any and every method of shaping human behavior by imparting techniques of self-control. Some techniques were obvious enough, for they had marked turning points in human history. 'Love your enemies' is an example—a psychological invention for easing the lot of an oppressed people. The severest trial of oppression is the constant rage which one suffers at the thought of the oppressor. What Jesus discovered was how to avoid these inner devastations. His technique was to *practice the opposite emotion.* If a man can succeed in 'loving his enemies' and 'taking no thought for the morrow,' he will no longer be assailed by hatred of the oppressor or rage at the loss of his freedom or possessions. He may not get his freedom or possessions back, but he's less miserable. It's a difficult lesson. It comes late in our program."

"I thought you were opposed to modifying emotions and instincts until the world was ready for it," said Castle. "According to you, the principle of 'love your enemies' should have been suicidal."

"It would have been suicidal, except for an entirely unforeseen consequence. Jesus must have been quite astonished at the effect of his discovery. We are only just beginning to understand the power of love because we are just beginning to understand the weakness of force and aggression. But the science of behavior is clear about all that now. . . .

"When Simmons and I had collected our techniques of control, we had to discover how to teach them. That was more difficult. Current educational practices were of little value, and religious practices scarcely any better. Promising paradise or threatening hell-fire is, we assumed, generally admitted to be unproductive. It is based upon a fundamental fraud which, when discovered, turns the individual against society and nourishes the very thing it tries to stamp out. What Jesus offered in return for loving one's enemies was heaven *on earth,* better known as peace of mind.

"We found a few suggestions worth following in the practices of the clinical psychologist. We undertook to build a tolerance for annoying experiences. The sunshine of midday is extremely painful if you come from a dark room, but take it in easy stages and you can avoid pain altogether. The analogy can be misleading, but in much the same way it's possible to build a tolerance to painful or distasteful stimuli, or to frustration, or to situations which arouse fear, anger, or rage. Society and nature throw these annoyances at the individual with no regard for the development of tolerances. Some achieve tolerances; most fail. Where would the science of immunization be if it followed a schedule of accidental dosages?

"Take the principle of 'Get thee behind me, Satan,' for example," Frazier continued. "It's a special case of self-control by altering the environment. Subclass A_3, I believe. We give each child a lollipop which has been dipped in powdered sugar so that a single touch of the tongue can be detected. We tell him he may eat the lollipop later in the day, provided it hasn't already been licked. Since the child is only three or four, it is a fairly diff——"

"Three or four!" Castle exclaimed.

"All our ethical training is completed by the age of six," said Frazier quietly. "A simple principle like putting temptation out of sight would be acquired before four. But at such an early age the problem of not licking the lollipop isn't easy. Now, what would you do, Mr. Castle, in a similar situation?"

"Put the lollipop out of sight as quickly as possible."

"Exactly. I can see you've been well trained. Or perhaps you discovered the principle for yourself. We're in favor of original inquiry wherever possible, but in this case we have a more important goal and we don't hesitate to give verbal help. First of all, the children are urged to examine their own behavior while looking at the lollipops. This helps them to recognize the need for self-control. Then the lollipops are concealed, and the children are asked to notice any gain in happiness or any reduction in tension. Then a strong distraction is arranged—say, an interesting game.

Later the children are reminded of the candy and encouraged to examine their reaction. The value of the distraction is generally obvious. Well, need I go on? When the experiment is repeated a day or so later, the children all run with the lollipops to their lockers and do exactly what Mr. Castle would do—a sufficient indication of the success of our training."

"I wish to report an objective observation of my reaction to your story," said Castle, controlling his voice wtih great precision. "I find myself revolted by this display of sadistic tyranny."

"I don't wish to deny you the exercise of an emotion which you seem to find enjoyable," said Frazier. "So let me go on. Concealing a tempting but forbidden object is a crude solution. For one thing, it's not always feasible. We want a sort of psychological concealment—covering up the candy by paying no attention. In a later experiment the children wear their lollipops like crucifixes for a few hours."

" 'Instead of the cross, the lollipop,
    About my neck was hung.' "
said Castle.

"I wish somebody had taught me that, though," said Rodge, with a glance at Barbara.

"Don't we all?" said Frazier. "Some of us learn control, more or less by accident. The rest of us go all our lives not even understanding how it is possible, and blaming our failure on being born the wrong way."

"How do you build up a tolerance to an annoying situation?" I said.

"Oh, for example, by having the children 'take' a more and more painful shock, or drink cocoa with less and less sugar in it until a bitter concoction can be savored without a bitter face."

"But jealousy or envy—you can't administer them in graded doses," I said.

"And why not? Remember, we control the social environment, too, at this age. That's why we get our ethical training in early. Take this case. A group of children arrive home after a long walk tired and hungry. They're expecting supper; they find, instead, that it's time for a lesson in self-control: they must stand for five minutes in front of steaming bowls of soup.

"The assignment is accepted like a problem in arithmetic. Any groaning or complaining is a wrong answer. Instead, the children begin at once to work upon themselves to avoid any unhappiness during the delay. One of them may make a joke of it. We encourage a sense of humor as a good way of not taking an annoyance seriously. The joke won't be much, according to adult standards—perhaps the child will simply pretend to empty the bowl of soup into his upturned mouth. Another may start a song with many verses. The rest join in at once, for they've learned that it's a good way to make time pass."

Frazier glanced uneasily at Castle, who was not to be appeased.

"That also strikes you as a form of torture, Mr. Castle?" he asked.

"I'd rather be put on the rack," said Castle.

"Then you have by no means had the thorough training I supposed. You can't imagine how lightly the children take such an experience. It's a rather severe biological frustration, for the children are tired and hungry and they must stand and look at food; but it's passed off as lightly as a five-minute delay at curtain time. We regard it as a fairly elementary test. Much more difficult problems follow."

"I suspect as much," muttered Castle.

"In a later stage we forbid all social devices. No songs, no jokes— merely silence. Each child his forced back upon his own resources—a very important step."

"I should think so," I said. "And how do you know it's successful? You might produce a lot of silently resentful children. It's certainly a dangerous stage."

"It is, and we follow each child carefully. If he hasn't picked up the necessary techniques, we start back a little. A still more advanced stage"— Frazier glanced again at Castle, who stirred uneasily—"brings me to my point. When it's time to sit down to the soup, the children count off— heads and tails. Then a coin is tossed and if it comes up heads, the 'heads' sit down and eat. The 'tails' remain standing for another five minutes."

Castle groaned.

"And you call that envy?" I said.

"Perhaps not exactly," said Frazier. "At least there's seldom any aggression against the lucky ones. The emotion, if any, is directed against Lady Luck herself, against the toss of the coin. That, in itself, is a lesson worth learning, for it's the only direction in which emotion has a surviving chance to be useful. And resentment toward things in general, while perhaps just as silly as personal aggression, is more easily controlled. Its expression is not socially objectionable." . . .

"May you not inadvertently teach your children some of the very emotions you're trying to eliminate?" I said. "What's the effect, for example, of finding the anticipation of a warm supper suddenly thwarted? Doesn't that eventually lead to feelings of uncertainty, or even anxiety?"

"It might. We had to discover how often our lessons could be safely administered. But all our schedules are worked out experimentally. We watch for undesired consequences just as any scientist watches for disrupting factors in his experiments.

"After all, it's a simple and sensible program," he went on in a tone of appeasement. "We set up a system of gradually increasing annoyances and frustrations against a background of complete serenity. An easy environment is made more and more difficult as the children acquire the capacity to adjust."

"But *why?*" said Castle. "Why these deliberate unpleasantnesses—to put it mildly? I must say I think you and your friend Simmons are really very subtle sadists."

"You've reversed your position, Mr. Castle," said Frazier in a sudden flash of anger with which I rather sympathized. Castle was calling names, and he was also being unaccountably and perhaps intentionally obtuse. "A while ago you accused me of breeding a race of softies," Frazier continued. "Now you object to toughening them up. But what you don't understand is that these potentially unhappy situations are never very annoying. Our schedules make sure of that. You wouldn't understand, however, because you're not so far advanced as our children."

Castle grew black.

"But what do your children get out of it?" he insisted, apparently trying to press some vague advantage in Frazier's anger. . . .

"If I must spell it out," Frazier began with a deep sigh, "what they get is escape from the petty emotions which eat the heart out of the unprepared. They get the satisfaction of pleasant and profitable social relations on a scale almost undreamed of in the world at large. They get immeasurably increased efficiency, because they can stick to a job without suffering the aches and pains which soon beset most of us. They get new horizons, for they are spared the emotions characteristic of frustration and failure. They get—" His eyes searched the branches of the trees, "Is that enough?" he said at last.

"And the community must gain their loyalty," I said, "when they discover the fears and jealousies and diffidences in the world at large."

"I'm glad you put it that way," said Frazier. "You might have said that they must feel superior to the miserable products of our public schools. But we're at pains to keep any feeling of superiority or contempt under control, too. Having suffered most acutely from it myself, I put the subject first on our agenda. We carefully avoid any joy in a personal triumph which means the personal failure of somebody else. We take no pleasure in the sophistical, the disputative, the dialectical." He threw a vicious glance at Castle. "We don't use the motive of domination, because we are always thinking of the whole group. We could motivate a few geniuses that way—it was certainly my own motivation—but we'd sacrifice some of the happiness of everyone else. Triumph over nature and over oneself, yes. But over others, never."

"You've taken the mainspring out of the watch," said Castle flatly.

"That's an experimental question, Mr. Castle, and you have the wrong answer." . . .

"Are your techniques really so very new?" I said hurriedly. "What about the primitive practice of submitting a boy to various tortures before granting him a place among adults? What about the disciplinary techniques of Puritanism? Or of the modern school, for that matter?"

"In one sense you're right," said Frazier. "And I think you've nicely answered Mr. Castle's tender concern for our little ones. The unhappinesses we deliberately impose are far milder than the normal unhappinesses from which we offer protection. Even at the height of our ethical training, the unhappiness is ridiculously trivial—to the well-trained child. "But there's a world of difference in the way we use these annoyances," he continued. "For one thing, we don't punish. We never administer an unpleasantness in the hope of repressing or eliminating undesirable behavior. But there's another difference. In most cultures the child meets up with annoyances and reverses of uncontrolled magnitude. Some are imposed in the name of discipline by persons in authority. Some, like hazings, are condoned though not authorized. Others are merely accidental. No one cares to, or is able to, prevent them.

"We all know what happens. A few hardy children emerge, particularly those who have got their unhappiness in doses that could be swallowed. They become brave men. Others become sadists or masochists of varying degrees of pathology. Not having conquered a painful environment, they become preoccupied with pain and make a devious art of it. Others submit—and hope to inherit the earth. The rest—the cravens, the cowards—live in fear for the rest of their lives. And that's only a single field—the reaction to pain. I could cite a dozen parallel cases. The optimist and the pessimist, the contented and the disgruntled, the loved and the unloved, the ambitious and the discouraged—these are only the extreme products of a miserable system.

"Traditional practices are admittedly better than nothing," Frazier went on. "Spartan or Puritan—no one can question the occasional happy result. But the whole system rests upon the wasteful principle of selection. The English public school of the nineteenth century produced brave men—by setting up almost insurmountable barriers and making the most of the few who came over. But selection isn't education. Its crops of brave men will always be small, and the waste enormous. Like all primitive principles, selection serves in place of education only through a profligate use of material. Multiply extravagantly and select with rigor. It's the philosophy of the 'big litter' as an alternative to good child hygiene.

"In Walden Two we have a different objective. We make every man a brave man. They all come over the barriers. Some require more preparation than others, but they all come over. The traditional use of adversity is to select the strong. We control adversity to build strength. And we do it deliberately, no matter how sadistic Mr. Castle may think us, in order to prepare for adversities which are beyond control. Our children eventually experience the 'heartache and the thousand natural shocks that flesh is heir to.' It would be the cruelest possible practice to protect them as long as possible, especially when we *could* protect them so well."

Frazier held out his hands in an exaggerated gesture of appeal.

"What alternative *had* we?" he said, as if he were in pain. "What else could we do? For four or five years we could provide a life in which no important need would go unsatisfied, a life practically free of anxiety or frustration or annoyance. What would *you* do? Would you let the child enjoy this paradise with no thought for the future—like an idolatrous and pampering mother? Or would you relax control of the environment and let the child meet accidental frustrations? *But what is the virtue of accident?* No, there was only one course open to us. We had to *design* a series of adversities, so that the child would develop the greatest possible self-control. Call it deliberate, if you like, and accuse us of sadism; there was no other course." . . .

The living quarters and daily schedules of the older children furnished a particularly good example of behavioral engineering. At first sight they seemed wholly casual, almost haphazard, but as Frazier pointed out their significant features and the consequences of each, I began to make out a comprehensive, almost Machiavellian design.

The children passed smoothly from one age group to another, following a natural process of growth and avoiding the abrupt changes of the home-and-school system. The arrangements were such that each child emulated children slightly older than himself and hence derived motives and patterns for much of his early education without adult aid.

The control of the physical and social environment, of which Frazier had made so much, was progressively relaxed—or, to be more exact, the control was transferred from the authorities to the child himself and to the other members of his group. . . .

When we returned to our shade tree, I was primed with questions, and so, I am sure, was Castle. But Frazier had other plans. He had either forgotten how remarkable was the spectacle we had just witnessed, or he was intentionally allowing our wonderment and curiosity to ferment. He began from a very different point of view.

"When we discussed the economics of community life," he said, "I should have mentioned education. Teachers are, of course, workers, and I'm willing to defend all that I said about our economic advantage as specifically applied to education. God knows, the outside world is not exactly profligate in the education of its children. It doesn't spend much on equipment or teachers. Yet in spite of this penny-wise policy, there's still enormous waste. A much better education would cost less if society were better organized.

"We can arrange things more expeditiously here because we don't need to be constantly re-educating. The ordinary teacher spends a good share of her time changing the cultural and intellectual habits which the child acquires from its family and surrounding culture. Or else the teacher duplicates home training, in a complete waste of time. Here we can almost say that the school *is* the family, and vice versa.

"We can adopt the best educational methods and still avoid the administrative machinery which schools need in order to adjust to an unfavorable social structure. We don't have to worry about standardization in order to permit pupils to transfer from one school to another, or to appraise or control the work of particular schools. We don't need 'grades.' Everyone knows that talents and abilities don't develop at the same rate in different children. A fourth-grade reader may be a sixth-grade mathematician. The grade is an administrative device which does violence to the nature of the developmental process. Here the child advances as rapidly as he likes in any field. No time is wasted in forcing him to participate in, or be bored by, activities he has outgrown. And the backward child can be handled more efficiently too.

"We also don't require all our children to develop the same abilities or skills. We don't insist upon a certain set of courses. I don't suppose we have a single child who has had a 'secondary school education,' whatever that means. But they've all developed as rapidly as advisable, and they're well educated in many useful respects. By the same token we don't waste time in teaching the unteachable. The fixed education represented by a diploma is a bit of conspicuous waste which has no place in Walden Two. We don't attach an economic or honorific value to education. It has its own value or none at all.

"Since our children remain happy, energetic, and curious, we don't need to teach 'subjects' at all. We teach only the techniques of learning and thinking. As for geography, literature, the sciences—we give our children opportunity and guidance, and they learn them for themselves. In that way we dispense with half the teachers required under the old system, and the education is incomparably better. Our children aren't neglected, but they're seldom, if ever, *taught* anything.

"Education in Walden Two is part of the life of the community. We don't need to resort to trumped-up life experiences. Our children begin to work at a very early age. It's no hardship; it's accepted as readily as sport or play. And a good share of our education goes on in workshops, laboratories, and fields. It's part of the Walden Two Code to encourage children in all the arts and crafts. We're glad to spend time in instructing them, for we know it's important for the future of Walden Two and our own security."

"What about higher education?" I said.

"We aren't equipped for professional training, of course," said Frazier. "Those who want to go on to graduate study in a university are given special preparation. Entrance requirements are always tyrannical, though perhaps inevitable in a mass-production system. So far, we've been able to find graduate schools that will take our young people as special students, and as they continue to make excellent records, we expect fewer difficulties. If worse comes to worst, we shall organize as a college and get ourselves accredited. But can you imagine the stupid changes we should have to make?" Frazier snorted with impatience. "Oh, well. Tongue in cheek. Tongue in cheek."

"Don't you mean 'chin up?' " I asked.

"We'd have to set up a 'curriculum,' require a 'C average,' a 'foreign language,' 'so many years of residence,' and so on, and so on. It would be most amusing. No, 'tongue in cheek' was what I meant." . . .

"I'm still skeptical," said Castle. "Of course, I'm still at a disadvantage in arguing against an accomplished fact." Frazier nodded his head violently. "But not everything has been accomplished," Castle went on. "Your pleasant schoolrooms, your industrious and contented children—these we must accept. But it would take us a long time to find out how well-educated your children really are, according to our standards." Frazier made a move to speak, but Castle hurried on. "I'll admit these standards won't tell us everything. We couldn't ask your children to take our examinations, because they haven't been learning the same things, even in such a field as French. Your students would probably do no better on a second-year French examination than the average Parisian. I'll admit that, and I confess with all the humility I can muster that the kind of learning you've described is the better—if a comparison is possible. It's the ideal which every college teacher glimpses now and then when he looks up from the dance of death in which he has been caught. But I can't swallow the system you've described because I don't see what keeps the motors running. Why do your children learn anything at all? What are your substitutes for our standard motives?"

"Your 'standard motives'—exactly," said Frazier. "And there's the rub. An educational institution spends most of its time, not in presenting facts or imparting techniques of learning, but in trying to make its students learn. It has to create spurious needs. Have you ever stopped to analyze them? What are the 'standard motives,' Mr. Castle?"

"I must admit they're not very attractive," said Castle. "I suppose they consist of fear of one's family in the event of low grades or expulsion, the award of grades and honors, the snob value of a cap and gown, the cash value of a diploma."

"Very good, Mr. Castle," said Frazier. "You're an honest man. And now to answer your question—our substitute is simply the absence of these devices. We have had to *uncover* the worthwhile and truly productive motives—the motives which inspire creative work in science and art outside the academies. No one asks how to motivate a baby. A baby naturally explores everything it can get at, unless restraining forces have already been at work. And this tendency doesn't die out, it's *wiped* out.

"We made a survey of the motives of the unhampered child and found more than we could use. Our engineering job was to *preserve* them by fortifying the child against discouragement. We introduce discouragement as carefully as we introduce any other emotional situation, beginning at about six months. Some of the toys in our air-conditioned cubicles are designed to build perseverance. A bit of a tune from a music box, or a pattern of flashing lights, is arranged to follow an appropriate response— say, pulling on a ring. Later the ring must be pulled twice, later still three or five or ten times. It's possible to build up fantastically perseverative behavior without encountering frustration or rage. It may not surprise you to learn that some of our experiments miscarried; the resistance to discouragement became almost stupid or pathological. One takes some risks in work of this sort, of course. Fortunately, we were able to reverse the process and restore the children to a satisfactory level.

"Building a tolerance for discouraging events proved to be all we needed," Frazier continued. "The motives in education, Mr. Castle, are the motives in all human behavior. Education should be only life itself. We don't need to create motives. We avoid the spurious academic needs you've just listed so frankly, and also the escape from threat so widely used in our civil institutions. We appeal to the curiosity which is characteristic of the unrestrained child, as well as the alert and inquiring adult. We appeal to that drive to control the environment which makes a baby continue to crumple a piece of noisy paper and the scientist continue to press forward with his predictive analyses of nature. We don't need to motivate anyone by creating spurious needs."

"I've known a few men with the kind of motivation you mean," I said.

"The contemporary culture produces a few by accident," said Frazier quickly, "just as it produces a few brave or happy men."

"But I've never understood them," I said. . . .

"Why should you, any more than unhappy people can understand the happy ones?"

"But isn't there a real need for the spurious satisfactions?" I said. "Little signs of personal success, money—personal domination, too, if you like. Most of what I do, I do to avoid undesirable consequences, to evade unpleasantnesses, or to reject or attack forces which interfere with my freedom."

"All the unhappy motives," said Frazier.

"Unhappy, perhaps, but powerful. I think the very thing which seems most unpromising in your system is its happiness. Your people are going to be too happy, too successful. But why won't they just go to sleep? Can we expect real achievements from them? Haven't the great men of history been essentially unhappy or maladjusted or neurotic?"

"I have little interest in conclusions drawn from history," said Frazier, "but if you must play that game, I'll play it too. For every genius you cite whose greatness seems to have sprung from a neurosis, I will undertake to cite similar acts of greatness without neurosis. Turn it around and I'll agree. A man with a touch of genius will be so likely to attack existing institutions that he'll be called unbalanced or neurotic. The only geniuses produced by the chaos of society are those who do something about it." Frazier paused, and I wondered if he were thinking of himself. "Chaos breeds geniuses. It offers a man something to be a genius about. But here, we have better things to do."

"But what about the cases where unhappiness has led to artistic or scientific achievement?" I asked.

"Oh, I daresay a few first-rate sonnets would have remained unwritten had the lady yielded," said Frazier. "But not so many, at that. Not many works of art can be traced to the lack of satisfaction of the basic needs. It's not plain sex that gives rise to art, but personal relations which are social or cultural rather than biological. Art deals with something less obvious than the satisfaction to be found in a square meal. . . . We shall never produce so satisfying a world that there will be no place for art," he continued. "On the contrary, Walden Two has demonstrated very nicely that as soon as the simple necessities of life are obtained with little effort, there's an enormous welling up of artistic interest. And least of all do we need to fear that simple satisfactions will detract from the scientific conquest of the world. What scientist worth the name is engaged, as scientist, in the satisfaction of his own basic needs? He may be thinking of the basic needs of others, but his own motives are clearly cultural. There can be no doubt of the survival value of the inquiring spirit—of curiosity, of exploration, of the need to dominate media, of the urge to control the forces of nature. The world will never be wholly known, and man can't help trying to know more and more of it."

The topic seemed to have grown too vague to stimulate further discussion, but Castle soon offered a substitute.

"I'm torn between two questions which seem incompatible yet equally pressing," he said. "What do you do about differences among your children in intellect and talent? And what do you do to avoid producing a lot of completely standardized young people? Which question should I ask, and what's your answer?"

"They're both good questions," said Frazier, "and quite compatible." I made a move to speak and Frazier said, "I see that Mr. Burris wants to help with the answers."

"My guess is," I said, "that differences are due to environmental and cultural factors and that Mr. Frazier has no great problem to solve. Give all your children the excellent care we have just been witnessing and your differences will be negligible."

"No, you're wrong, Burris," said Frazier. "That's one question we have answered to our satisfaction. Our ten-year-olds have all had the same environment since birth, but the range of their IQ's is almost as great as in the population at large. This seems to be true of other abilities and skills as well."

"And of physical prowess, of course," said Castle. . . .

"All differences are physical, my dear Mr. Castle. We think with our bodies, too. You might have replied that differences in prowess have always been obvious and impossible to conceal, while other differences have customarily been disguised for the sake of prestige and family pride. We accept our gross physical limitations without protest and are reasonably happy in spite of them, but we may spend a lifetime trying to live up to a wholly false conception of our powers in another field, and suffer the pain of a lingering failure. Here we accept ourselves as we are."

"Aren't the untalented going to be unhappy?"

"But we don't go in for personal rivalry; individuals are seldom compared. We never develop a taste much beyond a talent. Our parents have little reason to misrepresent their children's abilities to themselves or others. It's easy for our children to accept their limitations—exactly as they have always accepted the gross differences which Mr. Castle called physical prowess. At the same time our gifted children aren't held back by organized mediocrity. We don't throw our geniuses off balance. The brilliant but unstable type is unfamiliar here. Genius can express itself." . . .

Frazier stood up and straightened his knees with care. The rest of us also got up—except Castle, who stayed stubbornly in his place.

"I can't believe," he began, looking at the ground and apparently not caring whether he was heard or not, "I can't believe you can really get spontaneity and freedom through a system of tyrannical control. Where does initiative come in? When does the child begin to think of himself as a free agent? What is freedom, anyway, under such a plan?"

"Freedom, freedom," said Frazier, stretching his arms and neck and almost singing the words, as if he were uttering them through a yawn. "Freedom is a question, isn't it? But let's not answer it now. Let's let it ring, shall we? . . ."

36   Summerhill: A Radical Approach
to Child-Rearing*

BY ALEXANDER S. NEILL

EDITOR'S NOTE: Unlike the Walden Two *explained in the previous selection, this is not a fictional story but a real one. The effectiveness of the techniques used by Dr. Neill may depend not so much on how they are applied but the extent to which they are valued. Which of the two, Summerhill or Walden Two, would you like to live in? Teach in? Raise children in? How do Skinner and Neill differ in their conceptions of human nature? Consider your answers carefully. As you search out, discuss and debate the major issues related to these two articles, you will very likely find yourself coming closer to your own ideas about human nature.*

This is a story of a modern school—Summerhill.

Summerhill was founded in the year 1921. The school is situated within the village of Leiston, in Suffolk, England, and is about one hundred miles from London.

Just a word about Summerhill pupils. Some children come to Summerhill at the age of five years, and others as late as fifteen. The children generally remain at the school until they are sixteen years old. We generally have about twenty-five boys and twenty girls.

The children are divided into three age groups: The youngest range from five to seven, the intermediates from eight to ten, and the oldest from eleven to fifteen.

* Reprinted and abridged from *Summerhill: A Radical Approach to Child-Rearing* (New York: Hart Publishing Company, copyright 1960), 3–55, by permission of the publisher.

Generally we have a fairly large sprinkling of children from foreign countries. At the present time (1960) we have five Scandinavians, one Hollander, one German and one American.

The children are housed by age groups with a house mother for each group. The intermediates sleep in a stone building, the seniors sleep in huts. Only one or two older pupils have rooms for themselves. The boys live two or three or four to a room, and so do the girls. The pupils do not have to stand room inspection and no one picks up after them. They are left free. No one tells them what to wear: they put on any kind of costume they want to at any time.

Newspapers call it a *Go-as-you-please School* and imply that it is a gathering of wild primitives who know no law and have no manners.

It seems necessary, therefore, for me to write the story of Summerhill as honestly as I can. That I write with a bias is natural; yet I shall try to show the demerits of Summerhill as well as its merits. Its merits will be the merits of healthy, free children whose lives are unspoiled by fear and hate.

Obviously, a school that makes active children sit at desks studying mostly useless subjects is a bad school. It is a good school only for those who believe in *such* a school, for those uncreative citizens who want docile, uncreative children who will fit into a civilization whose standard of success is money.

Summerhill began as an experimental school. It is no longer such; it is now a demonstration school, for it demonstrates that freedom works.

When my first wife and I began the school, we had one main idea: *to make the school fit the child* —instead of making the child fit the school.

I had taught in ordinary schools for many years. I knew the other way well. I knew it was all wrong. It was wrong because it was based on an adult conception of what a child should be and of how a child should learn. The other way dated from the days when psychology was still an unknown science.

Well, we set out to make a school in which we should allow children freedom to be themselves. In order to do this, we had to renounce all discipline, all direction, all suggestion, all moral training, all religious instruction. We have been called brave, but it did not require courage. All it required was what we had—a complete belief in the child as a good, not an evil, being. For almost forty years, this belief in the goodness of the child has never wavered; it rather has become a final faith.

My view is that a child is innately wise and realistic. If left to himself without adult suggestion of any kind, he will develop as far as he is capable of developing. Logically, Summerhill is a place in which people who have the innate ability and wish to be scholars will be scholars; while those who are only fit to sweep the streets will sweep the streets. But we have not produced a street cleaner so far. Nor do I write this snobbishly, for I would rather see a school produce a happy street cleaner than a neurotic scholar.

What is Summerhill like? Well, for one thing, lessons are optional.

Children can go to them or stay away from them—for years if they want to. There *is* a timetable—but only for the teachers.

The children have classes usually according to their age, but sometimes according to their interests. We have no new methods of teaching, because we do not consider that teaching in itself matters very much. Whether a school has or has not a special method for teaching long division is of no significance, for long division is of no importance except to those who *want* to learn it. And the child who *wants* to learn long division *will* learn it no matter how it is taught.

Children who come to Summerhill as kindergarteners attend lessons from the beginning of their stay; but pupils from other schools vow that they will never attend any beastly lessons again at any time. They play and cycle and get in people's way, but they fight shy of lessons. This sometimes goes on for months. The recovery time is proportionate to the hatred their last school gave them. Our record case was a girl from a convent. She loafed for three years. The average period of recovery from lesson aversion is three months.

Strangers to this idea of freedom will be wondering what sort of madhouse it is where children play all day if they want to. Many an adult says, "If I had been sent to a school like that, I'd never have done a thing." Others say, "Such children will feel themselves heavily handicapped when they have to compete against children who have been made to learn."

I think of Jack who left us at the age of seventeen to go into an engineering factory. One day, the managing director sent for him.

"You are the lad from Summerhill," he said. "I'm curious to know how such an education appears to you now that you are mixing with lads from the old schools. Suppose you had to choose again, would you go to Eton or Summerhill?"

"Oh, Summerhill, of course," replied Jack.

"But what does it offer that the other schools don't offer?"

Jack scratched his head. "I dunno," he said slowly; "I think it gives you a feeling of complete self-confidence."

"Yes," said the manager dryly, "I noticed it when you came into the room."

"Lord," laughed Jack, "I'm sorry if I gave you that impression."

"I liked it," said the director. "Most men when I call them into the office fidget about and look uncomfortable. You came in as my equal. By the way, what department did you say you would like to transfer to?"

This story shows that learning in itself is not as important as personality and character. Jack failed in his university exams because he hated book learning. But his lack of knowledge about *Lamb's Essays* or the French language did not handicap him in life. He is now a successful engineer.

All the same, there is a lot of learning in Summerhill. Perhaps a group of our twelve-year-olds could not compete with a class of equal age in handwriting or spelling or fractions. But in an examination requiring originality, our lot would beat the others hollow.

We have no class examinations in the school, but sometimes I set an exam for fun. The following questions appeared in one such paper:

> *Where are the following:—Madrid, Thursday Island, yesterday, love, democracy, hate, my pocket screwdriver (alas, there was no helpful answer to that one).*
>
> *Give meanings for the following: (the number shows how many are expected for each)—Hand (3) . . . only two got the third right—the standard of measure for a horse. Brass (4) . . . metal, cheek, top army officers, department of an orchestra. Translate Hamlet's To-be-or-not-to-be speech into Summerhillese.*

These questions are obviously not intended to be serious, and the children enjoy them thoroughly. Newcomers, on the whole, do not rise to the answering standard of pupils who have become acclimatized to the school. Not that they have less brain power, but rather because they have become so accustomed to work in a serious groove that any light touch puzzles them.

This is the play side of our teaching. In all classes much work is done. If, for some reason, a teacher cannot take his class on the appointed day, there is usually much disappointment for the pupils.

David, aged nine, had to be isolated for whooping cough. He cried bitterly. "I'll miss Roger's lesson in geography," he protested. David had been in the school practically from birth, and he had definite and final ideas about the necessity of having his lessons given to him. David is now a lecturer in mathematics at London University.

A few years ago someone at a General School Meeting (at which all school rules are voted by the entire school, each pupil and each staff member having one vote) proposed that a certain culprit should be punished by being banished from lessons for a week. The other children protested on the ground that the punishment was too severe.

My staff and I have a hearty hatred of all examinations. To us, the university exams are anathema. But we cannot refuse to teach children the required subjects. Obviously, as long as the exams are in existence, they are our master. Hence, the Summmerhill staff is always qualified to teach to the set standard.

Not that many children want to take these exams; only those going to the university do so. And such children do not seem to find it especially hard to tackle these exams. They generally begin to work for them seriously at the age of fourteen, and they do the work in about three years. Of course they don't always pass at the first try. The more important fact is that they try again.

Summerhill is possibly the happiest school in the world. We have no truants and seldom a case of homesickness. We very rarely have fights—

quarrels, of course, but seldom have I seen a stand-up fight like the ones we used to have as boys. I seldom hear a child cry, because children when free have much less hate to express than children who are downtrodden. Hate breeds hate, and love breeds love. Love means approving of children, and that is essential in any school. You can't be on the side of children if you punish them and storm at them. Summerhill is a school in which the child knows that he is approved of.

Mind you, we are not above and beyond human foibles. I spent weeks planting potatoes one spring, and when I found eight plants pulled up in June, I made a big fuss. Yet there was a difference between my fuss and that of an authoritarian. My fuss was about potatoes, but the fuss an authoritarian would have made would have dragged in the question of morality—right and wrong. I did not say that it was wrong to steal my spuds; I did not make it a matter of good and evil—I made it a matter of *my spuds*. They were *my* spuds and they should have been left alone. I hope I am making the distinction clear.

Let me put it another way. To the children, I am no authority to be feared. I am their equal, and the row I kick up about my spuds has no more significance to them than the row a boy may kick up about his punctured bicycle tire. It is quite safe to have a row with a child when you are equals.

Now some will say: "That's all bunk. There can't be equality. Neill is the boss; he is bigger and wiser." That is indeed true. I am the boss, and if the house caught fire the children would run to me. They know that I am bigger and more knowledgeable, but that does not matter when I meet them on their own ground, the potato patch, so to speak.

When Billy, aged five, told me to get out of his birthday party because I hadn't been invited, I went at once without hesitation—just as Billy gets out of my room when I don't want his company. It is not easy to describe this relationship between teacher and child, but every visitor to Summerhill knows what I mean when I say that the relationship is ideal. One sees it in the attitude to the staff in general. Rudd, the chemistry man, is Derek. Other members of the staff are known as Harry, and Ulla, and Pam. I am Neill, and the cook is Esther.

In Summerhill, everyone has equal rights. No one is allowed to walk on my grand piano, and I am not allowed to borrow a boy's cycle without his permission. At a General School Meeting, the vote of a child of six counts for as much as my vote does.

But, says the knowing one, in practice of course the voices of the grownups count. Doesn't the child of six wait to see how you vote before he raises his hand? I wish he sometimes would, for too many of my proposals are beaten. Free children are not easily influenced; the absence of fear accounts for this phenomenon. Indeed, the absence of fear is the finest thing that can happen to a child.

Our children do not fear our staff. One of the school rules is that after ten o'clock at night there shall be quietness on the upper corridor. One night, about eleven, a pillow fight was going on, and I left my desk, where I was writing, to protest against the row. As I got upstairs, there was a scurrying of feet and the corridor was empty and quiet. Suddenly I heard a disappointed voice say, "Humph, it's only Neill," and the fun began again at once. When I explained that I was trying to write a book downstairs, they showed concern and at once agreed to chuck the noise. Their scurrying came from the suspicion that their bedtime officer (one of their own age) was on their track.

I emphasize the importance of this absence of fear of adults. A child of nine will come and tell me he has broken a window with a ball. He tells me, because he isn't afraid of arousing wrath or moral indignation. He may have to pay for the window, but he doesn't have to fear being lectured or being punished.

There was a time some years back when a School Government resigned, and no one would stand for election. I seized the opportunity of putting up a notice: "In the absence of a government, I herewith declare myself Dictator. Heil Neill!" Soon there were mutterings. In the afternoon Vivien, aged six, came to me and said, "Neill, I've broken a window in the gym."

I waved him away. "Don't bother me with little things like that," I said, and he went.

A little later he came back and said he had broken two windows. By this time I was curious, and asked him what the great idea was.

"I don't like dictators," he said, "and I don't like going without my grub." (I discovered later that the opposition to dictatorship had tried to take itself out on the cook, who promptly shut up the kitchen and went home.)

"Well," I asked, "what are you going to do about it?"

"Break more windows," he said doggedly.

"Carry on," I said, and he carried on.

When he returned, he announced that he had broken seventeen windows. "But mind," he said earnestly, "I'm going to pay for them."

"How?"

"Out of my pocket money. How long will it take me?"

I did a rapid calculation. "About ten years," I said.

He looked glum for a minute; then I saw his face light up. "Gee," he cried, "I don't have to pay for them at all."

"But what about the private property rule?" I asked. "The windows are my private property."

"I know that but there isn't any private property rule now. There isn't any government, and the government makes the rules."

It may have been my expression that made him add, "But all the same I'll pay for them."

But he didn't have to pay for them. Lecturing in London shortly afterward, I told the story; and at the end of my talk, a young man came up and handed me a pound note "to pay for the young devil's windows." Two years later, Vivien was still telling people of his windows and of the man who paid for them. "He must have been a terrible fool, because he never even saw me."

Children make contact with strangers more easily when fear is unknown to them. English reserve is, at bottom, really fear; and that is why the most reserved are those who have the most wealth. The fact that Summerhill children are so exceptionally friendly to visitors and strangers is a source of pride to me and my staff.

We must confess, however, that many of our visitors are people of interest to the children. The kind of visitor most unwelcome to them is the teacher, especially the earnest teacher, who wants to see their drawing and written work. The most welcome visitor is the one who has good tales to tell—of adventure and travel or, best of all, of aviation. A boxer or a good tennis player is surrounded at once, but visitors who spout theory are left severely alone.

The most frequent remark that visitors make is that they cannot tell who is staff and who is pupil. It is true: the feeling of unity is that strong when children are approved of. There is no deference to a teacher as a teacher. Staff and pupils have the same food and have to obey the same community laws. The children would resent any special privileges given to the staff.

When I used to give the staff a talk on psychology every week, there was a muttering that it wasn't fair. I changed the plan and made the talks open to everyone over twelve. Every Tuesday night, my room is filled with eager youngsters who not only listen but give their opinions freely. Among the subjects the children have asked me to talk about have been these: The Inferiority Complex, The Psychology of Stealing, The Psychology of the Gangster, The Psychology of Humor, Why Did Man Become a Moralist?, Masturbation, Crowd Psychology. It is obvious that such children will go out into life with a broad clear knowledge of themselves and others.

The most frequent question asked by Summerhill visitors is, "Won't the child turn round and blame the school for not making him learn arithmetic or music?" The answer is that young Freddy Beethoven and young Tommy Einstein will refuse to be kept away from their respective spheres.

The function of the child is to live his own life—not the life that his anxious parents think he should live, nor a life according to the purpose of the educator who thinks he knows what is best. All this interference and guidance on the part of adults only produces a generation of robots.

You cannot *make* children learn music or anything else without to some degree converting them into will-less adults. You fashion them into accepters of the *status quo*—a good thing for a society that needs obedient sitters at dreary desks, standers in shops, mechanical catchers of the 8:30

suburban train—a society, in short, that is carried on the shabby shoulders of the scared little man—the scared-to-death conformist.

SUMMERHILL EDUCATION VS. STANDARD EDUCATION

I hold that the aim of life is to find happiness, which means to find interest. Education should be a preparation for life. Our culture has not been very successful. Our education, politics, and economics lead to war. Our medicines have not done away with disease. Our religion has not abolished usury and robbery. Our boasted humanitarianism still allows public opinion to approve of the barbaric sport of hunting. The advances of the age are advances in mechanism—in radio and television, in electronics, in jet planes. New world wars threaten, for the world's social conscience is still primitive.

If we feel like questioning today, we can pose a few awkward questions. Why does man seem to have many more diseases than animals have? Why does man hate and kill in war when animals do not? Why does cancer increase? Why are there so many suicides? So many insane sex crimes? Why the hate that is anti-Semitism? Why Negro hating and lynching? Why back-biting and spite? Why is sex obscene and a leering joke? Why is being a bastard a social disgrace? Why the continuance of religions that have long ago lost their love and hope and charity? Why, a thousand whys about our vaunted state of civilized eminence!

I ask these questions because I am by profession a teacher, one who deals with the young. I ask these questions because those so often asked by teachers are the unimportant ones, the ones about school subjects. I ask what earthly good can come out of discussions about French or ancient history or what not when these subjects don't matter a lot compared to the larger question of life's natural fulfillment—of man's inner happiness.

How much of our education is real doing, real self-expression? Handwork is too often the making of a pin tray under the eye of an expert. Even the Montessori system, well-known as a system of directed play, is an artificial way of making the child learn by doing. It has nothing creative about it.

In the home, the child is always being taught. In almost every home, there is always at least one ungrown-up grownup who rushes to show Tommy how his new engine works. There is always someone to lift the baby up on a chair when baby wants to examine something on the wall. Every time we show Tommy how his engine works we are stealing from that child the joy of life—the joy of discovery—the joy of overcoming an obstacle. Worse! We make that child come to believe that he is inferior, and must depend on help.

Parents are slow in realizing how unimportant the learning side of school is. Children, like adults, learn what they want to learn. All prize-giving and marks and exams sidetrack proper personality development. Only pedants claim that learning from books is education.

Books are the least important apparatus in a school. All that any child needs is the three R's; the rest should be tools and clay and sports and theater and paint and freedom.

SELF-GOVERNMENT

Summerhill is a self-governing school, democratic in form. Everything connected with social, or group, life, including punishment for social offenses, is settled by vote at the Saturday night General School Meeting.

Each member of the teaching staff and each child, regardless of his age, has one vote. My vote carries the same weight as that of a seven-year-old.

One may smile and say, "But your voice has more value, hasn't it?" Well, let's see. Once I got up at a meeting and proposed that no child under sixteen should be allowed to smoke. I argued my case: a drug, poisonous, not a real appetite in children, but mostly an attempt to be grown up. Counterarguments were thrown across the floor. The vote was taken. I was beaten by a large majority.

The sequel is worth recording. After my defeat, a boy of sixteen proposed that no one under twelve should be allowed to smoke. He carried his motion. However, at the following weekly meeting, a boy of twelve proposed the repeal of the new smoking rule, saying, "We are all sitting in the toilets smoking on the sly just like kids do in a strict school, and I say it is against the whole idea of Summerhill." His speech was cheered, and that meeting repealed the law. I hope I have made it clear that my voice is not always more powerful than that of a child.

Once, I spoke strongly about breaking the bedtime rules, with the consequent noise and the sleepy heads that lumbered around the next morning. I proposed that culprits should be fined all their pocket money for each offense. A boy of fourteen proposed that there should be a penny reward per hour for everyone staying up after his or her bedtime. I got a few votes, but he got a big majority.

Summerhill self-government has no bureaucracy. There is a different chairman at each meeting, appointed by the previous chairman, and the secretary's job is voluntary. Bedtime officers are seldom in office for more than a few weeks.

Our democracy makes laws—good ones, too. For example, it is forbidden to bathe in the sea without the supervision of lifeguards, who are always staff members. It is forbidden to climb on the roofs. Bedtimes must be kept or there is an automatic fine. Whether classes should be called off on the Thursday or on the Friday preceding a holiday is a matter for a show of hands at a General School Meeting.

The success of the meeting depends largely on whether the chairman is weak or strong, for to keep order among forty-five vigorous children is no easy task. The chairman has power to fine noisy citizens. Under a weak chairman, the fines are much too frequent.

The staff takes a hand, of course, in the discussions. So do I; although there are a number of situations in which I must remain neutral. In fact, I have seen a lad charged with an offense get away with it on a complete alibi, although he had privately confided to me that he had committed the offense. In a case like this, I must always be on the side of the individual.

I, of course, participate like anyone else when it comes to casting my vote on any issue or bringing up a proposal of my own. Here is a typical example. I once raised the question of whether football should be played in the lounge. The lounge is under my office, and I explained that I disliked the noise of football while I was working. I proposed that indoor football be forbidden. I was supported by some of the girls, by some older boys, and by most of the staff. But my proposal was not carried, and that meant my continuing to put up with the noisy scuffle of feet below my office. Finally, after much public disputation at several meetings, I did carry by majority approval the abolition of football in the lounge. And this is the way the minority generally gets its rights in our school democracy; it keeps demanding them. This applies to little children as much as it does to adults.

On the other hand, there are aspects of school life that do not come under the self-government regime. My wife plans the arrangements for bedrooms, provides the menu, sends out and pays bills. I appoint teachers and ask them to leave if I think they are not suitable.

The function of Summerhill self-government is not only to make laws but to discuss social features of the community as well. At the beginning of each term, rules about bedtime are made by vote. You go to bed according to your age. Then questions of general behavior come up. Sports committees have to be elected, as well as an end-of-term dance committee, a theater committee, bedtime officers, and downtown officers who report any disgraceful behavior out of the school boundaries.

The most exciting subject ever brought up is that of food. I have more than once waked up a dull meeting by proposing that second helpings be abolished. Any sign of kitchen favoritism in the matter of food is severely handled. But when the kitchen brings up the question of wasting food, the meeting is not much interested. The attitude of children toward food is essentially a personal and self-centered one.

In a General School Meeting, all academic discussions are avoided. Children are eminently practical and theory bores them. They like concreteness, not abstraction. I once brought forward a motion that swearing be abolished by law, and I gave my reason. I had been showing a woman around with her little boy, a prospective pupil. Suddenly from upstairs came a very strong adjective. The mother hastily gathered up her son and went off in a hurry. "Why," I asked at a meeting, "should my income suffer because some fathead swears in front of a prospective parent? It isn't a moral question at all; it is purely financial. You swear and I lose a pupil."

My question was answered by a lad of fourteen. "Neill is talking rot," he said. "Obviously, if this woman was shocked, she didn't believe in Summerhill. Even if she had enrolled her boy, the first time he came home saying damn or hell, she would have taken him out of here." The meeting agreed with him, and my proposal was voted down.

A General School Meeting often has to tackle the problem of bullying. Our community is pretty hard on bullies; and I notice that the school government's bullying rule has been underlined on the bulletin board: *"All cases of bullying will be severely dealt with."* Bullying is not so rife in Summerhill, however, as in strict schools, and the reason is not far to seek. Under adult discipline, the child becomes a hater. Since the child cannot express his hatred of adults with impunity, he takes it out on smaller or weaker boys. But this seldom happens in Summerhill. Very often, a charge of bullying when investigated amounts to the fact that Jenny called Peggy a lunatic.

Sometimes a case of stealing is brought up at the General School Meeting. There is never any punishment for stealing, but there is always reparation. Often children will come to me and say, "John stole some coins from David. Is this a case for psychology, or shall we bring it up?"

If I consider it a case for psychology, requiring individual attention, I tell them to leave it to me. If John is a happy, normal boy who has stolen something inconsequential, I allow charges to be brought against him. The worst that happens is that he is docked all of his pocket money until the debt is paid.

How are General School Meetings run? At the beginning of each term, a chairman is elected for one meeting only. At the end of the meeting he appoints his successor. This procedure is followed throughout the term. Anyone who has a grievance, a charge, or a suggestion, or a new law to propose brings it up.

Here is a typical example: Jim took the pedals from Jack's bicycle because his own cycle is in disrepair, and he wanted to go away with some other boys for a week-end trip. After due consideration of the evidence, the meeting decides that Jim must replace the pedals, and he is forbidden to go on the trip.

The chairman asks, "Any objections?"

Jim gets up and shouts that there jolly well are! Only his adjective isn't exactly "jolly." "This isn't fair!" he cries. "I didn't know that Jack ever used his old crock of a bike. It has been kicking about among the bushes for days. I don't mind shoving his pedals back, but I think the punishment unfair. I don't think I should be cut out of the trip."

Follows a breezy discussion. In the debate, it transpires that Jim usually gets a weekly allowance from home, but the allowance hasn't come for six weeks, and he hasn't a bean. The meeting votes that the sentence be quashed, and it is duly quashed.

But what to do about Jim? Finally it is decided to open a subscription fund to put Jim's bike in order. His schoolmates chip in to buy him pedals for his bike, and he sets off happily on his trip.

Usually, the School Meeting's verdict is accepted by the culprit. However, if the verdict is unacceptable, the defendant may appeal, in which case the chairman will bring up the matter once again at the very end of the meeting. At such an appeal, the matter is considered more carefully, and generally the original verdict is tempered in view of the dissatisfaction of the defendant. The children realize that if the defendant feels he has been unfairly judged, there is a good chance that he actually has been.

No culprit at Summerhill ever shows any signs of defiance or hatred of the authority of his community. I am always surprised at the docility our pupils show when punished.

One term, four of the biggest boys were charged at the General School Meeting with doing an illegal thing—selling various articles from their wardrobes. The law forbidding this had been passed on the ground that such practices are unfair to the parents who buy the clothes and unfair as well to the school, because when children go home minus certain wearing apparel, the parents blame the school for carelessness. The four boys were punished by being kept on the grounds for four days and being sent to bed at eight each night. They accepted the sentence without a murmur. On Monday night, when everyone had gone to the town movies, I found Dick, one of the culprits, in bed reading.

"You are a chump," I said. "Everyone has gone to the movies. Why don't you get up?"

"Don't try to be funny," he said.

This loyalty of Summerhill pupils to their own democracy is amazing. It has no fear in it, and no resentment. I have seen a boy go through a long trial for some antisocial act, and I have seen him sentenced. Often, the boy who has just been sentenced is elected chairman for the next meeting.

The sense of justice that children have never ceases to make me marvel. And their administrative ability is great. As education, self-government is of infinite value.

Certain classes of offenses come under the automatic fine rule. If you ride another's bike without permission, there is an automatic fine of sixpence. Swearing in town (but you can swear as much as you like on the school grounds), bad behavior in the movies, climbing on roofs, throwing food in the dining room—these and other infractions of rules carry automatic fines.

Punishments are nearly always fines: hand over pocket money for a week or miss a movie.

An oft-heard objection to children acting as judges is that they punish too harshly. I find it not so. On the contrary, they are very lenient. On no occasion has there been a harsh sentence at Summerhill. And invariably the punishment has some relation to the crime.

Three small girls were disturbing the sleep of others. Punishment: they must go to bed an hour earlier every night for a week. Two boys were accused of throwing clods at other boys. Punishment: they must cart clods to level the hockey field.

Often the chairman will say, "The case is too silly for words," and decide that nothing should be done.

When our secretary was tried for riding Ginger's bike without permission, he and two other members of the staff who had also ridden it were ordered to push each other on Ginger's bike ten times around the front lawn.

Four small boys who climbed the ladder that belonged to the builders who were erecting the new workshop were ordered to climb up and down the ladder for ten minutes straight.

The meeting never seeks advice from an adult. Well, I can remember only one occasion when it was done. Three girls had raided the kitchen larder. The meeting fined them their pocket money. They raided the kitchen again that night and the meeting fined them a movie. They raided it once more, and the meeting was graveled what to do. The chairman consulted me. "Give them tuppence reward each," I suggested. "What? Why, man, you'll have the whole school raiding the kitchen if we do that." "You won't," I said. "Try it."

He tried it. Two of the girls refused to take the money; and all three were heard to declare that they would never raid the larder again. They didn't—for about two months.

Priggish behavior at meetings is rare. Any sign of priggishness is frowned upon by the community. A boy of eleven, a strong exhibitionist, used to get up and draw attention to himself by making long involved remarks of obvious irrelevance. At least he tried to, but the meeting shouted him down. The young have a sensitive nose for insincerity.

At Summerhill we have proved, I believe, that self-government works. In fact, the school that has no self-government should not be called a progressive school. It is a compromise school. You cannot have freedom unless children feel completely free to govern their own social life. When there is a boss, there is no real freedom. This applies even more to the benevolent boss than to the disciplinarian. The child of spirit can rebel against the hard boss, but the soft boss merely makes the child impotently soft and unsure of his real feelings.

Good self-government in a school is possible only when there is a sprinkling of older pupils who like a quiet life and fight the indifference or opposition of the gangster age. These older youngsters are often outvoted, but it is they who really believe in and want self-government. Children up to, say, twelve, on the other hand, will not run good self-government on their own, because they have not reached the social age. Yet at Summerhill, a seven-year-old rarely misses a General Meeting.

One spring we had a spate of bad luck. Some community-minded seniors had left us after passing their college entrance exams, so that there were very few seniors left in the school. The vast majority of the pupils were at the gangster stage and age. Although they were social in their speeches, they were not old enough to run the community well. They passed any amount of laws and then forgot them and broke them. The few older pupils left were, by some chance, rather individualist, and tended to live their own lives in their own groups, so that the staff was figuring too prominently in attacking the breaking of the school rules. Thus it came about that at a General School Meeting I felt compelled to launch a vigorous attack on the seniors for being not antisocial but asocial, breaking the bedtime rules by sitting up far too late and taking no interest in what the juniors were doing in an antisocial way.

Frankly, younger children are only mildly interested in government. Left to themselves, I question whether younger children would ever form a government. Their values are not our values, and their manners are not our manners.

Stern discipline is the easiest way for the adult to have peace and quiet. Anyone can be a drill sergeant. What the ideal alternative method of securing a quiet life is I do not know. Our Summerhill trials and errors certainly fail to give the adults a quiet life. On the other hand they do not give the children an overnoisy life. Perhaps the ultimate test is happiness. By this criterion, Summerhill has found an excellent compromise in its self-government.

Our law against dangerous weapons is likewise a compromise. Air guns are forbidden. The few boys who want to have air guns in the school hate the law; but in the main, they conform to it. When they are a minority, children do not seem to feel so strongly as adults do.

In Summerhill, there is one perennial problem that can never be solved; it might be called the problem of *the individual vs. the community*. Both staff and pupils get exasperated when a gang of little girls led by a problem girl annoy some people, throw water on others, break the bedtime laws, and make themselves a perpetual nuisance. Jean, the leader, is attacked in a General Meeting. Strong words are used to condemn her misuse of freedom as license.

A visitor, a psychologist, said to me: "It is all wrong. The girl's face is an unhappy one; she has never been loved, and all this open criticism makes her feel more unloved than ever. She needs love, not opposition."

"My dear woman," I replied, "we *have* tried to change her with love. For weeks, we rewarded her for being antisocial. We have shown her affection and tolerance, and she has not reacted. Rather, she has looked on us as simpletons, easy marks for her aggression. We cannot sacrifice the entire community to one individual."

I do not know the complete answer. I know that when Jean is fifteen, she will be a social girl and not a gang leader. I pin my faith on public opinion. No child will go on for years being disliked and criticized. As for the condemnation by the school meeting, one simply cannot sacrifice other children to one problem child.

Once, we had a boy of six who had a miserable life before he came to Summerhill. He was a violent bully, destructive and full of hate. The four- and five-year-olds suffered and wept. The community had to do something to protect them; and in doing so, it had to be against the bully. The mistakes of two parents could not be allowed to react on other children whose parents had given them love and care.

On a very few occasions, I have had to send a child away because the others were finding the school a hell because of him. I say this with regret, with a vague feeling of failure, but I could see no other way.

Have I had to alter my views on self-government in these long years? On the whole, no. I could not visualize Summerhill without it. It has always been popular. It is our show piece for visitors. But that, too, has its drawbacks, as when a girl of fourteen whispered to me at a meeting, "I meant to bring up about girls blocking the toilets by putting sanitary napkins in them, but look at all these visitors." I advised her to damn the visitors and bring the matter up—which she did.

The educational benefit of practical civics cannot be overemphasized. At Summerhill, the pupils would fight to the death for their right to govern themselves. In my opinion, one weekly General School Meeting is of more value than a week's curriculum of school subjects. It is an excellent theater for practicing public speaking, and most of the children speak well and without self-consciousness. I have often heard sensible speeches from children who could neither read nor write.

I cannot see an alternative method to our Summerhill democracy. It may be a fairer democracy than the political one, for children are pretty charitable to each other, and have no vested interests to speak of. Moreover, it is a more genuine democracy because laws are made at an open meeting, and the question of uncontrollable elected delegates does not arise.

After all, it is the broad outlook that free children acquire that makes self-government so important. Their laws deal with essentials, not appearances. The laws governing conduct in the town are the compromise with a less free civilization. "Downtown"—the outside world—wastes its precious energy in worrying over trifles. As if it matters in the scheme of life whether you wear dressy clothes or say hell. Summerhill, by getting away from the outward nothings of life, can have and does have a community spirit that is in advance of its time. True, it is apt to call a spade a damn shovel, but any ditchdigger will tell you with truth that a spade *is* a damn shovel.

PART FOUR

Toward Understanding Maladaptive
Behavior and Disadvantaged Youth

"If all the misfortunes of mankind were cast into a public stock, in order to be equally distributed among the whole species, those who now think themselves the most unhappy would prefer the share they are already possessed of before that which would fall to them by such a division." Socrates (469–399 B.C.)

Understanding maladaptive behavior and disadvantaged youth in this day and age is not just a requirement for the psychologist and altruist, but a challenge for every thoughtful person working with young people who come from little and who have little. It is a challenge because what one comes from is far less important than what one can *become*. The readings in Chapters Nine and Ten are included to broaden the range of your understanding and sensitivity to some of the problems, issues, and unanswered questions frequently associated with maladaptive behavior and disadvantaged youth.

Chapter Nine, which explores the dynamics of maladjusted and delinquent behavior, begins with Dr. Redl challenging some of our preconceived thinking about "defiant youth." Delinquent behavior doesn't just happen by chance. It is for a reason and usually with a purpose. Dr. Haimowitz suggests that some delinquents behave as delinquents because *they get the idea that they are expected to by those whom they take seriously.*

What is and what is not a behavior problem depends not only on the behaver but also on the perceiver. Dr. Beilin examines what 30 years of research has to say about the differences between how teachers and clinicians view the behavior problems of children and explains why, in fact, there are differences. Behavior problems do exist and Dr. Morse outlines an interview technique designed to help the teacher and student inquire together about the attitudes, feelings, and motivations behind problem behavior. Just as there are punitive and nonpunitive students, there are these kinds of adults as well. And some are teachers. What kind of influence do these kinds of teachers have on the students? Drs. Kounin and Gump explore this and related questions in the last paper in Chapter Nine, and you will see that a punitive teacher, like a punitive parent, like a punitive dictator, like a punitive you-name-it, gets pretty much the same results.

Probably no single educational or social issue in recent times has attracted as much attention, time, and money as our educational programs for the disadvantaged. Chapter Ten is aimed at presenting some ideas, points of view, and speculations relevant to the education of the disadvantaged. First, you will see some of the problems of the disadvantaged from the point of view of a psychologist. It is one thing to insist that all children, including the disadvantaged, go to school until a certain age, but it is quite another to present them with a curriculum that has no meaning in terms of the way they see the world. Those characteristics most commonly associated with the disadvantaged are discussed by Millard Black. You will discover that the disadvantaged child is of no single race or color. Poverty, illiteracy, delinquency are shared by peoples of all colors and national origins.

School integration and the dropout issue remain as two major social-psychological problems we are still working to cure, and in readings 43 and 44 Dr. Green and Bernard Bard explore the implications and overtones of each. We hear a lot these days about dropout campaigns, but how successful are they? Mr. Bard doubts if they're as successful as we may want to believe and offers some ideas why campaigns of this sort may, indeed, fail.

The last reading in this section speaks for itself with a kind of poetic eloquence. If you are thinking seriously about becoming a teacher, read it carefully—you, too, may have some "poor scholars" in your classes.

CHAPTER NINE

DYNAMICS OF MALADJUSTED AND DELINQUENT BEHAVIOR

*37   Our Troubles with Defiant Youth**

BY FRITZ REDL

EDITOR'S NOTE: *The following article points out the fallacy of the "delinquent" stereotype and shows the diversity of motivation and causes behind four kinds of "defiant" behavior. Too often we act as if "defiant" behavior is symbolic of exploding aggression when, in fact, it may mean passive submission. Our management or mismanagement may make the difference between a healthy solution and a dismal failure for growing youth. This selection will help you better understand the various expressions of defiance.*

The term "delinquency" is used these days generally in vague and confusing ways. Clinically the behavior referred to as "delinquent" may cover a wide range of entirely different afflictions. Sometimes the word is as loosely applied as the popular term "bellyache" which may cover anything from temporary upset after eating too much ice cream to stomach ulcers or acute appendicitis. Nobody in the medical field today would attempt to answer the question "what should be done about it" before finding out concretely just which of the afflictions gave rise to the "bellyache." Unfortunately, however, in the field of human behavior and mental health, the public has not yet reached as wise an acceptance of the variety of ills which may result in excessive aggression or as much respect for the need for specific diagnosis.

The concept of "defiant youth" does *not* coincide with the delin-

---

* Reprinted from *Children*, January-February, 1955, Vol. 2, 5–9, by permission of the author and the Children's Bureau, Social Security Administration, U.S. Department of Health, Education, and Welfare.

quency problem. Some "defiance" is part and parcel of the normal growth process. It may even be a desirable though an uncomfortable forerunner of a character trait commonly referred to as "integrity" or "spine." Other forms of defiance, however, do overlap with the kind of trouble usually referred to as "delinquency" and constitute a great strain on our communities. On the other hand, not all delinquents show overt defiant behavior. In fact some of the hardest to reach cases exhibit a very "slick" surface conformity as a safe cover for the cultivation of a totally immoral outlook on life or a safe buildup for a long-prepared criminal "splurge."

These facts leave persons concerned with the behavior of today's youth facing two important questions:

1. In what areas are confused public opinion and juvenile delinquency most seriously blocking clinical progress and preventive planning?

2. What types of youthful defiance need to be differentiated in order to begin wise preventive and therapeutic planning?

AREAS OF CONFUSION

There are three main areas of confusion:

1. *The Individual and the Symbol*

Most of us have been annoyed at one time or another by the fact that children go through a phase where they suddenly consider us, their parents and teachers, as just a general symbol of "the adult." They seem suddenly to have emptied us of all personal relationships with them. We stop being Mary's dad or Johnny's older friend and represent simply "those adults," the power group from whose grip they are trying to emancipate themselves.

However, we adults don't usually recognize that we begin to do the same thing to our children as soon as they enter the development phases of preadolescence and adolescence. In these periods Daddy does have moments of reacting to his son not so much as a person, but as though he represented the "world of adults" pitched against "youth" which is getting out of hand. Dad's little boy suddenly becomes not his son whom he knows and loves so well, but just an "example" of the way postwar young people act when you don't "keep them in line."

This peculiar phenomenon, natural and harmless within limits, often becomes a real block to wise handling of youthful behavior. It is responsible for much avoidable antagonism between the generations. The more we feel threatened by what youngsters do, the more we fall into this form of stereotyping. As a result many situations grow into sham battles over a "cause," when the immediate problem could have been easily solved if the two adversaries had remained what they were to begin with: two *people* having it out.

2. Some of My Best Friends Are Teenagers

There seems to be a tendency in the adult world toward hostility to youth as such which is in striking contrast to the fact that we all "like kids," especially our own or those entrusted to our care. Something seems to happen to the most child-acceptant of us when we suddenly switch from personal involvement with a child to a collective view of the youth problem. This shift in focus tends especially to occur when a youngster becomes involved in some rather atrocious crime—although the act has so obviously grown out of extreme disorganization within the world surrounding him, such a long and involved chain of disturbing events that nobody could logically regard the outcome as "typical" youthful behavior.

A 14-year-old boy tries to defend his mother against the onslaughts of his drunken father and hits him a bit too hard with the piece of pipe he grabs in despair. Why are our newspapers so ready to call this a "teenage crime"? By doing so aren't they implying that this boy is "typical" of the youth of our time, or at least that something about being a "teenager" has brought about the unfortunate event which so obviously stemmed from the pathology of the adults in the boy's life? On the other hand, do the papers write up as a typical teenage deed the heroism of Bobby, an Eagle Scout, who rescued a little girl from drowning? On the contrary Bobby Smith, aged 15, remains Bobby Smith, not a representative of his age, and the heroism is credited to himself. In other words, teenagers are regarded as a breed suspect until proven innocent. Their bad deeds redound on the whole age group. Their good deeds point only to the exceptions that prove the rule.

When public attitudes incline toward stereotyping of this sort there is cause for deep concern. Collective suspicion and negativism of one group toward another always backfire by engendering conscious or unconscious collective counter-aggression and distrust from the other side. To increase intergroup tensions between the "world of grown-ups" and the "youth of our time" is the last thing we should do at this point in history. Since we have paid such prices in the past for collective prejudices in the areas of race, religion, class, and caste we should know something about the high cost of group psychological pathology.

3. An Optical Illusion

Adult disgust with "youth" is easily aroused when the young people gather in mobs. Their boisterous and rather inconsiderate behavior gets on our nerves and reinforces our suspicious stereotypes. Thus, unfortunately, we are taken in by a kind of "optical illusion," for loud and thoughtless behavior is often more typical of the group situation individuals are in than of the individuals themselves. If you doubt this, just remember the last large convention held in your town. Many riotous teenagers would have trouble living up to what otherwise dignified adults can do to hotel-room towels, ashtrays, and doorknobs when they are convening in somebody else's city.

While much remains to be learned about the impact of group psychological excitement on the behavior of the human individual, age, or "teenage," as such is not the main factor involved. The problem of how to predict which person's self-control and value system will melt under a certain amount of group psychological heat and how to help individuals keep sense and control intact under free-floating contagion is one of the most urgent research issues before us. Instead of allowing ourselves to become irritated at an "age range," we should take steps to investigate thoroughly this larger problem of group pathology.

In summary, it seems as important for the fields of mental hygiene and preventive psychiatry to tackle the collective confusions about youthful behavior in which the present adult generation indulges as to cope with the problems of youth itself. We have made wonderful strides with analogous problems in the field of physical medicine and health. Through the astounding successes of public-health education on a variety of levels, present public opinion is enlightened about the nature of invisible germs, accepts even unpleasant facts about the nutritive values of certain foods, and no longer quarrels with the wisdom of certain "first aid" directives even where these contradict deeply ingrained popular myths or personal feelings. But in the field of human behavior the major task of "deconfusing the public" lies ahead.

WHAT ABOUT "DEFIANCE"?

Without attempting anything as ambitious as an outline of symptomatology and etiology of the "defiant child," we can differentiate a few of the outstanding problems that usually sail under this heading. Here too conceptual confusion, while not the core of the difficulty, is a dangerous roadblock on the way to progress.

1. Developmental Defiance

In spite of all the talk about "adjustment," we would not really want children to "adjust" to everything all the time. If they did we would think they lacked "spine." Healthy development on the part of a child is fostered by strengthening not only his ability to adjust to outside demands, but also his ability to defend his own integrity against wrong demands made by others. We want Johnny to be respectful to his teacher but we don't want him to run after the first designing bum that offers him candy just because the man is an adult and looks like a mixture of Abe Lincoln and Santa Claus. On the contrary, we want our children to retain the capacity for *intelligent rebellion*—courage to stick to what they believe in even against strong-armed pressure and the fear of becoming unpopular with the mob. All traits that we want eventually to see in our children must grow through a range of developmental phases. "Intelligent rebellion," too, needs leeway to be learned and practiced. Of course, while being practiced it often looks anything but intelligent and can be very annoying to the adult who has to live with it. We know from our studies of child development that certain age ranges seem to be especially cut out for the practice of "emancipation acrobatics." The negativism of the child between 3 and 5 as well as the strong "emancipation" efforts of the young adolescent are normal phases in child development. While uncomfortable for educator and parent, these rebellious phases are important as preparation for independence. We also know that defiance which is part of this developmental process is *not habit forming*. It tones down by itself as soon as the character trait of integrity, for the sake of which it was displayed, is sufficiently secured.

Although we have many books that tell us how to cultivate "intelligent rebellion" in the well-adjusted child in relation to the child's dependence on individuals, we have little information on how to help him keep his integrity when confronted with gang and mob pressure. One of the Nation's greatest problems at this time is to find out how to help our young people stick to what they believe in, even in defiance of whatever opinion or action might be popular at the moment with the rest of the youthful crowd. Actually a lot of behavior usually termed "defiance" is exactly the opposite. The 16-year-old who participates in an incident of vandalism because he is afraid of being called a sissy is not a *defiant* child. He is a coward, an overconformist, a spineless lickspittle for public acclaim. The fact that he is overdependent on the wrong opinions does not change the fact that submission rather than defiance is the real problem at hand.

Clinically speaking, then, we have to look a few inches below the surface before we can know what the problems in any specific "defiant act" really are. Where behavior falls into the category of "developmental defiance," it presents us with an educational challenge, but we must not be fooled into regarding it as "delinquency."

2. Reactive Defiance

Some youthful defiant behavior may be compared to the process of regurgitation. If you pour poison or stuff pins down somebody's throat, his organism will probably rebel by choking reactions to ward off the hurtful intrusion. Vomiting under such conditions is not symptomatic of illness. On the contrary, it is the defense of a healthy organism against hurt from the outside.

A lot of youthful "defiant" behavior falls into the same category. It is *not* the outcropping of a corrupt or morbid personality, but the defense of a healthy one against the kind of treatment that shouldn't happen to a dog, but often does happen to children. At close inspection even many of the rather frightening and disgusting outbursts of youthful defiance are of this type. In a group of normal schoolchildren bored beyond limit by stupid teaching methods, the intelligent ones will be the first to become "hard to handle." Their misbehavior is a defense against the demoralizing impact of excessive boredom. If a child with deep-seated anxieties is put into solitary confinement under frightening circumstances, the resulting temper tantrum will not be his "warped personality" coming to the fore but his desperate defense against total breakdown into mental disease. His frantic muscle spasms and aggressive mauling of the surrounding outside world are the expression of his inward terror.

Such "reactive defiance" calls for consideration not only of what's wrong with the child but also of what is wrong with what we are doing to him. Every case of really pathological and dangerous defiance which I have had a chance to study closely has had its origin at some time in "reactive" defiance. Many people had to do the wrong things consistently for a long time to the children involved to produce such a severe degree of disturbance. This means that one of our greatest preventive opportunities lies in developing and applying greater knowledge about the most advantageous setting for growing youngsters and in helping adults toward a maximum of wisdom in their reaction to youthful behavior.

3. *Defiance as a Wrapping*

Some defiant behavior is quite clearly "unprovoked," or at least seems so at first sight. Why should Billy, a well-loved and well-cared-for child, one day suddenly act up, hanging on to furniture and kicking and biting when you try to make him go to school? His unwarranted behavior toward you looks dangerously like the "rebellious child" in the making. It looks and feels like that, until you learn that Billy has deep-seated fears of any "crowd" situation—fears that are irrational but extremely intense. The panic aroused in Billy's mind is in itself a "sickness," an anxiety neurosis. This is the affliction, not the "disrespectful disobedience" which he displays when confronted with it.

Other "defiant acts" by youthful offenders may be the secondary accompaniment of any of a variety of mental diseases. I once knew a child who when compulsively hit by sudden intense spurts of fantasy images would get up during class and wander around, impervious to threats of punishment. He *seemed* to do all this "just in order to spite authority." Yet nothing was further from the truth. At these moments, he did not even *perceive* the teacher's presence nor any of the world around him. He had no thought of being "spiteful." It would have been easier to help him if he had, for this child was out of contact with reality far beyond the normal degree of childish daydreaming. This sickness is worse than the usual "defiance." But the important point is that it is *different* and calls for entirely different treatment and preventive measures.

Defiance which comes as a "wrapping" around some other disease is especially frustrating. Because in such cases the techniques so often found helpful in dealing with other defiant children are totally ineffectual, the adult's wrath at the defiant behavior is apt to be increased by his fury at his helplessness. The result is a loud cry for some form of physical punishment. Unfortunately, in these cases physical punishment is the most futile and most damaging technique we could use. Where defiance is a "wrapping" no matter how smell-proof or loose, the only thing to do is to tackle the disease behind the wrapping. All other efforts are useless.

THE DEFIANT EGO

By a "defiant ego" I mean the ego that has thrown itself on the side of the child's impulsivity, defending it against reason and the voice of his "better self" with enormous skill and strength.

This, unfortunately, is the most neglected although the most serious form of defiance. While from the outside it looks very much like other types of defiant behavior, at closer range it reveals itself as a most pernicious and serious affliction which educator and psychiatrist so far are completely helpless to change.

Children with "defiant egos" act destructively any time they so desire because they enjoy it. If they want their "fun" they are going to have it. Either they have not developed that "voice from within" that would make them feel bad about "fun" that is unjustly had at somebody else's expense; or they have developed very skillful tricks of putting that "voice" out of commission should it tend to interfere. Diagnosis, however, is not easy. The size of the offense or the intensity of the defiance gives no clue as to what type of defiance is involved. It is not true that rowdyism marks a child as sickest or worst, while milder or even "cute" forms of rebellion can be passed by as harmless. Nuisance value to others, or intensity and degree of defiance are only a few of the criteria for sizing things up for what they really are.

I know of actions close to murder, which have had little to do with real defiance, but are reactive or psychoneurotic in origin. I also know of cases where as mild a symptom as polite withdrawal from arts and crafts activities—but always exactly when whim dictated and always accompanied by total disinterest and bland imperviousness to the persuasiveness of others—proved to be the forerunner of very severe character disorders which later blossomed into openly recognizable symptom displays.

A detailed description of the "defiant ego" is not possible in the space available. However, this is the type of affliction which may justifiably be classified as "delinquency," even if the defiance displayed does not seem to have any "legal" implications. The early recognition of such afflictions and the determination of conditions for preventive and therapeutic work with them constitute the main themes of the present project at the Psychiatric Children's Unit at the National Institute of Mental Health. [See "Child Study in a New Setting," *Children*, Vol. 1, No. 1.]

IN SUMMARY

The problem of "defiant youth" is complicated by the fact that the adult generation generally lacks conceptual clarity in discussing the issues involved. Furthermore, "defiant" behavior by children seems to bring out the worst in adults, provoking them to react with their own feelings rather than with deliberate thought. The collective "suspicious antagonism" which communities often display against the "teenagers" as a "caste and class" is likely to foster or increase a collective spirit of defiance among youth itself.

The actual phenomenon of "defiance" has many degrees ranging from "light" to "severe and dangerous," from "cute" to "morbidly obnoxious." Unfortunately, the degree does not indicate in any given case what lies behind the behavior. No matter which specific form of behavior defiance may take, it may derive from any one, or a mixture of, at least four types of afflictions. . . .

The answer to the problem of defiant youth must be sought in the direction of more practice-geared research, greater concerted effort toward the education of the public to the causes of defiance, and more courage to think straight even under the impact of panic and wrath.

FOOTNOTE:

[1] Redl, F., and D. Wineman, *The Aggressive Child*, The Free Press, 1957.

38   *Criminals Are Made, Not Born**

BY MORRIS L. HAIMOWITZ

EDITOR'S NOTE: We have always heard a lot of talk about how society or environment helps make a criminal "criminal," but seldom is there any specific discussion about how this may happen. This paper describes some of the specific and critical experiences which conceivably could lead a boy into a criminal career. This is not to suggest that all criminals go into a life of crime because of the dynamics outlined in this article, but we could reasonably speculate that more than just a few boys learn that being a delinquent "somebody" is better than being a nondelinquent "nobody." The way they learn this is adroitly discussed in this selection.

I. INTRODUCTION

A number of theories attempt to explain how people become professional criminals: poverty causes crime; "bad" neighborhoods cause crime; movies, TV, comic books, or radio crime stories cause crime; criminal associates cause crime; broken homes cause crime; race, nationality, neuroses, or crowded housing cause crime. These theories do not explain why most poor people never become professional criminals. Nor do most people from bad neighborhoods, or most children of broken homes, or most members of any race or nationality, or most neurotics become criminals. If crowded housing caused crime, all Eskimos would be criminals; actually, very few are.

* Reprinted from *Human Development: Selected Readings*, 2nd edition, Morris L. Haimowitz and Natalie R. Haimowitz (Eds.), (New York: Thomas Y. Crowell Company, 1966), 391–403, by permission of the author.

Some studies show these factors to be associated with criminality. But science aims at generalizations which account for *all* cases, and not one of these theories accounts for even a majority of cases. What they do indicate is some *associated* factors, not the *causes* of crime. Let us illustrate the difference. Suppose we didn't know how a child is conceived and were seeking an explanation. We might make a survey and find the following factors associated with having children: poverty, illiteracy, race, religion, marriage, wedding rings, rural dwellings. Could we therefore state that poverty, illiteracy, and so on, were the causes of conception? Such a conclusion would completely overlook the crucial role of the sperm and ovary. Marriage is an associated factor, but it is not the cause of conception. The theories that poverty or race cause crime are as untrue as the ones that poverty or a wedding ring cause conception.

II. HYPOTHESIS

This paper seeks to develop the hypothesis that the only way a person can become a professional criminal is by getting the idea that he is expected to be an outlaw by those whom he takes seriously: his parents, friends, neighbors, teachers, clergymen, police, social workers, or judges. He must form a mental picture of himself as different from others, different in a way requiring a different vocational career and requiring that he associate with persons ostracized as he is.

This hypothesis refers to professional criminals, not to occasional lawbreakers or alcoholics, or persons who murder or steal in a passionate outbreak. It applies to those persons who belong to professional criminal societies and whose trade or occupation is criminal, with "professional" standards or skills. It is not always easy to tell which criminal is the professional and which is the amateur because many criminals have conflicting self-conceptions. And it is not easy to study the professional because he rarely goes to jail. Our jails are filled by the amateurs or neurotics, who play cops and robbers, who get a kick out of tearing up a place or doing something to get caught.

We like to think that there are two classes of occupations, the legal and the illegal, but the actual situation is not so simple. There are many gradations between the strictly honest and the strictly criminal. Many activities of business or professional men, repairmen, or governmental workers fall into criminal categories. In addition, there are other activities, not definitely criminal, nor yet definitely honest, in the shady or unethical category. Moreover, there are perfectly legal activities which are of questionable value, such as manufacturing, advertising, or selling hydrogen bombs, white flour, candy, alcohol, tobacco, patent medicines, or firearms, and which may be declared illegal in the future. Finally there are ideas which may be considered dangerous or illegal because they are new or different.

Some parents teach their children methods of stealing, but the usual delinquent cannot be explained so easily. Usually, his mother is frightened and embarrassed by his notoriety, even though she also may be secretly proud of her little rascal. This seems to be especially true of the mother whose husband is dead, divorced, or absent. The lonely mother is titillated by the adventures of her two-, three-, ten-, or twenty-year-old boy, and subtly encourages them by her exciting laughter or other reactions. Some criminals put on a "tough-baby" mask with an exaggerated masculinity.[1]

It is popular to explain socially disapproved behavior by labeling it neurotic. Suppose a man steals or damages property and finds himself waiting, terrified and yet wanting to be caught. He may experience an anxiety, like the child playing hide-and-seek, with excitement reaching a climax when he is discovered. Such a person would be a neurotic criminal. However, one can not say all criminals are neurotic, especially the one who performs his acts because he, his family, and his associates consider them proper and desirable. Furthermore, criminal law changes from time to time and is differently enforced from place to place. Betting is illegal in Chicago; legal in the suburbs. George Washington was a hero in America; a criminal in England.

III. THE SETTING: SOME FACTORS ASSOCIATED WITH CRIME

When we study criminals we find certain factors statistically associated with crime.

Most delinquents are found in the slums, yet most slum children never become delinquents. Most delinquents come from broken homes, yet most children from broken homes never become delinquents. Most delinquents are of a different racial or ethnic stock than the majority, yet race or ethnic affiliation is no guarantee of law-abiding or criminal behavior. Most delinquents are probably neurotic, but so are most non-delinquents. Most delinquents, finally, come from low-income families, but most persons with low incomes are law-abiding. A recent study of 2,000 white teenagers by Nye and Short showed that delinquency was not as closely related to income, religion, or to broken homes, as to the feeling, "My parents hate me."

Most people who steal are not professional criminals. The act of stealing something probably involves a conscious decision. But the act of becoming a professional criminal appears to involve a long series of experiences in which a pattern of behavior occurs, a drifting into an unplanned habit of life which could have only one ending. The criminal may never have made a conscious decision to enter on a career of crime.

The people living in the slums and rooming house areas of the city are different from others not only in being on the average less well educated, earning less money, having higher mortality and morbidity rates, in appearing to have a higher rate of criminality, but also in being of different ethnic, racial, or national stocks. They are the newcomers. The immigrants usually settle in the slums; they bring with them not only poverty but also opinions as to what's right and what's wrong which were appropriate in the environment from which they came. It is a crime for the newcomer in Chicago to throw his garbage out the window; but home in the South it was perfectly proper to so feed the chickens and hogs. Prohibition was incomprehensible to Europeans accustomed to wine with dinner.

The rapid growth of the factories and of the slums housing the factory workers, the high rate of immigration, and the rapid technological developments have made this country, as well as other countries of our time, an area of cultural ferment, with rapidly changing ideas of what is criminal and what is proper. What is legal today may be criminal tomorrow.

All children get into mischief. Technically, you could say they violate the law. A little boy two years old pulls down the curtains in the living room. When they fall they knock over a lamp, dust flies all over the room, and his mother, hearing the commotion, runs in from the kitchen and helps him out of difficulty. He has behaved in utter disregard for life and property and is thus a lawbreaker, but no one calls him a criminal. His mother is caring for him all the time, getting him out of the refrigerator, turning off the gas which he has turned on, rescuing his toy rabbit from the toilet bowl. Like adults, all little children err, but few become gangsters.

Not all children, especially slum children, have a mother at home caring for them. They live in the "zones of transition," called such because these areas are changing from big homes to rooming houses, from residential to business, from native citizens to immigrants, from white to Negro to Mexican and Puerto Rican. But in one way such a zone is not changing. It always has had the highest crime rate of any area in the city. When the father is sick, dead, in jail, or shut out of home because he is unable to find a job and bring home money, the mother has to work, and cannot be home supervising the children; or perhaps she is sick or doesn't like caring for children.

A very high proportion of professional criminals come from the slums. Occasionally they come from nicer neighborhoods, but here too we find the unsupervised child. The child who steals and is caught and arrested is delinquent; if he steals and is not caught or not arrested, he is not delinquent. Of course, police act more courteously to accused children of middle class or wealthy families. The policeman here says "naughty, naughty." He neither wants to give the child a record nor be sued for false arrest.

There are many ways a child may react to the fears and loneliness resulting from parental neglect. He can become a dreamer; he can become sick or develop an inferiority complex; or he can become a fighter, and demand attention, stating in effect, "Love me or fear me." The self-conception he forms is determined by the way he perceives certain crucial experiences.

IV. THE CRUCIAL EXPERIENCES

With Parents

Let's see what happens. A boy is involved in an incident during which someone is hurt or property is damaged or stolen. The injured party usually talks to the boy or his parents, and they make an amicable settlement. But sometimes the injured party feels frightened, angry with himself and his neighbors, and unable to deal with the situation alone, and so he calls the police. The boys see the police, and they all run away. One who did not run away, or was too slow, or had nothing to do with it, or has a bad reputation is caught. The parents are called in and they protect or spank the boy and everyone is satisfied. Or for some reason parents and sons are brought in for questioning. What concerns us is how the child learns that people expect him to be untrustworthy.

There are many ways parents may tell their children they are not to be trusted. They may be direct and say, "You are becoming a little hoodlum." Or they may be subtle and say, "My boy is good," and the boy knows they mean, "He is bad."

Here is an example of this. A juvenile officer was told that a fifteen-year-old boy had been committing delinquencies with a girl of his age. The girl had admitted relations with him. So the boy, accompanied by his mother, was brought in for questioning.

> POLICE OFFICER: Did you see Miss X on December 15?
> MOTHER: No, he didn't.
> POLICE OFFICER: Did you meet Miss X after school that day?
> MOTHER: No, why don't you leave him alone?
> POLICE OFFICER: Did you have relations with her?
> MOTHER: Why do you keep picking on him? He's a good boy; he would never do such a thing!
> POLICE OFFICER: Why don't you let him talk for himself. I've been asking him questions for thirty minutes and you haven't let him answer once.

Was this mother so convinced of her son's innocence? It is natural for a mother to defend her son. Her words said, "He is a good boy," but her manner said, "He can't be trusted to speak; he is either too stupid to say the right thing, or he is terribly guilty." Thus she became an accessory to the crime.

And how would the boy feel in a spot like this? "To die, to sink through the floor, where can I hide? It's even harder when she lies. Why don't the police mind their own business?"

When persons important to the child don't trust him, he may come to distrust himself. The conception of oneself as a law-violator, or just a hateful, worthless, public nuisance does not usually develop full-blown in a few minutes. We don't know precisely how it happens. Little children interact thousands of times with others, thereby learning what is expected of them. Little children of two, three, or four years like to help their mothers in the kitchen—wash the dishes, peel the potatoes, string the beans, crack the nuts, mop the floor. They like to help their father repair the clock, fix the furnace, paint the chairs, drive the car. Some mothers and fathers find this "help" more than they can bear. They tell the child, "Go away! You can't wash the dishes, you'll break them; you can't paint the furniture; you can't mop the floor, scram!"

We have observed eleven-year-old children who could not clear the table or wash a dish ("She might break them," the mother would say); and we have observed other children, five years old, who could clear the table and wash and dry the dishes. One mother expects the child to break the dishes; the other mother expects the child to do a good job. Both children do what is expected of them, and by doing so, each is developing a self-conception.

Parents are very worried when their children are destructive. One mother who asked us for help could not understand her child: "Come see for yourself; that little boy was impossible." We went to her home, and she was right. He was impossible. But he wasn't learning how to be impossible all by himself; he was getting lots of help from his mother, and from his older brothers. During the hour of the visit we heard them tell him forty times, "Don't break the wall down; don't tear up your clothes; don't scream so loud; don't sweep the floor; don't be a bad boy; don't run; don't carry the tray. For God's sake, don't be impossible!" The boy told us, "I just wanted to help, and every time I try to help they make me do it wrong." His family wanted him to be good, but they told him they expected him to be bad. It appears that some children are more likely to act as people *expect* them to act than as they want to act. How many times a day may a parent tell the child, "I expect you to be bad." One hundred? and how many times by the child's sixth birthday? One hundred thousand? Some parents are more patient and can even enjoy the child's attempts to be useful. When the child strings one bean, they say, "Thank you," because they consider the child's age when judging his craftsmanship.

What is important is not so much just what words the parents say to the child as the way they act and the way their acts are interpreted by the child. The parents may say, "You are bad," but act as though the child were the most precious object in the world. Both the words and the other feelings are communicated. So the child may feel, "I am capable, but my parents are sometimes impatient."

If neglect, cruelty, or constant criticism indicate to the child he is the least *precious* object in the world, he will learn to see himself as no good. It may happen because the child is often neglected, left uncared for, unfed. Or no one takes time for the child or every time the child wants to help wash dishes, they say, "Go away, dishes are not for you, you just make a mess." This may happen thousands of times between his second and sixth year. And one day his mother decides he is now old enough to help, and she calls him in—but now he has learned "Dishes are not for me." He refuses to help wash the dishes, or gets a headache, or has to go to the bathroom. More extreme situations, such as the parent's leaving the child alone for days at a time, or beating him frequently, convey to him a sense of his worthlessness or undesirability.

With Police

Sometimes the boy is unsupervised, out on the streets. His parents prefer earning money to staying home and taking care of him. Something happens. He borrows a friend's bicycle, rides to the grocery store, goes inside, and buys an ice cream bar. As he comes out some bigger boys, wanting to share the ice cream, are waiting for him; he runs away from them, leaving the bicycle.

Meanwhile, the owner of the bicycle starts screaming, "Someone stole my bike." Fred says, "Tommy took it. I saw him." They find Tommy. He says he left it at the grocery store, but it is no longer there. The police are called. They try to locate Tommy's parents, but they are not at home. Now it is up to the police.

Usually the policeman is friendly but firm; he has children of his own who might have done the same thing, and he wouldn't want anyone roughing them up. He tells the boy, "You're a good boy. I know it was an accident. Be more careful next time," and let him go. If he has the time and the desire, if he is well trained, if he has been assigned to that neighborhood long enough to know it well, if he is patient, the policeman will talk to the natural leaders of the boys to convert the leaders from delinquent to productive activities. The policeman knows that most leaders of boys' gangs will cooperate if they are given a chance to participate in the planning and that these leaders can influence their followers better than anyone else. Or the policeman may recognize the need for community aid for these boys and will talk to local adult leaders—the clergyman, teacher, school principal, businessman, YMCA, or Lions Club officials for the purpose of getting more supervised activities underway. A number of studies have shown that participation in supervised activities deters juvenile delinquency. Even when such facilities are available, however, some supervisors refuse to permit delinquents to participate.

Often the policeman can't do these things. He doesn't have the time or the training. Perhaps he is under strain because it has happened several

times before, or the citizen wronged is very angry or influential, or the
policeman was recently reprimanded for being lax, or another child hit him
in the ear with a snowball ten minutes earlier. Or, most important of all,
the lad is impertinent. Then our young citizen—five, ten, fifteen years
old—may be taken in and detained. The policeman may feel less likely to
get into trouble by such action. Or he may feel, "Today I am starting a boy
off on the wrong road, but I can't help it."

Until this time the boy is like all the other kids; full of energy, going
through many different kinds of activities all day long, singing, jumping,
screaming, playing cops and robbers, tearing clothes, crying, fighting—just
like everyone else. But once arrested he becomes different. He is asked
questions which imply a difference—name, father's name, religion, age,
father's occupation, nationality, race. Ordinary things become extraordinary. He never thought about such things before. He was just like
everyone else until now. He wonders about himself. He is frightened but
also may be very impressed with the whole procedure and perhaps with his
own importance. He wants his mother. He is taken to a social worker. She
is expected to ask questions. Tell me about your home, your father and
mother, the implication being something is wrong with them. She might
even go home and find out for herself. He is taken to a psychologist or
sociologist. His intelligence is measured. His emotions are wondered at. He
is taken to a judge: he hears lawyers talking about him. He is getting an
education that his brothers and sisters and neighbors never dreamed about.
Being in a detention home or jail can terrify a child. Everyone is saying,
"Something's wrong with you."

He may be interrogated. Did you ever hear a policeman interrogating
a teenager alleged to be guilty of a crime? The policeman acts and speaks
as though the prisoner is guilty. It's his duty to clear up the crime. He is
usually courteous, but sometimes he is filthy with insults, especially if the
boy is a member of an ethnic group the policeman doesn't trust:

POLICE: What were you doing at that house?
BOY: I went there to collect $5.00 a man owed me.
POLICE: Don't you know they're a pack of thieves?
BOY: I didn't know that.
POLICE: If you sleep in a stable, you will smell like—.
BOY: I just went to collect my $5.00.
POLICE: Who did you lend it to?
BOY: Fred Johnson.
POLICE: Fred Johnson! He's an old-timer. Been in jail a dozen times.
Why did you lend him $5.00?
BOY: He asked me for it. He lent me money when we were in school
together.
SECOND POLICE: Oh boy! what a tale! [*Sarcastically*] They were plan-
ning another A&P job.

BOY: I never had anything to do with any A&P. I go to Brundy
  School.
POLICE: Who went through the transom, you or Fred?
BOY: I never robbed any store in my life!
POLICE: [*All laugh*] You're a damned liar!
  [Boy cries.][2]

Some policemen treat him like a son. Others, like a step-son. The
policeman has a tough job. It sounds easy, "Just enforce law and order."
But what does he do when John Doe, age eight, is caught for the third
time stealing a bike? Scold him, let him go, arrest him? There must be an
answer.

Why should a poorly paid, often semi-trained policeman be permitted
to bear the burden of such a major decision? Many people are involved;
many should help decide—maybe a community council, including teen-
agers as well as adults. One thing the police could do to give the boy some
idea of the problems of policemen would be to invite delinquents to patrol
the city a few hours a week in a police squad car. Most cities have enough
squad cars to keep many delinquents occupied several hours a week. It
might work, properly supervised so that the officers are instructed to try to
be friendly, courteous, to explain their jobs, to listen to the problems of the
boys as a sort of get-acquainted, how-do-you-do gesture, or as a long-term
intensive activity.

In Court

The boy may be taken to court. What happens in the court room?
The state's attorney may appear if enough publicity is involved, and he
makes a speech, such as: "[Crime] by teen-agers must be stopped. The
energetic measures taken by police to deal with *these future hoodlums* will
be backed to the limit by the state's attorney's office." (In this particular
case, the judge in Boy's Court ordered bond increases from $100 to $4,000
for each of the six young men arrested.) The state's attorney continued his
speech. "Either those boys will have a chance to reflect in jail while they
are waiting trial, or their parents, through the expense of getting them out
on bond, will realize that *parental irresponsibility dosen't pay.*"[3] His speech
was longer. The boys might remember part of it, but we are sure they
would like to forget that such a prominent man considered them "future
hoodlums" and publicly proclaimed that not only they, but their parents as
well, are tainted. Could the boys think: "He's important; he says we'll be
criminals. He ought to know. I never thought I'd be a criminal; but he's a
very important man." The public doesn't expect the state's attorney to
furnish adequate homes, parents, playgrounds, and psychologists for these
boys. But the public doesn't expect him to teach these boys that they are
permanent public enemies either.

The judge at the Boy's Court has many problems. Among some boys who had been arrested for participating in a riot, two were dismissed. Here's what the newspapers said about these two: "John _____, 21, of Chicago, a laborer, and his brother, 19, of Chicago, unemployed, were dismissed. They said they merely stopped nearby to see what the trouble was and were arrested. Judge _____ told the defendants: 'We're going to give you a break. We operate on the theory that every dog is entitled to one bite.' "[4] Here were two bystanders arrested, taken to jail, and then instead of getting an apology for being inconvenienced, the judge says he will invoke a canine justice. But this is no dog's court. These boys, like the judge, are human. What can the judge do? The police say, "They are guilty—we saw them rioting." The boys say, "We broke no law." Citizens, relatives, and neighbors testify, orate, hiss, and applaud both sides. The judge doesn't know who is right or what to do. The boys are our concern here. They may get the impression: "We are not like other human beings. We are bad."

What can the judge do? The voters are angry because there was a riot; the police are angry because the boys were not convicted; the boys, because they were arrested and scolded; the judge, because he too is on public trial in a difficult situation. Because of this many judges try to protect themselves and the public by utilizing medical, sociological, psychological, or other professional advice. Sometimes, though, they lose their tempers.

The writer has no quarrel with these officials. Thousands of such items appear in the papers every year. The point is that the police, state's attorney, and judges may not lead the defendants to expect honest, law-abiding behavior of themselves. If this were the end of it, probably the defendants would go back home and be upright citizens. The suggestions from the officials that they are disreputable might not be taken seriously. But this may not be the end.

Why should a solitary judge with fifty to one hundred cases in one day be permitted to make such vital decisions? Crime hurts everyone. These decisions are too important for any one person to make.

Back Home

The boy goes back home. Whether or not he was found guilty, he is not quite like his friends any more, but is an object of curiosity: "What did they do to you?" "My lawyers defended me," he says. "I saw the judge." An object of adoration: his picture was in the paper; he has had his IQ measured; he has talked to lots of policemen. An object of scorn—he was arrested, put in jail with crooks—he is vicious. For some of his friends he is a hero; for others he must never be played with again. If he should see them, they turn away: "My mother says not to play with you. The state's attorney says you're a hoodlum."

Little boys soon forget. They play together as usual, except for those whose mothers are constantly reminding them, protecting them from the "criminal," the bad apple in the neighborhood. Then something happens again. The newspapers have a heyday. Who did it? The citizens are upset and impatient. They put pressure on the police. The police have to do something. Well, everyone knows who did it. Didn't someone just leave the detention home? Wasn't his name in the paper? It makes no difference that he was at school or visiting in another city when it happened. He is apprehended because he is convenient. He is found not guilty, but everyone suspects him just the same. He is getting a reputation, and a self-conception.

Lots of boys find their home life uncomfortable. Pick a child up off the street some night—say, at midnight. Take him home and you will see why he doesn't want to be home. His home may be physically repulsive; or it may be a lovely house but a miserable home. To say that it's the parent's fault misses the point. Most parents of delinquents are helpless, sorely in need of psychological, medical, religious, or economic aid. Responsibility lies not with irresponsible parents but with the community.

We assume that parents mean well but many just do not have the energy and skills necessary to win the confidence of their children and to make plans together. Parents expect their children to mature gradually and become independent. That this can be done gracefully is proved by many happy parents who help their children settle on their own. Even in the better neighborhoods a barrier often develops between the parents and children. Most children on the street go home after a while and play inside, but some can't go home. In many instances help for the parents would prevent a child from going to the street.

On the Street

Our young citizen may find friends on the street where things are more pleasant, where he can be a hero. We assume everyone wants to be liked; everyone wants a word of praise, and if it is not available at home and is available on the street, then one goes to the street. A little boy knows where he is afraid to breathe and where he is a regular guy like all the rest.

The boys he plays with on the street may like to play volleyball. They have a volleyball and play all the time. They don't get into trouble. Or they may not have a volleyball. Slum children have less equipment than other children. What can you do on the street?

Everyone needs someone to idealize, someone to be like, someone to dream he is like. These street children could idealize their parents, but it is not likely since they don't enjoy their parents. Their hero could be a policeman who saves a man's life; but not if the policeman hurts them or depreciates them. We don't know enough about whom the street boys idealize. Maybe it's a famous boxer who can beat anyone in the whole world; or a cowboy movie star. These boys can't be cowboys; but they can fight, they can be brave, not afraid of their parents, not afraid of the police. They can learn to be tough.

If the street boy could get along with his mother, he might be home with her, learning to keep his room straight: "Freddie, hang up your clothes. Freddie, wash your hands; Freddie, shine your shoes this minute. Freddie, here's some new crayons. That's a sweet boy." His mother cannot be at ease until she knows he is responding to her attempts at socialization.

The boys on the street are learning a different moral code: Who can throw the stone the straightest. Who can run faster. Who is a sissy. Who can do things and not get caught. Hundreds of times a day a boy is learning the code of the street: Be loyal to friends—never betray a comrade. Find out who you can trust. Avoid the police.

Street boys go to school. The teacher knows they have been in trouble and if anything out of the ordinary occurs in the classroom, she knows who is to blame. Even if they are not really to blame, she can guess who were the agitators. Because the street boys have more than average trouble at home, they may be more restless than the average pupils and not perform well in school. You can't want to please a teacher if this makes you a sissy, especially if this teacher is always picking on you or your friends. The teacher is not going to be his ideal or model. She could if she had a class of fifteen children instead of thirty to sixty and if her salary made it unnecessary to hold down an extra job or two, and if teachers had high morale, and if she had time to consult with parents, social workers, religious workers, a physician, a psychologist, a reading specialist, to discuss the boy's problems, and if she had professional training and attitudes. Sometimes she can do it without all these. But aren't we foolish to expect miracles of semitrained overworked teachers?

It takes most people years to settle down to one ego ideal. Little boys play at being policemen or cowboys or gangsters. When they are growing up they decide to be truck drivers or ambulance drivers or doctors. In school they want to be teachers or janitors or a principal or the coach. In college they want to be lawyers or scientists or philosophers or business-men. After they leave college, they are deciding one day this, one day that. Who do I want to be like? What am I going to do? It takes years for the average citizen to decide.

Lots of people are helping the street boy to decide on his career. His mother and father and his home life are unbearable to him, so he joins the street boys. His friends on the street give him fellowship and praise for doing a good job. His teacher tells him he is too jumpy. The police suggest that he is a liar. The social worker suggests his family is tainted. The psychologist tells him he is not like other boys. The judge says, "Every dog deserves one bite." The state's attorney says, "You are the future hoodlums." Can one's career be that of a hoodlum?

Reform School

One day he is arrested, found guilty and goes to reform school. He is frightened and angry. He wishes he were home. He wants out: "Who are my friends and who are enemies?" He learns that some of the inmates are regular guys; others snitch on you. The guards, the hired hands around the place, can't be trusted; they are against you. "What are you here for?" a friend asks. "I grabbed a pocketbook and ran." "Is that all? Boy! I robbed five filling stations! You know that kid with the glasses, the tall blond one? He killed a policeman! When he says something, you'd better jump."

How do you rob a filling station? What do you do with the tires? Which lawyers will help you if you get caught? Which is the easiest way to rob the A&P? How do you steal a car? Where can you sell it? Who buys the parts? How can you be successful? This sounds like an exciting career. He never realized so many people are in this business. The reform school teaches much about crime, but little about reform.

The guards are afraid the boys will run away, hurt each other or hurt the guards. The superintendent has his job to do. He has to keep the boys clean, working, in school, has to buy the groceries, get a new psychologist to replace the one leaving for a better job, get three new attendants, make out dozens of reports, read what the wardens at other schools are doing, go to meetings, see visitors from the Rotary Club, decide what to do about a boy who is always fighting. If he is strict, the boys hate him more. If he is less strict, the place gets dirty and citizens complain; newspapers take pictures. There is never enough money. The superintendent does what he can. The boys are learning a career. They can't help it, and he can't help it. And the respectable citizens back home are not aware of the fact that they are paying $500 to $5,000 per year to train each child to become a more professional criminal. Foster homes may be a better risk, especially if foster parents get special training in ways to handle these children; however it's hard to find parents who will take disturbed children.

After Reform School

When the boy leaves the reform school, he goes home. He has been a disgrace to the family, and his welcome is thin: "Your mother is ashamed to walk down the street!" "We hope they reformed you." He is now perhaps nine, twelve, or fifteen years old. His sister says, "You have ruined my life." He wonders who his friends are. Maybe a brother is friendly to him. Maybe his mother. She gives him a new necktie. But can she give him what will save him from the electric chair or from a life sentence? If she can give him the trust and patience and ability to be responsible, and skill in holding a job—what every boy needs much and he needs immensely—she can save him. Usually she cannot, any more than she could before reform school. If he is to be helped, it will be by foster parents or officials of the institutional kingdoms, school, church, scouts, PTA, settlement house, working as an integrated unit. Today these kingdoms often work in competition and at odds with one another.

It is easy in the neighborhood to tell who can be trusted. Plenty of guys make nasty remarks. They go to school; they go to Sunday school; they brush their teeth and say, "Good afternoon," to the corner policeman. When their mothers see the returned "criminal" in the drug store, they say: "Look who's out! If I see my boy playing with you I'll call the police. Stay away." You can understand that such mothers are trying to protect their own boys. But they are helping another boy to become a criminal. If good boys won't play with him, who will? Underworld characters?

Other mothers don't know much about him. They are working or sick or preoccupied. Their sons are the street boys. The boys want to know about reform school. Did they beat you? Let me show you what I learned. Let's pull a job tonight. I'll show you how to do it. I can chin with one hand.

He has to go to school. That's the law. The principal talks to him, the teacher talks to him, some kids talk to him, and what they say adds up to one thing: They are not his friends. They expect him to start something. It doesn't have to be that way. They could invite him to join the Scouts, or write on the school paper, or sing in the choir, or play on the team. If they did, it might save him.

His mother wants him to go to church. She has talked to the clergyman, who says he needs religion. He may not be as clean, as well dressed as the next boy—or he may be cleaner. The boy out of reform school wonders how his new clothes look. They feel strange. The people in Sunday school may not feel hostile toward him, but they are strangers. One looks at him in a friendly way; another says, "He just got out of reform school."

There is still a chance he won't go back to reform school or graduate into prison, but the chance is slim. Let a window be broken, a store burglarized, a car stolen, and the neighbors will know who to blame. A nice neighborhood finds it easy to blame someone for its troubles, not only because the accused may be guilty, but because he is the one expected to perform such acts in this community. If he does not expect of himself what they expect of him, he will go straight, perhaps leaving the community, perhaps even changing the community, but that is unlikely.

Even after he comes to expect vicious or criminal behavior of himself, he may still act like a good citizen most of the time. But it appears that the self-concept, the picture of himself inside, is more powerful than anything else in determining his behavior. Here is part of an interview between a prisoner and a prison counselor to illustrate this:

PRISONER: Why do I keep getting in trouble? I want to go straight, but I'll go out and before you know it I'm with the same crowd. I know it's wrong and yet there I am.

COUNSELOR: Maybe you are forced back to the old crowd.[5] Have you ever been treated like an ex-con?

PRISONER: I was going with a girl and couldn't get the nerve to tell her I'd been in the pen. I knew she'd find out sooner or later. I finally did in a way. I took to drinking.

COUNSELOR: You had to. It's too much to bear. You knew she wouldn't understand.

PRISONER: I began to hate her. She kept asking what was wrong and all that. In fact I don't think I minded it too much when I had to leave her, knowing what she would think of me.

COUNSELOR: It's hard to love a person when you expect her to hate you.

PRISONER: You know, she still comes to see me, so I was wrong about how she would feel.

The prisoner could not bring himself to tell his girl friend that he had been in jail for fear that she would hate him. Since it was not true that she hated him, we must conclude that the hatred was in himself, that he hated himself because he felt he was a criminal or because he expected her to hate him because he was a criminal. Of course, it is difficult for one who has been arrested many times to feel, "I'm an honest and respected man." He wanted to go straight but felt he was not honest. In not telling the girl, he was in fact dishonest. If he had felt he was an honest man, it would have been much easier for him to say, "I was convicted of a crime and spent some time in jail, but now I am honest." But his self-conception must have been: "I'm a criminal. She would hate criminals like everyone else hates them, perhaps even as I myself do. So I can't tell her." With such a self-conception, he could not be comfortable around law-abiding citizens.

Gradually, over the years, if he comes to expect of himself what his neighbors expect of him, he becomes a professional criminal. But if along the way he can find satisfactions and social approval from legitimate activities, he will obey the law. When he has learned over and over again that he can find no satisfaction this way, he welcomes the greetings of his professional associates in the underworld. As a professional criminal, he has standards of performance to live up to, friends who will help him when in trouble, visit him in prison, send him presents at Christmas, give him a home when he is sick, tell him where the police are lax and where strict—hideouts, fences, and lawyers. At twelve, fourteen, sixteen, or eighteen he has come to a conclusion about his career that ordinary boys may not make until they are twenty or even forty. And he could not have drifted into this career without the help of his family and neighbors who sought a scapegoat and unwittingly suggested to him that he become an outlaw.

V. IMPLICATIONS

When a crime is committed in a community, it is, in a sense, caused by everyone. No one grows up and lives alone; the criminal grows up with people. He is affected by his social experiences. If he wants to murder, people have made him want to murder; if he wants to break school windows, his environment has taught him how and given him a reason. And if he is punished by the community, it is because the community feels guilty for his crime, for failing to provide positive experiences in schools, for not protecting him from severe cruelty, neglect, starvation, and rejection. Those in the community who most demand his punishment are usually those who feel most guilty for their own failures, real or imaginary. They punish the criminal as they have been punished themselves. If they could forgive themselves, accept themselves, they could forgive the delinquent, accept and teach him, and, in so doing, convert him before he becomes a hardened unconvertible criminal. This conversion process is usually too big a job for any one school, teacher, policeman, judge, psychologist or social worker. It takes many people to make an ordinary little boy into a hardened criminal. It will take a lot of people to make a criminal into a good citizen. Every little boy or girl in trouble should be examined by a physician, a psychologist, a reading specialist, a social worker, and his home and neighborhood should be studied. Intelligent steps can then be taken by this team of people working with the community council, with the cooperation of the boy and taking into consideration his preferences, to give this boy what everybody needs: security, affection, adventure, a chance to get recognition, to learn, and to give to others the best that he has to give.

Every city and hamlet has some special programs for handling delinquents. Every program in every city is different from the next. Naturally, some are more effective than others. Study and systematic evaluation of these programs are required to find out what works and what does not.

Statistics show considerable increase in juvenile crime, just as they show increase in divorce rate. This is not clear evidence of increase in juvenile crime or in broken marriages. The first could be a result of more accurate reporting or because there are more policemen; the second, of greater resort to legal processes because there is more money for divorce lawyers. In a rural community or village where everyone is known, the community is aware when a child takes another child's bicycle and tries private means to have it returned. No police are notified. In the secular, impersonal, anonymous city, a bicycle theft is more likely to be reported to the police. As our society becomes more secular, the official agencies are used more often. Two hundred years ago, divorce was rare: When a couple could not get along they either separated, the husband left, the wife ran away, they lived together but did not speak to one another, or they took lovers. The rise in the divorce rate does not necessarily mean a rise in unsuccessful marriages. In a friendly neighborhood, when children at play break a window, the parents may talk it over and decide who pays; but in an anonymous neighborhood, they may call the police. The two misdeeds are the same, but the "crime rate" is higher in one place than another.

PUNISHMENT

Sometimes a youth commits a crime which so angers the community that letting him go without "punishment" is impossible. Punishment in our society is either a fine, imprisonment, or the death penalty. There are no other punishments within our legal system. When I ask some of my legal advisers why we might not try out some other forms of punishment, they ask me to name one. I name several: for the youth who breaks windows and street lights, let him pick up glass and other debris from the streets for a few days. For the youth who breaks someone's jaw, let him take care of patients who have been injured. For those bigots who have been involved in racial demonstrations, let them meet with bigots on the other side. The attorney said about picking up debris, "That would be involuntary servitude, which would be illegal." I asked about prisoners in jails who work for 15 cents a day. They are not forced to work. If they don't work they don't get the 15 cents a day they need for cigarettes and candy." How about asking the tough to pick up debris or work in a hospital? My lawyer said "No."

The problem is that what punishment is to one may be reward to another. Sending a person to jail may be just what he has been hoping for, an opportunity to get away from his mother or wife or gang, relax, and get three square meals a day.

A good deal of evidence is accumulating to show that the majority of juvenile delinquents and criminals have been neglected or otherwise punished as infants and children. What will reduce crime, therefore, will be prevention of such punishment of these infants and small children, for it seems that by the age of four or five a child may believe "I am no good; people are no good; it is a dog-eat-dog world, and I'll take what I can get. The only mistake is getting caught." Those of us who assume that delinquency is an act of free will might contemplate this: We know a great deal about how persons become delinquent, and how delinquents may be converted into law-abiding citizens.[6] We know that if someone accepts the delinquent and is sufficiently persuasive in attempts to redirect him, the delinquent may discover a new self and a new model to follow. We know that if the delinquent is educated and trained in salable skills, and if opportunities for dignified work at acceptable wages are available, he will go to work.

If we know how to turn a delinquent into a law-abiding citizen—by voting more money for schools and for mental health research, by helping the Boy Scouts and the Girl Scouts, by providing parks and playgrounds supervised by professionally trained personnel, by volunteering our services as tutor or referee or big brother, by helping the parents of the potentially delinquent find suitable training and jobs—if we know this and refuse to act, arguments about free will fall on deaf ears. If we are free to cure the delinquent and do not, how ghastly incredible is our crime. Only determinism theory exonerates us: We are not free to change the delinquent even though we know how, just as he is not free to change himself unless we help him.

FOOTNOTES:

[1] See M. K. Bacon, Irvin L. Child, and Herbert Barry III, "A Cross-Cultural Study of Correlates of Crime," *Journal of Abnormal and Social Psychology*, LXVI (1963), 291–300.

[2] This dialogue is quoted verbatim. Only names and obscenity are changed. The writer is grateful to many policemen in Chicago and prison officials in New York whose cooperation helped to formulate the ideas here.

[3] Chicago Sunday *Tribune*, August 23, 1953, part 1, p. 25.

[4] Chicago *Daily News*, August 17, 1953, p. 3.

[5] In trying to be sympathetic, the counselor may be destructive. He suggests that the prisoner is not responsible for his behavior. A more constructive response would be, "Let's outline activities you can do when you leave the prison," although this would not be successful until the prisoner and counselor are involved with one another.

[6] See William Glasser, *Reality Therapy* (New York: Harper and Row, 1965) for a description of highly skilled teams that convert the most delinquent girls and 20-year veterans of psychoses into responsible citizens.

39   Teachers' and Clinicians' Attitudes Toward the Behavior Problems of Children: A Reappraisal*

BY HARRY BEILIN[1]

EDITOR'S NOTE: *Since 1927, teachers have come to more closely approximate the attitudes of clinicians when it comes to ranking behavior problems of children. If we are to more effectively identify, diagnose, and assist students with behavior problems of one sort or other, we must first of all have some agreement as to what is and what is not a problem. Dr. Beilin cites research evidence which has tracked teachers' and clinicians' attitudes over the years and speculates about why there were differences in the first place and why there seem to be fewer now.*

The contrast between contemporary American education and that of 40 or 50 years ago is striking in at least one respect, the influence of psychology, in particular, clinical psychology.[2] It would require little effort to detail the many and diverse ways teacher training, parent education and child care reflect the consequences of psychology's influence. The future historian will undoubtedly dwell upon the part played by E. K. Wickman's 1928 Commonwealth Fund monograph, "Children's Behavior and Teachers' Attitudes" in this development (43). Wickman's report, which contrasts teachers' and "mental hygienists'" attitudes toward the behavior problems of children evoked an assault upon the teacher's mode of dealing with children when it made evident that teachers' attitudes were widely at

---

* Reprinted and abridged from *Child Development*, 1959, Vol. 30, 9–25, by permission of the author and the Society for Research in Child Development.

477

variance with those of clinicians. The effect of its publication is still felt. The contiguity of events might suggest to some a causal relationship between widespread knowledge of the Wickman findings and the emergence of clinical psychology as a force in contemporary education. However, a more temperate and realistic appraisal would accept the ubiquitous penetration of psychology into American life and not as a condition unique to education. The impact of the monograph was in actuality only one of a series of challenges to the values and attitudes of educational personnel. But irrespective of its true role—whether as reflection, or as initiator of a Zeitgeist—the place of the Wickman study in education and child psychology has been significant and will probably continue to be.

Wickman's results, in the main, suggested that mental hygienists were primarily concerned with *withdrawing* and other nonsocial forms of behavior in children of elementary school age, whereas teachers of these same children were more concerned with *classroom management, authority,* and *sex problems.* The results influenced many (starting with Wickman) to urge teachers to adopt a hierarchy of attitudes closer to that of the clinician. This view presumed that the clinician's judgment should be accepted as the criterion for adequate and inadequate behavior. Few have challenged this thesis.

The intent of the present review is to examine what the result of 30 years of research suggests for continued accceptance of this point of view. To anticipate, it will be suggested that Wickman's findings be reinterpreted and his prescription for change in educational policy modified.

THE WICKMAN STUDY

The Wickman studies were begun in Minneapolis in 1924, but a more ambitious program was undertaken in Cleveland in 1925–1926, where the following was done:

1. In a single pilot school, teachers' characterizations of undesirable behavior, with indications of "sensitiveness" to their occurrence, were elicited by questionnaire.

2. Teachers' attitudes toward various types of problems were obtained by three measures (detailed in part below).

3. On rating scales, teachers noted their reactions to problems themselves, then to pupils in whom the problems were observed, and finally to the total adjustment of their pupils.

4. Subsequently, the teachers from 13 schools in six communities and two additional teacher groups enrolled in graduate school were studied using the rating scale method developed for the pilot study. The most important feature of this involved the rating of a number of behaviors obtained from the teachers' original freely-given characterizations of prob-

lem behavior. The results are reported as mean ratings and rankings of mean ratings.

5. Finally, 30 "mental hygienists" (8 psychiatrists, 4 psychologists, 13 psychiatric social workers and 5 teachers with social work background) from child guidance clinics in three cities were studied for their attitudes toward 50 of the same behaviors rated by teachers. The mean ratings and rankings of ratings were then contrasted and correlated with those of teachers.

The rating instructions for teachers stressed: (a) *present* problems, (b) "seriousness" of the problems or "difficulties" created by them, and (c) rapid responses to the rating scale. With clinicians, the emphasis was on (a) relevance of the problem behavior for *future* adjustment, (b) though "seriousness" and "difficulty" were retained, the focus was on the "importance" of the behavior, and (c) no time limit was imposed for response to the rating scale.

The principal results can be summarized as follows:

1. Teachers were most aware of overt and aggressive behaviors, inattention to school tasks, and behaviors which violated their standards of morality. They were much less concerned with behaviors indicative of social or emotional maladjustment not directly related to school routine.

2. Boys were reported more frequently than girls for behavior problems.

3. Teachers preferred the less active, more compliant behavior of girls to the more aggressive behavior of boys. Desirable conduct for teachers, then, took on the distinguishing characteristics of girl behavior.

4. "Mental hygienists" considered withdrawing and other nonsocial forms of behavior most serious and discounted the teachers' stress on antisocial behavior and violations of school rules.

5. There was a rank order correlation of $-.22$ between the rankings by mental hygienists of 50 behavior problems and the original Cleveland teachers' ($N = 28$) rankings of the same behaviors. The correlation was $-.11$ when the full sample was used ($N-511$).

These findings were interpreted by Wickman in Thorndikian stimulus-response terms. The teachers distinguish, he said, between the attacking and withdrawing types of behavior problems. Their attitudes are principally determined, however, by the attacking nature of the child's conduct. The aggressive behaviors are identified and considered more serious because the teacher is aroused to counterattack by virtue of the frustration in him. On the other hand, the responses to withdrawing forms of behavior are modified by sympathy and protective feelings.

On the basis of these findings Wickman then proposed that:

1. Teachers' attitudes should be influenced to become more like the "ideal" clinicians. (Clinicians' attitudes are considered ideal because their

judgments are (ostensibly) based upon knowledge of research in child adjustment.)

2. Teacher attitudes should be changed not by exhortation but by (a) information about child behavior through seminars and other learning experiences; and (b) practice in therapy with children.

3. Teachers' functions be less concerned with intellectual learnings and more with life adjustment.

After the appearance of the 1928 monograph some serious limitations in method and conception were pointed out by G. Watson (42) in a critical note[3] which are as cogent now as when first offered. The majority of efforts to rectify the deficiencies have concerned only some of the criticisms. The others, however, may be of as great issue as those treated.

Watson's objections were:
1. *The procedures themselves are open to criticism.*
a. The directions given teachers and clinicians were not the same. Teachers were instructed to rank behaviors for *present* seriousness; clinicians, for *future* adjustment.
b. The time given to respond to the questionnaires was not identical. Teachers were under the control of the experimenter; clinicians were allowed an extended period to respond.
c. No definitions were given for the behavioral terms to be rated leaving to each subject the interpretation of the terms, and thus further reducing comparability of the results.

The issues raised by Watson's concern with methodology are intimately related to other criticisms.

2. *The choice of mental hygienists' attitudes toward the behavior problems of children as a criterion for evaluating teachers' attitudes toward the same problems is open to question.*

The Wickman study and others that follow (though not all) accept the clinicians' judgments as a criterion either implicitly or explicitly. Watson observes that there is no reason to suppose clinicians to be "correct" and teachers not, rather than vice versa. Wickman is questioned for not even considering this possibility.

3. *There has been too ready an acceptance of a causal relationship between withdrawing behavior in childhood and maladjustment in adulthood.*

In addition to questioning whether the term "withdrawing" means the same thing to teachers and clinicians, Watson questioned whether withdrawing behavior in childhood is causally related to, or predictive of, maladjustment in adulthood. Although this is contended in more than one theoretical position, there was very little evidence for the validity of this claim in 1928, and little more is available now. In Watson's paper there is reference to a pilot study which, for all its limitations, casts some doubt on the aforementioned assumption.

THE LITERATURE

After the Watson critique there was concern for the validity of the results and replications were undertaken with one or another modification in design, ultimately making comparability difficult.[4]

The studies, in the main, fall into the following groupings according to procedures used:

A. *Studies Employing Descriptions of Problem Behavior*

    1. Teacher nomination of children with problems, followed by description and classification of problem behaviors (3, 5, 16, 26, 41).
      a. In addition to all or part of the above, some use is made of a rating scale of problem behaviors (7, 14, 22, 23, 33, 40, 45, 46).
    2. Teacher description of problem behavior (with no reference to specific children) from which a rating scale is developed or the descriptions themselves are used (9, 10, 20, 32, 37, 39, 43).
    3. Children identified and described as problems by a social or therapeutic agency (6, 29).

B. *Studies Employing the Wickman Rating Scales*

    1. With Wickman's directions (1, 18, 31).
    2. With modifications of Wickman's directions (13, 17, 24, 34, 35, 36).

Confirmation of Wickman findings. . . . Holding the question of the validity of Wickman's methodology aside for the moment, [we would conclude from a number of studies (1, 7, 10, 12, 14, 15, 20, 31, 33, 39, 45, 46) that there is] considerable evidence to indicate agreement with Wickman's original findings. Furthermore, there has been an observable shift in the intervening years in the attitudes of teachers in the direction of being more like those of "mental hygienists." In spite of greater congruence, however, a sizeable difference remains between the attitudes of teachers and clinicians toward behavior problems of children.

The methodical issue. Modifications as a rule have aimed at introducing uniformity in the administration of the problem rating scales. This has meant either modifying the directions given clinicians or teachers so that both groups could respond under the same stimulus conditions. . . .

[From several studies (3, 13, 17, 24, 34, 35, 36, 40)] it appears that the differences in directions that were a part of the Wickman procedure quite clearly contributed to the differences demonstrated between teachers and mental hygienists. When this is controlled, however, differences still emerge and these are of the kind originally observed.

It is also apparent that there has been a change in the direction of greater congruence between the attitudes of teachers and clinicians. That that congruence is not consistent for all levels of teachers has been made explicit in recent studies. It is likely that differences between elementary and secondary teachers have always existed vis-à-vis the matters here reviewed, but, where teacher and clinician attitudes appear to be the same, differences in meaning may still attach to the behaviors.

Teacher "expertness."   The specific criteria employed by teachers and clinicians in assessing maladjustment in children have been mentioned. As already indicated, most investigators have shown teachers to be most concerned with children's behaviors that are *aggressive, disruptive of school routines,* or generally reflecting *lack of interest in school activities.* In addition, teachers are, or have been, less concerned with withdrawing and other nonsocial behaviors. Some investigators have characterized this as indicative of a middle class value pattern; e.g., *stealing* is the teacher's consistent concern in MacClenathan's (22) study. The emphasis upon these school disrupting traits has not been unanimous, however. Peck (26) found *undesirable personality traits* to be the greatest concern of the teacher, *regressive* traits somewhat less so, and *aggressive* behaviors least. Of only moderate import were *violations of school work demands.* Clark (9) differs from the usual view, too, in concluding that teachers are actually more annoyed by children's behaviors which annoy other children than by behaviors which affect teachers themselves.

In most of the cited studies it is implied or explicitly stated that the teacher is "wrong" in reacting as she does to the problems of children. Teachers have been criticized as untutored in the scientific facts concerning child development and are thus seen as generally being incapable of assessing children's adjustment.

Stewart (38) rejects this thesis. With 184 boys and 193 girls as subjects, a comparison was made between ratings of problem students and non-problem students. Identification was also attempted of those with and without "whole life" problems. From ratings of these youngsters she concludes that teachers are capable of distinguishing between problems as school problems or "whole life" problems. She insists that teachers possess much more insight into children's behavior than they are credited with by some investigators.

In spite of the few studies that report different patterns of teachers' attitudes, the hierarchy of attitudes seems to be quite close to Wickman's formulation. The Stewart report is important not so much because it rejects this hierarchy but rather in its highlighting the difference between clinicians and teachers as not being a matter of ignorance. What the difference is attributable to remains to be discussed.

Sex differences.   There seems to be universal agreement that boys are more likely to be identified as maladjusted or behavior problems than girls (6, 7, 14, 15, 16, 18, 23, 25, 26, 29, 33, 43, 45, 47). The proportion of boys (in contrast to girls) so identified ranges in these reports from 66 to 88 per cent. Not only is there a difference in proportion but behaviors which form the bases for these identifications are in part different for each sex (5, 14, 43). Ullmann's (47) interpretation is of some interest. It is *not*, he says, that "desirable conduct for teachers takes the distinguishing characteristics of girl behavior as suggested by Wickman but rather teachers assign girls more favorable ratings because they lack awareness of the manner in which girls are making their adjustment" (p. 39). Ullmann explains that boys' patterns of adjustment are more manifest to the observer, whereas girls deal with problems on an intrapsychic level. This interpretation is in the tradition of imputing lack of insight to teachers. Stewart's (38) results are again cogent. Her data do not suggest that teachers lack insight into their adjustment, but rather that they distinguish a different *kind* of adjustment for girls. Another study with young adults suggests the same (5). In this instance, sex differences in degree of adjustment are supplemented by differences in the types of behavior identified with the maladjustments of each sex.

Why should the nature of adjustment be different for boys and girls? Whatever the *ultimate* reasons (whether biological or social), the temptation is to say that the differences, in an *immediate* sense at least, result from different *expectations*. It is evident from the cited studies that boys and girls are expected to act in prescribed ways in our culture. The reasons girls are considered better adjusted by teachers is that teachers have certain expectations of what good adjustment *in school* should be and the prescription for girls' adjustment is more consistent with these expectations than the prescription for boys' good adjustment. As Wickman makes evident, the teacher is concerned with getting what she is teaching "across," and behaviors which facilitate this are more likely to be valued. The behaviors of girls are of this kind.

This approach is more acceptable to us, from the evidence, than the interpretation that teachers' attitudes are based on a lack of sophistication.

There is some evidence that men and women teachers evaluate the problems of children differently. Women are found by one investigator to rate problem behaviors as more serious than do men (13). Another study (17) reports, however, that specific problem behaviors are treated differently by each sex. Men teachers consider *sex* problems as less serious than do women; women consider *appearance* and *destruction of property* as less serious than do men. Others (4, 37) report similar findings, although in the former case it is emphasized that the similarities are greater than the differences.

Age and grade influences. The sixth grade appears to be modal for the nomination of children with problems, with the first and second grades offering the least. The fifth, seventh, and eighth grades also give the teacher some difficulty (16, 18, 23, 33). Differences in maladjustments of elementary and secondary school youngsters were reported early in the literature (16) and somewhat neglected till recently. Hildreth (16) observed that maladjusted elementary school children are more likely to be identified as *unstable, nervous,* or *shy;* the secondary school pupil, as *aggressive* or demonstrating *poor study habits.* Peck (26) finds the differential effect of sex of students in these identifications, however. Grade differences in problem type are reported by others as well (5, 36, 37). The differences found by Stouffer (36) have already been described. Griffiths (15) states that certain behavior difficulties (as reported by teachers and parents) increase with age; others decrease.

Socioeconomic status. There are limited data relating socioeconomic status of the child to his identification as a problem. Levy (21) finds "socially high grade children have personality or emotional problems . . . children of lower classes have social problems" (p. 158). Yourman (46) reports a larger proportion of problem children are of lower socioeconomic status. Snyder (33) found that schools differentiated by their level of socioeconomic status yielded different numbers of problems with more from the lower groups. There was no statistically significant difference, however, in socioeconomic status between a problem group and a control group.

The study by Griffiths (15) makes the most ambitious attempt to relate socioeconomic status to the identification of behavior problems. There were few significant differences among children of different socioeconomic levels in teachers' ratings of their problems. More differences appear, however, according to the parents' ratings and the child's own ratings. Griffiths concludes that some differences exist between middle socioeconomic level children and others. In particular, they are more submissive and less aggressive.

It is apparent that few data are available as to the relationship between socioeconomic status and the behavior problems of children.

DISCUSSION

The studies reviewed suggest strongly that differences in teachers' and clinicians' attitudes existed in 1927. From that time to the present changes appear to have taken place among teachers' attitudes so that they approximate more closely those of clinicians. There is some possibility that clinicians have tempered their evaluations as well.

Despite the shift toward congruence, teachers' attitudes remain different, and different in ways not dissimilar from what they were in Wickman's day. Why? First, let us recall that Wickman and others made much of this difference. It was suggested, even insisted, that the teacher should change. Such an injunction could rest only on the premise that the clinician's attitudes were more legitimate or more correct. This view was accepted though G. Watson was the first and not the last to question it. Watson's position was not that the clinician was necessarily incorrect or that he should not serve as a criterion. Rather, Wickman was chided for not even considering the alternatives to accepting the clinician as criterion. For Wickman, the virtue of choosing the clinicians' attitudes as an ideal was recommended by his expert knowledge of children's adjustment. Let us examine this claim.

For one, Wickman asked clinicians to rate behaviors in light of their possible future consequences. Would the clinician, with any validity, know the future consequences of the appearance of a behavior in childhood? The answer is doubtful. In 1927 there were few if any studies which had indicated with even low degrees of certainty the outcome in adolescence or adulthood of a child's particular behavior (e.g., *withdrawing* behavior). In fact, if anything, there was some doubt that this could be done (27, 42). Evidence since then leads to even greater uncertainty (2, 19). According to some theories a withdrawn child is more likely to become maladjusted than one who is not. Yet the proof of how true this is and in what proportion for any population is almost non-existent. Although it has been shown that in an adult *psychotic* group (44) there was a tendency for maladjustive behaviors to be present in childhood (information was obtained from retrospective reports), this tells us little about the prevalence of withdrawing behavior in a population of children or about the likelihood of such behaviors resulting in maladjustment, neurosis, or psychosis in adulthood.

However, there is a more important issue, in light of the functions of the therapist qua therapist: withdrawing behaviors present a problem to be dealt with at the time of their appearance. Such behaviors can be a basis for a visit to a therapist—in childhood as well as adulthood. The clinician is more likely to attempt some therapy than to postpone action till adolescence or adulthood (although, in some instances, this might reasonably be done). The clinician is often forced to act by immediate criteria; for he cannot wait for ultimate validation. It is thus part of his role as a therapist to be concerned about these behaviors. In essence, the behaviors with which a clinician is concerned are related to his status and the functions that accompany that status. If these behaviors were of equal relevance to the functions of the teacher, they would be equally valued. However, they are not. This has been so even in the period of "life-adjustment" programs and through the era of the "whole child," except possibly for some special groups of teachers. In spite of much pressure, teachers on the whole continue to be concerned with behaviors that facilitate or interfere with their teaching. A number of investigators recognize the difference in function between clinician and teacher (11, 16, 22, 31, 38, 42, 46) even though the teacher's role is not simple to define. It is, after all, a reflection of an educational philosophy. The prevailing philosophy of education in 1927, whether explicit or implicit, was oriented to the training of intellectual skills. In the interim the function of the teacher has broadened considerably to include training in social and other skill. There has been much pressure on the teacher to be a counselor and in some ways something of a psychotherapist as well—but, at the least, to focus more on the emotional life and adjustment of the child. The question of which role is "better" is a question of values. At present, the trend is back again toward the training of intellectual skills. The trend of increasing teacher sophistication in psychology will probably continue, and will probably not revert to the level of 1927. To urge (e.g., 35, 36) that the teacher's attitudes approximate the clinician's is unrealistic unless the teacher's role becomes one with the clinician—and this seems unlikely.

Other considerations recommend themselves as well. The teacher has a vital role in the socialization of the child. She is, after all, a culture carrier and to some extent a parental surrogate. Her own behaviors are significant in the child's development of self-control, character traits, values, and work habits. These functions are certainly as important as any. There is no question that the teacher needs to be aware of withdrawing and other undesirable personality characteristics. What is questioned is the need for the teacher to concern herself with them to the same extent and in the same way as the clinician.

To summarize, the difference reported by Wickman in attitudes toward the behavior problems of children should be interpreted as reflecting differences in the roles of teachers and clinicians and the discharge of functions of the role incumbents (8, 30). The efforts of many have been directed to alter the prescription of the teacher's role and performance in this role. The effort has in part been successful, as witnessed by the greater congruence in attitudes between teacher and clinician. In spite of the partial change in prescription, the teacher's role remains principally task-oriented; the clinician's, more adjustment-oriented. It seems unrealistic and possibly even undesirable to expect the teacher's behaviors reflected in her attitudes and values to become congruent with those of clinicians. Other results reviewed here are consistent with this thesis. The reported disparity between elementary and secondary teachers results from differences in role. The high school teacher is even more subject matter-oriented than the elementary school teacher. The greatest impact of the "child-oriented" or "life-adjustment" philosophy in turn has been in the elementary school. This has resulted in a modification of role prescription for the elementary school teacher which is reflected in greater similarity between the attitudinal hierarchies of elementary teachers and clinicians. The observed differences are due not only to the teacher's role but result from the actions of the children themselves. The pupil's role-related behaviors change with progress through school as the youngster assumes new responsibilities and loses old ones. Behavior differences are not only bound to their age but also their sex. The same behavior is not expected or demanded of boys and girls. The attitudes of teachers in turn will reflect differences in age and sex role expectations.

SUMMARY AND CONCLUSIONS

The studies concerning teachers' and clinicians' attitudes toward the behavior problems of children, which have emerged principally from the initiative of the Wickman 1928 monograph, are reviewed. The following conclusions are drawn:

1. Differences existed in 1927 between the attitudes of teachers and clinicians toward the behavior problems of children. This seems to have been true in spite of the methodological limitations of the Wickman study.

2. Since 1927 there has been a shift in the hierarchy of teachers' attitudes to approximate more closely those of clinicians. This shift is not due to an artifact of research methodology. Those studies which incorporate adequate controls and consistent instructions show even greater congruence between the attitudes of the two groups.

3. There has been some change in the attitudes of clinicians although this is based upon the conclusions of one study.

4. Criteria employed in evaluating the behavior problems of children differ for elementary and secondary school teachers.

5. More boys are identified as maladjusted than girls and the criteria of maladjustment (and adjustment) differ in part for each sex.

6. The sex of the teacher affects, in part, attitudes toward children's problems.

7. Studies of the relationship of socioeconomic factors to the evaluation of children's behavior problems are inadequately dealt with in the literature.

Differences in attitudes between teachers and clinicians are interpreted in the framework of role theory. The attitudinal hierarchies of teachers and clinicians are seen as reflecting their respective roles and the ways these roles influence the organization of their respective experiences. Wickman's findings of 1927 are interpreted as indicative of the role of the teacher in that era. The role expectations of teachers have changed. Replications of the Wickman study indicate these changes have resulted in greater congruence between teachers' and clinicians' attitudes. It is suggested by virtue of the teachers' essential task-orientation and the clinicians' adjustment-orientation and the clinicians' adjustment-orientation that complete or nearly complete congruence is not likely to be achieved.

The relationship of sex and age to attitudes toward behavior problems in also explained in the light of role theory.

REFERENCES:

1. BAIN, W. E. A study of the attitudes of teachers toward behavior problems. *Child Develpm.*, 1934, 5, 19–35.

2. BEILIN, H. The prediction of adjustment over a four-year interval. *J. Clin. Psychol.*, 1957, 13, 270–274.

3. BEILIN, H. Effects of social (occupational) role and age upon the criteria of mental health. *J. Soc. Psychol.*, 1958, 48, 247–256.

4. BEILIN, H., and WERNER, E. Sex differences among teachers in the use of criteria adjustment. *J. Educ. Psychol.*, 1957, 48, 426–436.

5. BEILIN, H., and WERNER, E. Sex role expectations and the criteria of social adjustment for young adults. *J. Clin. Psychol.*, 1957, 13, 341–343.

6. BLANCHARD, P., and PAYNTER, R. H. The problem child. *Ment. Hyg.*, 1924, 8, 26–54.

7. BOYNTON, P. L., and MC GAW, B. H. The characteristics of problem children. *J. Juv. Res.*, 1934, 18, 215–222.

8. BRIM, O. G. The parent-child relation as a social system: 1. Parent and child roles. *Child Develpm.*, 1957, 28, 343–364.

9. CLARK, E. J. Teacher reactions toward objectionable pupil behavior. *Elem. Sch. J.*, 1951, 51, 446–449.

10. DEL SOLAR, C. *Parents and Teachers View the Child; a Comparative Study of Parents' and Teachers' Appraisals of Children* (New York: Bureau of Publications, Teachers College, Columbia Univer., 1949).

11. DAVIS, E. A., and MC GINNIS, E. *Parent Education; a Survey of the Minnesota Program* (Minneapolis: Univer. of Minnesota Press, 1939).

12. DICKSON, V. E. Behavior difficulties that baffle teachers. *J. Juv. Res.*, 1932, 16, 93–101.

13. ELLIS, D. B., and MILLER, L. W. Teachers' attitudes and child behavior problems. *J. Educ. Psychol.*, 1936, 27, 501–511.

14. EPSTEIN, L. J. An analysis of teachers' judgments of problem children. *J. Genet. Psychol.*, 1941, 59, 101–107.

15. GRIFFITHS, W. *Behavior Difficulties of Children as Perceived and Judged by Parents, Teachers and Children Themselves* (Minneapolis: Univer. of Minnesota Press, 1952).

16. HILDRETH, G. A survey of problem pupils. *J. Educ. Res.*, 1928, 18, 1–14.

17. HUNTER, E. C. Changes in teachers' attitudes toward children's behavior over the last thirty years. *Ment. Hyg.*, 1957, 41, 3–11.

18. HURLOCK, E. B., and MC DONALD, L. C. Undesirable behavior traits in junior high school students. *Child Develpm.*, 1934, 5, 278–290.

19. IVES, O. L. *A Critique of Teachers' Ratings of High School Boys as*

an Indication of Later Neuro-Psychiatric Rejection for the Armed Services (New York: Bureau of Publications, Teachers College, Columbia Univer., 1949).

20. LAYCOCK, S. R. Teachers' reactions to maladjustments of school children. *Brit. J. Educ. Psychol.*, 1934, 4, 11–29.

21. LEVY, J. A quantitative study of the relationship between intelligence and economic status as factors in the etiology of children's behavior problems. *Amer. J. Orthopsychiat.*, 1931, 1, 152–162.

22. MAC CLENATHAN, R. H. Teachers and parents study children's behaviors. *J. Educ. Sociol.*, 1934, 7, 325–333.

23. MC CLURE, W. E. Characteristics of problem children based on judgments of teachers. *J. Juv. Res.*, 1929, 13, 124–140.

24. MITCHELL, J. C. A study of teachers' and mental hygienists' ratings of certain behavior problems of children. *J. Educ. Res.*, 1942, 36, 292–307.

25. NEUMEYER, M. H. *Juvenile Delinquency in Modern Society* (New York: D. Van Nostrand, 1949).

26. PECK, L. Teachers' reports of the problems of unadjusted school children. *J. Educ. Psychol.*, 1935, 26, 123–138.

27. PRESTON, G. H., and SHEPLER, W. MC L. A study of the problems of "normal" children. *Amer. J. Orthopsychiat.*, 1931, 1, 245–256.

28. ROGERS, C. R. The criteria used in a study of mental health problems. *Educ. Res. Bull.*, 1942, 21, 29–40.

29. ROGERS, C. R. Mental health findings in three elementary schools. *Educ. Res. Bull.*, 1942, 21, 69–79.

30. SARBIN, T. R. Role theory. In G. Lindzey (Ed.), *Handbook of Social Psychology* (Cambridge: Addison-Wesley), 1954. Pp. 223–258.

31. SCHRUPP, M. H., and GJERDE, C. M. Teacher growth in attitudes toward behavior problems of children. *J. Educ. Psychol.*, 1953, 44, 203–214.

32. SEIDMAN, J. M., and KNAPP, L. B. Teacher likes and dislikes of student behavior and student perceptions of these attitudes. *J. Educ. Res.*, 1953, 47, 143–149.

33. SNYDER, L. M. The problem child in the Jersey City elementary schools. *J. Educ. Sociol.*, 1934, 7, 343–352.

34. SPARKS, J. N. Teachers' attitudes toward the behavior problems of children. *J. Educ. Psychol.*, 1952, 43, 284–291.

35. STOUFFER, G. A. W., JR. Behavior problems of children as viewed by teachers and mental hygienists. *Ment. Hyg.*, 1952, 36, 271–285.

36. STOUFFER, G. A. W., JR. The attitudes of secondary school teachers toward certain behavior problems of children. *Sch. Rev.*, 1956, 64, 358–362.

37. STOUFFER, G. A. W., JR., and OWENS, J. Behavior problems of children as identified by today's teachers and compared with those reported by E. K. Wickman. *J. Educ. Res.*, 1955, 48, 321–331.

38. STEWART, N. Teachers' concepts of "behavior problems." In *Growing Points in Educational Research* (Washington: American Educ. Res. Ass. Rep., 1949).

39. THOMPSON, C. E. The attitudes of various groups toward behavior problems of children. *J. Abnorm. Soc. Psychol.*, 1940, 35, 120–125.

40. ULLMANN, C. A. *Identification of Maladjusted School Children.* Public Hlth. Monogr. No. 7 (Washington: U.S. Govt. Printing Office, 1952). Rev. 1957.

41. WANDT, E. Measurement and analysis of teachers' attitudes. *Calif. J. Educ. Res.*, 1952, 3, 10–13.

42. WATSON, G. A critical note on two attitude scales, *Ment. Hyg.*, 1933, 17, 59–64.

43. WICKMAN, E. K. *Children's Behavior and Teachers' Attitudes.* (New York: Commonwealth Fund, 1928).

44. WITMER, H. L. Childhood personality and parent-child relationships of dementia praecox and manic depressive patients. *Smith Coll. Stud. Soc. Wk.*, 1934, 4, 287–378.

45. YOUNG-MASTEN, I. Behavior problems of elementary school children: a descriptive and comparative study. *Genet. Psychol. Monogr.*, 1938, 20, 123–181.

46. YOURMAN, J. Children identified by their teachers as problems. *J. Educ. Sociol.*, 1932, 5, 334–343.

47. U.S. Children's Bureau. *Juvenile Court Statistics 1946–49.* Statistical Series No. 8 (Washington: U.S. Govt. Printing Office, 1949).

FOOTNOTES:

[1] The author is indebted to Martin Hamburger and Louis Rosenzweig for their critical reading of this paper.

[2] Although the period following the first World War saw the impact of the testing movement and the effects of Behaviorism, it was not till the 1930's and 1940's that clinical psychology became a part of the child development and educational scene in a major way.

[3] One writer has even wondered how the study could have been so widely and uncritically accepted with these limitations. The answer probably rests in the fact that its thesis was part of a powerfully developing movement.

[4] We shall consider all studies found that bear upon the problems focused on by Wickman and his critics in spite of the lack of comparability. Some studies are included which antedate Wickman because the data they offer are relevant.

40   Training Teachers in Life Space Interviewing*

BY WILLIAM C. MORSE

EDITOR'S NOTE: It is one thing to be able to identify problem
children, but it is another thing to deal with them once trouble starts.
A moralistic lecture seldom reaches the offender(s), and the therapeutic interview commonly associated with psychotherapy is too long
and involved to be efficiently used by teachers. This paper outlines a
special interviewing technique which can be used to enable a teacher
and student to inquire together about the student's feelings, attitudes, behavior and about their consequences.

    The key to improved school mental health lies in the ability of the
classroom teacher to deal effectively and hygienically with day-by-day life
events. To that end the present program focuses on the core skill of life
space or reality interviewing, following the conceptual framework of Redl
(1959).
    The original practice was termed "crisis interviewing," since the
technical development was derived in camp setting for disturbed, acting-
out boys where this method was used in individual and group situations
ranging from minor disagreements to major mayhem. While a teacher
might start working with such critical behavior situations, once these were
under control, action would be directed to such perennial vexing problems
as motivation, helping the unhappy and withdrawn children and inter-
pretating typical growth-related problems of youngsters.

* Training Teachers in Life Space Interviewing," *American Journal of Ortho-
psychiatry,* Vol. XXXIII, No. 4, July, 1963, pp. 727–730, by William C.
Morse, Ph.D. Copyright, The American Orthopsychiatric Association, Inc.
Reprinted by permission.

Teachers need concrete help on specific stituations, but they also need a theoretical framework so that their efforts are not idiosyncratic. Life space interviewing embodies a theory and method uniquely suited to the teacher's responsibility in group management, social adjustment and social learning.

We first introduce teachers to Redl's concept of milieu as a design for the analysis of life space. The teacher finds cues through reading the child's reactions in the setting. Little by little the nature of the pupil's perceptual bias and distortion become evident: The teacher sees life through the eyes of the pupil. Detailed studies are made to see how a child gives evidence of his inner feelings through his gesture, language and style of social interaction. While it is simple to appreciate aggressive intent when a pupil uses sarcasm or hits another, the signs are less obvious when the child defends against fear of failure, has covert mistrust of adults, and so on.

Settings for Training Teachers

There are two essential conditions for this training. First, the teacher must start with a recognized group or individual problem that he is interested in trying to work out. Frequently the initial problem chosen proves not to be the true critical problem and redirection is accomplished. The second essential condition is ample supervisory time. The teacher may at first take the child to work jointly with the supervisor, or, at second best, take tapes or notes.

We employ more direct focus on the teacher's own reactions than is usual. Central fustration results when one avoids obvious aspects of the teacher's behavior. In fact, if there is a most subtle aspect of this work, it is the trainer's ability to approach the significance of such personal reactions without giving psychological insult, the very thing we are hoping to teach the teachers to do. Most teachers have been far more ready to deal directly with elements of their behavior than we had originally judged. This has introduced a quality of psychological realism in the relationship that enhances rather than inhibits the supervisor's function. On those infrequent occasions when the teacher's behavior implied the need for therapeutic treatment, referrals were suggested. Parenthetically, the level of technical perfection and pureness of self-insight stated in the literature as necessary for therapists is unrealistic to expect of teachers. In place of this, it is possible to capitalize on the deep, intuitive capacities found in many teachers. Pupils do not await perfection in their teachers: They often respond well to moderation or mitigation of negative forces. This is not to say that the course is always smooth, for at times there are outcroppings of human relationships that makes one wince. However, in our experience, most teachers are reasonable and, when they respond in poor fashion, it is usually out of frustration regarding their inability rather than serious personal maladjustment.

Training Procedures

We start by having the teacher describe the way the world looks through the eyes of the pupil under study. This description is worked over with particular attention to how one judges what the child's life space looks like to him. Consideration is given to properly limited goals for the teacher-pupil relationship, and to what eventual outcome might be anticipated. In many instances, the teacher must first clear plans with the administration or special personnel.

Life space interviewing has its own integrity and meaning as a process that will enable the on-the-line adult to come to grips with a problem without indulging in the typical morass of moralistic preachment. Our theoretical scheme illustrates how the instigating conditions, content, process, goals and closure of reality interviewing differ from those of traditional interviewing. Stress is put on the empathic nature of the teacher relationship, coupled with a non-interpreted recognition of deeper dynamics.

But teachers seek more than a theoretical framework: operational steps are needed. First, the teacher makes certain conversational progress in a nonthreatening and nonjudgmental way. The perception of the pupil must be clearly expressed by him and on his own terms, distorted though it may be. When more than one pupil is involved, special attention is given to balanced or rotated listening. The pupil's psychological perception is sought rather than the usual "legal" truth of who did what first. The empathic manner of listening is the process by which trust is established.

Second, the teacher tests for depth and spread of the behavior: Are there other related problems? Is this really the central issue? Here the teacher assesses how the incident is an expression of the pupil's personality. Children frequently give deep and meaningful material at this stage, and teachers can learn to listen without probing or accepting responsibility for resolving that which is beyond their sphere of influence.

Third, comes the critical state, when the teacher asks, "Well what do you think ought to be done about this?" Here the interest is to explore how the pupil's value system is applied in the given situation. Of course, there is far more to this, including the sensing of pupil anxiety and dealing with resistance that the pupil puts up to prevent any self-commitment.

Frequently, even at this early stage in the interview, the problem resolution is produced by the juxtaposition of various factors brought into the open through reasonable discussion. If not, then the teacher as a responsible adult goes to step four. By this time, aware of psychological ramifications in this situation, the teacher begins to highlight reality factors in the school milieu that have implications should the behavior continue. This is done by objective examination of various real features of the school environment in a factual manner.

Step five is the exploration of pupil motivation for change; that is, how does the pupil think he might be helped, and what role might the teacher play in supporting reasonable subsequent management of the behavior impulse in question? No one-shot magic or instant therapy is expected, and the need to return again and again to significant problems is emphasized.

Finally, in step six, the teacher develops a follow-through plan with the pupil. What will we have to do if this happens again? This must be both realistic and relevant. Any plan must be designed within the limitations of the school resources, and must acknowledge possible escape hatches. Pretense in the school milieu, or reluctance to come to proper grips with issues must be faced frankly. For example, a teacher cannot set up a "removal" plan if no one in this school is ever suspended, or suggest referral to therapy if none is available. Thus we are again at the point of beginning, the school milieu in which teachers' efforts take place. A clear recognition of this fact prevents a teacher from expecting to solve all the problems, or even thinking he should be able to solve them all.

In all stages, the specific content of the teacher's life space interviews are analyzed and next steps are proposed, even to answers for anticipated specific response on the part of the pupil. Planning for anticipated responses is used to trial-test adult answers before actual confrontation occurs.

REFERENCE:

REDL, F. "The Life-Space Interview," *American Journal of Orthopsychiatry*, 1959, 29, 1–18.

41 The Comparative Influence of Punitive and Nonpunitive Teachers Upon Children's Concepts of School Misconduct*

BY JACOB S. KOUNIN AND PAUL V. GUMP

EDITOR'S NOTE: *We have known for a long time that the behavior of a teacher can influence how a student behaves in school, but we have not always been clear about how this influence works. Dr. Kounin and Dr. Gump attempt to analyze more specifically just what particular behaviors of teachers have the greatest influence on a student's concept about school misconduct. Perhaps as we move closer to understanding the role that adults play in encouraging maladjusted school behavior, we will be in a better position to change not only the student but ourselves as well.*

This paper reports a portion of a research project pertaining to the management of childrens' behavior in classroom settings. Because so many teachers, especially beginners, verbalize considerable concern about discipline and control, we are focusing our current research in this area. While there is some relevant literature, based upon experience and insightfulness, we have been unable to locate any generalizations based upon data from research.

In a previous study by Kounin and Gump (1958) specimen-record types of observations were gathered of discipline incidents during the first

* Reprinted from the *Journal of Educational Psychology*, 1961, Vol. 52, 44–49, by permission of the senior author and the American Psychological Association.

week of kindergarten, focusing upon the triad of: a misbehaving child (target), a teacher doing something to stop the misbehavior, and a watching audience-child. Limiting our dependent variables to overt behavior we found that teachers' techniques of handling a misbehaving kindergarten child (target) did have different degrees of socializing success upon audience-children. A socializing success was defined as an observable reduction of overt misbehavior or an increase in conforming behavior (standing up "even straighter" in line). Control techniques high in clarity (defining the deviancy, specifying how to stop) were most successful. Control techniques high in firmness (standing closer to the misbehaving child, continuing to look at him until he stopped misbehaving) were successful only for audience-children who were themselves deviancy-oriented at the time. Control techniques high in roughness (anger, physical handling) were least successful and tended to be followed by behavior disruption (less involvement in work, overt signs of anxiety) rather than conformity on the part of audience-children. In terms of their effects, it is evident that roughness is a different dimension than firmness. . . .

It is postulated that aggression leads to counteraggression; it is further postulated that a punitive teacher has more power over her pupils than they have over her and that she blocks overt manifestation of pupils' aggression (observations in the classrooms of the punitive teachers selected for this study indicate that this second assumption is tenable). From these two postulations, we derive the following hypotheses:

1. That the school misconduct preoccupations of children with punitive teachers will contain more aggression than those of children with nonpunitive teachers.

2. That children with punitive teachers will be more conflicted about school misconduct than will children with nonpunitive teachers.

3. That the aggression needs and the conflict relating to misconduct hypothesized to exist among children with punitive teachers will detract from their concern with school-unique values that are not directly related to misconduct.

4. The question may also be raised as to whether or not the amount of tension generated in the children with these particular punitive teachers is sufficiently great to reduce the rational qualities of their attitudes toward misconduct.

METHOD

Subjects

The subjects were 74 boys and 100 girls attending their first semester of the first grade in the public schools of a large city. They represented all the children from six home rooms of three schools, in from upper-lower to middle-middle socioeconomic neighborhoods.

Procedure

Overall school climate was controlled by selecting pairs of punitive vs. nonpunitive teachers from the same school. Three such pairs were obtained from three elementary schools.

The initial selection of punitive and nonpunitive teachers was obtained from the principal and assistant principal. Following this the classes were observed by both principal investigators. At approximately a week later the teachers were further rated by a supervisor of student teachers who visited each class twice.

The raters checked along a continuum from Extremely Punitive (threatens children with consequences that really hurt; makes threats that imply sharp dislike, real willingness to harm child; ever-readiness to punish) to Not Punitive (does not punish and does not threaten). A punitive vs. nonpunitive pair of teachers was used for the study only when all five persons agreed on their dichotomizations. All the teachers were rated as having good organization, well-behaved classes, and as achieving the learning objectives for their grade. Eighty-four of the children were in classes with punitive teachers and 90 children were in classes with nonpunitive teachers.

The children were interviewed individually during the third month of attendance at school. The interview consisted of the questions: "What is the worst thing a child can do at school?" and, following the reply, "Why is that so bad?" Identical questions were asked regarding home as the milieu for misbehavior.

Coding the Replies

The misconducts mentioned by the children were coded for content and for certain qualities or dimensions.

The content code (obtained from the question of "What is the worst thing to do?") contained two parts: the misconducts and the explanations given for why these were bad. The misconduct included: the act type (physical or psychological assaults, noncompliance, etc.) and the object of the misconduct (parents or teachers, other children, institutional laws or custom, etc.).

The code for the explanation of misconduct was designed to answer three questions: Who is involved in the consequence (the child himself, parent or teacher, a peer, etc.)? What kind of sufferings result to others from the misconduct (physical pain, achievement loss, property loss, etc.)? What kinds of retributions occur to the misbehaver (work imposal; character loss, physical punishment, etc.)?

RESULTS AND CONCLUSIONS

Children probably answer the question of "What's the worst thing a child can do in school?" with a report of acts that reflect their preoccupations. It is not likely that our subjects' answers would have been the same if they were presented with a forced-choice of alternative acts. Given a choice, most children would probably rate "stabbing someone" as more serious than "talking in class." If the misconducts the children talked about are taken to represent tension systems and preoccupations, we may infer from these the comparative impact of punitive and nonpunitive teachers.

In a concurrent study of childrens' attitudes toward misconduct (201 boys and 214 girls in the first grade of six public schools representing a range of socioeconomic backgrounds), Gump and Kounin (1959) found both sex differences and differences between home and school milieus. For example, home misconducts included more breaking of objects while school misconducts included more rule violations; parents suffered more than teachers in consequences but teachers retributed more frequently. However, parents were reported as retributing with more corporal punishment and with more severe punishment than teachers. There were also differences in the responses of boys and girls, especially in school. For example, girls reported "talking" as a school misconduct eight times more frequently than boys, whereas boys reported physical assaults on peers in school more frequently than did girls.

Consequently, the comparison of the responses of children with punitive and nonpunitive teachers was made separately for sexes and also for home and school milieus. However, on *all* comparisons of school responses the direction of differences between children with punitive and nonpunitive teachers was the same for both boys and girls. The report of results, therefore, combines both boys and girls. Insofar as the differences between children with punitive and non-punitive teachers are concerned, only 2 of the 48 comparisons of home responses were statistically significant: home misconducts of the children with punitive teachers were rated as more serious ($p < .05$, for girls only) and retributions to the subject were more serious ($p < .02$, for boys only). It is uncertain whether these represent some spillover of the influence of punitive teachers onto attitudes toward home misconducts, or whether they are chance differences for the number of comparisons made.

The results to be reported here, then, refer to boys and girls combined and to school misconducts only. Intercoder reliabilities ranged from 73–95% agreement, with a median of 90. The p levels of differences are based on the x^2 test. . . .

Following are definitions of the codes used which are not self-explanatory both for the misconducts and for the subjects' explanations for the wrongness of the act. These codes appear in Table 1.

I.

A. Physical assaults include all physical attacks on other persons (pushing, hitting).

B. Milieu-seriousness refers to the length to which the milieu would go to prevent such an act. The school would practically ignore "scratching head," would mildly frown at "whispering," and would go to any length to stop burning down buildings.

C. Coder seriousness refers to the general immorality or danger in the misconduct considered from the point of view of the overall culture. (The only frame of reference which produced high intercoder agreement was when the coders took the position of an understanding Reformed rabbi or a Unitarian minister. Taking an unspecified role, or that of either a parent or a teacher produced low intercoder agreement.) "Studying spelling lessons at the wrong time" is morally trivial while "maiming someone" is morally very serious.

D. Abstractness of misconduct refers to the size of coverage. It may range from a unique, "one time" misbehavior, such as, "cut a climbing rope in gym," to an abstract one, such as, "be mean to other people."

II.

A. A central adult is the responsible leader: teacher at school.

B. A psychological loss to another is exemplified by "It would make her worry."

C. Seriousness of consequences to others range from trivial harm, such as, "She'd be annoyed" to serious ones, such as, "He'd die."

D. A reality-centered retribution (this is scored only when the perpetrator himself suffers in the consequence) is coded when the consequence of a misconduct follows naturally from the act-type, such as: "not study because you'll get behind in your work." This contrasts with the response in which the connection between act and consequence is dependent upon a personal intervention of another, such as: "not study because teacher will make you stand in the corner."

E. "Reflexive justification" was coded when the child gave no consequence for either himself or others in his explanation of why the act was bad. When he said the act is bad because "It's not nice" or "It's bad" it was called a reflexive justification.

III.

A. On ego-acceptability, we sought to determine the degree to which the respondent could see himself as the perpetrator of the misconduct. In an ego-alien act, the respondent expresses abhorrence, such as: "It's dirty to hit little kids who didn't do nothing to you." An ego-attractive act is one in which the child indicates its seductive quality for him, such as: "Tell off a teacher—boy, I'd like to do that."

B. On the premeditation category, we sought to learn the extent to which the child sought to do wrong. If premeditated, the child plans the act and intends the consequences ahead of time, such as: "Put thumb tacks on teacher's chair when she is out." If intentional, the child accepts his part in the wrongdoing but does not plan it, such as, "talk during a lesson."

IV.

Aggression ("blood and guts") refers to the amount of aggression the respondent expresses in his misconducts and consequences. "Play in the storage bin because somebody might get hurt" expresses less aggression than "Play in the storage bin because you might push a kid off and there could be a sharp rock down there and he could hit his head against it and crash open his skull and he would bleed and his brains would fall out and he'd die."

V.

A. A learning or achievement loss is coded when interference with learning is the misconduct or the explanation, such as: "It's bad to make noise because somebody could make a mistake in his work," or ". . . because then he couldn't read good."

B. An institutional law violation is a violation of the rules of the school, such as: "talk when you're supposed to study," "not take your seat when the bell rings."

The results presented in Table 1 may be summarized around the three hypotheses and the one question raised in the introduction:

Punitive teachers will create or activate more aggression-tension than will nonpunitive teachers. This is strongly supported by the data. The children who have punitive teachers have more sheer aggression in their sins and consequences, they give both more milieu-serious and more coder-serious misconducts, their targets suffer more harm, they give more physical assaults as act-types, and their targets suffer more physical harm. The targets of children with nonpunitive teachers are more inclined to suffer psychological losses as consequences. As an example of the results: of 84 respondents with punitive teachers, 31 give physical assaults on other children and 40 mention school rule violations; while of 90 children with nonpunitive teachers, 15 talk about physical assaults and 56 about rule violations. (The remainder of the act-types are non-conformances and "miscellaneous.")

Children with punitive teachers will be more unsettled and conflicted about misbehavior in school. This hypothesis is supported by the findings related to the role of self in misbehavior. The children from nonpunitive teachers give misconducts in which their own role is intentional whereas children from punitive teachers give both premeditated and ego-alien misconducts. We may say that children with punitive teachers express more abhorrence for the misdeeds which they have selected and yet select misdeeds which require "malice and forethought."

Punitiveness of teachers will detract from children's concern with school-unique values. This hypothesis is supported. Children from punitive teachers talk more about physical attacks on peers—misbehavior by no means unique to the classroom setting. Children with nonpunitive teachers talk more about learning, achievement losses, and violations of school-unique values and rules.

Do children from nonpunitive teachers show more rational qualities in their responses? The answer to this question is not clear. Fairly direct attempts to measure this—codes for milieu likelihood of misconducts, for likelihood of consequences, and for appropriateness of consequences to the misconduct—did *not* show significant differences between the two groups. On the other hand, children with punitive teachers gave fewer abstract misconducts which result, in our camp study, was negatively correlated with age. But these same children also gave fewer reflexive justifications which result was positively correlated with chronological age. One interpretation of the findings that children of punitive teachers gave fewer abstract misconducts and fewer reflexive justifications is to regard these as indications of the unsettled and conflicted state of the attitudes regarding misconduct held by children with punitive teachers. When a child is inclined to misbehave but fears to, then a concrete act occurs to him—"hit George in the mouth"; when he is not pressed by his needs to misbehave, then an abstraction occurs to him—"be mean to people." Similarly, when he expresses this verbal act, a real consequence occurs—the target gets hurt or the perpetrator suffers a consequence; when he is not preoccupied with wrongdoing then a reflexive justification occurs to him—"it's not nice." A reflexive justification at this age may not be a primitive reply but a reflection of a settled issue: "You just don't do this because it's not nice."

Another interpretation is to regard the greater use of reflexive justification by the children with nonpunitive teachers as evidence of their greater trust and faith in school, i.e., of their internalization of school values more than children with punitive teachers. Inspection of the data showed the reflexive justification was used predominately in connection with rule violations (talking, running in halls, not taking seat, and the like). These misconducts are milieu-inconvenient which are disturbing to the milieu but which are without direct harm to either the actor or to others and do not

TABLE 1: *A comparison of attitudes toward school misconducts held by children with punitive and nonpunitive first-grade teachers* $(N = 176)$

Misconducts and Explanations	% of Pu[a]	% of NPu[a]
I. Content and quality of the misconducts:		
A. Physical assaults on others	38	17
B. Milieu-serious misconducts	89	63
C. Coder-serious misconducts	48	27
D. Abstract misconducts	27	52
II. Content and quality of the explanations:		
A. Peers as objects of consequences	94	61
B. Physical damage to objects of consequences	60	23
C. Serious harm to others	45	18
D. Reality-centered retributions	21	48
E. "Reflective justifications" as explanations	11	26
III. Role of self in misconducts:		
A. Ego-alien misconducts	26	11
B. Premeditated misconducts	29	15
IV. Aggression:		
A. Overall aggression ("blood and guts")	49	24
V. Concern with school-unique objectives:		
A. Learning and achievement losses	20	43
B. Institutional law violations	49	62

Note.—All differences in percentages are significant at the .05 level or beyond.

[a] *Pu stands for those children who have punitive teachers; NPu refers to those children who have nonpunitive teachers.*

violate an important moral code. Such misconducts to the first grade child have no real explanation except that "they're bad because they say so." As such, they express a sort of naive faith and trust in the rightness of what the teacher says.

SUMMARY

Three pairs of punitive vs. nonpunitive first grade teachers were selected from three elementary schools. The 174 children in these teachers' classrooms were individually interviewed about what they thought was "the worst thing to do in school" together with their explanations of why these misconducts were bad. Regarding their responses as expressions of their preoccupations it was concluded that, as compared with children who have nonpunitive teachers, children who have punitive teachers: manifest more aggression in their misconducts, are more unsettled and conflicted about misconduct in school, are less concerned with learning and school-unique values, show some, but not consistent, indication of a reduction in rationality pertaining to school misconduct. A theory that children with punitive teachers develop less trust of school than do children with nonpunitive teachers was also presented to explain some of the findings.

REFERENCES:

GUMP, P. V. and KOUNIN, J. S. Sex and milieu influences in children's concepts of misconduct. *Amer. Psychologist*, 1959, *14*, 346. (Abstract)

KOUNIN, J. S., and GUMP, P. V. The ripple effect in discipline. *Elem. Sch. J.*, 1958, *59*, 158–162.

CHAPTER TEN

EDUCATING AND UNDERSTANDING
THE DISADVANTAGED

*42   As a Psychologist Sees Pressures on
Disadvantaged Teen-agers**

BY ARTHUR PEARL[1]

EDITOR'S NOTE: Sometimes the misbehavior of disadvantaged youth is a reaction against the good intentions of advantaged adults who have little idea about how the world is perceived by young people of less standing and fewer means. We frequently hear that "love" is what disadvantaged children need most. Dr. Pearl challenges this. Is it possible that our time-tested middle-class conceptions of what is good or acceptable as opposed to what is bad or unacceptable get in the way of doing a better job with our disadvantaged youth? Maybe. In any case, this reading outlines ideas which could help any person working with disadvantaged youth to be more effective in his relationships with them.

The greatest pressure on the disadvantaged youth is caused not so much by his environmental deficit as by what he feels is his lack of a future. The truth of the matter is that our society provides little opportunity for a low-income youth to find a place in the world. As a result, most of his formal education and other kinds of social intervention are not only ineffective but often humiliating or debasing.

For example, he is compelled to go to school, but what he is presented with there has no meaning to him in terms of the way he sees the world. He is told to stay in school so that eventually he can get a better job, but in actuality being a high school graduate offers him little if any more in terms of access to the opportunity structure than being a high school dropout. He knows friends and relatives who have graduated from high school and are

* Reprinted from the *N.E.A. Journal*, February, 1965, Vol. 19, p. 21, by permission of the author and the publisher.

either unemployed or in some undignified, degrading, and debasing jobs. His real choice is often boiled down to becoming an unemployed high school graduate or an unemployed dropout.

Although society today is geared to favor the college graduate, a higher education is an impossible goal to most disadvantaged young people. Even if they could conceive of the possibility of going to college, there is little in their educational activity and nothing in their home background that prepares them for it. Many of them are in basic tracks that do not prepare for college. The slightly more fortunate are placed in a so-called general curriculum, which does not prepare them for college either.

What the schools need to do is to find some way to offer these disadvantaged youth the possibility of going to college or, at the very least, some hope for a future.*

Another kind of pressure on the disadvantaged youth is exerted by love—the undiscriminating sort dispensed by well-meaning teachers. Not all of these kids are lovable, and they can see through any false posture.

Not long ago I heard the dean of a school of education say that the one thing disadvantaged children need is love. If we could only give them enough love, we could solve all of our problems, he implied. He became furious with me, however, when I tried to explain to him that love given so promiscuously is known in the streets as prostitution.

By trying to give universal love, the teacher actually punishes the disadvantaged student. In effect, the teacher is asking him to feel guilty for anything he does that displeases her because he is hurting or disappointing one who loves him.

For example, take the fifth grade teacher in a Chicago slum school who, shortly after the mass demonstrations against de facto segregation, found some salacious comments scrawled on her record book. Turning to the class, she asked, "After all I've done for you, why are you being so mean to me?"

After a long silence, one of the boys finally answered, "Because you're white."

The teacher, although she had just witnessed two racial school boycotts, was dumbfounded. With tears in her eyes, she told the class that she could not teach them any more that morning; she was too upset.

Her self-righteousness was the most excruciating punishment that she could have used against the boy. He had presented himself honestly and courageously and, if anything, should have been rewarded for his contribution. Instead, he was humiliated. Not surprisingly, at the end of the class he walked up to the teacher and stamped as hard as he could on her feet.

The object lesson here is quite clear. The teacher had established a love relationship that no one had asked for. By failing to acknowledge the boy's honesty and by humiliating him, she drove him to the only kind of face-saving action he knew how to express. If she had handled the situation honestly, say by discussing this particular problem with the class, she could have built up this boy's self-respect and her own effectiveness as a teacher.

It is not love that disadvantaged children need so much as honest respect. Anything phony will force them to lash out against the teacher and whatever else the school imposes upon them.

Another pressure the schools have got to do away with if they are to deal effectively with the disadvantaged is the fierceness of individual competition. Most disadvantaged children have nothing in their backgrounds to prepare them for school, and as a consequence they are unable to complete equally with most other children.

If the school continues to punish such children with failing grades and other forms of humiliation, these youngsters will be disaffected with the whole educational process. Even if they are not actually told they are stupid, the school implies it. They are asked to read when they can't read well; they have to stand at the board and face the laughter and ridicule of their friends. If they finally decide not to go to school, they are arrested as truants.

Admittedly, some of these children are not of high or even average intelligence—in the ways that we normally measure intelligence—but they can learn to do many useful things in society.

One of the interesting results of a recent experiment in programed learning reveals that IQ does not truly indicate how *much* a person can learn but how *fast* he can learn. Experiments with programed learning in physics and chemistry indicate that a person with an IQ of 80 can learn just as much as a person with an IQ of 140, although it may take the person with the low IQ a much longer time. (Incidentally, when tested a year later, the low IQ students, who had invested much more time in learning, scored higher than the high IQ students.)

Although their rate of learning is generally slower than that of the more fortunate children, disadvantaged students need not be placed in special groups. Homogeneous grouping, I believe, is done more often for the benefit of the teacher than for his students.

Instead of depending on such gimmicks, educators ought to be moving toward what I would call team learning. We have had team learning for a long time, but we have called it cheating. In the context I am speaking of, however, all students work together to help each other learn instead of working to beat the system. The effectiveness of this type of learning has been proven in scores of experiments, particularly some conducted by the Army.

In short, we have got to be less concerned with the outcomes of education and more concerned with the process of education.

Obviously, putting the right type of teacher in the classroom is a key to relieving many of the pressures on the disadvantaged child in school. Unfortunately, we have a lot of teachers in predominantly disadvantaged schools who should not be there. A lot of them are prejudiced, not necessarily because of their children's racial or ethnic background but because the values and mores of these children are opposed to the values and mores of the middle class from which most of their teachers come.

A teacher in a disadvantaged school should be nonjudgmental. He should recognize that his students may have a different approach to life, one perhaps more suitable to the kind of world they live in than the one in which he lives.

The teacher should also be attuned to the fact that while these children have many deficits, they have assets as well. The kinds of assets a child is likely to have will largely be in tune with the kind of world with which he has learned to deal.

The disadvantaged child lives in a very physical world, one which places little value on reflective thinking. His assets, therefore, are going to be largely physical—the ability to act out his emotions and feelings freely and honestly. This is one reason why Frank Reissman and others place a great deal of emphasis on the role playing as part of the learning experience of these children.

The teacher must recognize that children learn differently—that some learn by reading, some by listening, some by feeling, and some by acting out or projecting themselves.

Finally, the teacher should have a sense of humor. He should not take himself so seriously that he becomes outraged at a child's inability to respond in some preconceived way. A child should be able to come into a classroom knowing that he is going to have some fun. Even if the child looks upon learning as something incidental, it is surprising how much he learns in a relaxed atmosphere in which he is enjoying himself.

There is no reason why education has to be unenjoyable. If the teacher is nonjudgmental and free from prejudices, if he is willing to recognize the good qualities of his students, he can make of education what it is supposed to be—preparation for living in a democratic society where everyone has a chance to achieve dignity and status.

FOOTNOTE:

[1] Dr. Pearl, in association with Beryce MacLennan, Jacob Fishman, Lonnie Mitchell, and others, is involved in a pilot project which has successfully trained youngsters from grossly disadvantaged backgrounds to handle responsible jobs in day care, recreation, and research—three fields which are presently understaffed and which are sure to expand greatly in the years to come. Their project suggests one way to offer disadvantaged young people some hope for the future.

43 Characteristics of the Culturally Disadvantaged Child*

BY MILLARD H. BLACK

EDITOR'S NOTE: Before we can treat anything, be it a disease or disadvantaged student, we must first know as much about what or who it is as possible. This article will help focus into keener perspective the dominant social and learning characteristics commonly associated with the disadvantaged.

Who is the educationally or culturally disadvantaged child? What are his characteristics? What are some of the factors of his environment which affect his educational achievement? These questions, together with a determination of procedures which will compensate for or ameliorate his disadvantage, are areas of great and grave concern, not only in Chicago, Los Angeles, New York, and other great cities, but in many other areas which are in economic and social transition.

Who Is the Educationally or Culturally Disadvantaged Child?

The answer varies from state to state, from city to city. He lives not only in the central area of our great cities. One southern governor in January 1964 declared that 20 per cent of the citizens of his state can neither read nor write, that 50 per cent of the state's young people fail to complete high school. The disadvantaged child is of no single race or color: poverty, delinquency, failure to achieve athe goals established by the main stream of society are shared by peoples of all colors and national origins.

* Reprinted from *The Reading Teacher,* March, 1965, 465–470, by permission of Millard H. Black and the International Reading Association.

The disadvantaged individual may derive from a culture which is rich in its own tradition, but which no longer prepares its members for successful participation in society. The change in economic patterns apparent over the past half-century was intensified by World War II. People from submarginal farms have been forced into cities, while in the cities jobs for the unskilled are decreasing. Thousands have learned that their older ways of life no longer are effective.

What Are the Characteristics of the Culturally Disadvantaged Child?

He is no stranger to failure and to the fear that continued failure engenders. He knows the fear of being overpowered by teachers who are ignorant of the culture and mores of his society, and who may not expect success of him. He fears lack of recognition and understanding from teachers whose backgrounds are totally dissimilar and who either misinterpret or fail to recognize many of his efforts to achieve and to accommodate himself to demands which are basically alien.

Riessman (8) describes these characteristics of the deprived individual: (a) is relatively slow at cognitive tasks, but not stupid; (b) appears to learn most readily through a physical, concrete approach (often is slow, but may be persistent when the content is meaningful and valued); (c) often appears to be anti-intellectual, pragmatic rather than theoretical; (d) is traditional, superstitious, and somewhat religious in a traditional sense; (e) is from a male-centered culture, except for a major section of the Negro subculture; (f) is inflexible and not open to reason about many of his beliefs (morality, diet, family polarity, and educational practice are examples of these beliefs); (g) feels alienated from the larger social structure, with resultant frustration; (h) holds others to blame for his misfortunes; (i) values masculinity and attendant action, viewing intellectual activities as unmasculine; (j) appreciates knowledge for its practical, vocational ends, but rarely values it for its own sake; (k) desires a better standard of living, with personal comforts for himself and his family, but does not wish to adopt a middle-class way of life; (l) is deficient in auditory attention and interpretation skills; (m) reads ineffectively and is deficient in the communication skills generally, has wide areas of ignorance, and often is suggestible, although he may be suspicious of innovations. Other delimiting characteristics reported by Riessman have been included among the factors discussed in later paragraphs.

In assessing some of the strengths of this group of children, Riessman describes them as: (a) being relatively free of the strains which accompany competitiveness and the need to establish oneself as an individual; (b) having the cooperativeness and mutual aid which marks an extended family; (c) being free of self-blame; (d) enjoying other members of the family and not competing with them; (e) having the security deriving from an extended family and a traditional outlook; (f) enjoying games, music, sports, and cars.

The following factors, reflecting the conclusions of many persons who have studied the causes and results of cultural disadvantage, are believed by Dr. Newton S. Metfessel (6) to be operative in the lives of children from disadvantaged homes.[1] The grouping of these factors and the remarks relative to them are the work of this writer.

Language factors. One such grouping may be termed language factors:

1. Culturally disadvantaged children understand more language than they use. This comparison between understanding and usage does not imply a wide hearing or understanding vocabulary. Figurel (5) reports that at grade two the vocabulary of such children is approximately one-third that of normal children, while at grade six it is about one-half.

2. Culturally disadvantaged children frequently use a great many words with fair precision, but not those words representative of the school culture. Figurel states that "less than half of the words in the vocabulary of pre-school children are known by second-grade children in slum areas." He also states that "common name words, such as *sink, chimney, honey, beef,* and *sandwich* are learned by culturally disadvantaged children one or two years later than by other children."

3. Culturally disadvantaged children frequently are crippled in language development because they do not perceive the concept that objects have names, and that the same objects may have different names. The impoverished economic conditions under which these pupils are reared, with a scarcity of objects of all types, and the absence of discussion which characterizes communication in the substandard home prejudice against the development of labels and of the concept of a specific name (or names) for everything.

4. Culturally disadvantaged kindergarten children use fewer words with less variety to express themselves than do kindergarten children of higher socioeconomic classes. The use of language by the child chiefly to express his concrete needs, and by parents and other adults to command the child to perform some function, may contribute to the severe limitation of self-expression.

5. Culturally disadvantaged children use a significantly smaller proportion of mature sentence structures, such as compound, complex, and more elaborate constructions. This is not limited to the non-English-speaking child, but occurs among most children who come from culturally disadvantaged areas.

6. Culturally disadvantaged children learn less from what they hear than do middle-class children. The importance of teaching all children the skills of listening has often been pointed out. This appears to be particularly true for disadvantaged children, who come from a milieu in which the radio, television, and the sounds made by many people living in crowded

quarters provide a background of noise from which the individual must retreat.

Learning patterns. The next grouping of the factors assembled by Metfessel have to do with learning patterns:

1. Culturally disadvantaged children tend to learn more readily by inductive than by deductive approaches. It appears reasonable to assume that low self-esteem, induced by long economic deprivation, discrimination, or both, may cause pupils to distrust their own judgment or conclusions; they need the support of an authoritarian figure in the classroom. The difficulties in using a discovery technique in teaching disadvantaged pupils are obvious.

2. Culturally disadvantaged children generally are unaccustomed to "insight building" by external use of lectures and discussions at home. In homes where families are preoccupied with supplying the elemental needs, there may be little opportunity to help children learn the techniques of discussion or to move from observation to conclusions. Deutsch (3) reports that "the lower class home is not verbally oriented," and the result is a diminution of the child's general level of responsiveness.

3. Culturally disadvantaged children are frequently symbolically deprived; for example, imaginary playmates are much less acceptable to the parents of culturally disadvantaged children when compared to their middle-class counterparts. The average middle-class parent appears to accept the imaginations of his children, whether or not he understands their educational and psychological import. On the other hand, parents from less affluent circumstances tend to look upon such imagining, even in very young children, as "lying" and to punish when it is observed.

4. Culturally disadvantaged children need to see concrete application of what is learned to immediate sensory and topical satisfaction. This is of particular importance in a school culture in which primary emphasis is placed on long-term goals, which can be met only by foregoing immediate satisfactions. The importance of a series of well defined instructional tasks and attendant goals, continued verbalization, and frequent evaluation of progress is implied by this factor.

5. Culturally disadvantaged children tend to have poor attention span and consequently experience difficulty in following the orders of a teacher. Several authorities have reported the great amount of time children spend listening in the classroom. Research shows that pupils "tune in and out" on the teacher, supplying from context and from their own experience much that they miss during these brief periods of inattention. The lack of connected discourse and generally inadequate communication processes in the disadvantaged home foster the inability of children to attend. This environmental deficiency is reinforced by differences in the vocabulary and syntax used in the classroom and in the home. The pupil whose cultural

background is the same as that of the teacher is in a position to supply through context much that he may have missed during intermittent periods of inattention. The sparseness of furnishings in the homes of the very poor, the general drab visual quality of the environment, tend to deny the pupil needed exercise in organization, perception, and reorganization of the objects in the environment.

Readiness for instruction. Four additional factors included by Metfessel are related to this concept:

1. The culturally disadvantaged child often is characterized by significant gaps in knowledge and learning. Entering school from a background which has not adequately prepared him for success in a traditional curriculum, the pupil participates in communication procedures and patterns alien to him. These disadvantages are multiplied by frequent changes of residence and school, particularly in the lower grades.

2. Culturally disadvantaged children generally have had little experience of receiving approval for success in a task. Born into a community in which relatively few adults have been successful in school, the disadvantaged child hardly can be expected to be self-motivated in his work in the classroom. The teacher's commonest motivation—"You read that well, John," or "Mary, that was a good report"—fails with this pupil because he has rarely experienced praise in his home. Lack of responsibility in the home is not to be inferred. Child care and housekeeping tasks are assumed regularly and successfully by many of these children who are not yet in their teens.

3. Culturally disadvantaged children are characterized by narrow experience outside the home. Children's participation in activities which are assumed by almost every teacher may be nonexistent among lowest-income groups. Without background to promote understanding, how much will the pupil gain from studying about these activities?

4. Culturally deprived children have very little concept of relative size. Limited in the communication skills, deprived of many experiences which help to build concepts of things to which he must react in the classroom, comprehension of much about which he studies will be severely limited.

School behavior. Three factors are directly related to behavior in school:

1. Culturally deprived children generally are unaware of the "ground rules" for success in school. The ignorance of *how* to be successful does not imply unawareness of the values of education. Although their reasons may differ from those given by persons in other social groups, many adults and adolescents among low-income groups express their need for education.

2. Culturally disadvantaged children frequently end the reading habit before it is begun. Metfessel continues, saying that "the cycle of skill mastery which demands that successful experiences generate more motivation to read which in turn generates levels of skill sufficient to prevent discouragement, and so on, may be easily reversed in direction and end the reading habit prior to its beginning." Books, magazines, and newspapers are more easily dispensable than food and clothing; among very low income groups they do not represent necessities.

3. Culturally disadvantaged children are placed at a marked disadvantage in timed test situations. Efforts to apply objective measures to almost every phase of school interest and activity have doubtful value for the children from a very low income home. Accurate determination of their potential and their achievement must be obtained through some technique which does not penalize them with rigidly defined time limitations.

4. Culturally disadvantaged children need assistance in perceiving an adult as a person of whom you ask questions and receive answers. The growing tendency of teachers to act as *directors* of classroom activity and to perceive themselves as resource persons implies an area in which culturally disadvantaged children will need specific help. They must be helped to accommodate themselves to an adult role which is unfamiliar to them.

What Are the Characteristics of a Disadvantaged Area?

We can round out the description of our culturally disadvantaged children by citing some characteristics of a large area in Los Angeles County, which appear to be similar to the characteristics of other very low income areas. Agencies which are seeking to ameliorate cultural disadvantage state that in this area: (a) the percentage of broken homes is almost three times that of the total county; (b) family income is 25 per cent below the county median; (c) population density is approximately double that of the entire county; (d) housing is substandard, and continues to decline in quality; (e) the school dropout rate is 2.2 times as large as the average of the city; and (f) youth delinquency rates are higher in almost all offense categories than for the county generally.

REFERENCES:

1. AUSUBEL, DAVID P., and PEARL AUSUBEL. "Ego Development Among Segregated Negro Children," in A. Harry Passow (ed.), *Education in Depressed Areas* (New York: Bureau of Publications, Columbia University, 1963). Pp. 109–141.
2. CONANT, JAMES B. *Slums and Suburbs* (New York: McGraw-Hill Book Co., 1961).

3. DEUTSCH, MARTIN P. "The Disadvantaged Child and the Learning Process," in A. Harry Passow (ed.), *Education in Depressed Areas* (New York: Bureau of Publications, Columbia University, 1963). Pp. 163–179.

4. EDUCATIONAL POLICIES COMMISSION, NATIONAL EDUCATION ASSOCIATION. *Education and the Disadvantaged American* (Washington: The Association, 1962).

5. FIGUREL, J. ALLEN. "Limitations in the Vocabulary of Disadvantaged Children: A Cause of Poor Reading," in *Improvement of Reading Through Classroom Practice*, Proceedings of the Annual Convention of the International Reading Association, Vol. 9 (New York: Scholastic Magazines, Inc., 1964).

6. METFESSEL, NEWTON S. Unpublished research, Center for the Study of the Education of Disadvantaged Youth, University of Southern California, 1964.

7. PASSOW, A. HARRY (ed.), *Education in Depressed Areas* (New York: Bureau of Publications, Columbia University, 1963).

8. RIESSMAN, FRANK. *The Culturally Deprived Child* (New York: Harper & Row, 1962).

9. ———. "The Culturally Deprived Child: A New View," *Education Digest, 29*, 12–15; November, 1963.

FOOTNOTE:

[1] Reported with the permission of Dr. Metfessel, Director of the Center for the Study of the Education of Disadvantaged Youth at the University of Southern California.

44   *After School Integration—What?*
*Problems in Social Learning**

BY ROBERT LEE GREEN

EDITOR'S NOTE: *If we really value an "education for all," then open and positive communication at all social and educational levels is necessary in dealing with the inevitable problems connected with the transition from segregated to integrated education. Dr. Green raises questions crucial to us all if we are truly interested in maintaining quality education. It is one thing to integrate a school, but as the title of this paper suggests, then what?*

The premise of this paper is that incorporating Negro or other minority students into an all-white school for the first time may bring about an interracial school but not necessarily an integrated school. An interracial school is one in which students of varying racial backgrounds are found; an integrated school is one in which students of varying racial backgrounds are found *and* a mutual interaction between them occurs. Mutual interaction between all segments of the student population is necessary if meaningful social and academic learning is to occur.

An observer of an elementary school, a secondary school, or a college that has a large white student population and a substantial number of Negro students can readily find clusters of Negro students in the school cafeteria, the school library, or the student union, although there is no official policy restricting them to certain areas. One explanation may be that Negro students for some reason segregate themselves from the white

* Reprinted from *Personnel and Guidance Journal*, March, 1966, Vol. 45, 704–710, by permission of the author and the publisher.

population although it is equally likely that white students sit together and segregate themselves from their Negro peers. The same pattern of group voluntary segregation can be observed in the union buildings or cafeterias of many eastern, western, or midwestern colleges and universities that, in some instances, have had substantial Negro student populations for years, a fact which suggests that voluntary group segregation does not necessarily decrease even though minority group students are consistent members of the school population.

Given these observations, how can school integration result in meaningful social learning for all children? What are the most effective roles for educators in promoting positive mutual interaction between all segments of the student population?

TRANSITIONAL OPPORTUNITIES

A crucial stage in bringing about meaningful social learning between white and Negro students is the transitional period when Negro students are first introduced into a formerly all-white school. As a result of living in an all-Negro community and attending predominantly Negro schools, which in most instances are admittedly educationally inferior to exclusively white schools, many Negro children experience difficulty in meeting the educational standards of the "new school" when integration first occurs. Numerous research studies indicate that Negro students score lower on standardized achievement and aptitude tests than their white counterparts (Bullick, 1950) and initially achieve at a lower level in their course work (Green and Farquhar, 1965). Many educators, in attempting to cope with this problem, group youngsters on the basis of their measured achievement level on nationally standardized tests. When this is done, one finds within such schools a "special class" for "slow learners" which, in many cases, is simply an all-Negro class. These youngsters are often labeled as "slow learners," "retardates," or youngsters unable to benefit from regular classroom instruction. Rather than regarding these youngsters as being *educationally* retarded, teachers frequently perceive them as being *intellectually* retarded and therefore incapable of benefiting from new and meaningful school experiences. As a consequence, what is in effect initially planned as school integration results in intraschool *de facto* segregation (Riessman, 1964). The latter approach inhibits and may actually reverse meaningful integration and social learning.

One suburban school district in the Detroit area is currently facing this problem. When grouping on the basis of the students' performance on standardized achievement tests, it was found that a high percentage of Negro students in the eleventh and twelfth grades were in special classes for "slow learners." School counselors in this situation were not aware of the fact that correlations between standardized achievement test scores and actual achievement (grade-point average) of Negro students are often low. In a recent study (Green and Farquhar, 1965), no correlation was found between the verbal score of the School and College Ability Tests (SCAT) and grade-point achievement for a sample of eleventh-grade Negro high school students. With the same sample, academic motivation was a more crucial factor and a much better predictor of school achievement than standardized aptitude test scores.

A similar phenomenon is being observed in Prince Edward County, Virginia (Green, Hofmann, Morse, Hayes, & Morgan, 1964) with a group of Negro students who were deprived of formal schooling for a four-year period. Many of these students performed from three and one-half to five years below grade level on standardized achievement tests, yet their present actual achievement level is inconsistent with their standardized achievement test scores. When grouping solely on the basis of standardized achievement test scores brings about intraschool *de facto* segregation, white students tend to regard Negro students as being "different," and Negro students perceive themselves as being "different," since they are in special classes. The notion of "difference" frequently centers around feelings of inferiority on the part of the Negro student and feelings of superiority on the part of the white student. In other words, the Negro group is not only considered to be different, but is also considered to be intellectually inferior to the white student population. Intraschool *de facto* segregation on the academic level which comes about during this transitional period leads to other forms of segregation, i.e., students who attend classes together are more likely to become friends with youngsters in their own classrooms, and these friendships are apt to be carried over to cafeteria, library situations, athletic events, and school assemblies.

Another adverse effect of intraschool *de facto* segregation is the reinforcement of the negative self-perception of many Negro students. A considerable body of research associated with the self-concept indicates that good concepts of self are associated with such desirable characteristics as low anxiety (Lipsitt, 1958), and generally good adjustment, popularity, and effectiveness (Mussen and Porter, 1959) in group relations. Furthermore, poor self-concepts are associated with academic underachievement. Recent research (Grambs, 1964) also indicates that many Negro students have developed very negative self-images as a result of the experiences that they have had with the dominant society. They perceive themselves as being worthless, ineffectual, and in general, not wanted by society. When placed in a school system in which their educational limitations are emphasized, this tends to reinforce their low self-esteem. Teachers in the latter school situation are aware of the fact that Negro students are in special classes and the notion that the deprived students are intellectually inferior may be reinforced. This also may become a rationale or an excuse for classroom teachers to provide inadequate instruction for such youngsters, i.e., "they cannot profit from quality instruction." Furthermore, teachers who regard certain students as being unable to benefit from quality instruction may not encourage them to become involved in aspects of the school situation which would more likely result in positive social learning (i.e., French club, band, etc.).

THE ROLE OF THE SCHOOL ADMINISTRATION

One problem that has come about over a period of time is related to the perception that teachers have concerning an integrated school. There are teachers who perceive an assignment to an integrated school as an academic affliction. An assignment to such a school is frequently perceived as a loss in status; i.e., the greater the number of Negroes or non-whites in such schools, the lower the school is ranked on the academic status pole.

In a large urban school community in which a prospective teacher was being interviewed for a position, there was some question as to whether or not she should be hired since her undergraduate school record was rather inadequate, as was her student teaching evaluation. After a lengthy discussion by the school hiring committee, it was decided to offer her a probationary position in a school which had the highest Negro population, the highest dropout rate, and whose members ranked high in family disorganization, physical illness, and residential mobility. The prospective teacher was told that if she did an excellent job of teaching during her probationary period at this school, she would be promoted to a higher prestige school within the system. In effect, the school administrators in this case had perceived this integrated school as being one of low status and communicated this attitude to prospective teachers by consequently assigning teachers to it who were low in academic qualifications. Communicating negative attitudes to teachers who will work in depressed areas reinforces the perceptions that they may already hold concerning students who attend such schools. Grambs indicates that recent studies show many teachers to entertain a Negro stereotype:

> Studies of their attitudes toward children show that the Negro child is rated lowest in all rankings of groups of a Bogardus-type social-distance scale (Grambs, 1950). The original study was completed 13 years ago; teachers in training in 1963 gave the same responses. Attempts to change teachers' attitudes through human-relations workshops and special courses have reached very few (Grambs, 1964).

Gottlieb (1963), in assessing the views of Negro and white teachers toward students in a northern urban school community, found differential perceptions of those students by their teachers. White teachers typically selected test items indicating that Negro students are "talkative, lazy, high-strung, rebellious, and fun-loving," while Negro teachers perceived the same students as being "happy, cooperative, energetic, ambitious, and fun-loving." However, most teachers agreed that the children did not possess qualities usually associated with middle-class children. They were not perceived as being "cultured, poised, or sophisticated." The above findings support the notion that Negro and white teachers in depressed schools may have differential impressions of the students, but, in general, they both perceive that the children do not possess the "desirable qualities of middle-class school children."

Furthermore, Negro and white teachers who teach in depressed areas are aware of the fact that their schools are perceived as being "low status" and "low prestige" schools which may cause them to have lower self-esteems when assigned to disadvantaged areas. School administrators should reassess their perceptions of schools that become integrated or that are located in depressed areas of the city and attempt to change the negative attitude and perceptions that teachers might have pertaining to such schools. The professional challenge of teaching in such schools should be stressed, higher salaries offered, and special consultative assistance by school personnel experienced in dealing with school-learning problems should be a part of the regular school program. It is crucial that educators foster the idea that an assignment to a school in a depressed area can be a worthwhile experience rather than a form of punishment.

COMMUNICATION AND INTEGRATION

During and immediately after the transitional period, an attempt to open communications between Negro and white students might alter intraschool *de facto* segregation. During this period it is crucial that school administrators encourage Negro students to become involved in the total school life. There seems to be no problem in getting Negroes involved in the athletic aspect of social learning. However, athletics is only a minute segment of the total school activities. A general ethic of American society is that we should be athletically excellent. Athletics, as a route to social mobility, have long been extolled. However, it should now be clear that while it is a desirable outcome that students achieve athletically, it is undesirable to focus the Negro students' attention on athletics to the detriment of other methods of achievement.

Indicative of the major society's regard for athletics was a United States Senator's recent comments on the effect that professional boxing had on social mobility for certain disadvantaged youth. Boxing, however, has possibly been least effective in this regard, and the ratio of successes to failures is probably far lower than in any other sport where Negroes actively compete. It would be an exceedingly interesting project to find out whether Cassius Clay and Sonny Liston are more popular models for Negro youth than Elgin Baylor, Arthur Ashe, Bill Russell, and Henry Carr (since education was related to the athletic push of the latter four athletes).

Boxing models, if found more popular, may be as much related to the lack of necessary educational qualifications, as they are related to the intrinsic popularity of the most successful participants. Educators should be wary of limiting the alternatives of successful Negro athletes. There may often be a press on the part of teachers in disadvantaged schools toward excellence in the field house rather than in the classroom.

Negro students should be encouraged to join various language and literary clubs, art clubs, band, future teachers club, etc., rather than assuming that "deprived students" are uninterested in such activities.

Another significant factor is the involvement of Negro parents in the activities of the school. It can be met by actively encouraging them to attend and become active in the PTA and other school related activities. Encouraging parents to become more personally involved in the activities of the school might promote more academic and social interest on the part of the students.

CURRICULUM

Another significant factor related to a lack of communication, awareness, and positive perception on the part of the Negro and white students is related to curriculum development and the absence of the role of minority groups in our history. Many Negro and white students are totally ignorant of the historical role that the American Negro has played in the development of America. As a matter of fact, it may be safe to say that the history of the Negro has been systematically excluded from our school textbooks. A more realistic appraisal of the Negro involvement in the development of our society would in itself allow the Negro student to develop a more favorable self-perception, and at the same time, allow white students to develop a more accurate perception and understanding of the Negro's participation. Rather than devote a special paragraph to only the contributions of George Washington Carver, Booker T. Washington, and Ralph Bunche, the technological and scientific contributions of the Negro throughout his entire history should be presented in an objective manner. Pressures from civil rights organizations such as the Detroit NAACP have recently caused school administrators to become concerned about the problem. In the latter case, supplementary materials were provided regarding the historical achievements of the American Negro.

However, historians make a basic error when they assume that Negroes should receive a special place or annex in our history and literature books. Historians have the obligation to present the Negro as a part of the whole rubric and not as a special group with its own aims, goals, and accomplishments. This might be accomplished more adequately by showing pictures of past Negro leaders without any attempt to render this a special issue. Only when racial characteristics are a necessary part of the history (the Civil War, the Underground Railway, etc.) should the race of the individual be emphasized.

TEACHER PREPARATION FOR DEPRESSED AREAS

An important factor related to teacher effectiveness in integrated schools is the ability and desire on the part of the teacher to work with children of varying social, religious, ethnic, and racial backgrounds. Needless to say, teachers who have the ability but not the desire to work in integrated areas will experience difficulty.

Teacher training programs should not overlook the special social and academic problems that often result when minority group students first integrate a school or school district. Language difficulties, lack of academic motivation, and poor home situations are well known. Haubrich (1963) recognizes this problem when he says: "One discovers very quickly just how interrelated is the social and educational context when the unique relationship between money, occupation, home and school comes to the teacher's classroom."

One meaningful approach in teacher training programs would be to expose education majors to integrated school settings early in their academic training career. Too often young people complete their college careers with minimal or no exposure to the "inner-city" school with its multitude of problems. Early exposure would allow students to assess their ability and desire to teach in other than a middle-class, racially homogeneous school. Programs such as the Student Education Corps at Michigan State University and the Hunter College Project in New York allow early teaching experience with more than the usual amount of professional assistance. In addition to the regular student teaching program, the Hunter College Project allows for weekly school conferences in which all subject-matter areas meet—a close relationship between college and school personnel in order to continually assist the student teacher in becoming a more adequate teacher and a regular program of community visits discussed with supervisors and other student participants. In the final analysis, the most crucial factors related to teacher success in integrated school areas are the ability to learn and benefit from one's experience and the desire and motivation to work in such areas.

COUNSELING

Counselors should recognize that when counseling the Negro student in Detroit, the Puerto Rican youngster in Harlem, or any non-white student, he will be confronted with an individual presenting a unique and complex set of needs and problems. So unique are the needs of the non-white student that some writers have proposed that white counselors are unable to see society as Negroes do, which prevents a positive counseling relationship from developing (Phillips, 1960). Negro students, due to their experiences in a predominantly white and often hostile world, may view a sympathetic white counselor with suspicion. In other special circumstances, a white counselor confronted with a Negro may find it difficult to develop rapport. However, this is not to say that only Negro counselors can counsel Negro students. This notion would be almost commensurate with the thesis that only Negro teachers can teach Negro students. (Such an argument could be reversed.) With a special knowledge of the needs of the Negro gained by studying his psychological and sociological background, a sensitive and sympathetic white counselor can structure an atmosphere that will allow the non-white student to express himself freely. A meaningful relationship with a representative of the group that he perceives as being hostile and rejecting could well bring about a positive attitudinal change.

Among the many psychological needs of the Negro student, basic acceptance is paramount. A recent study (Blodgett and Green, 1966) found that the Negro high school students felt basically rejected by both their school and home environment. Their feelings of rejection were complicated by a high rate of broken homes and material deprivation. The latter problems of non-white students often lead them to expect the "worst" in their relationships with adults. A well-trained, sensitive counselor, irrespective of race, may be able to offset the non-white students' past negative experiences with society.

EARLY SCHOOL INTEGRATION

School integration should come about at the early elementary levels so that Negro students can profit from quality education and social interaction throughout their elementary school careers, rather than being introduced into an all-white school situation at the junior or senior high school level. Present data indicates that there is a systematic decline in aptitude and achievement test scores with time when students remain in a school environment that is not stimulating, and there is enough evidence to support the contention that predominantly Negro schools are not academically stimulating (Green, et al., 1964).

When school integration does come about relatively late in the youngster's school career, these children may need special educational assistance in achieving the educational objective of the school. The research of Deutsch (1960) indicates that the lower-class Negro child at times receives about one-half to one-third less instructional time in the elementary grades than does the white child even when socio-economic status is controlled. In the same schools that Deutsch sampled, as much as 80 per cent of the school day focused on discipline problems and organizational detail. If similar students are integrated into a white junior or senior high school level, a significant portion of the assumed academic training that most youngsters receive at this period is completely lacking and must be accounted for. Frank Riessman (1964) points out that certain activities that could be put into effect can help the youngster through the crucial transitional period:

> Most of the catching up should be done in intensive after-school programs—afternoons, weekends, summers, vacations—can all be utilized. Homework helpers, tutors, teachings machines, educational TV, specially trained teachers, and the best existing teachers and supervisors (master teachers) should be utilized. These programs should key on reading, basic knowledge and school know-how, test-taking skills, how to do homework, make outlines, participate in class, take notes, etc. The assumption should be made that these students are ignorant and uninformed rather than unintelligent, non-verbal, lacking in motivation and the like. The parents must be intensively involved in supporting these after-school programs. Dr. Samuel Shepard's approach to involving parents in the Banneker District of St. Louis might provide an excellent model.

However, integration at the early school levels will prevent many of the educational deficiencies that are so apparent at the later elementary and upper school levels without diluting the academic program and might allow adequate social learning for both Negro and white students.

The general question of this paper was "After School Integration—What?" Certainly, educators must seek to minimize rather than maximize differences between the minority and majority student when integration occurs. Remedial programs during the transitional period should be carefully scrutinized in order to decrease the negative psychological effects of "special classes" which might make "catching up" more difficult. Students who need extra or remedial help should spend a good portion of the school day in regular classrooms. Furthermore, constant evaluation and careful counseling should be a part of the program to allow disadvantaged students to move rapidly to a regular academic schedule. Finally, teacher and in-service training programs are crucial and should focus on the educational challenge of teaching in integrated schools rather than on the pitfalls of such an experience.

REFERENCES:

BLODGETT, E., and GREEN, R. A junior high school group counseling program. *J. Negro Educ.*, Winter, 1966 (in press).

BULLOCK, H. A. A comparison of the academic achievements of white and Negro high school graduates. *J. Educ. Res.,* 1950, *44,* 179–192.

DEUTSCH, M. Minority group and class status as related to social and personality factors in scholastic achievement. *Soc. Appl. Anthropology Monograph,* 1960, *2,* 1–32.

GOTTLIEB, D. Teaching and students: the views of Negro and white teachers. Unpublished paper, Michigan State Univ., 1963.

GRAMBS, JEAN D. Are we training prejudiced teachers? *Sch. Soc.,* 1950, *71,* 196–198.

GRAMBS, JEAN D. The self-concept: basis for re-education of Negro youth. In Kvaraceus (Ed.), *Negro Self-concept: Implications for School and Citizenship.* Cooperative Research Project G-020, United States Office of Education, Department of Health, Education, and Welfare, 1964.

GREEN, R., and FARQUHAR, W. W. Negro academic motivation and scholastic achievement. *J. Educ. Psychol.,* 1965, *56,* 241–243.

GREEN, R., HOFMANN, L., MORSE, R. HAYES, MARILYN, and MORGAN, R. *The Educational Status of Children in a District without Public Schools.* Cooperative Research Project No. 2321, United States Office of Education, Department of Health, Education, and Welfare, 1964.

HAUBRICH, V. F. Teachers for big-city schools. In Passow (Ed.), *Education in Depressed Areas* (New York: Columbia Univ., 1963).

LIPSITT, L. P. A self-concept scale for children and its relationship to the children's form of manifest anxiety scale. *Child Develpm.,* 1958, *29,* 463–472.

MUSSEN, P. H., and PORTER, L. W. Personal motivations and self-conceptions associated with effectiveness and ineffectiveness in emergent groups. *J. Abnor. Soc. Psychol.,* 1959, *59,* 23–27.

PHILLIPS, W. B. Counseling Negro pupils: an educational dilemma. *J. Negro Educ.,* 1960, *29,* 504–507.

RIESSMAN, F. Integration: the key to quality education for all. Unpublished paper presented at Michigan State Univ. Symposium on School Integration, May, 1964.

45   Why Dropout Campaigns Fail*

BY BERNARD BARD

EDITOR'S NOTE: The dropout represents a special kind of social-educational-psychological problem in our society. Even though the dropout problem is probably more talked about and better understood than most school-related problems, schools are hard-pressed to know how to keep a potential dropout in school once he is identified or what to do with dropouts who are lured back after having been gone for awhile. One has to wonder how effective—and how sincere—our dropout programs really are. The author questions the effectiveness of most dropout campaigns and suggests that schools may ". . . give youngsters a hypocritical runaround instead of the 'Second Chance' their posters advertise." Maybe—what do you think?

Two years ago the U.S. Office of Education spent a quarter of a million dollars in twenty major cities to identify dropouts, and to persuade them back to school. Some 30,411 dropouts were identified, of whom 10,015 agreed to come back. To this date, no one knows how many of those ten thousand stayed until graduation, and how many dropped out again. "There has been no followup," said Leroy V. Goodman, information director for the Office of Education. "School districts operated on their own."

The information gap about the fate of the ten thousand typifies much that has been said, written, and researched (or not researched) about the multiplicity of anti-dropout drives in progress across the nation. On the whole, there has been no systematic evaluation of their success or failure.

* Reprinted from *Saturday Review*, September 17, 1966, 78–79, 95–97, by permission of the author and the publisher.

The campaigns come in many packages, from the rehabilitative Dropouts Anonymous to the humanitarian Operation Second Chance to the mundane Stay-in-School. Virtually all suffer from the same basic weaknesses. The school officials who mount these efforts are often more concerned with the image than the reality of their dropout drives. And, in many major cities, while the bus placards warn marginal students not to chuck it all, principals are chucking them out of school by the tens of thousands. Often the school districts are either unable or unwilling to follow up on their own propaganda. The returning dropout may be confronted with red tape, hostility, and constant reminders that he failed once and no one in authority expects much more from him the second time around.

Washington, D.C., persuaded hundreds of dropouts to come back in the fall of 1963, but didn't know what to do with them once they got there. At Spingarn High School, overcrowding was so severe, ninety dropouts were shoe-horned into a room. Some sat on radiators or stood in the rear. Other classrooms were overloaded with fifty and sixty students. At McKinley and Eastern High Schools, the dropouts were assigned to the same schools they had quit, depositing them, in effect, into the same environment of failure. Six out of ten quit again.

A premise of the anti-dropout mechanism is that getting the victim back to school is most of the battle. It is wrong, if nothing significant has changed about school to keep him there. And, as a rule, nothing has been changed. A growing body of expert opinion among youth specialists and sociologists holds that working on the dropout problem via the dropout is rather phony. Such an approach assumes the dropout is at fault, when actually he may have made his own shrewd appraisal of what school and the high-school diploma is worth in terms of his own future. Negroes and Puerto Ricans know that their diploma is often useless on the job market. Statistically, there is practically no difference in the unemployment rates of minority-group youngsters who finish high-school and those who drop out.

Dr. Abraham Tannenbaum, a consultant to New York's Mobilization for Youth and an associate professor at Teachers College, Columbia University, says, "Society is resorting to the Big Lie and using a convenient excuse when it employs the label—'the dropout problem.' We tell youngsters to stay in school so they can earn more money. This is all very well if you're talking to a white kid, but for the Negro it will only make a little bit of difference, not much. By conning the sixteen-year-old to stay in school for another year or two, we know or should know that it's not going to make a great deal of difference in his chances. This is balony; it's like putting a Band Aid on cancer."

The scope of the dropout problem dulls the senses. The statistics are already a cliché. Of the 3,800,000 Americans who reach age eighteen every year, at least 1,200,000 will be dropouts. Ten per cent will be chronically jobless. A year ago, the number of jobless youths between sixteen and twenty-one stood at 730,000. In five years, if present trends hold up, the figure will more than double.

What schools are doing about it—while often irrelevant—covers a wide range of approaches. Galveston, Texas, organized a Dropouts Anonymous, with groups meeting once a week. When a member shows signs of defeatism, a group leader talks him out of dropping out again. Of those participating, there is an 85 per cent holding-power. Denver runs a Metropolitan Youth Education Center, which arranges a flexible work-study program. Potential dropouts can proceed through school without grades, and without time limit. Houston has a Talent Preservation Program; Albuquerque a Lincoln Project; Memphis a Youth Corps; and Chicago an EE (Education-Employment) Program. The list goes on and on, but what does it add up to? Frequently, nothing.

At the root of the so-called dropout problem, of course, is this statistical indictment—schools in the big cities spawn far more dropouts than can be salvaged. The nation's five largest cities, New York, Los Angeles, Chicago, Detroit, and Philadelphia, have a combined average dropout rate of 24 per cent. (Philadelphia is the champ, with a whopping 46.6 per cent.) In general, the larger the city, the higher the dropout rate, according to the NEA. Even the job of compiling dependable dropout statistics is made next to impossible by the duplicity of some school districts. The NEA, in its dropout project, found that some school officials only keep dropout records on a nine-month basis. Since about 25 per cent of the dropouts occur over the summer, the nine-month casualty list is artificially depressed.

Some other systems compute the dropout percentage against the "total school population," which means first grade through high school. Since few pupils are precocious enough to call it quits in the third, or fourth, or sixth grade—even if compulsory attendance laws allowed them to—this approach is a statistical lie. To obtain accurate dropout percentages—measured against high-school enrollments—the NEA found it had to throw out figures supplied by many districts and work instead from raw U.S. census data. The same schoolmen who are in part responsible for the dropout tried, in other words, to camouflage the number of victims.

How great is the distance between what school officials say and what they do concerning the dropout? The case of Laura M., from the files of Mobilization for Youth, suggests the disparity. She became pregnant, and dropped out of Washington Irving High School in lower Manhattan. After she had her child, she tried to go back under Operation Return, a city program aimed at the 27,000 city students who quit school each year. At first, she was told by an assistant principal at Irving to try another school. She did. The new school sent for her records, but weeks elapsed before their arrival. Meanwhile, Laura was advised to seek counseling from one of the maze of agencies working on dropouts. She selected MFY, which bombarded Irving with phone calls in an effort to obtain her records.

Finally, as a last desperate act, a project director called Board of Education headquarters, and was told: "Laura is not acceptable because of motherhood status." MFY had never heard of such a regulation. A check with the Bureau of Attendance produced the information that it did not exist. "In fact, we encourage them to come back," said a functionary. "No one can take that right away from her."

Laura's rights had been taken from her, of course. Her enthusiasm for school had long vanished, crushed by the "get-lost" attitude at her old school and the inertia of the record-keepers. She abandoned the idea of returning to high school, and became a dropout statistic.

The biggest stumbling block is the school principal. In Harlem, a youth worker reported that "ninety-nine times out of a hundred the principal won't take the kid back." Similar conclusions were reported by the NEA in connection with its Project: School Dropout, despite the assertions of the official propaganda issued by various boards of education. Daniel Schreiber, former director of the project, found the prevailing attitude among principals to be one of hostility and suspicion. "The principals were most afraid the dropout would become a discipline problem," said Schreiber. "Their biggest worry was that the dropout might endanger the education of the others if he came back."

What about the dropout who doesn't drop out a second time? Does his perseverance pay off? Rarely. Pittsburgh recently inaugurated a month-long course for dropouts on how to get and hold a job. Ten Negroes signed up. At the windup, only one found employment. This, despite the fact that the course was planned by Pittsburgh businessmen who said they would help place the dropouts. School officials decided it would be cruel and pointless to bring dropouts back for more of the same.

The business community is ambivalent toward the dropout. On the one hand, hundreds of the nation's leading firms are cooperating with work-study programs aimed at luring him back to school while giving him a part-time job. On the other hand, there is substantial resistance on the part of many industrial giants. The rub apparently is that there aren't enough jobs to go around. In a recent nationwide sampling, the *Wall Street Journal* found a fear on the part of some firms of creating ill-will if dropouts were signed on. "If we let it be known we were hiring dropouts and then have to turn down a youngster who's got a high-school diploma, how do we explain it to him?" asked a personnel officer for a large insurance company. One of the nation's Big Three auto manufacturers (Ford) proposed that each of its 9,000 dealers provide a part-time job for a dropout, provided he returned to school. But dealer reaction was "pretty negative," so the plan was put on the shelf. "I'm frankly disappointed," said a company executive, "it would have helped 9,000 boys get back on the right track."

The anti-dropout effort, no matter how novel the approach or what combination of alphabet-soup the agency is packaged in, invariably comes at least five years too late. The dropout usually becomes visible in the third through the fifth grades. From that point on, he usually keeps stumbling—right out the schoolhouse door. It is quite often the school that has failed as much as the dropout.

"They are bored, tremendously bored," says Aramis Gomez, director of the East Harlem center of Job Orientation in Neighborhoods (JOIN) in Manhattan, a $3,000,000 program co-sponsored by the city and the U.S. Labor Department. "They yawn their way through school," says Dr. Tannenbaum of MFY.

Despite New York's many-sided approach to the problem, counselors still find in talking to dropouts that principals and teachers are "throwing them out arbitrarily." Many counselors at anti-dropout agencies fault the Board of Education on several counts—shoving out dropouts in filing-case batches, offering outmoded courses in obsolete skills at vocational schools, and permitting near-illiterates to get as far as the sophomore and junior years of high school. "We shouldn't be in business," asserted an official of a dropout agency with branches in the five boroughs. "Why should we have to offer courses in remedial reading and arithmetic? This is supposed to be done by the Board of Education—and yet it forms the biggest part of our job. We're taking on what they messed up in the first place."

A high Board of Education official admitted that it was standard practice to promote children who should be left back. She conceded, in fact, that as many as 25 per cent of the "graduates" of junior highs do not graduate at all, but are merely handed certificates of attendance, stating they have been there, and that's about all. "This is a fake," she said.

The pupil who is too old, then, for junior high is passed into senior high school without a diploma, and further shoved along the route to becoming a dropout. It is left for such as JOIN, MFY, and others, to pick up the pieces. MFY, for instance, runs a nonprofit service station and luncheonette to give realistic training to youngsters who need help in finding a job. But it has been found that many flunk the training courses because they can't handle enough arithmetic to add the city sales tax to a customer's bill. Much of the work of anti-dropout agencies boils down to patchwork educational remediation, or random efforts at finding jobs for a handful of trainees whose numbers are dwarfed by new "push-outs" and "squeeze-outs" and other categories of school rejects.

For the agencies, it is an up-mountain fight. New York's Neighborhood Youth Corps, for instance, obtained 4,500 full-time and 900 part-time jobs for dropouts last year—but the city that year produced five times that number of new dropouts. "This program is intended specifically as an aid to the high-school dropouts. Yet it would not affect the total dropout problem if it were magnified five-fold," said Professor Robert A. Dentler of the Center for Urban Education and a faculty member at Teachers College, Columbia University. "It is hard to grasp how it could be magnified at all, or even repeated in a second or third year of operation, since 40 per cent of the jobs being offered are for posts in city departments.

There is a fallacy inherent in such programs. They may supply a limited number of jobs for pupils fresh out of pilot programs, but they are very apt to be like the jobs available now for dropouts, scarce in number and good for one filling per generation."

While most dropout campaigns are too little and too late, there are some rays of light in the generally dismal picture. They may be seen, usually, in more imaginative school districts that saw past mistakes and completely overhauled programs. Washington, D.C., which muffed its earlier drive, tried again last year and found it was able to hold on to virtually all the returnees. Instead of shipping dropouts back to their old schools, they were installed in special night classes at Spingarn High School. The program is called STAY (School to Aid Youth). Classes run from 3:30 to 10 P.M., some lasting two hours so a student can take more credits in fewer trips to school. Classes are small (under twenty), all homework is done in school in recognition of the fact that many dropouts have no desk at home, and a full range of academic courses is offered. Students may take as many or as few courses as they wish. "There isn't any formula," said STAY director William F. Carpenter. "That's just the point. We find out what the kids need and give it to them. It's simple."

STAY officials made an interesting discovery—one that may have national implications. Students came into the program weeks before transcripts arrived from their former schools. They were asked to write down their own grades, so they could be placed accordingly. Later, when the records arrived, teachers were astonished to find that some of the hardest working students had been rated "absolute incorrigible" or otherwise hopeless. Knowing that their past records of failure had, in effect, been erased the dropouts gave themselves a clean slate and made good. School officials decided to ignore the old records altogether and to judge each returnee on the basis of current performance.

One of the miracles wrought by Assistant Superintendent Samuel Shepard, Jr., in the 95 per cent Negro Banneker District in St. Louis, has been a reversal of dropout trends among the 15,000 pupils in his twenty-three schools. Shepard reduced the rate from more than a third to less than one in ten by motivating parents as well as pupils. Parents were signed up as homework managers, as aids on field trips, as counselors to run study-ins. "You've heard of sit-ins and teach-ins," said Shepard. "Well, these are the same, except they're for studying." The parents were asked to sign pledges to turn off the radio or television during homework hours. They promised to sign each day's homework, or to check with the school when a child said there was none. Teachers who complained of too-large classes were told the class size would be cut, and it was now up to them to "deliver or get out." Dropouts in Banneker today average well below the St. Louis citywide average of 13 per cent.

B. Frank Brown, principal of the 1,500-student Melbourne High School, Melbourne, Florida, faced a different sort of problem. His school, near the Cape Kennedy space center, accommodates children of mechanics as well as those of propulsion experts with Ph.D.'s. In 1959, he had an 18 per cent dropout rate. Today it is down to 4 per cent. He combatted dropouts through a non-graded high school program in which traditional grade levels are abolished and "phases of learning" are substituted. Students are taught in small and large study groups, and encouraged to progress at their own pace. Time is made available for individual research projects.

"If a fifteen-year-old reads at fourth grade level, we put him into a reading course at that level," said Brown. "Also we have a gimmick—a student dropout committee. It's composed of one good guy, such as the leader of the Student Council, and two bad buys, youngsters who dropped out and re-entered and are now making the grade. If a boy is about to drop out, the committee meets with him and hotboxes him. He's got to respect the ex-dropouts on the committee, and if he drops out anyway, the committee visits him at the filling station or wherever he's working and puts more pressure on him. Many dropouts return."

Dropouts can be helped—but not the way most school districts are trying to do it. To begin with, the effort must start years earlier. The dropout is "a victim of some alien middle-class culture," said Edgar Z. Friedenberg, the author of *The Vanishing Adolescent* and now a member of the faculty at the University of California at Davis. "They know quite well what we can do with it. Dropping out is one way of telling us. It is about time we turned our attention to the things about the school that are bugging them. The school is the arena in which these youngsters encounter middle-class life. This is where the dropouts fight the ten-year ideological war that ends in their defeat and rout."

For those who do walk out on school—assuming the school has done its best to keep them there—something more must be offered than an editorial in the high-school paper or a placard in the subway inviting them back. Most of the authorities in the field believe that there must be either some form of scholarship aid or a subsidized work-study program. The conventional back-to-school pitch—without such a financial sweetener—is a public-relations fraud and a hoax on the children who literally must leave school because their parents can't afford to keep them there. If necessary, schools must pay to keep impoverished youngsters from dropping out. This will show the dropout that more than words stands behind the stay-in-school progaganda.

And, most important, the economy must produce more jobs. Dr. Dentler and Mary Ellen Warshauer, in a just-published study, *Big City Dropouts and Illiterates,* discovered that the dropout rate in any community is almost always directly linked to the level of job opportunity. Cities with the most expensive educational programs or the most elaborate anti-dropout drives produced massive numbers of dropouts if they were in an economic slump. The converse was also true. "Anti-dropout programs were irrelevant," Dentler said. "If they were having any impact, we would have found a correlation. There wasn't even a flicker."

The dropout has too long been the whipping boy. The schools have told him he is not wanted, and shown him the door. The economy has told him he is "surplus" and unskilled. And the public-relations lures that have been set forth to draw him back to classes have led him instead to a head-butting contest with school officials who don't really want him, and don't know what to do with him when he shows up. Part of the problem, of course, lies with the dropout himself. But a major source of trouble lies in schools that don't teach, an economy without enough jobs, and school officials who give youngsters a hypocritical runaround instead of the "Second Chance" their posters advertise.

46   *A Poor Scholar's Soliloquy**

BY STEPHEN M. COREY

EDITOR'S NOTE: *Although written over 20 years ago, this article still carries a timely and relevant message. It is, in many ways, the soliloquy of thousands of so-called "disadvantaged" youth and from that point of view seemed the most appropriate selection to end this chapter of the book. Read it carefully. Depending on the professional work you do, youngsters of this sort may end up either on your caseload or in your classroom and it is imperative that we try to understand them from their point of view.*

No, I'm not very good in school. This is my second year in the seventh grade and I'm bigger and taller than the other kids. They like me all right, though, even if I don't say much in the schoolroom, because outside I can tell them how to do a lot of things. They tag me around and that sort of makes up for what goes on in school.

I don't know why the teachers don't like me. They never have very much. Seems like they don't think you know anything unless you can read the book it comes out of. I've got a lot of books in my own room at home—books like Popular Science, Mechanical Encyclopedia, and the Sears' and Ward's catalogues, but I don't very often just sit down and read them through like they make us do in school. I use my books when I want to find something out, like whenever Mom buys anything secondhand I

* "The Poor Scholar's Soliloquy" by Stephen M. Corey. From *Childhood Education*, January, 1944, Vol. 20, No. 5. Reprinted by permission of the author and the Association for Childhood Education International, 3615 Wisconsin Avenue, N.W., Washington, D.C., 20016.

look it up in Sears' or Ward's first and tell her if she's getting stung or not. I can use the index in a hurry to find the things I want.

In school, though, we've got to learn whatever is in the book and I just can't memorize the stuff. Last year I stayed after school every night for two weeks trying to learn the names of the Presidents. Of course I knew some of them like Washington and Jefferson and Lincoln, but there must have been thirty altogether and I never did get them straight.

I'm not too sorry though because the kids who learned the Presidents had to turn right around and learn all the Vice Presidents. I'm taking the seventh grade over but our teacher this year isn't so interested in the names of Presidents. She had us trying to learn the names of all the great American inventors.

I guess I just can't remember names in history. Anyway, this year I've been trying to learn about trucks because my uncle owns three and he says I can drive one when I'm sixteen. I already know the horsepower and number of forward and backward speeds of twenty-six American trucks, some of them Diesels, and I can spot each make a long way off. It's funny how the Diesel works. I started to tell my teacher about it last Wednesday in science class when the pump we were using to make a vacuum in a bell jar got hot, but she said she didn't see what a Diesel engine had to do with our experiment on air pressure so I just kept still. The kids seemed interested, though. I took four of them around to my uncle's garage after school and we saw the mechanic, Gus, tearing a big truck Diesel down. Boy, does he know his stuff!

I'm not very good in geography either. They call it economic geography this year. We've been studying the imports and exports of Chile all week but I couldn't tell you what they are. Maybe the reason is I had to miss school yesterday because my uncle took me and his big trailer truck down state about two hundred miles and we brought almost ten tons of stock to the Chicago market.

He had told me where we were going and I had to figure out the highways to take and the mileage. He didn't do anything but drive and turn where I told him to. Was that fun! I sat with a map in my lap and told him to turn south or southeast or some other direction. We made seven stops and drove over five hundred miles round trip. I'm figuring now what his oil cost and also the wear and tear on the truck—he calls it depreciation—so we'll know how much we made.

I even write out all the bills and send letters to the farmers about what their pigs and beef cattle brought at the stockyards. I only made three mistakes in 17 letters last time, my aunt said—all commas. She's been through high school and reads them over. I wish I could write school themes that way. The last one I had to write was on, "What a Daffodil Thinks of Spring," and I just couldn't get going.

I don't do very well in school in arithmetic either. Seems I just can't keep my mind on the problems. We had one the other day like this: If a

57 foot telephone pole falls across a cement highway so that 17 3/5 feet extend from one side and 14 9/17 feet from the other, how wide is the highway? I don't even try to answer it because it didn't say whether the pole had fallen straight across or not.

Even in shop I don't get very good grades. All of us kids made a broom holder and a book end this term and mine were sloppy. I just couldn't get interested. Mom doesn't use a broom anymore with her new vacuum cleaner, and our books are in a bookcase with glass doors in the parlor. Anyway, I wanted to make an end gate for my uncle's trailer but the shop teacher said that meant using metal and wood both and I'd have to learn to work with wood first. I didn't see why, but I kept still and made a tie rack at school and the tail gate after school at my uncle's garage. He said I saved him $10.00.

Civics is hard for me, too. I've been staying after school trying to learn the "Articles of Confederation" for almost a week because the teacher said we couldn't be good citizens unless we did. I really tried, because I want to be a good citizen. I did hate to stay after school, though, because a bunch of us boys from the south end of town have been cleaning up the old lot across from Taylor's Machine Shop to make a playground out of it for the little kids from the Methodist Home. I made the jungle gym from old pipe and the guys made me Grand Mogul to keep the playground going. We raised enough money collecting scrap this month to build a wire fence clear around the lot.

Dad says I can quit school when I'm fifteen and I'm sort of anxious to because there are lots of things I want to learn how to do, and as my uncle says, I'm not getting any younger.

PART FIVE

Toward Understanding What Happens Within One's Self

"I am a human being, whatever that may be. . . . I am like a man journeying through a forest, aware of occasional glints of light overhead, with recollections of the long trail I have already traveled, and conscious of wider spaces ahead. I want to see more clearly where I have been and where I am going, and above all I want to know why I am where I am and why I am traveling at all."*

Interesting creatures, we humans. We can see where we've been, but we're not always sure what it means. We can see where we are, but we're not always certain how we got there. We can state the direction in which we would like to head, but we're not always sure how to go about it. We can tell people our names, but not our identity. We find it easier to describe what we have than to explain who we are. We have the unique talent for being able to think about what we've already thought about and still be puzzled. Indeed, in each of our individual pursuits for answers, for values, for whatever you want to call it, we are inescapably confronted with the problem of *meaning*—with the question of what life is all about. And in this context we may think in terms of three basic questions which each of us must attempt to answer if we are to become more personally effective in the sense of being more open to our experiences and more capable of developing our potentialities:

Who am I?
Where am I going?
Why?

Each of these questions, in its own way, deals with our sense of self, our goals, our means, our values, our strengths and weaknesses, and our way of life or "life style."

This section of the book, then, is one small step in the direction of not only raising questions but also answering questions related to the three basic questions listed above. It is an interesting, if not a lamentable, facet of our educational system that we study almost everything else before getting around to studying ourselves. The three chapters in this section are designed to probe and explore the question, "What do I mean to myself and how can I get to know myself better?"

Chapter Eleven treats the twin concepts, freedom and control, and the implications of these concepts or, if you will, "possibilities" for education and personal growth. The points of view range from Rogerian Freedom to Skinnerian Determinism. To a large extent, the intellectual encounters between the "free will" adherents and the "determinism" supporters have been noteworthy for what seems to be the panting (albeit myopic) passion with which each side embraces its own point of view. It is hoped that the selections in this chapter will encourage the sort of discussion which allows us to put into better perspective the usual monolithic oppositions between freedom and determinism.

Chapter Twelve attempts to go a step deeper by examining not only the concept but also the meaning of personality in terms of its origins, its organization, its growth, and its defenses. The men contributing to this chapter (Drs. Coleman, Maslow, Rogers, and Symonds) have spent their entire professional lives studying and trying to understand people and are eminently qualified to comment on the dynamics of personality and personal adjustment.

Chapter Thirteen, "Toward Understanding Self," seemed to be a logical conclusion to this section of the book. Both Drs. Fromm and Rogers contribute ideas about the meaning of personal existence and personal identity which have a kind of universal quality—that is, universal in the sense that each of us must answer the "Who am I?" and "What does it all mean?" questions before moving on to higher levels of actualization. The selections by William James and Miss Williams will speak for themselves. They are included to provoke not just thought but thoughtfulness as well.

When we are able to arrive at that point in life where we know pretty much who we are, and what we believe in, and what we stand for, and what we don't, we will be a step closer to the outlook stated so well by an unknown author:

"A master in the art of living draws no sharp distinction between his work and his play, his labour and his leisure, his mind and his body, his education and his recreation. He hardly knows which is which. He simply pursues his vision to excellence through whatever he is doing and leaves others to determine whether he is working or playing. To himself he always seems to be doing both."

In the final analysis, if we really desire to understand ourselves better, then perhaps we ought to allow life itself to be our laboratory for discovering who we are, with experience as our evidence.

CHAPTER ELEVEN

FREEDOM TO BECOME: ILLUSION OR REALITY?

47   Implications of Recent Advances in Prediction and Control of Behavior*

BY CARL R. ROGERS

EDITOR'S NOTE: Psychology has involved itself for many years with the problem of how to control and predict behavior. As Dr. Rogers points out in this article, there seems to be little question but that people can be controlled and predicted. The question is not so much whether control or prediction is possible but rather for what ends knowledge about human behavior is used. This reading will set the stage for the four subsequent readings in this chapter. As you read, be thinking about the implications for teacher behavior and the variety of techniques available to teachers (or anyone else, for that matter) to either control or free students.

The science of psychology, in spite of its immaturities and its brashness, has advanced mightily in recent decades. From a concern with observation and measurement, it has moved toward becoming an "if-then" science. By this I mean it has become more concerned with the discernment and discovery of lawful relationships such as that *if* certain conditions exist, *then* certain behaviors will predictably follow.

I believe that few people are aware of the breadth, depth, and extent of the advances in psychology and the behavioral sciences, and still fewer seem to be aware of the profound social, political, economic, ethical, philosophical, and educational problems posed by these advances. In this discussion I should like to focus on the educational implications of these advances in the science of psychology (which inevitably will involve me in

* Reprinted from *Teachers College Record,* 1956, Vol. 57, 316–322, by permission of the author and the publisher.

some concern with the philosophical implications as well) and to review a few selected examples of what I mean by the increased ability of psychology to understand and predict or control behavior. Each illustration I will give is supported by reasonably rigorous and adequate research, though like all scientific findings, each is open to modification or correction through more exact or imaginative future studies.

What, then, are some of the behaviors or learnings for which we now know how to supply the antecedent conditions?

We know how to set up the conditions under which many members of a group will report judgments which are contrary to the evidence of their senses. They will, for example, report that Figure A covers a larger area than Figure B, when the evidence of their senses *plainly* indicates that the reverse is true. Experiments by Asch (2), later refined and improved by Crutchfield (7), show that when a person is led to believe that everyone else in the group sees B as larger than A, then he has a strong tendency to go along with this judgment, and in many instances does so with a real belief in his false report.

We know a great deal about how to establish conditions which will influence consumer responses and/or public opinion. I refer you to the advertisements in any magazine, or to the TV program, "The $64,000 Question," and the sales of the sponsor's lipsticks.

We know how to influence the buying behavior of individuals by setting up conditions which provide satisfaction for needs of which they are unconscious, but which we have been able to determine. It has been shown that some women who do not buy instant coffee because of "a dislike for its flavor" actually dislike it at a subconscious level because it is associated in their minds with laziness, spendthrift qualities, and being a poor housekeeper (11). This type of study has led to sales campaigns based upon appealing to the unconscious motives of the individual—his unknown sexual, aggressive, or dependent desires.

We know how to predict which members of an organization will be troublesome and delinquent. On the basis of a paper and pencil test, Gough (11) has predicted which department store employees will be unreliable and dishonest or otherwise difficult. He freely states that it is quite possible to identify, with a good deal of accuracy, the potential troublemakers of any organized group.

This ability to identify troublemakers is only an extension of the knowledge we have about prediction in other fields—predicting which individual is most likely to become a good salesman, or typesetter, or physician, or student in college.

We know how to provide conditions in a work group, whether in industry or in education, which will be followed by increased productivity, originality, and morale. Conversely we know how to provide the conditions which lead to low productivity and low morale. Studies by Coch and French (5), and by Katz, Maccoby, and Morse (13) show in general that when workers in industry participate in planning and decisions, and when they are not supervised in a suspicious or authoritarian way, production and morale increase. The reverse conditions produce a reverse effect. A study reported by Corey (6) indicates that when the leader of a teacher group acts in a manner which is understanding, and which facilitates participation, the group is more productive in making and carrying through plans.

We know how to provide the conditions of leadership which will be followed by personality growth in the members of the group, as well as by increased productivity and improved group spirit. Richard (14), in his experience as manager of an industrial plant, and Gordon (10), in his study of leadership of a workshop, have shown that where the leader or leaders hold the attitudes customarily thought of as therapeutic, the results are good. In other words, if the leader is understanding, acceptant, and permissive toward his group and also acceptant of his own feelings in the situation, then the members of the group show evidence of personality growth and function more effectively and with better spirit.

We know how to provide the psychological conditions in the class-room which will result not only in the usual learning of academic content, but in improved personal adjustment as well. Studies by Asch (1) and Faw (8) show that if the attitudes of the teacher are similar to those described above for the leader, and hence responsible participation by the student is permitted and encouraged, then academic learning proceeds about as usual as measured by conventional tests, and personal growth and adjustment improve significantly.

We know how to provide an interpersonal relationship with qualities such that it enables the individual to meet stress with more serenity, less anxiety. Thetford (19), in an experiment with group therapy, and Faw (9), in a recent study of teacher-pupil relationships in the classroom, came to similar conclusions, though using very different methods and instruments. When individuals—clients or students—have experienced for a time a relationship of warmth, understanding, and acceptance, they are able to meet stress situations with less physiological upset and quicker recovery of physiological balance [Thetford] and are less upset psychologically by the stress [Faw].

We know the attitudes which, if provided by a counselor or a therapist, will be predictably followed by certain constructive personality and behavior changes in the client. Studies which in recent years have been completed in the field of psychotherapy justify this statement (17,

15, 16). The findings from these studies may be very briefly summarized in the following terms:

If the therapist provides a relationship in which he is (a) genuine, internally consistent; (b) acceptant, prizing the client as a person of worth; (c) empathically understanding of the client's private world; then the client becomes (a) more realistic in his self-perceptions; (b) more confident and self-directing; (c) more positively valued by himself; (d) less likely to repress elements of his experience; (e) more mature, socialized, and adaptive in his behavior; (f) more like the healthy, integrated, well-functioning person in his personality structure.

It is obvious that the essence of these findings in the field of therapy is closely related to the three previous illustrations.

We now know how, I believe, to disintegrate a man's personality structure, dissolving his self-confidence, destroying the concept he has of himself, and making him completely dependent upon another. This example has not been, so far as I know, verified by objective research. I make this statement after having studied, as far as one is able, the methods used in preparing prisoners for confession in various purge trials in Russia, and the brainwashing procedures applied in Communist China. It seems rather evident that these methods use many of the principles of psychotherapy, but use them in reverse fashion to bring about the disintegration of the autonomous personality, rather than integration. In a curious and abhorrent way this tends to validate the principles of psychotherapy mentioned above, because it indicates that the lawfulness of the process of therapy may be used to build or destroy personality.

We know how to provide psychological conditions which will produce vivid hallucinations and other abnormal reactions in the thoroughly normal individual in the waking state. This knowledge came about as the unexpected by-product of research at McGill University (4). It was discovered that if all channels of sensory stimulation are cut off or muffled, abnormal reactions follow. If healthy subjects lie relatively motionless, to reduce kinesthetic stimuli, with eyes shielded by translucent goggles which do not permit perception, with hearing largely stifled by foam-rubber pillows as well as by being in a quiet cubicle, and with tactile sensations reduced by cuffs over the hands, then hallucinations and ideation bearing some resemblance to that of the psychotic occur within forty-eight hours in many of these subjects. What the results would be if the sensory stifling were continued longer is not known.

We know how to influence psychological moods, attitudes, and behaviors through drugs. For this illustration we have stepped over into the rapidly developing borderline area between chemistry and psychology. From "truth serum," to the chemotherapy now practiced in psychiatric wards, to drugs for the normal citizen there are many ways of changing psychological states. We may take a drug to mobilize our energy to cram for an exam, or a drug to allay our anxiety about the exam. Drugs have reportedly been given to soldiers before a battle to eliminate fear. While much is still unknown in this field, Dr. Skinner of Harvard states that "In the not-too-distant future, the motivational and emotional conditions of normal life will probably be maintained in any desired state through the use of drugs."(18)

We know the psychological conditions of family life which, if established in a home, will tend to produce emotionally secure children with many socially valuable characteristics. Here we go to a very different field, that of personality development in children, for our example. We can measure the attitudes and emotional climate which parents are creating for their children, and from these measurements we can predict that Home A will in all probability produce children who will grow somewhat brighter over the years, will be emotionally secure, original, relatively unexcitable; who will be liked by their peers, likely to be leaders, and well-adjusted to adults. On the other hand we can predict that Home B will be likely to produce emotional, excitable children, with little emotional control, and with less of originality than the children from Home A. The studies done by Baldwin and others (3) at the Fels Research Institute are the basis for these statements. Home A is the home in which the parents' attitudes and behaviors cluster in what the investigators have termed the "democratic" category, and parental attitudes and behaviors in Home B cluster in what they term the "actively rejectant" group.

My purpose in the above examples has been to point up the wide-ranging power, the very diverse potentialities for control and prediction, which psychological knowledge is giving us. When we project ourselves into the future, and try to imagine the further developments which will inevitably come, the prospect arouses uneasiness. Small wonder that Dr. Robert Oppenheimer, in speaking of the points of similarity between his own profession, physics, and the profession of psychology, says that one of these points "is the extent to which our progress will create profound problems of decision in the public domain. The physicists have been quite noisy about their contributions in the last decade. The time may well come—as psychology acquires a sound objective corpus of knowledge about human behavior and feeling—when the powers of control thus made available will pose far graver problems than any the physicists have posed."[1]

Inherent in this development of the psychological or behavioral sciences are, I believe, two profound questions for educators. They are: How do educators propose to use these rapidly increasing potentialities for influencing and altering human learning and human behavior? How shall we prepare students to live in a world where the possibilities for such control of human behavior exist?

I shall not attempt to answer either of these questions, but shall only comment on each one. As to how educators propose to use this accumulating knowledge, I believe it is clear that it will depend entirely on their philosophy of education, as that philosophy is operationally defined in action. We are rapidly acquiring the knowledge and the skills which will enable us to turn out passive followers or independent citizens. Many teachers and educators, if we take account of their actions rather than their words, have the former as their goal. They will be able to implement this purpose much more adequately in the future. On the other hand, if the aim is to turn out self-directing, inquiring minds which will form their own judgments as to the truth, then knowledge exists which can facilitate this purpose also. It will be up to the educators, and even more broadly, up to the community, to choose the direction in which we shall go.

With regard to how we shall prepare students to live in this fearsome future world, I believe some of the research I have cited suggests possible answers.

In the investigation by Crutchfield (7), it was found that about one-third of the responses made by a group of individuals were strongly influenced by the majority opinion, even when that majority opinion was clearly false. However, not all individuals were equally influenced. Some persons were swayed on almost every item by what they thought to be a solid group opinion, but others were influenced scarcely at all. They "called the shots as they saw them," regardless of what others might think.

When Crutchfield analyzed the personality characteristics of these two groups on the basis of extensive personality assessment, the differences were sharp. The conforming group, who were swayed by the majority opinion, tended to be individuals who had little understanding of themselves, were defensive, had to put up a good "front." They were rigid, moralistic, and had great respect for authority. They were somewhat anxious, guilty, suggestible, and unable to tolerate ambiguity. They lacked self-confidence were vacillating, and tended to become confused under stress.

The independent group, on the other hand, were active, effective, persuasive leaders. They were individuals in whom others felt confidence, and they had confidence in themselves. They were natural, unaffected, nondefensive, and expressive. They were unconventional and adventurous.

To generalize somewhat speculatively from Crutchfield's study to some of the others, I believe it may be tentatively said that the individuals who may be most easily "managed" through the psychological know-how I have tried to sketch in this paper are those who are passive, rigid, insecure, and authoritarian. On the other hand, those who resist being "managed," who are able to deal intelligently with these possible influences, are confident, open, secure, independent, and spontaneous.

But here again we face an exciting fact. The individuals who were not overwhelmed by the majority opinion in Crutchfield's experiment bear a very strong resemblance to individuals produced in a democratic home atmosphere, to workers who have developed in a group-centered industrial situation, to students who have been exposed to an acceptant teacher-pupil relationship, to clients who have experienced a warm and empathic relationship in therapy. In other words, we already know to a considerable degree how to provide the conditions in which such individuals develop. And though the reverse evidence is not quite so clear, I believe it may be said that in large measure we also know how to provide the conditions in which the passive, insecure followers develop.

What I have been trying to say is that the growing body of knowledge in the behavioral sciences gives to our modern culture an astonishing power of choice. We know how to influence and mold behavior and personality in a great many significant ways. We also have available the choice of whether to set the conditions which develop a suggestible, submissive, unsure individual who can be easily influenced to behave in any way that "we" think wise, or the conditions which will develop an open, adaptive, independent, free-thinking, self-respecting individual. It is this latter person who will perhaps be able to use with intelligence and sensitivity to human values the enormous powers which the physical and behavioral sciences are putting at his disposal. The issue of what choice to make in this regard constitutes, I believe, the challenge of tomorrow both for education and for our whole culture.

It might well be pointed out that with few exceptions the psychological know-how which I have sketched has not been widely used or exploited by society. Hence it might seem that the challenge as I have described it is greatly exaggerated.

It is quite true that this knowledge has not been widely used. In this respect the status of the physical sciences is very different from that of the behavioral sciences. The physical sciences have become so greatly respected that if scientists from these fields report that they can create a satellite in space, the only question in the public mind is, How soon will it be done? There is no tendency to scoff at the possibility, as the public in 1906 scoffed at the Wright brothers' "ridiculous" predictions that a machine could fly. As of 1955 the behavioral sciences occupy, in the public mind, a status similar to that of the physical sciences in 1906. The community does not as yet believe that the behavioral sciences can achieve results. Yet this attitude is changing with remarkable rapidity. Who would have supposed, a few years ago, that our military forces would invest millions of dollars in research in the behavioral sciences, that industrial leaders would employ consultants whose main task is to provide a therapeutic relationship for the executives, that research in consumer attitudes would be a big business?

So I conclude that knowledge in the science of psychology will in the near future be used and exploited as fully as knowledge in the physical sciences is used today. The challenge for educators is unreal only if we are looking a year or two ahead. From the long view I know of no problem holding greater potentiality of growth and of destruction than the question of how to live with the increasing power the behavioral sciences will place in our hands and the hands of our children.

FOOTNOTE:

1 From a speech to the American Psychological Association, San Francisco, September 5, 1955.

REFERENCES:

1. ASCH, MORTON J. "Nondirective Teaching in Psychology: An Experimental Study." *Psychological Monographs*, 1951, 65, 4, 24 pp.
2. ASCH, SOLOMON E., *Social Psychology* (New York: Prentice-Hall, 1952). pp. 450–83.
3. BALDWIN, A. L., JOAN KALHORN, and F. H. BREESE. "Patterns of Parent Behavior." *Psychological Monographs*, No. 268, 1945, 58, No. 3, pp. 1–75.
4. BESTON, W. H., WOODBURN HERON, and T. H. SCOTT. "Effects of Decreased Variation in the Sensory Environment." *Canadian Journal of Psychology*, 1954, 8, pp. 70–76.
5. COCH, LESTER, and J. R. P. FRENCH, JR., "Overcoming Resistance to Change." *Human Relations*, 1948, 1, 512–32.
6. COREY, S. M., *Action Research to Improve School Practices*. New York, Bureau of Publications, Teachers College, 1953, pp. 47–61.
7. CRUTCHFIELD, RICHARD S. "Conformity and Character." *American Psychology*, 1955, 10, 191–98.
8. FAW, VOLNEY E. "A Psychotherapeutic Method of Teaching Psychology." *American Psychology*, 1949, 4, pp. 104–9.
9. FAW, VOLNEY E., *Evaluation of Student-Centered Teaching*. Unpublished manuscript.
10. GORDON, THOMAS. *Group-Centered Leadership*, (Boston, Houghton Mifflin, 1955). Chapters 6 to 11.
11. GOUGH, H. E., and D. R. PETERSON. "The Identification and Measurement of Predispositional Factors in Crime and Delinquency." *Journal of Consulting Psychology*, 1952, 16, pp. 207–12.
12. HAIRE, M. "Projective Techniques in Marketing Research." *Journal of Marketing*, April 1950, vol. 14, pp. 649–56.
13. KATZ, D., N. MACCOBY, and N. C. MORSE. *Productivity, Supervision, and Morale in an Office Situation*. Part I. Ann Arbor, Survey Research Center, University of Michigan, 1950.
14. RICHARD, JAMES, in *Group-Centered Leadership*, by Thomas Gordon, (Boston: Houghton Mifflin, 1955), Chapters 12 and 13.

15. ROGERS, CARL R. *Client-Centered Therapy* (Boston: Houghton Mifflin, 1951).
16. ROGERS, CARL R., and ROSALIND F. DYMOND (editors). *Psychotherapy and Personality Change* (Chicago: University of Chicago Press, 1954).
17. SEEMAN, JULIUS, and NATHANIEL J. RASKIN. "Research Perspectives in Client-Centered Therapy," in O. H. Mowrer (ed.), *Psychotherapy: Theory and Research,* (New York: Ronald Press, 1953), Chapter 9.
18. SKINNER, B. F. "The Control of Human Behavior." Paper presented to the New York Academy of Sciences, April 18, 1955, and published in the transactions of that body, pp. 547–51.
19. THETFORD, WILLIAM N. "An Objective Measure of Frustration Tolerance in Evaluating Psychotherapy," in W. Wolff (ed.), *Success in Psychotherapy,* (New York: Grune & Stratton, 1952), Chapter 2.

48   Freedom and the Control of Men*

BY B. F. SKINNER

EDITOR'S NOTE: If you have read selection 35 in Chapter Eight, you will recall that Dr. Skinner constructed a mythical utopia in which behavior was controlled via known scientific principles. As we move into an era of increasing anxiety and greater introspection, questions of freedom and control, of "Can I really be me?" become accordingly more important. Dr. Skinner asserts that it is possible to produce proper, or right, or desirable behavior by simply arranging the proper conditions. He elaborates how we can do this and why we must do it. You will find this contrasting sharply with the emphasis in the preceding Rogers article. To give the problems and questions raised in readings 47 and 48 even greater perspective, read carefully the next two selections.

The second half of the twentieth century may be remembered for its solution of a curious problem. Although Western democracy created the conditions responsible for the rise of modern science, it is now evident that it may never fully profit from that achievement. The so-called "democratic philosophy" of human behavior to which it also gave rise is increasingly in conflict with the application of the methods of science to human affairs. Unless this conflict is somehow resolved, the ultimate goals of democracy may be long deferred.

* Reprinted from *American Scholar*, Winter, 1955–1956, Vol. 25, special issue, 47–65, by permission of the author.

I

Just as biographers and critics look for external influences to account for the traits and achievements of the men they study, so science ultimately explains behavior in terms of "causes" or conditions which lie beyond the individual himself. As more and more causal relations are demonstrated, a practical corollary becomes difficult to resist: it should be possible to *produce* behavior according to plan simply by arranging the proper conditions. Now, among the specifications which might reasonably be submitted to a behavioral technology are these: Let men be happy, informed, skillful, well behaved, and productive.

This immediate practical implication of a science of behavior has a familiar ring, for it recalls the doctrine of human perfectibility of eighteenth- and nineteenth-century humanism. A science of man shares the optimism of that philosophy and supplies striking support for the working faith that men can build a better world and, through it, better men. The support comes just in time, for there has been little optimism of late among those who speak from the traditional point of view. Democracy has become "realistic," and it is only with some embarrassment that one admits today to perfectionistic or utopian thinking.

The earlier temper is worth considering, however. History records many foolish and unworkable schemes for human betterment, but almost all the great changes in our culture which we now regard as worthwhile can be traced to perfectionistic philosophies. Governmental, religious, educational, economic, and social reforms follow a common pattern. Someone believes that a change in a cultural practice—for example, in the rules of evidence in a court of law, in the characterization of man's relation to God, in the way children are taught to read and write, in permitted rates of interest, or in minimal housing standards—will improve the condition of men: by promoting justice, permitting men to seek salvation more effectively, increasing the literacy of a people, checking an inflationary trend, or improving public health and family relations, respectively. The underlying hypothesis is always the same: that a different physical or cultural environment will make a different and better man.

The scientific study of behavior not only justifies the general pattern of such proposals; it promises new and better hypotheses. The earliest cultural practices must have originated in sheer accidents. Those which strengthened the group survived with the group in a sort of natural selection. As soon as men began to propose and carry out changes in practice for the sake of possible consequences, the evolutionary process must have accelerated. The simple practice of making changes must have had survival value. A further acceleration is now to be expected. As laws of behavior are more precisely stated, the changes in the environment required to bring about a given effect may be more clearly specified. Conditions which have been neglected because their effects were slight or unlooked for may be shown to be relevant. New conditions may actually be created, as in the discovery and synthesis of drugs which affect behavior.

This is no time, then, to abandon notions of progress, improvement or, indeed, human perfectibility. The simple fact is that man is able, and now as never before, to lift himself by his own bootstraps. In achieving control of the world of which he is a part, he may learn at last to control himself.

II

Timeworn objections to the planned improvement of cultural practices are already losing much of their force. Marcus Aurelius was probably right in advising his readers to be content with a haphazard amelioration of mankind. "Never hope to realize Plato's republic," he sighed, ". . . for who can change the opinions of men? And without a change of sentiments what can you make but reluctant slaves and hypocrites?" He was thinking, no doubt, of contemporary patterns of control based upon punishment or the threat of punishment which, as he correctly observed, breed only reluctant slaves of those who submit and hypocrites of those who discover modes of evasion. But we need not share his pessimism, for the opinions of men can be changed. The techniques of indoctrination which were being devised by the early Christian Church at the very time Marcus Aurelius was writing are relevant, as are some of the techniques of psychotherapy and of advertising and public relations. Other methods suggested by recent scientific analyses leave little doubt of the matter.

The study of human behavior also answers the cynical complaint that there is a plain "cussedness" in man which will always thwart efforts to improve him. We are often told that men do not want to be changed, even for the better. Try to help them, and they will outwit you and remain happily wretched. Dostoevsky claimed to see some plan in it. "Out of sheer ingratitude," he complained, or possibly boasted, "man will play you a dirty trick, just to prove that men are still men and not the keys of a piano. . . . And even if you could prove that a man is only a piano key, he would still do something out of sheer perversity—he would create destruction and chaos—just to gain his point. . . . And if all this could in turn be analyzed and prevented by predicting that it would occur, then man would deliberately go mad to prove his point."

This is a conceivable neurotic reaction to inept control. A few men may have shown it, and many have enjoyed Dostoevsky's statement because they tend to show it. But that such perversity is a fundamental reaction of the human organism to controlling conditions is sheer nonsense.

So is the objection that we have no way of knowing what changes to make even though we have the necessary techniques. That is one of the great hoaxes of the century—a sort of booby trap left behind in the retreat before the advancing front of science. Scientists themselves have unsuspectingly agreed that there are two kinds of useful propositions about nature—facts and value judgments—and that science must confine itself to "what is," leaving "what ought to be" to others. But with what special sort of wisdom is the non-scientist endowed? Science is only effective knowing, no matter who engages in it. Verbal behavior proves upon analysis to be composed of many different types of utterances, from poetry and exhortation to logic and factual description, but these are not all equally useful in talking about cultural practices. We may classify useful propositions according to the degrees of confidence with which they may be asserted. Sentences about nature range from highly probable "facts" to sheer guesses. In general, future events are less likely to be correctly described than past. When a scientist talks about a projected experiment, for example, he must often resort to statements having only a moderate likelihood of being correct; he calls them hypotheses.

Designing a new cultural pattern is in many ways like designing an experiment. In drawing up a new constitution, outlining a new educational program, modifying a religious doctrine, or setting up a new fiscal policy, many statements must be quite tentative. We cannot be sure that the practices we specify will have the consequences we predict, or that the consequences will reward our efforts. This is in the nature of such proposals. They are not value judgments—they are guesses. To confuse and delay the improvement of cultural practices by quibbling about the word *improve* is itself not a useful practice. Let us agree, to start with, that health is better than illness, wisdom better than ignorance, love better than hate, and productive energy better than neurotic sloth.

Another familiar objection is the "political problem." Though we know what changes to make and how to make them, we still need to control certain relevant conditions, but these have long since fallen into the hands of selfish men who are not going to relinquish them for such purposes. Possibly we shall be permitted to develop areas which at the moment seem unimportant, but at the first signs of success the strong men will move in. This, it is said, has happened to Christianity, democracy, and communism. There will always be men who are fundamentally selfish and evil, and in the long run innocent goodness cannot have its way. The only evidence here is historical, and it may be misleading. Because of the way in which physical science developed, history could until very recently have "proved" that the unleashing of the energy of the atom was quite unlikely, if not impossible. Similarly, because of the order in which processes in human behavior have become available for purposes of control, history may seem to prove that power will probably be appropriated for selfish purposes. The first techniques to be discovered fell almost always to strong, selfish men. History led Lord Acton to believe that power corrupts, but he had probably never encountered absolute power, certainly not in all its forms, and had no way of predicting its effect.

An optimistic historian could defend a different conclusion. The principle that if there are not enough men of good will in the world the first step is to create more seems to be gaining recognition. The Marshall Plan (as originally conceived), Point Four, the offer of atomic materials to power-starved countries—these may or may not be wholly new in the history of international relations, but they suggest an increasing awareness of the power of governmental good will. They are proposals to make certain changes in the environments of men for the sake of consequences which should be rewarding for all concerned. They do not exemplify a distinterested generosity, but an interest which is the interest of everyone. We have not yet seen Plato's philosopher-king, and may not want to, but the gap between real and utopian government is closing.

III

But we are not yet in the clear, for a new and unexpected obstacle has arisen. With a world of their own making almost within reach, men of good will have been seized with distaste for their achievements. They have uneasily rejected opportunities to apply the techniques and findings of science in the service of men, and as the import of effective cultural design has come to be understood, many of them have voiced an outright refusal to have any part in it. Science has been challenged before when it has encroached upon institutions already engaged in the control of human behavior; but what are we to make of benevolent men, with no special interests of their own to defend, who nevertheless turn against the very means of reaching long-dreamed-of goals?

What is being rejected, of course, is the scientific conception of man and his place in nature. So long as the findings and methods of science are applied to human affairs only in a sort of remedial patchwork, we may continue to hold any view of human nature we like. But as the use of science increases, we are forced to accept the theoretical structure with which science represents its facts. The difficulty is that this structure is clearly at odds with the traditional democratic conception of man. Every discovery of an event which has a part in shaping a man's behavior seems to leave so much the less to be credited to the man himself; and as such explanations become more and more comprehensive, the contribution which may be claimed by the individual himself appears to approach zero. Man's vaunted creative powers, his original accomplishments in art, science, and morals, his capacity to choose and our right to hold him responsible for the consequences of his choice—none of these is conspicuous in this new self-portrait. Man, we once believed, was free to express himself in art, music, and literature, to inquire into nature, to seek salvation in his own way. He could initiate action and make spontaneous and capricious changes of course. Under the most extreme duress some sort of choice remained to him. He could resist any effort to control him, though it might cost him his life. But science insists that action is initiated by forces impinging upon the individual, and that caprice is only another name for behavior for which we have not yet found a cause.

In attempting to reconcile these views it is important to note that the traditional democratic conception was not designed as a description in the scientific sense but as a philosophy to be used in setting up and maintaining a governmental process. It arose under historical circumstances and served political purposes apart from which it cannot be properly understood. In rallying men against tyranny it was necessary that the individual be strengthened, that he be taught that he had rights and could govern himself. To give the common man a new conception of his worth, his dignity, and his power to save himself, both here and hereafter, was often the only resource of the revolutionist. When democratic principles were put into practice, the same doctrines were used as a working formula. This is exemplified by the notion of personal responsibility in Anglo-American law. All governments make certain forms of punishment contingent upon certain kinds of acts. In democratic countries these contingencies are expressed by the notion of responsible choice. But the notion may have no meaning under governmental practices formulated in other ways and would certainly have no place in systems which did not use punishment.

The democratic philosophy of human nature is determined by certain political exigencies and techniques, not by the goals of democracy. But exigencies and techniques change; and a conception which is not supported for its accuracy as a likeness—is not, indeed, rooted in fact at all—may be expected to change too. No matter how effective we judge current democratic practices to be, how highly we value them or how long we expect them to survive, they are almost certainly not the *final* form of government. The philosophy of human nature which has been useful in implementing them is also almost certainly not the last word. The ultimate achievement of democracy may be long deferred unles we emphasize the real aims rather than the verbal devices of democratic thinking. A philosophy which has been appropriate to one set of political exigencies will defeat its purpose if, under other circumstances, it prevents us from applying to human affairs the science of man which probably nothing but democracy itself could have produced.

IV

Perhaps the most crucial part of our democratic philosophy to be reconsidered is our attitude toward freedom—or its reciprocal, the control of human behavior. We do not oppose all forms of control because it is "human nature" to do so. The reaction is not characteristic of all men under all conditions of life. It is an attitude which has been carefully engineered, in large part by what we call the "literature" of democracy. With respect to some methods of control (for example, the threat of force), very little engineering is needed, for the techniques or their immediate consequences are objectionable. Society has suppressed these methods by branding them "wrong," "illegal," or "sinful." But to encourage these attitudes toward objectionable forms of control, it has been necessary to disguise the real nature of certain indispensable techniques, the commonest examples of which are education, moral discourse, and persuasion. The actual procedures appear harmless enough. They consist of supplying information, presenting opportunities for action, pointing out logical re-lationships, appealing to reason or "enlightened understanding," and so on. Through a masterful piece of misrepresentation, the illusion is fostered that these procedures do not involve the control of behavior; at most, they are simply ways of "getting someone to change his mind." But analysis not only reveals the presence of well-defined behavioral processes, it demonstrates a kind of control no less inexorable, though in some ways more acceptable, than the bully's threat of force.

Let us suppose that someone in whom we are interested is acting unwisely—he is careless in the way he deals with his friends, he drives too fast, or he holds his golf club the wrong way. We could probably help him by issuing a series of commands: don't nag, don't drive over sixty, don't hold your club that way. Much less objectionable would be "an appeal to reason." We could show him how people are affected by his treatment of them, how accident rates rise sharply at higher speeds, how a particular grip on the club alters the way the ball is struck and corrects a slice. In doing so we resort to verbal mediating devices which emphasize and support certain "contingencies of reinforcement"—that is, certain relations between behavior and its consequences—which strengthen the behavior we wish to set up. The same consequences would possibly set up the behavior without our help, and they eventually take control no matter which form of help we give. The appeal to reason has certain advantages over the authoritative command. A threat of punishment, no matter how subtle, generates emotional reactions and tendencies to escape or revolt. Perhaps the controllee merely "feels resentment" at being made to act in a given way, but even that is to be avoided. When we "appeal to reason," he "feels freer to do as he pleases." The fact is that we have exerted *less* control than in using a threat; since other conditions may contribute to the result, the effect may be delayed or, possibly in a given instance, lacking. But if we have worked a change in his behavior at all, it is because we have altered relevant environmental conditions, and the processes we have set in motion are just as real and just as inexorable, if not as comprehensive, as in the most authoritative coercion.

"Arranging an opportunity for action" is another example of disguised control. The power of the negative form has already been exposed in the analysis of censorship. Restriction of opportunity is recognized as far from harmless. As Ralph Barton Perry said in an article which appeared in the Spring, 1953, *Pacific Spectator,* "Whoever determines what alternatives shall be made known to man controls what that man shall choose *from.* He is deprived of freedom in proportion as he is denied access to *any* ideas, or is confined to any range of ideas short of the totality of relevant possibilities." But there is a positive side as well. When we present a relevant state of affairs, we increase the likelihood that a given form of behavior will be emitted. To the extent that the probability of action has changed, we have made a definite contribution. The teacher of history controls a student's behavior (or, if the reader prefers, "deprives him of freedom") just as much in *presenting* historical facts as in suppressing them. Other conditions will no doubt affect the student, but the contribution made to his behavior by the presentation of material is fixed and, within its range, irresistible.

The methods of education, moral discourse, and persuasion are acceptable not because they recognize the freedom of the individual or his right to dissent, but because they make only *partial* contributions to the control of his behavior. The freedom they recognize is freedom from a more coercive form of control. The dissent which they tolerate is the possible effect of other determiners of action. Since these sanctioned methods are frequently ineffective, we have been able to convince ourselves that they do not represent control at all. When they show too much strength to permit disguise, we give them other names and suppress them as energetically as we suppress the use of force. Education grown too powerful is rejected as propaganda or "brainwashing," while really effective persuasion is decried as "undue influence," "demagoguery," "seduction," and so on.

If we are not to rely solely upon accident for the innovations which give rise to cultural evolution, we must accept the fact that some kind of control of human behavior is inevitable. We cannot use good sense in human affairs unless someone engages in the design and construction of environmental conditions which affect the behavior of men. Environmental changes have always been the condition for the improvement of cultural patterns, and we can hardly use the more effective methods of science without making changes on a grander scale. We are all controlled by the world in which we live, and part of that world has been and will be constructed by men. The question is this: Are we to be controlled by accident, by tyrants, or by ourselves in effective cultural design?

The danger of the misuse of power is possibly greater than ever. It is not allayed by disguising the facts. We cannot make wise decisions if we continue to pretend that human behavior is not controlled, or if we refuse to engage in control when valuable results might be forthcoming. Such measures weaken only ourselves, leaving the strength of science to others. The first step in a defense against tyranny is the fullest possible exposure of controlling techniques. A second step has already been taken successfully in restricting the use of physical force. Slowly, and as yet imperfectly, we have worked out an ethical and governmental design in which the strong man is not allowed to use the power deriving from his strength to control his fellow men. He is restrained by a superior force created for that purpose—the ethical pressure of the group, or more explicit religious and governmental measures. We tend to distrust superior forces, as we currently hesitate to relinquish sovereignty in order to set up an international police force. But it is only through such counter-control that we have achieved what we call peace—a condition in which men are not permitted to control each other through force. In other words, control itself must be controlled.

Science has turned up dangerous processes and materials before. To use the facts and techniques of a science of man to the fullest extent without making some monstrous mistake will be difficult and obviously perilous. It is no time for self-deception, emotional indulgence, or the assumption of attitudes which are no longer useful. Man is facing a difficult test. He must keep his head now, or he must start again—a long way back.

V

Those who reject the scientific conception of man must, to be logical, oppose the methods of science as well. The position is often supported by predicting a series of dire consequences which are to follow if science is not checked. A recent book by Joseph Wood Krutch, The Measure of Man, is in this vein. Mr. Krutch sees in the growing science of man the threat of an unexampled tyranny over men's minds. If science is permitted to have its way, he insists, "we may never be able really to think again." A controlled culture will, for example, lack some virtue inherent in disorder. We have emerged from chaos through a series of happy accidents, but in an engineered culture it will be "impossible for the unplanned to erupt again." But there is no virtue in the accidental character of an accident, and the diversity which arises from disorder can not only be duplicated by design but vastly extended. The experimental method is superior to simple observation just because it multiplies "accidents" in a systematic coverage of the possibilities. Technology offers many familiar examples. We no longer wait for immunity to disease to develop from a series of accidental exposures, nor do we wait for natural mutations in sheep and cotton to produce better fibers; but we continue to make use of such accidents when they occur, and we certainly do not prevent them. Many of the things we value have emerged from the clash of ignorant armies on darkling plains, but it is not therefore wise to encourage ignorance and darkness.

It is not always disorder itself which we are told we shall miss but certain admirable qualities in men which flourish only in the presence of disorder. A man rises above an unpropitious childhood to a position of eminence, and since we cannot give a plausible account of the action of so complex an environment, we attribute the achievement to some admirable faculty in the man himself. But such "faculties" are suspiciously like the explanatory fictions against which the history of science warns us. We admire Lincoln for rising above a deficient school system, but it was not necessarily something *in him* which permitted him to become an educated man in spite of it. His educational environment was certainly unplanned, but it could nevertheless have made a full contribution to his mature behavior. He was a rare man, but the circumstances of his childhood were rare too. We do not give Franklin Delano Roosevelt the same credit for becoming an educated man with the help of Groton and Harvard, although the same behavioral processes may have been involved. The founding of Groton and Harvard somewhat reduced the possibility that fortuitous combinations of circumstances would erupt to produce other Lincolns. Yet the founders can hardly be condemned for attacking an admirable human quality.

Another predicted consequence of a science of man is an excessive uniformity. We are told that effective control—whether governmental, religious, educational, economic, or social—will produce a race of men who differ from each other only through relatively refractory genetic differences. That would probably be bad design, but we must admit that we are not now pursuing another course from choice. In a modern school, for example, there is usually a syllabus which specifies what every student is to learn by the end of each year. This would be flagrant regimentation if anyone expected every student to comply. But some will be poor in particular subjects, others will not study, others will not remember what they have been taught, and diversity is assured. Suppose, however, that we someday possess such effective educational techniques that every student will in fact be put in possession of all the behavior specified in a syllabus. At the end of the year, all students will correctly answer all questions on the final examination and "must all have prizes." Should we reject such a system on the grounds that in making all students excellent it has made them all alike? Advocates of the theory of a special faculty might contend that an important advantage of the present system is that the good student learns *in spite of* a system which is so defective that it is currently producing bad students as well. But if really effective techniques are available, we cannot avoid the problem of design simply by preferring the status quo. At what point should education be deliberately inefficient?

Such predictions of the havoc to be wreaked by the application of science to human affairs are usually made with surprising confidence. They not only show a faith in the orderliness of human behavior; they presuppose an established body of knowledge with the help of which it can be positively asserted that the changes which scientists propose to make will have quite specific results—albeit not the results they foresee. But the predictions made by the critics of science must be held to be equally fallible and subject also to empirical test. We may be sure that many steps in the scientific design of cultural patterns will produce unforeseen consequences. But there is only one way to find out. And the test must be made, for if we cannot advance in the design of cultural patterns with absolute certainty, neither can we rest completely confident of the superiority of the status quo.

VI

Apart from their possibly objectionable consequences, scientific methods seem to make no provision for certain admirable qualities and faculties which seem to have flourished in less explicitly planned cultures; hence they are called "degrading" or "lacking in dignity." (Mr. Krutch has called the author's Walden Two an "ignoble Utopia.") The conditioned reflex is the current whipping boy. Because conditioned reflexes may be demonstrated in animals, they are spoken of as though they were exclusively subhuman. It is implied, as we have seen, that no behavioral processes are involved in education and moral discourse or, at least, that the processes are exclusively human. But men do show conditioned reflexes (for example, when they are frightened by all instances of the control of human behavior because some instances engender fear), and animals do show processes similar to the human behavior involved in instruction and moral discourse. When Mr. Krutch asserts that " 'Conditioning' is achieved by methods which by-pass or, as it were, short-circuit those very reasoning faculties which education proposes to cultivate and exercise," he is making a technical statement which needs a definition of terms and a great deal of supporting evidence.

If such methods are called "ignoble" simply because they leave no room for certain admirable attributes, then perhaps the practice of admiration needs to be examined. We might say that the child whose education has been skillfully planned has been deprived of the right to intellectual heroism. Nothing has been left to be admired in the way he acquires an education. Similarly, we can conceive of moral training which is so adequate to the demands of the culture that men will be good practically automatically, but to that extent they will be deprived of the right to moral heroism, since we seldom admire automatic goodness. Yet if we consider the end of morals rather than certain virtuous means, is not "automatic goodness" a desirable state of affairs? Is it not, for example, the avowed goal of religious education? T. H. Huxley answered the question unambiguously: "If some great power would agree to make me always think what is true and do what is right, on condition of being a sort of clock and wound up every morning before I got out of bed, I should close instantly with the offer." Yet Mr. Krutch quotes this as the scarcely credible point of view of a "proto-modern" and seems himself to share T. S. Eliot's contempt for ". . . systems so perfect/That no one will need to be good."

"Having to be good" is an excellent example of an expendable honorific. It is inseparable from a particular form of ethical and moral control. We distinguish between the things we *have* to do to avoid punishment and those we *want* to do for rewarding consequences. In a culture which did not resort to punishment we should never "have" to do anything except with respect to the punishing contingencies which arise directly in the physical environment. And we are moving toward such a culture, because the neurotic, not to say psychotic, by-products of control through punishment have long since led compassionate men to seek alternative techniques. Recent research has explained some of the objectionable results of punishment and has revealed resources of at least equal power in "positive reinforcement." It is reasonable to look forward to a time when man will seldom "have" to do anything, although he may show interest, energy, imagination, and productivity far beyond the level seen under the present system (except for rare eruptions of the unplanned).

What we have to do we do with *effort*. We call it "work." There is no other way to distinguish between exhausting labor and the possibly equally energetic but rewarding activity of play. It is presumably good cultural design to replace the former with the latter. But an adjustment in attitudes is needed. We are much more practiced in admiring the heroic labor of a Hercules than the activity of one who works without having to. In a truly effective educational system the student might not "have to work" at all, but that possibility is likely to be received by the contemporary teacher with an emotion little short of rage.

We cannot reconcile traditional and scientific views by agreeing upon *what* is to be admired or condemned. The question is whether anything is to be so treated. Praise and blame are cultural practices which have been adjuncts of the prevailing system of control in Western democracy. All peoples do not engage in them for the same purposes or to the same extent, nor, of course, are the same behaviors always classified in the same way as subject to praise or blame. In admiring intellectual and moral heroism and unrewarding labor, and in rejecting a world in which these would be uncommon, we are simply demonstrating our own cultural conditioning. By promoting certain tendencies to admire and censure, the group of which we are a part has arranged for the social reinforcement and punishment needed to assure a high level of intellectual and moral industry. Under other and possibly better controlling systems, the behavior which we now admire would occur, but not under those conditions which make it admirable, and we should have no reason to admire it because the culture would have arranged for its maintenance in other ways.

To those who are stimulated by the glamorous heroism of the battlefield, a peaceful world may not be a better world. Others may reject a world without sorrow, longing, or a sense of guilt because the relevance of deeply moving works of art would be lost. To many who have devoted their lives to the struggle to be wise and good, a world without confusion and evil might be an empty thing. A nostalgic concern for the decline of moral heroism has been a dominating theme in the work of Aldous Huxley. In *Brave New World* he could see in the application of science to human affairs only a travesty on the notion of the Good (just as George Orwell, in *1984*, could foresee nothing but horror). In a recent issue of *Esquire*, Huxley has expressed the point this way: "We have had religious revolutions, we have had political, industrial, economic and nationalistic revolutions. All of them, as our descendants will discover, were but ripples in an ocean of conservatism—trivial by comparison with the psychological revolution toward which we are so rapidly moving. *That* will really be a revolution. When it is over, the human race will give no further trouble." (Footnote for the reader of the future: This was not meant as a happy ending. Up to 1956 men had been admired, if at all, either for causing trouble or alleviating it. Therefore—)

It will be a long time before the world can dispense with heroes and hence with the cultural practice of admiring heroism, but we move in that direction whenever we act to prevent war, famine, pestilence, and disaster. It will be a long time before man will never need to submit to punishing environments or engage in exhausting labor, but we move in that direction whenever we make food, shelter, clothing, and labor-saving devices more readily available. We may mourn the passing of heroes but not the conditions which make for heroism. We can spare the self-made saint or sage as we spare the laundress on the river's bank struggling against fearful odds to achieve cleanliness.

VII

The two great dangers in modern democratic thinking are illustrated in a paper by former Secretary of State Dean Acheson. "For a long time now," writes Mr. Acheson, "we have gone along with some well-tested principles of conduct: That it was better to tell the truth than falsehoods; . . . that duties were older than and as fundamental as rights; that, as Justice Holmes put it, the mode by which the inevitable came to pass was effort; that to perpetrate a harm was wrong no matter how many joined in it . . . and so on. . . . Our institutions are founded on the assumption that most people follow these principles most of the time because they want to, and the institutions work pretty well when this assumption is true. More recently, however, bright people have been fooling with the machinery in the human head and they have discovered quite a lot. . . . Hitler introduced new refinements [as the result of which] a whole people have been utterly confused and corrupted. Unhappily neither the possession of this knowledge nor the desire to use it was confined to Hitler. . . . Others dip from this same devil's cauldron."

The first dangerous notion in this passage is that most people follow democratic principles of conduct "because they want to." This does not account for democracy or any other form of government if we have not explained why people *want* to behave in given ways. Although it is tempting to assume that it is human nature to believe in democratic principles, we must not overlook the "cultural engineering" which produced and continues to maintain democratic practices. If we neglect the conditions which produce democratic *behavior,* it is useless to try to maintain a democratic *form* of government. And we cannot expect to export a democratic form of government successfully if we do not also provide for the cultural practices which will sustain it. Our forebears did not discover the essential nature of man; they evolved a pattern of behavior which worked remarkably well under the circumstances. The "set of principles" expressed in that pattern is not the only true set or necessarily the best. Mr. Acheson has presumably listed the most unassailable items; some of them are probably beyond question, but others—concerning duty and effort—may need revision as the world changes.

The second—and greater—threat to the democracy which Mr. Acheson is defending is his assumption that knowledge is necessarily on the side of evil. All the admirable things he mentions are attributed to the innate goodness of man, all the detestable to "fooling with the machinery in the human head." This is reminiscent of the position, taken by other institutions engaged in the control of men, that certain forms of knowledge are in themselves evil. But how out of place in a democratic philosophy! Have we come this far only to conclude that well-intentioned people cannot study the behavior of men without becoming tyrants or that informed men cannot show good will? Let us for once have strength and good will on the same side.

VIII

Far from being a threat to the tradition of Western democracy, the growth of a science of man is a consistent and probably inevitable part of it. In turning to the external conditions which shape and maintain the behavior of men, while questioning the reality of inner qualities and faculties to which human achievements were once attributed, we turn from the ill-defined and remote to the observable and manipulable. Though it is a painful step, it has far-reaching consequences, for it not only sets higher standards of human welfare but shows us how to meet them. A change in a theory of human nature cannot change the facts. The achievements of man in science, art, literature, music, and morals will survive any interpretation we place upon them. The uniqueness of the individual is unchallenged in the scientific view. Man, in short, will remain man. (There will be much to admire for those who are so inclined. Possibly the noblest achievement to which man can aspire, even according to present standards, is to accept himself for what he is, as that is revealed to him by the methods which he devised and tested on a part of the world in which he had only a small personal stake.)

If Western democracy does not lose sight of the aims of humanitarian action, it will welcome the almost fabulous support of its own science of man and will strengthen itself and play an important role in building a better world for everyone. But if it cannot put its "democratic philosophy" into proper historical perspective—if, under the control of attitudes and emotions which it generated for other purposes, it now rejects the help of science—then it must be prepared for defeat. For if we continue to insist that science has nothing to offer but a new and more horrible form of tyranny, we may produce just such a result by allowing the strength of science to fall into the hands of despots. And if, with luck, it were to fall instead to men of good will in other political communities, it would be perhaps a more ignominious defeat; for we should then, through a miscarriage of democratic principles, be forced to leave to others the next step in man's long struggle to control nature and himself.

49   Fostering Self-Direction*

BY ARTHUR W. COMBS

EDITOR'S NOTE: Dr. Combs is a leading proponent of maximizing freedom in the classroom, and in this succinct, no-nonsense
paper he suggests specific ways in which self-direction can be encouraged. You have, up to this point, been exposed to various points
of view regarding control versus freedom. Of all things, Dr. Combs
suggests that if we are to provide people with increased opportunity
for self-direction, we must expect them to make mistakes! How is
this related to self-direction? As you read, you may become clearer
about the relationship between the two.

Schools which do not produce self-directed citizens have failed everyone—the student, the profession, and the society they are designed to serve.
The goals of modern education cannot be achieved without self-direction.
We have created a world in which there is no longer a common body of
information which everyone must have. The information explosion has
blasted for all time the notion that we can feed all students the same diet.
Instead, we have to adopt a cafeteria principle in which we help each
student select what he most needs to fulfill his potentialities. This calls for
student cooperation and acceptance of major responsibility for his own
learning.

As Earl Kelley has suggested, the goal of education in the modern
world must be the production of increasing uniqueness. This cannot be

* Arthur W. Combs, "Fostering Self-Direction," Educational Leadership, 23:
373–376, February, 1966. Reprinted with permission of the Association for
Supervision and Curriculum Development and Arthur W. Combs. Copyright
© 1966 by the Association for Supervision and Curriculum Development.

achieved in autocratic atmospheres where all decisions are made by the teachers and administration while students are reduced to passive followers of the established patterns. Authoritarian schools are as out of date in the world we live in as the horse and buggy. Such schools cannot hope to achieve our purposes. Worse yet, their existence will almost certainly defeat us.

The world we live in demands self-starting, self-directing citizens capable of independent action. The world is changing so fast we cannot hope to teach each person what he will need to know in twenty years. Our only hope to meet the demands of the future is the production of intelligent, independent people. Even our military establishment, historically the most authoritarian of all, has long since discovered that fact. For twenty years the armed forces have been steadily increasing the degree of responsibility and initiative it expects of even its lowest echelons. The modern war machine cannot be run by automatons. It must be run by *thinking* men.

Much of the curriculum of our current schools is predicated on a concept of learning conceived as the acquisition of right answers and many of our practices mirror this belief. Almost anyone can pick them out. Here are a few which occur to me:

> Preoccupation with right answers; insistence upon conformity; cook-book approaches to learning; overconcern for rules and regulations; preoccupation with materials and things instead of people; the solitary approach to learning; the delusion that mistakes are sinful; emphasis on memory rather than learning; emphasis on grades rather than understanding and content details rather than principles.

Meanwhile, psychologists are telling us that learning is a *personal* matter; individual and unique. It is not controlled by the teacher. It can only be accomplished with the cooperation and involvement of the student in the process. Providing students with information is not enough. People rarely misbehave because they do not know any better. The effectiveness of learning must be measured in behavior change: whether students *behave differently* as a consequence of their learning experience. This requires active participation by the student. So learning itself is dependent upon the capacity for self-direction.

TOWARD SELF-DIRECTION

What is needed of us? How can we produce students who are more self-directed?

1. *We need to believe this is important.* If we do not think self-direction is important, this will not get done. People are too pressed these

days to pay much attention to things that are not important. Everyone does what seems to him to be crucial and urgent. It seems self-evident that independence and self-direction are necessary for our kind of world. Why then has self-direction been given such inadequate attention? It is strange we should have to convince ourselves of its importance.

Unfortunately, because a matter is self-evident is no guarantee that people will really put it into practice. It must somehow be brought into clear figure in the forefront of our striving if it is to affect behavior. Everyone knows it is important to vote, too, yet millions regularly fail to vote. To be effective as an objective, each of us must hold the goal of self-direction clear in our thinking and high in our values whenever we are engaged in planning or teaching of any kind.

This is often not easy to do because self-direction is one of those goals which *everyone* is supposed to be working for. As a result, almost no one regards it as urgent! For each person, his own special duties are so much clearer, so much more pressing and his derelictions so much more glaring if he fails to produce. The goals we hold in common do not rebound so immediately to our credit or discredit. They are therefore set aside while we devote our energies to the things that *really* matter to us.

To begin doing something about self-direction we must, therefore, begin by declaring its importance; not as a lofty sentiment, but as an absolute essential. It must be given a place of greater concern than subject matter itself, for a very simple reason: It is far more important than subject matter. Without self-direction no content matters much. It is not enough that it be published in the handbook as a "Goal of Education." Each of us at every level must ask himself: Do I really think self-direction is important and what am I doing about it?

2. *Trust in the human organism.*   Many of us grew up in a tradition which conceived of man as basically evil and certain to revert to bestial ways if someone did not control him. Modern psychologists tell us this view is no longer tenable. From everything we can observe in humans and animals the basic striving of the organism is inexorably toward health both physical and mental. It is this growth principle on which doctors and psychotherapists depend to make the person well again. If an organism is free to do so—it can, will, it *must* move in positive ways. The organism is not our enemy. It wants the same things we do, the achievement of adequacy. Yet alas, how few believe this and how timid we are to trust our students with self-direction.

A recent best selling book, *Summerhill*, by A. S. Neill has fascinated many educators. In it Neill describes the absolute trust he placed in the children under his care. Many teachers are shocked by his unorthodox procedures and the extreme behavior of some of the children. But whether one approves of Neill's school or not, the thing which impressed me most was this: Here was a man who dared to trust children far beyond what most of us would be willing to risk. Yet, all the things we are so afraid might happen if we did give them such freedom, never happened! For forty years the school continued to turn out happy, effective citizens as well as, or better than, its competitors. It is time we give up fearing the human organism and learn to trust and use its built-in drives toward self-fulfillment. After all, the organism has had to be pretty tough to survive what we have done to it through the ages.

Responsibility and self-direction are learned. They must be acquired from experiences, from being given opportunities to be self-directing and responsible. You cannot learn to be self-directing if no one permits you to try. Human capacities are strengthened by use but atrophy with disuse. If young people are going to learn self-direction, then it must be through being *given* many opportunities to exercise such self-direction throughout the years they are in school. Someone has observed that our schools are operated on a directly contrary principle. Children are allowed more freedom of choice and self-direction in kindergarten (when they are presumably least able to handle it) and each year thereafter are given less and less, until, by the time they reach college, they are permitted practically no choice at all! This overdraws the case, to be sure, but there is enough truth in the statement to make one uncomfortable. If we are to produce independent, self-starting people we must do a great deal more to produce the kinds of experiences which will lead to these ends.

3. *The experimental attitude.* If we are going to provide young people with increased opportunity for self-direction, we must do it with our eyes open *expecting* them to make mistakes. This is not easy, for the importance of "being right" is in our blood. Education is built on right answers. Wrong ones are regarded as failures to be avoided like the plague. Unfortunately, such attitudes stand squarely in the way of progress toward self-direction and independence.

People too fearful of mistakes cannot risk trying. Without trying, self-direction, creativity and independence cannot be discovered. To be so afraid of mistakes that we kill the desire to try is a tragedy. Autonomy, independence and creativity are the products of being willing to look and eager to try. If we discourage these elements we do so at our peril. In the world we live in, victory is reserved only for the courageous and inventive. It is possible we may lose the game by making mistakes. We will not even get in the game if we are afraid to try.

Experimentation and innovation must be encouraged everywhere in our schools, in teachers as well as students. Each of us needs to be engaged in a continuous process of trying something new. The kind of experimentation which will make the difference to education in the long run is not that produced by the professional researcher with the aid of giant computers but by the everyday changes in goals and processes brought about by the individual teacher in the classroom.

To achieve this, teachers need to be freed of pressures and details by the administration for the exercise of self-direction and creativity. In addition, each of us must accept the challenge and set about a systematic search for the barriers we place in the path of self-direction for ourselves, our colleagues and our students. This should suggest all kinds of places for experimentation where we can begin the encouragement of self-direction. One of the nice things about self-direction is that it does not have to be taught. It only needs to be encouraged and set free to operate.

4. *The provision of opportunity.* The basic principle is clear. To produce more self-directed people it is necessary to give more opportunity to practice self-direction. This means some of us must be willing to give up our traditional prerogatives to make all the decisions. Education must be seen, not as providing right answers, but as confrontation with problems; not imaginary play problems either, but *real* ones in which decisions count.

Experiences calling for decision, independence and self-direction must be the daily diet of children, including such little decisions as what kinds of headings and margins a paper should have and big ones like the courses to be taken next year. They must also include decisions about goals, techniques, time, people, money, meals, rules, and subject matter.

If we are to achieve the objective of greater self-direction, I see no alternative to the fuller acceptance of students into partnership in the educative endeavor. Our modern goal for education, "the optimal development of the individual," cannot be achieved without this. Such an aim requires participation of the student and his wholehearted cooperation in the process. This is not likely to be accomplished unless students have the feeling they matter and their decisions count. Few of us are deeply committed to tasks imposed upon us; and students are not much different. Self-direction is learned from experience. What better, more meaningful experience could be provided than participation in the decisions about one's own life and learning?

The basic belief of democracy is that when people are free they can find their own best ways. Though all of us profess our acceptance of this credo, it is distressing how few of us dare to put it to work. Whatever limits the capacity of our young people to accept both the challenge and the responsibilities of that belief is destructive to all of us. It is time we put this belief to work and to expression in the education of our young as though we really meant it.

50 Three Forces in Psychology and Their Ethical and Educational Implications*

BY PAUL BRUCE

EDITOR'S NOTE: *If through psychology people can be influenced (for better or for worse) to behave in certain ways, and if through psychology the process of education toward certain goals can be made more effective, then it is important that these goals and their determination be carefully examined. To a large extent, psychological viewpoints about the nature of man have their roots in either Associationism, Classical Psychoanalysis, or Humanistic Psychology and it is the purpose of this paper to describe the basic tenets of each of these three broad frameworks. Think about it. Which of the three theories do you feel close to? What implications do you think your identification with any one of these psychological viewpoints will have for your personal and professional lives?*

Practically all strands of our society are being influenced by theories and research from the field of psychology. Probably the most blatant example of this influence is seen in the women's magazines which month after month headline lead articles by "experts" advising and analyzing the psychological problems of our day: sex, marriage, child-rearing, narcotics, alcoholism, etc. Even more significant than this is the more subtle influence psychology is having in such fields as advertising (à la Vance Packard's *The Wastemakers*), human engineering in industry, psychotherapy and

---

* Reprinted from *The Educational Forum*, March, 1966, Vol. 30, No. 3, 227–285, by permission of the author and Kappa Delta Pi, an Honor Society in Education.

counseling, and, of course, in our schools. Maybe one measure of this impact is the amount of critical attention psychology (in the name of mental health) is getting from the ultra-conservative elements who, indeed, find the influence from psychology to be threatening the status quo of a bygone era.

The point I want to make is that if through psychology humans can be influenced in certain directions, then the ethical problem arises of evaluating these directions in terms of their being desirable or not. And if through psychology the process of education toward certain goals becomes more effective, then it becomes imperative that these goals and the determination of these goals be carefully evaluated.

Now, the typical psychologist (or I might better say the typical scientific psychologist does not like to admit the ethical implications of his discipline; he prefers to don the robes of scientific impartiality and limit his consideration to the quest for truth as he finds it. But I don't think we should let him get away with this. We need to face up to the ethical implications ourselves, and we need to ask the psychologists to face up to the ethical implications of their theories and research and even to take a stand regarding them.

To illustrate and further define this issue, I want to discuss three forces or schools of influence in psychology today and indicate the ethical and educational implications of their formulations as I see them. These are associationism—particularly as represented by reinforcement (S-R) theory; Freudianism or classical psychoanalytic theory; and the third force which is relatively new and has no consistent label as yet, but goes under the names of humanistic psychology, perceptual psychology, existential psychology or neo-Freudianism. I will present these three schools of thought briefly as theoretical models and ask the reader to realize, as with everything else, that the adherents and practitioners who represent these models modify the theory to fit their own needs and perceptions.

ASSOCIATIONISM

Associationism in psychology developed during the latter part of the nineteenth century out of the thinking of such philosophers as Herbart, who described the mind as a complex of isolated sensations, ideas, thoughts, decisions, and feelings bound together by the process of association. With the aid of a new interest in the use of animals for observation and experimentation, psychologists, first under the leadership of E. L. Thorndike, developed theories of behavior most familiarly represented by the stimulus-response formula. Thus, Thorndike proposed that every new idea, every new feeling or sensation is a response to a preceding idea, feeling, or sensation. Under this system, memory or learning was explained as a series of stimulus-response connections, particular stimuli calling forth the specific responses. Various laws or principles of learning were developed which explained the establishment of a bond or association between stimulus and response. For example, reward or punishment, repetition, need satisfaction, reinforcement, conditioning, etc., were postulated as effecting learning and could be used to elicit certain desired behavior patterns.

This school of thought has persisted though modified and developed, and today it remains the most popular theory (at least among scientific and academic psychologists) and perhaps the most influential force representing psychology in society today. In our schools and colleges, the prevalent use of repetition as in drills (e.g., write each spelling word five times), the use of workbooks and tests which provide the stimulus and require the student to provide the "right" response which is subsequently approved or disapproved; the extensive use of a system of rewards and penalties (as in the way grades are typically given); all of these reflect the influence of this school of thought. More recently a whole new medium has been developed and is currently being promoted—that of programed learning or more popularly termed teaching machines. Based primarily on B. F. Skinner's reinforcement theory (a refinement of associationism), programed learning involves the careful presentation and division of the subject matter into extremely small units so that the student is frequently rewarded by correct answers and can move along independently at his own pace.

In advertising, political campaigns, public relations programs, etc., the principle of conditioning is used very effectively. Briefly, the principle of conditioning states that if a stimulus and response are associated enough times together, this association will be learned. Thus, if you hear a brand name associated with a product enough times, you will automatically think of the brand whenever you think of the product; and if the terms "liberal," "socialist," "civil libertarian," "progressive education," "life adjustment," are associated with the concept of the Communist menace enough times, then these labels and those to whom they apply become tainted with the same attitudes ascribed to Communism.

Thus, when addressing themselves to the problems and issues of our times, these psychologists, believing that people's behavior is a result of the forces exerted upon them, find their answers in terms of the manipulation of these forces. The ethical problem implicit in this system, of course, is that somebody, other than the persons affected, must decide the desired direction the behavior is to take. This necessarily calls for a "great man" philosophy of dealing with people—somebody who knows where the people should go. This system calls for leaders who are supermen of a sort, skilled in the manipulation of forces to get people to behave in the ways desired by the knowing few.

And so in schools, for example, we have developed specialists and experts who are determining what the children should learn in the various subject areas, and other experts who are predigesting what will be programed in the teaching machines. In the Midwest they now have airborne educational television by which one *expert* teacher can serve schools in six states (7000 school districts; over five million children); meaning that where used, all the children are getting the *same* presentation of the *same* curriculum at the *same* time!

One of my students wrote the following, which perhaps overstates the kind of teaching which follows from this system wherein learning is thought to result from having students respond to well-ordered stimuli:

> Teaching too often becomes the process of carrying, pulling, showing, and assisting pupils along to the end of the course. *Teachers* do the reading, the explaining, the thinking, the talking, the appreciating, the devising, the planning; the problems are *teacher*-worked, the reasons are *teacher*-thought-out; the beautiful is *teacher*-selected. All the pupils do is to remain passive, to listen, to copy, to memorize, and finally to recite or to write at a stated time what they have managed to cull out of an extended dictation!

B. F. Skinner, a prominent scientist from this force in psychology, wrote a novel some years ago (1948) entitled *Walden Two* in which he gives a fictional account of what he regards as a Utopian community in which the learnings of the behavioral sciences are fully utilized in all aspects of life—marriage, child rearing, ethical conduct, work, play, and artistic endeavor. Skinner's conception of paradise is a large rural colony where democracy is replaced by behavioral engineering. The common theme of this novel and of some of his other treatises is that the psychologist possesses the means of social control and must use these means effectively for the welfare of society. Let me quote what Skinner has his hero say in this novel:

> Well, what do you say to the design of personalities? Would that interest you? The control of temperament? Give me the specifications, and I'll give you the man! What do you say to the control of motivation, building the interests which will make men most productive and most successful? Does that seem to you fantastic? Yet some of the techniques are available, and more can be worked out experimentally. Think of the possibilities! . . . Let us control the lives of our children and see what we can make of them. . . . (p. 243).

In another paper (1955–56), Skinner elaborates the implications of his theories; he states,

> We must accept the fact that some kind of control of human affairs is inevitable. We cannot use good sense in human affairs unless *someone* engages in the design and construction of environmental conditions which affect the behavior of men. . . . (p. 56)

As you can see, Skinner's projection of his system is garbed in benevolence; however, the ethical question still remains as to who is to determine the *desired* direction behavior should take. And presumably this molding of human behavior would be the function of the schools, and we ask if this is the function we want education to perform.

CLASSICAL PSYCHOANALYSIS

If associationism is the most popular force among academic and scientific psychologists, Freudianism (classical psychoanalysis) has been the most influential among the clinical psychologists, and psychotherapists and counselors. Although few accept the theories exactly as Freud postulated them (which would be impossible anyway, since Freud modified and even contradicted his own theories throughout his lifetime), yet the main tenor of his system remains and poses some ethical questions.

Psychoanalysis originated in the field of medicine as a result of attempts to find some cure for the neuroses and in revolt against the dominant somatic or physiological explanations which were popular in the nineteenth century. Some psychiatrists were becoming convinced that such causal factors as brain lesions were not to be found in their patients, and they began to substitute such factors as emotional stress, weakness of will, suggestibility, and irrational habits as explanations. Soon hypnotism was introduced and accepted by some elements of the medical profession particularly when dealing with such neurotic conditions as hysteria. It was on this medical scene with an interest in neurology that Freud began his productive but controversial practice in Vienna. Influenced by the French schools in Paris under Charcot and later in Nancy under Janet, Freud built up a practice dealing primarily with hysteric patients, experimenting with hypnosis and eventually, giving this up, developing his own techniques and corresponding theoretical formulations.

The point I want to bring out in this very brief historical sketch is that psychoanalytic theory originated and was developed as a result of studying and treating mentally disturbed, upper-class Europeans during a period referred to as the Victorian era. In other words, Freud's sampling from which he drew his conclusions was anything but representative of the human race.

With his medical background, it is not surprising to learn that Freud believed that the nature of man is essentially biological; man is born with certain instinctual drives which can (though they frequently don't) work themselves out as a person grows. Freud classified the instincts under two main headings: the *life* instincts (*Eros*) and the *death* instincts (*Thanatos*). The life instincts include hunger, thirst, and sex, the latter being considered the most driving. The principle operating here is the pleasure principle of self-gratification. The death instincts include hate, aggressiveness, and self-destruction.

According to Freud, the *psyche* is divided horizontally into *conscious* and *unconscious;* and vertically into what he labels the *id, ego,* and *superego*. Gradually the child's unconscious fills with things forgotten or suppressed because they are unpleasant, and more importantly, with emotions and drives which are too painful to be tolerated in the consciousness. The *id*, entirely unconscious, is the most primitive and concerned only with the gratification of drives. The *ego*, almost entirely conscious, develops from experience and reason, interacts with the environment and acts as a check on the *id*. The *superego*, largely unconscious, is the restraining force, the conscience, and consists of the attitudes and moral codes absorbed unwittingly in childhood. Neuroses, then, result from a lack of harmony among the *id, ego,* and *superego*. Neuroses can develop as a result of lack of gratification of the instinctual drives (the *id*), or as a result of a weak *ego* structure and thus poor reality contact, or as a result of a too severe *superego*, which is the product of too strenuous socialization of the child at the hands of harsh, punitive parents.

In spite of the magical, fable-like quality of the theory, its distinctive, widely-accepted contribution to our understanding of human behavior is the significance the theory attributes to the unconscious.

The ethical implications of this theory are of greater or lesser significance depending on how literally we accept its assumptions and principles. Probably the most crucial implication stems from the proposition concerning the instinctual drives. Freud (1930) wrote,

> . . . Men are not gentle, friendly creatures wishing for love, who simply defend themselves if they are attacked, but . . . a powerful measure of desire for aggression has to be reckoned as part of their instinctual endowment. The result is that their neighbor is to them not only a possible helper or sexual object, but also a temptation to them to gratify their aggressiveness, . . . to seize his possessions, to humiliate him, to cause him pain, to torture and to kill him; . . . who has the courage to dispute it in the face of all the evidence in his own life and in history? (pp. 85–86).

According to this view, man's *finer* sentiments and strivings are only sublimations of animal instincts which lurk beneath the surface of his civilized veneer.

If this be the nature of man, then we cannot look to nature to provide us answers to our ethical question—the definition of good and evil. Traditional Christian doctrine provides an out with its supernatural definition of good and evil. But Freud rejected religion and referred to it as the "mass obsessional neurosis," and deplored society's religion-based concept of morality. Furthermore, denial, or even worse, restriction of man's nature (as viewed by Freud) leads to mental illness indicating we cannot look to the antithesis of the Freudian assumption for a solution.

Interestingly enough, much of the recent clamor against permissiveness and "life adjustment" in the schools (neither of which ever existed to any great extent in actual school practice) has been misdirected when "Progressive education" and John Dewey are blamed. (Dewey argued for an experimental, experience-centered, activity, problem-solving approach to education.) Actually the permissive, life adjustment emphasis stems largely from the Freudian influence whereby parents and teachers are admonished not to thwart or deny the expression of a child's instinctual drives or else his *psyche* will become crippled and pave the way for adult neuroses.

On the other hand, acceptance of the Freudian notion of the inherent primitive, animalistic, aggressive nature of the child leads many teachers and administrators to be preoccupied with the problem of control and discipline sometimes to the exclusion of concern over the learning process.

Another implication derives from the deterministic nature of the theory. The underlying causal factors of behavior are primarily unconscious and irrational. Man's motives are something other than they appear on the surface, and his thinking is easily distorted by inner desires and passions of which he is not aware. How then, with the minimizing of man's rational powers, with the denial of free will, can the individual be held responsible for his actions or behavior? Anna Russell catches the spirit of the problem posed by Freud's psychic determinism when she sings in her "Psychiatric Folksong,"

> At three I had a feeling of
>   Ambivalence toward my brothers,
> And so it follows naturally,
>   I poisoned all my lovers.
> But now I'm happy; I have learned
>   the lesson this has taught;
> That everything I do that's wrong,
>   Is someone else's fault. (Mowrer, 1960).

This view (shared with associationism) that man is the product of forces beyond his control, undercuts the basic convictions underlying democracy and democratic relations among men. Democracy just doesn't make sense (and wouldn't work) unless man is basically free, and active (and not just reactive), and capable to some degree of making rational choices and decisions and being responsible for his actions.

THIRD FORCE: HUMANISTIC PSYCHOLOGY

Throughout the development of psychology as a formal discipline during the past 60–75 years a number of psychologists have started rebellions of some importance against what they considered the dominant deterministic and analytic trends in psychology represented by associationism and psychoanalysis. Until recently, these psychologists did not represent a unified system or school. In the last few years, however, these various groups have been coalescing into an increasingly comprehensive theory of human nature, into what Abraham Maslow calls a "Third Force." This group includes the so-called neo-Freudians who emphasize man's nature as being primarily social and cultural rather than biological or instinctual; the Gestalt or field theorists who emphasize man's interaction with his environment as a unitary function which cannot be understood in a piecemeal fashion, as they claim the associationists would have us do; the organismic psychologists who, like the Gestaltists, insist on considering the individual as a whole; the perceptual psychologists and existential psychologists who emphasize the uniqueness and integrity of the individual and of his very personal and unique interpretation of his life and environment. As all of these movements place great significance on the individual human being and on distinctively human qualities (as opposed to animalistic or mechanistic qualities of the other two forces discussed above) the label *Humanistic Psychology* seems appropriate.

In contrast to the other two forces, many of the propositions of this third force stem from a study of man (as opposed to animals) and a study of psychologically healthy (rather than neurotic or sick) men. For example, A. H. Maslow, although beginning his career in the study of abnormal psychology, developed his present theories while studying psychologically healthy people and while studying the healthiest experiences and moments (which he called peak experiences) in the lives of average people.

Basic to this humanistic force in psychology is the conviction that man is essentially *good* if permitted to develop his natural humanistic qualities. Only when his nature is distorted by pathological conditions, rejecting parents, constant failure and rebuff, or a repressive culture does man become aggressive and cruel. *Good* in this context is equated with *nature,* thus anything conducive to bringing out man's inner nature is desirable. *Bad* or abnormal is anything that frustrates or blocks or denies the essential nature of man. Putting it another way, Maslow (1954) equates what we *ought* to be with we *can* be, and he states further that by substituting the concept of what one *can* become for the term *ought* or *should,* the matter becomes open to empirical, scientific investigation.

Space does not permit me to be more definitive regarding the inner nature (and thus what would be defined as desirable) in man. Writers such as A. Combs, A. Maslow, and C. Rogers do this well in their writings.[1] Suffice it to say that research being done in anthropology, psychiatry, sociology as well as psychology is coming up with some consistent findings. For example, there is wide-spread agreement that the following are characteristics of psychologically healthy (self-actualized) people: they can be described as loving, self-accepting, well integrated, fully functioning, creative, autonomous, reality-centered, adaptable, among other characteristics.

The other two forces we have discussed have built systems describing man as he *is*. Humanistic psychology has added the dimension of looking at what man can *become*—a look at not only the *actualities* but the *potentialities* as well. Also in contract to the other two forces which look upon man as *reactive* to the forces in the environment or to the *psyche*, humanistic psychology looks upon man as being active and having the capacity, at least to some degree, to evaluate and choose. While agreeing that human behavior is influenced by the environment and culture, humanistic psychology emphasizes that the ultimate effect of the environment and culture is in large part determined by the individual's unique view and attitudes of these external factors. That is, I am influenced by my world as I see it, not as you or anyone else sees it nor as the world may *really* be.

This view of man as having a large potential for freedom is consistent with the democratic conviction that the ordinary man given access to factual information *can* evaluate public issues with some degree of objectivity and rationality rather than as a robot conditioned to think and behave in certain ways. It is assumed that the freedom granted by democracy to the individual to make decisions is not just an illusion.

Similarly, the view of man as free and active is basic to a philosophy of education which emphasizes the development of young adults capable of rational problem solving, creativity, and critical evaluation. Applying the insights of this force in psychology (compared to those of associationism), teaching would involve facilitating learning rather than directing learning; it would involve uncovering new vistas rather than covering what is already known; it would involve asking pertinent questions rather than telling what is already thought out; it would involve helping children learn rather than making children go through the motions of learning. (Combs & Snygg, 1959).

Obviously, the ethical implications of this third force are part and parcel of the system it proposes. Unlike the other two forces, it does not beg the question of values. A commitment to a criterion for determining value—that which corresponds to basic human nature—underlies the entire movement. Some will claim that this takes the movement out of the jurisdiction of science. Maslow argues otherwise. He claims that the scientific approach can and should be used to develop greater understanding of man's basic nature, and thus a science of values *is* possible. Erich Fromm writes:

> The thesis is that values are rooted in the very conditions of human existence; hence that our knowledge of these conditions, that is of the "human situation," leads us to establishing values which have objective validity; this validity exists only with regard to the existence of man; outside of him there are no values. (Maslow, 1959, p. 131).

In summary, let me make this observation. The diverse views of human nature as neutral, evil, or good have important ethical and educational implications. Whichever view one accepts, it is apparent that man is a highly educable creature and that his development for good or evil can be greatly influenced by environmental conditions. But here agreements ends. If man is by nature hostile and aggressive, society through the school must shape him by exerting stringent controls; if, on the other hand, man's natural tendencies are for good, society through the school can best achieve its purposes by structuring the environment in such a way as to allow the child considerable freedom for creativity and self-development.

REFERENCES:

COMBS, A. W., and D. SNYGG. *Individual Behavior* (New York: Harper and Brothers, 1959). (Rev. Ed.)

FREUD, S. *Civilization and Its Discontents* (London: Hogarth Press, 1930).

MASLOW, A. H. *Motivation and Personality* (New York: Harper and Brothers, 1954).

MASLOW, A. H., ed. *New Knowledge in Human Values* (New York: Harper and Brothers, 1959).

MOWRER, O. H. "Sin, the Lesser of Two Evils." *American Psychologist, 15,* 301–304, 1960.

SKINNER, B. F. *Walden Two* (New York: Macmillan, 1948).

SKINNER, B. F. "Freedom and the Control of Men." *American Scholar, 25,* 47–65, Winter, 1955–56.

FOOTNOTE:

[1] See the 1962 Yearbook of the Association for Supervision and Curriculum Development (N.E.A.), *Perceiving, Behaving, Becoming,* which includes papers on this topic by Combs, Kelley, Maslow, and Rogers.

CHAPTER TWELVE

Personality Dynamics and Personal Adjustment

51   Origins of Personality*

by Percival M. Symonds

EDITOR'S NOTE: Personality is a complex thing. It is one person's brashness and another person's shyness; it is one person's self-confidence and another person's lack of it. Interestingly, the term "personality" came from the Latin word "persona," which was associated with the ancient Greek theater. A Greek player commonly held a mask before his face while performing so that he revealed himself only through his actions and his speech. The mask was called a "persona" because the actor talked through it. In time, the word "persona" came to apply to the actor and eventually to individuals in general. Hence, the term "personality" which has come to refer to an individual's characteristics and way of behaving. This article very effectively explores the origins of "personality" and implications for education.

It is the purpose of this discussion to review some of the findings of psychology that deal with the origin and development of personality, to discuss their implications for education, and to suggest some of the practical steps that may be taken by teachers, if the conclusion is reached that education has some responsibility for the development of personality.

Before we get involved in the subject, it is necessary to clarify what is meant by personality. Freud, in one of his letters to Karl Abraham, wrote, "Personality is a rather indefinite expression taken from surface psychology, and it doesn't contribute much to our understanding of the real processes. Only one can easily believe that by using it one has said something

* Reprinted from *Teachers College Record*, 1960, Vol. 61, 301–317, by permission.

substantial (22, p. 438). Personality is approached from the point of view of surface rather than depth psychology in this discussion, and its indefiniteness is quite acceptable. Personality refers to those personal characteristics which define the individual. It may be seen from a number of points of view. It refers to behavior which may be observed by another person (cooperative, boorish, systematic, untidy) or to the ways in which a person experiences himself (I feel uncomfortable in the presence of those whom I recognize as my superiors, I feel confident, I am discouraged, I am successful). These different observations may not agree, but they all must be taken into account in defining the complex of characteristics which is personality. Personality refers to the behavior, thoughts and feelings, motives, fantasies, defenses, and self-concepts of an individual.

As we are using the term, personality refers primarily to the typical ways in which a person reacts to other persons. We are thinking of personality less in terms of temperament and more in terms of his characteristic modes of managing and carrying himself, particularly in his relationships with others. We are mainly concerned with those aspects of personality which define the individual's capacity to be successful, to adapt himself in a socially acceptable way to others, to carry on the business of living in today's society in a competent and approved fashion, and to be comfortable with himself.

Character, often coupled with personality, refers to those aspects of personality that have moral implications, particularly those that relate to respect for persons and property. Here, we are considering personality in its wider aspects, and not limiting it to those with moral implications.

Attention of psychologists to personality is distinctly a modern phenomenon. Galton may be looked upon as the father of the psychology of personality, for in 1884 he published an article on the "Measurement of Character," but it was not until many decades later that psychologists developed methods for the study of personality along lines suggested by Galton (13).

James's only references to personality concerned highly pathological aberrations, always fascinating to him, which he classifies under three headings: insane delusions, alternating selves, and mediumships or possessions (20). Thorndike does not deal with personality as such, but many of his illustrations in duscussing instinct deal with personality, and one gathers that he would consider personality as largely a matter of original nature or inheritance. References to personality or character or the self may be found in older texts on psychology, but they are of a philosophical nature and are not based on experimental or observational evidence. MacDougall discussed personality under the heading of "sentiments." The beginnings of a scientific approach to the study of personality may be dated at 1918, when Woodworth constructed his "Personal Data Sheet," a questionnaire for studying neurotic tendencies in soldiers in World War I.

The first large-scale study of personality was undertaken by the Character Education Inquiry under the direction of Hartshorne and May from 1922 to 1930 (17). The main emphasis in these studies was on the measurement of character looking toward a description of its organization, and little attention was paid to the formation of character. This emphasis on measurement and the organization of personality persists to the present day, witness two recent comprehensive treatises by Cattell (5) and Guilford (15). Psychologists have been more interested in the problem of selection than in the formation and modification of personality. Accordingly, most of our information about the development of personality has come from clinical workers and the observations made by students of child development.

Every clinical worker becomes impressed with the persistence of personality. A client mentions some personality trend that is bothering him; for example, he is unable to hold a job for any length of time. Things seem at first to be going satisfactorily, and then he finds that he is being taken advantage of by his employer, who does not trust him and gives preference to others in his office. Matters become intolerable until he is forced to quit in a huff. But as he reviews his life, it appears that he reacted the same way toward one of his college instructors, although he had not previously noticed the similarity. And then sometime later it is revealed that as a boy he had similar thoughts toward his stepfather, who favored his stepbrother. There seems to be a persistence of personality trends extending back not just weeks and months, but apparently over much of the life span.

Recently, evidence of a more systematic nature that verifies such clinical observations has been supplied by psychologists. Madorah Smith (33), reporting from the University of Hawaii, had access to a journal kept by a missionary mother of six children which enabled Dr. Smith to compare ratings of character traits judged from entries in the journal with ratings made of these same individuals fifty years later by persons who knew them all well. Seventy per cent of the ratings differed by not more than one step on the five-step rating scale used, indicating a high degree of stability in the personality traits studied. E. L. Kelly (23) made a follow-up study of individuals twenty years after he had originally studied them as engaged couples. He found considerable consistency in personality test scores and self-ratings represented by correlations in the neighborhood of .30 to .60. He is careful to point out that these correlations also indicate an important amount of change in these same personality traits, even allowing for the unreliability of the measures.

The writer (with A. F. Jensen) has had the privilege of studying, after an interval of thirteen years, 28 out of the original 40 adolescents who were subjects in an investigation of adolescent fantasy (41). In the initial study the subjects were from thirteen to seventeen years of age; in the follow-up study they were from twenty-six to thirty. We found that there is considerable persistence of observed characteristics of personality as well as of fantasy, but shifts in personality and fantasy were noted which have been related to experiences in the intervening years (44).

McKinnon reported that ten children who were seen by her when they were three years old showed the same dominant personality characteristics at age eight or nine that they had exhibited at the earlier age (24).

Shirley (31) in 1933 reported on an intensive study of twenty-five babies who had been seen at frequent intervals from birth through the first two years. She was able to conclude that "each baby exhibits a characteristic pattern of personality traits that changes little with age."

Fifteen years later Neilon (25) was able to prepare personality sketches of 15 adolescents who had originally been among the 25 babies studied by Shirley. These were matched against Shirley's original sketches, and it was found that the matching could be accomplished well above chance expectancy, more successfully with certain subjects than with others, which made Neilon willing to conclude "personality similarities in an individual persist over a period of time."

This review of evidence that personality resists change over long periods of time is almost certain to be countered by instances in which personality shows sudden and sometimes dramatic changes. One young lady who came to my attention described herself as anything but pretty in early adolescence—cross-eyed, thin and gawky, the tallest in her class. A minor operation helped to straighten her eyes. When she went to high school a transformation took place. She had left off glasses, got a permanent wave, and used lipstick for the first time. She suddenly realized that she "had possibilities" and set out to make herself the most popular and sought-after girl in school, a marked transformation from the shy, retiring girl of a few years before. In her case, however, these characteristics which bloomed into reality in high school were present earlier in unexpressed fantasies and longings. Personality exists on more than one level and many wishes and yearnings, very much a part of personality, may not be expressed in overt behavior.

Probably the most famous illustration of personality change is Saint Paul. From one who "breathed threatening and slaughter against the disciples of the Lord" (Acts 9:1) he became one who could write, "If I speak with the tongues of men and angels, but have not love, I am become sounding brass or a clanging cymbal." (I Corinthians 13:1) But Paul after his conversion was very much the same personality that he had been before. He was the adventurous personality who could claim, "Thrice was I beaten with rods, once I was stoned, thrice I suffered shipwreck, a night and a day have I been in the deep" (II Corinthians 11:25). Paul's shift shows how closely related are love and hate. I would much prefer to have Paul on my side than against me.

It should be pointed out that the prediction of personality was not perfect in Smith's six cases; that Kelly's correlations leave much room for shifts in personality; that in my thirteen-year follow-up of 28 adolescents into adulthood, changes in personality were noted; that McKinnon did find changes in her children followed from age three to age eight or nine; and that Neilon noted changes in the adolescents who were babies in Shirley's study. But these shifts in personality in childhood, adolescent, and adult years do not alter the main fact that there is a pronounced consistency in personality in most individuals throughout life.

The evidence which is available points not only to the persistence of traits of personality throughout life but also to the great resistance of personality traits to change. The evidence for this comes largely from the experience of clinical workers who find that after months and even years of concentrated efforts to change personality in clients, basic personality patterns remain unchanged.

Both the clinical evidence and reports of longitudinal studies by psychologists point to the unescapable conclusion that for the majority of persons and for the majority of characteristics, the dominant characteristics of personality persist throughout life from infancy to old age. One gathers the impression after reviewing these studies that there is a natural history to personality. The man with whom you just talked has had a long period of development. The qualities of personality that you have just observed have been in the process of formation over many years. The foundation of many of his traits was laid down in early childhood or infancy, and he can be recognized as the same person as when he was a little child—demanding, patient, relaxed, excitable, gracious, quarrelsome, or whatever it may be. What does this mean? Of course it means that normally the mold of personality is fixed very early and does not change—for most persons—throughout life. Does it mean that personality is inherited?

The conclusion reached by Galton from his study of twins was that personality is inherited. He made inquiry of eighty pairs of twins who were "extremely similar" and twenty pairs who were "extremely dissimilar" and reached the conclusion that "man is so educable an animal that it is difficult to distinguish between that part of his character which has been acquired through education and circumstance, and that which was in the original grain of his constitution" (12, p. 128). Also "In solution of the question whether a continual improvement in education might not compensate for a stationary or even retrograde condition of natural gifts, I made inquiry into the life history of twins, which resulted in proving the vastly preponderating effects of nature over nurture" (12, pp. 216–17). Again, "There is no escape from the conclusion that nature prevails enormously over nurture when the differences of nurture do not exceed what is commonly to be found among persons of the same rank of society and in the same country" (12, p. 172).

Coming down from the past, then, were two main theories of personality development. One, and the most popular (the Judean-Christian), held that personality was formed through influences in the family and the church, but this took place through discipline and instruction after the years of understanding and the rational powers had been reached. The other, growing out of the biological-scientific position of the nineteenth century, held that personality is largely inherited.

It seemed utter heresy, then, for Freud to announce that the basic elements of character are formed before the end of the fifth year of life in most instances.

Freud's original statement concerned the development of sexual impulses. However, his emphasis on the early appearance of sexual behavior has been interpreted to include the development of all aspects of personality, as the following quotation from Ernest Jones indicates:

> [Freud] regards the mental processes, and particularly the wishes, of early childhood life as the permanent basis for all later development. . . . Freud looks upon the whole of a subject's life as a continuity, as a series of associated trends. . . . These views naturally have great importance in their bearing on education, for it is substantially maintained that the main traits of character are permanently determined for good or ill before the end of the fifth year of life. Freud holds in general that, owing to our ignorance of the most important mental processes of early childhood, and our own personal amnesia for this period, the significance for later life of these early trends is vastly underestimated (21).

It is difficult for us to capture the trend of thinking at the beginning of the century, but Freud's position that the "main traits of character are permanently determined before the end of the fifth year of life" before powers of reason have developed seemed utterly inconceivable when he announced it. This is particularly true because Freud's evidence was gathered from recaptured memories of adult patients and by "reconstructions" based on psychoanalytic theory. A psychoanalyst even goes so far as to talk and think about his adult client's behavior as though it were the behavior of an infant nursing with its mother or resisting its mother's attempts to train it in toilet cleanliness. So this Freudian point of view was discounted for many years and still is by many persons.

But the clinical evidence continued to verify Freud's observation. After 1921, when the Joint Committee on Methods of Preventing Delinquency established by the Commonwealth Fund initiated the child guidance movement, there was systematic clinical study of children, and some of the things that Freud learned from his analysis of adult patients about personality development were observed in the process of formation. Gradually it became clear that personality is formed through infantile experiences, primarily in the interaction between mother and child. Out of the child guidance movement such terms as "acceptance," "rejection," "overprotection" appeared to indicate attitudes of the mother, in particular, that have influence on the personality formation of the child. Kenworthy and David Levy, psychoanalysts and child psychiatrists, were influential in introducing these concepts as early as 1929.

An early study that electrified the psychological world by demonstrating how emotional responses could be learned in infancy was reported by the behaviorist John B. Watson. Watson and his wife were able to demonstrate that it was possible to condition fear in an eleven-month-old infant by "showing him a rat and as soon as he reached for it and touched it to strike a heavy steel bar behind him." At the eighth presentation "the instant the rat was shown the baby began to cry. Almost instantly he turned strongly to the left, fell over, raised himself on all fours and began to crawl away so rapidly that he was caught with difficulty before he reached the edge of the table" (45).

But it was not until two decades later that empirical evidence was reported that bore more closely on the influence of infantile experiences on personality formation. One of the early objective studies of the influence of parental attitudes on personality formation was made by the writer (39). I was able to secure data on the personalities of 31 so-called accepted children and 31 rejected children. Each clinical worker who contributed a pair of cases was requested to send in data for an accepted child who was as nearly as possible like the rejected child selected for the study in age, sex, school grade, social background, and intelligence level. A comparison of the two groups showed striking differences in personality, the rejected children exhibiting more emotional instability, an excess of activity and restlessness, and antagonism against society and its institutions.

Spitz (34), a psychoanalyst, spent much time in hospitals observing and photographing babies. He described a state which he called "hospitalism" in infants that were placed in an institutional setting separated from their mothers during the first year of life, a state which is characterized by severe retardation in personality development. Similar findings have been reported by Durfee and Wolf in Austria (6), and by several other investigators in this country.

Spitz and Wolf (36) also found that if the deprivation of the mother starts at a later date, a condition will result which greatly resembles depression in the adult. These same authors (37) studied a group of 153 mothers who showed periodic mood swings, and found that their children showed strange, disturbed personalities, many of them indulging in fecal play. Other mothers, whose personalities were described as infantile, had children who were "retarded in social responses and manipulative ability expressing a diminished capacity to relate to human beings or to manipulate inanimate objects."

In spite of the fact that Spitz has given inadequate statistical treatment to his data, the results have not been controverted. Spitz concludes from his studies that "the mother or her substitute transmits literally every experience to the infant. Barring starvation, disease or actual physical injury, no other factor is capable of so influencing the child's development in every field as its relation to its mother." (35).

Goldfarb was able to compare institutionally reared children with

586   UNDERSTANDING WHAT HAPPENS WITHIN ONE'S SELF

children reared in foster homes from age three to twelve. He concluded that "infant deprivation results in a basic defect in total personality" (15).

Another psychiatrist who has made close observations of infants is Margaret Ribble (28). Although Ribble presents no data, she states that her conclusions are based on the observation of some 600 healthy infants. She also reported studying mentally ill adult patients in Vienna of whom "the earliest upbringing of the individual as well as something of the parents were known, in order to determine, if possible, what part these factors played in the evolution of the mental illness." She concludes that "invariably the child who is deprived of individual mothering shows disordered behavior, with a compensatory retardation in general alertness" (28, p. 82). And again,

> Poor relationships with the parents result in reactions in the infant which tend to become the basis of adult personality disorders. The most important asset of the baby as he begins life is two emotionally healthy parents. His deepest need by far is the understanding care of one consistent individual—his mother. Perhaps in time we shall recognize the danger of the emotionally unhealthy personality and shall see that emotional disturbance in the parents is as damaging to the baby as is tuberculosis or syphilis. If this sounds shocking to any reader, let it be taken to heart (28, pp. 109–110).

Two psychologists, Orlansky and Pinneau, have reacted strongly against Ribble's assertions, in scholarly and highly documented articles (26, 27).

Orlansky says,

> It is unfortunate that such an influential writer has not attempted to draw a line between her empirical findings and her personal opinions. There is so much panegyric and so little satsifactory evidence in her writing that it is difficult for an impartial critic to evaluate many of her statements objectively.

If the foregoing studies are not convincing, particularly Ribble's (perhaps hers should not be called a study at all), because of the paucity of data and the subjective way in which the conclusions were arrived at, it may be helpful if better controlled studies are reported. Shirley, whose earlier study of twenty-five babies has been referred to, some years later reported a study that attempted to trace some of the factors which may have accounted for differences in the way in which two-year-old children reacted to being taken for an all-day visit to a center for research on child health and development. Some of the children adjusted well to the strange situation; others were much upset. Shirley eliminated such factors as age, sex, illness, and finally concluded that

> . . . a child's level of adjustment depends little upon the extrinsic features of the day, and little even upon his health. It depends much

more upon the wholesomeness of his upbringing in the home, and the security and confidence and affection given him by his parents. A secure and wholesomely loved child goes forth to meet new experience in a spirit of adventure and comes out triumphant in his encounters with new places, new materials, and new friends, young and old. A child that is oversheltered and underloved goes forth from home with misgivings and doubts, and gives an impression of inadequacy and immaturity in his encounter with new experiences that makes him unwelcome either in the society of adults or children (32).

Sears, Maccoby, and Levin have assembled a report of their researches in this field (29). Sears and his associates were able to question 379 American mothers about their methods of bringing up their children from birth to kindergarten age. These authors say, "[It is] ou. opinion that child-rearing practices are important determiners [of personality]" (29, p. 453). Every interaction between two people has an effect both on their present actions and on their potentialities for future action" (29, p. 458). "Every moment of a child's life that he spends in contact with his parents has some effect on both his present behavior and his potentialities for future action" (29, p. 466). These authors present much evidence concerning the reactions of children to the attitudes and behavior of their parents.

Vigorous research on parent-child relationships is still going on. As an example, Earl S. Schaefer, Richard Bell and Nancy Bayley are carrying on a study, the results of which are not yet available, at the National Institute of Mental Health on Quantification of Maternal Relations and Consistency of Mother-Child Interactions.

In most discussions the mother is assumed to be the key figure in determining personality formation in the child, simply because, normally, children are with their mothers more than with anyone else in the early years. To the extent that little children interact with their fathers they become an influence, and the nurse or caretaker becomes an influence if the children are with them for any considerable period.

"The essence of parent–child relations lies more in how a parent feels than in what a parent does" or says (42, p. xiii). This point of view has been difficult for many to understand and accept because a child can react only to parental behavior in the broad sense and not to unexpressed feeling. But any behavior may mean different things according to its context and concomitant expression. A parent may keep a child in the house on a rainy afternoon out of concern for a child's health, but also as a form of punishment. A child reacts to the parental response in terms of what it means to him rather than arbitrarily and blindly as a response to a stimulus.

In general it may be said that the responses acquired by the infant which are the forerunners of later personality characteristics are learned according to the same laws that govern all learning. At the beginning the infant tends to repeat responses which give it pleasure. These are the responses made in the nursing situation in connection with fondling, cuddling, handling, and other manipulations. Later, other responses and characteristics of responses are made when parental control is exercised, particularly in connection with toilet training. Personality is also formed as a result of punishment and deprivations. Indeed, it is believed that delinquency and neurosis find much of their origin in punishment and other negative phases of parental response.

One important determinant of personality is simply the presence or absence of the mother. This is clearly seen in the extreme separation from the mother reported by Spitz in his study of hospitalism, but the emotional insecurity of the child is also influenced by even momentary separations. A young baby shows the importance of being able to see the mother by his excitement in playing a simple game of hide-and-seek. Although pleasure is found in the nursing and fondling situations, the main factor soon becomes and continues throughout life to be the reaction of other persons, particularly the mother, to the infant and his responses to them.

The terms acceptance and rejection have been used to describe significant expressions in the mother-child relationship. By acceptance is meant a feeling of living, wanting, liking, being fond and proud of a child, and consequently doing things that nourish, protect, and encourage him. Rejection, on the other hand, refers to negative feelings of hate or dislike toward a child which may be expressed in a variety of ways; for instance, by extreme forms of separation, denial, neglect, or cruelty. Punishment and threat of punishment frequently are expressions of these negative feelings of the parent. More subtly, a parent can show rejection by ridicule and other methods of humiliating a child, and by preference for a sib or siblings. But these two attitudes of love and hate represent only one dimension of a parent's attitude. A parent may exhibit stability or anxiety, greater or less self-love, greater or less indulgence, greater or less authority and domination, greater or less ambition, and so on. Each of these attitudes when expressed contributes to the child's personality. And it should be added that these feelings are not strictly under the voluntary control of a parent, but are residues in his (the parent's) personality of his (or her) earlier experiences in childhood or infancy.

From my recent studies of adolescent fantasy and its impact on changes in personality in subsequent years, it has become clear that fantasy is a factor in the determination of later overt trends in personality (43). What a person yearns and strives for he may later work out in actual living. Personality is, then, in part, a precipitate of fantasy. As I have previously stated, "Behavior or personality is not wholly a direct response to the accepting or rejecting situation, but is also a response to the inner attitude of the child" (39, p. 84). This is as true, no doubt, in the formation of the earliest trends of personality in infancy as it is in childhood and adolescence. Always accompanying or preceding actual behavior are inner urges, strivings, promptings that determine the direction that personality will take. Very early, as Sullivan (38, p. 9) suggests, personality takes the character that coincides with one's concept of oneself.

Personality is also learned through identification—called imitation by psychologists of several generations ago. But it is not a simple matter of imitation. Early in life a baby recognizes its parents and older brothers and sisters as bigger, stronger, and more skillful than he, and he strives to satisfy some of his basic needs by being like them. So the little boy is said to be a "chip off the old block."

In order to grasp the full significance of Watson's experiment, one must be willing to recognize that personality is formed by virtue of the reactions that the infant or child makes without benefit of his awareness or appreciation of his reactions. Personality is formed by the infant's reactions to situations long before he develops conscious awareness of his reactions. By the time the child has acquired the language and concepts with which to understand his personality it has been formed so firmly that there is little that he can do to direct or modify it.

Because personality in all its ramifications is learned, we hold that the formation of personality is the task and responsibility of education. Only too often education is made synonymous with schooling. But if education is concerned with learning, then much of education must take place before the school years and in the home. Again, education is often thought of as a process of instruction, largely through language. But much of learning, and most of learning in infancy, takes place without benefit of instruction or language. Parents must learn to think of themselves as the child's first teachers, the teaching taking place not through formal, planned instruction, but by every changing response and attitude that the mother takes toward her child.

The contributions of heredity and experience have never been determined, and a precise answer to this issue is extremely difficult to establish. The point of view generally held today is that there are hereditary-constitutional determinants of personality, but that these are broad and general. Soon after birth, experiences tend to differentiate responses through learning on the broad foundation provided by heredity, and the distinguishing characteristics of personality are learned.

What are the constitutional elements of personality? New-born babies and babies seen shortly after birth have been observed to differ in a number of characteristics which may represent hereditary differences or differences that originate during the gestation period, and which are presumed to be the basis for fundamental personality differences in later life. The most outstanding of these differences is what has been termed *activity level*. This was noted by a New York psychoanalyst, Fries (10), who not only reported her findings in the literature but also recorded her observations in very convincing motion pictures. Newborn babies will differ in the amount of kicking and thrashing about and in particular in the vigor with which they nurse.

After following these same children (who had been observed periodically from the moment of birth) for five years, it was found that the activity pattern of the so-called normal child can be modified, but only within certain limits; and that the most important factor responsible for modifying it (excluding organic pathology) is the parents' emotional adjustment, their relations to each other and to the child (11).

Neonates also differ, according to observations by Bergman and Escalona, in their sensitivity to various sensory modalities, and they have been observed to respond differently to colors, bright lights, noises, unusual sounds, qualities of material, experiences of equilibrium, taste, smell, and temperature (4). In the same report these authors also note that infants differ in their ability to protect themselves by inattention and lowered response to stimuli as "protective barriers against stimuli." This seems to be related to the capacity to tolerate frustration and delay in having their wants satisfied. In another report, Escalona mentioned a related characteristic which she has noted in babies in earliest infancy—"the capacity to focus and channel energies upon a given task" (7).

To this list of possible constitutional factors which are observable in the first weeks of life may be added "social responsiveness," that is, the capacity and tendency of the infant to respond to the mother who nurses it (14).

What are some of the characteristics that are learned in the early months and years? Some of the characteristics of personality that are formed in the first year of life can best be stated in the form of dichotomies —being a boy or girl, being active or passive, socially responsive or self-centered, assertive or receptive, aggressive or submissive, independent or dependent, spontaneous or repressed. It will be noted that each of these seems to be a variant of the general constitutional tendency to be active or passive. But the precise uniqueness of the personality in the earliest years depends on the reactions of the individual to the mother and other individuals who are with it. It is on the basis of these fundamental trends that the later diffentiations of personality take place.

A boy or a girl accepts his or her sex role from the early months of life by virtue of the fact that he or she is given a boy's or a girl's name, is dressed appropriately for his or her sex, and is treated as befits a boy or a girl. Soon there are inner promptings that tend to reinforce the direction staked out, and the child begins to take on his individual character as a boy or a girl. Likewise, according to his initial energy and assertiveness, the infant will approach the nursing situation in his own unique way; and according to the mother's promptings will develop personality characteristics of assertiveness or passivity, independence or dependence.

To the extent that a baby is loved and his needs are met by affectionate handling, he acquires friendly responses. It is in infancy, largely through punishment, that hostile, aggressive attitudes are formed that may last through life. Tendencies toward anxiety, sometimes called "basic anxiety," and later guilt also have their origins in infancy (18).

In the first year of life the infant is more or less helpless and dependent on others for the gratification of his needs, and his reaction to this state of helplessness becomes the origin of many personality trends such as passivity, a fatalistic attitude, submissiveness. But if the infant strives to overcome his helpless position, he may develop characteristic modes of behavior which serve as the roots for later ambition, competition, envy, jealousy, rivalry, courage, and optimism. The Freudians have called this the oral stage of development (2). As the need for parental control arises in the second year, when the infant has greater powers of locomotion, such traits as stubbornness, obstinacy, cooperation, independence, responsibility, and the unwillingness to submit and conform have their beginnings. In this period the so-called authoritarian personality finds its first roots (3). In connection with toilet training, such traits as cleanliness, stinginess and generosity, reticence and openness appear (8, 1).

Infancy is the time when attitudes toward sex behavior are formed. The infant may find sex pleasurable, or if it is punished because of autoerotic acts—thumbsucking or play with the genitals—then sexual pleasure may be repressed. The objects or persons that one seeks for satisfaction in later life are determined in infancy, and it is during this period that essential heterosexual or homosexual orientations are formed (9).

An important aspect of personality is found in the attitudes of an individual as well as in his behavior. Of particular importance is the self-concept. Even in the first year the first mental processes of the infant are concerned with the reactions of others toward him, and out of these reactions of others he builds his concept of himself. The self-concept typically reflects the characteristics that he is forming or, at least, the way in which these characteristics impress others. This phenomenological aspect of personality is fully as important as the more objective impressions that a person makes on others. In fact, the self-concept interacts with the behavioral aspects of personality. One's behavioral tendencies help in a roundabout way to form the self-concept, and the self-concept helps to guide and control behavior.

In thinking about personality one must not forget the whole world of fantasy which includes the wishes, hopes, and aspirations, as well as the fears and anxieties. Fantasy does not consist of mere static images, but of images which have an impulsive quality with a pressure to erupt into active expression. But many fantasies have no counterpart in behavior. Most persons can enjoy the play or novel or mystery story in which characters do things that the reader or onlooker would not permit himself to do. Our ideals belong to this great realm of fantasy which may or may not find expression in actual accomplishment.

Finally an important aspect of personality that has its origin in infancy is what is called by the psychoanalysts "ego strength." This somewhat vague and ill-defined concept refers principally to the capacity to govern one's actions by reason. Of course this capacity is not fully formed until reason has developed, and this takes place gradually throughout childhood. Ego strength also refers to the capacity to postpone action, the roots of which are laid down early. Ego strength enables the individual to meet crises, threats, deprivations, and traumatic experiences with equanimity, but low ego strength makes the individual susceptible to neurotic adjustment.

Those aspects of personality which are present at birth or are formed during the first years are the ones which are most deeply rooted and which will be the most permanent and the most difficult to change in later years.

If the foundations of personality are laid in infancy, one may well ask what part of its development takes place after the first five or six years of life. Observation reveals that throughout the growth period there is a differentiation of personality along the lines determined by the early formations. The precise direction that personality will take, the persons toward whom it will be directed, the objects and activities that will give personality its unique flavor for each individual are determined by the environment and experiences of an individual. One can teach a child manners, rules of conduct, and etiquette, but the way in which these are expressed is determined by the basic personality. A child forms political and religious affiliations during his growing years, but even the roots for these in terms of essential conservatism, liberalism, reverence, and devotion are laid down in the earliest years. The personality trends formed in infancy are neither desirable nor undesirable, but they may be strong or weak. Whether they become good or bad depends on the direction that a person's activities and efforts, allegiances and affiliations take. Aggressive trends are laid down in infancy, but whether they will lead to delinquency and criminality or to socially constructive efforts is determined not only by infantile experiences but also by the influences of later years. A person with strong repressive trends, easily made anxious, and with low ego strength becomes an easy prey to neurotic adjustments in later life, but if he lives in a protected environment and is not subjected to stress and strain he may be able to work out tolerably satisfactory adjustments.

These facts about the early formation of personality are very difficult for many persons to accept and assimilate into their thinking. This is seen most clearly when some problem involving personality comes to a crisis and steps must be taken to meet the situation. When such circumstances arise many, if not most, persons will tend to decry the possibility that personality has been learned. The parents of Hal, the college student mentioned earlier, are puzzled by his behavior. Have they not been good parents and provided a good home with all possible comforts and conveniences? Are they not highly respected by the members of their community? Why should they have a son who presents such a problem? And their friends are puzzled. It could not possibly be the fault of the parents and the home. Hal's father is a successful lawyer. His mother is devoted to her family. His older brother is doing well in college. And Hal himself is troubled and perplexed—he has had to leave his classmates and concede that he is a failure. He is probably irritated at his parents because he cannot have things all his own way.

It is only natural in such circumstances to turn to other possible explanations. Many persons will search for a physical basis for a personality difficulty. Seeking medical assistance relieves one of the sense of responsibility for one's troubles, for what is physical seems so inexorable. So a person with a personality difficulty may have a physical examination and with hope clutch at the possibility that his troubles may be eased by vitamins, allergy treatment, building up the blood, tranquilizers, electric shock, or even by surgery. Belief in the hereditary basis for personality persists in part because people can evade responsibility for their behavior if they believe that it is inherited. The assertions of Sheldon (30) that morphology (relating to the form and structure of the human body) and temperament correlate in the neighborhood of .80 have attracted much more attention than the facts warrant, for it is obvious that in spite of the well-known temperamental differences between endomorphs (fleshy individuals), mesomorphs (muscular individuals), and ectomorphs (lean individuals), these differences in physical structure cannot begin to account for the differences in personality. Likewise, assertions that glands exert an influence on personality always receive hopeful attention, even though such an authority as Hoskins has said,

> Some things we know regarding the direct influence of the hormones upon the personality. By and large, however, the problem remains mostly for future solution. Even in broad outline, the picture is somewhat indeterminate and, in detail, is definitely confused (19, p. 364).

To return to the case of Hal, in spite of the assertions of family and friends, there is strong presumption that Hal's behavior and attitudes are a result of earlier reactions to parent-child and sibling relationships in the home.

Out of these facts follow important and far-reaching implications. The main responsibility for the development of personality falls on parents. The personality of the child develops out of the interaction of parent and infant. The expectant mother may be in trepidation lest she be unfit for the responsibility of child rearing that lies ahead, and child-rearing methods can cause regret and guilt to those whose children have been disappointing to them. As facts concerning parent–child relations become better known, mothers in the future can be more sensitive to the influence that their behavior has on the personality of the child. But it should be recognized that such information can have only minor influence in determining maternal practices in child rearing. As has been mentioned above, a mother's behavior and her responses toward her child are primarily a matter of attitude and feeling, which are to only a small extent under control by what the mother knows and by her conscious intentions. A mother's attitude toward her child is a function of *her* personality which was formed in *her* infancy and childhood. It would seem as though we are dealing here with closed circuits into which there is no penetration. This point of view is, of course, a highly fatalistic and deterministic docrine, but such conclusions seem inevitable from what we now know about the development of personality.

There are two possible ways in which this closed circle can be breached. One is through change in social arrangements which leads to a reduction in friction or tensions in the home. To the extent that housing is improved, for example, one source of tension and friction in families is removed with the result that impulses and feelings of hate and hostility will be less stimulated and positive emotions of love and affection can find freer expression. To the extent that there is freedom from want and greater social security there will be less anxiety in family relations. And to the extent that a society has social goals toward which its members can collectively strive, purposeful living will align the force within the family as a magnet aligns the molecules in an iron bar.

The other method, certainly more expensive, but increasingly popular, is through direct methods of personality reorganization, such as psychotherapy. Such direct methods, to have influence on personality development, must be undertaken in the young man or woman before parenthood.

Schools may be listed as one of the precipitating factors in the determination of the direction that personality will take, but they must work with the basic personalities of the children who come to them—they cannot hope to modify these basic personalities. If strength is there, education can help the individual grow in worth-while directions; it cannot overcome weakness in the basic personality structure. The school is one of the agencies of society that helps to determine the direction of the expression of personality in character.

And what is the function of the teacher in the development of personality? Teachers are, in part, responsible for the development of character; that is, the direction that personality should take in order that boys and girls may become responsible and moral members of society. This is done, in some measure, by the teaching of ideals. But the psychologist believes that more important than precept are the relations between teachers and pupils. Pupils will identify with teachers whom they like and admire. The teacher wields influence by what she *is* and *does;* that is, by what she stands for, what she approves of, what she holds valuable and honorable. Personalities are formed by interaction of teacher with pupil and pupil with pupil, so a program of social participation is essential if the school is to have any influence on character formation. I look with some reservation on the modern trend in the use of machines for teaching, in carrying on instruction in larger classes by "master teachers," and in the use of audio-visual devices, because none of these provides for necessary social participation. Children need more freedom for spontaneous expression and, in particular, opportunities to express emotions. To make this possible, teachers must cultivate attitudes of greater acceptingness, yet at the same time they should continue to exercise strictness and firmness in control, but without punishment. Pupils need more encouragement and greater satisfaction when their behavior meets with approval (40).

In summary, while there is evidence that the roots of personality are constitutional, the structure of personality, particularly as it is expressed in human relationships, is the result of learning—learning which begins shortly after birth and continues through infancy and early childhood. The basic patterns of personality are formed in the first five or six years of life. These facts place a great responsibility on parents, for personality is formed largely through parent-child relationships.

REFERENCES:

1. ABRAHAM, KARL. "Contributions to the Theory of the Anal Character," *Collected Papers*, Chapter 23, The International Psychoanalytical Library, No. 13 (London: Hogarth Press, 1927), pp. 370–92.
2. ABRAHAM, KARL. "The Influence of Oral Emotions on Character Formation," *Collected Papers*, Chapter 24, The International Psychoanalytical Library, No. 13 (London: Hogarth Press, 1927), pp. 393–406.
3. ADORNO, T. W. et al. *The Authoritarian Personality* (New York: Harper and Brothers, 1950).
4. BERGMAN, PAUL and S. K. ESCALONA. "Unusual Sensitivities in Very Young Children," *The Psychoanalytic Study of the Child*, Vols. 3, 4 (New York: International Universities Press, 1949), pp. 333–52.
5. CATTELL, R. B. *Personality and Motivation: Structure and Measurement* (Yonkers-on-Hudson: World Book Company, 1957).
6. DURFEE, H. and K. WOLF. "Abstaltspflegeund Entwicklung im ersten Lebanjähr," *Zeitschrift für Kinderforschung*, 42, 3: 1933.
7. ESCALONA, S. K. "The Use of Infant Tests for Predictive Purposes," *Bulletin of the Menninger Clinic*, 14: 117–28, 1950.
8. FREUD, SIGMUND. "Character and Anal Erotism," *Collected Papers*, Vol. II, Chapter 4, The International Psychoanalytical Library, No. 8 (London: Hogarth Press, 1924), pp. 45–50.
9. FREUD, SIGMUND. *Three Contributions to the Theory of Sex*, Nervous and Mental Disease Monograph Series, No. 7 (New York: Nervous and Mental Disease Publishing Company, 1910; first published in German in 1905). Also reprinted in *The Basic Writings of Sigmund Freud* (New York: The Modern Library, Inc., 1938), Book III, pp. 553–620.

10. FRIES, M. E. "Interrelated Factors in Character Development, Neuroses, Psychoses, and Delinquency," *American Journal of Orthopsychiatry,* 7: 142– 81, 1937.
11. FRIES, M. E. "Psychosomatic Relationships Between Mother and Child," *Psychosomatic Medicine,* 6: 159–62, 1944.
12. GALTON, FRANCIS. *Inquiries into Human Faculty and Its Development* (New York: E. P. Dutton and Company, 1883, 1907), Everyman's Library, No. 163.
13. GALTON, FRANCIS. "Measurement of Character," *Fortnightly Review,* 42: 179–85, 1884.
14. GESELL, ARNOLD, and L. B. AMES. "Early Evidences of Individuality in the Human Infant," *Scientific Monthly,* 45: 217–25, 1937.
15. GOLDFARB, WILLIAM. "Psychological Privation in Infancy and Subsequent Adjustment," *American Journal of Orthopsychiatry,* 15: 247–55, 1945.
16. GUILFORD, J. P. *Personality* (New York: McGraw-Hill Book Company, 1959).
17. HARTSTONE, HUGH, M. A. MAY, J. B. MALLER, and F. K. SHUTTLEWORTH, *Studies in the Nature of Character,* "Studies in Deceit," Vol. I; "Studies in Service and Self-Control," Vol. II; "Studies in the Organization of Character," Vol. III (New York: The Macmillan Company, 1928, 1929, 1930).
18. HORNEY, KAREN. *The Neurotic Personality of Our Time* (New York: W. W. Norton and Company, 1937).
19. HASKINS, R. G. *Endocrinology* (New York: W. W. Norton and Company, 1941), p. 364.
20. JAMES, WILLIAM. *Psychology,* Vol. I (New York: Henry Holt and Company, 1890), pp. 375–400.
21. JONES, ERNEST. "Freud's Psychology," *Psychological Bulletin,* 7: 109–28, 1911.
22. JONES, ERNEST. *The Life and Works of Sigmund Freud,* Vol. II (New York: Basic Books, 1955).
23. KELLY, E. L. "Consistency of the Adult Personality," *The American Psychologist,* 10: 659–81, 1955.
24. MCKINNON, K. M. *Consistency and Change in Behavior Manifestations,* Child Development Monographs, No. 30 (New York: Bureau of Publications, Teachers College, Columbia University, 1942).
25. NEILON, PATRICIA (NAKA), "Shirley's Babies after Fifteen Years: A Personality Study," *Journal of Genetic Psychology,* 73: 175–86, 1948.
26. ORLANSKY, HAROLD. "Infant Care and Personality," *Psychological Bulletin,* 46: 1–48, 1949.
27. PINNEAU, S. R. "A Critique of the Articles by Margaret Ribble," *Child Development,* 21: 203–28, 1950.

28. RIBBLE, MARGARET. *The Rights of Infants* (New York: Columbia University Press, 1943).
29. SEARS, R. R., E. E. MACCOBY, and HARRY LEVIN. *Patterns of Child Rearing* (Evanston, Illinois: Row, Peterson and Company, 1957).
30. SHELDON, W. H. *The Varieties of Temperament* (New York: Harper and Brothers, 1942).
31. SHIRLEY, M. M. *The First Two Years: A Study of Twenty-five Babies*, Vol. III, "Personality Manifestations," Institute of Child Welfare Monograph Series, No. 8 (Minneapolis: University of Minnesota Press, 1933).
32. SHIRLEY, M. M. "Children' Adjustment to a Strange Situation," *Child Development*, 37: 201–17, 1942.
33. SMITH, M. E. "A Comparison of Certain Personality Traits as Rated on the Same Individuals in Childhood and Fifty Years Later," *Child Development*, 23: 159–80, 1952.
34. SPITZ, RENE A. "Hospitalism" in *The Psychoanalytic Study of the Child*, Vol. I (New York: International Universities Press, 1945), pp. 53–74.
35. SPITZ, R. A. "The Role of Ecological Factors in Emotional Development in Infancy," *Child Development*, 20: 145–55, 1949.
36. SPITZ, R. A., and K. M. WOLF. "Analclitic Depression: An Inquiry into the Genesis of Psychiatric Conditions in Early Childhood," *The Psychoanalytic Study of the Child*, Vol. 2 (New York: International Universities Press, 1946), pp. 313–42.
37. SPITZ, R. A., and K. M. WOLF, "Autoerotism, Some Empirical Findings and Hypotheses on Three of its Manifestations in the First Year of Life," *The Psychoanalytic Study of the Child*, Vols. 3, 4 (New York: International Universities Press, 1949), pp. 85–119.
38. SULLIVAN, H. S. *Conceptions of Modern Psychiatry* (Washington, D.C.: The William Alanson White Psychiatric Foundation, 1947).
39. SYMONDS, P. M. *The Psychology of Parent-Child Relationships* (New York: D. Appleton-Century Company, 1939).
40. SYMONDS, P. M. "Education for the Development of Personality," *Teachers College Record*, 50: 163–69, 1948.
41. SYMONDS, P. M. *Adolescent Fantasy* (New York: Columbia University Press, 1949).
42. SYMONDS, P. M. *The Dynamics of Parent-Child Relationships* (New York: Bureau of Publications, Teachers College, Columbia University, 1949).
43. SYMONDS and JENSEN. *Out of Adolescence into Adulthood*.
44. SYMONDS, P. M., and A. F. JENSEN, *Out of Adolescence into Maturity*, to be published by the Columbia University Press.
45. WATSON, J. B., and R. R. WATSON. "Studies in Infant Psychology," *Scientific Monthly*, 13: 493–515, 1921.

52   *The Organization of Personality**

BY CARL R. ROGERS

EDITOR'S NOTE: Before one can hope to understand himself or others better, it is first necessary to examine how the personality is organized. Speaking from a perceptual psychology point of view, Dr. Rogers discusses the relationship between perceptions and behavior and between self-perceptions and adjustment. He calls attention to personality as a process, as a fluid state rather than a set of fixed charateristics, and discusses the conditions of change which would be necessary in order for self-perception to change. Have you ever thought of that possibility—that is, the possibility of a personality being able to change? Have you ever wanted to change your own personality from its current organization? Whether you agree or disagree with Dr. Rogers, this paper will stimulate your thinking.

In various fields of science rapid strides have been made when direct observation of significant processes has become possible. In medicine, when circumstances have permitted the physician to peer directly into the stomach of his patient, understanding of digestive processes has increased and the influence of emotional tension upon all aspects of that process has been more accurately observed and understood. In our work with non-directive therapy we often feel that we are having a psychological opportunity comparable to this medical experience—an opportunity to observe directly a number of the effective processes of personality. Quite aside from

* Reprinted from *The American Psychologist*, 1947, Vol. 2, 358–368, by permission of the author and the American Psychological Association.

598

any question regarding nondirective therapy as therapy, here is a precious vein of observational material of unusual value for the study of personality.

Characteristics of the Observational Material

There are several ways in which the raw clinical data to which we have had access is unique in its value for understanding personality. The fact that these verbal expressions of inner dynamics are preserved by electrical recording makes possible a detailed analysis of a sort not heretofore possible. Recording has given us a microscope by which we may examine at leisure, and in minute detail, almost every aspect of what was, in its occurrence, a fleeting moment impossible of accurate observation.

Another scientifically fortunate characteristic of this material is the fact that the verbal productions of the client are biased to a minimal degree by the therapist. Material from client-centered interviews probably comes closer to being a "pure" expression of attitudes than has yet been achieved through other means. One can read through a complete recorded case or listen to it, without finding more than a half-dozen instances in which the therapist's views on any point are evident. One would find it impossible to form an estimate as to the therapist's views about personality dynamics. One could not determine his diagnostic views, his standards of behavior, his social class. The one value or standard held by the therapist which would exhibit itself in his tone of voice, responses, and activity, is a deep respect for the personality and attitudes of the client as a separate person. It is difficult to see how this would bias the content of the interview, except to permit deeper expression than the client would ordinarily allow himself. This almost complete lack of any distorting attitide is felt, and sometimes expressed by the client. One woman says:

> It's almost impersonal. I like you—of course I don't know why I should like you or why I shouldn't like you. It's a peculiar thing. I've never had that relationship with anybody before and I've often thought about it. . . . A lot of times I walk out with a feeling of elation that you think highly of me, and of course at the same time I have the feeling that "Gee, he must think I'm an awful jerk" or something like that. But it doesn't really—those feelings aren't so deep that I can form an opinion one way or the other about you.

Here it would seem that even though she would like to discover some type of evaluational attitude, she is unable to do so. Published studies and research as yet unpublished bear out this point that counselor responses which are in any way evaluational or distorting as to content are at a minimum, thus enhancing the worth of such interviews for personality study.

The counselor attitude of warmth and understanding, well described by Snyder (1946) and Rogers (1946), also helps to maximize the freedom of expression by the individual. The client experiences sufficient interest in him as a person, and sufficient acceptance, to enable him to talk openly, not only about surface attitudes, but increasingly about intimate attitudes and feelings hidden even from himself. Hence in these recorded interviews we have material of very considerable depth so far as personality dynamics is concerned, along with a freedom from distortion.

Finally the very nature of the interviews and the techniques by which they are handled give us a rare opportunity to see to some extent through the eyes of another person—to perceive the world as it appears to him, to achieve at least partially the internal frame of reference of another person. We see his behavior through his eyes, and also the psychological meaning which it had for him. We see also changes in personality and behavior, and the meanings which those changes have for the individual. We are admitted freely into the backstage of the person's living where we can observe from within some of the dramas of internal change, which are often far more compelling and moving than the drama which is presented on the stage viewed by the public. Only a novelist or a poet could do justice to the deep struggles which we are permitted to observe from within the client's own world of reality.

This rare opportunity to observe so directly and so clearly the inner dynamics of personality is a learning experience of the deepest sort for the clinician. Most of clinical psychology and psychiatry involves judgments *about* the individual, judgments which must, of necessity, be based on some framework brought to the situation by the clinician. To try continually to see and think *with* the individual, as in client-centered therapy, is a mindstretching experience in which learning goes on apace because the clinician brings to the interview no predetermined yardstick by which to judge the material.

I wish in this paper to try to bring you some of the clinical observations which we have made as we have repeatedly peered through these psychological windows into personality, and to raise with you some of the questions about the organization of personality which these observations have forced upon us. I shall not attempt to present these observations in logical order, but rather in the order in which they impressed themselves upon our notice. What I shall offer is not a series of research findings, but only the first step in that process of gradual approximation which we call science, a description of some observed phenomena which appear to be significant, and some highly tentative explanations of these phenomena.

The Relation of the Organized Perceptual Field to Behavior

One simple observation, which is repeated over and over again in each successful therapeutic case, seems to have rather deep theoretical implications. It is that as changes occur in the perception of self and in the perception of reality, changes occur in behavior. In therapy, these perceptual changes are more often concerned with the self than with the external world. Hence we find in therapy that as the perception of self alters, behavior alters. Perhaps an illustration will indicate the type of observation upon which this statement is based.

A young woman, a graduate student whom we shall call Miss Vib, came in for nine interviews. If we compare the first interview with the last, striking changes are evident. Perhaps some features of this change may be conveyed by taking from the first and last interviews all the major statements regarding self, and all the major statements regarding current behavior. In the first interview, for example, her perception of herself may be crudely indicated by taking all her own statements about herself, grouping those which seem similar, but otherwise doing a minimum of editing, and retaining so far as possible, her own words. We then come out with this as the conscious perception of self which was hers at the outset of counseling.

> I feel disorganized, muddled; I've lost all direction; my personal life has disintegrated.
> I sorta experience things from the forefront of my consciousness, but nothing sinks in very deep; things don't seem real to me; I feel nothing matters; I don't have any emotional response to situations; I'm worried about myself.
> I haven't been acting like myself; it doesn't seem like me; I'm a different person altogether from what I used to be in the past.
> I don't understand myself; I haven't known what was happening to me.
> I have withdrawn from everything, and feel all right only when I'm all alone and no one can expect me to do things.
> I don't care about my personal appearance.
> I don't know *anything* anymore.
> I feel guilty about the things I have left undone.
> I don't think I could ever assume responsibility for anything.

If we attempt to evaluate this picture of self from an external frame of reference, various diagnostic labels may come to mind. Trying to perceive it solely from the client's frame of reference, we observe that to the young woman herself she appears disorganized and not herself. She is perplexed and almost unacquainted with what is going on in herself. She feels unable and unwilling to function in any responsible or social way. This is at least a sampling of the way she experiences or perceives her self.

Her behavior is entirely consistent with this picture of self. If we abstract all her statements describing her behavior, in the same fashion as we abstracted her statements about self, the following pattern emerges—a pattern which in this case was corroborated by outside observation.

>I couldn't get up nerve to come in before; I haven't availed myself of help.
>Everything I should do or want to do, I don't do.
>I haven't kept in touch with friends; I avoid making the effort to go with them; I stopped writing letters home; I don't answer letters or telephone calls; I avoid contacts that would be professionally helpful; I didn't go home though I said I would.
>I failed to hand in my work in a course though I had it all done; I didn't buy clothing that I needed; I haven't even kept my nails manicured.
>I didn't listen to material we were studying; I waste hours reading the funny papers; I can spend the whole afternoon doing absolutely nothing.

The picture of behavior is very much in keeping with the picture of self, and is summed up in the statement that "Everything I should do or want to do, I don't do." The behavior goes on in ways that seem to the individual beyond understanding and beyond control.

If we contrast this picture of self and behavior with the picture as it exists in the ninth interview, thirty-eight days later, we find both the perception of self and the ways of behaving deeply altered. Her statements about self are as follows:

>I'm feeling much better; I'm taking more interest in myself.
>I do have some individuality, some interests.
>I seem to be getting a newer understanding of myself. I can look at myself a little better.
>I realize I'm just one person, with so much ability, but I'm not worried about it; I can accept the fact that I'm not always right.
>I feel more motivation, have more of a desire to go ahead.
>I still occasionally regret the past, though I feel less unhappy about it; I still have a long ways to go; I don't know whether I can keep the picture of myself I'm beginning to evolve.
>I can go on learning—in school or out.
>I do feel more like a normal person now; I feel more I can handle my life myself; I think I'm at the point where I can go along on my own.

Outstanding in this perception of herself are three things—that she knows herself, that she can view with comfort her assets and liabilities, and finally that she has drive and control of that drive.

In this ninth interview the behavioral picture is again consistent with the perception of self. It may be abstracted in these terms.

>I've been making plans about school and about a job; I've been working hard on a term paper; I've been going to the library to trace down a topic of special interest and finding it exciting.

> I've cleaned out my closets; washed my clothes.
> I finally wrote my parents; I'm going home for the holidays.
> I'm getting out and mixing with people; I am reacting sensibly to a fellow who is interested in me—seeing both his good and bad points.
> I will work toward my degree; I'll start looking for a job this week.

Her behavior, in contrast to the first interview, is now organized, forward-moving, effective, realistic and planful. It is in accord with the realistic and organized view she has achieved of her self.

It is this type of observation, in case after case, that leads us to say with some assurance that as perceptions of self and reality change, behavior changes. Likewise, in cases we might term failures, there appears to be no appreciable change in perceptual organization or in behavior.

What type of explanation might account for these concomitant changes in the perceptual field and the behavioral pattern? Let us examine some of the logical possibilities.

In the first place, it is possible that factors unrelated to therapy may have brought about the altered perception and behavior. There may have been physiological processes occurring which produced the change. There may have been alterations in the family relationships, or in the social forces, or in the educational picture or in some other area of cultural influence, which might account for the rather drastic shift in the concept of self and in the behavior.

There are difficulties in this type of explanation. Not only were there no known gross changes in the physical or cultural situation as far as Miss Vib was concerned, but the explanation gradually becomes inadequate when one tries to apply it to the many cases in which such change occurs. To postulate that some external factor brings the change and that only by chance does this period of change coincide with the period of therapy, becomes an untenable hypothesis.

Let us then look at another explanation, namely that the therapist exerted, during the nine hours of contact, a peculiarly potent cultural influence which brought about the change. Here again we are faced with several problems. It seems that nine hours scattered over five and one-half weeks is a very minute portion of time in which to bring about alteration of patterns which have been building for thirty years. We would have to postulate an influence so potent as to be classed as traumatic. This theory is particularly difficult to maintain when we find, on examining the recorded interviews, that not once in the nine hours did the therapist express any evaluation, positive or negative, of the client's initial or final perception of self, or her initial or final mode of behavior. There was not only no evaluation, but no standards expressed by which evaluation might be inferred.

There was, on the part of the therapist, evidence of warm interest in the individual, and thoroughgoing acceptance of the self and of the behavior as they existed initially, in the intermediate stages, and at the conclusion of therapy. It appears reasonable to say that the therapist established certain definite conditions of interpersonal relations, but since the very essence of this relationship is respect for the person as he is at that moment, the therapist can hardly be regarded as a cultural force making for change.

We find ourselves forced to a third type of explanation, a type of explanation which is not new to psychology, but which has had only partial acceptance. Briefly it may be put that the observed phenomena of change seem most adequately explained by the hypothesis that *given certain psychological conditions, the individual has the capacity to reorganize his field of perception, including the way he preceives himself, and that a concomitant or a resultant of this perceptual reorganization is an appropriate alteration of behavior.* This puts into formal and objective terminology a clinical hypothesis which experience forces upon the therapist using a client-centered approach. One is comelled through clinical observation to develop a high degree of respect for the ego-integrative forces residing within each individual. One comes to recognize that under proper conditions the self is a basic factor in the formation of personality and in the determination of behavior. Clinical experience would strongly suggest that the self is, to some extent, an architect of self, and the above hypothesis simply puts this observation into psychological terms.

In support of this hypothesis it is noted in some cases that one of the concomitants of success in therapy is the realization on the part of the client that the self has the capacity for reorganization. Thus a student says:

> You know I spoke of the fact that a person's background retards one. Like the fact that my family life wasn't good for me, and my mother certainly didn't give me any of the kind of bringing up that I should have had. Well, I've been thinking that over. It's true up to a point. But when you get so that you can see the situation, then it's really up to you.

Following this statement of the relation of the self to experience, many changes occurred in this young man's behavior. In this, as in other cases, it appears that when the person comes to see himself as the perceiving, organizing agent, then reorganization of perception and consequent change in patterns of reaction take place.

On the other side of the picture we have frequently observed that when the individual has been authoritatively told that he is governed by certain factors or conditions beyond his control, it makes therapy more difficult, and it is only when the individual discovers for himself that he can organize his perceptions that change is possible. In veterans who have been given their own psychiatric diagnosis, the effect is often that of making the individual feel that he is under an unalterable doom, that he is unable to control the organization of his life. When, however, the self sees itself as capable of reorganizing its own perceptual field, a marked change in basic confidence occurs. Miss Nam, a student, illustrates this phenomenon when she says, after having made progress in therapy:

> I think I do feel better about the future, too, because it's as if I won't be acting in darkness. It's sort of, well, knowing somewhat why I act the way I do . . . and at least it isn't the feeling that you're simply out of your own control and the fates are driving you to act that way. If you realize it, I think you can do something more about it.

A veteran at the conclusion of counseling puts it more briefly and more positively: "My attitude toward myself is changed now to where I feel I *can* do something with my self and life." He has come to view himself as the instrument by which some reorganization can take place.

There is another clinical observation which may be cited in support of the general hypothesis that there is a close relationship between behavior and the way in which reality is viewed by the individual. It has been noted in many cases that behavior changes come about for the most part imperceptibly and almost automatically, once the perceptual reorganization has taken place. A young wife who has been reacting violently to her maid, and has been quite disorganized in her behavior as a result of this antipathy, says "After I . . . discovered it was nothing more than that she resembled my mother, she didn't bother me any more. Isn't that interesting? She's still the same." Here is a clear statement indicating that through the basic perceptions have not changed, they have been differently organized, have acquired a new meaning, and that behavior changes then occur. Similar evidence is given by a client, a trained psychologist, who after completing a brief series of client-centered inteviews, writes:

> Another interesting aspect of the situation was in connection with the changes in some of my attitudes. When the change occurred, it was as if earlier attitudes were wiped out as completely as if erased from a blackboard. . . . When a situation which would formerly have provoked a given type of response occurred, it was not as if I was tempted to act in the way I formerly had but in some way found it easier to control my behavior. Rather the new type of behavior came quite spontaneously, and it was only through a deliberate analysis that I became aware that I was acting in a new and different way.

Here again it is of interest that the imagery is put in terms of visual perception and that as attitudes are "erased from the blackboard" behavioral changes take place automatically and without conscious effort.

Thus we have observed that appropriate changes in behavior occur when the individual acquires a different view of his world of experience, including himself; that this changed perception does not need to be dependent upon a change in the "reality," but may be a product of internal reorganization; that in some instances the awareness of the capacity for reperceiving experience accompanies this process of reorganization; that the altered behavioral responses occur automatically and without conscious effort as soon as the perceptual reorganization has taken place, apparently as a result of this.

In view of these observations a second hypothesis may be stated, which is closely related to the first. It is that *behavior is not directly influenced or determined by organic or cultural factors, but primarily* (and perhaps only) *by the perception of these elements.* In other words, the crucial element in the determination of behavior is the perceptual field of the individual. While this perceptual field is, to be sure, deeply influenced and largely shaped by cultural and physiological forces, it is nevertheless important that it appears to be only the field as it is *perceived* which exercises a specific determining influence upon behavior. This is not a new idea in psychology, but its implications have not always been fully recognized.

It might mean, first of all, that if it is the perceptual field which determines behavior, then the primary object of study for psychologists would be the person and his world *as viewed by the person himself.* It could mean that the internal frame of reference of the person might well constitute the field of psychology, an idea set forth persuasively by Snygg and Combs (1949). It might mean that the laws which govern behavior would be discovered more deeply by turning our attention to the laws which govern perception.

Now if our speculations contain a measure of truth, if the *specific* determinant of behavior is the perceptual field, and if the self can reorganize that perceptual field, then what are the limits of this process? Is the reorganization of perception capricious, or does it follow certain laws? Are there limits to the degree of reorganization? If so, what are they? In this connection we have observed with some care the perception of one portion of the field of experience, the portion we call the self.

The Relation of the Perception of the Self to Adjustment

Initially we were oriented by the background of both lay and psychological thinking to regard the outcome of successful therapy as the solution of problems. If a person had a marital problem, a vocational problem, a problem of educational adjustment, the obvious purpose of counseling or therapy was to solve that problem. But as we observe and study the recorded accounts of the conclusion of therapy, it is clear that the most characteristic outcome is not necessarily solution of problems, but a freedom from tension, a different feeling about, and perception of, self. Perhaps something of this outcome may be conveyed by some illustrations. Several statements taken from the final interview with a twenty-year-old young woman, Miss Mir, give indications of the characteristic attitude toward self, and the sense of freedom which appears to accompany it.

> I've always tried to be what the others thought I should be, but now I am wondering whether I shouldn't just see that I am what I am.
> Well, I've just noticed such a difference. I find that when I feel things, even when I feel hate, I don't care. I don't mind. I feel more free somehow. I don't feel guilty about things.
> You know it's suddenly as though a big cloud has been lifted off. I feel so much more content.

Note in these statements the willingness to perceive herself as she is, to accept herself "realistically," to perceive and accept her "bad" attitudes as well as "good" ones. This realism seems to be accompanied by a sense of freedom and contentment.

Miss Vib, whose attitudes were quoted earlier, wrote out her own feelings about counseling some six weeks after the interviews were over, and gave the statement to her counselor. She begins:

> The happiest outcome of therapy has been a new feeling about myself. As I think of it, it might be the only outcome. Certainly it is basic to all the changes in my behavior that have resulted.

In discussing her experience in therapy she states:

> I was coming to see myself as a whole. I began to realize that I am *one* person. This was an important insight to me. I saw that the former good academic achievement, job success, ease in social situations, and the present withdrawal, dejection, apathy and failure were all adaptive behavior, performed by *me*. This meant that I had to reorganize my feelings about myself, no longer holding to the unrealistic notion that the very good adjustment was the expression of the real "me" and this neurotic behavior was not. I came to feel that I am the same person, sometimes functioning maturely, and sometimes assuming a neurotic role in the face of what I had conceived as insurmountable problems. The acceptance of myself as one person gave me strength in the process of reorganization. Now I had a substratum, a core of unity on which to work.

As she continues her discussion there are such statements as

> I am getting more happiness in being myself. I approve of myself more, and I have so much less anxiety.

As in the previous example, the outstanding aspects appear to be the realization that all of her behavior "belonged" to her, that she could accept both the good and bad features about herself and that doing so gave her a release from anxiety and a feeling of solid happiness. In both instances there is only incidental reference to the serious "problems" which had been initially discussed.

Since Miss Mir is undoubtedly above average intelligence and Miss Vib is a person with some psychological training, it may appear that such results are found only with the sophisticated individual. To counteract this opinion a quotation may be given from a statement written by a veteran of limited ability and education who had just completed counseling, and was asked to write whatever reactions he had to the experience. He says:

> As for the counseling I have had I can say this, It really makes a man strip his own mind bare, and when he does he knows then what he really is and what he can do. Or at least thinks he knows himself party [sic] well. As for myself, I know that my ideas were a little too big for what I really am, but now I realize one must try start out [sic] at his own level.
>
> Now after four visits, I have a much clearer picture of myself and my future. It makes me feel a little depressed and disappointed, but on the other hand, it has taken me out of the dark, the load seems a lot lighter now, that is I can see my way now, I know what I want to do, I know about what I can do, so now that I can see my goal, I will be able to work a whole lot easyer [sic], at my own level.

Although the expression is much simpler, one notes again the same two elements—the acceptance of self as it is, and the feeling of easiness, of lightened burden, which accompanies it.

As we examine many individual case records and case recordings, it appears to be possible to bring together the findings in regard to successful therapy by stating another hypothesis in regard to that portion of the perceptual field which we call the self. It would appear that *when all of the ways in which the individual perceives himself—all perceptions of the qualities, abilities, impulses, and attitudes of the person, and all perceptions of himself in relation to others—are accepted into the organized conscious concept of the self, then this achievement is accompanied by feelings of comfort and freedom from tension which are experienced as psychological adjustment.*

This hypothesis would seem to account for the observed fact that the comfortable perception of self which is achieved is sometimes more positive than before, sometimes more negative. When the individual permits all his perceptions of himself to be organized into one pattern, the picture is sometimes more flattering than he has held in the past, sometimes less flattering. It is always more comfortable.

It may be pointed out also that this tentative hypothesis supplies an operational type of definition, based on the client's internal frame of reference, for such hitherto vague terms as "adjustment," "integration," and "acceptance of self." They are defined in terms of perception, in a way which it should be possible to prove or disprove. When all of the organic perceptual experiences—the experiencing of attitudes, impulses, abilities and disabilities, the experiencing of others and of "reality"—when all of these perceptions are freely assimilated into an organized and consistent system, available to consciousness, then psychological adjustment or integration might be said to exist. The definition of adjustment is thus made an internal affair, rather than dependent upon an external "reality."

Something of what is meant by this acceptance and assimilation of perceptions about the self may be illustrated from the case of Miss Nam, a student. Like many other clients, she gives evidence of having experienced attitudes and feelings which are defensively denied because they are not consistent with the concept or picture she holds of herself. The way in which they are first fully admitted into consciousness, and then organized into a unified system may be shown by excerpts from the recorded interviews. She has spoken of the difficulty she has had in bringing herself to write papers for her university courses.

> I just thought of something else which perhaps hinders me, and that is that again it's two different feelings. When I have to sit down and do (a paper), though I have a lot of ideas, underneath I think I always have the feeling that I just can't do it. . . . I have this feeling of being terrifically confident that I can do something, without being willing to put the work into it. At other times I'm practically afraid of what I have to do. . . .

Note that the conscious self has been organized as "having a lot of ideas," being "terrifically confident" but that "underneath," in other words not freely admitted into consciousness, has been the experience of feeling "I just can't do it." She continues:

> I'm trying to work through this funny relationship between this terrific confidence and then this almost fear of doing anything . . . and I think the kind of feeling that I can really do things is part of an illusion I have about myself of being, in my imagination, sure that it will be something good and very good and all that, but whenever I get down to the actual task of getting started, it's a terrible feeling of—well, incapacity, that I won't get it done either the way I want to do it, or even not being sure how I want to do it.

Again the picture of herself which is present in consciousness is that of a person who is "very good," but this picture is entirely out of line with the actual organic experience in the situation.

Later in the same interview she expresses very well the fact that her perceptions are not all organized into one consistent conscious self.

> I'm not sure about what kind of a person I am—well, I realize that all of these are a part of me, but I'm not quite sure of how to make all of these things fall in line.

In the next interview we have an excellent opportunity to observe the organization of both of these conflicting perceptions into one pattern, with the resultant sense of freedom from tension which has been described above.

> It's very funny, even as I sit here I realize that I have more confidence in myself, in the sense that when I used to approach new situations I would have two very funny things operating at the same time. I had a fantasy that I could do anything, which was a fantasy which covered over all these other feelings that I really couldn't do it, or couldn't do it as well as I wanted to, and it's as if now those two things have merged together, and it is more real, that a situation isn't either testing myself or proving something to myself or anyone else. It's just in terms of doing it. And I think I have done away both with that fantasy and that fear. . . . So I think I can go ahead and approach things— well, just sensibly.

No longer is it necessary for this client to "cover over" her real experiences. Instead the picture of herself as very able, and the experienced feeling of complete inability, have now been brought together into one integrated pattern of self as a person with real, but imperfect abilities. Once the self is thus accepted the inner energies making for self-actualization are released and she attacks her life problems more efficiently.

Observing this type of material frequently in counseling experience would lead to a tentative hypothesis of maladjustment, which like the other hypothesis suggested, focuses on the perception of self. It might be proposed that the tensions called psychological maladjustment exist when the organized concept of self (conscious or available to conscious awareness is not in accord with the perceptions actually experienced.

This discrepancy between the concept of self and the actual perceptions seems to be explicable only in terms of the fact that the self concept resists assimilating into itself any percept which is inconsistent with its present organization. The feeling that she may not have the ability to do a paper is inconsistent with Miss Nam's conscious picture of herself as a very able and confident person, and hence, though fleetingly perceived, is denied organization as a part of her self, until this comes about in therapy.

The Conditions of Change of Self-Perception

If the way in which the self is perceived has as close and significant a relationship to behavior as has been suggested, then the manner in which this perception may be altered becomes a question of importance. If a reorganization of self-perceptions brings a change in behavior; if adjustment and maladjustment depend on the congruence between perceptions as experienced and the self as perceived, then the factors which permit a reorganization of the perception of self are significant.

Our observations of psychotherapeutic experience would seem to indicate that absence of any threat to the self-concept is an important item in the problem. Normally the self resists incorporating into itself those experiences which are inconsistent with the functioning of self. But a point overlooked by Lecky and others is that when the self is free from any threat of attack or likelihood of attack, then it is possible for the self to consider these hitherto rejected perceptions, to make new differentiations, and to reintegrate the self in such a way as to include them.

An illustration from the case of Miss Vib may serve to clarify this point. In her statement written six weeks after the conclusion of counseling Miss Vib thus describes the way in which unacceptable percepts become incorporated into the self. She writes:

> In the earlier interviews I kept saying such things as, "I am not acting like myself," "I never acted this way before." What I meant was that this withdrawn, untidy, and apathetic person was not myself. Then I began to realize that I was the same person, seriously withdrawn, etc. now, as I had been before. That did not happen until after I had talked out my self-rejection, shame, despair, and doubt, in the accepting situation of the interview. The counselor was not startled or shocked. I was telling him all these things about myself which did not fit into my picture of a graduate student, a teacher, a sound person. He responded with complete acceptance and warm interest without heavy emotional overtones. Here was a sane, intelligent person wholeheartedly accepting this behavior that seemed so shameful to me. I can remember an organic feeling of relaxation. I did not have to keep up the struggle to cover up and hide this shameful person.

Note how clearly one can see here the whole range of denied perceptions of self, and the fact that they could be considered as a part of self only in a social situation which involved no threat to the self, in which another person, the counselor, becomes almost an alternate self and looks with understanding and acceptance upon these same perceptions. She continues:

> Retrospectively, it seems to me that what I felt as "warm acceptance without emotional overtones" was what I needed to work through my difficulties. . . . The counselor's impersonality with interest allowed me to talk out my feelings. The clarification in the interview situation presented the attitude to me as a "ding an sich" which I could look at, manipulate, and put in place. In organizing my attitudes, I was beginning to organize me.

Here the nature of the exploration of experience, of seeing it as experience and not as a threat to self, enables the client to reorganize her perceptions of self, which as she says was also "reorganizing me."

If we attempt to describe in more conventional psychological terms the nature of the process which culminates in an altered organization and integration of self in the process of therapy it might run as follows. The individual is continually endeavoring to meet his needs by reacting to the field of experience as he perceives it, and to do that more efficiently by differentiating elements of the field and reintegrating them into new patterns. Reorganization of the field may involve the reorganization of the self as well as of other parts of the field. The self, however, resists reorganization and change. In everyday life individual adjustment by means of reorganization of the field exclusive of the self is more common and is less threatening to the individual. Consequently, the individual's first mode of adjustment is the reorganization of that part of the field which does not include the self.

Client-centered therapy is different from other life situations inasmuch as the therapist tends to remove from the individual's immediate world all those aspects of the field which the individual can reorganize except the self. The therapist, by reacting to the client's feelings and attitudes rather than to the objects of his feelings and attitudes, assists the client in bringing from background into focus his own self, making it easier than ever before for the client to perceive and react to the self. By offering only understanding and no trace of evaluation, the therapist removes himself as an object of attitudes, becoming only an alternate expression of the client's self. The therapist by providing a consistent atmosphere of permissiveness and understanding removes whatever threat existed to prevent all perceptions of the self from emerging into figure. Hence in this situation all the ways in which the self has been experienced can be viewed openly, and organized into a complex unity.

It is then this complete absence of any factor which would attack the concept of self, and second, the assistance in focusing upon the perception of self, which seems to permit a more differentiated view of self and finally the reorganization of self.

Relationship to Current Psychological Thinking

Up to this point, these remarks have been presented as clinical observations and tentative hypotheses, quite apart from any relationship to past or present thinking in the field of psychology. This has been intentional. It is felt that it is the function of the clinician to try to observe, with an open-minded attitude, the complexity of material which comes to him, to report his observations, and in the light of this to formulate hypotheses and problems which both the clinic and the laboratory may utilize as a basis for study and research.

Yet, though these are clinical observations and hypotheses, they have, as has doubtless been recognized, a relationship to some of the currents of theoretical and laboratory thinking in psychology. Some of the observations about the self bear a relationship to the thinking of G. H. Mead (1934) about the "I" and the "me." The outcome of therapy might be described in Mead's terms as the increasing awareness of the "I," and the organization of the "me's," by the "I." The importance which has been given in this paper to the self as an organizer of experience, and to some extent as an architect of self, bears a relationship to the thinking of Allport (1943) and others concerning the increased place which we must give to the integrative function of the ego. In the stress which has been given to the present field of experience as the determinant of behavior, the relationship to Gestalt psychology, and to the work of Lewin (1935) and his students is obvious. The theories of Angyal (1941) find some parallel in our observations. His view that the self represents only a small part of the biological organism which has reached symbolic elaboration, and that it often attempts the direction of the organism on the basis of unreliable and insufficient information, seems to be particularly related to the observations we have made. Lecky's posthumous book (1945), small in size but large in the significance of its contribution, has brought a new light on the way in which the self operates, and the principle of consistency by which new experience is included in or excluded from the self. Much of his thinking runs parallel to our observations. Snygg and Combs (1949) have recently attempted a more radical and more complete emphasis upon the internal world of perception as the basis for all psychology, a statement which has helped to formulate a theory in which our observations fit.

It is not only from the realm of theory but also from the experimental laboratory that one finds confirmation of the line of thinking which has been proposed. Tolman (1938) has stressed the need of thinking as a rat if fruitful experimental work is to be done. The work of Snygg (1936) indicates that rat behavior may be better predicted by inferring the rat's field of perception than by viewing him as an object. Krech (Krechevsky, 1932) showed in a brilliant study some years ago that rat learning can only be understood if we realize that the rat is consistently acting upon one hypothesis after another. Leeper (1946) has summarized the evidence from a number of experimental investigations, showing that animal behavior cannot be explained by simple S-R mechanisms, but only by recognizing that complex internal processes of perceptual organization intervene between the stimulus and the behavioral response. Thus there are parallel streams of clinical observation, theoretical thinking, and laboratory experiment, which all point up the fact that for an effective psychology we need a much more complete understanding of the private world of the individual, and need to learn ways of entering and studying that world from within.

Implications

It would be misleading however if I left you with the impression that the hypotheses I have formulated in this paper, or those springing from the parallel psychological studies I have mentioned, are simply extensions of the main stream of psychological thinking, additional bricks in the edifice of psychological thought. We have discovered with some surprise that our clinical observations, and the tentative hypotheses which seem to grow out of them, raise disturbing questions which appear to cast doubt on the very foundations of many of our psychological endeavors, particularly in the fields of clinical psychology and personality study. To clarify what is meant, I should like to restate in more logical order the formulations I have given, and to leave with you certain questions and problems which each one seems to raise.

If we take first the tentative proposition that the specific determinant of behavior is the perceptual field of the individual, would this not lead, if regarded as a working hypothesis, to a radically different approach in clinical psychology and personality research? It would seem to mean that instead of elaborate case histories full of information about the person as an object, we would endeavor to develop ways of seeing his situation, his past, and himself, as these objects appear to him. We would try to see with him, rather than to evaluate him. It might mean the minimizing of the elaborate psychometric procedures by which we have endeavored to measure or value the individual from our own frame of reference. It might mean the minimizing or discarding of all the vast series of labels which we have painstakingly built up over the years. Paranoid, preschizophrenic, compulsive, constricted—terms such as these might become irrelevant because they are all based in thinking which takes an external frame of reference. They are not the ways in which the individual experiences himself. If we consistently studied each individual from the internal frame of reference of that individual, from within his own perceptual field, it seems probable that we should find generalizations which could be made, and principles which were operative, but we may be very sure that they would be of a different order from these externally based judgments *about* individuals.

Let us look at another of the suggested propositions. If we took seriously the hypothesis that integration and adjustment are internal conditions related to the degree of acceptance or nonacceptance of all perceptions, and the degree of organization of these perceptions into one consistent system, this would decidedly affect our clinical procedures. It would seem to imply the abandonment of the notion that adjustment is dependent upon the pleasantness or unpleasantness of the environment, and would demand concentration upon those processes which bring about self-integration within the person. It would mean a minimizing or an abandoning of those clinical procedures which utilize the alteration of environmental forces as a method of treatment. It would rely instead upon the fact that the person who is internally unified has the greatest likelihood of meeting environmental problems constructively, either as an individual or in cooperation with others.

If we take the remaining proposition that the self, under proper conditions, is capable of reorganizing, to some extent, its own perceptual field, and of thus altering behavior, this too seems to raise disturbing questions. Following the path of this hypothesis would appear to mean a shift in emphasis in psychology from focusing upon the fixity of personality attributes and psychological abilities, to the alterability of these same characteristics. It would concentrate attention upon process rather than upon fixed status. Whereas psychology has, in personality study, been concerned primarily with the measurement of the fixed qualities of the individual, and with his past in order to explain his present, the hypothesis here suggested would seem to concern itself much more with the personal world of the present in order to understand the future, and in predicting that future would be concerned with the principles by which personality and behavior are altered, as well as the extent to which they remain fixed.

Thus we find that a clinical approach, client-centered therapy, has led us to try to adopt the client's perceptual field as the basis for genuine understanding. In trying to enter this internal world of perception, not by introspection, but by observation and direct inference, we find ourselves in a new vantage point for understanding personality dynamics, a vantage point which opens up some disturbing vistas. We find that behavior seems to be better understood as a reaction to this reality-as-perceived. We discover that the way in which the person sees himself, and the perceptions he dares not take as belonging to himself, seem to have an important relationship to the inner peace which constitutes adjustment. We discover within the person, under certain conditions, a capacity for the restructuring and the reorganization of self, and consequently the reorganization of behavior, which has profound social implications. We see these observations, and the theoretical formulations which they inspire, as a fruitful new approach for study and research in various fields of psychology.

REFERENCES:

ALLPORT, GORDON W. The ego in contemporary psychology. Psychol. Rev., 1943, 50, 451–478.

ANGYAL, ANDRAS. Foundations for a science of personality. New York: Commonwealth Fund, 1941.

KRECHEVSKY, I. Hypotheses in rats. Psychol. Rev., 1932, 39, 516–532.

LECKY, PRESCOTT. Self-consistency: A theory of personality. New York: Island Press, 1945.

LEEPER, ROBERT. The experimental psychologists as reluctant dragons. Paper presented at APA meeting, September 1946.

LEWIN, KURT. *A dynamic theory of personality*. New York: McGraw-Hill, 1935.

MEAD, GEORGE H. *Mind, self, and society*. Chicago: Univ. of Chicago Press, 1934.

ROGERS, CARL R. Significant aspects of client-centered therapy. *Amer. Psychologist*, 1946, *1*, 415–422.

SNYDER, W. U. "Warmth in nondirective counseling. *J. abnorm. soc. Psychol.*, 1946, *41*, 491–495.

SNYGG, DONALD. Mazes in which rats take the longer path to food. *J. Psychol.*, 1936, *1*, 153–166.

SNYGG, DONALD, and COMBS, ARTHUR W. *Individual behavior: A new frame of reference for psychology*. New York: Harper, 1949.

TOLMAN, E. C. The determiners of behavior at a choice point. *Psychol. Rev.*, 1938, *45*, 1–41.

53   *Types of Adjustive Reactions**

BY JAMES C. COLEMAN

EDITOR'S NOTE: Whether we are always aware of it or not, each of us uses certain defense mechanisms to help us "preserve" or "protect" our personalities. Indeed, our effectiveness in using certain "adjustive reactions" has a lot to do with how successful we are in meeting the daily stress and strains of living. Although defense mechanisms are necessary, they can prove debilitating if one uses them, however consciously or unconsciously, to avoid assuming responsibility, to avoid taking risks now and then, or to manufacture excuses for constantly behaving in an immature, self-defeating manner. In this excellent article, Dr. Coleman discusses the various kinds of defense mechanisms, how and under what conditions they are used.

Adjustive reactions can best be understood in terms of the total personality organization of the individual and his specific life situation. The particular adjustive reaction that occurs will vary widely depending upon these two sets of factors. However, even the most divergent attempts at adjustment follow certain basic dynamic principles and can be understood as attempts to cope with actual or perceived stress in such a way as to maintain psychobiological integrity by satisfying basic needs.

* Reprinted from *Abnormal Psychology and Modern Life* by James C. Coleman. Copyright © 1950 by Scott, Foresman and Company, Glenview, Illinois.

General Patterns

In general the individual deals with his adjustive problems by either attack, withdrawal, or compromise, complicated by various ego defense mechanisms and by varying degrees of emotional involvement.

Attack, aggression, hostility.   In attack behavior we attempt to remove or surmount the obstacles through the increased effort or a variation in mode of approach. We have seen that biological frustration' leads to various compensatory or corrective activities such as the release of stored energy to allow increased activity by the organism in an attempt to meet the need and restore equilibrium. This increased tension and variant activity is apparently the primary origin of aggressive or attack-type behavior (Schilder, 1942). In primitive form it is seen in the restless behavior of the infant deprived of food; such behavior is at first relatively uncoordinated and generalized, but as motor and intellectual abilities increase, the individual learns to evaluate and deal directly with an ever-increasing variety of specific obstacles.

Despite these improvements in efficiency, only a small number of stress situations can be adequately dealt with by means of direct aggression. This means that in infancy, as well as later in life, direct attack may be unsuccessful, the frustration continues, and the irritation, pain, and unpleasantness connected with it become attached to the objects or persons viewed as obstacles and sources of frustration. Such conditions, of course, lead to the arousal of emergency emotional reactions, particularly hostility. Thus aggressive reactions, which at first involve only a tendency toward increased activity and variation in mode of attack, may eventually be reinforced by hate or hostility (Cushing and Cushing, 1949).

Attack behavior may be primarily constructive or destructive in nature. With hostility there is a tendency to destroy as well as attack; hence we find that where hostility is extremely intense, attack behavior may be primarily destructive. For example, an individual who feels unwanted, unjustly treated, and deprived of opportunities afforded to others may build up intense resentment and hostility which may be manifested in hostile, aggressive activities, perhaps of a delinquent or criminal nature. Stealing, destroying property, setting fires, sexual misbehavior, and assault frequently represent attack patterns involving defiant hostile reactions of this sort.

The way in which hostility is discharged is very important in personality dynamics. For example, it may be expressed directly in overt behavior (physical or verbal), in fantasies (in which the individual may machine-gun or otherwise attack and destroy his enemies), or in competitive sports and other activities; or it may be discharged internally through the visceral organs. Although hostility is ordinarily directed toward external objects and persons viewed as sources of frustration, it may be evoked by personal limitations and mistakes and directed toward the self in terms of self-recrimination, self-punishment, and even self-mutilation and suicide.

Where the hostility is felt toward more powerful persons—authority figures—the individual may inhibit any actual outward manifestations. However, such hostile tensions may build up to high levels of intensity and become extremely difficult to manage; for we may not only view hostility as morally wrong, particularly if it is directed toward parents or siblings, but we know from unpleasant experience that overt hostile acts toward others lead to retaliation in the form of punishment and frustration. So, as we shall see, such hostility may come to be expressed in various deviant but "safe" ways.

Flight, withdrawal, fear. Simple withdrawal is the second fundamental type of reaction to stress. Many animals seem capable of fairly well-coordinated withdrawal or flight reactions shortly after birth, but the human infant is relatively helpless for a long period and is unable to execute any well-coordinated withdrawal reaction. However, he is able to withdraw a bodily part from a painful stimulus such as a hot object and as Watson has demonstrated, he may on the occasion of sudden, unexpected stimuli tend to curl up into a ball, which appears to be sort of a primitive fear reaction.

As the growing infant learns to associate certain objects and situations with frustration and hurt, he may avoid instead of attacking them. His action tendency to withdraw in the face of such dangerous situations is typically reinforced by emotional processes involving fear. With time, his fears involve a wide range of real and imagined dangers as well as being usually induced by any strong, sudden, unexpected stimulation. And in a related way his withdrawal behavior becomes more complicated; in addition to mere physical withdrawal, he may withdraw in various psychological ways; he may inhibit dangerous internal desires, or consciously suppress them, or abandon goals, or restrict the situations to which he reacts, or even become emotionally passive.

So just as simple aggression becomes complicated by hostility we find simple withdrawal or flight reactions becoming complicated by fear. In both cases the individual's action tendencies are reinforced by mobilization of reserve resources, with a high degree of psychobiological tension demanding discharge. But here again social living provides few situations in which such mobilized energy can be utilized in direct physical action. Taking final examinations, being interviewed for jobs, excessive competition, cannot ordinarily be met by direct physical withdrawal. Rather the individual is forced to face the dangerous situation despite fears and anticipated frustration. It is of interest here to note that Shaffer found, in a study of fear in aerial combat, that situations permitting no adjustive response, such as "being fired upon when you have no chance to shoot back," were the most frequently reported causes of increased fear (Shaffer,

1947). On the other hand, he found that engaging in some effective activity was frequently conducive to reducing fear, even though such activities did not make possible the avoidance of the real danger.

Anxiety is very similar to fear, involving the same general pattern of emergency physiological changes and arising in connection with anticipated frustration or hurt. However, it differs from fear in certain essential respects. Fear is usually related to some immediate concrete situation, whereas the stress giving rise to anxiety is usually vague and ill-defined. Often the individual is unaware of what is causing his anxiety. Likewise, fear involves a definite action tendency of flight whereas anxiety is more in the nature of diffuse apprehension not leading to any action tendency. Thus anxiety seems to be a sort of preliminary or primitive fear reaction which mobilizes energy reserves to meet some threat, but in which neither the threat nor the appropriate direction of response is clearly discernible by the individual. Perhaps this feeling of vagueness and uncertainty adds to the unpleasantness of anxiety; in any event anxiety is one of the most painful and intolerable of all conscious experiences.

Compromise, substitution. Since most situations cannot be dealt with successfully by either direct attack or withdrawal, it usually becomes necessary to work out some sort of compromise. This represents our most common method of dealing with conflicts. Such compromises may mean accepting substitute goals or lowering one's aspirations or internal ethical or reality restraints. An individual faced with starvation may compromise with his conscience and steal "just this one time" because of the special

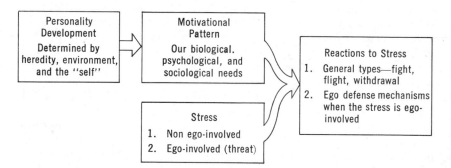

Fig. 1. *Personality Development Determines Motivational Patterns. Motivational Pattern and Stress Jointly Determine Reactions to Stress, which will include Ego Defensive Mechanisms if the Stress Is Ego-involved.*

nature of the conditions, or he may resort to eating worms, bugs, spiders, and even human flesh, or he may revise his ethical standards. Often, too, we resort to symbolic satisfactions under conditions of severe frustration.

Thus a soldier may gain some substitutive satisfaction out of pin-up pictures or out of wish-fulfilling daydreams. In fact, Masserman (1946) has shown that under frustration, the individual becomes increasingly willing to accept substitutive goals—both symbolic and nonsymbolic ones. Hate, fear, and other emotional reactions may, of course, also reinforce or be involved in compromise reactions, as well as in attack or withdrawal reactions.

Ego Defense Mechanisms

As we have noted, the self is the integrating core of the personality and any threat to its worth or adequacy is a threat to the individual's very center of existence. Consequently various psychological defenses are gradually built up around the self which are designed to protect it from insult and to enhance it as much as possible. These are then called into play when we find ourselves in an ego-involved stress situation, in which threat to the integrity or worth of the self is present. The "we won today" of the football fan may help him to achieve some measure of importance by "identifying himself with a successful team; the student who flunks a test may "project" the blame for his performance onto the poor quality of instruction and the unfairness of the test; the person who feels guilty about his unethical business dealings may "rationalize" that others would take similar advantage of him if they were smart enough. In more extreme cases an individual may insist that his failure is due to the fact that other people are working against him, or a person with unacceptable sexual fantasies may insist that others are making immoral sexual advances toward him.

All of us use these ego defense mechanisms to some extent. They are essential for softening failures, alleviating guilt, preserving internal harmony, and maintaining our feelings of personal worth and adequacy. At the same time they perform a vital function in protecting us from the intolerable anxiety aroused by threats to the value of the self. Failure, guilt, inferiority are all self-devaluating and hence threatening and anxiety-arousing. The protection of the self from overwhelming devaluation and thus from anxiety is the very essence of the defensive functions of these mechanisms.

Thus we must consider these mechanisms as normal adjustive reactions unless they are used to such an extreme degree that they actually interfere with the maintenance of self-integrity instead of aiding it. In a sense, the self, like a nation devoting its major energies to armaments, may break down under the very load of its defensive activities. In addition, these mechanisms, as necessary as they are, have certain drawbacks. They are not usually adaptive in the sense of realistically coping with the adjustment problems. The individual who continually rationalizes away his mistakes is not apt to profit from them on subsequent occasions. In this sense these mechanisms may be said to involve a high degree of self-deception and reality distortion. Also they operate on relatively unconscious levels and hence are not subject to normal conscious checks and evaluations. In fact, the individual usually resents having his attention called to them, for once they become conscious they do not serve their defensive purposes as well.

But whether or not they lead to adjustive behavior, they can be understood in the light of the *purpose* for which they are used, which is to protect the integrity and worth of the ego. Thus it is only as we conceive of an active, striving "self" that they make sense. Only in this framework are we able to understand our ability to change "facts" to fit our needs and evaluations and utilize these mechanisms to protect ourselves from anxiety.

With this brief introduction, let us now turn to a consideration of the more important of these ego defense mechanisms.

Denial of reality. We manage to evade many disagreeable realities by ignoring or refusing to acknowledge them. Very few of us, for example, accept the full inevitability of death. Of course, we act as if we were quite resigned to the idea, but the full realization of the actual physical decay of our bodies is usually mercifully obscured by vague feelings of our omnipotence—everybody else dies but not us—and by various religious and philosophical convictions about continuation of life after death. This tendency to avoid or deny unpleasant reality is exemplified in a great many of our everyday activities. We turn away from unpleasant sights, we refuse to discuss unpleasant topics, we ignore or deny criticism, we refuse to face our real problems, and even in old age we are prone to deny to ourselves the evidence of physical and mental decline. Proud parents are notoriously blind when it comes to the defects of their offspring. One mother, whose nine-year-old son had been diagnosed by several psychologists and psychiatrists as mentally deficient, developed the firm belief that her son was a member of a new species which matured at a slower rate and would in the long run achieve a higher level of mental development. The common sayings, "None is so blind as he who will not see" and "Love is blind," perhaps exemplify even more clearly our tendency to ignore things which are not compatible with our desires and wishes.

By means of this mechanism of ignoring or denying unpleasant reality we do protect ourselves from a great deal of traumatic stress. But like the proverbial ostrich who buries his head in the sand when danger approaches, we may fail to take cognizance of many things which are essential for effective adjustment.

Fantasy. Not only do we often deny unpleasant reality, but we also tend to construct the world in fantasy as we would like it to be. We fall for various half-baked get-rich-quick schemes, we accept flattery eagerly, and we are highly susceptible to selling techniques based on telling us what we want to hear about the merchandise.

Fantasy grows essentially out of mental images associated with need gratification. It is stimulated by frustrated desires, for in fantasy the person achieves his goals and gratifies his needs, albeit in substitute fashion. Such fantasies may take many forms. Starving men commonly have mental images of food; the merchant beginning his first business venture has fantasies of wealth and success.

Of course, fantasy imaginings may be either productive or nonproductive. Productive fantasy is used constructively in the solution of immediate problems, as in creative imagination, whereas nonproductive fantasy is merely a wish-fulfilling activity, compensating for lack of achievement rather than stimulating or promoting achievement.

Two common varieties of wish-fulfilling fantasy are the "conquering hero" and the "suffering hero." The first imagines himself a great and courageous soldier, an athlete, a surgeon, or some other remarkable figure who performs the most incredible feats and wins the admiration and respect of all, the essential idea being that he is rich, powerful, and respected—the fulfillment of wished-for status. James Thurber used this theme as the basis for his "Secret Life of Walter Mitty" (Thurber, 1946). Hostility is frequently dissipated safely and conveniently through conquering-hero fantasies in which the individual destroys or punishes all who stand in his way. Most students report fantasies involving the physical injury or destruction of others, such as fisticuffs, shooting, machine-gunning, and even running over people in tanks; undoubtedly all these act as safety valves for the release of hostility.

The suffering hero does not have to admit any personal inferiority because he imagines himself suffering from some terrible affliction, handicap, or visitation from unjust fate. If others only knew about his difficulties and realized how nobly and with what courage he has carried on, they would accord him the sympathy and admiration he deserves. Thus inferior accomplishments are explained away without any threat to the individual's feeling of adequacy or basic worth.

As Ruch (1948) has pointed out, many of our fantasies are ready-made for us in the form of movies, soap operas, magazine stories, and books in which we escape from our own status and identify ourselves in fantasy with the hero or heroine, bravely facing and surmounting their problems with them, and sharing in their adventures and triumphs.

The ability to escape temporarily from unpleasant reality into a more pleasant fantasy world has considerable adjustive value. It may add the dash of excitement and interest which enables us to bear up under an otherwise drab and uninteresting existence, or our fantasy achievements and their rewards may spur us on to greater efforts toward our goals in real life. We often return to work with increased vigor and enthusiasm after seeing a movie. However, wish-fulfilling fantasies are divorced from reality, and thus present a danger for adequate personality adjustment. For it may become increasingly easy to retreat to a dream world when the going gets tough. Particularly under conditions of extreme frustration are our fantasies apt to get out of hand. For example, at the concentration camps of Dachau and Buchenwald, it was found that "The longer the time a prisoner had spent in camp, the less true to reality were his daydreams; so much so that the hopes and expectations of the old prisoners often took the form of eschatological or messianic hopes (Bettelheim, 1943, p. 443).

Compensation. Compensatory reactions are defenses against feelings of inferiority and inadequacy growing out of real or imagined personal defects or weaknesses as well as out of our inevitable actual failures and setbacks. Such defensive reactions may take many forms. In the case of a physical handicap the individual may attempt to overcome his handicap directly through increased effort and persistence. Demosthenes, the great orator, had to overcome his early stuttering, and Theodore Roosevelt waged a valiant fight against early ill health and became noted for his physical daring and robustness. Many great athletes have had to overcome initial deformities or injuries which would have been incapacitating for most people. Compensatory reactions of this type may be a deciding factor in success, as biographers are quick to point out. However, failures probably overwhelmingly outnumber successes in such efforts, and the increased effort and striving may make the eventual failure more bitter.

More commonly, compensatory reactions are more indirect; there is an attempt to substitute for the defect in some way or to draw attention away from it. The physically unattractive boy or girl may develop an exceptionally pleasing personality, the puny boy may turn from athletics to scholastics, the mediocre nobody may become the Grand Imperial Potentate of some secret order. A whole science of dress has developed which centers around the concealing of undesirable physical features and the emphasizing of desirable ones. The short girl is made to look tall, the fat girl thin, the colorless one glamorous.

Unfortunately, not all compensatory reactions are desirable or useful. The individual who feels insecure and rejected may show off to try to get more attention and raise his status in the eyes of others and himself. The boy who feels inferior and unpopular may become the local bully; the person who feels unloved and frustrated may eat too much, or resort to excessive fantasy satisfactions. Many people brag about their illustrious ancestors and exaggerate their own accomplishments, while others resort to criticism or innuendoes in an attempt to cut others down to their own size. In extreme cases the individual may engage in antisocial behavior or develop marked eccentricities in an attempt to get some attention and evidence of interest and concern from others.

Conpensatory reactions are greatly stimulated by our highly competitive society. We constantly compare ourselves with others and too often measure our worth and that of others largely by status, achievements, and possessions. Such social values lead to the development of strong psychological motivation toward at least average, and if possible superior, achievement. In meeting these conditions, compensatory reactions may be of great adjustive value but where they result in increased anxiety or become exaggerated or take antisocial forms, they hinder rather than help us.

Identification. The growing child soon realizes that his evaluation by others is to a large extent dependent upon his family and other group memberships. The position of his father, the size of his house, the importance of his relatives all help to determine his personal prestige and status. Exaggerating the strength, importance, and money of his father early becomes a common means of enhancing his own prestige.

This mechanism of identification is expanded in later life to include a wide variety of situations and persons and enables the individual to experience vicarious achievements, feelings of adequacy, and other satisfactions through his various identifications. Not only does society evaluate him in terms of his various group identifications, but he comes to evaluate himself in the light of them. College students bask in the reflected glory of their football teams—"we" won today. Fraternity and sorority members enjoy the social prestige of their groups, adults identify themselves with their occupations, the size of their homes, their membership in exclusive clubs, the size of their bank accounts and cars. Parents identify themselves with the accomplishments of their children. Most employees identify themselves with the power and prestige of the companies for which they work. By so doing the individual takes unto himself some of the desirable attributes of the groups and institutions with which he identifies himself.

We are probably all prone to a certain amount of fantasy identification in which we gain vicarious satisfaction through identifying ourselves with the leading characters in novels, movies, and radio serials. As we have noted, such identifications enable us to share in the adventures and triumphs of our heroes. It is interesting to note that in those rare pictures in which the hero dies, members of the audience slump down in their seats and figuratively or symbolically die themselves. Such identifications, particularly in the form of "hero worship," may play an important role in shaping the personality development of the child, who strives to be like his hero in dress and manner.

Most people identify themselves with the hero or winner and thus achieve increased feelings of adequacy or worth. However, some identifications are consistently with the loser or with the villain. Such negative identifications may be based upon the acceptance of undesirable models such as gangsters, which are common in slum areas, or upon strong guilt feelings, leading to a need for punishment, or upon suppressed asocial tendencies.

In general, individuals tend to associate themselves with others who are most like themselves or who possess the qualities which they most desire. The athlete identifies himself with the athletic hero, the scholar with the great scientist, the co-ed with the glamorous cinema beauty. Of course, where there is compensatory identification, the meek, timid individual may become the great and brave detective, or the uneducated man the renowned scholar and scientist. However, all such identifications have to conform to the individual's ego values.

Identifications are of great value in enhancing our feelings of adequacy and worth and in the reduction of frustrations through fantasy identifications with the adventures and achievements of our heroes. We all use identifications. But like the other ego defense mechanisms it is potentially dangerous. We see identification in extreme form in certain psychotic reactions, with a loss of personal identification and the firm belief that one is some famous person such as Jesus Christ or Abraham Lincoln.

Introjection (internalization).   Introjection is, in a way, a primitive form of identification, in which the individual internalizes the threatening situation. This is exemplified early in life when the child gradually learns and accepts as his own, various social regulations and value attitudes. He can then control his own behavior in the light of his internalized values, and protect himself from possible infractions of regulations and thus avoid social retaliation and punishment. If the individual's only restraints were based on reality considerations, he would be continually in danger of getting caught and being punished by society. But by internalizing society's values and using them to guide and control his own behavior he can protect himself from frustration and punishment.

Bettelheim (1943), in his report of his experiences at the German concentration camps of Dachau and Buchenwald, tells of the gradual breakdown of previous values under the insidious camp experiences and the development and internalization of new norms—Nazi norms:

> A prisoner had reached the final stage of adjustment to the camp situation when he had changed his personality so as to accept as his own the values of the Gestapo. . . . Practically all prisoners who had spent a long time in the camp took over the Gestapo's attitude toward the so-called unfit prisoners. . . . So old prisoners were sometimes instrumental in getting rid of the unfit, in this way making a feature of Gestapo ideology a feature of their own behavior. This was one of the many situations in which old prisoners demonstrated toughness and molded their way of treating other prisoners according to the example set by the Gestapo. That this was really a taking-over of Gestapo attitudes can be seen from the treatment of traitors. Self-protection asked for their elimination, but the way in which they were tortured for days and slowly killed was taken over from the Gestapo.
>
> Old prisoners who seemed to have a tendency to identify themselves with the Gestapo did so not only in respect to aggressive behavior. They would try to arrogate to themselves old pieces of Gestapo uniforms. If that was not possible, they tried to sew and mend their uniforms so that

they would resemble those of the guards. The length to which prisoners would go in these efforts seemed unbelievable, particularly since the Gestapo punished them for their efforts to copy Gestapo uniforms. When asked why they did it they admitted that they loved to look like the guards.

The identification with the Gestapo did not stop with the copying of their outer appearance and behavior. Old prisoners accepted their goals and values, too, even when they seemed opposed to their own interests. It was appalling to see how far formerly even politically well-educated prisoners would go in this identification. . . . When old prisoners accepted Nazi values as their own they usually did not admit it, but explained their behavior by means of rationalizations (Bettelheim, 1943, pp. 447, 448, 449).

Similarly, as Sherif and Cantril (1947) point out, many lighter Negroes internalize the color values of the white world and look upon darker Negroes as inferior and exclude them from the "upper class" social groupings.

Introjection, or internalization, is thus a defensive reaction which seems to follow the general idea: if you can't defeat your enemies, join them. Apparently it is preferable, from an ego-defensive point of view, to be good or bad oneself rather than to be continually at the mercy of good or bad objects or forces from without.

Projection. Projection is a defensive reaction by means of which we (1) transfer the blame for our own shortcomings, mistakes, and misdeeds to others, and (2) attribute to others our own unacceptable impulses, thoughts, and desires.

Projection is perhaps most commonly evidenced in our tendency to blame others for our own mistakes. The student who fails an examination may feel sure the examination was unfair, the erring husband may blame his moral lapse on the girl "who led me on." "It wasn't my fault, he hit me first" or "If I hadn't taken advantage of him he would have taken advantage of me," and so it goes. Fate and bad luck are particularly over-worked objects of projection. Even inanimate objects are not exempt from blame. The tennis player who misses the ball may look at his racquet with a puzzled expression as if there must be a hole in it, and the basketball player who slips may return to inspect the imaginary slippery spot. A three-year-old boy who falls off his hobby horse may attack it with blows and kicks.

Such projections help to maintain our feelings of adequacy and self-esteem in the face of failure, and probably develop frmm our early realization that placing the blame on others for our own mistakes helps us to avoid social disapproval and punishment. And as we internalize society's value attitudes, such projections protect us from self-devaluation. In ex-treme cases, however, the individual may become convinced that his failures and difficulties are not his fault while at the same time they seem to follow some sort of pattern which cannot be entirely attributed to bad luck or chance. It seems to him that other persons or forces are systematically working against him. Out of such initial ideas delusions of persecution may develop, involving the supposed plots and conspiracies of his enemies.

In other projective reactions we attribute to others our own unacceptable impulses, desires, wishes, and thoughts. In an elementary way this is evidenced by our tendency to see others in the light of our own personality make-up. If we are honest, we tend to think others are too, whereas if we are deceitful we are prone to attribute this characteristic to others. Individuals who are tempted to be dishonest or to lapse morally are quick to detect similar tendencies in others. This, of course, may enable the individual to justify his proposed behavior since others have the same tendencies. Or he may be quick to condemn such tendencies in others, thereby in a way protecting himself from such moral lapses. Often the individual may ascribe ethically unacceptable desires and impulses to others while he remains totally unaware of their internal origin. The individual with homosexual leanings may accuse other males of attempting to seduce him. It is common for mental patients who are obsessed by ethically unacceptable sexual ideas to accuse others of "pouring filth into their minds." Thus the individual protects himself against facing his own dangerous and unacceptable impulses by attributing them to others instead.

Rationalization.   Rationalization has two major defensive values: (1) it helps us to justify what we do and what we believe, and (2) it aids us in softening the disappointment connected with unattainable goals.

Typically, rationalization involves thinking up logical, socially approved reasons for our past, present, or proposed behavior. With a little effort we can soon justify to ourselves the absolute necessity of purchasing a new car, of going to a show instead of studying, or even marrying someone with whom we are not in love. Carrying matters a step further, we may find it equally easy to justify most selfish and antisocial behavior. "Why should we yield the right of way to an oncoming motorist? He wouldn't yield it to us if he could help it, so why should we show him any consideration either?" "Suppose we did misrepresent the facts in making a sale—the other fellow has to learn sometime not to be so gullible and this provided a cheap lesson." "Yes, we did cheat on the test, but so would everyone else if he thought he could get away with it." One of the most notorious bootleggers and gangsters of American history sincerely insisted that he was being persecuted by the government when all he was trying to do was bring people the "lighter pleasures" of life. Thus we justify our behavior and protect our adequacy and self-esteem. For were we to face the real reasons or motivations for our behavior, we might feel ashamed and guilty. Of course, many rationalizations such as these, where we laud our own motives and condemn the other fellow's, overlap with the use of projection.

In a similar way we may justify our political, religious, and economic beliefs and prejudices. "Why should we worry about the unemployed? If they had any initiative they would go out and find a job! And anyway they are too lazy to work even if a job were offered to them." Similarly, a wealthy landowner in Italy who received an income from 700 peasants who tilled his estate and permitted him to live in luxury was not at all interested in helping to improve their terribly wretched farming and housing conditions. "We aren't concerned with production," he said. "We collect rents. Anyway, the peasants are retrograde. If we built clean, good homes, they'd only dirty them" (*Time*, 1949, p. 22).

In protecting ourselves from the disappointment of unattainable goals, we often resort to two additional types of rationalization—the so-called "sour grapes" and "sweet lemon" mechanisms. The "sour grapes" mechanism is based upon the fable of the fox, who, unable to reach clusters of luscious grapes, decided that they were sour and not worth having anyway. A new automobile may not be worth having because it costs more than it is worth, the insurance on it is exorbitant, it would lead to increased driving, which isn't worth while in view of the high cost of gasoline and the increased possibility of accidents, and anyway if people don't like you well enough to enjoy riding in your old car, they aren't worth having as friends. Similarly, we may view business success as requiring more effort than it is worth or point out that the girl we couldn't get talks too much and will probably lose her figure at an early age.

The "sweet lemon" attitude is in a sense an extension of sour grapes. Not only is the unattainable not worth while, but what we have is remarkably satisfactory. Not only are the disadvantages of a new car obvious but the many virtues of our old one would make such an exchange extremely silly. We find comfort in our poverty, for money is the root of all evil and would probably distort our political and economic views. Such sweet-lemon mechanisms may involve more generalized pollyanna attitudes so that "every dark cloud has a silver lining" and "everything happens for the best."

Frequently, of course, it is difficult to tell where the objective consideration of facts and problems leaves off and rationalization begins. Rather conclusive indications of rationalization are (1) hunting for reasons to justify our behavior or beliefs, (2) being unable to recognize inconsistencies and rationalizing them away, and (3) becoming emotional when our rationalizations are questioned. The questioning of our rationalizations, of course, is a threat to the defenses we have managed to construct against self-devaluation and would, if we were to permit our defenses to be destroyed, lead to the arousal of anxiety. For we would be faced with threats to our needs without any adequate defenses with which to protect ourselves.

Even the young child soon learns to justify questionable behavior by advancing reasons for it which he has learned are socially approved. And as he internalizes the value attitudes of society he follows the same procedures in justifying his behavior to himself. In this way rationalization becomes an important adjustive reaction in helping us to avoid unnecessary frustrations and to maintain a reasonable degree of self-integrity in a dangerous world. The price of this defensive reaction, however, is self-deception, for we accept reasons for our behavior which are not the true ones. As a result we are less likely to profit from our errors, but may instead spend our energy in trying to justify them or in proving that they weren't errors or misdeeds at all. When used to an extreme degree, rationalization may lead to the development of false beliefs or delusions which are maintained despite contradictory objective evidence.

Repression.   Repression is a defensive reaction by means of which painful or dangerous thoughts and desires are excluded from consciousness. It has often been referred to as selective forgetting, but it is more in the nature of selective remembering. For although the material is denied admission to consciousness, it is not really forgotten. For example, the soldier who has seen his best friend killed by shrapnel may find this experience so terribly painful and disruptive to ego values that it must be excluded from consciousness if he is to maintain his ego-integrity. As a result he becomes "amnesic" for the battle experience. However, by means of hypnosis or sodium amytal interviews, the repressed experience may be brought into consciousness.

It is of value dynamically to distinguish repression from *inhibition* and *suppression*. Early in life we learn the necessity for inhibiting the overt expression of various desires in order to avoid social disapproval and punishment, and, as we internalize ethical attitudes, to avoid lowered self-esteem and guilt feelings. Such inhibitions operate on a relatively conscious level, e.g., an individual may be tempted to seduce his best friend's wife, but inhibits any overt action. Suppression differs from inhibition in that the individual consciously "puts the idea out of mind" and thinks of other things. Repression, however, takes place without the individual's awareness. Now the dangerous and immoral thought is spontaneously and unconsciously excluded from consciousness.

Repression is by no means always complete: often desires and thoughts are only partially excluded from consciousness. Vague feelings of unworthiness, insecurity, and guilt often indicate incomplete repression. Also with continued frustration, the repressed desires may increase in strength and threaten to break directly through repression defenses into consciousness and overt action. Such threats lead to arousal of anxiety and to the implementation of existing ego defenses by means of other defense mechanisms such as projection and rationalization.

Furthermore, dangerous wishes continue to play a part in the actual motivation of behavior, even though the repressive defenses may success-fully prevent their direct expression. Although they are refused admission to consciousness, their continued operation is frequently revealed in dreams, reverie, jokes, and slips of the tongue and under the influence of alcohol or drugs. Here they manage to escape ego defenses and find expression in behavior or consciousness (Freud, 1916, 1948, 1949).

In helping the individual to control dangerous desires and in minimiz-ing the disruptive effects of painful experiences, repression plays a vitally important and often valuable role. Like other defensive reactions, however, repression is self-deceptive and may be used to an exaggerated degree or to protect the individual from desires or problems that could better be met by a realistic facing and "working through" than by evasion. Since the repression of dangerous desires not only requires considerable energy but also interferes with a stable and healthy personality integration, a more realistic facing of problems whenever possible would appear more con-ducive to long-range mental health.

Reaction formation.   Reaction formation refers to the development of conscious attitudes and behavior patterns which are the opposite of various suppressed or repressed wishes and impulses. Dynamically speaking, it involves the erection of obstacles or barriers to assist in repressing these dangerous desires and in preventing them from being carried out in overt behavior.

Usually reaction formation can be easily recognized by its extreme and intolerant characteristics, which are out of all proportion to the importance of the situation. The most militant crusaders against vice are often fighting their own repressed impulses as well as condemning the outcome of such impulses in others. Self-appointed protectors of the public's morals who voluntarily devote their lives to reading obscene literature, attending burlesque shows, and investigating the younger generation and who obses-sively condemn homosexuality, alcohol, and other alleged vices are usually found to have dangerously strong impulses in the same direction them-selves. By making such activities their "duty" they both partially satisfy their repressed desires and at the same time hold them in check by their energetic condemnations.

In everyday behavior, reaction formation may take the form of being excessively polite to a person we don't like—so much so that we make him uncomfortable—of developing a "don't care" attitude to conceal feelings of rejection and a craving for affection, of assuming an air of bravado when one is fearful, and of developing a puritanical attitude toward sexual and other pleasures. Extreme solicitousness over someone's health may conceal repressed hostility and even an actual wish for his death. The individual may develop various exaggerated fears, as for example of syphilis, which may help him to keep his dangerous impulses in check. Reaction formation in extreme form is well illustrated by excerpts from an interesting and self-diagnostic letter which Masserman received from a "kind-hearted" anti vivisectionist:

> . . . I read [a magazine article] . . . on your work on alcoholism [cf. Exp. 16] . . . I am surprised that anyone who is as well educated as you must be to hold the position that you do would stoop to such a depth as to torture helpless little cats in the pursuit of a cure for alcoholics. . . . A drunkard does not want to be cured—a drunkard is just a weak minded idiot who belongs in the gutter and should be left there. Instead of torturing helpless little cats why not torture the drunks or better still exert your would-be noble effort toward getting a bill passed to *exterminate* the drunks. They are not any good to anyone or themselves and are just a drain on the public, having to pull them off the street, jail them, then they have to be fed while there and it's against the law to feed them arsenic so there they are. . . . If people are such weaklings the world is better off without them. . . . My greatest wish is that you have brought home to you a torture that will be a thousand fold greater than what you have, and are doing to the little animals. . . . If you are an example of what a noted psychiatrist should be I'm glad I am just an ordinary human being without a letter after my name. I'd rather be just myself with a clear conscience, *knowing I have not hurt any living creature*, and can sleep without seeing frightened, terrified dying cats— because I know they must die after you have finished with them. No punishment is too great for you and I hope I live to read about your mangled body and long suffering before you finally die—and I'll laugh long and loud (Masserman, 1946).

Reaction formation, like repression, has adjustive value in helping us to maintain socially approved behavior and to avoid facing our unacceptable desires with the consequent self-devaluation that would be involved. To all intents and purposes we are pure—it is the other fellow who has the vices. But because this mechanism, too, is self-deceptive, it often results in exaggerated and rigid fears or beliefs which may complicate the individual's adjustive reactions and may lead to excessive harshness or severity in dealing with the lapses of others.

Displacement. Displacement refers to the shift of emotion, symbolic meaning, or fantasy from a person or object toward which it was originally directed to another person or object. Typically it involves the discharge of aroused emotions toward neutral or less dangerous objects. A child who has been spanked or thwarted by his mother may kick his little sister or a young playmate, or he may break up his toys. Many times a minor situation may act as a sort of trigger which releases the pent-up emotional feelings in a torrent of displaced anger and abuse surprising to everyone involved and out of all proportion to the immediate incident. A young housewife had been upbraided by her husband for not being more efficient and later in the day lost a bridge tournament to a disliked social rival. On her way home she was stopped by a traffic policeman for speeding. That was the final straw and she loosed a torrent of abuse on the poor fellow ranging from such questions as "Haven't you anything better to do than spy on innocent women?" to blaming him for the generally sad traffic condition of the city which he should have been working on instead of wasting his time persecuting busy civic-minded citizens for barely exceeding the speed limit.

Through a process of symbolic association or spread, displacement may become extremely complex and deviant. Swearing is commonly used as a means of discharging pent-up feelings. "Beating" a disliked rival at bridge or golf may symbolically represent his destruction. Destructive criticism and vindictive gossip are frequently only disguised methods of expressing hostility. Repressed fears of murdering a hated husband may be displaced to all sorts of dangerous weapons such as guns, knives, or poison. Such apparently irrational fears or phobias act as additional defenses by protecting the individual from situations in which his dangerous impulses might be carried out in action. Frequently displacement is combined with projection, as in Nazi Germany, where the blame for all the country's ills was projected upon the Jews and the Communists, and pent-up feelings of frustration and hostility were displaced upon these two groups.

Displacement is of considerable adjustive value because it enables the individual to discharge dangerous emotional tensions without risking loss of love and possible retaliation, and without the necessity of even recognizing the person at whom such feelings were originally directed. In this way it enables the individual to avoid the conflict of ambivalent feelings toward some powerful or loved person. By displacing his pent-up hostility on his wife, the little clerk maintains relatively pure feelings, consciously, of respect and cordiality toward his domineering boss. The boy who displaces his hostility onto his toys or playmates can maintain relatively pure feelings of love toward the mother who has just punished or frustrated him. Similarly the husband with considerable hostility toward his wife because of her sloppy housekeeping can wholeheartedly love her by displacing the blame both for her behavior and for his hostility onto his mother-in-law. In such instances displacement is often accompanied by repression (particularly where hostility is directed toward some loved person such as the mother) and this combination is an extremely potent ego defense.

Unfortunately, however, displacements can become too deviant, and they can result in the persistent avoidance of situations which could be more efficiently handled by a more direct approach, e.g., displacing hostility and blame onto one's mother-in-law may make it possible to maintain the marriage but unless a more direct and realistic approach to the wife's sloppy housekeeping is worked out, this behavior may show little improvement. In general it is much more healthful to face and work through hostility-arousing situations whenever this is feasible, rather than to avoid them through displacement.

Emotional insulation.   In emotional insulation the individual reduces the tensions of need and anxiety by withdrawing into a sort of shell of passivity.

As a result of previous frustrations and disappointments, we all learn to protect ourselves not only by lowering our level of aspiration but by restricting emotional involvement in the attainment of our goals. This reaction is well expressed in the common saying "I didn't dare to even hope" (that a particular desired event would come about). Similarly, the boy who has been terribly disappointed in his first great love may be very careful not to allow himself to become so emotionally involved on subsequent occasions. In fact, he may find it very difficult or impossible to "let himself go" in the sense of entering into intimate affectional relationships. Many individuals who have been badly bruised by life's blows become cold, detached, and aloof and are often unable to either give or receive normal affection. Many times they seem highly self-sufficient, but privately such persons usually complain of intense feelings of inadequacy, loneliness, and tension. In more extreme conditions of long-continued frustration, as in chronic unemployment or prison confinement, many persons lose hope, become resigned and apathetic, and adapt themselves to a restricted way of living with an extremely low level of aspiration. Such "broken" individuals protect themselves from the bitter hurt of sustained frustration and disappointment by giving up and becoming disinterested and passive.

Another method of insulating ourselves emotionally is to avoid competitive activities or situations in which we might not compare favorably with others. Many people will not engage in sports such as bowling or ping-pong unless they feel that they excel in them. In this way they protect themselves from the unpleasantness and devaluation that might result from doing less well than others. This may be carried to the point of choosing both a vocation and leisure interests which are as noncompetitive and impersonal as possible.

Permitting ourselves to become emotionally involved in life's affairs does involve certain "calculated risks." For example, the giving of affection to other people does expose us to possible hurt in that they may reject us or may be taken from us by death. Ordinarily, of course, we operate on the assumption that the rewards of emotional involvement are worth the risks, even though, if we are realistic, we all know that we shall experience some disappointments in life.

Used to a mild degree, emotional insulation is an important means of defense against disappointment and hurt. Unfortunately, when used in more marked degree, it reduces the individual's healthy vigorous participation in life's problems and leads to shallowness and blunting of affect.

Isolation.   This defense mechanism involves some measure of emotional insulation by distorting or cutting off the affective charge which normally accompanies hurtful situations. The hurt concerning Mother's

death is reduced by saying that she lived a "full" life or that she died
mercifully without pain. Catastrophes are interpreted within the framework of "It is the Will of the Lord!" Cynicism becomes a convenient means
of withdrawing emotional support from our ideals. Guilt feelings over
unethical behavior may be reduced by emphasizing the cultural relativity
of our ideas of right and wrong. Often the glib admission that "we should
work harder" or that "we should be less selfish and more interested in the
welfare of others" seems to cut off a good deal of the guilt that normally
accompanies unethical behavior without, however, leading to any positive
action.

In such isolation reactions, rationalization and other ego defense
mechanisms may play a prominent role, but it is the cutting off of the
normal affective charge by means of "intellectualization" that we are
primarily concerned with here.

Emotional conflicts may also be reduced through the process of isolat-
ing certain attitudes and dimensions of the personality. The confirmed
believer in democracy may also believe firmly in racial discrimination. The
ruthless and dishonest businessman may be a kind father and a pillar of the
church. Such contradictory beliefs and attitudes are maintained in "logic-
tight compartments" of the mind without emotional conflict. Of course the
individual may resort to rationalization to make such incompatible values
seem more consistent, but the essential process seems to be one of unconscious isolation in which one attitude is dissociated or segregated from the
other. A passage from Sheila Cousins (1938), a London prostitute, well
illustrates this type of dissociative or isolation reaction. She writes,

> The act of sex I could go through because I hardly seemed to be
> taking part in it. It was merely something happening to me, while my
> mind drifted inconsequentially away. Indeed, it was scarcely happening
> even to me; it was happening to something lying on a bed that had a
> vague connection with me, while I was calculating whether I could afford
> a new coat or impatiently counting sheep jumping over a gate (pp. 150–
> 151).

In this way situations which would ordinarily give rise to strong
emotional conflicts are kept, as it were, in isolated ego positions. In more
extreme cases, we may find the isolation or dissociation of entire sections of
the ego, as in multiple personality or certain psychotic reactions where the
patient looks up from scrubbing the floor to tell you in a sort of detached
way that he is a multimillionaire.

Regression. Regression is a defensive reaction involving a retreat, in
the face of stress, to the use of reaction patterns which were appropriate
at an earlier level of development. It involves a modification of behavior in
the direction of more primitive, infantile modes of behavior. When a new
addition to the family has seemingly undermined his status, a child may

revert to bed-wetting, baby talk, thumb-sucking, and other infantile behavior which once brought him parental attention. The frustrated adult may return to the temper tantrums which were useful during childhood; the bride may run home to mother at the first sign of trouble. Perhaps regression is best typified by the tendency of the aged to live more and more in the pleasures of the past. In fact, regression has been called the "old oaken bucket" delusion because of its emphasis on the superior joys of "the good old days."

Regression can be readily understood if we remember the child's gradual shift from a position of helplessness and dependency on the parents to one of independent action and responsibility. This developmental process from dependency to independency is by no means an easy accomplishment, and it is common for all of us in the face of adult difficulties to yearn for the carefree and sheltered days of infancy and childhood. Consequently it is not surprising that in the face of severe stress we may retreat from adult reaction patterns to a less mature level of adjustment. Of course, we might expect something akin to regression to occur merely on the basis of the frequent failure of more recently learned reactions to bring satisfaction: in looking for other, more successful modes of adjustment it would be only natural that we should try out discarded patterns which previously brought satisfaction. However, regression is a more comprehensive reaction than merely trying out older modes of response when new ones have failed. For in regression the individual retreats from reality to a less demanding personal status—one which involves *lowered aspiration* and more readily accomplished satisfactions. This point is well illustrated by Bettelheim's (1943) reference to a general "regression to infantile behavior" seen in nearly all the prisoners at Dachau and Buchenwald.

> The prisoners lived, like children, only in the immediate present; . . . they became unable to plan for the future or to give up immediate pleasure satisfactions to gain greater ones in the near future. . . . They were boastful, telling tales about what they had accomplished in their former lives, or how they succeeded in cheating foreman or guards, and how they sabotaged the work. Like children they felt not at all set back or ashamed when it became known that they had lied about their prowess (p. 443).

The collapse of adult attitudes under the strain of frustration or conflict is a very common form of ego breakdown and underlies a great deal of psychopathology. In its most dramatic form, it is seen in mentally ill adults who show extreme regression to infantile levels of behavior so that they are unable to wash, dress, or feed themselves or take care of their eliminative needs. In some cases they even curl up in a position similar to that of the fetus in the womb.

The defensive nature of the reaction is readily apparent in this severe case.

A seventeen-year-old girl was brought to a psychiatric clinic by her mother with the complaint that for the preceding five months her behavior had become increasingly destructive and irrational. The history revealed that after the patient was about four years old her parents had begun to quarrel violently, making her early environment extremely contentious and unstable.

At about this age she first developed various neurotic traits: nail-biting, temper-tantrums, enuresis and numerous phobias. When the patient was seven the mother refused further sexual relations with the father and left the marital bed, but the patient continued to sleep with the father until she was thirteen. At this time the mother suspected that the patient was being incestuously seduced, obtained legal custody of the girl and moved away with her to a separate home. The patient resented this, quarreled frequently with her mother, became a disciplinary problem at home and at school and acquired a police record for various delinquencies. Three years later, at the patient's insistence, she and her mother paid an unexpected visit to the father and found him living with a girl in questionable circumstances. In a violent scene, the mother denounced the father for unfaithfulness and, again contrary to the patient's wishes, took her home. There the patient refused to attend school and rapidly became sullen, withdrawn, and non-communicative. During her mother's absence at work she would throw the house into disorder, destroy clothes her mother had made for her, and throw her mother's effects out of the window. During one of these forays she discovered a photograph of herself at the age of five, which, incidentally, was so poorly lighted and faded that, for one detail, it did not show her eyebrows. Using this as a pattern, she shaved off her own eyebrows, cut her hair to the same baby bob, and began to affect the facial expression and sitting posture of the pictured child. When brought to the hospital her general behavior was correspondingly childish; she was untidy and enuretic, giggled incessantly or spoke in simple monosyllabic sentences, spent most of her time on the floor playing with blocks or paper dolls, and had to be fed, cleaned, and supervised as though she were an infant. In effect, she appeared to have regressed to a relatively desirable period in life antedating disruptive jealousies and other conflicts; moreover, she acted out this regression in unconsciously determined but strikingly symbolic patterns of eliminating the mother as a rival and regaining the father she had lost in her childhood. (Masserman, 1946, case of Dr. John Romano).

Sublimation.   Sublimation, as it has been traditionally conceived, involves the acceptance of a socially approved substitute goal for a drive whose normal channel of expression or normal goal is blocked. The girl who fails to marry may find a substitute sexual outlet in nursing or becoming a masseuse. The individual with sadistic impulses may become a surgeon.

There is considerable doubt as to whether any real process of sublimation actually takes place. For example, can a desire as basic as the sexual desire actually be sublimated? Kinsey (1948) finds evidence of repression but hardly any evidence of sublimation in sexual behavior. Apparently sublimation, in so far as it does occur, is based upon the utilization of general bodily energy in constructive activities which indirectly reduce the tension built up around frustrated sexual or other drives. Also, constructive activities keep the individual too busy to dwell on the frustration. Thus even though sublimation is limited in its scope, it does have a great deal of individual and social value in producing socially approved activity when strong drives are frustrated.

Undoing. This is a defensive reaction designed to negate or annul some disapproved thought, impulse, or act. It is as if the individual has spelled a word wrong and used an eraser to clear the paper and start over. Apologizing for wrongs committed against others, penance, repentance, and being punished are all forms of undoing.

Undoing apparently develops out of our early training in which we are made to apologize or to make some restitution, or are punished in some way commensurate with our socially disapproved behavior. Once the apology or restitution or punishment has taken place, our misdeed is negated and we can start over with a clean slate and with renewed parental approval and affection. In this sequence of events, we also learn that repentance, penance, or restitution may enable us to avoid more serious punishment. For example, by returning Johnny's toys with considerable alacrity, we may avoid being spanked, although we may of course be scolded. By saying we are sorry and offering to do something to make up for our misdeed, we may escape punishment and rejection.

Since we have all been taught that evil and wrongdoing inevitably lead to punishment, we have all developed various methods of atoning for or undoing our misdeeds—methods designed to avoid or ameliorate the punishment that would otherwise accrue. The unfaithful husband may bring his wife presents, the unethical businessman may give huge sums of money to charitable organizations, the rejecting mother may buy her child toys.

Sometimes we feel that the only atonement for our misdeeds is punishment itself, and we may confess them in order that we may be punished and thereby pay for and erase our sins. Not infrequently people who have committed crimes years earlier will confess to the police in order to regain their self-esteem and security. Where sins seem so great to the individual that he sees no hope of undoing or atoning for them, he may suffer such intense guilt, anxiety, and self-devaluation that suicide seems the only way out.

Since undoing is fundamental to the maintenance of ethical human relations, as well as to our self-esteem, it is one of our most valuable ego defenses. Particularly in combination with rationalization and projection is it a potent ego defense against self-devaluating guilt feelings. . . . how-

SUMMARY CHART OF EGO DEFENSE MECHANISM

Denial of reality	Protects self from unpleasant reality by refusal to perceive it
Fantasy	Gratification of frustrated desires in imaginary achievements
Compensation	Covering up weakness by emphasizing desirable trait or making up for frustration in one area by overgratification in another
Identification	Increasing feelings of worth by identifying self with person or institution of illustrious standing
Introjection	Incorporation of external values and standards into ego structure so individual is not at their mercy as external threats
Projection	Placing blame for difficulties upon others or attributing one's own unethical desires to others
Rationalization	Attempting to prove that one's behavior is "rational" and justifiable and thus worthy of self and social approval
Repression	Preventing painful or dangerous thoughts from entering consciousness
Reaction formation	Preventing dangerous desires from being expressed by exaggerating opposed attitudes and types of behavior and using them as "barriers"
Displacement	Discharging pent-up feelings, usually of hostility, on objects less dangerous than those which initially aroused the emotions
Emotional insulation	Withdrawal into passivity to protect self from hurt
Isolation	Cutting off affective charge from hurtful situations or separating incompatible attitudes by logic-tight compartments
Regression	Retreating to earlier developmental level involving less mature responses and usually a lower level of aspiration
Sublimation	Gratification of frustrated sexual desires in substitutive nonsexual activities
Undoing	Atoning for and thus counteracting immoral desires or acts

ever, in . . . psychotic patterns, undoing is subject to exaggerated and unhealthy usage.

In the preceding discussion we have dealt with the major ego defense mechanisms. It is worth re-emphasizing that these defense mechanisms are learned adjustive reactions, that they function in both individual and group behavior, that they operate on relatively habitual and unconscious levels, and that they involve self-deception and reality distortion. However, these mechanisms are essential for the maintenance of ego integrity and we all use them in various degrees and patterns. Consequently they may be considered quite normal and desirable except in cases where they are used to an extreme degree, at the expense of the ultimate adaptive efficiency and happiness of the individual.

REFERENCES:

BETTELHEIM, BRUNO. "Individual and Mass Behavior in Extreme Situations." *J. abnorm. soc. Psychol.*, 38, 417–452, 1943.

COUSINS, SHEILA (pseud.). *To Beg I Am Ashamed* (New York: Vanguard Press, Inc., 1938).

CUSHING, J. G. N., and MARY MCK. CUSHING. "A Concept of the Genesis of Hostility." *Bulletin of the Menninger Clinic*, 13, 94–99, 1949.

FREUD, SIGMUND. *General Introduction to Psychoanalysis* (new ed.) (New York: Garden City, 1949).

FREUD, SIGMUND. *The Psychopathology of Everyday Life* (London: Ernest Benn, Ltd., 1948).

FREUD, SIGMUND. *Wit and Its Relation to the Unconscious* (New York: Moffatt, Yard, 1916).

KINSEY, ALFRED C. *Sexual Behavior in the Human Male* (Philadelphia: W. B. Saunders Company, 1948).

MASSERMAN, JULES H. *Principles of Dynamic Psychiatry* (Philadelphia: W. B. Saunders Company, 1946).

RUCH, FLOYD L. *Psychology and Life* (3rd ed.) (Chicago: Scott, Foresman, 1948).

SCHILDER, PAUL. *Goals and Desires of Man* (New York: Columbia University Press, 1942).

SCHAFFER, LAURANCE. "Fear and Courage in Aerial Combat." *J. consult. Psychol.*, 11, 137–143, 1947.

SHERIF, M., and H. CANTRIL. *The Psychology of Ego-involvements* (New York: Wiley, 1947).

THURBER, JAMES. "The Secret Life of Walter Mitty." In *A Treasury of Laughter*. (Louis Untermeyer, ed.) (New York: Simon and Schuster, 1946).

Time, May 30, 1949.

54 Personality Problems and Personality Growth*

BY A. H. MASLOW

EDITOR'S NOTE: Dr. Maslow has spent the better part of his professional life studying and trying to understand what it is that makes healthy people healthy, what it is that brings out the best in some people, and what it is that enables some persons to transcend the everyday, the ordinary, and the mundane in an effort to become what they have the potential to become. In this selection, Dr. Maslow outlines some basic assumptions about personality growth and describes the various kinds of personality problems which can interfere with one becoming a more productive, healthy person. Is it true that we don't really know how to have fun, that we lack meditativeness, that we lack a value system, that we have given up individual decision and choice? Dr. Maslow maintains that disorders of this sort are our basic personality problems and concludes with some suggestions for doing something about them.

I must tell you that the normal way in which most psychologists would approach these topics would be to list and describe each of the classical psychoses and neuroses and then in the last analysis admit that the sick person can do little for himself. This is also what happens in most books on Mental Hygiene. They, too, end not with a bang but a whimper.

Supposing we try something different this time. Not only do I feel dissatisfied with the helpless labelling of neuroses but also I and many

* From A. H. Maslow, "Personality Problems and Personality Growth." In *The Self*, edited by Clark Moustakas, Harper and Row, Inc., 1956. Copyright © by Clark Moustakas. Reprinted by permission.

other psychologists feel excited and hopeful because there is now emerging over the horizon, a new conception of human sickness and of human health, a psychology that I find so thrilling and so full of wonderful possibilities that I yield to the temptation to present it publicly even *before* it is checked and confirmed, and before it can be called reliable scientific knowledge.

Assumptions About Personality Growth

Call it an expert guess, if you like, or a set of theories, but remember, I speak for only one school of psychologists and not for all. In any case, here it is!

The basic assumptions of this point of view are:

1. We have, each of us, an essential inner nature, which is to some degree "natural," intrinsic, given, and, in a certain sense, unchangeable, or, at least, unchanging.
2. Each person's inner nature is in part unique to himself and in part species-wide.
3. It is possible to study this inner nature scientifically and to discover what it is like—(not *invent—discover*).
4. This inner nature, as much as we know of it so far, seems not to be intrinsically evil, but rather either neutral or positively "good." What we call evil appears most often to be a secondary reaction to frustration of this intrinsic nature.
5. Since this inner nature is good rather than bad, it is best to bring it out, and to encourage it rather than to suppress it. If it is permitted to guide our life, we grow healthy, fruitful and happy.
6. If this essential core of the person is denied or suppressed, he gets sick, sometimes in obvious ways, sometimes in subtle ways, sometimes immediately, sometimes later.
7. This inner nature is not strong and overpowering and unmistakeable like the instincts of animals. It is weak and delicate and subtle and easily overcome by habit, cultural pressure and wrong attitudes toward it.
8. Even though weak, it never disappears in the normal person— perhaps not even in the sick person. Even though denied, it persists underground forever pressing for actualization.
9. Somehow, these conclusions must all be articulated with the necessity of discipline, deprivation, frustration, pain, and tragedy. To the extent that these experiences reveal and foster and fulfill our inner nature, to that extent they are desirable experiences.

Observe that if these assumptions are proven true, they promise a scientific ethics, a natural value system, a court of ultimate appeal for the determination of good and bad, of right and wrong. The more we learn about man's natural tendencies, the easier it will be to tell him how to be good, how to be happy, how to be fruitful, how to respect himself, how to love, how to fulfill his highest potentialities. This amounts to automatic solution of many of the personality problems of the future. The thing to do seems to be to find out what *you* are *really* like, inside, deep down, as a member of the human species and as a particular individual.

Personality Problems

How can we encourage free development? What are the best educational conditions for it? Sexual? Economic? Political? What kind of world do we need for such people to grow in? What kind of world will such people create? Sick people are made by a sick culture; healthy people are made possible by a healthy culture. But it is just as true that sick individuals make their culture more sick and that healthy individuals make their culture more healthy. Improving individual health is one approach to making a better world. To express it in another way, encouragement of personal growth is a real possibility; cure of actual neurotic symptoms is far less possible without outside help. It is relatively easy to try deliberately to make oneself a more honest man; it is very difficult to try to cure one's own compulsions or obsessions.

The classical approach to personality problems considers them to be problems in an undesirable sense. Struggle, conflict, guilt, bad conscience, anxiety, depression, frustration, tension, shame, self-punishment, feeling of inferiority or unworthiness—they all cause psychic pain, they disturb efficiency of performance, and they are uncontrollable. They are, therefore, automatically regarded as sick and undesirable and they get "cured" away as soon as possible.

But all of these symptoms are found also in healthy people, or in people who are growing towards health. Supposing you *should* feel guilty and don't? Supposing you have attained to a nice stabilization which, while good because it cuts your pain, is also bad because development toward a higher ideal ceases?

If this is a startling thought, let me give you a more detailed example. Erich Fromm, in a very important book, attacked the classical Freudian notion of a superego because this concept was entirely authoritarian and relativistic. That is to say, your superego or your conscience was supposed by Freud to be primarily the internalization of the wishes, demands and ideal of the father and mother, whoever they happen to be. But supposing they are criminals? Then what kind of conscience do you have? Or supposing you have a rigid moralizing father who hates fun? Or a psychopath? This conscience exists—Freud was right. We do get our ideals largely from such early figures and not from Sunday School books. But there is also another element in conscience, or, if you like, another kind of conscience which we all have either weakly or strongly. And this is the "intrinsic conscience." This is based upon the unconscious or preconscious perception of our own nature, of our own destiny, or our OWN capacities, of our own "call" in life. It insists that we be true to our inner nature and that we not deny it out of weakness or advantage or for any other reason. He who belies his talent, the born painter who sells stockings instead, the intelligent man who lives a stupid life, the man who sees the truth and keeps his mouth shut, the coward who gives up his manliness, all these people perceive in a deep way that they have done wrong to themselves and despise themselves for it. Out of this self-punishment may come only neurosis, but there may equally well come renewed courage, righteous indignation, increased self-respect, because of thereafter doing the right thing; in a word, growth and improvement can come through pain and conflict.

Supposing we stand by and watch such a person in such a conflict, as students of personality or as therapists or simply as friends? What is our duty? What shall we say? I am afraid that our newer conception means trouble, for it already implies that people who have done wrong to their own nature as human beings or as specific individuals ought to feel guilty and if they don't, perhaps we should help them to feel so. What else am I trying to do right now?

Another consequence of our problem can be pointed out. In essence, I am deliberately rejecting our present, easy distinction between sickness and health, at least as far as symptoms are concerned. Does sickness mean having symptoms? I maintain now that sickness might consist of not having symptoms when you should. Does health mean being symptom-free? I deny it. Which of the Nazis at Auschwitz or Dachau were healthy? Those with stricken conscience or those with a nice, clear, happy conscience? Was it possible for a profoundly human person not to feel conflict, suffering, depression, rage, etc.?

In a word, if you tell me you have a personality problem, I am not certain until I know you better, whether to say "Good!" or "I'm sorry." It depends on the reasons. And these, it seems, may be bad reasons, or they may be good reasons.

An example is the changing attitude of psychologists toward popularity, toward adjustment, even toward delinquency. Popular with whom? Perhaps it is better for a youngster to be unpopular with the neighboring snobs or with the local country club set. Adjusted to what? To a bad culture? To a dominating parent? What shall we think of a well-adjusted slave? A well-adjusted prisoner? Even the behavior problem boy is being looked upon with new tolerance. *Why* is he delinquent? Most often it is for sick reasons. But occasionally it is for good reasons and the boy is simply resisting exploitation, domination, neglect, contempt, and trampling upon.

Clearly what will be called personality problems depends on who is doing the calling. The slave owner? The dictator? The patriarchal father?

The husband who wants his wife to remain a child? It seems quite clear that personality problems may sometimes be loud protests against the crushing of one's psychological bones, of one's true inner nature. What is sick then is that most people do not protest under such treatment. They take it and pay years later, in neurotic and psychosomatic symptoms of various kinds, or perhaps in some cases never become aware that they are sick, that they have missed true happiness, true fulfillment of promise, a rich emotional life, and a serene, fruitful old age, that they have never known how wonderful it is to be creative, to react aesthetically, to find life thrilling.

The question of desirable grief and pain or the necessity for it must also be faced. Is growth and self-fulfillment possible at all without pain and grief and sorrow and turmoil? If these are to some extent necessary and unavoidable, then to what extent? Now, if grief and pain are sometimes necessary for growth of the person, then we must learn not to protect people from them automatically as if they were always bad. Sometimes they may be good and desirable in view of the ultimate good consequences. Not allowing people to go through their pain, and protecting them from it, may turn out to be a kind of over-protection, which in turn implies a certain lack of respect for the integrity and the intrinsic nature and the future development of the individual.

There are many such subtle diseases with which many average Americans are afflicted. They don't think of themselves as sick because everybody else has the same sickness. Where everyone is blind, the sighted man is suspect.

Average Americans don't *really* have fun, and as a matter of fact, don't really know what it is. They don't know how to enjoy themselves, to idle, to saunter. Getting drunk, going to night clubs, watching someone else play games, gambling, insulting women, changing wives at the Saturday night dance are not fun. These are *real* personality problems.

American men and women are not yet friendly enough and respectful enough of each other, nor can they love each other as a rule. The war between the sexes is not yet a partnership. Any man who doesn't know how to love a woman, fuse with her into a unit, is a cripple, a personality problem. He is not whole and completed. Neither is his wife.

Americans are too often anti-intellectual and anti-aesthetic. Poets, theoretical scientists, painters, sculptors, dancers, cannot easily make a living if they are creative. Their social status is poor with the average American. Goodwill ambassadors, selected to represent the best in our culture to other countries, are generally movie stars, the poorer ones at that. More money can be gathered to combat infantile paralysis by television comics than by the greatest researchers. To mistrust your highest intellectual powers, to stifle your creativeness, these are *real* personality problems and not spurious ones. Your own Museum of Modern Art has classes in which your creativeness can be taught to come to life, as I have seen with my own eyes in their television broadcasts, and yet only a few hundred people take advantage of this opportunity to remedy a very basic personal defect, the starvation of creativeness.

The lack of meditativeness and inwardness, of real conscience and real values is a standard American personality defect; a shallowness, a superficial living on the surface of life, a living by other people's opinions rather than by one's own native, inner voice. These are the other-directed men who live, or rather are directed, by publicity campaigns, by testimonials, by majority vote, by public opinion, by what other people think. They don't really know what they want, what they feel, what they, themselves, think right and wrong. Mind you, when everything goes well, these are the adjusted people. They feel fine. They never go to the psychotherapist for help, thinking until it is too late that they need none. And yet they are sick, deep down sick, for they have lost their individuality, their uniqueness. They have become robots.

Loss of the value system is in general a serious worldwide disease, not just American. The cynical, the despairing, the disillusioned, the wise guys, the mistrustful, the swindled ones, the ones who live rootlessly, without zest and without purpose, these too are profoundly serious personality problems even if they don't know they are. The world is too full of them. And they are *very* dangerous, not only to themselves, but to others as well. Since every person needs a value system and yearns for it until he finds one, these are the ones who can be caught up by any offer of absolute truth, by the lunatic groups, by the fanatics who "know" what's right.

Another widespread personality problem is our conventionality, which is to say, the giving up altogether of individual decision and choice. The person who accepts all the conventions, not only the sensible ones, but the stupid and vicious ones as well, commits himself to stifling his conscience and to inevitable guilt and shame and loss of inner self-respect.

American hypocrisy about the naked body, about pregnancy, about sex, about the bowels, about menstruation, and about the other natural functions is notorious in other countries. Less well known is our fear of our own hostility, of tenderness, of grief and of weeping, of rich emotions, of sentiment. Our embarrassment when confronted by our best impulses, altruism, charity, kindness, honesty, unselfishness, cooperation, love, dedication, devotion, impractical benevolence is notorious. The response too frequently is "Hm! A Boy Scout!" We have turned our backs on our own nature and it takes its revenge upon us. As Lewis Mumford says, this shows our fundamental fear of life.

The Basic Needs

Even though the overall and ultimate problem for each human being is his self-fulfillment and the living up to his potentialities, there are many steps along the path to this goal, many needs which have to be fulfilled and gratified so that he is able to go on to a higher and higher level of living, closer and closer to self-fulfillment. These sub-goals are called basic needs. Each of them represents a special and basic and universal personality problem which must be managed or solved before higher development can take place. In a certain sense these are *the* basic personality problems, and solving them nicely makes possible good healthy growth. Furthermore, when we break them down in this way and separate them out from each other, we can be more practical. We can see more clearly what to do about these problems.

1. Most basic of all are the animal needs, those which we share with most of the other higher animals, the needs for food, for water, for sleep, for rest, for sex, for warmth, and so on.

2. Then comes the necessity for safety and for security, for the absence of danger and threat, for being cared for when necessary, being able to be dependent and helpless and weak without feeling endangered.

3. To belong to a group of some sort, and more specifically to be able to love and to be loved, these also are needs in the sense that their fulfill-ment makes further and higher growth possible and their frustration tends to block it and to make us sick.

4. We need to respect ourselves, to be strong, to have a good sound self-esteem. Generally this good self-esteem rests on three foundations; first, respect and approval from other people; second, on actual capacity, achievement and success and third, on the acceptance of and acting upon our own inner nature.

5. In addition to these needs we also have the so-called cognitive needs and the aesthetic needs. Unfortunately the psychologists don't know enough about these needs to prove their case. But most philosophers, most artists, and indeed also most psychologists are willing to concede the clinical fact that these needs do in fact exist. If they are not satisfied, certain forms of sickness result.

The growth of knowledge, of understanding, and the development of a philosophy of values therefore seem to be necessities rather than luxuries. Fortunately, each human being has these possibilities within his own grasp. Creativeness too, especially in the arts, can be fostered and encouraged and taught, it would seem. And I must now agree with these art educators that this is a step in the direction of psychological health, perhaps even a prerequisite or a necessity for full psychological health. My therapeutic recommendations here would be obvious.

Characteristics of Healthy People

The satisfaction of all these basic needs sets the stage for the fullest development of the human being. They are generally prerequisite satisfactions to the full development of the potentialities of the individual. Self-actualization ordinarily implies not only all that has so far been set forth, but also several other characteristics that have self-therapeutic implications for each individual.

For one thing, in order to achieve the fullest growth and development of the personality we must develop what Carl Rogers calls the open self. This phrase is the opposite of sensitiveness, or of distorting experiences or rejecting them or repressing them or suppressing them out of fear of what they may do to us and to our picture of ourselves. Most people are not open in this sense. They pick over their experiences and their sensations and perceptions, accepting some, rejecting others, distorting a few and so on. As examples of this I may cite prejudice, stereotyping, and the like. The healthy person is aware of what actually is happening to him. If he feels pain, he isn't afraid to know that he is feeling pain. The same is true for grief or for happiness or tenderness or love or even feelings of weakness and confusion and conflict and guilt. He can accept his own experiences rather than shutting them out of consciousness. I may add finally that this openness of awareness applies both to our inner selves and also to the external world. I have found that healthy people can perceive the external world more efficiently than can other people.

Another characteristic of healthy people which has lessons for us by way of self-improvement is that of spontaneity. Spontaneity means that the behavior of this individual tends to be natural, easy, unself-conscious, and to flow automatically without design and without intent. It comes easy. Perhaps the best example of spontaneity is the behavior of animals. They simply behave without thinking the matter over first, without being self-conscious about it, or without being deliberate and designed and planned. One consequence is that the spontaneous person is easy, effortless and tends to be graceful, well-coordinated, in his motor behavior. The person who is fully integrated behaves in this sense quite easily and without design and without planning it to be so. I do not imply that spontaneity can be self-willed. It cannot. I mention it here not as a model to follow necessarily because this is rarely possible but rather as an indicator that all is going well within us. When we are in fact spontaneous, we should be pleased and glad and recognize that this is a sign that we are behaving well in the situation. If we feel spontaneous with one person rather than with another, then we can learn from this that we are more compatible, more at ease, less anxious with this first person than with the other.

If a person is open to himself and to his self-experiences, then when he looks within himself, not being afraid, he need not distort. Quite easily then, and without effort, he will automatically have more self-knowledge than those people who are afraid to look or who when they do look, must distort and change and reshape. Self-knowledge either in a conscious or an unconscious form is an ultimate necessity for psychological health. If we are to live with our own inner nature and to fulfill it in its own style, then we must in some fashion or other, know what it is and be aware of it. I think for most people that this self-awareness is at an unconscious or semi-conscious level. But there is no reason in the world why it should not be made more conscious.

What then can we do about these subtle value illnesses which represent a falling away from perfection, a cessation of growth, a stunting and crippling of our inborn potentialities? For one thing, I have indicated that prophylaxis or prevention is far easier than cure or undoing of already formed illnesses. It is also quite important before closing to point out that the classical neurotic symptoms are another matter altogether. I hope no one will get the idea from what I have said that people can cure their own compulsions or anxiety attacks or depressions. For all practical purposes, they can *not*. What is within our power in principle is the improvement of personality, the turn toward honesty, affection, self-respect, intellectual and aesthetic growth, acceptance of our own nature, and turning away from hypocrisy, from meanness, prejudice, cruelty, cowardice, and smallness.

CHAPTER THIRTEEN

TOWARD UNDERSTANDING ONE'S SELF

55   *To Be That Self Which One Truly Is:*
*A Therapist's View of Personal Goals**

BY CARL ROGERS

EDITOR'S NOTE: Although we are not always certain what it means, each of us in our own way seeks to be that self which he truly is. In this sensitive paper, Dr. Rogers reaches deep into his experience as a teacher, therapist, and counselor to describe the directions that he has seen people take when they move closer to understanding and accepting themselves as individuals. As teachers, we need to comprehend as fully as possible those processes which free and release students to reach their potentials. As individuals, we need to know as much about how to truly be ourselves as we can if we are to reach our potentials (and maybe be more effective teachers for it). In Rogers' words, each person must learn to ". . . listen sensitively to himself." This paper may enhance that possibility.

THE QUESTIONS

"What is my goal in life?" "What am I striving for?" "What is my purpose?" These are questions which every individual asks himself at one time or another, sometimes calmly and meditatively, sometimes in agonizing uncertainty or despair. They are old, old questions which have been asked and answered in every century of history. Yet they are also questions which every individual must ask and answer for himself, in his own way. They are questions which I, as a counselor, hear expressed in many

* From *On Becoming a Person* (Boston: Houghton-Mifflin Company, 1961). Chap. Eight, 163–82. Copyright © 1961 by Carl Rogers. Reprinted by permission.

differing ways as men and women in personal distress try to learn, or understand, or choose, the directions which their lives are taking.

In one sense there is nothing new which can be said about these questions. Indeed the opening phrase in the title I have chosen for this paper is taken from the writings of a man who wrestled with these questions more than a century ago. Simply to express another personal opinion about this whole issue of goals and purposes would seem presumptuous. But as I have worked for many years with troubled and maladjusted individuals I believe that I can discern a pattern, a trend, a commonality, an orderliness, in the tentative answers to these questions which they have found for themselves. And so I would like to share with you my perception of what human beings appear to be striving for, when they are free to choose.

SOME ANSWERS

Before trying to take you into this world of my own experience with my clients, I would like to remind you that the questions I have mentioned are not pseudo-questions, nor have men in the past or at the present time agreed on the answers. When men in the past have asked themselves the purpose of life, some have answered, in the words of the catechism, that "the chief end of man is to glorify God." Others have thought of life's purpose as being the preparation of oneself for immortality. Others have settled on a much more earthy goal—to enjoy and release and satisfy every purpose of life as being to achieve—to gain material possessions, status, knowledge, power. Some have made it their goal to give themselves completely and devotedly to a cause outside of themselves such as Christianity, or Communism. A Hitler has seen his goal as that of becoming the leader of a master race which would exercise power over all. In sharp contrast, many an Oriental has striven to eliminate all personal desires, to exercise the utmost of control over himself. I mention these widely ranging choices to indicate some of the very different aims men have lived for, to suggest that there are indeed many goals possible.

In a recent important study Charles Morris investigated objectively the pathways of life which were preferred by students in six different countries—India, China, Japan, the United States, Canada, and Norway (5). As one might expect, he found decided differences in goals between these national groups. He also endeavored, through a factor analysis of his data, to determine the underlying dimensions of value which seemed to operate in the thousands of specific individual preferences. Without going into the details of his analysis, we might look at the five dimensions which emerged, and which, combined in various positive and negative ways, appeared to be responsible for the individual choices.

The first such value dimension involves a preference for a responsible, moral, self-restrained participation in life, appreciating and conserving what man has attained.

The second places stress upon delight in vigorous action for the overcoming of obstacles. It involves a confident initiation of change, either in resolving personal and social problems, or in overcoming obstacles in the natural world.

The third dimension stresses the value of a self-sufficient inner life with a rich and heightened self-awareness. Control over persons and things is rejected in favor of a deep and sympathetic insight into self and others.

The fourth underlying dimension values a receptivity to persons and to nature. Inspiration is seen as coming from a source outside the self, and the person lives and develops in devoted responsiveness to this source.

The fifth and final dimension stresses sensuous enjoyment, self-enjoyment. The simple pleasures of life, an abandonment to the moment, a relaxed openness to life, are valued.

This is a significant study, one of the first to measure objectively the answers given in different cultures to the question, what is the purpose of my life? It has added to our knowledge of the answers given. It has also helped to define some of the basic dimensions in terms of which the choice is made. As Morris says, speaking of these dimensions, "it is as if persons in various cultures have in common five major tones in the musical scales on which they compose different melodies." (5, p. 185)

ANOTHER VIEW

I find myself, however, vaguely dissatisfied with this study. None of the "Ways to Live" which Morris put before the students as possible choices, and none of the factor dimensions, seems to contain satisfactorily the goal of life which emerges in my experience with my clients. As I watch person after person struggle in his therapy hours to find a way of life for himself, there seems to be a general pattern emerging, which is not quite captured by any of Morris' descriptions.

The best way I can state this aim of life, as I see it coming to light in my relationship with my clients, is to use the words of Søren Kierkegaard—"to be that self which one truly is." (3, p. 29) I am quite aware that this may sound so simple as to be absurd. To be what one is seems like a statement of obvious fact rather than a goal. What does it mean? What does it imply? I want to devote the remainder of my remarks to those issues. I will simply say at the outset that it seems to mean and imply some strange things. Out of my experience with my clients, and out of my own self-searching, I find myself arriving at views which would have been very foreign to me ten or fifteen years ago. So I trust you will look at these views with critical scepticism, and accept them only in so far as they ring true in your own experience.

DIRECTIONS TAKEN BY CLIENTS

Let me see if I can draw out and clarify some of the trends and tendencies which I see as I work with clients. In my relationship with these individuals my aim has been to provide a climate which contains as much of safety, of warmth, of empathic understanding, as I can genuinely find in myself to give. I have not found it satisfying or helpful to intervene in the client's experience with diagnostic or interpretative explanations, nor with suggestions and guidance. Hence the trends which I see appear to me to come from the client himself, rather than emanating from me.[1]

Away From Façades

I observe first that characteristically the client shows a tendency to move away, hesitantly and fearfully, from a self that he is *not*. In other words even though there may be no recognition of what he might be moving toward, he is moving away from something. And of course in so doing he is beginning to define, however negatively, what he *is*.

At first this may be expressed simply as a fear of exposing what he is. Thus one eighteen-year-old boy says, in an early interview: "I know I'm not so hot, and I'm afraid they'll find it out. That's why I do these things. . . . They're going to find out some day that I'm not so hot. I'm just trying to put that day off as long as possible. . . . If you know me as I know myself—. (*Pause*) I'm not going to tell you the person I really think I am. There's only one place I won't cooperate and that's it. . . . It wouldn't help your opinion of me to know what I think of myself."

It will be clear that the very expression of this fear is a part of becoming what he is. Instead of simply *being* a façade, as if it were himself, he is coming closer to being *himself*, namely a frightened person hiding behind a façade because he regards himself as too awful to be seen.

Away From "Oughts"

Another tendency of this sort seems evident in the client's moving away from the compelling image of what he "ought to be." Some individuals have absorbed so deeply from their parents the concept "I ought to be good," or "I have to be good," that it is only with the greatest of inward struggle that they find themselves moving away from this goal. Thus one young woman, describing her unsatisfactory relationship with her father, tells first how much she wanted his love. "I think in all this feeling I've had about my father, that *really* I *did* very much want a good relationship with him. . . . I wanted so much to have him care for me, and yet didn't seem to get what I really wanted." She always felt she had to meet all of his demands and expectations and it was "just too much. Because once I meet one there's another and another and another, and I never really meet them. It's sort of an endless demand." She feels she has been like her mother, submissive and compliant, trying continually to meet his demands. "And really *not* wanting to be that kind of person. I find it's not a good way to be, but yet I think I've had a sort of belief that that's the way you *have* to be if you intend to be thought a lot of and loved. And yet who would *want* to love somebody who was that sort of wishy washy person?" The counselor responded, "Who really would love a door mat?" She went on, "At least I wouldn't want to be loved by the kind of person who'd love a door mat!"

Thus, though these words convey nothing of the self she might be moving toward, the weariness and disdain in both her voice and her statement make it clear that she is moving away from a self which *has* to be good, which *has* to be submissive.

Curiously enough a number of individuals find that they have felt compelled to regard themselves as bad, and it is this concept of themselves that they find they are moving away from. One young man shows very clearly such a movement. He says: "I don't know how I got this impression that being ashamed of myself was such an *appropriate* way to feel. . . . Being ashamed of me was the way I just *had* to be. . . . There was a world where being ashamed of myself was the best way to feel. . . . If you are something which is disapproved of very much, then I guess the only way you can have any kind of self-respect is to be ashamed of that part of you which isn't approved of. . . .

"But now I'm adamantly refusing to do things from the old viewpoint. . . . It's as if I'm convinced that someone said, 'The way you will *have* to be is to be *ashamed* of yourself—so *be* that way!' And now I'm standing up against that somebody, saying, 'I don't care *what* you say. I'm *not* going to feel ashamed of myself!' " Obviously he is abandoning the concept of himself as shameful and bad.

Away From Meeting Expectations

Other clients find themselves moving away from what the culture expects them to be. In our current industrial culture, for example, as Whyte has forcefully pointed out in his recent book (7), there are enormous pressures to become the characteristics which are expected of the "organization man." Thus one should be fully a member of the group, should subordinate his individuality to fit into the group needs, should become "the well-rounded man who can handle well-rounded men."

In a newly completed study of student values in this country Jacob summarizes his findings by saying, "The main overall effect of higher education upon student values is to bring about general acceptance of a body of standards and attitudes characteristic of collegebred men and women in the American community. . . . The impact of the college experience is . . . to *socialize* the individual, to refine, polish, or 'shape up' his values so that he can fit comfortably into the ranks of American college alumni." (1, p. 6).

Over against these pressures for conformity, I find that when clients are free to be any way they wish, they tend to resent and to question the tendency of the organization, the college or the culture to mould them to any given form. One of my clients says with considerable heat: "I've been so long trying to live according to what was meaningful to other people, and what made no sense at *all* to me, really. I somehow felt so much *more* than that, at some level." So he, like others, tends to move away from being what is expected.

Away From Pleasing Others

I find that many individuals have formed themselves by trying to please others, but again, when they are free, they move away from being this person. So one professional man, looking back at some of the process he has been through, writes, toward the end of therapy: "I finally felt that I simply *had* to begin doing what I *wanted* to do, not what I thought I *should* do, and regardless of what other people feel I *should* do. This is a complete reversal of my whole life. I've always felt I *had* to do things because they were expected of me, or more important, to make people like me. The hell with it! I think from now on I'm going to just be me—rich or poor, good or bad, rational or irrational, logical or illogical, famous or infamous. So thanks for your part in helping me to rediscover Shakespeare's—'To thine own *self* be true.' "

So one may say that in a somewhat negative way, clients define their goal, their purpose, by discovering, in the freedom and safety of an understanding relationship, some of the directions they do *not* wish to move. They prefer not to hide themselves and their feelings from themselves, or even from some significant others. They do not wish to be what they "ought" to be, whether that imperative is set by parents, or by the culture, whether it is defined positively or negatively. They do not wish to mould themselves and their behavior into a form which would be merely pleasing to others. They do not, in other words, choose to be anything which is artificial, anything which is imposed, anything which is defined from without. They realize that they do not value such purposes or goals, even though they may have lived by them all their lives up to this point.

Toward Self-Direction

But what is involved positively in the experience of these clients? I shall try to describe a number of the facets I see in the directions in which they move.

First of all, the client moves toward being autonomous. By this I mean that gradually he chooses the goals toward which *he* wants to move. He becomes responsible for himself. He decides what activities and ways of behaving have meaning for him, and what do not. I think this tendency toward self-direction is amply illustrated in the examples I have given.

I would not want to give the impression that my clients move blithely or confidently in this direction. No indeed. Freedom to be oneself is a frighteningly responsible freedom, and an individual moves toward it cautiously, fearfully, and with almost no confidence at first.

Nor would I want to give the impression that he always makes sound choices. To be responsibly self-directing means that one chooses—and then learns from the consequences. So clients find this a sobering but exciting kind of experience. As one client says—"I feel frightened, and vulnerable, and cut loose from support, but I also feel a sort of surging up or force or strength in me." This is a common kind of reaction as the client takes over the self-direction of his own life and behavior.

Toward Being Process

The second observation is difficult to make, because we do not have good words for it. Clients seem to move toward more openly being a process, a fluidity, a changing. They are not disturbed to find that they are not the same from day to day, that they do not always hold the same feelings toward a given experience or person, that they are not always consistent. They are in flux, and seem more content to continue in this flowing current. The striving for conclusions and end states seems to diminish.

One client says, "Things are sure changing, boy, when I can't even predict my own behavior in here anymore. It was something I was able to do before. Now I don't know what I'll say next. Man, it's quite a feeling. . . . I'm just surprised I even said these things. . . . I see something new every time. It's an adventure, that's what it is—into the unknown. . . . I'm beginning to enjoy this now, I'm joyful about it, even about all these old negative things." He is beginning to appreciate himself as a fluid process, at first in the therapy hour, but later he will find this true in his life. I cannot help but be reminded of Kierkegaard's description of the individual who really exists. "An existing individual is constantly in process of becoming, . . . and translates all his thinking into terms of process. It is with (him) . . . as it is with a writer and his style; for he only has a style who never has anything finished, but 'moves the waters of the language' every time he begins, so that the most common expression comes into being for him with the freshness of a new birth." (2, p. 79) I find this catches excellently the direction in which clients move, toward being a process of potentialities being born, rather than being or becoming some fixed goal.

Toward Being Complexity

It also involves being a complexity of process. Perhaps an illustration will help here. One of our counselors, who has himself been much helped by psychotherapy, recently came to me to discuss his relationship with a very difficult and disturbed client. It interested me that he did not wish to discuss the client, except in the briefest terms. Mostly he wanted to be sure that he was clearly aware of the complexity of his own feelings in the relationship—his warm feelings toward the client, his occasional frustration and annoyance, his sympathetic regard for the client's welfare, a degree of fear that the client might become psychotic, his concern as to what others would think if the case did not turn out well. I realized that his overall attitude was that if he could *be,* quite openly and transparently, all of his complex and changing and sometimes contradictory feelings in the relationship, all would go well. If, however, he was only part of his feelings, and partly façade or defense, he was sure the relationship would not be good. I find that this desire to be *all* of oneself in each moment—all the richness and complexity, with nothing hidden from oneself, and nothing feared in oneself—this is a common desire in those who have seemed to show much movement in therapy. I do not need to say that this is a difficult, and in its absolute sense an impossible goal. Yet one of the most evident trends in clients is to move toward becoming all of the complexity of one's changing self in each significant moment.

Toward Openness to Experience

"To be that self which one truly is" involves still other components. One which has perhaps been implied already is that the individual moves toward living in an open, friendly, close relationship to his own experience. This does not occur easily. Often as the client senses some new facet of himself, he initially rejects it. Only as he experiences such a hitherto denied aspect of himself in an acceptant climate can he tentatively accept it as a part of himself. As one client says with some shock after experiencing the dependent, small boy aspect of himself, "That's an emotion I've never felt clearly—one that I've never been!" He cannot tolerate the experience of his childish feelings. But gradually he comes to accept and embrace them as a part of himself, to live close to them and in them when they occur.

Another young man, with a very serious stuttering problem, lets himself be open to some of his buried feelings toward the end of his therapy. He says, "Boy, it was a terrible fight. I never realized it. I guess it was too painful to reach that height. I mean I'm just beginning to feel it now. Oh, the *terrible* pain. . . . It was *terrible* to talk. I mean I wanted to talk and then I didn't want to. . . . I'm feeling—I think I know—it's just plain strain—terrible strain—*stress,* that's the word, just so much *stress* I've been feeling. I'm just beginning to *feel* it now after all these years of it. . . . it's terrible. I can hardly get my breath now too, I'm just all choked up inside, all *tight* inside. . . . I just feel like I'm *crushed. (He begins to cry.)* I never realized that, I never knew that." (6) Here he is opening himself to internal feelings which are clearly not new to him, but which up to this time, he has never been able fully to experience. Now that he can permit himself to experience them, he will find them less terrible, and he will be able to live closer to his own experiencing.

Gradually clients learn that experiencing is a friendly resource, not a frightening enemy. Thus I think of one client who, toward the close of therapy, when puzzled about an issue, would put his head in his hands and say, "Now what *is* it I'm feeling? I want to get next to it. I want to learn what it is." Then he would wait, quietly and patiently, until he could discern the exact flavor of the feelings occurring in him. Often I sense that the client is trying to listen to himself, is trying to hear the messages and meanings which are being communicated by his own physiological re-actions. No longer is he so fearful of what he may find. He comes to realize that his own inner reactions and experiences, the messages of his senses and his viscera, are friendly. He comes to want to be close to his inner sources of information rather than closing them off.

Maslow, in his study of what he calls self-actualizing people, has noted this same characteristic. Speaking of these people, he says, "Their ease of penetration to reality, their closer approach to an animal-like or child-like acceptance and spontaneity imply a superior awareness of their own impulses, their own desires, opinions, and subjective reactions in general." (4, p. 210)

This greater openness to what goes on within is associated with a similar openness to experiences of external reality. Maslow might be speaking of clients I have known when he says, "self-actualized people have a wonderful capacity to appreciate again and again, freshly and naively, the basic goods of life with awe, pleasure, wonder, and even ecstasy, however stale these experiences may be for other people." (4, p. 214)

Toward Acceptance of Others

Closely related to this openness to inner and outer experience in general is an openness to and an acceptance of other individuals. As a client moves toward being able to accept his own experience, he also moves toward the acceptance of the experience of others. He values and appreci-ates both his own experience and that of others for what it *is*. To quote Maslow again regarding his self-actualizing individuals: "One does not complain about water because it is wet, nor about rocks because they are hard. . . . As the child looks out upon the world with wide, uncritical and innocent eyes, simply noting and observing what is the case, without either arguing the matter or demanding that it be otherwise, so does the self-actualizing person look upon human nature both in himself and in others." (4, p. 207) This acceptant attitude toward that which exists, I find developing in clients in therapy.

Toward Trust of Self

Still another way of describing this pattern which I see in each client is to say that increasingly he trusts and values the process which is himself. Watching my clients, I have come to a much better understanding of creative people. El Greco, for example, must have realized as he looked at some of his early work, that "good artists do not paint like that." But somehow he trusted his own experiencing of life, the process of himself, sufficiently that he could go on expressing his own unique perceptions. It was as though he could say, "Good artists do not paint like this, but I paint like this." Or to move to another field, Ernest Hemingway was surely aware that "good writers do not write like this." But fortunately he moved toward being Hemingway, being himself, rather than toward some one else's conception of a good writer. Einstein seems to have been unusually oblivious to the fact that good physicists did not think his kind of thoughts. Rather than drawing back because of his inadequate academic preparation in physics, he simply moved toward being Einstein, toward thinking his own thoughts, toward being as truly and deeply himself as he could. This is not a phenomenon which occurs only in the artist or the genius. Time and again in my clients, I have seen simple people become significant and creative in their own spheres, as they have developed more trust of the processes going on within themselves, and have dared to feel their own feelings, live by values which they discover within, and express themselves in their own unique ways.

The General Direction

Let me see if I can state more concisely what is involved in this pattern of movement which I see in clients, the elements of which I have been trying to describe. It seems to mean that the individual moves toward *being*, knowingly and acceptingly, the process which he inwardly and actually *is*. He moves away from being what he is not, from being a façade. He is not trying to be more than he is, with the attendant feelings of insecurity or bombastic defensiveness. He is not trying to be less than he is, with the attendant feelings of guilt or self-depreciation. He is increasingly listening to the deepest recesses of his physiological and emotional being, and finds himself increasingly willing to be, with greater accuracy and depth, that self which he most truly is. One client, as he begins to sense the direction he is taking, asks himself wonderingly and with incredulity in one interview, "You mean if I'd really be what I feel like being, that that would be all right?" His own further experience, and that of many another client, tends toward an affirmative answer. To be what he truly is, this is the path of life which he appears to value most highly, when he is free to move in any direction. It is not simply an intellectual value choice, but seems to be the best description of the groping, tentative, uncertain behaviors by which he moves exploringly toward what he wants to be.

SOME MISAPPREHENSIONS

To many people, the path of life I have been endeavoring to describe seems like a most unsatisfactory path indeed. To the degree that this involves a real difference in values, I simply respect it as a difference. But I have found that sometimes such an attitude is due to certain misapprehensions. In so far as I can I would like to clear these away.

Does It Imply Fixity?

To some it appears that to be what one is, is to remain static. They see such a purpose or value as synonymous with being fixed or unchanging. Nothing could be further from the truth. To be what one is, is to enter fully into being a process. Change is facilitated, probably maximized, when one is willing to be what he truly is. Indeed it is the person who is denying his feelings and his reactions who is the person who tends to come for therapy. He has, often for years, been trying to change, but finds himself fixed in these behaviors which he dislikes. It is only as he can become more of himself, can be more of what he has denied in himself, that there is any prospect of change.

Does It Imply Being Evil?

An even more common reaction to the path of life I have been describing is that to be what one truly is would mean to be bad, evil, uncontrolled, destructive. It would mean to unleash some kind of a monster on the world. This is a view which is very well known to me, since I meet it in almost every client. "If I dare to let the feelings flow which are dammed up within me, if by some chance I should live in those feelings, then this would be catastrophe." This is the attitude, spoken or unspoken, of nearly every client as he moves into the experiencing of the unknown aspects of himself. But the whole course of his experience in therapy contradicts these fears. He finds that gradually he can be his anger, when anger is his real reaction, but that such accepted or transparent anger is not destructive. He finds that he can be his fear, but that knowingly to be his fear does not dissolve him. He finds that he can be self-pitying, and it is not "bad." He can feel and be his sexual feelings, or his "lazy" feelings, or his hostile feelings, and the roof of the world does not fall in. The reason seems to be that the more he is able to permit these feelings to flow and to be in him, the more they take their appropriate place in a total harmony of his feelings. He discovers that he has other feelings with which these mingle and find a balance. He feels loving and tender and considerate and cooperative, as well as hostile or lustful or angry. He feels interest and zest and curiosity, as well as laziness or apathy. He feels courageous and venturesome, as well as fearful. His feelings, when he lives closely and acceptingly with their complexity, operate in a constructive harmony rather than sweeping him into some uncontrollably evil path.

Sometimes people express this concern by saying that if an individual were to be what he truly is, he would be releasing the beast in himself. I feel somewhat amused by this, because I think we might take a closer look at the beasts. The lion is often a symbol of the "ravening beast." But what about him? Unless he has been very much warped by contact with humans, he has a number of the qualities I have been describing. To be sure, he kills when he is hungry, but he does not go on a wild rampage of killing, nor does he overfeed himself. He keeps his handsome figure better than some of us. He is helpless and dependent in his puppyhood, but he moves from that to independence. He does not cling to dependence. He is selfish and self-centered in infancy, but in adulthood he shows a reasonable degree of cooperativeness, and feeds, cares for, and protects his young. He satisfies his sexual desires, but this does not mean that he goes on wild and lustful orgies. His various tendencies and urges have a harmony within him. He is, in some basic sense, a constructive and trustworthy member of the species *felis leo*. And what I am trying to suggest is that when one is truly and deeply a unique member of the human species, this is not something which should excite horror. It means instead that one lives fully and openly the complex process of being one of the most widely sensitive, responsive, and creative creatures on this planet. Fully to be one's own uniqueness as a human being, is not, in my experience, a process which would be labeled bad. More appropriate words might be that it is a positive, or a constructive, or a realistic, or a trustworthy process.

SOCIAL IMPLICATIONS

Let me turn for a moment to some of the social implications of the path of life I have attempted to describe. I have presented it as a direction which seems to have great meaning for individuals. Does it have, could it have, any meaning or significance for groups or organizations? Would it be a direction which might usefully be chosen by a labor union, a church group, an industrial corporation, a university, a nation? To me it seems that this might be possible. Let us take a look, for example, at the conduct of our own country in its foreign affairs. By and large we find, if we listen to the statements of our leaders during the past several years, and read their documents, that our diplomacy is always based upon high moral purposes; that it is always consistent with the policies we have followed previously; that it involves no selfish desires; and that it has never been mistaken in its judgments and choices. I think perhaps you will agree with me that if we heard an individual speaking in these terms we would recognize at once that this must be a façade, that such statements could not possibly represent the real process going on within himself.

Suppose we speculate for a moment as to how we, as a nation, might present ourselves in our foreign diplomacy if we were openly, knowingly, and acceptingly being what we truly are. I do not know precisely what we are, but I suspect that if we were trying to express ourselves as we are, then our communications with foreign countries would contain elements of this sort.

We as a nation are slowly realizing our enormous strength, and the power and responsibility which go with that strength.

We are moving, somewhat ignorantly and clumsily, toward accepting a position of responsible world leadership.

We make many mistakes. We are often inconsistent.

We are far from perfect.

We are deeply frightened by the strength of Communism, a view of life different from our own.

We feel extremely competitive toward Communism, and we are angry and humiliated when the Russians surpass us in any field.

We have some very selfish foreign interests, such as in the oil in the Middle East.

On the other hand, we have no desire to hold dominion over peoples.

We have complex and contradictory feelings toward the freedom and independence and self-determination of individuals and countries: we desire these and are proud of the past support we have given to such tendencies, and yet we are often frightened by what they may mean.

We tend to value and respect the dignity and worth of each individual, yet when we are frightened, we move away from this direction.

Suppose we presented ourselves in some such fashion, openly and transparently, in our foreign relations. We would be attempting to be the nation which we truly are, in all our complexity and even contradictoriness. What would be the results? To me the results would be similar to the experiences of a client when he is more truly that which he is. Let us look at some of the probable outcomes.

We would be much more comfortable, because we would have nothing to hide.

We could focus on the problem at hand, rather than spending our energies to prove that we are moral or consistent.

We could use all of our creative imagination in solving the problem, rather than in defending ourselves.

We could openly advance both our selfish interests, and our sympathetic concern for others, and let these conflicting desires find the balance which is acceptable to us as a people.

We could freely change and grow in our leadership position, because we would not be bound by rigid concepts of what we have been, must be, ought to be.

We would find that we were much less feared, because others would be less inclined to suspect what lies behind the façade.

We would, by our own openness, tend to bring forth openness and realism on the part of others.

We would tend to work out the solutions of world problems on the basis of the real issues involved, rather than in terms of the façades being worn by the negotiating parties.

In short what I am suggesting by this fantasied example is that nations and organizations might discover, as have individuals, that it is a richly rewarding experience to be what one deeply is. I am suggesting that this view contains the seeds of a philosophical approach to all of life, that it is more than a trend observed in the experience of clients.

SUMMARY

I began this talk with the question each individual asks of himself—what is the goal, the purpose, of my life? I have tried to tell you what I have learned from my clients, who in the therapeutic relationship, with its freedom from threat and freedom of choice, exemplify in their lives a commonality of direction and goal.

I have pointed out that they tend to move away from self-concealment, away from being the expectations of others. The characteristic movement, I have said, is for the client to permit himself freely to be the changing, fluid, process which he is. He moves also toward a friendly openness to what is going on within him—learning to listen sensitively to himself. This means that he is increasingly a harmony of complex sensings and reactions, rather than being the clarity and simplicity of rigidity. It means that as he moves toward acceptance of the "is-ness" of himself, he accepts others increasingly in the same listening, understanding way. He trusts and values the complex inner processes of himself, as they emerge toward expression. He is creatively realistic, and realistically creative. He finds that to be this process in himself is to maximize the rate of change and growth in himself. He is continually engaged in discovering that to be all of himself in this fluid sense is not synonymous with being evil or uncontrolled. It is instead to feel a growing pride in being a sensitive, open, realistic, inner-directed member of the human species, adapting with courage and imagination to the complexities of the changing situation. It means taking continual steps toward being, in awareness and in expression, that which is congruent with one's total organismic reactions. To use Kierkegaard's more aesthetically satisfying terms, it means "to be that self which one truly is." I trust I have made it evident that this is not an easy direction to move, nor one which is ever completed. It is a continuing way of life.

In trying to explore the limits of such a concept, I have suggested that this direction is not a way which is necessarily limited to clients in therapy, nor to individuals seeking to find a purpose in life. It would seem to make the same kind of sense for a group, an organization, or a nation, and would seem to have the same kind of rewarding concomitants.

I recognize quite clearly that this pathway of life which I have outlined is a value choice which is decidedly at variance with the goals usually chosen or behaviorally followed. Yet because it springs from individuals who have more than the usual freedom to choose, and because it seems to express a unified trend in these individuals, I offer it to you for your consideration.

FOOTNOTE:

1 I cannot close my mind, however, to the possibility that someone might be able to demonstrate that the trends I am about to describe might in some subtle fashion, or to some degree, have been initiated by me. I am describing them as occurring in the client in this safe relationship, because that seems the most likely explanation.

REFERENCES:

1. JACOB, P. E. Changing Values in College (New Haven: Hazen Foundation, 1956).
2. KIERKEGAARD, S. Concluding Unscientific Postscript (Princeton University Press, 1941).
3. KIERKEGAARD, S. The Sickness Unto Death (Princeton University Press, 1941).
4. MASLOW, A. H. Motivation and Personality (Harper and Bros., 1954).
5. MORRIS, C. W. Varieties of Human Value (University of Chicago Press, 1956).
6. SEEMAN, JULIUS. The Case of Jim (Nashville: Educational Testing Bureau, 1957).
7. WHYTE, W. H., JR. The Organization Man (Simon and Schuster, 1956).

56   *Values, Psychology, and Human Existence**

BY ERICH FROMM

EDITOR'S NOTE: Without a system of values, some personal framework for living, it is difficult to know who one is because there is nothing to which one can attach his sense of identity. Dr. Fromm addresses himself to what he sees as four distinct needs of man and discusses how man's search for the answers to these needs can mean the difference between mental health and mental sickness or between suffering and joy. This article is a good cross-section of the thoughts and ideas of a man who has had a significant impact on the mood and tenor of psychology for many years.

    In this paper, I want to present some substantiation and evidence for a thesis that is shared by a number of us.

    The thesis is that *values are rooted in the very conditions of human existence; hence that our knowledge of these conditions, that is, of the "human situation," leads us to establishing values which have objective validity; this validity exists,* only with regard to the existence of man; outside of him there are no values.

Man and the Conditions of Human Existence

    What is the nature of man, what are the special conditions of human existence, and what are the needs which are rooted in these conditions?

* "Values, Psychology, and Human Existence" by Erich Fromm, from *New Knowledge in Human Values,* edited by Abraham H. Maslow. Copyright © 1959, Research Society for Creative Altruism. Reprinted by permission of Harper and Row, Publishers.

Man is torn away from the primary union with nature, which characterizes animal existence. Having at the same time reason and imagination, he is aware of his aloneness and separateness, of his powerlessness and ignorance, of the accidentalness of his birth and of his death. He could not face this state of being for a second if he could not find new ties with his fellow man which replace the old ones, regulated by instincts. . . . The necessity to unite with other living beings, to be related to them, is an imperative need on the fulfillment of which man's sanity depends. This need is behind all phenomena which constitute the whole gamut of intimate human relations, of all passions which are called love in the broadest sense of the word.

There are several ways in which this union can be sought and achieved. Man can attempt to become one with the world by *submission* to a person, to a group, to an institution, to a God. In this way he transcends the separateness of his individual existence by becoming part of somebody or something bigger than himself and experiences his identity in connection with the power to which he has submitted. Another possibility of overcoming separateness lies in the opposite direction: man can try to unite himself with the world by having power over it, by making others a part of himself, and thus transcending his individual existence by domination.

The common element in both submission and domination is the symbiotic nature of relatedness. Both persons involved have lost their integrity and freedom; they live on each other and from each other, satisfying their craving for closeness, yet suffering from the lack of inner strength and self-reliance which would require freedom and independence, and furthermore constantly threatened by the conscious or unconscious hostility which is bound to arise from the symbiotic relationship. . . .

There is only one passion which satisfies man's need to unite himself with the world and to acquire at the same time a sense of integrity and individuality, and this is *love. Love is union* with somebody, or something, outside oneself, *under the condition of retaining the separateness and integrity of one's own self*. It is an experience of sharing, of communion, which permits the full unfolding of one's own inner activity. The experience of love does away with the necessity of illusions. There is no need to inflate the image of the other person, or of myself, since the reality of active sharing and loving permits me to transcend my individualized existence and at the same time to experience myself as the bearer of the active powers which constitute the act of loving. What matters is the particular *quality* of loving, not the object. Love is in the experience of human solidarity with our fellow creatures, it is in the erotic love of man and woman, in the love of the mother for her child, and also in the love for oneself as a human being; it is in the mystical experience of union. In the act of loving, I am one with All, and yet I am myself, a unique, separate, limited, mortal human being. Indeed, out of the very polarity between separateness and union, love is born and reborn.

Another aspect of the human situation, closely connected with the need for relatedness, is man's situation as a *creature* and his need to *transcend* this very state of the passive creature. Man is thrown into this world without his consent or will. In this respect he is not different from the animal, from the plants, or from inorganic matter. But being endowed with reason and imagination, he cannot be content with the passive role of the creature, with the role of dice cast out of a cup. He is driven by the urge to transcend the role of the creature, the accidentalness and passivity of his existence, by becoming a "creator."

Man can create life. This is the miraculous quality which he indeed shares with all living beings, but with the difference that he alone is aware of being created and of being a creator. Man can create life, or rather, woman can create life, by giving birth to a child and by caring for the child until it is sufficiently grown to take care of his own needs. Man—man and woman—can create by planting seeds, by producing material objects, by creating art, by creating ideas, by loving one another. In the act of creation man transcends himself as a creature, raises himself beyond the passivity and accidentalness of his existence into the realm of purposefulness and freedom. In man's need for transcendence lies one of the roots for love, as well as for art, religion, and material production.

To create presupposes activity and care. It presupposes love for that which one creates. How then does man solve the problem of transcending himself if he is not capable of creating, if he cannot love? *There is another answer to this need for transcendence; if I cannot create life, I can destroy it. To destroy life makes me also transcend it.* Indeed, that man can destroy life is just as miraculous a feat as that he can create it, for life is *the* miracle, the inexplicable. In the act of destruction, man sets himself above life; he transcends himself as a creature. Thus, the ultimate choice for man, inasmuch as he is driven to transcend himself, is to create or to destroy, to love or to hate. The enormous power of the will for destruction which we see in the history of man, and which we have witnessed so frightfully in our own time, is rooted in the nature of man, just as the drive to create is rooted in it. To say that man is capable of developing his primary potentiality for love and reason does not imply the naive belief in man's goodness. Destructiveness is a secondary potentiality, rooted in the very existence of man, and having the same intensity and power as any passion can have. But—and this is the essential point of my argument—it is the *alternative* to creativeness. Creation and destruction, love and hate, are not two instincts which exist independently. They are both answers to the same need for transcendence, and the will to destroy must rise when the will to create cannot be satisfied. However, the satisfaction of the need to create leads to happiness, destructiveness to suffering—most of all, for the destroyer himself.

A third need, again following the conditions of human existence, is that for *rootedness*. Man's birth as man means the beginning of his emergence from his natural home, the beginning of the severance of his natural ties. Yet this very severance is frightening; if man loses his natural roots, where is he and who is he? He would stand alone, without a home, without roots; he could not bear the isolation and helplessness of this position. He would become insane. He can dispense with the natural roots only insofar as he finds new *human* roots and only after he has found them can he feel at home again in this world. Is it surprising, then, to find a deep craving in man not to sever the natural ties, to fight against being torn away from nature, from mother, blood and soil?

The most elementary of the natural ties is the tie of the child to the mother. The child begins life in the mother's womb and exists there for a much longer time than is the case with most animals; even after birth, the child remains physically helpless and completely dependent on the mother; this period of helplessness and dependence again is much more protracted than with any animal. In the first years of life no full separation between child and mother has occurred. The satisfaction of all his physiological needs, of his vital need for warmth and affection depend on her; she has not only given birth to him, but she continues to give life to him. Her care is not dependent on anything the child does for her, on any obligation which the child has to fulfill; it is unconditional. She cares because the new creature is her child. The child, in these decisive first years of his life, has the experience of his mother as the fountain of life, as an all-enveloping, protective, nourishing power. Mother is food; she is love; she is warmth; she is earth. To be loved by her means to be alive, to be rooted, to be at home.

Just as birth means to leave the enveloping protection of the womb, growing up means to leave the protective orbit of the mother. Yet, even in the mature adult, the longing for this situation as it once existed never ceases completely, in spite of the fact that there is, indeed, a great difference between the adult and the child. The adult has the means to stand on his own feet, to take care of himself, to be responsible for himself and even for others, whereas the child is not yet capable of doing all this. But, considering the increased perplexities of life, the fragmentary nature of our knowledge, the acidentalness of adult existence, the unavoidable errors we make, the situation of the adult is by no means as different from that of the child as it is generally assumed. Every adult is in need of help, of warmth, of protection, in many ways differing and yet in many ways similar to the needs of the child. It is surprising to find in the average adult a deep longing for the security and rootedness which the relationship to his mother once gave him? Is it not to be expected that he cannot give up this intense longing unless he finds other ways of being rooted? . . .

Living is a process of continuous birth. The tragedy in the life of most of us is that we die before we are fully born. Being born, however, does not only mean to be free *from* the womb, the lap, the hand, etc., but also to be free *to* be active and creative. Just as the infant must breathe once the umbilical cord is cut, so man must be active and creative at every moment of birth. To the extent that man is fully born, he finds a new kind of rootedness; that lies in his creative relatedness to the world, and in the ensuring experience of solidarity with all men and with all nature. From being *passively* rooted in nature and in the womb, man becomes one again—but this time actively and creatively with all life.

Fourth, man needs to have a *sense of identity*. Man can be defined as the animal that can say "I," that can be aware of himself as a separate entity. The animal, being within nature and not transcending it, has no awareness of himself, has no need for a sense of identity. Man, being torn away from nature, being endowed with reason and imagination, needs to form a concept of himself, needs to say and to feel: "I am I." Because he is not *lived,* but *lives,* because he has lost the original unity with nature, has to make decisions, is aware of himself and of his neighbor as different persons, he must be able to sense himself as the subject of his actions. As with the need for relatedness, rootedness, and transcendence, this need for a sense of identity is so vital and imperative that man could not remain sane if he did not find some way of satisfying it. Man's sense of identity develops in the process of emerging from the "primary bonds" which tie him to mother and nature. The infant, still feeling one with mother, cannot yet say "I," nor has he any need for it. Only after he has conceived of the outer world as being separate and different from himself does he come to the awareness of himself as a distinct being, and one of the last words he learns to use is "I," in reference to himself.

In the development of *the human race* the degree to which man is aware of himself as a separate self depends on the extent to which he has emerged from the clan and the extent to which the process of individuation has developed. The member of a primitive clan might express his sense of identity in the formula "I am we"; he cannot yet conceive of himself as an "individual," existing apart from his group. In the medieval world, the individual was identified with his social role in the feudal hierarchy. The peasant was not a man who happened to be a peasant, the feudal lord not a man who happened to be a feudal lord. *He was a* peasant or a lord, and this sense of his unalterable station was an essential part of his sense of identity. When the feudal system broke down, this sense of identity was shaken and the acute question "Who am I?" arose—or, more precisely, "How do I know that I am I?" . . .

The development of Western culture went in the direction of creating the basis for the full experience of individuality. By making the individual free politically and economically, by teaching him to think for himself and freeing him from an authoritarian pressure, one hoped to enable him to feel "I" in the sense that he was the center and active subject of his powers and experienced himself as such. But only a minority achieved the new experience of "I." For the majority, individualism was not much more than a facade behind which was hidden the failure to acquire an individual sense of identity.

Many substitutes for a truly individual sense of identity were sought for and found. Nation, religion, class, and occupation serve to furnish a sense of identity. "I am an American," "I am a Protestant," "I am a businessman," are the formulae that help a man experience a sense of identity after the original clan identity has disappeared and before a truly individual sense of identity has been acquired. These different identifications are, in contemporary society, usually employed together. They are in a broad sense status identifications, and they are more efficient if blended with older feudal remnants, as in European countries. In the United States, in which so little is left of feudal relics and in which there is so much social mobility, these status identifications are naturally less efficient, and the sense of identity is shifted . . . to the experience of conformity.

Inasmuch as I am not different, inasmuch as I am like the others and recognized by them as "a regular fellow," I can sense myself as "I." I am—"as you desire me"—as Pirandello put it in the title of one of his plays. Instead of the pre-individualistic clan identity, a new herd identity develops in which the sense of identity rests on the sense of an unquestionable belonging to the crowd. That this uniformity and conformity are often not recognized as such, and are covered by the illusion of individuality, does not alter the facts.

The problem of the sense of identity is not, as it is usually understood, merely a philosophical problem, or a problem concerning only our mind and thought. The need to feel a sense of identity stems from the very condition of human existence, and it is the source of the most intense strivings. Since I cannot remain sane without the sense of "I," I am driven to do almost anything to acquire this sense. Behind the intense passion for status and conformity is this very need, and it is sometimes even stronger than the need for physical survival. What could be more obvious than the fact that people are willing to risk their lives, to give up their love, to surrender their freedom, to sacrifice their own thoughts for the sake of being one of the herd, of conforming, and thus of acquiring a sense of identity, even though it is an illusory one.

Reason and Orientation in the World

The fact that man has reason and imagination leads to the necessity not only for having a sense of his own identity but also for *orienting himself in the world intellectually*. This need can be compared with the process of physical orientation that develops in the first years of life and that is completed when the child can walk by himself, touch and handle things, knowing what they are. But when the ability to walk and to speak has been acquired, only the first step in the direction of orientation has been taken. Man finds himself surrounded by many puzzling phenomena and, having reason, he has to make sense of them, has to put them in some context which he can understand and which permits him to deal with them in his thoughts. The further his reason develops, the more adequate becomes his system of orientation, that is, the more it approximates reality. But even if man's frame of orientation is utterly illusory, it satisfies his need for some picture which is meaningful to him. Whether he believes in the power of a totem animal, in a rain god, or in the superiority and destiny of his race, his need for some frame of orientation is satisfied. Quite obviously, the picture of the world that he has depends on the development of his reason and of his knowledge. Although biologically the brain capacity of the human race has remained the same for thousands of generations, it takes a long evolutionary process to arrive at *objectivity*, that is, to acquire the faculty to see the world, nature, other persons, and oneself as they are and not distorted by desires and fears. The more man develops this objectivity, the more he is in touch with reality, the more he matures, the better can he create a human world in which he is at home. Reason is man's faculty for *grasping* the world by thought, in contradiction to intelligence, which is man's ability to *manipulate* the world with the help of thought. Reason is man's instrument for arriving at the truth, intelligence is man's instrument for manipulating the world more successfully; the former is essentially human, the latter belongs also to the animal part of man.

Reason is a faculty which must be practiced in order to develop, and it is indivisible. By this I mean that the faculty for objectivity refers to the knowledge of nature as well as to the knowledge of man, of society, and of oneself. If one lives in illusions about one sector of life, one's capacity for reason is restricted or damaged, and thus the use of reason is inhibited with regard to all other sectors. Reason in this respect is like love. Just as love is an orientation which refers to all objects and is incompatible with the restriction to one object, so is reason a human faculty which must embrace the whole of the world with which man is confronted. . . .

Feeling and Orientation to the World

If man were only a disembodied intellect, his aim would be achieved by a comprehensive thought system. But since he is an entity endowed with a body as well as a mind, he has to react to the dichotomy of his existence not only in thinking but in the total process of living, in his feelings and actions. Hence any satisfying system of orientation contains not only intellectual elements but elements of feeling and sensing which are expressed in the relationship to an object of devotion.

The answers given to man's need for a system of orientation and an object of devotion differ widely both in content and in form. There are primitive systems such as animism and totemism in which natural objects or ancestors represent answers to man's quest for meaning. There are nontheistic systems, such as Buddhism, which are usually called religions although in their original form there is no concept of God. There are purely philosophical systems, such as Stoicism, and there are the monotheistic religious systems that give an answer to man's quest for meaning in reference to the concept of God.

But whatever their contents, they all respond to man's need to have not only some thought system but also an object of devotion that gives meaning to his existence and to his position in the world. Only the analysis of the various forms of religion can show which answers are better and which are worse solutions to man's quest for meaning and devotion, "better" or "worse" always considered from the standpoint of man's nature and his development.

Choices and Fulfillment

In discussing the various needs of man as they result from the conditions of his existence, I have tried to indicate that they have to be satisfied in some way or other lest man should become insane. But there are several ways in which each of these needs can be satisfied; the difference between these ways is the difference in their appropriateness for the development of man. The need to be related can be satisfied by submission, or by domination; but only in love is another human need fulfilled—that of independence and integrity of the self. The need for transcendence can be satisfied either by creativeness or by destructiveness; but only creativeness permits of joy—whereas destructiveness causes suffering for oneself and others. The need for rootedness can be satisfied regressively by fixation in nature and mother, or progressively by full birth in which new solidarity and oneness is achieved. Here again only in the latter case are individuality and integrity preserved. A frame of orientation may be irrational or rational; yet only the rational one can serve as a basis for the growth and development of the total personality. Eventually, the sense of identity can be based on primary ties with nature and clan, on adjustment to a group, or, on the other hand, on the full, creative development of the person. Again, only in the latter case can man achieve a sense of joy and strength.

The difference between the various answers is the difference between mental health and mental sickness, between suffering and joy, between stagnation and growth, between life and death, between good and evil. All answers that can be qualified as good have in common that they are consistent with the very nature of life, which is continuous birth and growth. All answers that can be qualified as bad have in common that they conflict with the nature of life, that they are conducive to stagnation and eventually to death. . . .

Well-being I would describe as the *ability to be creative, to be aware, and to respond;* to be independent and fully active, and by this very fact to be one with the world. To be concerned with *being,* not with *having;* to experience joy in the very act of living—and to consider living creatively as the only meaning of life. Well-being is not an assumption in the *mind* of a person. It is expressed in his whole body, in the way he walks, talks, in the tonus of his muscles.

Certainly, anyone who wants to achieve this aim must struggle against many basic trends of modern culture. I want to mention very briefly only two. One, the idea of a *split between intellect and affect,* an idea which has been prevalent from Descartes to Freud. In this whole development (to which there are, of course, exceptions) the assumption is made that only the intellect is rational and that affect, by its very nature, is irrational. . . . We cannot understand man fully nor achieve the aim of well-being unless we overcome the idea of this split, restore to man his original unity, and recognize that the split between affect and thought, body and mind, is nothing but a product of our own thought and does not correspond to the reality of man.

The other obstacle to the achievement of well-being, deeply rooted in the spirit of modern society, is the fact of man's dethronement from his supreme place. The nineteenth century said: God is dead; the twentieth century could say: man is dead. Means have been transformed into ends, the production and consumption of things has become the aim of life, to which living is subordinated. We produce things that act like men and men that act like things. Man has transformed himself into a thing and worships the products of his own hands; he is alienated from himself and has regressed to idolatry, even though he uses God's name. Emerson already saw that "things are in the saddle and ride mankind." Today many of us see it. The achievement of well-being is possible only under one condition: *if we put man back into the saddle.*

57   *Chronology of a Self** *

BY JAYNIE WILLIAMS

EDITOR'S NOTE: This is a 20-year-old girl's look-back over the significant events and people in her life. It was written in response to an assignment made in an undergraduate educational psychology class which asked students to examine and analyze themselves from their point of view. Although it is just one girl's look at self, it seems to have the sort of universal quality about it which may allow you to see bits and pieces of yourself reflected in it. In Miss Williams' words, "How do you tell anyone 'This is me'?"

How do you tell anyone:
"This is me.
I am this and that
and—then again—
I am not"?
Can you put down
in black and white
why you are as you are
if sometimes it is not clear to you
that you are at all?
Once—oh, just a year or two ago—
I could have laughed and said:
"Oh, me? That's easy!
I'm young and I'm vulnerable . . .

---

* "Chronology of a Self," unpublished term paper, Summer, 1966, College of Education, Michigan State University. Reproduced by permission.

People hurt my feelings by a look or a word
or an expression . . .
I'm hypersensitive, really."
Once I could have said:
"Emotional? But of course I am!
I cry at movies and stare out at the rain
and find myself in moods that—sometimes—frighten me."
Once I could tell the world:
"Here I am . . . I'm a romanticist!
I like Keats and Shelley and Byron.
I love the sun shining through the trees
and a warm spring night
makes me thoughtful and at peace."
And once I could have called myself patient
and an easy mark for sympathy
and an unselfish person.
And then, too,
without thinking twice,
I would have said:
"Dependent?
I can't stand on my own two feet.
The corner drugstore is too far to walk
alone."
Then, too, I could add that I have been babied
and sheltered and protected
because I have always been the child of my friends.
"Be quiet! Don't talk that way! Jaynie's here."
and the talk became more polite
and the atmosphere less charged
because they delighted in innocence
among so much experience
and I was proud they never pushed me
but wanted me as I was.
Once I could have told a tale
of a desperate young teenager
who lashed out at her mother
and cringed before her father
and blamed the world's wrongs on them
and blamed herself for blaming them.
I could have cried a little
as I told of a child
who tried to push her way into an adult world
but found she couldn't compete
because she didn't know the rules of the game
and, on learning them, turned back

because she didn't want to play that way.
And I could tell you how partings
used to leave me lost
because I fell in love with people too easily
and I lost them just as easily
and then I was standing in the rain (alone)
listening to train whistles grow higher and thinner
until they faded away like curls of smoke
that disappear in the air . . . drifting toward
their final resting-place and settling there,
without me . . .
I cried.

All this I could tell,
and, in the telling,
you would know my self-concept.
But would I?
For this is what I once was,
and I knew it,
and I strove to change it.
Now I am in a period
of my own personal Renaissance
and things are changing
and things are shifting
and I have not yet sorted the chaff from the grain
and realized why I do what I do
or how I feel as I feel,
or if I feel.
Too much is happening too fast.
But, perhaps, if I show you glimpses—
brief and unconnected, but chronological—
you will see why I am as I am now
and, maybe, I will,
too.

MY FRESHMAN YEAR . . . off in a world of dates and hourlies with
never a moment to stop and look at myself until one quiet Sunday during
Winter Term:

February, 1965

Whirl around,
Settle down,
Just for a minute,
Never forever.
Carousel with purple horses—

all of them purple—
but when the white one appears,
It disappears.
It blends in with the purple.
Lavendar now . . .
lavendar sky,
lavendar day,
lavendar mood.
Quick! Grab the brass ring!
But make sure it isn't a smoke ring.
It could be, you know.
"But of course I care"
For candy canes
and pumpkin pie
and chalk on sidewalks.
"I love being with you"
but I'd rather run barefoot in the grass
or listen to Frankie croon
or hold a cloud in my hands.
All over again now.
Twelve o'clock and time to turn . . .
to turn into what?

*****A LESSON LEARNED . . . discretion. I found that my time
was too valuable to be thrown away on the folly of "dating just to date." I
priced myself as a human being and found myself too valuable to follow
the crowd, to throw myself away on trivia that led nowhere and people
that meant nothing.

THE FOLLOWING SUMMER . . . a time of thinking back on my
actions in the past year . . . a time of whipping myself into shape . . .
of learning to show myself where I had gone wrong.

July, 1965

Today my past floated by
and I was shocked at the hunched back
and gnarled hands
and sunken eyes—
so strangely old in one so young.
I tasted my own heart today
and it was bittersweet and lemon-coated
and not pleasant.

*****A LESSON LEARNED . . . to take experience and turn it to my
advantage. To keep my eyes open and benefit from all I saw, whether right

or wrong. To learn from the smallest things around me . . . from the most insignificant people. For who or what is, after all, insignificant?

MY SOPHOMORE YEAR . . . one of my best years of self-revelation. Is it true—"sophomore slump"—does it really exist? For me it did . . . a rough time with a boyfriend all year long . . . grades that were miserably low . . . arguments with roommates . . . friends dropping out of school . . . a melee of engagements that made you wonder what was wrong with you . . . letters from home that made you wonder what was wrong with them because they loved you so much and you seemed to give back so little. The following show my state of mind and the changes it underwent from all the above and more . . .

October, 1965

I wish . . .
that time was nothing,
and words were less
and you and I stood face-to-face
without our masks . . .
that souls could open
and shine the truth
and fear never entered
where it should not . . .
that people cried
and laughed with ease
and no one denied anyone
because there was no need . . .
that friends spoke softly
and God could smile
and hope settled peacefully
where it belonged . . .
that I could feel
and love again,
and forget a something
that should be nothing . . .
that I could tell you
what I want . . .
that you could show me
why you are . . .
that we could know
where we had failed . . .
that it was later
so we could laugh . . .
that I could know
if I am right . . .

that you could be
yourself sometimes . . .
that all could be
forgiven now . . .
that both of us
will not forget . . .
that it was yesterday
again . . .
that wishes could
come true.

*****A LESSON LEARNED . . . many of them. Forgiveness, the most valuable. Willingness to let down pride for the sake of keeping a friend. The ability to give the other person a chance to explain instead of my usual immature stubbornness to be anything other than right. The value of insight into another human being. The finding that nobody was perfect, that I could no longer hero-worship, that everyone I knew was as vulnerable as I only in their own ways. And this made me more self-confident, knowing that I was not alone in uncertainty.

November, 1965

please tell me why
people say things
they really mean
at the time
and then change their minds
and don't tell you
and you have to find it out
through somebody
who would just as soon
not be the one to carry the news.
it doesn't help
to just be hurt
and not to know
the reason for it.
how can you learn
from your mistakes
if people will not tell you
what your mistakes are?
and why are people
so afraid
that honesty is not
the best policy
when you know
it's what you need

and all you want.
but, most of all,
please let me know
why in this world
there can be
no trust.

*****A LESSON LEARNED . . . or should I say "a wall built"? My childish illusion, my unquestioning faith in all people finally disintegrated. I learned to show myself to only those I felt would care and I learned quickly that there are very few that really *do* care. I learned honesty. I feel now that "playing the game" is not only a ridiculous waste of time, but can harm someone more than help them. I say what is to be said with a certain amount of tact and avoid beating about the bush. And I learned that those who run and hide from telling the truth are not always nasty and stupid, but sometimes merely afraid to hurt another person. Although I understánd this, I feel a little bit of contempt for these people, anyhow. For people who run away cannot face life . . . or themselves. And I learned to face myself.

And in a letter to my friend, my confusion at these changes in me shows quite clearly:

April, 1966

Dear David,
Where are you
and why
did you leave?
Sometimes I have
the need to talk with you
and sometimes
I know
I can't talk with anyone.
What has happened?
Why don't I care anymore
that Phil came back to Helen
or that my roommate got engaged
or that Karen solved her problem?
Why is his love my life
and not my life?
Why don't I miss anyone?
Why don't I cry?
Why do I try to tell myself I'm lonely
when I'm not—really—
and why do I worry

because I'm not?
I wanted to be independent
and now I am
and now I wonder
if I should feed people more.
I hated being a doormat,
an Ann Landers,
and everybody's sister;
now I hate that I care
for just myself.
I liked to hate myself
and now I hate liking myself.
I once felt immature
and now I feel some of age's weight
and I cry for my immaturity.
And oh! I dreamed of weddings
and diamond rings
and now I don't want marriage
or any of that—
or do I scorn it
because I feel I'll be
one of the unchosen ones?
David,
this isn't a letter
and it isn't
a poem—
these are simply
thoughts I have daily in my mind.
Do you realize
that you and I
may never see each other
again?
It's an odd—
a frighteningly odd—
feeling.
But then,
so is
love.

*****A LESSON LEARNED . . . that I could not break the world into black and white. That there is gray. And so I found myself to be a meditator. Before I had simply said, "I believe such-and-such" without wondering why. Now I find I must question endlessly before finding a solid basis for a belief. Solid bases are hard to come by, thus, I have no set value or belief, which makes me also an extremely frustrated individual.

THIS SUMMER . . . and I have learned now that I am basically a pensive person, prone to be a bit cynical, having—at times—a strong melancholy streak in me. Although my outward actions do not support this, I am really a quiet person. I tend to watch others and learn from them quite a bit about myself. I draw from their actions a source of amusement that is quite often bitter. I find musing to myself better entertainment than a Saturday night party and I much prefer a good book in an empty house to swimming at the university pool.

July, 1966

A summer morning and the first thing I see . . .
the girl next door
bending over a stove and hoping
she won't break the egg yolk
and be embarrassed in front of her boyfriend.
I laugh
because I know how she feels.
How many yolks have I slopped in the skillet
before I learned to make a perfect egg?
Sometimes
I still break a few
but now I know why
and I know how to prevent it and then
Sometimes
I like breaking a few
so I can start again.
Kathy never breaks hers
and Kathy wears a diamond ring,
but she has years ahead of her
to break all the yolks she wants
and I have just this fleeting summer
because I seek Perfection
that she has found
or that she is not striving for,
depending on her definition of Perfection.
The kitten is trying to reach a spot on the wall
and get it in her paws to toy with it,
and I laugh at this, too,
because I have learned the spot will stay there . . .
but it was fun when I used to think
it would fall off into my hands,
even when it was frustrating, too;
Youth, I think,
is a funny time.

*****A LESSON LEARNED . . . all my life, possibly because of my ridiculous height of 4' 11", people have babied me and treated me as a child. I reacted in the only way—acting as a child, and giving myself no real chance to grow mentally. This summer—completely on my own—I learned more than budgeting or cooking . . . I learned independence and I learned maturity. I feel that I am by far more mature than many of my friends, that I have come out from under all protective wings offered me. This, the last summer of my teens, was not a teenage summer to me at all, but one in which I have finally made myself feel ready to take that step into adulthood whenever I feel I must, with the single regret that childhood comes but once and mine will be gone forever.

58   What Makes Life Significant?*

BY WILLIAM JAMES

EDITOR'S NOTE: We all have our own peculiar way of perceiving and experiencing the world around us and the people in it. Our attitudes, values, and life experiences serve as screening devices through which all of our perceptions are filtered. Ultimately, we behave, learn, and grow personally in terms of what seems to be true and right as we see it. One of the things which may help make our lives significant is the extent to which we can share more or less similar outlooks with people who are meaningful to us. In that sense, every Jack does, indeed, need a Jill, and every Jill a Jack. As suggested by William James, "Where would any of us be, were there no one willing to know us as we really are . . . ?"

The first thing to learn in intercourse with others is non-interference with their own peculiar ways of being happy, provided those ways do not assume to interfere by violence with ours. No one has insight into all the ideals. No one should presume to judge them off-hand. The pretension to dogmatize about them in each other is the root of most human injustices and cruelties, and the trait in human character most likely to make the angels weep.

Every Jack sees in his own particular Jill charms and perfections to the enchantment of which we stolid onlookers are stone-cold. And which has the superior view of the absolute truth, he or we? Which has the more vital insight into the nature of Jill's existence, as a fact? Is he in excess,

* From *Talks to Teachers* by William James. All rights reserved. Reprinted by permission of Holt, Rinehart and Winston, Inc.

being in this matter a maniac? Or are we in defect, being victims of a pathological anaesthesia as regards Jill's magical importance? Surely the latter; surely to Jack are the profounder truths revealed; surely poor Jill's palpitating little life-throbs *are* among the wonders of creation, *are* worthy of this sympathetic interest; and it is to our shame that the rest of us cannot feel like Jack. For Jack realizes Jill concretely, and we do not. He struggles toward a union with her inner life, divining her feelings, anticipating her desires, understanding her limits as manfully as he can, and yet inadequately, too; for he is also afflicted with some blindness, even here. Whilst we, dead clods that we are, do not even seek after these things, but are contented that that portion of eternal fact named Jill should be for us as if it were not. Jill, who knows her inner life, knows that Jack's way of taking it—so importantly—is the true and serious way; and she responds to the truth in him by taking him truly and seriously, too. May the ancient blindness never wrap its clouds about either of them again! Where would any of *us* be, were there no one willing to know us as we really are or ready to repay us for *our* insight by making recognizant return? We ought, all of us, to realize each other in this intense, pathetic, and important way.

INDEX